Resourcebook in

Macro
Organizational
Behavior

The Goodyear Series in
Administration and Business Management

Lyman W. Porter
Joseph W. McGuire
Series Editors

Resourcebook in
Macro
Organizational
Behavior

Robert H. Miles

Harvard University

Goodyear Publishing Company, Inc., Santa Monica, California

Library of Congress Cataloging in Publication Data

Main entry under title:

Resourcebook in macro organizational behavior.

(The Goodyear series in administration and business management)
1. Organization—Addresses, essays, lectures.
2. Organizational behavior—Addresses, essays, lectures.
I. Miles, Robert H.   II. Series: Goodyear series in administration and business management.
HD 31.R463   658.4   79–26187
ISBN 0–8302–5113–8

Current Printing (last number):
10   9   8   7   6   5   4   3   2   1

ISBN: 0–8302–5113–8

Y–5113–9

Printed in the United States of America

CONTRIBUTORS

HOWARD ALDRICH, Associate Professor of Organizational Behavior, New York State School of Industrial and Labor Relations, Cornell University

PAUL BERSTEIN, Associate Professor of Sociology, Boston College

CHARLES G. BURCK, Associate Editor, *Fortune* magazine

TOM BURNS

ROBERT CALLAHAN, Assistant Professor of Organizational Behavior, School of Management, Case Western Reserve University

JOHN CHILD, Professor, University of Aston Management Centre, England

HENRY J. COLEMAN, JR., Ph.D. Candidate in Organizational Behavior, University of California–Berkeley

FRED E. EMERY, Professor, Australian National University, Canberra, Aus- School, University of Pennsylvania

COLIN L. FOX, Graduate Teaching Fellow of Management, The Wharton School, University of Pennsylvania

JAY R. GALBRAITH, Associate Professor of Management, The Wharton School, University of Pennsylvania

WILLIAM C. GOGGIN, Chairman of the Board and Chief Executive Officer, Dow Corning

DIANE HERKER STRICKER, Assistant Professor of Management, School of Economics and Management, Oakland University

RAY JURKOVICH, Research Associate, Sociologisch Instituut, Leiden, Holland

JOHN R. KIMBERLY, Associate Professor of Organizational Behavior, Yale School of Organization and Management

KENNETH KNIGHT, Director, Management Programme, Institute of Organisation and Social Studies, Brunel University, England

JAMES L. KOCH, Associate Professor of Management, University of Oregon

JOHN P. KOTTER, Associate Professor of Organizational Behavior, Harvard Business School

JOSEPH A. LITTERER, Professor of Management, School of Business Administration, University of Massachusetts

JAY W. LORSCH, Louis E. Kirstein Professor of Human Relations, Harvard Business School

ALAN D. MEYER, Assistant Professor of Organizational Behavior, School of Business Administration, University of Wisconsin at Milwaukee

RAYMOND E. MILES, Professor of Business Administration and Associate Director of the Institute of Industrial Relations, University of California, Berkeley

ROBERT H. MILES, Associate Professor of Organizational Behavior, Harvard Business School

TED MILLS, Director, American Center for the Quality of Work Life, Washington, D.C.

HENRY MINTZBERG, Professor of Management, Faculty of Management, McGill University, Canada

DAVID A. NADLER, Associate Professor of Organizational Behavior, Graduate School of Business, Columbia University

BARRY NEWMAN, Staff Reporter, *The Wall Street Journal*

CHARLES PERROW, Professor of Sociology, Department of Sociology, State University of New York at Stoney Brook

LOUIS R. PONDY, Professor of Organizational Behavior, School of Business Administration, University of Illinois, Champagne–Urbana

W. ALAN RANDOLPH, Assistant Professor of Management, College of Business Administration, University of South Carolina

PAUL SALIPANTE, JR., Assistant Professor of Management, School of Management, Case Western Reserve University

CHARLES C. SNOW, Assistant Professor of Organizational Behavior, Pennsylvania State University

RICHARD M. STEERS, Associate Professor of Management, Graduate School of Management and Business, University of Oregon

HAROLD STIEGLITZ, President, National Industrial Conference Board

ERIC L. TRIST, Emeritus Professor of Social Systems Sciences, The Wharton School, University of Pennsylvania

MICHAEL L. TUSHMAN, Associate Professor of Organizational Behavior, Graduate School of Business, Columbia University

RICHARD E. WALTON, Professor of Organizational Behavior, Harvard Business School

Contents

PART III
UNDERSTANDING AND MANAGING ORGANIZATION–ENVIRONMENT RELATIONS   **225**

PART IV
EMERGING PERSPECTIVES AND NEW FRONTIERS IN MACRO ORGANIZATIONAL BEHAVIOR

CROSS-REFERENCE OF RESOURCEBOOK READINGS WITH CHAPTERS IN MACRO ORGANIZATIONAL BEHAVIOR TEXT

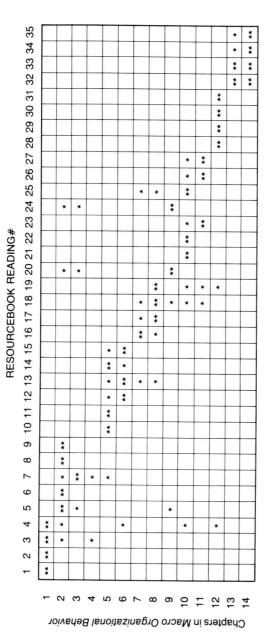

RESOURCEBOOK READING#

Chapters in Macro Organizational Behavior

KEY: ★★ - Primary cross-reference
★ - Secondary cross-reference

For cross-reference with *Macro Organizational Behavior* by Robert H. Miles (Goodyear Publishing Co., 1980).

Resourcebook in
Macro
Organizational
Behavior

An Introduction

Robert H. Miles

Organizational Behavior as an emerging applied discipline was developed for the purpose of understanding and more effectively managing the whole of *organizational* behavior. Yet, the traditional emphasis within the field has been on individuals, small groups, and their leaders, with less focus on the design and behavior of major subsystems and organizations themselves. This relative emphasis on the "micro" features of organizational behavior was no doubt influenced by the social psychological backgrounds of the founders of the discipline.

CREATION AND EVOLUTION OF THE FIELD

Virtually all of the founding figures were refugees from the older, social psychological discipline. Kurt Lewin, Elton Mayo, Rensis Likert, J. Stacy Adams, Edgar Schien, Victor Vroom, Robert Kahn, Harold Leavitt, and Daniel Katz, all psychologists by training and profession, are associated with the birth and early development of the organizational behavior field. A few left the psychology department to join applied social science institutes, but the main body of this first wave found a new home in schools of management.

Adapted from Robert H. Miles, *Macro Organizational Behavior*, Chapter 1. Goodyear Publishing Company, Santa Monica, Calif., 1980.

For a time, the new applied behavioral scientist, with an orientation toward general theory and scholarly research, coexisted in the management school with more traditional management faculty members, whose orientations were more particularistic and pragmatic. For a decade or so the two orientations rode in uneasy harness as both attempted to sort out their respective domains. Sparing details, which no doubt varied from setting to setting, three conditions now exist, at least within the management school setting: the organizational behaviorists have become applied enough to displace their management counterparts; or vice versa; or the two continue to coexist.

At the same time this contest was being waged in the management school, sociologists were developing a perspective on organizations that was much more structuralist and "macro" than the one characterizing the early stages of the field of organizational behavior. Led by the early writings of Max Weber and Talcott Parsons, sociologists began to develop models for understanding patterns of behaviors across collections of individuals and for predicting the behavior of organizations as wholes interacting with their larger contexts.

Gradually, the theoretical work of the sociologist and the pragmatism of the management theorist have become assimilated into parts of the field of organizational behavior. The result is that the field has evolved; it has become more complete in its conceptualization of organizational behavior, and it has begun to crystallize implications for practice affecting not only individuals and small groups within organizations, but the design and management of the behaviors of organizations as wholes.

This *Resourcebook in Macro Organizational Behavior* is a beginning reader for understanding, designing, and managing macro *organizational* behavior. Its purpose is not to displace or to diminish in any way the importance of understanding the micro aspects of organizational behavior, but rather to address the present imbalance in emphasis between the micro and macro features of organizational life. Moreover, instead of creating a dichotomy within the field, the theory and practice sampled in this volume is evidence of its evolution and growing maturity. (A similar division and elaboration has already evolved in older disciplines. For example, students of economics normally take an introductory course in general economics before proceeding to the more focused courses on microeconomics and macroeconomics.)

MICRO VERSUS MACRO ORGANIZATIONAL BEHAVIOR

Before proceeding with a discussion of the major components of macro organizational behavior, a few words are needed to clarify the distinction between the relative emphases of the micro and macro views. A comparative summary of the major differences between the traditional emphasis on organizational behavior and the one taken here is presented in Table 1. But it should be realized that these differences in issues, research, and applications serve to indicate relative emphases rather than a complete dichotomy.

For example, one cannot ignore the role of individual abilities and behaviors in the study of interunit conflict or politics any more than one can disregard the influence of the larger organization structure and culture on the character of interpersonal relations. But, the emphasis in macro organizational behavior is on the conflict or power of major subsystems or organizations and the contextual, as opposed to individual, factors that help explain and manage these features of organizational life.

Rather than focus on the design of individual jobs and role relations, the emphasis is placed on unit tasks and organizational technologies and their implications for the design of complex enterprise. Rather than focus on individual adjustment to social and technical influences, the emphasis is on the adjustment processes of major subsystems and whole organizations to their changing contexts.

TABLE 1   Micro vs. Macro Organizational Behavior: Issues, Research, and Applications

TRADITIONAL (MICRO) ORGANIZATIONAL BEHAVIOR	versus	MACRO ORGANIZATIONAL BEHAVIOR
Issue Emphasis		
Structures and processes (cognitive, emotional, and physical) within individuals, small groups and their leaders, and the linkages between them.		Structures and processes within major subsystems, organizations, and their environments, and the linkages between them.
Research Focus		
Study of the behaviors of individuals, small groups, and their leaders in the laboratory or in relatively isolated or immediate social settings.		Study of the behaviors of members of major subsystems, subsystems themselves, organizations, and their environments within their larger contexts.
Primary Applications		
Individual self-improvement and job design, intervention into interpersonal and group processes, training of leaders of small groups. Individual and group change.		Design and management of the structures and processes linking major subsystems, organizations, and their environments. Organizational and environmental change.

No doubt the reader will soon discover that people are not left out of macro organizational behavior. But, instead of focusing on individual behaviors *per se*, the attempt is to reveal patterns of behavior across collections of organizational members that are influenced by the larger social structures of organization and environment. Thus, the study of macro organizational behavior is much more sociological in perspective than the traditional psychological treatment of the field. Yet, again the reader will find that many of the models of individual and social psychology have worked their way into the macro end of the field, and to good purpose.

In addition, the subject matter in macro organizational behavior is more managerially oriented than the traditional psychological and sociological analyses of organizations. Throughout this *Resourcebook*, an attempt is made to bring the implications of the concepts and research findings into focus for organizational designers and practicing managers. To be sure, this is not an easy task, because the study of organizational behavior at any level of analysis is still only emerging from its infancy. But managers live in a world of ideas, and it is hoped that the *Resourcebook* will expose those who would design and manage complex organizations to the contemporary mainstream of "ideas in good currency."

Finally, the *Resourcebook in Macro Organizational Behavior* represents a mix of conceptual articles and supporting managerial situations. Because of this blending of theory and practice the book should have appeal to both future and practicing managers.

THE NATURE OF ORGANIZATIONS

It has become almost *passe* to say that large, complex organizations have become the ascendant social form in modern civilization. Not only do we spend more of our precious waking hours in organizations than we like to think, but many of us derive our personal identity from the roles we play in organizations. Our lives are touched by organizations not only during the times we work in them, but also when we are off the work premises. Many of us hold positions that require the performance of work-related behaviors off the job, and all of us have to contend with a wide assortment of organizations just to secure the basic requirements for existence. Moreover, our civilization is heavily influenced by the cultures that develop within organizations, and it is critically dependent upon both their effectiveness and the nature of relations between them.

In short, the modern complex organization has become both ubiquitous and essential. Given that it is so much a part of our lives, it is sometimes difficult for one who has focused on the study of these social and technical systems for many years to understand why (and how) the great majority of individuals attempt to go through life without pausing to carefully reflect on the nature and behavior of complex organizations. Therefore, it is hoped that the reader of this volume will experience a heightened awareness and greater sensitivity to the implications of organizational design and behavior and that he or she will put some of this appreciation into the development of these complex systems to the mutual benefit of both their members and the societies they serve.

Varieties of the Species

Organizations come in great variety. They may be distinguished on the basis of the *primary transformation processes* they employ (e.g., mass production, custom manufacture, continuous process), the basis of their *ownership* (e.g., public vs. private ownership), their *size*, the *primary recipients* of their goods and services (e.g., owners, members, etc.), the *goals* they pursue (e.g., economic, cultural, order goals), their *stage of development* (e.g., new venture vs. mature bureaucracy), the nature of the *criteria* used to assess their effectiveness (e.g., ''hard'' vs. ''soft'' performance measures), the basis of *member commitment* (e.g., remunerative, voluntary, involuntary), the nature of their *workforce* (e.g., unskilled, skilled, professional), and the nature of their *external environment* (e.g., stable vs. dynamic, simple vs. complex, receptive vs. hostile). And, all of these bases for "typing" organizations have an influence on the character of the culture and the system of design and management that prevail in an organization. We will deal with many of these influences in the chapters to follow, but what we need first is a means for describing the essential nature of all organizations—something to serve as both a definition and a point of departure.

Organization: A Definition and Point of Departure

An *organization* is defined as *a coalition of interest groups, sharing a common resource base, paying homage to a common mission, and depending upon a larger context for its legitimacy and development.* An organization is a *coalition* in the sense that the fates of the interest groups created by the division of work are substantially interdependent. These interest groups and the outcomes they derive from work are linked by the frequent circumstance that each performs only a "piece" of the product or mission of the organization as a whole and by the fact that they must share, and negotiate for portions of, a common resource base. These interest groups "pay homage" to a common mission in the sense that, while they must publicly acknowledge identification with some overall organizational mission or purpose, they frequently displace this common mission with goals more particular to their own interests. Finally, the collection of interest groups depends on a larger environment for support and legitimacy to continue operations and to grow and develop.

All of these facets of the nature of organization create certain tensions within the system—tensions that must be institutionalized and managed if the organization is to survive and prosper. The necessary division of work creates separate units that deal with different issues on behalf of the organization, develop different structures and cultures, and depend on members with different skills, orientations, and needs. This requisite variety within an enterprise creates a major tension for the organization that must be effectively managed to achieve success.

Dependence of units on a common resource base is another source of tension for organizations. Units and coalitions constantly jockey to acquire a larger share of the necessarily limited economic pie within an organization. And this process generates political as well as rational modes of organization decision making.

Subunit and coalition goals, which develop out of these differences, often serve to displace the more macro objectives of the organization as a whole. Therefore, the development and management of goals across levels is necessary to cope with this source of organizational tensions.

Finally, an organization is an open system, dependent on its environment for both legitimacy and needed resources. The indeterminateness and uncertainty created by this dependency also contribute to the tensions that must be managed from within. Organizations confronting dynamic, complex, and unreceptive environments must exert great energy in managing external relations. They may attempt to modify their goals, structures or processes to better conform to environmental demands or they may attempt to change the environment itself.

Given the nature of organization and the inevitable tensions created within it by internal and external forces, effective design and management requires the skillful application of three essential and intimately related activities: the internal *division of work,* the internal *control and coordination,* and the *management of relations with the external environment.* Therefore, the format of the *Resourcebook* is structured so that Part II deals with the broad topics of division and control of work, and their consequences for organization design and management, and Part III focuses on the design and management of organization-environment relations. Part IV concludes the volume by drawing attention to some larger contextual issues that are having an influence on these internal and external organizational dynamics.

FRAMEWORK FOR STUDYING MACRO ORGANIZATIONAL BEHAVIOR

The framework adopted in the *Resourcebook* for studying macro organizational behavior is illustrated in Figure 1. Having already presented an

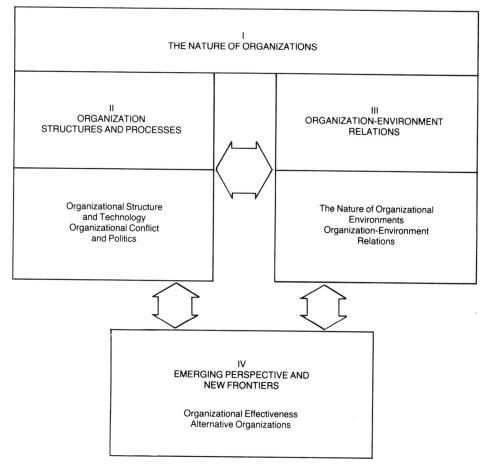

Figure 1   A Framework for Studying Macro Organizational Behavior

overview of the nature of organizations, we now need to sketch the macro organizational behavior domains sampled in the last three parts of the *Resourcebook*.

Understanding and Managing Organization Structures and Processes

Part II of the *Resourcebook* focuses on the need to understand and manage organizational structures and processes. The first section deals with the meaning and interactions of organizational structures and technologies. The second section focuses on the processes and outcomes of organizational conflicts and politics.

Organizational Structure and Technology. In general, *organizational structures* serve to both differentiate and integrate the components of complex organizations. Structures may be formal, as when management prescribes certain workflow patterns, creates subunits to perform portions of the overall mission, specifies the roles to be performed, and enforces a body of rules and standard operating procedures. Other features of structure within organizations are informal in nature. An organizational culture often emerges to sometimes complement, sometimes counter, the structures prescribed by higher managerial authority. In fact, informal social control exerted by members or coalitions of interest groups can powerfully constrain organizational behaviors. Effective organization design and management rests critically on an understanding of these organizational structures.

In addition, it is important to recognize that the effectiveness of an organization is contingent upon the degree of fit it achieves between the nature of the technology it employs and its structural design. Moreover, organizations are not internally uniform in the kinds of tasks their subunits and members perform. Therefore, different structural designs are required to coordinate and control the tasks performed by different subunits within the same organization.

The readings under "Organizational Structure and Technology" reveal the structural alternatives and technological contingencies that organization designers and managers must understand if they are to ensure the effectiveness and survival of their enterprise. The article by Galbraith treats organizations as information processing systems and discusses design options suited to different levels of information-processing demands. The next selection by Knight gives meaning to the most complex organization design, the "matrix," discusses the conditions that motivate managers to choose this form, and examines the pros and cons of its employment. The last reading by Randolph develops a typology of unit technologies and describes the mixes of structural design, human resources, and decision-making techniques that are most effective for each unit technology. Finally, the selections by Goggin and Steiglitz apply these concepts of organizational design to specific managerial situations.

Organizational Conflict and Politics. Conflicts and politics are inevitable parts of organizational life and, therefore, should be of concern to those who would design and manage complex organizations. Although the dysfunctional effects of *conflicts* on organizations and their members are well recognized, their potential benefits at both levels are not. Therefore, both the functions and dysfunctions of organizational conflict are examined in the selection by Litterer, who makes a case for the institutionalization and management of conflict rather than its repression. In addition there is a need to understand conflict as an organizational process that begins with a latent condition, moves through a period of manifest conflict, and continues in the form of conflict "aftermath." The conflict process is discussed in the article by Pondy.

Decision-making processes are treated next, with an objective of exposing both the political and rational sides of organizational choice. *Political processes* are often difficult to understand and manage. Organizational members are reluctant to discuss their political motives. Moreover, political processes are usually enacted covertly, often under the guise of objectivity and rationality. But the fact that political influences in organizational decision making are difficult to identify and measure in no way diminishes their role in organizational life. And, like conflict, organizational politics can serve both functional and dysfunctional ends.

Our purpose in the articles by Tushman and Nadler and by Kotter is to pierce the political veil by discussing the nature of organizational politics, identifying some political tactics frequently employed in organizations, and revealing those situations that encourage or dampen the emergence of political as opposed to rational decision-making behaviors. The focus is on how managers and subunits within organizations acquire, maintain, employ, and lose their ability to influence the course of organizational events.

The section on "Organizational Conflict and Politics" closes with two managerial situations. One reveals the conflicts inherent in the annual budgeting process within organizations. The other describes the politics that surround the decision at IBM to introduce a whole new line of computers.

Understanding and Managing
Organization-Environment Relations

Having surveyed some of the more important features of the internal dynamics of organizations, Part III shifts the emphasis to the design and management of relations between organizations and their external environments. We begin by focusing on the nature of the external environments of complex organizations, and then outline what kinds of relations between organizations and environments are most effective and what processes are available to managers for achieving them.

The articles by Emery and Trist and by Jurkovich discuss the nature of organizational environments and its impact on decision-maker uncertainty within organizations. Next, the selection by Lorsch outlines the relations between organizations and their environments that appear to lead to organizational effectiveness. The readings by Kotter and by Miles and associates turn toward the processes available to organizations for achieving and maintaining effective relations with the outside world.

These readings outline the *contingency* and *process* models of organization-environment relations and their implications for organization design and management.

The *contingency* perspective on organization-environment relations emphasizes the controlling and shaping influences exerted by environments on organizations. The major issue posed by the contingency perspective concerns how organizations can more closely conform their structures and processes to the nature and dictates of their confronting environment. The Lorsch article, therefore, provides some answers about the kinds of "fits" between organization design and environment that are likely to lead to organizational success or failure.

Instead of focusing on effective matches between organizations and environment, the perspective taken by Kotter and by Miles and his associates deals with the *processes* by which organizations manage relations with their environments. Thus, the contingency perspective emphasizes *what* organization-environment states tend to be relatively effective or ineffective, whereas the *process* perspective emphasizes *how* organizations go about achieving those states.

The processes of managing organization-environment relations involve organizational choices of strategy mixes. These strategic choices may be reactive or proactive. For example, organizations may attempt to change themselves in order to conform with the demands and contingencies posed by its external environment. But organizations are not wholly determined by their environments, and often they may be found actively engaged in attempts to alter the external environment in the direction of becoming more accommodative to organizational structures, processes, and objectives. These readings, therefore, examine the processes of strategic choice and provide a framework for understanding and managing organization-environment relations.

Finally, *organizations* do not transact with their environments. Instead, they design and staff a wide assortment of *boundary-spanning roles and units* to manage these activities on their behalf. The final conceptual article in this section, by Aldrich and Herker, reveals the structures and dynamics of organization units and roles that span the boundary between organization and environment and through which effective relations between the two domains are achieved.

Managerial situations in Part III focus on the attempts by managers to understand their changing environments, to develop strategies for enhancing the fit between organization and environment, and to staff and control the efforts of organization boundary-spanning units.

Emerging Perspectives and New Frontiers in Macro Organizational Behavior

Having surveyed the primary features of internal and external organizational dynamics and their implications for organizational behavior, design, and management, Part IV is an attempt to step back from contemporary organizations and their immediate environments in order to identify some major trends and events that are having an increasing effect on both organizations and their contexts.

Organizational Effectiveness. The concept of organizational effectiveness has been evolving since the emergence of complex organizations. From an early emphasis on efficiency of the primary transformation processes within organizations, the concept of effectiveness has undergone elaboration in ways that place additional pressures on organizational design and management. For example, because of the growing complexity and turbulence of contemporary environments, organizations can no longer be treated as closed systems. Indeed, concentrating exclusively on internal efficiency, as earlier schools of organization and management thought suggested, would almost surely lead to organizational demise in contemporary settings. The readings and managerial situations in this section provide an overview of the approaches to organizational assessment and some concrete settings in which to experiment with them.

Alternative Organizations. The concluding section of the *Resourcebook* surveys the major alternatives in organization design. These alternative organizations have emerged both in the United States and abroad, and the changes they have wrought in the character and outcomes of organizational life are beginning to diffuse into the mainstream of thought and practice of organization design and management.

These alternative organizations involve radically different forms of work design, decision-making processes, reward systems, and even organizational governance. Some confine organizational reform to the "shop floor," while others have literally turned the conventional organization pyramid upside down. In the latter, workers themselves own and manage their organizations. Managers are appointed or elected by the organization membership and administer the enterprise in accordance with the operations and policy decisions made by rank-and-file employees. In still other cases, management jobs are rotated among members of the workforce. In sum, these alternative organizations, and the successes they are achieving, are having a powerful influence on the field of macro organizational behavior, and hopefully these final chapters will provide some additional ideas for understanding, designing, and managing complex organizations.

SUMMARY

The *Resourcebook* should serve to introduce you to the "macro" features of organizational behavior, and the material that follows should facilitate a more balanced exposure to organizational behavior in the direction of understanding the design and management of organizations and their major subsystems.

In order to accomplish this objective, the *Resourcebook* is organized into four major parts: the first providing an overview of the nature of organizations; the second focusing on internal macro organizational dynamics; the third on external macro organizational dynamics; and the last part exposing the reader to new developments on the frontier of the field.

The Nature of Organizations

The selections in Part I focus on the nature and dynamics of complex organizations and the problems they pose for organization design and development. Perrow's account of "The Short and Glorious History of Organizational Theory" chronicles the rise, fall and persistence of the major schools of thought on the nature of organizations. Nadler and Tushman develop a framework for diagnosing organizational behavior and design. This section concludes with a case study of the creation of an innovative medical school that reveals some of the more important dynamics of organizational design and development.

The Short and Glorious History of Organizational Theory

Charles Perrow

From the beginning, the forces of light and the forces of darkness have polarized the field of organizational analysis, and the struggle has been protracted and inconclusive. The forces of darkness have been represented by the mechanical school of organizational theory—those who treat the organization as a machine. This school characterizes organizations in terms of such things as:

Centralized authority

Clear lines of authority

Specialization and expertise

Marked division of labor

Rules and regulations

Clear separation of staff and line

The forces of light, which by mid-twentieth century came to be characterized as the human relations school, emphasizes people rather than machines, accommodations rather than machine-like precision, and draws its inspiration from biological systems rather than engineering systems. It has emphasized such things as:

> Delegation of authority
>
> Employee autonomy
>
> Trust and openness
>
> Concerns with the "whole person"
>
> Interpersonal dynamics

THE RISE AND FALL OF SCIENTIFIC MANAGEMENT

The forces of darkness formulated their position first, starting in the early part of this century. They have been characterized as the scientific management or classical management school. This school started by parading simple-minded injunctions to plan ahead, keep records, write down policies, specialize, be decisive, and keep your span of control to about six people. These injunctions were needed as firms grew in size and complexity, since there were few models around beyond the railroads, the military, and the Catholic Church to guide organizations. And their injunctions worked. Executives began to delegate, reduce their span of control, keep records, and specialize. Planning ahead still is difficult, it seems, and the modern equivalent is Management by Objectives.

But many things intruded to make these simple-minded injunctions less relevant:

1. Labor became a more critical factor in the firm. As the technology increased in sophistication it took longer to train people, and more varied and specialized skills were needed. Thus, labor turnover cost more and recruitment became more selective. As a consequence, labor's power increased. Unions and strikes appeared. Management adjusted by beginning to speak of a cooperative system of capital, management, and labor. The machine model began to lose its relevancy.

2. The increasing complexity of markets, variability of products, increasing number of branch plants, and changes in technology all required more adaptive organization. The scientific management school was ill-equipped to deal with rapid change. It had presumed that once the proper structure was achieved the firm could run forever without much tampering. By the late 1930s, people began writing about adaptation and change in industry from an organizational point of view and had to abandon some of the principles of scientific management.

3. Political, social, and cultural changes meant new expectations regarding the proper way to treat people. The dark, satanic mills needed at

the least a white-washing. Child labor and the brutality of supervision in many enterprises became no longer permissible. Even managers could not be expected to accept the authoritarian patterns of leadership that prevailed in the small firm run by the founding father.

4. As mergers and growth proceeded apace and the firm could no longer be viewed as the shadow of one man (the founding entrepreneur), a search for methods of selecting good leadership became a preoccupation. A good, clear, mechanical structure would no longer suffice. Instead, firms had to search for the qualities of leadership that could fill the large footsteps of the entrepreneur. They tacitly had to admit that something other than either "sound principles" or "dynamic leadership" was needed. The search for leadership traits implied that leaders were made, not just born, that the matter was complex, and that several skills were involved.

ENTER HUMAN RELATIONS

From the beginning, individual voices were raised against the implications of the scientific management school. "Bureaucracy" had always been a dirty word, and the job design efforts of Frederick Taylor were even the subject of a congressional investigation. But no effective counterforce developed until 1938, when a business executive with academic talents named Chester Barnard proposed the first new theory of organizations: Organizations are cooperative systems, not the products of mechanical engineering. He stressed natural groups within the organization, upward communication, authority from below rather than from above, and leaders who functioned as a cohesive force. With the spectre of labor unrest and the Great Depression upon him, Barnard's emphasis on the cooperative nature of organizations was well-timed. The year following the publication of his *Functions of the Executive* (1938) saw the publication of F. J. Roethlisberger and William Dickson's *Management and the Worker*, reporting on the first large-scale empirical investigation of productivity and social relations. The research, most of it conducted in the Hawthorne plant of the Western Electric Company during a period in which the workforce was reduced, highlighted the role of informal groups, work restriction norms, the value of decent, humane leadership, and the role of psychological manipulation of employees through the counseling system. World War II intervened, but after the war the human relations movement, building on the insights of Barnard and the Hawthorne studies, came into its own.

The first step was a search for the traits of good leadership. It went on furiously at university centers but at first failed to produce more than a list of Boy Scout maxims: A good leader was kind, courteous, loyal, courageous, etc. We suspected as much. However, the studies did turn up a distinction between "consideration," or employee-centered aspects of leadership, and job-centered, technical aspects labeled "initiating structure." Both were important, but the former received most of the attention and the latter went undeveloped. The former led directly to an examination of group processes, an investigation that has culminated in T-group programs and is moving forward still with encounter groups. Meanwhile, in England, the Tavistock Institute sensed the importance of the influence of the kind of task a group had to perform on the social relations within the group. The first important study, conducted among coal miners, showed that job simplification and specialization did not work under conditions of uncertainty and nonroutine tasks.

As this work flourished and spread, more adventurous theorists began to extend it beyond work groups to organizations as a whole. We now knew that there were a number of things that were bad for the morale and loyalty of groups—routine tasks, submission to authority, specialization of task, segregation of task sequence, ignorance of the goals of the firm, centralized decision making, and so on. If these were bad for groups, they were likely to be bad for groups of groups—i.e., for organizations. So people like Warren Bennis began talking about innovative, rapidly changing organizations that were made up of temporary groups, temporary authority systems, temporary leadership and role assignments, and democratic access to the goals of the firm. If rapidly changing technologies and unstable, turbulent environments were to characterize industry, then the structure of firms should be temporary and decentralized. The forces of light, of freedom, autonomy, change, humanity, creativity, and democracy were winning. Scientific management survived only in outdated text books. If the evangelizing of some of the human relations school theorists was excessive, and if Likert's System 4 or MacGregor's Theory Y or Blake's 9×9 evaded us, at least there was a rationale for confusion, disorganization, scrambling, and stress: Systems should be temporary.

BUREAUCRACY'S COMEBACK

Meanwhile, in another part of the management forest, the mechanistic school was gathering its forces and preparing to outflank the forces of light. First came the numbers men—the linear programmers, the budget experts, and the financial analysts—with their PERT systems and cost-benefit analyses. From another world, unburdened by most of the scientific management ideology and untouched by the human relations school, they began to parcel things out and give some meaning to those truisms, "plan ahead" and "keep records." Armed with emerging systems concepts, they carried the "mechanistic" analogy to its fullest—and it was very productive. Their work still goes on, largely untroubled by organizational theory; the theory, it seems clear, will have to adjust to them, rather than the other way around.

Then the works of Max Weber, first translated from the German in the 1940s—he wrote around 1910, incredibly—began to find their way into social science thought. At first, with his celebration of the efficiency of bureaucracy, he was received with only reluctant respect, and even with hostility. All writers were against bureaucracy. But it turned out, surprisingly, that managers were not. When asked, they acknowledged that they preferred clear lines of communication, clear specifications of authority and responsibility, and clear knowledge of whom they were responsible to. They were as wont to say "there ought to be a rule about this," as to say "there are too many rules around here," as wont to say "next week we've got to get organized," as to say "there is too much red tape." Gradually, studies began to show that bureaucratic organizations could change faster than nonbureaucratic ones, and that morale could be higher where there was clear evidence of bureaucracy.

What was this thing, then? Weber had showed us, for example, that bureaucracy was the most effective way of ridding organizations of favoritism, arbitrary authority, discrimination, payola and kick-backs, and yes, even incompetence. His model stressed expertise, and the favorite or the boss' nephew or the guy who burned up resources to make his performance look good was *not* the one with expertise. Rules could be changed; they could be dropped in exceptional circumstances; job security promoted more innovation. The sins of bureaucracy began to look like the sins of failing to follow its principles.

ENTER POWER, CONFLICT, AND DECISIONS

But another discipline began to intrude upon the confident work and increasingly elaborate models of the human relations theorists (largely social psychologists) and the uneasy toying with bureaucracy of the "structionalists" (largely sociologists). Both tended to study economic organizations. A few, like Philip Selznick, were noting conflict and differences in goals (perhaps because he was studying a public agency, the Tennessee Valley Authority), but most ignored conflict or treated it as a pathological manifestation of breakdowns in communication or the ego trips of unreconstructed managers.

But in the world of political parties, pressure groups, and legislative bodies, conflict was not only rampant, but to be expected—it was even functional. This was the domain of the political scientists. They kept talking about power, making it a legitimate concern for analysis. There was an open acknowledgement of "manipulation." These were political scientists who were "behaviorally" inclined—studying and recording behavior rather than constitutions and formal systems of government—and they came to a much more complex view of organized activity. It spilled over into the area of economic organizations, with the help of some economists like R. A. Gordon and some sociologists who were studying conflicting goals of treatment and custody in prisons and mental hospitals.

The presence of legitimately conflicting goals and techniques of preserving and using power did not, of course, sit well with a cooperative systems view of organizations. But it also puzzled the bureaucratic school (and what was left of the old scientific management school), for the impressive Weberian principles were designed to settle questions of power through organizational design and to keep conflict out through reliance on rational-legal authority and systems of careers, expertise, and hierarchy. But power was being overtly contested and exercised in covert ways, and conflict was bursting out all over, and even being creative.

Gradually, in the second half of the 1950s and in the next decade, the political science view infiltrated both schools. Conflict could be healthy, even in a cooperative system, said the human relationists; it was the mode of resolution that counted, rather than prevention. Power became reconceptualized as "influence," and the distribution was less important, said Arnold Tannenbaum, than the total amount. For the bureaucratic school —never a clearly defined group of people, and largely without any clear ideology—it was easier to just absorb the new data and theories as something else to be thrown into the pot. That is to say, they floundered, writing books that went from topic to topic, without a clear view of organizations, or better yet, producing "readers" and leaving students to sort it all out.

Buried in the political science viewpoint was a sleeper that only gradually began to undermine the dominant views. This was the idea, largely found in the work of Herbert Simon and James March, that because man was so limited—in intelligence, reasoning powers, information at his disposal, time available, and means of ordering his preferences clearly—he generally seized on the first acceptable alternative when deciding, rather than looking for the best; that he rarely changed things unless they really got bad, and even then he continued to try what had worked before; that he limited his search for solutions to well-worn paths and traditional sources of information and established ideas; that he was wont to remain preoccupied with routine, thus preventing innovation. They called these characteristics "cognitive limits on rationality" and spoke of "satisficing" rather than maximizing or optimizing. It is now called the "decision making" school, and is concerned with the basic question of how people make decisions.

This view had some rather unusual implications. It suggested that if managers were so limited, then they could be easily controlled. What was necessary was not to give direct orders (on the assumption that subordinates were idiots without expertise) or to leave them to their own devices (on the assumption that they were supermen who would somehow know what was best for the organization, how to coordinate with all the other supermen, how to anticipate market changes, etc.). It was necessary to control only the *premises* of their decisions. Left to themselves, with those premises set, they could be predicted to rely on precedent, keep things stable and smooth, and respond to signals that reinforce the behavior desired of them.

To control the premises of decision making, March and Simon outline a variety of devices, all of which are familiar to you, but some of which you may not have seen before in quite this light. For example, organizations develop vocabularies, and this means that certain kinds of information are highlighted, and others are screened out—just as Eskimos (and skiers) distinguish many varieties of snow, while Londoners see only one. This is a form of attention directing. Another is the reward system. Change the bonus for salesmen and you can shift them from volume selling to steady-account selling, or to selling quality products or new products. If you want to channel good people into a different function (because, for example, sales should no longer be the critical function as the market changes, but engineering applications should), you may have to promote mediocre people in the unrewarded function in order to signal to the good people in the rewarded one that the game has changed. You cannot expect most people to make such decisions on their own because of the cognitive limits on their rationality, nor will you succeed by giving direct orders, because you yourself probably do not know whom to order where. You presume that once the signals are clear and the new sets of alternatives are manifest, they have enough ability to make the decision but you have had to change the premises for their decisions about their career lines.

It would take too long to go through the dozen or so devices, covering a range of decision areas (March and Simon are not that clear or systematic about them, themselves, so I have summarized them in my own book), but I think the message is clear.

It was becoming clear to the human relations school, and to the bureaucratic school. The human relationists had begun to speak of changing stimuli rather than changing personality. They had begun to see that the rewards that can change behavior can well be prestige, money, comfort, etc., rather than trust, openness, self-insight, and so on. The alternative to supportive relations need not be punishment, since behavior can best be changed by rewarding approved behavior rather than by punishing disapproved behavior. They were finding that although leadership may be centralized, it can function best through indirect and unobtrusive means such as changing the premises on which decisions are made, thus giving the impression that the subordinate is actually making a decision when he has only been switched to a different set of alternatives. The implications of this work were also beginning to filter into the human relations school through an emphasis on behavioral psychology (the modern version of the much maligned stimulus-response school) that was supplanting personality theory (Freudian in its roots, and drawing heavily, in the human relations school, on Maslow).

For the bureaucratic school, this new line of thought reduced the heavy weight placed upon the bony structure of bureaucracy by highlighting the muscle and flesh that make these bones move. A single chain of command, precise division of labor, and clear lines of communication are simply not enough in themselves. Control can be achieved by using alternative communication channels, depending on the situation; by increasing or decreasing the static or "noise" in the system; by creating organizational myths and organizational vocabularies that allow only selective bits of information to enter the system; and through monitoring performance through indirect means rather than direct surveillance. Weber was all right for a starter, but organizations had changed vastly, and the leaders needed many more means of control and more subtle means of manipulation than they did at the turn of the century.

THE TECHNOLOGICAL QUALIFICATION

By now the forces of darkness and forces of light had moved respectively from midnight and noon to about 4 A.M. and 8 A.M. But any convergence or resolution would have to be on yet new terms, for soon after the political science tradition had begun to infiltrate the established schools, another blow struck both of the major positions. Working quite independently of the Tavistock Group, with its emphasis on sociotechnical systems, and before the work of Burns and Stalker on mechanistic and organic firms, Joan Woodward was trying to see whether the classical scientific principles of organization made any sense in her survey of 100 firms in South Essex. She tripped and stumbled over a piece of gold in the process. She picked up the gold, labeled it "technology," and made sense out of her otherwise hopeless data. Job-shop firms, mass-production firms, and continuous-process firms all had quite different structures because the type of tasks, or the "technology," was different. Somewhat later, researchers in America were coming to very similar conclusions based on studies of hospitals, juvenile correctional institutions, and industrial firms. Bureaucracy appeared to be the best form of organization for routine operations; temporary work groups, decentralization, and emphasis on interpersonal processes appeared to work best for nonroutine operations. A raft of studies appeared and are still appearing, all trying to show how the nature of the task affects the structure of the organization.

This severely complicated things for the human relations school, since it suggested that openness and trust, while good things in themselves, did not have much impact, or perhaps were not even possible in some kinds of work situations. The prescriptions that were being handed out would have to be drastically qualified. What might work for nonroutine, high-status, interesting, and challenging jobs performed by highly educated people might not be relevant or even beneficial for the vast majority of jobs and people.

It also forced the upholders of the revised bureaucratic theory to qualify their recommendations, since research and development units should obviously be run differently from mass-production units, and the difference between both of these and highly programmed and highly sophisticated continuous-process firms was obscure in terms of bureaucratic theory. But the bureaucratic school perhaps came out on top, because the forces of evil—authority, structure, division of labor, etc.—no longer looked evil, even if they were not applicable to a minority of industrial units.

The emphasis on technology raised other questions, however. A can company might be quite routine, and a plastics division nonroutine, but there were both routine and nonroutine units within each. How should they be integrated if the prescription were followed that, say, production should be bureaucratized and R&D not? James Thompson began spelling out different forms of interdependence among units in organizations, and Paul Lawrence and Jay Lorsch looked closely at the nature of integrating mechanisms. Lawrence and Lorsch found that firms performed best when the differences between units were *maximized* (in contrast to both the human relations and the bureaucratic school), as long as the integrating mechanisms stood half-way between the two—being neither strongly bureaucratic nor nonroutine. They also noted that attempts at participative management in routine situations were counterproductive, that the environments of some kinds of organizations were far from turbulent and customers did not want innovations and changes, that cost reduction, price, and efficiency were trivial considerations in some firms, and so on. The technological insight was demolishing our comfortable truths right and left. They were also being questioned from another quarter.

ENTER GOALS, ENVIRONMENTS, AND SYSTEMS

The final seam was being mined by the sociologists while all this went on. This was the concern with organizational goals and the environment. Borrowing from the political scientists to some extent, but pushing ahead on their own, this "institutional school" came to see that goals were not fixed; conflicting goals could be pursued simultaneously, if there were enough slack resources, or sequentially (growth for the next four years, then cost-cutting and profit-taking for the next four); that goals were up for grabs in organizations, and units fought over them. Goals were, of course, not what they seemed to be, the important ones were quite unofficial; history played a big role; and assuming profit as the pre-eminent goal explained almost nothing about a firm's behavior.

They also did case studies that linked the organization to the web of influence of the environment; that showed how unique organizations were in many respects (so that, once again, there was no one best way to do things for all organizations); how organizations were embedded in their own history, making change difficult. Most striking of all, perhaps, the case studies revealed that the stated goals usually were not the real ones; the official leaders usually were not the powerful ones; claims of effectiveness and efficiency were deceptive or even untrue; the public interest was not being served; political influences were pervasive; favoritism, discrimination, and sheer corruption were commonplace. The accumulation of these studies presented quite a pill for either the forces of light or darkness to swallow, since it was hard to see how training sessions or interpersonal skills were relevant to these problems, and it was also clear that the vaunted efficiency of bureaucracy was hardly in evidence. What could they make of this wad of case studies?

We are still sorting it out. In one sense, the Weberian model is upheld because organizations are not, *by nature*, cooperative systems; top managers must exercise a great deal of effort to control them. But if organizations are tools in the hands of leaders, they may be very recalcitrant ones. Like the broom in the story of the sorcerer's apprentice, they occasionally get out of hand. If conflicting goals, bargaining, and unofficial leadership exists, where is the structure of Weberian bones and Simonian muscle? To what extent are organizations tools, and to what extent are they products of the varied interests and group strivings of their members? Does it vary by organization, in terms of some typological alchemy we have not discovered? We don't know. But at any rate, the bureaucratic model suffers again; it simply has not reckoned on the role of the environment. There are enormous sources of variations that the neat, though by now quite complex, neo-Weberian model could not account for.

The human relations model has also been badly shaken by the findings of the institutional school, for it was wont to assume that goals were given and unproblematical, and that anything that promoted harmony and efficiency for an organization also was good for society. Human relationists assumed that the problems created by organizations were largely limited to the psychological consequences of poor interpersonal relations within them, rather than their impact on the environment. Could the organization really promote the psychological health of its members when by necessity it had to define psychological health in terms of the goals of the organization itself? The neo-Weberian model at least called manipulation "manipulation" and was skeptical of claims about autonomy and self-realization.

But on one thing all the varied schools of organizational analysis now seemed to be agreed: organizations are systems—indeed, they are open systems. As the growth of the field has forced ever more variables into our consciousness, flat claims of predictive power are beginning to decrease and research has become bewilderingly complex. Even consulting groups need more than one or two tools in their kit-bag as the software multiplies.

The systems view is intuitively simple. Everything is related to everything else, though in uneven degrees of tension and reciprocity. Every unit, organization, department, or work group takes in resources, transforms them, and sends them out, and thus interacts with the larger system. The psychological, sociological, and cultural aspects of units interact. The systems view was explicit in the institutional work, since they tried to study whole organizations; it became explicit in the human relations school, because they were so concerned with the interactions of people. The political science and technology viewpoints also had to come to this realization, since they dealt with parts affecting each other (sales affecting production; technology affecting structure).

But as intuitively simple as it is, the systems view has been difficult to put into practical use. We still find ourselves ignoring the tenets of the open systems view, possibly because of the cognitive limits on our rationality. General systems theory itself has not lived up to its heady predictions; it remains rather nebulous. But at least there is a model for calling us to account and for stretching our minds, our research tools, and our troubled nostrums.

SOME CONCLUSIONS

Where does all this leave us? We might summarize the prescriptions and proscriptions for management very roughly as follows:

1. A great deal of the "variance" in a firm's behavior depends on the environment. We have become more realistic about the limited range of change that can be induced through internal efforts. The goals of organizations, including those of profit and efficiency, vary greatly among industries and vary systematically by industries. This suggests that the impact of better management by itself will be limited, since so much will depend on market forces, competition, legislation, nature of the work force, available technologies and innovations, and so on. Another source of variation is, obviously, the history of the firm and its industry and its traditions.

2. A fair amount of variation in both firms and industries is due to the type of work done in the organization—the technology. We are now fairly confident in recommending that if work is predictable and routine, the necessary arrangement for getting the work done can be highly structured, and one can use a good deal of bureaucratic theory in accomplishing this. If it is not predictable, if it is nonroutine and there is a good deal of uncertainty as to how to do a job, then one had better utilize the theories that emphasize autonomy, temporary groups, multiple lines of authority and communications, and so on. We also know that this distinction is important when organizing different parts of an organization.

We are also getting a grasp on the question of what is the most critical function in different types of organizations. For some organizations it is production; for others, marketing; for still others, development. Furthermore, firms go through phases whereby the initial development of a market or a product or manufacturing process or accounting scheme may require a non-bureaucratic structure, but once it comes on stream, the structure should change to reflect the changed character of the work.

3. In keeping with this, management should be advised that the attempt to produce change in an organization through managerial grids, sensitivity training, and even job enrichment and job enlargement is likely to be fairly ineffective for all but a few organizations. The critical reviews of research in all these fields show that there is no scientific evidence to support the claims of the proponents of these various methods; that research has told us a great deal about social psychology, but little about how to apply the highly complex findings to actual situations. The key word is *selectivity:* We have no broad-spectrum antibiotics for interpersonal relations. Of course, managers should be sensitive, decent, kind, courteous, and courageous, but we have known that for some time now, and beyond a minimal threshold level, the payoff is hard to measure. The various attempts to make work and interpersonal relations more humane and stimulating should be applauded, but we should not confuse this with solving problems of structure, or as the equivalent of decentralization or participatory democracy.

4. The burning cry in all organizations is for "good leadership," but we have learned that beyond a threshold level of adequacy it is extremely difficult to know what good leadership is. The hundreds of scientific studies of this phenomenon come to one general conclusion: Leadership is highly variable or "contingent" upon a large variety of important variables such as nature of task, size of the group, length of time the group has existed, type of personnel within the group and their relationships with each other, and amount of pressure the group is under. It does not seem likely that we'll be able to devise a way to select the best leader for a particular situation. Even if we could, that situation would probably change in a short time and thus would require a somewhat different type of leader.

Furthermore, we are beginning to realize that leadership involves more than smoothing the paths of human interaction. What has rarely been studied in this area is the wisdom or even the technical adequacy of a leader's decision. A leader does more than lead people; he also makes decisions about the allocation of resources, type of technology to be used, the nature of the market, and so on. This aspect of leadership remains very obscure, but it is obviously crucial.

5. If we cannot solve our problems through good human relations or through good leadership, what are we then left with? The literature sug-

gests that changing the structures of organizations might be the most effective and certainly the quickest and cheapest method. However, we are now sophisticated enough to know that changing the formal structure by itself is not likely to produce the desired changes. In addition, one must be aware of a large range of subtle, unobtrusive, and even covert processes and change devices that exist. If inspection procedures are not working, we are now unlikely to rush in with sensitivity training, nor would we send down authoritative communications telling people to do a better job. We are more likely to find out where the authority really lies, whether the degree of specialization is adequate, what the rules and regulations are, and so on, but even this very likely will not be enough.

According to the neo-Weberian bureaucratic model, as it has been influenced by work on decision making and behavioral psychology, we should find out how to manipulate the reward structure, change the premises of the decision-makers through finer controls on the information received and the expectations generated, search for interdepartmental conflicts that prevent better inspection procedures from being followed, and after manipulating these variables, sit back and wait for two or three months for them to take hold. This is complicated and hardly as dramatic as many of the solutions currently being peddled, but I think the weight of organizational theory is in its favor.

We have probably learned more, over several decades of research and theory, about the things that do *not* work (even though some of them obviously *should* have worked), than we have about things that do work. On balance, this is an important gain and should not discourage us. As you know, organizations are extremely complicated. To have as much knowledge as we do have in a fledgling discipline that has had to borrow from the diverse tools and concepts of psychology, sociology, economics, engineering, biology, history, and even anthropology is not really so bad.

SELECTED BIBLIOGRAPHY

This paper is an adaptation of the discussion to be found in Charles Perrow, *Complex Organizations: A Critical Essay*, Scott, Foresman & Co., Glenville, Illinois, 1972. All the points made in this paper are discussed thoroughly in that volume.

The best overview and discussion of classical management theory, and its changes over time is by Joseph Massie—"Management Theory" in the *Handbook of Organizations* edited by James March, Rand McNally & Co., Chicago, 1965, pp. 387–422.

The best discussion of the changing justifications for managerial rule and worker obedience as they are related to changes in technology, etc., can be found in Reinhard Bendix's *Work and Authority in Industry*, John Wiley & Sons, Inc., New York, 1956. See especially the chapter on the American experience.

Some of the leading lights of the classical view—F. W. Taylor, Col. Urwick, and Henry Fayol—are briefly discussed in *Writers on Organizations* by D. S. Pugh, D. J. Hickson and C. R. Hinings, Penguin, 1971. This brief, readable, and useful book also contains selections from many other schools that I discuss, including Weber, Woodward, Cyert and March, Simon, the Hawthorne Investigations, and the Human Relations Movement as represented by Argyris, Herzberg, Likert, McGregor, and Blake and Mouton.

As good a place as any to start examining the human relations tradition is Rensis Likert, *The Human Organization*, McGraw-Hill, New York, 1967. See also his *New Patterns of Management*, McGraw-Hill Book Company, New York, 1961.

The Buck Rogers school of organizational theory is best represented by Warren Bennis. See his *Changing Organizations*, McGraw-Hill Book Company, New York, 1966, and his book with Philip Slater, *The Temporary Society*, Harper & Row, Inc., New York, 1968. Much of this work is linked into more general studies, e.g., Alvin Toffler's very popular paperback *Future Shock*, Random House, 1970, and Bantam Paperbacks, or Zibigniew Brzezinsky's *Between Two Ages: America's Role in the Technitronic Era*, The Viking Press, New York, 1970. One of the first intimations of the new type of environment and firm and still perhaps the most perceptive is to be found in the volume by Tom Burns and G. Stalker, *The Management of Innovation*, Tavistock, London, 1961, where they distinguished between "organic" and "mechanistic" systems. The introduction, which is not very long, is an excellent and very tight summary of the book.

The political science tradition came in through three important works. First, Herbert Simon's *Administrative Behavior*, The MacMillan Co., New York, 1948, followed by the second half of James March and Herbert Simon's *Organizations*, John Wiley & Sons, Inc., New York, 1958, then Richard M. Cyert and James March's *A Behavioral Theory of the Firm*, Prentice-Hall, Inc. Englewood Cliffs, N.J., 1963. All three of these books are fairly rough going, though chapters 1, 2, 3, and 6 of the last volume are fairly short and accessible. A quite interesting book in this tradition, though somewhat heavy-going, is Michael Crozier's *The Bureaucratic Phenomenon*, University of Chicago, and Tavistock Publications, 1964. This is a striking description of power in organizations, though there is a somewhat dubious attempt to link organization processes in France to the cultural traits of the French people.

The book by Joan Woodward *Industrial Organisation: Theory and Practice*, Oxford University Press, London, 1965, is still very much worth reading. A fairly popular attempt to discuss the implications for this for management can be found in my own book, *Organizational Analysis: A Sociological View*, Tavistock, 1970, Chapters 2 and 3. The impact of technology on structure is still fairly controversial. A number of technical studies have found both support and nonsupport, largely because the concept is defined so differently, but there is general agreement that different structures and leadership techniques are needed for different situations. For studies that support and document this viewpoint see James Thompson, *Organizations in Action*, McGraw-Hill Book Company, New York, 1967 and Paul Lawrence and Jay Lorsch, *Organizations and Environment*, Harvard University Press, Cambridge, Mass., 1967.

The best single work on the relation between the organization and the environment and one of the most readable books in the field is Philip Selznick's short volume *Leadership in Administration*, Row, Peterson, Evanston, Illinois, 1957. But the large number of these studies are scattered about. I have summarized several in my *Complex Organizations: A Critical Essay.*

Lastly, the most elaborate and persuasive argument for a systems view of organizations is found in the first 100 pages of the book by Daniel Katz and Robert Kahn, *The Social Psychology of Organizations,* John Wiley and Co., 1966. It is not easy reading, however.

A Congruence Model for Diagnosing Organizational Behavior

David A. Nadler
Michael L. Tushman

Managers perform their jobs within complex social systems called organizations. In many senses, the task of the manager is to influence behavior in a desired direction, usually towards the accomplishment of a specific task or performance goal. Given this definition of the managerial role, skills in the diagnosis of patterns of organizational behavior become vital. Specifically, the manager needs to be able to *understand* the patterns of behavior that are observed, to *predict* in what direction behavior will move (particularly in the light of managerial action), and to use this knowledge to *control* behavior over the course of time.

Managers attempt to predict and control behavior in organizations every day. The problem, however, is that the understanding-prediction-control sequence frequently is based solely on the intuition of the individual manager. This intuitive approach builds on implicit models of behavior or organization which the manager carries around in his or her head—models that are often naive and simplistic. If managers are to be more effective, they must examine their implicit models and test them against other models. Given this perspective, the goal of this paper is to

Adapted from "A Diagnostic Model for Organizational Behavior," by D. A. Nadler and M. L. Tushman, in J. R. Hackman, E. E. Lawler, and L. W. Porter (eds.), *Perspectives on Behavior in Organizations.* New York: McGraw-Hill, 1977, pp. 83–100. Reprinted by permission.

present a model of organizations, based on behavioral science research, that is both systematic and useful.

Effective managerial action requires that the manager be able to diagnose the system he or she is working in. Since all elements of social behavior cannot be dealt with at once, the manager facing this "blooming-buzzing" confusion must simplify reality—that is, develop a road map or model of organizational functioning. The model presented here reflects one way of simplifying social reality that still retains the dynamic nature of organizations. The model will focus on a set of key organizational components (or variables) and their relationships as the primary determinants of behavior. The examination of these key components will provide a concise snapshot of the organization and how it functions. The model does not consider all the complexity of organizational behavior. To be useful in real settings, it must be supplemented with clinical data and managerial insight.

A model can also serve as a vehicle to organize a substantial portion of research on and knowledge about organizational behavior. An increased awareness of the research results concerning the relationships between the key components should help the manager make the link between diagnosing the situation and making decisions for future action. The model, then, can not only help the manager diagnose and describe organizational behavior, but it should be able to provide an effective way to organize and discuss behavioral science research results that may be of use in practice.

While the model that will be discussed is a potentially valuable managerial tool, it must be seen as a developing tool. It represents one view of how total patterns of organizational behavior might be analyzed. As research in the field advances, so too should the development of this model. Finally, no claim is made that this particular diagnostic model is the most effective way of organizing reality. It is but one attempt to develop a useful "walking stick" to aid in analysis and action.

The basic premise of this paper therefore is that effective management requires that the manager be able to systematically diagnose, predict, and control behavior. Our goal is to present a research based (as opposed to intuitive) model of organizational behavior which can be used to diagnose organizations as well as to integrate different perspectives on organizational behavior. The model is intended to be of use to practitioners in organizations as well as to students in the classroom.

BASIC ASSUMPTIONS OF THE MODEL

The perspective on organizations which will be developed here is based on a number of assumptions about organizational life. These assumptions are as follows:

1. Organizations Are Dynamic Entities. Organizations exist over time and space, and the activities which make up organizations are dynamic. There are many definitions of organizations like Schein's (1970) statement that

> An organization is the rational coordination of the activities of a number of people for the achievement of some common explicit purpose or goal, through division of labor and function, and through a hierarchy of authority and responsibility.

While definitions like this are adequate to define what an organization is, they are static in nature and do not enable one to grasp how the different components of organization interact with each other over time. An adequate model of organizations must reflect the dynamic nature of organizational behavior.

2. Organizational Behavior Exists at Multiple Levels. There are different levels of abstraction at which organizational behavior can be examined. Specifically, behavior occurs at the *individual,* the *group,* and the *organizational systems* levels. Behavior that is attributable to each of these levels can be identified and isolated (that is, one can see the behavior of individuals as different from the behavior of groups or of organizations themselves). At the same time, these three levels interact with each other, organizational level behavior being affected by the behavior of individuals, group level behavior being affected by the organizational level phenomena, etc.

3. Organizational Behavior Does Not Occur in a Vacuum. Organizations are made up of both social and technical components and thus have been characterized as socio-technical systems (Emery & Trist, 1960). The implication of this is that any approach to looking at behavior must also take into account the technical components of the organization—such issues as the nature of the task and the technology. Since the organization is dependent on inputs, knowledge, and feedback from the environment, our model must also take into account the constraints of the organization's task environment (e.g., to what extent is the market changing).

4. Organizations Have the Characteristics of Open Social Systems. Organizations have the characteristics of systems which are composed of interrelated components and conduct transactions with a larger environment (Aldrich & Pfeffer, 1976). Systems have a number of unique behavioral characteristics and thus, a model of organizational behavior must take into account the systemic nature of organizations.

OPEN SYSTEMS THEORY

The point made above about open systems theory is a crucial one, which needs to be explored in more depth. The basic premise is the characteristics of systems which are seen in both the physical and social sciences (Von Bertalanffy, 1962; Buckley, 1967) are particularly valuable when looking at organizations. Social organizations, it is claimed, can be viewed as systems (Katz & Kahn, 1966, 1978) with a number of key systems characteristics.

What is a system, and what are systems characteristics? In the simplest of terms, a system is a "set of interrelated elements." These elements are interdependent such that changes in the nature of one component may lead to changes in the nature of the other components. Further, because the system is embedded within larger systems, it is dependent on the larger environment for resources, information, and feedback. Another way of looking at a system is to define it as a mechanism that imports some form of energic input from the environment, which submits that input to some kind of transformation process, and which produces some kind of energic output back to the environment (Katz & Kahn, 1966). The notion of open systems also implies the existence of some boundary differentiating the system from the larger environment in which it is embedded. These system boundaries are usually not rigid. This familiar view of a system can be seen in Figure 1. Closed systems, on the other hand, are not dependent on the environment and are more deterministic in nature. Closed systems tend to have more rigid boundaries and all of its transactions take place within the system, guided by unitary goals and rationality. (An example approaching a closed system would be a terrarium, completely self-contained and insulated from the larger environment.)

A more extensive definition of open systems has been presented by Katz & Kahn (1966) in the form of a listing of characteristics of open social systems. An adapted list of these characteristics is as follows:

1. *Importation of energy*—a system functions by importing energy (information, products, materials, etc.) from the larger environment.

2. *Throughput*—systems move energy through them, largely in the form of transformation processes. These are often multiple processes (i.e., decisions, material manipulation, etc.)

3. *Output*—systems send energy back to the larger environment in the form of products, services, and other kinds of outcomes which may be intended or not.

4. *Cycles of events over time*—systems function over time and thus are dynamic in nature. Events tend to occur in natural repetitive cycles of input, throughput, and output with events in sequence occurring over and over again.

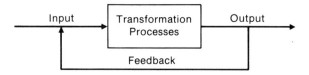

Figure 1   The Elementary Systems Model

5. *Equilibrium seeking*—systems tend to move towards the state where all components are in equilibrium, where a steady state exists. When changes are made which result in an imbalance, different components of the system move to restore the balance.

6. *Feedback*—systems use information about their output to regulate their input and transformation processes. These informational connections also exist between system components and thus changes in the functioning of one component will lead to changes in other system components (second order effects).

7. *Increasing differentiation*—as systems grow, they also tend to increase their differentiation; more components are added, more feedback loops, more transformation processes. Thus, as systems get larger, they also get more complex.

8. *Equifinality*—different system configurations may lead to the same end point, or conversely, the same end state may be reached by a variety of different processes.

9. *System survival requirements*—because of the inherent tendency of systems to "run down" or dissipate their energy, certain functions must be performed (at least at minimal levels) over time. These requirements include: (a) goal achievement, (b) adaptation (the ability to maintain balanced successful transactions with the environment).

A SPECIFIC SYSTEMS MODEL

Open systems theory is a general framework for conceptualizing organizational behavior over time. It sensitizes the manager to a basic model of organizations (i.e., input-throughput-output-feedback) as well as to a set of basic organizational processes (e.g., equilibrium, differentiation, equifinality). While systems concepts are useful as an overall perspective, they do not necessarily help the manager systematically diagnose specific situations or help him or her apply research results to specific problems. A more concrete model must be developed that takes into account system theory concepts and processes and helps the manager deal with organizational reality.

According to Figure 1, organizations (or some other unit of interest, e.g., a department or factory) take some set of inputs, work on these inputs through some sort of transformation process, and product output which is evaluated and responded to by the environment. While managers must attend to the environment and input considerations, a major focus of the managerial job is on what the organization does to produce output. That is, managers are intimately involved in what systems theory terms the *transformation processes*. It is the transformation processes, then, that the model will emphasize. Given the cycle of processes from input to feedback, the model will propose a more specific set of variables and processes that affect how the organization takes a given set of inputs and produces a set of organizational outputs (e.g., productivity, innovation, satisfaction). While the model focuses on the determinants of the transformation processes and their relationships to outputs, it must be remembered that these processes are part of a more general model of organizational behavior that takes inputs, outputs, and the environment into account (see Figure 1).

The model emphasizes the critical system characteristic of interdependence. Organizations are made up of components or parts which interact with each other. These components exist in states of relative balance, consistency, or "fit" with each other. The different parts of the organization can fit well together and thus function effectively, or fit poorly, thus leading to problems, dysfunctions, or performance below potential. Given the central nature of fit in the model, we will talk about it as a *congruence model* of organizational behavior, since effectiveness is a function of the congruence of the various components.

This concept of congruence between organizational components is not a new one. Leavitt (1965) for example identifies four major components of organization as being people, tasks, technology, and structure. The congruence model presented here builds on this view and also draws from fit models developed and used by Seiler (1967), Lawrence & Lorsch (1969), and Lorsch & Sheldon (1972).

What we are concerned about is modeling the *behavioral* system of the organization—the system of elements that ultimately produce patterns of behavior. In its simplest form, what inputs does the system have to work with, what are the major components of the system and the nature of their interactions, and finally what is the nature of the system output.

The congruence model is based on the systems assumptions outlined above. The inputs to the system (see Figure 2) are those factors that at any time are relatively fixed or given. Four major classes of inputs can be identified, including 1) the environment of the system, 2) the resources available to the system, 3) the history of the system, and 4) the organizational strategies that are developed over time.

The transformation process of the system is seen as the interaction between four major components on the organizational system. These com-

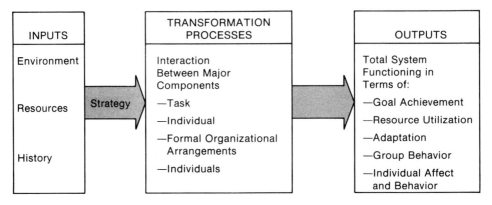

Figure 2   The Systems Model as Applied to Organizational Behavior

ponents are (1) the tasks of the organization, (2) the individuals in the organizational system, (3) the organizational arrangements, and (4) the informal organization.

The outputs are the results of the interactions among the components, given the inputs. Several major outputs can be identified including the effectiveness of total system functioning, individual affect and behavior, and group behavior. Looking at the total system, particular attention is paid to the system's ability to attain its goals, to utilize available resources, and to successfully adapt over time. Included in the model are feedback loops running from the outputs and the transformation process. The loops represent information flow about the nature of the system output and the interaction of system components. The information is available for use to make modifications in the nature of systems inputs or transformation processes.

THE NATURE OF INPUTS

Inputs are important since at any point in time they are the fixed or given factors which define the limits of organizational behavior. The inputs provide both constraints and opportunities for managerial action. The major classes of inputs which constrain organizational behavior are as follows:

A. Environmental Inputs.   Organizations as open systems carry on constant transactions with the environment. This includes the functioning of product, service, and capital markets, the behavior of competitors and suppliers, governmental regulation, and the effect of the larger culture. Second, the organization may be embedded within another larger formal system. For example, a factory which is being considered may be part of a larger multinational corporation or of a larger corporate division. These larger "supra-systems" form an important part of the environment of the organization. Third, both the internal and external environment can be described according to a number of dimensions which appear to impact the functioning of organizations (Emery & Trist, 1965). Specifically, the issues of stability and homogeneity of the environment are important.

B. Resources. Another input is composed of the resources which are available to the organization. Any organization has a range of resources available as inputs. Major categories for classifying resources would include capital resources (including liquid capital, physical plant, property, etc.), raw materials (the material on which the organization will perform the transformation process), technologies (approaches or procedures for performing the transformation), people, and various intangible resources.

C. History. At any point in time, the patterns of organizational behavior that we observe are to some degree products of the past. Thus an important input is the history of the organization. Key decisions, previous patterns of behavior, major crises, etc.—all are potential sources of influence on the present.

D. Strategy. Over time, organizations develop ways of utilizing their resources that deal effectively with the constraints, demands, and opportunities of the environment. They develop plans of action which centrally define what the organization will attempt to do in relation to the larger systems in which it is embedded. These plans of action are called strategies.

While all four inputs are important, strategy, however, has a very critical primary effect upon the nature of one of the components, and therefore it ultimately affects all of the components and their interactions.

As has been said, an organization as an open system functions within a larger environment. That environment provides opportunities for action, it provides constraints on activities, and it makes demands upon the organization's capacities. The organization faces the environment with a given set of resources of various kinds, human, technological, managerial, etc. The process of determining how these resources can best be used to function within the environment is generally called strategy determination (see Hofer & Schendel, 1978, or Andrews, 1971). The organization identifies opportunities in the environment where its distinctive competence of unique set of resources will provide it with a competitive advantage.

Some organizations develop strategies through formalized and complex processes of long range strategic planning, while other organizations may give little or no thought to strategy at all. Further, the process of strategy formulation can itself be seen as the output of intra-organizational processes (e.g., Bower, 1970; Mintzberg, 1973). The point is, however, that organizations have strategies, whether they be implicit or explicit, formal or informal. The point for organizational behavior is that the strategy of an organization is probably the single most important input (or constraint set) to the behavioral system. The strategy and the elements of that strategy (goals or plans) essentially define the *task* of the organization, one of the major components of the behavioral system (see Figure 3). From the managerial perspective, much of organizational behavior is concerned with implementation of strategies through the performance of tasks. Individuals, formal organizational arrangements, and informal organizational arrangements are all important because of their relationship to the tasks that need to be performed.

The above listed inputs therefore provide opportunities, provide constraints, and may even make demands upon the organization. Given these inputs, the issue of how the organization functions to make use of the opportunities and constraints provided by the inputs is perhaps the most central issue of managerial and organizational behavior.

THE NATURE OF ORGANIZATIONAL COMPONENTS

Assuming a set of inputs, the transformation process occurs through the interaction of a number of basic components of organization. The major components (listed with their sub-dimensions in Table 1) are as follows:

A. Task Component. This component concerns the nature of the tasks or jobs which must be performed by the organization, by groups, and by individuals. Major dimensions of tasks include the extent and nature of interdependence between task performers, the level of required skill, and

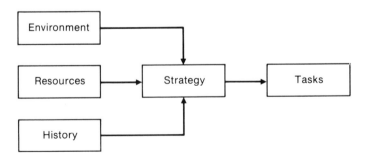

Figure 3   The Role of Strategy as the Primary Input to the Model

TABLE 1   Basic Characteristics of Behavioral System Components

TASK	INDIVIDUALS	ORGANIZATIONAL ARRANGEMENTS	INFORMAL ORGANIZATION
	Response Capabilities		
Complexity Predictability Required interdependence Skill demands	Intelligence Skills and abilities Experience Training	Organization design Work design Measurement and reward systems Methods and procedures Work resources Physical working conditions	Small group function Intergroup relations Communication patterns Emergent leadership and power Informal methods and procedures
	Psychological Differences		
	Needs strength Attitudes Expectations Background differences		

the types of information needed to adequately perform the task. It is important to note that the task is the work to be done and its *inherent* characteristics.

B. Individuals Component. This component obviously refers to the individuals who are members of the organization. The major dimensions of this component relate to the systematic differences in individuals which have relevance for organizational behavior. Such dimensions include background or demographic variables such as skill levels, levels of education, etc. and individual differences in need strength, personality, or perceptual biases.

C. Organizational Arrangements. This includes all of the formal mechanisms used by the organization to direct structure, or control behavior. Major elements include organization design (how units are composed and linked together), work design, measurement and reward systems, etc. They represent the formal and explicit decisions about how to organize to get the work done.

D. Informal Organization. In addition to the formal prescribed structure which exists in the system, there also is an informal social structure which tends to emerge over time. Relevant dimensions of the informal organization include the functioning of informal group structures, the quality of intergroup relations, and the operation of various political processes throughout the organization.

Organizations therefore can be looked at as a set of components including the task, the individuals, the organizational arrangements, and the informal organization. (For the complete model, see Figure 4.) To be useful, however, the model must go beyond the simple listing and description of these components and must describe the dynamic relationship that exists among the various components.

THE CONCEPT OF FIT

Between each pair of inputs there exists a degree of congruence, or "fit." Specifically, the congruence between two components is defined as follows:

The degree to which the needs, demands, goals, objectives, and/or structures of one component are consistent with the needs, demands, goals, objectives, and/or structures of another component.

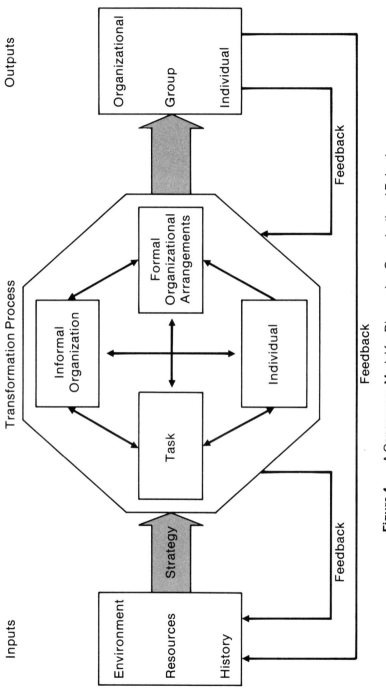

Figure 4   A Congruence Model for Diagnosing Organizational Behavior

Thus, fit (indicated by the double-headed arrows in the model in Figure 4) is a measure of the congruence between pairs of components. Because components cover a range of different types of phenomena, however, fit can be more clearly defined only by referring to specific fits between specific pairs of components. In each case, research results can be used as a guide to evaluate whether the components are in a state of high consistency or high inconsistency. An awareness of these fits is critical since inconsistent fits will be related to dysfunctional behavior.

Specific definitions of congruence are presented in Table 2. For each of the six fits among the components, more information is provided about the specific issues which need to be examined in order to determine the level of consistency between the components.

THE CONGRUENCE HYPOTHESIS

Just as each pair of components has a degree of high or low congruence, so does the aggregate model display a relatively high or low total system congruence. Underlying the model is a basic hypothesis about the nature of fits and their relationship to behavior. This hypothesis is as follows:

> Other things being equal, the greater the total degree of congruence or fit between the various components, the more effective will be organizational behavior at multiple levels. Effective organizational behavior is defined as behavior which leads to higher levels of goal attainment, utilization of resources, and adaptation.

The implications of the congruence hypothesis in this model are that the manager needs to adequately diagnose the system, determine the location and nature of inconsistent fits, and plan courses of action to change the nature of those fits without bringing about dysfunctional second order effects. The model also implies that different configurations of the key components can lead to effective behavior (consistent with the systems characteristic of equifinality). Therefore, the question is not finding the "one best way" of managing, but of determining effective combinations of inputs that will lead to congruent fits.

This process of diagnosing fit and identifying combinations of inputs to produce congruence is not necessarily an intuitive process. A number of situations which lead to consistent fits have been defined in the research literature. Thus, in many cases fit is something that can be defined, measured, and quantified in many organizational systems. The basic point is that goodness of fit is based upon theory and research rather than intuition. In most cases, the theory provides considerable guidance about what

TABLE 2 Definitions of Fits

FIT	THE ISSUES
Individual-organization	To what extent individual needs are met by the organizational arrangements. To what extent individuals hold clear or distorted perceptions of organizational structures. The convergence of individual and organizational goals.
Individual-task	To what extent the needs of individuals are met by the tasks, to what extent individuals have skills and abilities to meet task demands.
Individual-informal organization	To what extent individual needs are met by the informal organization, to what extent does the informal organization make use of individual resources, consistent with informal goals.
Task-organization	Whether the organizational arrangements are adequate to meet the demands of the task, whether organizational arrangements tend to motivate behavior consistent with task demands.
Task-informal organization	Whether the informal organization structure facilitates task performance or not, whether it hinders or promotes meeting the demands of the task.
Organization-informal organization	Whether the goals, rewards, and structures of the informal organization are consistent with those of the formal organization.

leads to congruent relationships (although in some areas the research is more definitive and helpful than others). The implication is that the manager who is attempting to diagnose behavior needs to become familiar with critical findings of the relevant research so that he or she can evaluate the nature of fits in a particular system.

The congruence model is thus a general organizing framework. The organizational analyst needs other more specific "submodels" to define high and low congruence. Example of such submodels that might be used are (1) Job characteristics theory (Hackman & Oldham, 1979) to explain the fit between individuals and tasks and individuals and formal organizational arrangements, (2) Expectancy theory (Vroom, 1964; Lawler, 1973) to explain the fit between individuals and the other three components, or (3) Information processing theory (Galbraith, 1977; Tushman & Nadler, 1978) to explain the task-formal organization and task-informal organization fit.

THE NATURE OF OUTPUTS

The model indicates that the outputs flow out of the interaction of the various components. Any organizational system produces a number of different outputs. For general diagnostic purposes, however, four major classes of outputs are particularly important:

A. System Functioning. At the highest level of abstraction is the question of how well the system as a whole is functioning. The key issues here include (1) how well is the system attaining its desired goals of production, output, return on investment, etc., (2) how well is the organization utilizing available resources, and (3) how well is the organization adapting (i.e., maintaining favorable transactions with the environment over time).

B. Group and Intergroup Behavior. Beyond the behavior of individuals, the organization is also concerned with the performance of groups or departments. Important considerations would include intergroup conflict or collaboration and the quality of intergroup communication.

C. Individual Behavior and Affect. A crucial issue is how individuals behave, specifically with regard to their organizational membership behavior (for example, absenteeism, lateness, turnover) and with regard to performance of designated tasks. Individuals also have affective responses to the work environment (levels of satisfaction, for example) which also are of consequence. Other individual behavior such as nonproductive behavior, drug usage, off-the-job activities, etc., are also outputs of the organization in many cases.

USING THE CONGRUENCE MODEL

Given the congruence model, the final question to be addressed here is how the model can be put to use. A number of authors have observed that the conditions facing organizations are always changing and that managers must therefore continually engage in problem identification and problem solving activities (Schein, 1970). These authors suggest that managers must gather data on the performance of their organization, compare the desired performance levels, identify causes of problems, develop and choose action plans, and then implement and evaluate these action plans. These phases can be viewed as a *problem solving process*. For long term organizational viability, this problem solving process must be continually in operation (Schein, 1970; Weick, 1969). The basic phases of this problem solving process are outlined in Figure 5.

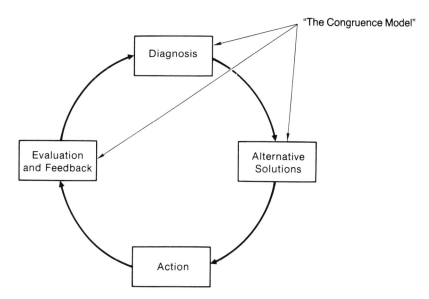

Figure 5   Basic Phases of Using the Congruence Model

How does the congruence model relate to this problem solving process? The problem solving process requires diagnosis, the generation of action plans, and the evaluation of the action plans. *Each of these steps requires a way of looking at organizations, a "theory base", to guide the analysis.* The congruence model can therefore be used as one framework to guide the diagnosis, the evaluation of alternative actions, and the evaluation and feedback of the results of a managerial action. Further, to the extent that the manager is familiar with the submodels bearing on the different fits in the general congruence model, then he or she will be better able to both diagnose the situation as well as evaluate alternative action plans. In short, a systematic problem solving process along with the informed application of the diagnostic model can be used as an effective managerial tool.

Given the problem solving process and the congruence model, it is possible to identify and describe a number of discrete steps in the problem solving cycle. These steps can be organized into three phases: (A) Diagnosis; (B) Alternative Solutions-Action; and (C) Evaluation-Feedback. The basic phases and their component steps will be outlined here.

A. The Diagnostic Phase.   This phase is premised on the idea that any managerial action must be preceded by a systematic diagnosis of the system under investigation. This phase can be broken into three distinct steps:

1. *Identify the system:* Before any detailed analyses can begin it is important to identify the system being considered. The unit of analysis must be clearly specified (i.e., project, division, organization). The boundaries of the focal unit, its membership, and what other units constitute the larger system should be considered.

2. *Determine the nature of the key variables:* Having defined the system, the next step is to use the available data to determine the nature of the inputs and the four key components. The diagnosis should focus not on an exhaustive description of each component, but rather should focus on the dimensions which the analyst considers most important in the particular situation. The question could be phrased: "In this situation, what are the most salient characteristics of the key components that are affecting the observed behavior?" The analysis should also focus on outputs, identifying desired outputs, actual outputs, and the discrepancy (if any) between them.

3. *Diagnose the state of fits:* This step is the most critical in the diagnosis phase. It really involves two related states, (a) diagnosing fits between the components, and (b) considering the link between the fits and system output.

   a. Using the experience, observations and relevant research knowledge, the manager must evaluate each of the fit lines in the congruence model. The analyst must focus on the extent to which the key components are congruent (or fit) with each other. For instance, to what extent do the organizational arrangements fit with the demands of the task?

   b. Identifying critical systems problems. Fits (or lack of fits) between the key components have consequences for individuals' behaviors. That is, given the diagnoses of the various fits, the analyst must then relate the fits to behaviors observed as outputs of the system (e.g., conflict, performance, stress, satisfaction). Based on the diagnosis of fits and their behavioral consequences, the final diagnostic step is to relate the set of behaviors to system outputs (goal achievement, resource utilization, adaptation of output discrepancies). Given these data, the manager must then evaluate which system fits require managerial attention and action.

The diagnostic phase forces the analyst to make a set of decisions. The analyst must decide the unit of analysis, make decisions as to the most salient characteristics of each of the key variables, make decisions as to the relationships between the key components and their effects on behavior, and finally, the manager must relate the system outputs to what has been observed in the transformation process and decide on the system's most pressing problems. None of the above decisions are completely clear cut —each involves some degree of judgment.

B. Alternative Solutions—Action Plan Phase. Diagnosis leads to a consideration of potential managerial actions. This evaluation-action phase can be separated into three stages.

4. *Generate alternative solutions:* Having identified critical problems and the relationship between fits and behavior, the next step is to generate a range of possible managerial actions. These actions or interventions will be directed at the inconsistent fits which will in turn affect the behaviors under consideration.

5. *Evaluating alternative strategies:* While there usually is not one single most appropriate managerial action to deal with a particular situation, the various alternatives can be evaluated for their relative merits. To what extent do the solutions deal with the inconsistent fits? Does one solution deal with the inconsistent fits more comprehensively? Are there dysfunctional second order (i.e., latent) consequences of the action—for instance, will changing the task dimensions deal with an inconsistent task-informal organization fit but adversely affect the task-individual fit? In short, given the highly interdependent nature of open systems, the manager must make predictions about the possible effects of different strategies. The manager should therefore focus on the extent to which the intervention deals with the critical system problem *as well as* deal with the possibilities of latent consequences of the intervention. This exercise of prediction should provide a way of evaluating the relative strengths and weaknesses of the alternative actions.

6. *Choice of strategies to be implemented:* Given the explicit evaluation of the different approaches, the final step in this phase is to weigh the various advantages and disadvantages of the alternative actions and choose an action plan to be implemented.

C. Evaluation and Feedback Phase. The diagnosis and alternative solution-action phases leave the manager with an action plan to deal with the critical system problem(s). The final phase in using the congruence model deals with the implementation of the action plan and with the importance of evaluation, feedback, and adjustment of strategy to meet emergent system requirements.

7. *Implementation of strategies:* This step deals explicitly with issues that arise in introducing change into an ongoing system. This step recognizes the need to deal with the response of organizations to change.

To what extent will the intervention be accepted and worked on as opposed to resisted and sabotaged? There is an extensive literature dealing with the implementation of change programs (e.g., Walton, 1974; Rogers and Shoemaker, 1971; French and Bell, 1973). While these considerations cannot be dealt with here, it is important to highlight the potential problems of translating plans and strategies into effective action.

8. *Evaluation and feedback:* After implementing a strategy it is important to continue the diagnostic activity and to explicitly evaluate the actual vs. the ideal (or predicted) impact of the intervention on the system. Feedback concerning the organization's or the environment's response to the action can then be used to adjust the intervention to better fit the system's requirements and/or deal with any unanticipated consequences of the change. In a sense then, step eight closes the loop and starts the diagnosis-alternatives-action-evaluation cycle again (see Figure 5).

The congruence model and the problem solving cycle are ways of structuring and dealing with the complex reality of organizations. Given the indeterminate nature of social systems, there is no one best way of handling a particular situation. The model and problem solving cycle do, however, force the manager to make a number of decisions and to think about the consequences of those decisions. If the congruence model and problem solving process have merit, then it is up to the manager to use these tools along with his or her experiences to make the appropriate set of diagnostic, evaluative and action decisions over time.

SUMMARY

This paper has attempted to briefly outline a model for diagnosing organizational behavior. The model is based on the assumption that organizations are open social systems and that an interaction of inputs leads to behavior and various outputs. The model presented is one based on the theory and research literature in organizational behavior and thus assumes that the manager using the model has some familiarity with the concepts coming out of this literature. Together with a process for its use, the model provides managers with a potentially valuable tool in the creation of more effective organizations.

REFERENCES

ALDRICH, H. E. and PFEFFER, J. Environments of organizations. *Annual Review of Sociology,* 1976, 2, 79–105.

ANDREWS, K. R. *The concept of corporate strategy.* Homewood, Ill.: Dow Jones-Irwin, 1971.

BOWER, J. L. *Managing the resource allocation process.* Cambridge, Mass.: Harvard University Graduate School of Business Administration, Division of Research, 1970.

BUCKLEY, W. *Sociology and modern systems theory.* Englewood Cliffs: Prentice-Hall, 1967.

EMERY, F. E. and TRIST, E. L. Socio-technical systems. In *Management sciences models and techniques,* Vol. W. London: Pergamon Press, 1960.

EMERY, F. E. and TRIST, E. L. The causal texture of organizational environments, *Human Relations,* 1965, *18,* 21–32.

FRENCH, W. L. and BELL, C. H. *Organization development.* Englewood Cliffs: Prentice-Hall, 1973.

GALBRAITH, J. *Organizational design.* Reading, Mass.: Addison-Wesley, 1977.

HACKMAN, J. R. and OLDHAM, G. R. *Work redesign.* Reading, Mass.: Addison-Wesley, 1979.

HOFER, C. W. and SCHENDEL, D. *Strategy formulation: Analytical concepts.* St. Paul: West, 1978.

KATZ, D. and KAHN, R. L. *The social psychology of organizations* (2nd edition). New York: John Wiley & Sons, 1978.

KATZ, D. and KAHN, R. L. *The social psychology of organizations.* New York: John Wiley, 1966.

LAWLER, E. E. *Motivation in work organizations.* Belmont, Calif.: Wadsworth, 1973.

LAWRENCE, P. R. and LORSCH, J. W. *Developing organizations: Diagnosis and action.* Reading, Mass.: Addison-Wesley, 1969.

LEAVITT, H. J. Applied organizational change in industry. In March, J. G. (ed.) *Handbook of organizations.* Chicago: Rand McNally, 1965, 1144–1170.

LORSCH, J. W. and SHELDON, A. The individual in the organization: A systems view. In Lorsch, J. W. and Lawrence, P. R. (eds.) *Managing group and intergroup relations.* Homewood, Ill.: Irwin-Dorsey, 1972.

MINTZBERG, H. *The nature of managerial work.* New York: Harper & Row, 1973.

ROGERS, E. M. and SHOEMAKER, F. F. *Communication of innovations: A cross-cultural approach.* New York: The Free Press, 1971.

SCHEIN, E. H. *Organizational psychology.* Englewood Cliffs: Prentice-Hall, 1970.

SEILER, J. A. *Systems analysis in organizational behavior.* Homewood, Ill.: Irwin-Dorsey, 1967.

TUSHMAN, M. L. and NADLER, D. A. Information processing as an integrating framework in organizational design, *Academy of Management Review,* 1978, *3,* 613–624.

Von Bertalanffy, L. *General systems theory: Foundations, development, applications.* (Revised ed.) New York: Braziller, 1968.

VROOM, V. H. *Work and motivation.* New York: Wiley, 1964.

WALTON, R. E. The diffusion of new work structures: Explaining why success didn't take, *Organizational Dynamics,* 1975 (Winter), 3–22.

WEICK, K. E. *The social psychology of organizing.* Reading, Mass.: Addison-Wesley, 1969.

Issues in the Creation of Organizations

John R. Kimberly

What makes some organizations more successful than others? This question is either implicitly or explicitly part of most research on organizations and management. There are obviously both practical and theoretical reasons for the salience of the issue. Managers are concerned with increasing the success of their organizations—and hence their own careers. To the extent that research can contribute to that end, it is welcomed and supported by them. The early history of organizational research, in fact, suggests that its origins were stimulated as much by the needs and concerns of industry as by those of researchers. Researchers, on the other hand, have recognized the importance of differing levels of success as a dependent variable in the study of organizational behavior and have devoted much time and

Reprinted by permission of the publisher from the Academy of Management Journal, *1979, vol. 22, pp. 437–57.* © *1979 by Academy of Management Journal.*

energy to attempting to understand both its correlates and determinants.

The measurement of success—or effectiveness—of course, has been problematic.[1] Although it is generally agreed that success is multi-dimensional, there has been little consensus about what its components are (Steers, 1975; Goodman and Pennings, 1977). Survival is one criterion which most researchers agree is a necessary—albeit not sufficient—condition for success.[2] There is less agreement about other dimensions, however, and many managers themselves are hard pressed to justify traditional measures and to suggest viable alternatives. And when the focus shifts from industrial to non-industrial or "people-processing" organizations, the problem of determining what success or effectiveness is is exacerbated (Kimberly, 1979). What distinguishes a successful from a less successful prison —or mental hospital—or educational institution? Debates over appropriate criteria are intense and few widely accepted ones have been developed.

One very real problem in research on organizations, then, has been determining what success is. This problem, however, does not appear to be insoluble, and researchers have made progress (Mahoney and Weitzel, 1969; Price, 1968; Yuchtman and Seashore, 1967). The most comprehensive statement of the current state of the art in conceptualizing and measuring effectiveness and of the problems that remain is found in the collection of papers edited by Goodman and Pennings (1977).

This paper is framed around an issue in the analysis of effectiveness which has received little attention but which has important implications, a sampling and research strategy issue. Most research on the question has been carried out in mature organizations that have existing structures, domains, control systems, and normative codes and has been based on cross-sectional designs. This means that the perspective is usually static and the possible relevance of what stage an organization is in in its "life cycle" (Kimberly, 1976a) is overlooked.

Researchers tend not to be involved with the organization except for a brief period at some—usually unspecified—point during its life. As a result, the question of what implications the conditions surrounding its birth and early development may have for levels of success or effectiveness later on is not considered. There is at least the possibility that, just as for a child, the conditions under which an organization is born and the course of its development in infancy have non-trivial consequences for its later life. Just as one might be interested in similarities and differences in the backgrounds of executives as one important element in an explanation of their personal success, so might one be analogously interested in the backgrounds of organizations. I would not argue that the analogy is perfect by any

means, only that it raises a question about the analysis of organizational effectiveness which has not been pursued to any great extent in the literature. Pursuing it might lead to some new insights.

This paper analyzes the question of effectiveness in the context of the birth and early development of an innovative organization. In so doing, it confronts the sampling and research design issue noted above directly. The organization studied is not "mature," and the analysis is not cross-sectional. It is a case study, and thus the usual *caveats* are in order. As Cummings (1977) has argued, however, intensive longitudinal analysis of individual cases is likely to enrich our perspectives on organizations and lead to theoretically more interesting conceptualizations of effectiveness and its etiology.

Three separate but related bodies of literature—apart from that on effectiveness—have influenced the development of the paper. First is the literature on organizational innovation, much of which has been summarized in Rogers and Shoemaker (1971), Zaltman, Duncan and Holbek (1973) and Kimberly (1979). This work highlights the effects of both internal and external factors on the fate of innovation. Second is the literature on organizational environments. The importance of this research, the leading edge of which is contained in the volumes by Meyer and his associates (1978), by Pfeffer and Salancik (1978), and by Aldrich (1979) is to demonstrate that both organizational process and outcomes are strongly influenced by environmental factors, factors which may be only partially within the control of any single organization. Finally, research on organizational growth and development, summarized and extended by Starbuck (1965, 1971), suggests that growth and development are not linear processes and may be influenced by a variety of political, economic, and social factors. The analysis presented in the following pages owes much to these literatures even as it attempts to move in some new directions.

THE SETTING AND RESEARCH DESIGN

New organizations are being created continuously in both the private and public sectors. Very little data exists regarding the rates of foundation of new organizations, although one has the impression that the rates are high. One also has the impression that the rates are higher in the private sector than in the public sector, although the rate of growth of government as an employer in recent years has risen rapidly, while that for industry has leveled off considerably. Whether this is indicative of a shift in rates of foundation of new organizations is unknown. All that can be said with certainty is that rates of organizational birth are non-trivial in both sectors.

The organizational subject of this paper is a new school of medical education which opened its doors to its first class of students in September, 1971. At the time it was started, there were 86 other medical schools in the United States. The majority of these schools were very similar in terms of both their organizational structure and the content of their curricula. They were all four-year programs in which the first two years consisted of basic science training (biochemistry, physiology, etc.) and the final two were spent in clinical training (direct contact with patients in the hospital setting). With very few exceptions, the basic science curricula were discipline-oriented lecture-laboratory experiences taught by Ph.D.'s in the particular disciplines. The students had no contact with patients during this time. This contact came during the clinical training.

Whether the remarkable similarity among the schools of medicine can be accounted for by the Stinchcombe (1965) hypothesis about structural stability and date of founding and/or by the widespread impact of the Flexner Report on the state of medical education in the United States at the beginning of this century, is debatable. What is interesting about the new school, however, is that it was both new and different. Its structure and curriculum departed significantly from the norm and thus it faced not only those problems which any new organization might be likely to confront, what Stinchcombe (1965) has called the "liability of newness," but also problems of being different. Being both new and different proved to be both an advantage and a disadvantage, as will be demonstrated later in the paper.

The observations which form the basis for the present paper were made during the application of a "process research" design for evaluating the birth, development and impact of the new school. This approach, which has been described in detail elsewhere (Kimberly, Counte and Dickinson, 1972), was based on the belief that significant learnings about organizational phenomena can result from intensive longitudinal analysis of organizational processes.

The researcher was a faculty member in a social science department on the campus where the medical school was started, and was contacted by the Dean of the new school during the spring of the year prior to its formal opening. The Dean was interested in a social science-oriented appraisal of his program by an outsider, and was willing to provide a modest amount of seed money to help launch such an effort. The researcher was interested by the opportunity to get in on the ground floor of the birth of an organization, to develop a longitudinal study, and to conduct research on organizational behavior in a non-industrial setting. An understanding was reached whereby the Dean agreed to provide access to those data sources defined as relevant by the researcher and the researcher agreed to share observations and findings with the Dean on a regular basis.

The research effort extended over a four-year period, with funding being obtained from a number of federal and state sources. The data collection strategy involved a variety of survey, interview, observational, and archival research techniques. Data collected systematically from community physicians, students, faculty, and administrators at multiple points in time were combined with data from conversations, observations made both formally and informally in and around the school, minutes from a variety of different kinds of meetings, and memoranda of all sorts to form a rich store of information. In addition to learning a great deal about organizational behavior, much was learned about the problems and opportunities associated with the process research approach to the assessment of organizations (Kimberly and Nielsen, 1977).

The observations and interpretations presented in this particular paper represent an effort to stand back from the specifics of the data that were collected and to piece together a more general mosaic based on, but not directly tied to, those data. It is an effort to understand some important things about the context in which the questions of birth and effectiveness were explored and to tease out their implications for organizational theory and research.

Any new organization faces two general problems, and the analysis of the birth and early development of the school deals with both. First is the problem of getting off the ground. Here the origins of the school will be considered and the conditions of its birth described. Second is the problem of institutionalization. Once off the ground, organizations must develop strategies for longer run survival and growth, strategies which basically involve, following Thompson's (1967) lead, sealing off their core technologies from the effects of environmental uncertainty. Here problems the school faced as it grew will be discussed and what I have chosen to call the "paradoxical nature of success" will be described. This section will be followed by discussion of the implications of the study for organizational theory and research.

GETTING OFF THE GROUND: THE BIRTH OF THE SCHOOL

The birth of any organization is affected by a complex set of political, economic, social, and psychological factors. It is beyond the scope of this paper to try to deal systematically with all of these; instead, the analysis will take into account what are felt on the basis of careful observation to be the two most important sets of factors involved in the birth of the new medical school, the situational constraints favoring its emergence at a particular point in history and the ambition and vision of its first dean which were largely responsible for defining the particular shape the school took and the directions it followed.

Situational Constraints

There was a particular mix of social, economic and political factors existing in the late 1960's and early 1970's which together created a favorable climate for the founding of a new medical school. For purposes of analysis, it is convenient to adopt Hall's (1972) distinction between general and specific environmental conditions and to distinguish between concerns at the national level—general environmental conditions—and those at the state and local level—specific environmental conditions.

On the national level in the middle and late sixties there was an increasing concern with the adequacy of existing supplies of physicians. Although there was much debate about whether a shortage of doctors did, in fact, exist, the federal government was persuaded and developed a number of policies designed to increase the production of new doctors. Particularly influential was its decision to make federal monies available to medical schools on a capitation basis, thus encouraging the schools themselves to admit and graduate increasing numbers of students. Money also became available from the federal government and a number of private foundations to help finance the establishment of new schools. Thus, the national mood favored the establishment of new medical schools at this time and this mood was reinforced by the availability of resources.

During this period there was also a national debate within the community of medical educators about the viability of traditional structures of medical education. This debate was influenced, of course, by the more general issues of that era related to education in general and higher education in particular. Traditional values and structures were being called into question and cries for reform came from many sources. Students were demanding more "relevance" in their education and a greater voice in determining the form and content of the educational process. The utility of grading systems was called into question and there was much experimentation with "pass-fail" systems and ungraded courses. Faculties were re-examining basic assumptions of their own careers, and much of the initiative for reform came from them. Medical education was not immune from these debates, in spite of the generally conservative character of most medical schools. Criticisms of the existing system abounded. It was argued that traditional structure with its lockstep approach was one in which time (4 years) was the constant and learning was the variable. It was also argued that the two years of basic science had negative effects on student motivation because it was simply more of what they had experienced as undergraduates in college. Not being able to see patients until their third year of medical school, it was argued, did not enable students to see the relevance of the basic sciences for the practice of medicine. The strong explicit and implicit emphasis on specialization as opposed to general practice resulted in pressures on most students not to consider general practice seriously as a career alternative. The socialization process in medical school, in other words, was a major contributor to the oft-cited imbalance between specialists and general practitioners on a national basis.

These two factors, increasing the supply of doctors as a national priority and widespread questioning of some of the basic assumptions and structures of medical education, provided a conducive general environmental climate for the founding of new medical schools.

Other things were happening on the state and local levels, in the specific environment, to favor the establishment of a new medical school. The University College of Medicine, headquartered in a major metropolitan area, had long been one of the largest medical schools in the country as measured by the number of doctors per year it graduated. It was the unchallenged leader in medical education in the state. Doctors and politicians in other parts of the state, however, had felt for some time that it cast an uncomfortably long shadow over medicine in the rest of the state, and looked upon developments nationally as an opportunity to initiate medical education programs outside the metropolis. Accordingly, there was a move to establish a new medical school in the state capital. Not to be outdone, the University College of Medicine proposed a substantial growth program of its own which involved establishing semi-autonomous branches in three other cities as well as increasing its own capacity at home. The existence of a campus of the University with a number of distinguished basic science departments, three hospitals and a sizeable medical community in another city made that city a logical site for one of the three branches. There was also a good deal of concern among policy-makers at the state level over the large numbers of state-trained doctors who were leaving the state to practice elsewhere. The major urban area was not affected by this exodus, but the rest of the state was. There was some hope expressed, therefore, that by establishing branches outside that area, students would be exposed to the practice of medicine in non-urban settings and would thus be more inclined to locate in those settings once their training had been completed.

For its part, the campus of the University which was the potential site of the new school looked on the possibility of a medical program with mixed emotions. It was clearly attractive in the short run, as a new medical school would undoubtedly help generate other new resources, and by the late sixties it was evident that the days of abundant resources and rapid growth were by. The longer run was less clear, and there was considerable uncertainty about how the administrative linkages with the College of Medicine could be established on the most favorable of terms. In the end, however, the advocates of potential overcame the proponents of caution, and it was agreed that one of the branches would be established there.

The Role of Entrepreneurship

A number of forces combined at a particular point in time to lead to the decision to establish a new medical school in the particular locale. An understanding of these forces alone, however, is not sufficient for an understanding of the kind of school that was established and the course of its early development. For this it is necessary to look carefully at the ambitions and character of the individual that was hired as the school's first dean.

There is a good deal of controversy among organizational theorists about the advisability of attributing organizational outcomes to the particular characteristics of particular individuals. Sociologists label such attribution psychological reductionism, and argue that organizational analysis is most fruitfully pursued apart from considerations of individual personalities and motivations. This position has been perhaps most forcefully argued by Perrow (1970: 5–14) in his critique of the "leadership" approach to organizational analysis. He contends that a structural approach is more useful. In reflecting on the development of the medical

school, however, I am led to conclude that Perrow's position needs to be emended. In the case examined here, an understanding of the entrepreneur and his values and objectives is necessary for an understanding of the school he developed. Purely structural explanations are inadequate. Whether this would be as true in the case of the birth of other organizations, I cannot say, but I suspect that were enough research available on organizational birth, one would find that the role of the early leaders was critical. Sarason's (1972) work on the creation of new settings tends to substantiate this view. As an organization matures, develops norms and acquires a history and identity, the importance of the person at the top diminishes in explaining organizational outcomes. Organizational mechanisms are designed to remove the equivocality which attaches to individual personalities. Thus, Perrow may be right insofar as mature organizations are concerned, but is less right where the interest is in brand new ones.

The new Dean, a cardiologist by training, was in full time private practice and a clinical assistant professor at a leading medical school when he was hired. This medical school was one of the first to break from the traditional structure of medical education and move in some new directions. He thus came to his job from an environment which encouraged innovation. He had had limited administrative experience, however, having served five years on the Board of Education in the city where he practiced and having founded and served on the executive committee of a prepaid group practice in the same city. His hiring thus represented a certain amount of risk both for the University and for him.

Five things about the man help to explain the nature of his influence on early development of the school. First, he had a deep-rooted dissatisfaction with traditional forms of medical education and a very real commitment to the importance of developing new structures. Second, he was a risk-taker, willing to experiment with new ideas in an often uncritical fashion. Third, he was a man of action as opposed to a man of reflection, and was given to making very quick decisions. Fourth, he was an idea man as opposed to a detail man, ready to paint scenarios for the future in very broad strokes, leaving his staff—often unprepared—to fill in the blanks. Finally, he was an optimist with very strong instincts for self-preservation, and quickly learned the often intricate rules of survival in the highly political and politicized university environment.

He came to the position with a budget and an associate dean. The school he developed was, in a very real sense, his school, and represented in concrete terms at the outset his vision of what medical education should consist of. In the beginning he was reacting instinctively and intuitively, and what he did—and what he did not do—had important consequences for the early life of the school. The major constraint imposed from without was the fact that the school was to start out as a one year basic science program. The intention was then to send students to one of the other three campuses of the College of Medicine for the three years of clinical training which were to follow. Another, initially latent, constraint was the fact that the school served two administrative masters, the College of Medicine located in another city and the University campus. As long as the school was small and neither commanded nor demanded large amounts of resources, it posed little threat and the Dean had a good deal of freedom to design the kind of program he wanted. As soon as it started to increase its visibility, however, the administrative constraints were activated and played an important role in the school's development.

The Dean's first commitment was to generate enthusiasm for the medical school in the medical community. This commitment was the direct result of his vision of what the program would do—expose new students to patients from the outset. He felt that this would enhance their motivation and would help demonstrate the relevance of the basic sciences to the practice of medicine. To do this, however, it was necessary to find doctors willing to work with the students, and the Dean turned to the medical community for help. His view was that community physicians represent an untapped resource for medical education. If they could be persuaded to participate in his program, they would not only provide important learning experiences for the students, but might in turn be motivated by their contact with the students to keep up with current developments in medicine themselves. And if they would be willing to participate on an unsalaried basis, that would result in considerable cost-effectiveness for the school. The inducement for participation was the status accompanying the title of Clinical Associate at the medical school. Thus, his major initial investment was in the community, an investment which was to have positive payoffs initially in terms of physician response but which had certain costs as well because of lack of attention to the importance of campus-based bridges.

Development of the curriculum was influenced by his views about learning medicine. He had strong feelings that (a) students do not all learn at the same rate and (b) that it made more sense from the perspective of medical practice to take a disease system approach rather than a discipline-centered curriculum. He also felt that he could reasonably devise a one-year basic science program to supplant the usual two-year one.

The program was designed to start small, with 16 students in the first year. That number was to double each of the next 3 years until the class size was 128, which was the target figure. Five faculty members were hired on the basis of their interest in the innovative character of the program and became involved in curriculum design. The curriculum was to consist of a number of disease-centered problems, and each student was to be assigned to a community physician who would act as an advisor, expose the student to patients, and let the student see individuals afflicted with the particular problem the student was currently studying. Progress was to be evaluated by another community physician who would examine the student orally. The role of the faculty was to provide advice, expertise, and counselling as the students felt they needed it.

When the school opened its doors, it was modest in size. It consisted of the Dean, an Associate Dean, an Assistant Dean, an Executive Secretary, two secretaries, five faculty members, sixteen students, commitments from over 100 physicians in the local community to participate if called upon, a curriculum which was not fully developed, and a structure which departed substantially from that of most basic science medical programs. The Dean had an enormous capacity for work, and often put in 16–18 hour days. The results were impressive. He managed to develop a high degree of credibility in the local medical community in a very short period of time. In fact, in a study of factors affecting their willingness to participate in the new program, it was found that the local physicians most frequently cited the influence of the Dean as singularly important (Counte and Kimberly, 1974). He was also able to begin to build a reputation for the innovative nature of the school both in the state (Sorlie *et al*, 1971) and nationally (Bloomfield *et al*, 1972).

Growth

Rapid growth is often equated with success. There is a value embedded deeply in our culture which places a strong positive evaluation on evidence of growth, and a negative evaluation on steady state and particularly on decline. Although recent stringencies in the general environment have forced many institutions, including higher education, to reconsider the relevance of this value, in the early days of the medical school the value was still occupying center stage. At that point in time, one way both members of the organization and its external constituencies evaluated performance was on the basis of growth. Use of growth as a criterion for success has persisted, even in the face of evidence that it may not be *the* or even *a* major factor.

Defined in terms of growth, the initial success of the school is readily apparent. As can be seen in Figure 1, numbers of students, numbers of faculty, numbers of administrators, numbers of support personnel and total budget expanded rapidly in the period from 1971–72 to 1975–76. In addition, a new building to house the school opened in the spring of 1975.

Available evidence indicated that its innovative curriculum was favorably received by the students, and that they performed as well as their peers in other basic science programs in the College on standard year-end exams. Thus it appeared that the school was doing both good and well at the same time. It was an institution whose time had come, headed by a man of ambition and vision, and this combination spawned an organization which could conceivably serve as a model for others to follow. Situational constraints and an entrepreneurial Dean had together given birth to an organization that gave every indication of being highly successful.

INSTITUTIONALIZING INNOVATION: THE PARADOXICAL NATURE OF SUCCESS

Does success breed success? This question is often asked, but observation of the case of the new medical school suggests that it may not be the right one to ask. Success, as noted earlier, is multi-faceted, and in the case of the medical school the composition of success changed as the process of institutionalization unfolded. For a variety of reasons which are described below, the early success of the organization as an in-

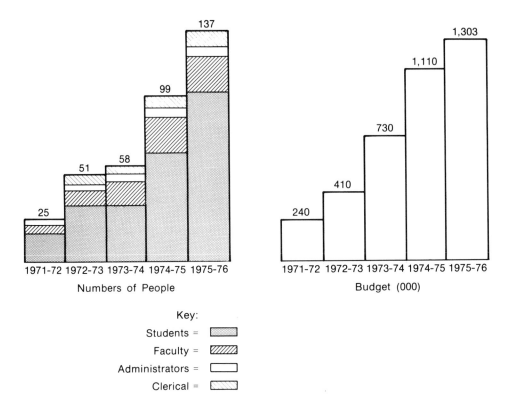

Key:

Students =

Faculty =

Administrators =

Clerical =

Figure 1   Early Growth

novation was difficult to sustain as the organization developed. The very reasons it was successful as an innovation were incompatible with what was needed to be successful in the long run. Paradoxically, those things that accounted for its early success were among those things that had to be changed to insure its long run success. The nature of the paradox is explained by the nature of the process of institutionalization, and indicates why it is that the question of success breeding success vastly oversimplifies the realities of organizational evolution.

The process of institutionalization is that process whereby new norms, values and structures become incorporated within the framework of existing patterns of norms, values and structures. This process is one which lends stability and predictability to social relationships and enables them to persist. It is especially visible in the context of

formal organizations, where a frequent problem is developing mechanisms to sustain planned change efforts (Goodman and Bazerman, 1979).

In the case of the medical school, the process was highly visible in the context of the way three problems in particular were dealt with. The problems of internal social control, of the structure of work, and of managing relationships with the environment are faced by all organizations (Kimberly, 1976b). As an organization is born and begins to develop, the process of institutionalization is inevitably joined in each of these areas. The organization seeks to increase the predictability of its own outcomes and, at the same time, organizations and institutions in its environment attempt to increase the predictability of its outcomes for them. Assessments of performance are both internal and external (Pfeffer, 1977). To trace the process of institutionalization and its effects, therefore, one needs to look both inside the organization and outside. How does it deal with the three problems noted above and with what consequences?

A complete description of the process in the case of the new medical school is beyond the scope of this paper. What will be presented instead is an example illustrating the nature of the response to each of the three problems. These illustrations can then serve as the basis for some more general observations.

Structural Differentiation as a Response to the Problem of Internal Social Control

The school's first year of existence was characterized by an atmosphere of experimentation and tolerance of each other's mistakes on the part of all of the participants —students, administrators, faculty and local physicians. The interest of each group in seeing the school get off the ground meant that there were important degrees of freedom for everyone. The Dean had been successful, for example, in enlisting the active participation of 20 local physicians on a non-salaried basis, getting them to agree to spend at least four hours per week with their student advisees. He had been less successful, however, in defining precisely what should happen during the time they spent with their advisees, because he and his staff had not had enough time to work on that problem and because he did not have a very specific vision of what should occur. Although the physicians often felt that they were in the dark regarding what they were supposed to be doing with their advisees, they were willing to continue through the year because it was important to them to have a medical school in the community. And the Dean made several efforts to reassure them personally, through phone conversations and meetings, that they were doing well and that a clearer set of guide-lines for their role would be provided as experience with the new format was gained.

The first 16 students also lived in an atmosphere of uncertainty. The curriculum was not fully developed, facilities were crude, there were few guidelines for their behavior and it was difficult for them to judge how "well" they were doing in the program. The Dean and his staff spent a great deal of time with the students during the year, fostering a sense of camaraderie and building up enough social capital to offset concerns about the lack of structure in the program itself. The students, in fact, responded positively to the program during the first year. Internal social control, then, was established and maintained during the early stages of development on an effective, personalized basis. The Dean devoted an enormous amount of time to pattern maintenance activities, maintaining an "open-door" policy and encouraging interaction. This provided much-needed support and encouragement to both physicians and students.

Two things happened to change the basis of internal social control from a highly personal one to a highly impersonal one. The number of students increased and other administrative demands reduced the amount of time the Dean could spend interacting with students and physicians. As the number of students increased over the next years from 16 to 100, the Dean hired people to perform the important linking role between the school and the local physicians and between the school and the students. But whereas in the first year the program had been the Dean, over time the program became the School. The metaphor changed from personal to impersonal, with consequent effects on the reactions of both physicians and students. Both groups were more willing to challenge and less willing to tolerate errors. The less time the Dean spent with them, the more true this became. Thus, structural differentiation—the hiring of staff to perform tasks formerly performed by the Dean—had the effect of producing a more highly bureaucratized system, a system which had a conservative impact on the initially innovative character of the school.

Structural differentiation did not occur solely in response to the increasing numbers of students. It also reflected changing administrative demands on the Dean. Whereas in the first year he could focus primarily on problems of internal social control, in ensuing years he had to devote increasing amounts of his time and energy to the structure of work and particularly to managing relations with the environment. These demands were independent of changes in size, and reflect, perhaps, an important aspect of the process of institutionalization. It is not a linear process, and is not one which involves a particular sequence. The Dean could have made different decisions about how to spend his time during the first year and the years following and attended to the three problems in any number of sequences and combinations. Ultimately, however, all of them had to be dealt with. The result of structural differentiation as a response to the problem of internal social control was that the Dean was able to devote his energies to other areas, and in that sense it represented an effective response. The cost, however, was a diminishing of the initially organic relationship between the Dean, the faculty, the students and the local physicians. There was thus less tolerance for experimentation and error and hence less willingness to accept the uncertainty that inevitably accompanies innovation.

Formalization as a Response to the Problem of the Structure of Work

One of the explicit objectives of the Dean was to create a medical school in which the students would be able to pace themselves, to learn at their own rate and to study independently. There was a deliberate effort to avoid the lock-step rigidity which characterized basic medical science education in most medical schools. Accordingly, during

the first year a curriculum was developed which was disease-centered and which required that the students learn those aspects of the basic sciences (e.g., biochemistry, physiology) that would apply to the specific problem (e.g., peptic ulcer). Students were able, after doing an introductory problem together, to do succeeding problems in any order and at any time they chose. Their physician advisors were to help them by showing them patients who had the particular problem they were studying, but the definition of when a student had mastered a particular problem came from his physician advisor. The faculty played a consultative role only, and was not directly involved in a major way in the learning process.

There was a good deal of anxiety and uncertainty created by the lack of structure of work during the first year. Physician advisors were not sure they were giving the students what they needed, the students were not sure they were getting what they needed, and the Dean and his staff were not sure that the students would perform adequately on the College-wide standard year-end exam or on the National Medical Boards, Part I. As it turned out, the students did very well on the exams, and 15 or 16 passed the Boards. This, it must be remembered, after only one year of basic sciences as opposed to the usual two.

Yet in spite of this "success," there were pressures from a number of sources to structure the work more highly. The uncertainty was not pleasant for anyone, and there was some concern that the students' performance was a fluke and ways needed to be found to insure that the performance would be as impressive in the future. Over the next three years, therefore, the physician advisors were given job descriptions and the curriculum developed to the point where students had a required number of problems to finish in a required sequence in a required amount of time. There was, in other words, a dramatic increase in the extent of formalization of the work. It is undoubtedly the case that formalization was required, in part, by the increase in the number of students. This is not the sole explanation, however. The level of uncertainty required by the innovative independent study format was simply not felt to be supportable over time. As the program began to attract national attention and requests for documentation of the curriculum were received, the professional motivations of the staff led to the production of such documentation. Paradoxically, however, this very production process itself represented a kind of formalization which limited degrees of freedom and constrained innovation in the program. And perhaps even more significant, the demands of accreditation bodies made formalization imperative. Thus, although the disease-centered concept underlying the content of the curriculum did not change, the independent study format changed dramatically. Those characteristics of the original structure of work which contributed to its success as an innovation were incompatible with the long run felt need for predictability and stability. Formalization as a response enhanced stability but diminished innovativeness.

Managing Relationships with the Specific Environment: The Role of the Faculty

Earlier it was noted that there were both specific and general environmental conditions creating a favorable climate for the establishment of a new medical school at the site of its birth. It was also the case that the school had to manage relationships with both. A good example of the process of institutionalization and its effects in the specific environment was the evolving role of the faculty. An important component of the specific environment of the school was its relationship to the basic science departments on campus. During the first year this was not an issue. The faculty was small, and everyone was busy trying to define their role. At the end of the first year, however, the faculty

felt that they were not as directly involved in educating the students as they should be and persuaded the Dean that they should have a broader and more clearly defined teaching and advising role. It was only natural that this role, over time, should evolve in the direction of the traditional conceptualization of teaching and research. The faculty was part of a large, traditional university where this role was the norm and where their role was clearly a low-status exception. More important still was the fact that all of the faculty from the beginning had joint appointments with the discipline departments on campus. Joint appointments enhanced their academic credibility among research colleagues at other universities. The Dean, too, realized the importance of the joint appointments as a mechanism for enhancing the legitimacy and reputation of his school both within the university and in the larger arena of academic medicine. In the short run, the university could welcome the innovative program as a potentially interesting addition. Over time, however, the school would have to prove its merit—on terms comparable to other campus units. The first real testing ground was the question of evaluation and promotion of faculty. What criteria should be used and who should be involved in the evaluation process? It was clear that the medical school would not be able to enjoy special privilege and that its faculty would be subject to general campus-wide criteria of research and publication. This was a way in which the specific environment could remove equivocality vis a vis the medical school. While not unexpected, the effect was a conservatizing one on the faculty. Because they were to be evaluated largely in terms of traditional criteria, there were few incentives to engage in nontraditional behavior.

Once again, one can see the paradox of institutionalization and success at work. The school attracted qualified faculty members both because of the personal persuasiveness of the Dean and the record of success of the first year. Although perhaps initially attracted by the innovative character of the program, the faculty responded to the traditional nature of the reward structure that emerged. Their attention became focused more on research and publication and less on developing their roles in ways which would help to maintain the innovative character of the program. Early success as an innovation created conditions which made continued success on that basis difficult.

Managing Relationships with the General Environment: The Creation of a Public Face

If building credibility in the specific environment of the university in which the new school was located led to important changes in the role of the faculty, creating a public face for the general environment required certain readjustments for the Dean. His interest was not in building an organization of local reputation only. That was important, but he was also interested in national recognition. National recognition would not only be personally rewarding but would make the job of fund raising less problematic.

The Dean had a personal conviction that one of the problems in medical education was an overemphasis on specialization, and he wanted to build a program which did not have such an emphasis. He felt that the best form of medical education produced good general physicians. Good general physicians could specialize in anything. Utilization of local physicians, many of whom were general practitioners, as participants in the program were designed, in part, to expose students to the physician's role from the very beginning of their training. The hope was that they would then become better general physicians once their training had been completed. This was another aspect of the school which, at the time of its birth, was innovative.

The need to create a public face and the desire to have a program which produced good general physicians led to a dilemma

for the Dean. The public face had to be legitimate first and foremost in the medical profession and particularly in the field of medical education. Yet the concept of a good general physician was somewhat vague, and was often confused with the concept of the general practitioner. General practice, however, did not rank high in the status hierarchy in the field. If his program was to become publicly identified as a general practice program, the Dean realized, it would by definition be a low status program. Status in the medical profession is highly prized, and for good reason, because resources tend to flow up the status hierarchy. Needing resources and hence recognition, the Dean could not afford a public face which had too strong an overtone of general practice attached to it. Thus, although the program initially was developed around the importance of producing good general physicians, over time the need to project an "acceptable" public image led to a diminishing emphasis on this aspect. On yet another dimension, the program became less successful as an innovation as it became more successful as a medical school.

And the Beat Goes On: Today's Hopes for Tomorrow

The first four years of the new organization's existence witnessed many interesting and dramatic changes—both quantitative and qualitative—in its structure and operations. As the school grew, it became more conservative. The initial period of heady enthusiasm gave way to a period of negotiating the terms for continued existence. Administrators, staff, faculty, community physicians and students all made extraordinary contributions to the development of the school, particularly during its first two years of existence. But the initial enthusiasm proved impossible to sustain for a variety of reasons and by the third year life at the school was characterized by many of the same conflicts, jealousies and problems that typify life in its more "mature" counterparts. Altruistic orientations were replaced by instrumental orientations as career imperatives began to intrude. Analytically, one might argue that the emerging dominance of instrumental orientations at the level of individual persons involved with the school was not only perhaps inevitable, but also a necessary condition for effectiveness. To the extent that each participant was able to maximize his or her own personal goals, the organization as a whole would be more effective (Cummings, 1977). In any case, people began to think more in terms of their own futures than of the school's, and this shift from a collective to an instrumental metaphor reinforced many of the dynamics that accompanied the shift from the personal to the impersonal metaphor within the school which was discussed earlier.

Our process research evaluation of the school continued on a formal basis for four years. Since that time, when I left the university, a new development has been unfolding in the school's biography that has already further complicated the evaluation of its success. In the back of the Dean's mind from the day he was hired was a vision of a full medical school. Although he was committed to getting a school of basic sciences started, he was also hoping that one day he would preside over a full program. His entrepreneurial appetites were not satisfied with the creation of a basic sciences program alone.

It is simply not possible in this paper to deal systematically with the implications of the launching of the clinical component of the school. The promise of such an addition has created a renewed sense of enthusiasm both in the school and in the local medical community. Interestingly, however, the enthusiasm is not comparable to that generated by the inauguration of the school itself. Although the new component is itself innovative, and although the Dean has continued to exercise his considerable entrepreneurial skills in its evolution, the enthusiasm is tempered by a history of un-

easy relations between the Dean and his faculty, by a decidedly wait and see posture on the part of the local medical community, and by apprehension and resistance both in other parts of the university and in the state legislature. This development will add new dimensions to the evaluation of the success of the school, a fact which underlines the often evanescent nature of the evaluation criteria used.

CONCLUSIONS AND IMPLICATIONS

What conclusions and implications can be drawn from these observations? Clearly, the birth and early development of the new medical school cannot be considered to be typical or to embody the full range of patterns and possibilities that confront the creation of organizations. Yet some of the dynamics are surely not idiosyncratic. The interaction between situational constraints and the personal characteristics of the founder as a significant constraint on the shape of the early chapters of an organization's biography; the tension between innovation and institutionalization; the transition from personal to impersonal and from collective to instrumental metaphors are themes which transcend any particular organizational setting.

Identification of general themes, of course, pushes one in the direction of elaborating general frameworks, but I will resist that temptation here. There may be differences in the process of creating nested organizations as opposed to free-standing, fully autonomous entities; public agencies as opposed to private organizations; organizational clones as opposed to innovative organizational forms; corporations as opposed to privately-held enterprises. The inventory of possible influences on the process is lengthy, and organizational researchers are only beginning to appreciate their range and complexity. In addition, there is an intricate web of institutional factors that need to be more fully integrated into theoretical perspectives on creation. The role of environmental legislation, of tax incentives, of governmental regulation and of patent law—to name just a few—are significant and should not be treated merely as a residual category of exogenous influences. As the process of creation captures the imagination of more researchers and more data are accumulated, the task of building more general frameworks will be facilitated.

Five more specific conclusions and implications are suggested by our analysis of the early history of the new medical school. First, entrepreneurial activity played an important part in shaping its early development. There appeared to be conditions in both the general and specific environments which combined at a particular point in time to favor the birth of a new medical school at a particular site. The decision to establish the school was made by individuals in the specific environment who responded to these conditions, and can be understood in macro structural terms. The school's early development, however, cannot be understood without some knowledge of the ambitions, visions and strengths and weaknesses of its first Dean. He was able to take advantage of the conditions which gave birth to the school and use them to help create an innovative program of his own design. Whether one chooses to call him an entrepreneur, a leader, or a guru, the fact is that his personality, his dreams, his flaws, and his talents were largely responsible for the school's early structure and results. One reason that organizational sociologists typically down play the influence of particular individuals on organizational outcomes is that they study organizations which have already gone through the process of institutionalization, a process which is designed to remove as much uncertainty as possible from organizational life. Mechanisms have already been developed, in other words, to reduce the amount of influence particular individuals can have on outcomes, and it is not

surprising that structural explanations are more efficacious. But for the early stages of organizational development and perhaps for certain periods of relatively major transformation at other points in an organization's biography, a more catholic approach is necessary.

Second, being both new and different creates short run opportunities and long run problems for organizations because of the uncertainty that accompanies the combination of newness and differentness. This uncertainty is both internal and external, and adds another dimension to the problem of evaluating success. Internally, individuals are in the process of negotiating new roles, with new people in unfamiliar surroundings where performance criteria are often unclear. Externally, other organizations do not know what to expect from the focal organization and are trying to negotiate relations which will result in greater predictability for them. Where an organization is only new, that is, where it is essentially a replication of an existing organizational form, roles are familiar even if the surroundings and people are not. Performance rules and criteria for evaluation of performance are clearer. The basic transition involves applying rules learned in one setting in another. Outside organizations know what to expect and know how—or believe they know how—to evaluate progress and performance. Thus, at the very least, studies of organizational birth and theories of organizational effectiveness should distinguish between the two kinds of cases.

Third, birth and early development on the one hand and institutionalization on the other are two relatively distinct chapters in the biography of an organization. When an organization is both new and different, as in the case of the new medical school, and thus where innovation is involved, the transition between the two stages is likely to be problematic, as those things which lead to an organization's success as an innovation are not the same as those which lead to longer run success. For the entrepreneur, the transition is likely to be particularly difficult because the institutionalization stage involves removing equivocality and reducing degrees of freedom, both of which are needed in an organization's infancy and both of which appear to be important entrepreneurial hallmarks. Although a public sector organization has been discussed here, private sector organizations no doubt go through similar stages. When an initially successful enterprise goes public to generate more funds for expansion, for example, there is bound to be a conservative effect on development because of the addition of investors with their concerns for predictability and stability to the decision-making process.

Fourth, the processes of initiation, innovation and institutionalization are not the particular province of new organizations. Many organizations go through similar processes at various points in their biographies (Kimberly, 1979), and thus many of the observations made about the new medical school may be applicable to existing organizations as well. What is different is that change in existing organizations has to come in the context of an established culture and an institutionalized set of norms, values and procedures, whereas in the creation of new organizations, new cultures develop, and new norms, values and procedures are established. A context, in other words, is created. For organizational researchers, the interesting question is why some organizations, once born, are more susceptible to substantial transformations than others and what circumstances create the possibility for transformations to occur. It appears that it is during such transformations that particular individuals can exert unusually large amounts of influence over organizational outcomes, whereas in periods of relative stability highly visible personal contributions are less likely.

Finally, an intensive, longitudinal research design was used to analyze the birth of the new school. The depth of understanding of organizational processes resulting from this approach more than offsets costs due to questions of external validity. The substantive significance of the study is directly traceable to its longitudinal design. The limitations of cross-sectional research are all too apparent and have been discussed elsewhere (Kimberly, 1976a). But what is more challenging for the field are the observations that organizational birth is a phenomenon about which relatively little is known but which may be an important constraint on later development, and that birth, although important, is only one chapter in an organization's biography. These observations suggest an exciting new agenda of research and theory building. Systematic, in-depth, comparative analysis of the birth, life, and death of organizations should lead both to a clearer understanding of the complex nature of organizational success and to more dynamic perspectives on organizations. Both would certainly be welcome.

NOTES

1. The terms "success" and "effectiveness" are used interchangeably in this paper, although it is recognized that there are theoretical debates about the appropriateness of doing so.

2. It is not even clear that survival is always a criterion for success. Organizations which are truly effective may put themselves out of business, in which case death is the ultimate criterion for success.

REFERENCES

ALDRICH, H. *Organization and Environment* (Englewood Cliffs, NJ: Prentice-Hall, 1979).

BLOOMFIELD, D. K., T. GAMBLE, W. SORLIE and J. A. ANDERSON. "A Role for Practicing Physicians in Basic Medical Education," *Journal of the American Medical Association*, Vol. 213 (1972), 187–188.

COUNTE, M. A. and J. R. KIMBERLY. "Organizational Innovation in a Professionally Dominated System: Responses of Physicians to a New Program in Medical Education," *Journal of Health and Social Behavior*, Vol. 15 (1974), 188–198.

CUMMINGS, L. L. "Emergence of the Instrumental Organization," In P. S. Goodman and J. M. Pennings (Eds.) *New Perspectives on Organizational Effectiveness* (San Francisco: Jossey-Bass, 1977).

GOODMAN, P. S. and M. BAZERMAN. "Institutionalization of Planned Organizational Change," In B. M. Staw and L. L. Cummings (Eds.) *Research in Organizational Behavior,* Vol. II (Greenwich, CT: JAI Press, 1979).

GOODMAN, P. S. and J. M. PENNINGS. *New Perspectives on Organizational Effectiveness* (San Francisco: Jossey-Bass, 1977).

HALL, R. H. *Organizations: Structure and Process* (Englewood Cliffs, NJ: Prentice-Hall, 1972).

KIMBERLY, J. R., M. A. COUNTE and R. O. DICKINSON. "Design for Process Research on Change in Medical Education," Proceedings: Eleventh Annual Conference on Research in Medical Education, AAMC (1972), 26–31.

KIMBERLY, J. R., and W. R. NIELSEN. "Assessing Organizational Change Strategies," In P. S. Nystrom and W. H. Starbuck (Eds.) *Prescriptive Models of Organizations* North-Holland/TIMS Studies in the Management Sciences, Vol. 5 (1977), 143–155.

KIMBERLY, J. R. "Issues in the Design of Longitudinal Organizational Research," *Sociological Methods & Research,* Vol. 4 (1976a), 321–347.

KIMBERLY, J. R. "Organizational Size and the Structuralist Perspective: A Review, Critique and Proposal," *Administrative Science Quarterly,* Vol. 21 (1976b), 571–597.

KIMBERLY, J. R. "Managerial Innovation," In P. S. Nystrom and W. H. Starbuck (Eds.) *Handbook of Organizational Design* (New York: 1979).

MAHONEY, T. A. and W. WEITZEL. "Managerial Models of Organizational Effectiveness," *Administrative Science Quarterly,* Vol. 14 (1969), 357–365.

MEYER, M. and Associates. *Environments and Organizations* (San Francisco: Jossey-Bass, 1978).

PENNINGS, J. M. and P. S. GOODMAN. "Toward a Workable Framework," In P. S. Goodman and J. M. Pennings (Eds.) *New Perspectives on Organizational Effectiveness* (San Francisco: Jossey-Bass, 1977).

PERROW, C. B. *Organizational Analysis: A Sociological View* (Belmont, CA: Wadsworth, 1970).

PFEFFER, J. and G. SALANCIK. *The External Control of Organizations* (New York: Harper & Row, 1978).

PFEFFER, J. "Usefulness of the Concept," in P. S. Goodman and J. M. Pennings (Eds.) *New Perspectives on Organizational Effectiveness* (San Francisco: Jossey-Bass, 1977).

PRICE, J. L. *Organizational Effectiveness: An Inventory of Propositions* (Homewood, IL: Richard D. Irwin, 1968).

ROGERS, E. M. and F. SHOEMAKER. *The Communication of Innovation* (New York: Free Press, 1962).

SARASON, S. *The Creation of Settings and the Future Societies* (San Francisco: Jossey-Bass, 1972).

SORLIE, W., D. K. BLOOMFIELD, T. GAMBLE, and J. A. ANDERSON. "An Innovative One-Year Basic Science Program in Medical Education," *Illinois Medicine,* Vol. 40 (1971), 206–209.

STARBUCK, W. H. "Organizational Growth and Development," In J. G. March (ed.) *Handbook of Organizations* (Chicago: Rand McNally, 1965).

STARBUCK, W. H. *Organizational Growth and Development* (Baltimore, MD: Penguin Books, Inc., 1971).

STEERS, R. "Problems in the Measurement of Organizational Effectiveness," *Administrative Science Quarterly,* Vol. 20 (1975), 546–558.

STINCHCOMBE, A. L. "Social Structure and Organizations," In J. G. March (Ed.) *Handbook of Organizations* (Chicago: Rand McNally, 1965).

THOMPSON, J. D. *Organizations in Action* (New York: McGraw Hill, 1967).

WARNER, W. K. and A. E. HAVENS. "Goal Displacement and the Intangibility of Organizational Goals," *Administrative Science Quarterly,* Vol. 12 (1968), 539–555.

YUCHTMAN, E. and S. E. SEASHORE. "A System Resource Approach to Organizational Effectiveness," *American Sociological Review,* Vol. 32 (1967), 891–903.

ZALTMAN, G., R. B. DUNCAN and J. HOLBEK. *Innovations and Organizations* (New York: Wiley, 1973).

PART II

Understanding and Managing Organization Structures and Processes

The selections in Part II are divided into two sections. The first set of articles and situations focuses on organization structure and technology and their implications for design and management. The first article by Galbraith develops a view of organizations as information processing systems and describes alternative designs for coping with different levels of managerial uncertainty. Knight's article focuses on the complex "matrix" organizational design and includes a discussion of its potential benefits and weaknesses. Finally, Randolph describes relationships between unit technologies, designs, and people that lead to overall unit effectiveness. The section on organizational structure and technology concludes with two situations; one features the management of a multidimensional organization design at Dow Corning, and the other develops a continuum of organizational types and describes the most appropriate design for each.

The second section under Part II focuses on understanding and managing organizational conflict and politics. Litterer discusses the positive features of organizational conflict, and Pondy conceptualizes conflict as a process that begins with latent conflict and ends with conflict aftermath. The final two articles by Kotter and by Tushman and Nadler shift the focus to the politics of power and dependence within and between organizations. The section concludes with two management situations. The first, by Pondy, describes interunit conflicts associated with the budgeting process, and "The Rocky Road to the Marketplace" describes the conflicts and power struggles that accompanied a major organizational change at IBM.

In summary, the readings in Part II represent a blend of conceptual articles and actual management situations that provide a basis for understanding and managing organizational design and the inevitable processes of interunit conflict and politics.

Organization Design: An Information Processing View

Jay R. Galbraith

THE INFORMATION PROCESSING MODEL

A basic proposition is that the greater the uncertainty of the task, the greater the amount of information that has to be processed between decision makers during the execution of the task. If the task is well understood prior to performing it, much of the activity can be preplanned. If it is not understood, then during the actual task execution more knowledge is acquired which leads to changes in resource allocations, schedules, and priorities. All these changes require information processing *during* task performance. Therefore *the greater the task uncertainty, the greater the amount of information that must be processed among decision makers during task execution in order to achieve a given level of performance.* The basic effect of uncertainty is to limit the ability of the organization to preplan or to make decisions about activities in advance of their execution. Therefore it is hypothesized that the observed variations in organizational forms are variations in the strategies of organizations to 1) increase their ability to preplan, 2) increase their flexibility to adapt to their inability to preplan, or, 3) to decrease the level of performance required for continued viability. Which strategy is chosen depends on the relative costs of the strategies. The function of the framework is to identify these strategies and their costs.

THE MECHANISTIC MODEL

This framework is best developed by keeping in mind a hypothetical organization. Assume it is large and employs a number of specialist groups and resources in providing the output. After the task has been divided into specialists subtasks, the problem is to integrate the subtasks around the completion of the global task. This is the problem of organization design. The behaviors that occur in one subtask cannot be judged as good or bad *per se*. The behaviors are more effective or ineffective depending upon the behaviors of the other subtask performers. There is a design problem because the executors of the behaviors cannot communicate with all the roles with whom they are interdependent. Therefore the design problem is to create mechanisms that permit coordinated action across large numbers of interdependent roles. Each of these mechanisms, however, has a limited range over which it is effective at handling the information requirements necessary to coordinate the interdependent roles. As the amount of uncertainty increases, and therefore information processing increases, the organization must adopt integrating mechanisms which increase its information processing capabilities.

1. Coordination by Rules or Programs.   For routine predictable tasks March and Simon have identified the use of rules or programs to coordinate behavior between interdependent subtasks [March and Simon, 1958, Chap. 6]. To the extent that job related situations can be predicted in advance, and behaviors specified for these situations, programs allow an interdependent set of activities to be performed without the need for inter-unit communication. Each role occupant simply executes the behavior which is appropriate for the task related situation with which he is faced.

2. Hierarchy.   As the organization faces greater uncertainty its participants face situations for which they have no rules. At this point the hierarchy is employed on an exception basis. The recurring job situations are programmed with rules while infrequent situations are referred to that level in the hierarchy where a global perspective exists for all affected subunits. However, the hierarchy also has a limited range. As uncertainty increases the number of exceptions increases until the hierarchy becomes overloaded.

3. Coordination by Targets or Goals.   As the uncertainty of the organization's task increases, coordination increasingly takes place by specifying outputs, goals or targets [March and Simon, 1958, p. 145]. Instead of specifying specific behaviors to be enacted, the organization undertakes processes to set goals to be achieved and the employees select the behaviors which lead to goal accomplishment. Planning reduces the amount of information processing in the hierarchy by increasing the amount of discretion exercised at lower levels. Like the use of rules, planning achieves integrated action and also eliminates the need for continuous communication among interdependent subunits as long as task performance stays within the planned task specifications, budget limits and within targeted completion dates. If it does not, the hierarchy is again employed on an exception basis.

The ability of an organization to coordinate interdependent tasks depends on its ability to compute meaningful subgoals to guide subunit action. When uncertainty increases because of introducing new products, entering new markets, or employing new technologies these subgoals are incorrect. The result is more exceptions, more information processing, and an overloaded hierarchy.

DESIGN STRATEGIES

The ability of an organization to successfully utilize coordination by goal setting, hierarchy, and rules depends on the combination of the frequency of exceptions and the capacity of the hierarchy to handle them. As the task uncertainty increases the organization must again take organization design action. It can proceed in either of two general ways. First, it can act in two ways to reduce the amount of information that is processed. And second, the organization can act in two ways to increase its capacity to handle more information. The two methods for reducing the need for information and the two methods for increasing processing capacity are shown schematically in Figure 1. The effect of all these actions is to reduce the number of exceptional cases referred upward into the organization through hierar-

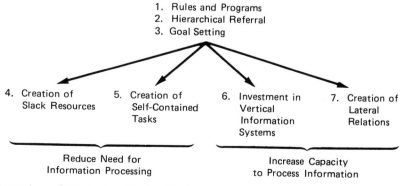

Figure 1   Organization Design Strategies

chical channels. The assumption is that the critical limiting factor of an organizational form is its ability to handle the non-routine, consequential events that cannot be anticipated and planned for in advance. The non-programmed events place the greatest communication load on the organization.

1. Creation of Slack Resources. As the number of exceptions begins to overload the hierarchy, one response is to increase the planning targets so that fewer exceptions occur. For example, completion dates can be extended until the number of exceptions that occur are within the existing information processing capacity of the organization. This has been the practice in solving job shop scheduling problems [Pounds, 1963]. Job shops quote delivery times that are long enough to keep the scheduling problem within the computational and information processing limits of the organization. Since every job shop has the same problem standard lead times evolve in the industry. Similarly budget targets could be raised, buffer inventories employed, etc. The greater the uncertainty, the greater the magnitude of the inventory, lead time or budget needed to reduce an overload.

All of these examples have a similar effect. They represent the use of slack resources to reduce the amount of interdependence between subunits [March and Simon, 1958, Cyert and March, 1963]. This keeps the required amount of information within the capacity of the organization to process it. Information processing is reduced because an exception is less likely to occur and reduced interdependence means that fewer factors need to be considered simultaneously when an exception does occur.

The strategy of using slack resources has its costs. Relaxing budget targets has the obvious cost of requiring more budget. Increasing the time to completion date has the effect of delaying the customer. Inventories require the investment of capital funds which could be used elsewhere. Reduction of design optimization reduces the performance of the article being designed. Whether slack resources are used to reduce information or not depends on the relative cost of the other alternatives.

The design choices are: 1) among which factors to change (lead time, overtime, machine utilization, etc.) to create the slack, and 2) by what amount should the factor be changed. Many operations research models are useful in choosing factors and amounts. The time-cost trade off problem in project networks is a good example.

2. Creation of Self-Contained Tasks. The second method of reducing the amount of information processed is to change the subtask groupings from resource (input) based to output based categories and give each group the resources it needs to supply the output. For example, the functional organization could be changed to product groups. Each group would have its own product engineers, process engineers, fabricating and assembly operations, and marketing activities. In other situations, groups can be created around product lines, geographical areas, projects, client groups, markets, etc., each of which would contain the input resources necessary for creation of the output.

The strategy of self-containment shifts the basis of the authority structure from one based on input, resource, skill, or occupational categories to one based on output or geographical categories. The shift reduces the amount of information processing through several mechanisms. First, it reduces the amount of output diversity faced by a single collection of resources. For example, a professional organization with multiple skill specialties providing service to three different client groups must schedule the use of these specialties across three demands for their services and determine priorities when conflicts occur. But, if the organization changed to three groups, one for each client category, each with its own full complement of specialties, the schedule conflicts across client groups disappear and there is no need to process information to determine priorities.

The second source of information reduction occurs through a reduced division of labor. The functional or resource specialized structure pools the demand for skills across all output categories. In the example above each client generates approximately one-third of the demand for each skill. Since the division of labor is limited by the extent of the market, the division of labor must decrease as the demand decreases. In the professional organization, each client group may have generated a need for one-third of a computer programmer. The functional organization would have hired one programmer and shared him across the groups. In the self-contained structure there is insufficient demand in each group for a programmer so the professionals must do their own programming. Specialization is reduced but there is no problem of scheduling the programmer's time across the three possible uses for it.

The cost of the self-containment strategy is the loss of resource specialization. In the example, the organization foregoes the benefit of a specialist in computer programming. If there is physical equipment, there is a loss of economies of scale. The professional organization would require three machines in the self-contained form but only a large time-shared machine in the functional form. But those resources which have large economies of scale or for which specialization is necessary may remain centralized. Thus, it is the degree of self-containment that is the variable. The greater the degree of uncertainty, other things equal, the greater the degree of self-containment.

The design choices are the basis for the self-contained structure and the number of resources to be contained in the groups. No groups are completely self-contained or they would not be part of the same organization. But one product divisionalized firm may have eight of fifteen functions in the divisions while another may have twelve of fifteen in the divisions. Usually accounting, finance, and legal services are centralized and shared. Those functions which have economies of scale, require specialization or are necessary for control remain centralized and not part of the self-contained group.

The first two strategies reduced the amount of information by lower performance standards and creating small autonomous groups to provide the output. Information is reduced because an exception is less likely to occur and fewer factors need to be considered when an exception does occur. The next two strategies accept the performance standards and division of labor as given and adapt the organization so as to process the new information which is created during task performance.

3. Investment in Vertical Information Systems. The organization can invest in mechanisms which allow it to process information acquired during task performance without overloading the hierarchical communication channels. The investment occurs according to the following logic. After the organization has created its plan or set of targets for inventories, labor utilization, budgets, and schedules, unanticipated events occur which generate exceptions requiring adjustments to the original plan. At some point when the number of exceptions becomes substantial, it is preferable to generate a new plan rather than make incremental changes with each exception. The issue is then how frequently should plans be revised —yearly, quarterly, or monthly? The greater the frequency of replanning the greater the resources, such as clerks, computer time, input-output devices, etc., required to process information about relevant factors.

The cost of information processing resources can be minimized if the language is formalized. Formalization of a decision-making language simply means that more information is transmitted with the same number of symbols. It is assumed that information processing resources are consumed in proportion to the number of symbols transmitted. The accounting system is an example of a formalized language.

Providing more information, more often, may simply overload the decision maker. Investment may be required to increase the capacity of the decision maker by employing computers, various man-machine combinations, assistants-to, etc. The cost of this strategy is the cost of the information processing resources consumed in transmitting and processing the data.

The design variables of this strategy are the decision frequency, the degree of formalization of language, and the type of decision mechanism which will make the choice. This strategy is usually operationalized by creating redundant information channels which transmit data from the point of origination upward in the hierarchy where the point of decision rests. If data is formalized and quantifiable, this strategy is effective. If the relevant data are qualitative and ambiguous, then it may prove easier to bring the decisions down to where the information exists.

4. Creation of Lateral Relationships. The last strategy is to employ selectively joint decision processes which cut across lines of authority. This strategy moves the level of decision making down in the organization to where the information exists but does so without reorganizing around self-contained groups. There are several types of lateral decision processes. Some processes are usually referred to as the informal organization. However, these informal processes do not always arise spontaneously out of the needs of the task. This is particularly true in multi-national organizations in which participants are separated by physical barriers, language differences, and cultural differences. Under these circumstances lateral processes need to be designed. The lateral processes evolve as follows with increases in uncertainty.

4.1. *Direct Contact* between managers who share a problem. If a problem arises on the shop floor, the foreman can simply call the design engineer, and they can jointly agree upon a solution. From an information processing view, the joint decision prevents an upward referral and unloads the hierarchy.

4.2. *Liaison Roles*—when the volume of contacts between any two departments grows, it becomes economical to set up a specialized role to handle this communication. Liaison men are typical examples of specialized roles designed to facilitate communication between two interdependent departments and to bypass the long lines of communication involved in upward referral. Liaison roles arise at lower and middle levels of management.

4.3. *Task Forces.* Direct contact and liaison roles, like the integration mechanisms before them, have a limited range of usefulness. They work when two managers or functions are involved. When problems arise involving seven or eight departments, the decision making capacity of direct contacts is exceeded. Then these problems must be referred upward. For uncertain, interdependent tasks such situations arise frequently. Task forces are a form of horizontal contact which is designed for problems of multiple departments.

The task force is made up of representatives from each of the affected departments. Some are full-time members, others may be part-time. The task force is a temporary group. It exists only as long as the problem remains. When a solution is reached, each participant returns to his normal tasks.

To the extent that they are successful, task forces remove problems from higher levels of the hierarchy. The decisions are made at lower levels in the organization. In order to guarantee integration, a group problem solving approach is taken. Each affected subunit contributes a member and therefore provides the information necessary to judge the impact on all units.

4.4. *Teams.* The next extension is to incorporate the group decision process into the permanent decision processes. That is, as certain decisions consistently arise, the task forces become permanent. These groups are labeled teams. There are many design issues concerned in team decision making such as at what level do they operate, who participates, etc. [Galbraith, 1973, Chapters 6 and 7]. One design decision is particularly critical. This is the choice of leadership. Sometimes a problem exists largely in one department so that the department manager is the leader. Sometimes the leadership passes from one manager to another. As a new product moves to the market place, the leader of the new product team is first the technical manager followed by the production and then the marketing manager. The result is that if the team cannot reach a consensus decision and the leader decides, the goals of the leader are consistent with the goals of the organization for the decision in question. But quite often obvious leaders cannot be found. Another mechanism must be introduced.

4.5. *Integrating Roles.* The leadership issue is solved by creating a new role—an integrating role [Lawrence and Lorsch, 1967, Chapter 3]. These roles carry the labels of product managers, program managers, project managers, unit managers (hospitals), materials managers, etc. After the role is created, the design problem is to create enough power in the role to influence the decision process. These roles have power even when no one reports directly to them. They have some power because they report to the general manager. But if they are selected so as to be unbiased with respect to the groups they integrate and to have technical competence, they have expert power. They collect information and equalize power differences due to preferential access to knowledge and information. The power equalization increases trust and the quality of the joint decision process. But power equalization occurs only if the integrating role is staffed with someone who can exercise expert power in the form of persuasion and informal influences rather than exert the power of rank or authority.

4.6. *Managerial Linking Roles.* As tasks become more uncertain, it is more difficult to exercise expert power. The role must get more power of the formal authority type in order to be effective at coordinating the joint decisions which occur at lower levels of the organization. This position power changes the nature of the role which for lack of a better name is labeled a managerial linking role. It is not like the integrating role because it possesses formal position power but is different from line managerial roles in that participants do not report to the linking manager. The power is added by the following successive changes.

a. The integrator receives approval power of budgets formulated in the departments to be integrated.

b. The planning and budgeting process starts with the integrator making his initiation in budgeting legitimate.

c. Linking manager receives the budget for the area of responsibility and buys resources from the specialist groups.

These mechanisms permit the manager to exercise influence even though no one works directly for him. The role is concerned with integration but exercises power through the formal power of the position. If this power is insufficient to integrate the subtasks and creation of self-contained groups is not feasible, there is one last step.

4.7. Matrix Organization. The last step is to create the dual authority relationship and the matrix organization [Galbraith, 1971]. At some point in the organization some roles have two superiors. The design issue is to select the locus of these roles. The result is a balance of power between the managerial linking roles and the normal line organization roles. Figure 2 depicts the pure matrix design.

The work of Lawrence and Lorsch is highly consistent with the assertions concerning lateral relations [Lawrence and Lorsch, 1967, Lorsch and Lawrence, 1968]. They compared the types of lateral relations undertaken by the most successful firm in three different industries. Their data are summarized in Table 1. The plastics firm has the greatest rate of new product introduction (uncertainty) and the greatest utilization of lateral processes. The container firm was also very successful but utilized only

TABLE 1

	PLASTICS	FOOD	CONTAINER
% new products in last ten years	35%	20%	0%

Integrating Devices	Rules
	Hierarchy
	Planning
	Direct
	  Contact
	Teams at 3
	  levels
	Integrating
	  Dept.
		Rules
		Hierarchy
		Planning
		Direct
		  Contact
		Task forces
		
		Integrators
			Rules
			Hierarchy
			Planning
			Direct
			  Contact

% Integrators/Managers	22%	17%	0%

Adapted from Lawrence and Lorsch, 1967, pp. 86–138 and Lorsch and Lawrence, 1968.

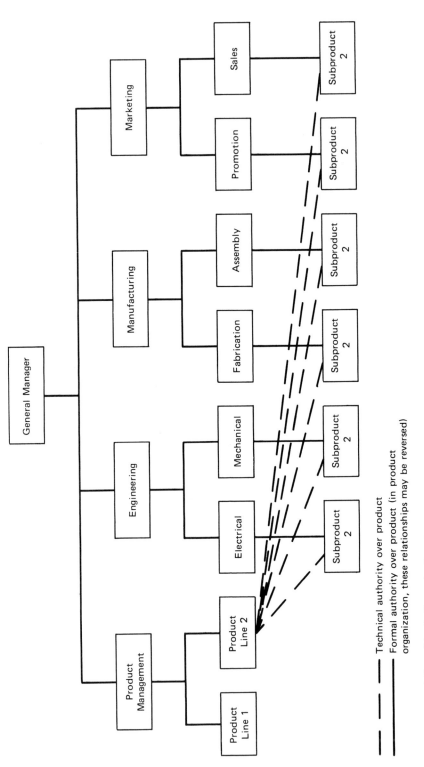

Figure 2   A Pure Matrix Organization

standard practices because its information processing task is much less formidable. Thus, the greater the uncertainty the lower the level of decision making and the integration is maintained by lateral relations.

Table 1 points out the cost of using lateral relations. The plastics firm has 22% of its managers in integration roles. Thus, the greater the use of lateral relations the greater the managerial intensity. This cost must be balanced against the cost of slack resources, self-contained groups and information systems.

CHOICE OF STRATEGY

Each of the four strategies has been briefly presented. The organization can follow one or some combination of several if it chooses. It will choose that strategy which has the least cost in its environmental context. [For an example, see Galbraith, 1970.] However, what may be lost in all of the explanations is that the four strategies are hypothesized to be an exhaustive set of alternatives. That is, if the organization is faced with greater uncertainty due to technological change, higher performance standards due to increased competition, or diversifies its product line to reduce dependence, the amount of information processing is increased. *The organization must adopt at least one of the four strategies when faced with greater uncertainty.* If it does not consciously choose one of the four, then the first, reduced performance standards, will happen automatically. The task information requirements and the capacity of the organization to process information are always matched. If the organization does not consciously match them, reduced performance through budget overruns, schedule overruns will occur in order to bring about equality. Thus the organization should be planned and designed simultaneously with the planning of the strategy and resource allocations. But if the strategy involves introducing new products, entering new markets, etc., then some provision for increased information must be made. Not to decide is to decide, and it is to decide upon slack resources as the strategy to remove hierarchical overload.

There is probably a fifth strategy which is not articulated here. Instead of changing the organization in response to task uncertainty, the organization can operate on its environment to reduce uncertainty. The organization through strategic decisions, long term contracts, coalitions, etc., can control its environment. But these maneuvers have costs also. They should be compared with costs of the four design strategies presented above.

SUMMARY

The purpose of this paper has been to explain why task uncertainty is related to organizational form. In so doing the cognitive limits theory of

Herbert Simon was the guiding influence. As the consequences of cognitive limits were traced through the framework various organization design strategies were articulated. The framework provides a basis for integrating organizational interventions, such as information systems and group problem solving, which have been treated separately before.

BIBLIOGRAPHY

CYERT, RICHARD, and MARCH, JAMES, *The Behavioral Theory of the Firm*, Prentice-Hall, Englewood Cliffs, N.J., 1963.

GALBRAITH, JAY, "Environmental and Technological Determinants of Organization Design: A Case Study" in Lawrence and Lorsch (eds.) *Studies in Organization Design*, Richard D. Irwin Inc., Homewood, Ill., 1970.

GALBRAITH, JAY, "Designing Matrix Organizations," *Business Horizons*, (Feb. 1971), pp. 29–40.

GALBRAITH, JAY, *Organization Design*, Addison-Wesley Pub. Co., Reading, Mass., 1973.

LAWRENCE, PAUL, and LORSCH, JAY, *Organization and Environment*, Division of Research, Harvard Business School, Boston, Mass., 1967.

LORSCH, JAY, and LAWRENCE, PAUL, "Environmental Factors and Organization Integration," Paper read at the Annual Meeting of the American Sociological Association, August 27, 1968, Boston, Mass.

MARCH, JAMES, and SIMON, HERBERT, *Organizations*, John Wiley & Sons, New York, N.Y., 1958.

POUNDS, WILLIAM, "The Scheduling Environment" in Muth and Thompson (eds.) *Industrial Scheduling*, Prentice-Hall Inc., Englewood Cliffs, N.J., 1963.

SIMON, HERBERT, *Models of Man*, John Wiley & Sons, New York, N.Y., 1957.

Matrix Organization: A Review

Kenneth Knight

A new type of organization structure is spreading through industry and parts of the public sector, which has so far been very inadequately documented. The common label used to describe it is 'Matrix' though there is at present no agreed definition of the term. Usually the name is applied to structures which involve some form of dual or multiple authority, a 'two boss' situation, but the range of interpretation of the term is fairly wide, and will be explored below.

Matrix structures have spread most rapidly in organizations where people work on projects,[1] such as research and development units,[2] advertising agencies[3] and management consultancies[4] but they have also begun to appear in non-project settings. An American report published some years ago[5] gave a list of prestigious companies like American Cyanamid, Avco, Carborundum, Caterpillar Tractor, General Telephone and Electronics, Hughes Aircraft, ITT, 3M's, Monsanto Chemical, National Cash Register, Prudential Insurance, TRW and Texas Instruments as users of matrix organization. In some of these only parts of the company, such as R and D, marketing, or construction activities may be structured on matrix lines, in others matrix organization extends to major divisions or the whole com-

From *Journal of Management Studies*, May 1976, vol. 13, no. 2, pp. 111–30. Reprinted by permission.

pany. Examples of the latter include Dow-Corning,[6] Corning Glass,[7] Lockheed Aircraft[8] and, in this country, the British Aircraft Corporation[9] and a number of the major divisions of ICI.[10]

In the public services sector matrix structures are turning up in some of the new establishments of higher education and have been identified or advocated in the administration of health and social services.[11]

Although organizations of this type are structurally complex and bristle with managerial and psychological problems, they have not as yet attracted a great deal of attention from either researchers or theoreticians and one must agree with Kingdon that '. . . it is really quite amazing how little organizational guidance is available either conceptually or pragmatically, to those who are currently involved in operating matrix organizations'.[12]

An extensive literature search has discovered only two books[13] which deal seriously with the theory and operating problems of matrix organization, together with a handful of articles which throw light on specific aspects. They are supplemented by a number of descriptions of specific matrix organizations, some extremely succinct, others more detailed, and various references-in-passing in books or articles on other subjects.[14]

This article attempts to review the literature on matrix organization, such as it is, in order to find answers to five questions:

1. What do people who use the term matrix organization mean by it?
2. What reasons are there for introducing such structures?
3. What advantages are claimed for them?
4. What problems do they encounter?
5. How can they be made to work effectively?

THE MEANING OF MATRIX ORGANIZATION

Despite the lack of accepted definition and occasional divergencies of viewpoint, there seems to be a fair measure of agreement among authors who use the term, about the essential character of matrix organization. It is seen as a 'mixed' organizational form[15] in which the normal vertical hierarchy is 'overlayed' by some form of lateral authority, influence or communication. As a result it contains roles which are subject to dual influence and it emphasizes coordination through lateral relationships which cross departmental boundaries.

The word 'overlay' is used frequently and expresses the same image as the word matrix itself. This is, that the normal hierarchical groupings of an organization (usually functional) can be represented by the columns, and the lateral, coordinating ones (often of project, product or business area) by the rows of a matrix or grid, *e.g.*

		FUNCTIONS			
		A	*B*	*C*	*D*
Projects or	1				
Products or	2				
Business areas	3				
	4				

The cells of the matrix contain people who belong to more than one grouping.

So far, however, we are dealing with a very general concept, so general indeed that it is possible for Kingdon to claim that

> It is obvious to anyone who has worked in even the most stringent hierarchy, or bureaucracy, that any organization is really a matrix or mixed model with multiple-channel communication. But in non-matrix organizations lateral channels are not necessarily 'legitimate'. More frequently they are viewed as informal or even underground forms of communication.[16]

It is in the form in which lateral groupings are legitimized that the main differences arise.

One interpretation is that the matrix is essentially a coordinative device added to an executive hierarchy which remains the true basis of managerial authority.

This gives rise to interdepartmental project teams,[17] coordinated groups,[18] and individuals acting as project coordinators.[19] In this form either a functional or an area organization predominates and the role of the project manager or team is to coordinate the efforts of people working in parallel heirarchies in relation to specific projects or areas of common concern.

A contrasting view of matrix organization is found occasionally.[20] In this, project teams and functional departments exist side by side, and individuals are working in either one or the other at any particular point in time. The functional organization, however, exists as a 'fall-back' for the project groups, both providing a home for people when they are not working full-time on a project, an opportunity for keeping in touch with colleagues in their own speciality and a base to return to when a project comes to an end. This situation is similar to the one advocated by Miller and Rice[21] as an answer to the increasingly common problem of creating and disbanding temporary organizations for the performance of specific tasks.

The most typical and widespread view, however, sees the matrix as an evenly balanced compromise between functional and project organization, between grouping by process and by purpose. This is the view of Galbraith[22] who in a diagram displaying the range of alternatives, confines matrix organization to a fairly narrow central portion of a continuum going from complete functional to complete product organization. In this model it is possible to talk of authority being shared between project and functional managers, and of individuals having roles which involve dual reporting relationships.[23] Typically, however, the authority of the two managers and the decisions and outcomes for which they can be held responsible are not the same and the definition of their respective roles is one of the recurring themes in the literature on matrix management, to which we shall return.

Thus overall agreement on the general meaning of matrix is accompanied by a good deal of disagreement concerning its practical embodiments and, while the three models mentioned seem to summarize the range of interpretations found in the literature, there are almost as many individual variants as there are examples.

REASONS FOR INTRODUCING MATRIX STRUCTURES

Matrix organizations do not just happen, they are introduced for a reason. The reasons given for their adoption seem to be of three kinds—the historical background to the development of matrix structures in the American aerospace industry, a set of analytic approaches to the new tasks and requirements facing complex organizations, and associated with the latter, the more general desire to develop new organizational forms which satisfy the motivational and ideological criteria of those who criticize bureaucratic hierarchies.

Historical reasons. According to Kingdon the development of matrix structures in the 1960s resulted from a quite specific state of affairs—the fact that the American government made it a condition of consideration for research and development contracts that the contracting firms should have a 'project management system'.[24] This ensured that representatives of government agencies could work with a specific person, the project manager, with full responsibility for meeting costs and deadlines over the project as a whole, rather than having to negotiate with a number of functional heads, each with only partial responsibility. In practice the condition could be met in one of two ways—by abandoning functional groupings and organizing entirely on a project basis, or by superimposing project management on top of the existing functional structure, thus creating a matrix.

Those firms who chose the latter and more difficult alternative did so, according to Kingdon, because while the project organization satisfied the customer's requirements for having project responsibility located in one place, the functional structure remained essential for the future of the firm, beyond the completion of current projects. It ensured continuity by preserving, updating and developing the firm's technical and human resources, its capability to compete for future projects as well as complete existing ones. Hence the matrix structure achieved a compromise between the customers' requirements for successful project completion and the shareholders' requirements for the continuing viability of the firm.

Moreover, as Marquis found in a detailed study of thirty-eight firms working on U.S. Government R and D contracts, while the existence of project teams increased the likelihood of meeting cost and time targets, the presence of a strong functional base was associated with higher technical excellence as rated by both managers and clients.[25]

Task requirements. The demands placed on aerospace firms by the American Government can be regarded as a special case, or as an example of the generally more complex demands which some organizations are having to face. The need to deal with increasing complexity is one of the main reasons given for the growth of matrix organization. The explanation comes in several forms. Greiner[26] sees matrix organization and the use of cross-functional teams as one of a series of responses to growing *internal* complexity, associated with increases in the size of organizations. It replaces coordination through a formal bureaucratic structure with a more flexible system of direct contacts. Argyris[27] relates similar developments to an increasingly competitive environment and 'the new administrative and information technology available to deal with complexity'. Kingdon[28] sees the matrix as the organization's response to a 'turbulent-field' environment (i.e. using the four-fold classification developed by Emery and Trist, an environment in which causal relationships are a great deal more complex than those arising in a purely competitive system).

It is left to Galbraith[29] to spell out in detail just how matrix organization constitutes a response to complexity. In the first instance, increased complexity, whether internal (size, technology) or external (markets, competitors, collaboration with other organizations) means that the organization has more information to process, and the point comes when the existing information processing capacity becomes overloaded. Galbraith identifies four possible responses.

1. *Creation of slack resources.* The organization extends its schedules, incurs higher costs. (A 'do-nothing' response also amounts to this.)

2. *Creation of self-contained tasks.* Complexity is reduced by delegation and decentralization, creating independent sub-units. This resembles the project-only solution rejected by Kingdon.

3. *Investment in vertical information systems.* This can mean the use of computers or extra people or both, to enable the vertical hierarchy to

cope with more information and more frequent changes of plan. It can be costly.

4. *Creation of lateral relations.* This off-loads part of the information processing task to lower levels of the organization, through direct interfunctional contacts. Galbraith envisages seven ways of achieving this, in an ascending order of cost. Matrix organization is the seventh, which he would expect to be reached only if the preceding six prove inadequate.[30]

What the matrix does, according to this analysis, is to deal with the kinds of communication and decision needs which arise in complex interdisciplinary projects, subject to critical time and cost constraints, which by definition, have neither the option of slack resources, nor that of self-contained tasks.

Motivational and ideological reasons. Matrix organizations seem to be attractive to some of those who are searching for alternatives to hierarchical organization, 'pyramidal' structures or 'bureaucracy'. This kind of reason can never be clearly distinguished from the task-related reasons that have just been discussed, because the very criticism of hierarchical organization as such tends to be based on the premise that this type of structure is unfitted for the requirements of complex technologies and rapidly changing environments (a premise which has still to be proved). Nevertheless, there is a distinctly 'value-laden' flavour in some of the matrix literature.

There are suggestions in Kingdon that matrix organizations will share some of the characteristics of the 'organic' form identified by Burns and Stalker[31] and contrasted by them with the 'mechanistic' form of extreme hierarchical control. Argyris (who unlike Kingdon or Burns and Stalker has argued elsewhere that pyramidal structures have now become inappropriate to *most* situations[32]) prefaces his discussion of the problems of introducing matrix organization by a strong plea for organizational forms which will increase free, reliable communication, trust, risk-taking and helping each other, and internalized long-term commitment.[33] The adaptive and organic nature of what he calls 'polyarchic organization' is stressed by Algie.[34] Davis sees matrix organization as more in line with the 'democratic norms' of scientific and professional staff and sees it as leading to improved motivation.[35] And in one of the most detailed accounts of the operation of a matrix structure, that of the Advanced Devices Centre of the Northern Electric Company, it is made quite explicit that the aim of the new organization was to create an environment conducive to 'increased commitment and participation of all those involved', making use of 'concepts from the behavioral sciences'.[36]

That matrix should be attractive to people who look for more humane, participative and flexible forms of organization should not surprise us. By its very nature it depends on greatly increased collaboration between a wider range of people, it emphasizes interdependence of departments rather than the boundaries between them, and it brings opportunities for enhanced discretion, a greater personal contribution and participation in decision-making to people at lower levels of the hierarchy.

ADVANTAGES CLAIMED FOR MATRIX ORGANIZATION

The main advantages which are claimed for matrix structures are:

> efficient use of resources
>
> flexibility in conditions of change and uncertainty
>
> technical excellence
>
> ability to balance conflicting objectives
>
> freeing top management for long-range planning
>
> improving motivation and commitment
>
> giving opportunities for personal development.

Some of these may have to be qualified when we come to look at the problems attendant on this type of structure, but first it is useful to look more closely at the basis for these claims.

Efficiency. The 'resources' which can be used more efficiently by a matrix structure are mainly specialized staff. Individual specialists or specialist groups, as well as their equipment, can be shared between a number of projects or products rather than having to be duplicated in order to provide independent cover for each. If a project requires half an astrophysicist, it does not need to support a whole one half-occupied. Parkinson's law is less likely to operate where a number of projects are competing for the time of the same person. Star performers and possessors of rare skills or knowledge can make their contribution where the need for their competence and expertise is greatest, and to more than one project at a time without loss of project control.

Flexibility. Matrix organizations are said to enjoy the same advantage as the 'organic' organizations described by Burns and Stalker, that of being able to respond quickly and adaptively to a changing and uncertain environment. This is due to the additional lateral communication channels, which in small 'organic' organizations arise from the fluid nature of relationships, but which are institutionalized in the matrix. Because of frequent contact between members of different departments, information permeates the organization and more quickly reaches those people who need to take account of it. Decisions can be made more rapidly, changes in the givens of a situation can quickly be translated into changes of plan and acted on.[37]

Technical excellence. Matrix structures are said to facilitate high quality and innovative solutions to complex technical problems. On the one hand they provide the advantage of interdisciplinary stimulation and cross-fertilization by bringing together the diverse viewpoints and perspectives of different specialities and departments in cross-functional, interdisciplinary project teams. At the same time, and this is regarded as more important by Marquis, they ensure the maintenance of high technical standards through the ongoing contact of specialists with members of their own discipline.[38]

Balance. The need to balance conflicting objectives lies at the origin of matrix organization. Cleland describes it as a principle of 'deliberate conflict'[39] which contains a set of built-in checks and balances on time, cost and performance.[40] Kingdon describes the matrix as a way of balancing the customer's requirement for project completion and cost control with the organization's need for economic operation and development of technical capability for the future. He sees project management as tending towards opportunism, functional towards utopianism, with the matrix holding the balance between the two.[41]

Freeing top management. A point made by Goggin describing the company-wide 'multi-dimensional' structure of Dow-Corning[42] is that it frees top management from the need to become involved in day-to-day operations, through the delegation of ongoing decision-making, thus giving more time for long range planning.

Motivation. Project teams tend to operate, whether by force of circumstances or by deliberate design, in a more participative and 'democratic' manner than functional hierarchies. Membership of the team is based on special knowledge and responsibility for given aspects of the work and hence the members have to be listened to irrespective of status and rank. This results in people at lower levels in the organization finding themselves with a greater say in significant decisions and is likely to enhance their commitment to the task. High levels of motivation are mentioned in many descriptions of matrix operation. The extreme case perhaps is Kingdon's description of the 'batcave', a strategy used by engineering and programming groups up against a deadline, where volunteers from the two groups worked together in a single large office, non-stop on a two shift basis, until the problem was solved and the programmes working.

Another aspect of motivation is treated by Miller and Rice who emphasize the need for psychological support from a group which has some permanence and with whom the individual can identify, the 'sentient group'.[43] Where people work on projects or tasks involving groupings of limited duration it is important to provide some more permanent organizational 'home' and this is one of the functions which a matrix organization can fulfil.

Development. There are three ways in which working in a matrix structure can help to develop individual employees. Firstly, it enlarges their experience and broadens their outlook, by putting them in situations where they have to take account of a wider range of considerations and issues than those arising within their own speciality. Next to the job rotation practised by some companies it is the best way of exposing people to the different facets of an operation and diverse criteria that have to be satisfied. Secondly, the matrix increases the responsibility of individuals representing their speciality within a mixed team, and involves them in challenges and decisions which are normally met at a higher level in a departmental hierarchy. Finally it exposes them in a wider arena and gives persons of high potential a chance to demonstrate their capabilities and make a name for themselves.

CAN THESE CLAIMS BE SUBSTANTIATED?

It should come as no surprise that 'hard' evidence for the claimed advantages of matrix is at present practically non-existent. Given the fact that there is as yet no agreed definition of what constitutes a matrix organization, that several types of bilateral and multilateral structure have been and are being tried, and that these tend to be introduced in situations of operational complexity and change, the circumstances for systematic investigation (as distinct from advocacy by committed managers or social scientists) have hardly begun to exist.

The main attempt so far to evaluate the effect of different forms of project organization in a comparative study seems to be the Sloan School Project on the Management of Science and Technology, the results of which have not been very fully, or accessibly, published.[44] This provides some evidence of superior technical performance on projects using a 'matrix' organization, compared with three other types of structure: complete project and complete functional organization, as well as a structure in which more than 50 per cent of technical staff were full-time in project teams with only a small functional back-up structure. The 'hybrid' structure which proved the most successful had less than 50 per cent of technical staff in full-time project teams, while 'most of the personnel were directly responsible to the project manager for work assignments but remained physically located with their functional manager .

Another study which provides some relevant evidence is reported by Corey and Star.[45] In a survey of some 500 among the 1000 largest U.S. manufacturing companies in 1968 it was found that those firms (a majority) which had a 'programme management' structure were more successful in developing and introducing new products than the rest. Moreover, 'in general, businesses whose programme manager had considerable authority and responsibility cutting across several areas (*e.g.* sales, advertising, engineering, logistics) were more successful in developing and introducing new products than businesses whose programme managers had more limited authority and responsibilities'.

Apart from these two studies and Argyris's negative findings from his survey of nine large organizations,[46] all the evidence at present seems to be anecdotal, and the benefits reported in specific cases tend to be in a fairly generalized form. Personally, I do not regard this as particularly damaging to the concept of matrix organization. How much 'evidence' do we have, after all, for the effectiveness of any of the other organizational options? Two decades of comparative organizational studies have left us with rather a limited, and highly generalized, stock of research-based knowledge. The main conclusion to emerge from this body of research (and even this is still controversial) is that 'organic' organizations, which emphasize lateral communications, individual discretion, and participative decision-making, are more appropriate to situations of uncertainty and rapid change, than more strongly hierarchical ones in which the emphasis is on vertical communications, prescribed rules and authority, while the latter are more effective in stable, predictable situations.

In so far as matrix represents an attempt to achieve the benefits of an 'organic' pattern of relationships in the more highly structured setting of the large organization, it can claim the backing of this body of research, for what it is worth. To expect more in the current state of organizational research would be unrealistic.

PROBLEMS OF MATRIX ORGANIZATION

It is usual to find that the benefits of a particular approach have to be offset against a corresponding set of costs. Decentralization increases individual accountability but reduces control, fragmented jobs may be more efficient in the short term but their incumbents suffer from low motivation, and so forth. With matrix organization the situation is much less clear-cut and rather curious. If we look through the published accounts for the problems and costs which users of matrix organization have experienced, we find that many of them are not so much complementary to the advantages we have listed, but contradictory—the same factors, but with the sign reversed. Thus matrix organizations have been reported as costly, cumbersome and bureaucratic, inhibiting technical achievement, overburdening top-management, demotivating employees and detrimental to their development. The balancing of conflicting objectives and authority, which is the *raison d'être* of the matrix proves also to be one of its major problems. Why is this?

I think there are two possible reasons for this odd situation. One is the lack of experience with matrix organization and the diversity of actual systems which are embraced by the single title. Eric Trist, in his *Foreword* to Kingdon's book, tells how matrix organizations emerged in the U.S. aerospace industry under the pressure of events, 'as hurried improvisations rather than as thought-through transformations'.[47] Hence the advantages and disadvantages found in a particular matrix structure may have a great deal to do with the way in which that structure was introduced, the actual system of management being used, and the skill with which it is being applied. No one has yet tried to relate structural and operational differences between various examples of matrix management to their respective costs and benefits.

But there may well be a second and more fundamental reason for the contradictions that are found. In most cases an innovation is assessed from a single implied reference point—profit centres from the point of view of functional organization, job enrichment from the point of view of fragmented and routinized work. But matrix organization, being a compromise between two or more existing alternatives always has to be looked at from at least two potential points of view and may, therefore, carry two diametrically opposed sets of costs and benefits. It is more flexible than functional organization but less so than a completely project-centered system. It uses resources more efficiently than a project structure but incurs administrative costs which would be unnecessary with a purely functional set-up. And so forth.

The main problems which arise in matrix organizations are most conveniently considered under four headings:

the conflicts that exist in them
achieving balance between their parts
the stresses on people in them
administrative and communication costs.

Conflict.   As we have seen, the matrix expresses a set of pre-existing conflicts between organizational needs and environmental pressures. It structures these conflicts, internalizes them within the organization, but does not remove them. The main institutionalized form of conflict within the matrix is that between functional managers and project managers who are in competition for the control of the same set of resources. This institutionalized conflict is liable to give rise to conflict at a more personal level, resulting from conflicting objectives and accountabilities, disputes about credit and blame, and attempts to redress an unequal power balance.

Argyris[48] describes how introducing a matrix intensified defensive and hostile attitudes between managers, which in his view it was intended to remove. He puts this down to the way in which the new systems were introduced, giving managers the impression of a new form of control, designed to help top management to check up on them. But Argyris' description also suggests that the organizational changes resulted in a breaking down of those organizational 'boundaries' which normally act as protective walls for the individual manager, safeguarding his undisputed control over a given sphere of operations.

It seems that whenever a matrix organization is introduced into what was a simple one-way authority structure, it leads to an increased sense of insecurity among managers, a sure recipe for defensive behaviour and personal conflict. Similar threats may be perceived by technicians, scientists and other specialists who are no longer left as sole judges in their own domain. The Northern Electric case study[49] demonstrates the resentment of technical specialists at the erosion of their autonomy through the insistence on 'democratic' group decision-making, which they perceived as a pressure to conform to inappropriate norms and detrimental to technical excellence.

Wilemon[50] in a detailed set of propositions based on his study of matrix management in the Apollo programme, lists those factors which increase the potential for conflict. These include:

diversity of disciplinary expertise
low power of project manager
poor understanding of project objectives by team
role ambiguity of team members
lack of agreement on superordinate goals
perception by functional staff that their roles are being usurped
low perception of interdependence
managerial level (more conflict at higher levels).

Wilemon sees the management of conflict as a key role of the project manager, and hence regards low project manager power as increasing the potential for conflict. This does not, however, take care of those situations where the project manager is himself a major protagonist in conflict.

Balance.   The difficulty of striking a balance between the authority of project heads and functional managers is illustrated by Kingdon's description of two systems for deploying staff at T.R.W., the 'job-shop' and the 'work package'. In the former the project managers largely control the movement of staff from functions into and out of project groups without a great deal of notice to functional management. It is like a 'hire and fire' situation within the company. In the 'work package' relationship by contrast the project manager negotiates the performance of given tasks with the functional head, who is left in control of staff assignment and the performance of the work.

In these two approaches the problem of conflict is solved by tilting the power balance decisively one way or the other. At the same time, of course, some of the major benefits of matrix organization are lost. The 'job shop' results in reduced efficiency in the use of resources, while the 'work package' may impair the flexibility and ultimately the viability of project management.

In the intervening situation where power is equally balanced between project and functional management, the assumption is that the managers concerned can resolve their conflicts amicably at their own level. Where this is not achieved conflicts often have to be taken up to the nearest 'cross-over point' for arbitration, and this may well be the chief executive. Under these circumstances, far from being freed for long-range planning, top management may find itself becoming overloaded with the task of resolving a succession of disputes.

The sources of the project manager's power, and hence of his ability to do the job for which he has been appointed, is a frequently discussed problem. Wilemon and Gemmill[51] discuss situations in which project managers are responsible for projects but have to work through functional management. They are seen as occupying an ambiguous position on the 'boundary', and their power to do their job depends on the rewards and punishments, direct or indirect, which they can bring into play, as well as on the respect inspired by their expertise and their personal skill at influencing others.

Kingdon highlights the difficulty of striking a stable balance between project and functional authority, horizontal and vertical influence. According to him the two kinds of influence are negatively correlated. The more successful lateral collaboration is achieved at a given level, the greater are the stresses up through the vertical hierarchy, with more senior managers resentful of being by-passed. And conversely, the better the vertical relationships in the line hierarchy, the more likely the lateral activities are to suffer from boundary disputes and communication blocks.[52]

Stress.   Matrix organizations can be stressful places to work in, not only for managers, for whom they can mean insecurity and conflict, but also for their subordinates. Kahn *et al.*[53] see stress at work arising from being in a 'boundary' position, which leads to the individual being subjected to conflicting or confusing expectations from others. Matrix organization creates many roles which are analogous to Kahn's boundary positions. The three conditions—role conflict, role ambiguity and role overload —identified by Kahn *et al.* as sources of stress are all to be found in the matrix.

Role conflict results directly from reporting to more than one superior, as is the case in the 'true' matrix as described for instance by Galbraith. If the superiors agree about one's role there is no role conflict, but as we have seen there is a likelihood that the two managers will themselves be in actual or potential conflict.

Role ambiguity results from a situation where expectations are unclear. In a matrix, staff at junior levels find themselves as members of project teams in a *de facto* decision-making situation, although they are theoretically liable to be overruled by their superiors outside the team. In this situation their authority, their ability to make decisions and their accountability can become very unclear. The increase in personal discretion and delegation which is typical of matrix structures is experienced as stressful by many.

Role overload arises from a situation in which the individual simply has too many demands placed on him. This arises most typically in a matrix organization where the normal operating responsibilities of individuals remain unchanged but they have to find additional time for meetings and discussions which are part of the new system. From these discussions arise new commitments and additional demands, thus leading to an increase in the overall workload.

Where such stresses exist matrix organizations can have an adverse effect on motivation rather than a positive one. For scientists in an R and D matrix even the enhanced opportunities for personal development may not be apparent. Where the project managers are in a very powerful position (as in T.R.W.'s 'job shop') specialists can get 'type-cast' and find themselves selected over and over again for the type of work in which they have demonstrated their competence, rather than being given an opportunity to expand their knowledge through a variety of tasks.

Administrative and communication costs. We have seen that the introduction of a matrix organization can lead to an increase in defensive behaviour by managers who feel their security and autonomy threatened. Unused to sharing responsibility they react by trying to erect alibis and cover themselves against blame by 'putting everything in writing'. This explains the perception that matrix organizations are 'bureaucratic'. They are, if operated with the attitudes and disciplines of a punitive single-channel hierarchy. It is in these circumstances also that matrix organizations seem to slow down decision-making, in contrast to those other situations of smooth collaboration at lower levels when the matrix is seen as 'a very efficient way of getting things done in a hurry'.

But even when allowances are made for the effects of defensive tactics by managers who are basically opposed to the matrix mode, it still seems that at the best of times, the matrix organization incurs greater administrative costs than a conventional hierarchy.

The system demands that people have to spend far more time at meetings, discussing rather than doing work, than in a simpler authority structure. There simply is more communicating to be done, more information has to get to more people either by written means or through meetings, or both. Given these extra costs it is most unlikely that matrix organizations will survive in the long run except in situations where they are essential. Kingdon reports, at the end of his book, a tendency to 'regress' to more conventional functional organization under the pressure of these higher costs and a reduced willingness to pay on the part of the Government. But as Galbraith has pointed out[54] matrix organization is a response to a problem of information processing. If the complexity of the situation is such that additional information processing is required, then the costs of this simply have to be paid in one way or another. Under these circumstances, matrix organization may be a cheaper or more acceptable solution than the alternative of large scale management information systems or of cost and time over-runs.

APPROACHES TO MAKING MATRIX WORK

Given the problems to which they are subject, the question of how matrix organizations can be made to work most effectively is one of obvious importance, and a number of approaches are suggested in the literature. There are four main approaches:

careful definition of organizational roles

modifying the organizational culture through training and organization development

setting up practical guidelines and ground rules for operating the matrix, and

creation of appropriate management systems to support it.

Definition of Roles. Many of the writers on matrix organization emphasize the importance of clearly defining the key roles in such a structure.

To encourage both communication and cooperation, prudent companies spell out every possible detail of a matrix project in advance—and in writing. Without some basic document to refer to, there are just too many chances for misunderstanding. Included in the agreement are such details as who does what, when and for whom.[55]

I have only come across one dissentient view, namely that of Goodman, who concluded from his research that ambiguous role definition is used deliberately in project and matrix organizations in order to preserve flexibility. But the data reported by Goodman do not support his argument.[56]

A number of writers suggest how the roles of project managers and functional managers in the typical R and D matrix should be defined.[57] A typical formulation is that the project manager decides *what* should be done, *when* and at *what cost*, while the functional manager is responsible for deciding *who* should do it and *how*.

A more radical approach to clarifying roles in dual (or multiple) influence situations has emerged from the organizational analysis work of the Glacier Project[58] further developed in a public services context by research teams at Brunel. This approach has given rise to a 'vocabulary' of role definitions which can be used to elucidate complex role relationships in a wide range of organizations.[59] By using this approach it might be found that in a particular organization certain *managerial* roles have to be distinguished from certain other *monitoring and coordinating* roles, while certain individuals are either *seconded, attached* or *outposted* to given units.[60] The use of these terms would be supported by a set of agreed definitions which specify the various aspects of authority and accountability in each of the roles.

Organization development. Many of the problems of operating a matrix seem to arise from inappropriate forms of behaviour, carried over from a departmentalized, functional structure and hence one approach to making matrix organizations work more effectively is to undertake activities aimed at changing the organization 'culture' and facilitating new forms of behaviour.

T.R.W. undertook sensitivity training and team-building activities in introducing their matrix,[61] and Kingdon also describes an intergroup O.D. project aimed at improving cross-functional collaboration.[62]

Argyris, who ascribes the 'failure' of the matrix organizations which he studied to faulty introduction by top management and the persistence of managers in inappropriate behaviour patterns, describes a detailed scheme for participative introduction of organizational change, involving participation from people at all levels, both in diagnosing problems and formulating plans.[63]

The use of team building approaches to making matrix organizations work better has also been described elsewhere.[64] Galbraith underlines the importance of training in group and interpersonal skills, and the adoption of appropriate conflict resolution practices.[65]

Guidelines. In a very useful section of his book headed 'Making Lateral Processes Effective', Galbraith provides a series of practical suggestions, all of them designed to make matrix and similar organizational forms work more effectively in practice. The following is a brief summary:

1. *Perceived reward and importance.* Participation in a task force or project team should be perceived as an important and rewarding assignment, rather than a chore imposed by higher authority, getting in the way of one's normal work and arousing the resentment of one's boss.

2. *Information and authority.* To be effective, project teams must contain people who have relevant information, and people who have authority to commit their departments. As information in technical departments tends to be held at lower levels, this requirement may result in 'diagonal slice' project teams with different departments represented by people of different status.

3. *Influence based on knowledge.* Under these circumstances it is important to establish a culture within the project team where influence on decisions is based not on rank, but on knowledge and information.

4. *Lateral processes integrated into vertical processes.* This seems to me to be one of Galbraith's most important suggestions. It is an attempt to counteract the tendency noted by Kingdon for the effectiveness of the vertical and horizontal influence patterns to be negatively correlated. Galbraith advocates that meetings of project teams should be preceded and followed by meetings within the functional departments who staff the team, and that members of a project group should systematically keep their superiors and colleagues informed and involved in developments relating to the project.

5. *Part-time, full-time composition.* On the basis of research by Marquis, Galbraith suggests that the best results will be obtained if project teams within a matrix structure are made up of less than 50 per cent full-time members, with the remainder being part-time in the project team and part-time in the functional department. This arrangement results in a mixed organization which is partly project and partly matrix.

6. *Leadership.* In versions of matrix organization where project groups are not headed up by a professional project manager, project leadership may rest with the most senior member of the group or a member from the most influential department. Galbraith suggests that it may well be appropriate for leadership to pass from one member to another, as the project moves from stage to stage in its progress, since different members of the team may at different times be in possession of key information or responsible for dominant activities. An example of this type of system is provided by Bergen.[66]

Supporting Management Systems. While it seems fairly obvious that a matrix organization will require matching control systems and could well be undermined by a set of accounting and reward systems based on assumptions of unitary authority, there is little reference to this aspect in the literature. Goggin mentions the importance of management systems and describes the systems used to support Dow-Corning's 'multidimensional' structure. These include M.B.O., personnel reviews, corporate planning, economic evaluation, profit reporting and a seven-stage approach to new product planning.[67] The article describes how these systems are adapted to support the operation of the multidimensional structure.

Bergen[68] describes a project planning system which pinpoints the varying responsibilities of different project members at different stages. Wilkinson[69] shows how financial control systems can be adapted to a matrix structure, costs and expenditure being themselves shown in the form of a matrix, in which the sum of the column totals must equal that of the rows.

Apart from these few examples, information on this important aspect of matrix organization is rather sparse as yet.

CONCLUSION

Looking at existing information about matrix organizations, one is particularly struck by the extremely tentative and diverse character of the implementations so far.

Very different types of multiauthority, multidimensional and mixed organizations have emerged in various areas, either in response to specific needs and pressures, or because someone thought it a good idea.

Their success and effectiveness has been extremely varied, ranging from structures which are viewed as flexible, efficient and motivating, to ones perceived as bureaucratic, conflict-ridden and stressful.

In spite of these inconsistencies, the idea of dual structures seems to be acquiring increasing momentum. Matrix or similar structures are springing up wherever one looks, and the sooner we find out how to organize and operate them harmoniously and effectively, the better it will be for people who work in them.

NOTES

1. Until the late sixties the term most commonly used for dual authority structures was 'project organization'; *e.g.* Janger, A. R., 'Anatomy of the Project Organization', *Business Management Record* (National Industrial Conference Board), November 1963, pp. 12–18.

2. For example, 'The Systems Group of TRW, Inc.' in Rush, H. M. F., *Behavioral Science*, New York: National Industrial Conference Board, 1969; *Personnel Policy Study No. 216*, pp. 157–71; Wilkinson, J. B., 'Management Structure in an Industrial Research Laboratory', *R and D Management*, Vol. 4, No. 3, 1974, pp. 135–9.

3. Reported by David Frankel, London Graduate School of Business Studies.

4. For example, Palmer, D., 'How Scicon had its Head Shrunk', *Financial Times*, 29th December 1970.

5. Perham, H., 'Matrix Management: a Tough Game to Play', *Dun's Review*, August 1970, pp. 31–4.

6. Goggin, W. C., 'How the Multi-dimensional Structure Works at Dow-Corning', *Harvard Business Review*, Vol. 52, No. 1, January–February 1974, pp. 54–65.

7. Hill, R., 'Corning Glass Reshapes its International Operations', *International Management*, Vol. 29, No. 10, October 1974.

8. Corey, E. R. and Star, S. H., *Organization Strategy: a Marketing Approach*, Boston, Mass.: Division of Research, Graduate School of Business Administration, Harvard University, 1971, pp. 61–108.

9. Brooks, P. W., 'Management and Marketing in Large Enterprises', *Aeronautical Journal*, Vol. 74, No. 720, 1970, pp. 936–47.

10. Talks given by A. V. Johnston at seminars organized by the Brunel University Management Programme in January and November 1975.

11. Social Services Organization Research Unit, Brunel Institute of Organization and Social Studies, *Social Services Departments*, London: Heinemann, 1974, pp. 30–2, 85–7; Gray, J. L., 'Matrix Organizational Design as a Vehicle for Effective Delivery of Public Health Care and Social Services', *Management International Review*, Vol. 14, No. 6, 1974, pp. 73–87; Algie, J., 'Management and Organization in the Social Services', *British Hospital Journal and Social Services Review*, Vol. LXXX, No. 4184, 26th June 1970, pp. 1245–8.

12. Kingdon, D. R., *Matrix Organization*. London: Tavistock, 1973, p. 26.

13. Kingdon, D. R., *ibid.*, and Galbraith, J. R., *Designing Complex Organizations*, Reading, Mass.: Addison-Wesley, 1973.

14. A useful review article is provided by Hendry, W. D., 'A General Guide to Matrix Management', *Personnel Review*, Vol. 4, No. 2, Spring 1975, pp. 33–9. A book mentioned by a number of colleagues as a source of information on matrix organization proved disappointing. This is Shull, F. A., Delbecq, A. L. and Cummings, L. L., *Organizational Decision-making*, New York: McGraw-Hill, 1970, pp. 171–226. Though its discussion of 'Matrix Organization' (p. 187) refers to 'multiple supervisors, committee overlays, task force groups, and project management designs' (p. 184), it quickly turns into a version of 'contingency theory' applied to task groups (i.e. a model relating management structures to tasks and group membership). The same applies to a later article: Grimes, A. J., Klein, S. M. and Shull, F. A., 'Matrix Model: A Selective Empirical Test', *Academy of Management Journal*, Vol. 15, No. 1, 1972, pp. 9–32.

15. That is, using more than one of the 'classical' management theorists' principles of grouping (*e.g.* by purpose, process, clientele, place). *Cf.* Massie, J. L.,

'Management Theory', in March, J. G. (Ed.), *Handbook of Organizations*, Chicago: Rand McNally, 1965, p. 400.

16. Kingdon, D. R., op. cit. (note 12), p. 5.

17. For example, Argyris, C., 'Today's Problems with Tomorrow's Organizations', *Journal of Management Studies*, Vol. 4, No. 1, February 1967, pp. 31–55.

18. For example, Social Services Organization Research Unit, op. cit.; (Algie, J., op. cit.) note.

19. For example, Bergen, S. A., 'The New Product Matrix', *R and D Management*, Vol. 5, No. 2, 1975.

20. For example, Marquis, D., 'Ways of Organizing Projects', *Innovation*, No. 5, 1969, pp. 26–33; Davis, K., *Human Relations at Work* (3rd edn), New York: McGraw-Hill, 1967, pp. 295–8; Moe, J. F., 'Matrix Organization', *Business Horizons*, Summer 1964, p. 70.

21. Miller, E. J. and Rice, A. K., *Systems of Organization*, London: Tavistock, 1967, pp. 165–8.

22. Galbraith, J. R., 'Matrix Organization Designs', *Business Horizons*, February 1971, pp. 29–40; also Galbraith, J. R., op. cit. (note 13), p. 114.

23. Others who define matrix organization in this way include: Cleland, D. I. and King, W. R., *Systems Analysis and Project Management*, New York: McGraw-Hill, 1968, pp. 168–84; Wilemon, D. L. and Gemmill, G. R., 'Interpersonal Power in Temporary Management Systems', *Journal of Management Studies*, Vol. 8, No. 3, October 1971, pp. 315–28. Examples of this model are found in: Brookes, P. W., op cit. (note 9); Goggin, W. C., op. cit. (note 6); Rush, H. M. F., op. cit. (note 1). In the last of these examples only a few individuals, the 'sub-project' managers' have dual reporting links.

24. Kingdon, D. R., op. cit., pp. 15, 19, 21.

25. Marquis, D., op. cit. (note 20).

26. Greiner, L. E., 'Evolution and Revolution as Organizations Grow', *Harvard Business Review*, Vol. 50, No. 4, July–August 1972, pp. 43–4.

27. Argyris, C., op. cit. (note 17).

28. Kingdon, D. R., op. cit., pp. 6–17.

29. Galbraith, J. R., 1973, op. cit. (note 13).

30. The six preceding methods of increasing lateral processes are in order: direct contact between managers, liaison roles, temporary task forces, permanent inter-departmental teams, creation of an integrating role, transforming this into a 'linking-managerial role'. The last three of these would probably be regarded as less powerful versions of matrix organization by some of our authors—all three involve dual influence of an ongoing kind.

31. Burns, T. and Stalker, G. M., *The Management of Innovation*, London: Tavistock, 1961.

32. Argyris, C., *The Applicability of Organizational Sociology*, Cambridge: Cambridge University Press, 1972.

33. Argyris, C., 1967, op. cit. (note 17).

34. Algie, J., op. cit. (note 11).

35. Davis, K., op. cit. (note 20).

36. Lorsch, J. W. and Lawrence, P. R., *Organization Planning: Cases and Concepts*, Homewood, Illinois: Irwin-Dorsey, 1972, pp. 210–57.

37. Perham, J., op. cit. (note 5), calls it 'a very efficient way of getting things done in a hurry'.

38. Marquis, D., op. cit. (note 20).

39. Cleland, D. I., 'The Deliberate Conflict', *Business Horizons*, February 1968, pp. 78–80.

40. Cleland, D. I. and King, W. R., op. cit. (note 23).

41. Kingdon, D. R., op. cit., p. 103.

42. Goggin, W. C., op. cit. (note 6).

43. Miller, E. J. and Rice, A. K., op. cit. (note 21).

44. The only publication of which I am aware is the article in *Innovation*, already quoted—Marquis, D., op. cit. (note 20). Galbraith also refers to a working paper of 1965, Marquis, D. G. and Straight, D. M., 'Organizational Factors in Project Performance', Sloane School of Management *Working Paper No. 133 –65*. In a lecture given at University College, London, Marquis elaborated somewhat on the data given in the *Innovation* article, and my interpretation of the data is partly based on this lecture.

45. Corey, E. R. and Star, S. H., op. cit. (note 8), pp. 52–7.

46. Argyris, C., 1967, op. cit. (note 17).

47. Kingdon, D. R., op. cit., p. xii.

48. Argyris, C., 1967, op. cit. (note 17).

49. Lorsch, J. W. and Lawrence, P. R., 1972, op. cit. (note 36).

50. Wilemon, D. L., 'Managing Conflict in Temporary Management Systems', *Journal of Management Studies*, Vol. 10, No. 3, October 1973, pp. 282–96.

51. Wilemon, D. L. and Gemmill, G. R., op. cit. (note 23).

52. Kingdon, D. R., op. cit., Chapter 5.

53. Kahn, R. L. et al., *Organizational Stress: Studies in Role Conflict and Ambiguity*, New York: Wiley, 1964.

54. Galbraith, J. R., 1973, op. cit. (note 13).

55. Perham, J., op. cit. (note 5).

56. Goodman, R. A., 'Ambiguous Authority Definition in Project Management', *Academy of Management Journal*, Vol. 10, 1967, pp. 395–407. Goodman's method involved asking a number of senior managers in three project and three matrix organizations which of a list of critical project decisions were or were not within the authority of the project manager. Goodman's claim that these roles are left deliberately ambiguous, is based on the finding that the average agreement about the responsibilities of the project manager was only 80 per cent instead of 100 per cent. Other studies in which perceptions of individuals' roles by their colleagues have been collected (e.g. Sadler, P. J. and Barry, B. A., *Organisational Development*, London: Longmans, 1970, pp. 109–12, and Kahn et al., op. cit. (note 53)) suggest that 80 per cent agreement is unusually high and corresponds to a very clear level of role definition.

57. For example, Cleland, D. I., op. cit. (note 39).

58. *Cf.* Brown, W., *Exploration in Management*, London: Heinemann, 1960, and Brown, W., *Organization*, London: Heinemann, 1971; Jaques, E., *Measurement of Responsibility*, London: Tavistock 1956; Newman, A. D. and Rowbottom, R. W., *Organization Analysis*, London: Heinemann, 1968.

59. Rowbottom, R. W. et al., *Hospital Organization*, London: Heinemann, 1973; Social Services Organization Research Unit, op. cit. (note 11).

60. *Cf.* Hey, A., 'Clarifying Responsibilities'. Paper given at a seminar organized by the *Brunel Management Programme* in March 1975.

61. Rush, H. M. F., op. cit. (note 2).

62. Kingdon, D. R., op. cit., Chapter 5.

63. Argyris, C., 1967, op. cit. (note 17), pp. 53–5.

64. For example, by D. Sheane of I.C.I. Ltd., at seminars organized by the *Brunel Management Programme*, 1975.

65. Galbraith, J. R., 1973, op. cit., pp. 61–3. Using the analysis provided by Lawrence and Lorsch, he advocates 'confrontation' as a preferred approach which would be backed up by occasional 'forcing'. (*Cf.* Lawrence, P. R. and Lorsch, J. W., *Organization and Environment, Managing Differentiation and Integration*, Boston: Harvard Business School, 1967.)

66. Bergen, S. A., op. cit. (note 19).

67. Goggin, W. C., op. cit. (note 6).

68. Bergen, S. A., op. cit. (note 19).

69. Wilkinson, J. B., op. cit. (note 2).

Technology and the Design of Organization Units

W. Alan Randolph

Organizations are complex entities, and most researchers and theoreticians now agree that the only realistic way to view them is as open systems. They consist of many input variables which interact with each other and with internal characteristics of the organization to determine the nature and eventually the effectiveness of the organization. The problems for managers relate to the proper choices for key variables. In other words, managers must design an organization with the proper mix of technology, structure, and human behaviors if it is to effectively achieve its goals and accomplish its tasks. It is therefore useful for managers to view organizations as shown in Figure 1.

Given this framework, the manager asks, "Where do I start in designing an effective organization?" Lupton (1976) suggests that we can view the choice of technology type as a primary choice, and the choice of technology is based on an understanding of the nature of the organization's task and the slice of external environment relevant to that task. For example, assume the managers choose, or are assigned, the task of providing help for abused and neglected children. The relevant subenvironment includes the legal

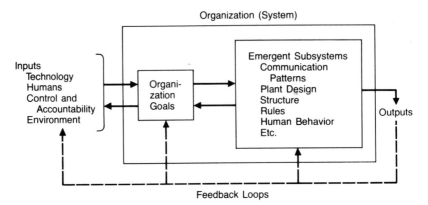

Figure 1   A Socio-Technical Systems Description of Organizations

aspects surrounding these children, the funding sources available, and so forth. With this knowledge, the managers can choose an appropriate technology for accomplishing the task. In turn then, technology choice helps determine the parameters of the organization's/unit's internal environment and thus influences the choices of structure, skill mix, functional interdependence of people, skill requirements of people, and so forth (see Figure 2). But before we go too far in this flow of events leading to effective organization/unit design, we need to back off and define what is meant by technology, task, structure, and processes, and what typologies of technologies might be useful.

UNDERSTANDING THE TECHNOLOGY CONSTRUCT

A search of the literature related to the study of organizations reveals many definitions of organizational technology, ranging from the general to the specific. Perrow (1967) defines technology as ". . . the actions that an individual performs on an object, with or without the aid of tools or mechanical devices, in order to make some change in that object." Thompson and Bates (1957) define it as ". . . those sets of man-machine activities which together produce a desired good or service." Davis (1971) says technology is ". . . the combination of skills, equipment and relevant technical knowledge needed to bring about desired transformations in materials, information, or people." Finally, Pugh, Hickson, Hinings and Turner (1969) refer to technology as " . . . the sequence of physical techniques of the organization, even if the physical techniques involve only pen, ink, and paper."

In all of these definitions the underlying concept is that technology is "how" the organization's task is accomplished (i.e., how are inputs trans-

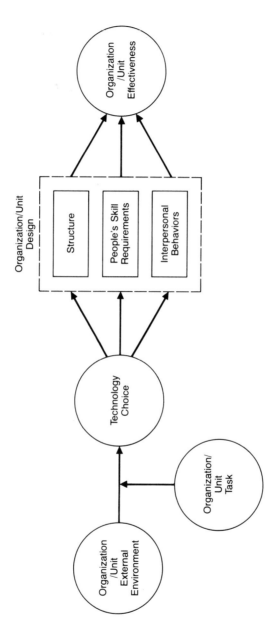

Figure 2   Sequential Relationship Between External Environment, Organization or Unit Technology, Design and Effectiveness, and Contingency Input of Organization or Unit Task

formed into desired outputs). This "how" may involve machines, tools, paper-pen, computers, procedures, medical equipment, knowledge utilization, information transfer, or other means which allow the organization/ unit to accomplish its appointed task or tasks. Technology also refers to the rationale and knowledge underlying the utilization of the means elaborated in the preceding sentence.

Distinguishing Technology from Task, Structure and Processes

Technology is different from "task" in that task is "what" has to be done while technology is "how" it is accomplished. Structure is also different from technology in that it is how the efforts of the people in a unit or organization are segregated for specialization and coordinated for overall goal accomplishment. Finally, processes differ from technology and structure in that processes are the activities that people engage in while utilizing the technology and structure to work on the task (e.g., decision making and communications).

An example may help to distinguish among these concepts. Suppose the task is to produce automobile engines. The technology choices include an assembly line or subassembly teams for building the entire engine. To complement the particular technology, jobs and hierarchies are designed and specific lines of responsibility and authority are established to create the structure. Once work on the task is under way, processes are introduced via decisions and communications regarding problems that arise.

Unit and Modal Technology

At this point in the explanation of the technology construct, it is appropriate to distinguish between unit and modal technology. Many of the early studies defined technology in terms of what was characteristic of the organization as a whole—really an aggregate of the various technologies represented in the organization's units. This modal measure of technology has been found in effective organizations to be related to overall measures of organization structure, such as job specialization, span of control, formalization of role performance, and percentage of nonproduction employees (Woodward, 1965). Recent studies, however, have found that organization size (i.e., number of employees) is a better predictor of such structural variables, especially in large organizations (Hickson, Pugh, and Pheysey, 1969). In other words, the modal measure of technology is sometimes of questionable use in explaining structure, behavior, and effectiveness, especially in large, complex organizations. The fact that this result occurs in large, complex organizations suggests that the modal technology measure may obscure variations in unit technologies.

Other studies by Hall (1963), Van de Ven, Delbecq, and Koenig

(1976), and Randolph (1975) did base the measure of technology at the unit level. They found that unit technology and unit size explained much of the variance in structure and behaviors of effective units, and they found that different units in the same organization had different technologies, structures and behaviors.

These findings suggest that unit, rather than modal, technology is probably more useful in terms of design, especially for large organizations which perform many tasks and utilize many technologies. In small organizations modal technology approaches the unit concept in that primary workflow and means of task performance more directly impinge on the characteristics of the organization, as in the units of large organizations. Hence, from a design perspective, unit technology appears to be the more useful of the two viewpoints in determining the appropriateness of organization structure and behavior at the unit level, and unit technology will be the analysis level assumed in the remainder of this paper.

DEVELOPING A USEFUL TYPOLOGY OF UNIT TECHNOLOGIES

Thompson's Technology Typology of Task Interdependence

Thompson (1967) has offered us a typology of technologies based on the nature of the task interdependence involved in performing the unit's primary task. Thompson's typology distinguishes three technologies as follows:

1. *Mediating*—linking in standardized ways parties who are or who wish to be interdependent, and the task interdependence is pooled meaning the various people in the unit can perform their function relatively independent of one another. Examples of this technology include loan departments in banks, supply departments, personnel units, and welfare agencies;
2. *Long linked*—performing well defined acts which are serially interdependent; that is, act A must be performed before act B, act B before act C, and so forth, in order to achieve the completion of the task. The best example of this technology is the mass production assembly line;
3. *Intensive*—using a variety of high skill techniques to achieve a change in some object or person, but the selection and ordering of the techniques are determined by feedback of information from the object or person. Thus the task interdependence is reciprocal in nature because of the act, get feedback, act cycle of activity. Examples of this technology include operating rooms in hospitals, construction units, mental health centers, and military combat teams.

Perrow's Routineness-Nonroutineness Technology Typology

Perrow (1970) offers another technology typology based on degree of non-routineness involved in performing the unit's primary task. Technologies can be distinguished along two basic dimensions: (1) *task predictability*, defined as the number of unexpected exceptions encountered in the work, and (2) *problem analyzability*, defined as the amount of search which must be engaged in to adequately deal with exceptions encountered in the work. Perrow argues that these two dimensions are essentially independent from one another, meaning that tasks may be nonroutine in terms of one dimension but not in terms of the other. This two dimensional aspect of Perrow's typology is depicted in Figure 3.

Two technological extremes exist in Perrow's typology. Nonroutine technologies (cell 2) are characterized by many exceptions and difficult-to-analyze problems. In other words, the unit faces many unanticipated problems in performing the primary task, and these problems do not have ready-made solutions but require an involved search procedure. For example, a psychiatric agency would likely employ this technology since each client is essentially an exception in that he/she will bring a unique set of problems to the agency and since it may take a great deal of work to develop solutions for the problems presented by the clients. At the other extreme, routine technologies (cell 4) are characterized by few exceptions and easy-to-analyze problems. Most of the exceptions encountered in the routine technology can be anticipated, and contingency plans developed for resolving these problems when they occur. An example of this technology would be a crude oil processing unit where once the raw materials are obtained, they can be fed into the system and will emerge at the other end in the form of gasoline, motor oil, asphalt, etc., with very few exceptions anticipated and the knowledge to resolve those that do occur.

The other technologies in Perrow's typology (cells 1 and 3) represent a mixture of nonroutineness in terms of the two dimensions of the typology. Craft technologies (e.g., furniture refinishing and restoring) deal with relatively difficult problems to solve, but the number of exceptions encoun-

	Few Exceptions	Many Exceptions
Unanalyzable Problems	Craft Industry 1	2 Non-routine
Analyzable Problems	4 Routine	3 Engineering

Figure 3   Perrow's Two Dimensional Technology Construct (Perrow, 1970)

tered are few in number (cell 1). On the other hand, an automobile assembly line (cell 3) may deal with a great variety of models and options on those models (i.e., many exceptions), but these exceptions do not represent problems for which the organization cannot preplan solutions.

Other typologies have been offered by various authors, but it appears that the typologies offered by Perrow and Thompson possess sufficient generalizability to be applied to many situations and can account for the typologies offered by other researchers. Indeed, the three dimensions offered by these two authors appear to be the basic dimensions underlying what is meant by the technology construct.

Given these dimensions of *task predictability, problem analyzability,* and *task interdependence,* we can picture a three dimensional typology of technology as shown in Figure 4. The descriptors of task predictability and task analyzability (ranging from low to high) are rather self explanatory, but the pooled, sequential, and reciprocal descriptors for the task interdependence need a little explanation. Referring to Thompson's typology (1967), pooled task interdependence means that the tasks assigned to a particular unit of the organization can be accomplished relatively independently of one another (as in the mediating technology). Sequential task interdependence means that the tasks of the unit must be performed in a particular order which means a one-way type of interdependence (as in the long-linked technology); worker B is dependent on worker A finishing his/her task, but worker A is not dependent on worker B. Finally, reciprocal task interdependence means that there is two-way interdependence between performers of the unit's tasks. The ordering of tasks depends on feedback from the object itself (as in the intensive technology).

Figure 4 also lays out in two dimensions the twelve-cubed, three dimensional typology and places descriptive labels on each of the twelve technology types. The basic descriptors of each technology (i.e., Routine, Nonroutine, Dynamic, Problematic) refer to the task predictability and problem analyzability dimensions, and the modifiers "pooled," "sequential" and "reciprocal" refer to the task interdependence dimension. Given a unit's mission, one can apply the typology to all technology situations by utilizing the general descriptors for *task predictability, problem analyzability,* and *task interdependence.* However, it may be helpful to relabel the technologies to fit each specific situation, in order to facilitate understanding. For example, an automobile plant might prefer to call the routine sequential technology an "assembly line."

UNIT DESIGN AND TECHNOLOGY

As Figure 2 showed, the choice of unit technology has a significant impact on the design which will be most effective for accomplishing the unit's tasks. In this section of the paper, we explore the designs which seem most

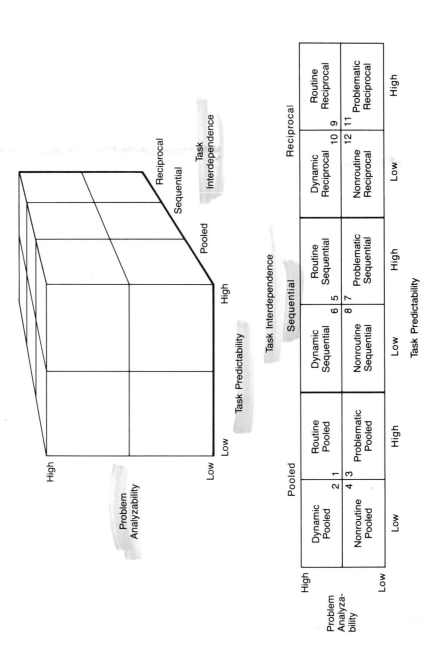

Figure 4   A Three Dimensional Technology Typology

appropriate for the various technologies which may be chosen. It will be important to remember that these design characteristics, like the technology characteristics, refer to the unit level of analysis in the organization and not to the interunit and overall organization structure characteristics.

Design Dimensions

The design dimensions utilized to prescribe the unit designs most appropriate for the twelve technology types consist of the following seven dimensions. First, the general design type is labeled as either mechanistic or organic, as per Burns and Stalker (1961). The second and third dimensions, differentiation and integration, utilize Lawrence and Lorsch's definitions (1969) to refer to the level of specialization and division of labor possible and desirable for the tasks that must be performed in the unit and the type of coordination desirable for the overall unit task. For this integration dimension, we utilize the means of coordination defined by Thompson (1967) and the means of information processing defined by Galbraith (1973), and they include coordination by categorization, plan, machine, rules, hierarchy, self-contained tasks, vertical systems, and lateral relations (examples of each are given later in the paper). The fourth dimension, discretion, is defined according to Perrow (1967) and greater discretion means that the people have choices about the means for completing the tasks. At times in the following pages, we will distinguish between the discretion of workers and that of supervisors, and we will also refer to the power of these people as part of their level of discretion. Power means the degree to which people in the unit have control over the unit's goals and basic strategies (Perrow, 1967). The fifth dimension, decision making, is categorized as either centralized in the hands of the unit's leaders or decentralized in the hands of many or all of the unit's members. The sixth dimension of design, communications, relates to the process level of the design. Communications are prescribed in terms of their frequency, their directionality—vertical or horizontal, and their media—verbal (V) or written (W) and also meetings (either scheduled or unscheduled). Seventh, and finally, the skills required of the people are prescribed in terms of their need for technical or content skills (such as might be obtained by more education in one's field) and their need for interpersonal or process skills (such as communications, group decision making, and leadership skills).

Now we are ready to turn to an exploration of the unit designs which are most appropriate for the various technologies. Each of the twelve designs has the basic objective of accomplishing the unit's task as effectively and efficiently as possible, given the unit's task and technology. The designs are summarized in Figure 5 and explained in the following pages.

Routine Technologies

We will discuss routine technologies at some length and will abbreviate our discussion of the dynamic, problematic, and nonroutine technologies. The

	TASK INTERDEPENDENCE						
	Pooled		Sequential		Reciprocal		PROBLEM ANALYZABILITY
General Type	Mechanistic	Mechanistic	Mechanistic	Mechanistic	Organic	Mechanistic	High
—Differentiation	—High	—High	—High	—High	—High	—High	
—Integration	—Categorization	—Closed system, Categorization	—Plan, Machine	—Rules, plan, machine	—Vertical system	—Rules, hierarchy	
—Discretion	—Moderate	—Low	—Moderate	—Low	—Moderate	—Moderate	
—Decision Making	—Centralized	—Centralized	—Centralized	—Centralized	—Centralized	—Centralized	
—Communications	—Mod frequency V,W vert.*	—Low frequency W vert.	—Mod frequency W vert., V horiz.	—Low frequency V horiz., W vert.	—High frequency V horiz., V, W vert.	—Mod frequency W, V vert., V horiz.	
—Skills of people	—Low Tech Mod. Interpers.	—Low Tech Low Interpers.	—Mod Tech Mod. Interpers.	—Low Tech Mod Interpers.	—Mod Tech High Interpers.	—Mod Tech Mod. Interpers.	
	2	1	6	5	10	9	
	4	3	8	7	12	11	
General Type	Organic	Mechanistic	Organic	Organic	Organic	Organic	Low
—Differentiation	—High	—High	—Moderate	—Moderate	—Low	—Moderate	
—Integration	—Hierarchy, vertical system	—Hierarchy & self contained tasks	—Lateral relations	—Vertical system	—Vert. & Lateral rel. (feedback)	—Vertical system; lateral rel.	
—Discretion	—High	—Moderate	—High	—Moderate	—High	—High	
—Decision Making	—Decentralized	—Decentralized	—Decentralized	—Centralized	—Decentralized	—Decentralized	
—Communications	—Mod. frequency V vert.	—Low frequency V,W vert.	—Mod. frequency V horiz., vert.	—Mod frequency V,W horiz., vert.	—High frequency V horiz., vert.	—High frequency V, W vert., V horiz.	
—Skills of people	—High Tech Mod. Interpers.	—High Tech Low Interpers.	—High Tech Mod. Interpers.	—High Tech Mod. Interpers.	—High Tech High Interpers.	—High Tech High Interpers.	
TASK PREDICTABILITY	Low	High	Low	High	Low	High	

Note: V = verbal, W = written

Figure 5 Unit Design and Process Characteristics Matched to Technology Types (see Figure 4)

first three technologies which we will discuss are all similar in their level of technological routineness. All three exhibit high task predictability and high problem analyzability—hence the name routine. The task interdependence, however, varies from pooled to sequential to reciprocal, thus increasing the complexity of the technological situation.

Routine-Pooled Technology (Cell 1—Figure 5)

The routine-pooled technology is characterized by high task predictability, high problem analyzability, and pooled task interdependence. An example of this kind of technology would be the bookkeeping/accounting unit found in many large organizations. Perrow (1967) prescribes several design characteristics for routine technology units (see Figure 6). Work managers should have low discretion in the choice of means for performing the unit's work since the work can be programmed, but they should have a great deal of power and sanction to carry out the planned activities of the unit. On the other hand unit workers should have both low discretion and low power; they should simply perform the work as programmed by specialists elsewhere in the organization. To use the terms of Burns and Stalker (1961), the unit should be mechanistic to be most effective. And to use the terms of Lawrence and Lorsch (1967) the tasks in the unit can be highly differentiated in a relatively closed system due to the low task interdependence.

Thompson (1967) found that pooled technologies depend on categorization and centralized decision making, and the high task predictability and problem analyzability would certainly make these design features more effective. Though not specifically dealing with pooled technologies, Woodward (1965) found that routine technologies tend to have small spans of control at the worker level, a high ratio of managers to workers, and high

	DISCRE-TION	POWER	COORDINATION WITHIN GROUPS	INTERDEPENDENCE OF GROUPS	DISCRE-TION	POWER	COORDINATION WITHIN GROUPS	INTERDEPENDENCE OF GROUPS
Tech. Mgt.	Low	Low	Plan		High	High	Feedbk.	
				Low				High
Super.	High	High	Feedbk. Decentralized		High	High	Feedbk. Flexible, polycentralized	
				1	2			
				4	3			
Tech. Mgt.	Low	High	Plan		High	High	Feedbk.	
				Low				Low
Super.	Low	Low	Plan Formal, centralized		Low	Low	Plan Flexible, centralized	

Figure 6 Comparison of Perrow's Four Technologies as Regards Task-Related Interactions (Perrow, 1967)

job specialization. Likewise, the Aston group (Hickson, *et al.*, 1969) found that effective routine technologies exhibited high job and functional specialization, extensive standardization of procedures, and highly mechanistic organizations accompanying routine technologies. Other studies (cf. Zwerman, 1970; Khandwalla, 1974) have replicated these findings leading to the conclusion that high structure can and does work well with routine technologies, especially if the task interdependence is of the pooled variety.

At an operating or process level Van de Ven, *et al.* (1976) offer some insight into the most desirable aspects of the routine-pooled technology unit (see Figures 7 and 8). In a study of state employment service agencies, they found that rules and plans are the primary sources of coordination of efforts and that vertical communications predominate in effective routine-pooled technologies. Also, these communications will tend not to be conducted in a group setting, such as meetings. Randolph (1975, 1978), in a study of a VA hospital, concurred in the finding about vertical communications for routine-pooled technologies and also found that communications tend to be infrequent and to utilize written and telephone media.

In short, a routine-pooled technology allows for and functions more effectively in conjunction with a highly structured, well-planned, well-ordered, mechanistic unit design. Moreover, unit members need not be highly skilled, either technically or interpersonally.

Routine-Sequential Technology (Cell 5—Figure 5)

The routine-sequential technology is also characterized by high task predictability and high problem analyzability, but the task interdependence is sequential. An example of this technology would be an assembly line making a limited number of product variations, such as a wine bottling unit. Thompson and Bates (1957) conclude that a high degree of mechanization, which is possible in the routine-sequential technology, results in functional specialization and integration of tasks primarily within the machine domain as opposed to the human domain. For example, on an assembly line the coordination of the sequential tasks can best be handled by the assembly line mechanical devices rather than the people working on the line, unless the line breaks down, which is seldom. And even when problems do arise, it is often quite possible to determine in advance how to resolve them, and a series of rules can be established to cover many of the infrequent, unplanned events that may arise (Galbraith, 1973). Another way of viewing this technology situation is that it emphasizes the planning function of management, and thus the use of staff units to assist management in planning is desirable in the routine-sequential technology.

To use the terms of Lawrence and Lorsch (1967), the unit design accompanying the automated technology should exhibit a relatively high

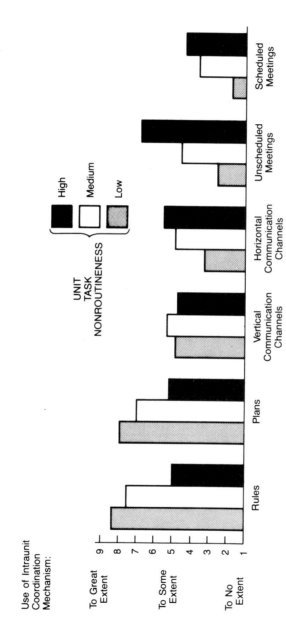

Figure 7 Profile of Intraunit Coordination Mechanisms on Types of Unit Task Nonroutiness *(Miles 1980, as adapted from Van de Ven, et al, 1976)*

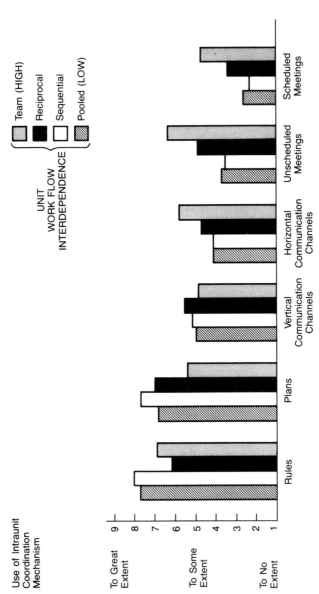

Figure 8 Profile of Intraunit Coordination Mechanisms on Types of Unit Work Flow Interdependence *(Miles, 1980, as adapted from Van de Ven, et al., 1976)*

degree of differentiation of tasks, and the integration of those tasks can be accomplished by the machinery employed and by rules and plans provided by specialists elsewhere in the organization. As Woodward (1965) found, the effective mass production technology exhibited separation of production administration from actual supervision of production operations, specialization between management functions, and use of control and sanction procedures based on established rules. She also found low role ambiguity regarding duties and responsibilities of the workers, which is desirable in unit design and achievable in a routine-sequential technology. Van de Ven's study (1976) supports the design consideration of using rules and plans as the means of coordination in a routine-sequential technology (see Figures 7 and 8).

At a process level, Woodward (1965) found that the effective routine-sequential technology was characterized by a high frequency of written communications as compared to verbal communications. Randolph (1977, 1978) found that routine-sequential technologies exhibited a low frequency of communications of any kind, when compared to less routine technologies, and his study also concurred with Woodward's in terms of written and verbal communications. In fact, he found that routine-sequential technologies utilize the horizontal direction for the infrequent communications which occur and that those communications tend to utilize written, sign and objective media. (Sign media was defined as using hand signals, body movements, and other non-verbal means of communication; object media was defined as using the work piece itself as the communication—e.g., a waiter in a restaurant hands the dishwasher a stack of dirty dishes—no words need be spoken for the message to be transmitted.)

Overall, then, the routine-sequential technology functions effectively with a highly structured and differentiated unit design, where the necessary coordination of tasks can be accomplished via rules, plans, and the machinery employed.

Routine-Reciprocal Technology (Cell 9—Figure 5)

Like the routine-pooled and routine-sequential technologies, the routine-reciprocal technology is also characterized by high task predictability and problem analyzability, but the task interdependence is of the more complex reciprocal variety. An example of this technology would be a chemical processing unit, which batch processes several similar chemicals. Thompson and Bates (1957) conclude that the reciprocal task interdependence necessitates more dependence on the human domain as opposed to the machine domain. Hence, coordination in the routine-reciprocal technology can be relatively prescribed, but in addition to rules it must depend on the hierarchy of the organization. In other words, the managers up the line need a moderate degree of discretion to invoke the appropriate rules to accomplish the integration of the highly interdependent tasks in the unit. Applying Lawrence and Lorsch's (1967) terms, the tasks can be highly differentiated within the unit, but attention must be given to integration of those tasks because of their high level of interdependence, and this integration can be accomplished via rules and the hierarchy (Galbraith, 1973). Van de Ven (1976) concurs in finding a somewhat decreased dependence on rules in reciprocal technologies as opposed to pooled or sequential technologies. However, there is still a heavy reliance on rules and plans in the reciprocal technology and an increased reliance on the hierarchy via group meetings (see Figure 8).

Woodward (1965) found that her process technologies, which approximate routine-reciprocal technologies, tended to have many levels of management in their hierarchies, small spans of control at the worker level, and a high ratio of managers to total personnel. Thus, we would expect that effective routine-reciprocal technologies would utilize relatively centralized decision making. On the other hand, Woodward (1965) and Randolph (1977) found that highly routine technologies with high task interdependence exhibit a tendency to utilize horizontal communications in addition to vertical communications. The reason for this is that once the tasks are prescribed by management (usually in written communications), the workers can effectively and more efficiently deal with the few and analyzable problems that they encounter by communicating among themselves rather than communicating with superiors.

Overall we would expect to see an increase in communications in the routine-reciprocal technology, as compared to the pooled and sequential technologies (Randolph, 1977). And as Van de Ven (1976) found, both vertical and horizontal communications increase in the high task interdependence situation, but a substantial increase in horizontal communications can and does occur in effective routine-reciprocal technologies: the workers simply go ahead and deal with the infrequent and simple problems usually encountered and save the very infrequent, more complex problems for vertical communications. Given these requirements on the employees, people who work in routine-reciprocal technologies need to have moderate skills both technically and interpersonally.

Overall, then, the more effective routine-reciprocal technology unit will be highly differentiated and integrated. Coordination will be accomplished via both rules and the hierarchy, and communications will begin to play an important role.

Dynamic Technologies (Cells 2, 6, 10—Figure 5)

We now turn to another level of technological routineness. The three dynamic technologies are alike in that they exhibit low task predictability and high problem analyzability. In other words, any nonroutineness arises from the unexpected occurrence of problems in performing the task and not from an inability to resolve the problems once they occur. Rather than discuss each of the three technologies separately, we will comparatively discuss all three proceeding in task interdependence complexity from pooled to sequential to reciprocal. First, though, let us give examples of each of the three technologies.

An example of the dynamic-pooled technology (cell 2) would be a bank office, where each customer brings a problem, the nature of which cannot be determined until the person arrives in the bank, but once the problem is presented the teller usually knows what to do and his/her task is relatively independent of what the other tellers are doing. A good example of the dynamic-sequential technology (cell 6) would be an automobile assembly line where many models and a myriad of options are produced based on consumer demands but using relatively well-defined techniques and procedures. An example of the dynamic-reciprocal technology (cell 10) would be a hospital chronic care or nursing home ward which must deal with a variety of patient types but can utilize a number of relatively well-defined techniques and procedures; however, these techniques must be performed in a highly interdependent fashion; i.e., dietary, medication, and therapy procedures must be coordinated in a reciprocal fashion.

Perrow (1967) says that work managers in a dynamic technology situation should have a great deal of discretion in the performance of the unit's work, because they must determine what type of problem has been encountered when one occurs in order to assign it to the proper category of resolution. Also, the managers should have a great deal of power and sanction to carry out the programmed problem solving techniques once the problems have been assigned to the proper category. On the other hand, the workers need little discretion and power in the unit; they simply perform the well-defined problem solutions once a problem is assigned to them. Indeed, centralized decision making can be effectively utilized to establish contingency plans for dealing with problems that will occur.

Referring to Lawrence and Lorsch (1967), the tasks in dynamic technology units can be highly differentiated because of the high problem analyzability. The integration of tasks varies depending on the level of task interdependence (Thompson, 1967). At the pooled level, the little integration that is necessary is induced by the uncertainty which arises when a problem is first encountered, but categorization of problems resolves the issue efficiently. At the sequential level, a high degree of mechanization can be utilized to help the coordination process proceed according to plan. For the dynamic-reciprocal unit, integration is achieved by mutual adjustment in the form of vertical systems (Galbraith, 1973). In the chronic care ward example, we might find person-machine combinations (like electrocardiograph equipment, computer analysis of feedback data from the patient, and assistants-to as a hierarchical form—e.g., registered nurses assisted by licensed practical nurses).

At a process level, the dynamic technologies should use an increased frequency of communications, compared to routine technologies, because of the increase in technological nonroutineness (Randolph, in press; Van de Ven, *et al.*, 1976). In the dynamic-pooled technology communications should combine both verbal and written media and utilize primarily the vertical direction. As we consider dynamic-sequential and dynamic-reciprocal technologies, we find an increased use of verbal, horizontal communications, and the dynamic-reciprocal technology exhibits the greatest frequency of communications of any of the designs thus far described. It also exhibits a greater number of meetings, both scheduled and unscheduled (Van de Ven, *et al.*, 1976).

The increasing demands for coordination and communications as we move from dynamic-pooled to dynamic-reciprocal suggest that the people employed in these technologies should have increasing technical and interpersonal skills. In the dynamic-pooled technology low technical skills and moderate interpersonal skills will suffice, but the dynamic-reciprocal technology needs people with moderate technical skills and highly developed interpersonal skills.

Overall, then, the dynamic technologies will be mechanistic except for the dynamic-reciprocal, which will be organic. All three will be highly differentiated and will utilize centralized decision making. As the task interdependence increases, we should find more sophisticated coordination mechanisms, as well as more dependence on people for horizontal communications, technical and interpersonal skills.

Problematic Technologies (Cells 3, 7, 11—Figure 5)

The next level of technological routineness is labeled problematic because the three technologies included are characterized by high task predictability but low problem analyzability. In other words, the nonroutineness arises not from the unexpected occurrence of problems but from the difficulty of resolving the problems once they occur. As with the previous technological level, we proceed in task interdependence complexity from pooled to sequential to reciprocal in a comparative fashion. First, however, we offer examples of the three problematic technologies.

An example of the problematic-pooled technology (cell 3) would be glass blowers working on specialty glass products. The tasks are predictable but developing the glass product to meet the customers' requirements requires the analysis of difficult problems, which can, however, be addressed by each glass blower as an individual rather than as an interdependent team. An example of the problematic-sequential technology would be a good secondary school. Students finishing secondary school need a relatively well established set of skills and knowledge, but the problems of accomplishing this sequential set of tasks are rather difficult to analyze, as any teacher can attest. An example of the problematic-reciprocal technology (cell 11) would be a building construction unit. Once the building site and type have been selected, the tasks can be predicted with relative certainty, but the problems encountered when exceptions arise can be quite difficult and usually require a highly interdependent resolution given the interdependence of the tasks comprising the building process.

At the problematic level of routineness the problems of design become increasingly complex. Only at the pooled level of task interdependence can the design be classified as mechanistic and can effective differentiation be accomplished. At the sequential and reciprocal task interdependence levels, the design must be organic, and while differentiation may be desirable it has become increasingly difficult to achieve due to the low problem analyzability.

Perrow (1970) suggests that discretion needs to be at the worker level in problematic technologies, rather than at the manager level (see Figure 6), and this suggests that a decentralized decision making system will be most appropriate. In the problematic-sequential technology centralization can be achieved in the decisions regarding task assignments, but decisions about how to achieve the tasks must remain in the hands of the worker.

In terms of integration efforts, these three technologies exhibit relatively complex needs regarding information processing, and as we consider the three task interdependence levels we find a broad range of coordination efforts being introduced (Galbraith, 1973). At the pooled level, the necessary coordination can be accomplished via the hierarchy and self-contained tasks. At the sequential level coordination can be achieved via vertical systems consisting of computer system support and assistants-to the teachers in our secondary school example. Finally, the problematic-reciprocal technology must utilize both vertical systems and lateral relations. The lateral relations enter the picture because of the discretion and power required at the worker level (Perrow, 1970) and because of the reciprocal nature of task interdependence.

At the process level of design, problematic technologies require increased levels of communication over more routine technologies. The low problem analyzability especially requires a great deal of effort directed at effective communications. However, the problematic-pooled technology is an exception due to the low task interdependence.

In the problematic-pooled technology communications will be infrequent and primarily vertical. Both the work of Van de Ven, *et al.* (1976) and Randolph (1977) tend to support this dependence on the vertical direction when the task interdependence is pooled. Their work suggests that verbal communications become more important as the technological nonroutineness increases, and Randolph's (1978) work suggests that written communications remain important when the task interdependence is pooled.

In the problematic-sequential technology, communications will need to exhibit a moderate frequency and be both verbal and written and both vertical and horizontal. Also, scheduled and unscheduled meetings will be utilized by the effective problematic-sequential technology (Van de Ven, *et al.*, 1976).

Finally, the problematic-reciprocal technology will need to utilize the highest frequency of communications of any technology thus far described (Randolph, 1977). Vertical communications will increase because of the problem solving difficulty and reciprocal task interdependence, and horizontal communications will increase because of the reciprocal task interdependence (Van de Ven, *et al.*, 1976). All of these communications will tend to utilize verbal media, especially unscheduled meetings, but because of the high task predictability written communications can be used in the vertical direction.

In terms of skill requirements of people, the low problem analyzability means that people in problematic technologies need high technical skills, and the need for interpersonal skills varies from low to high as the level of task interdependence increases from pooled to sequential to reciprocal.

In summary, the problematic technologies are a transitional stage in terms of design. At the pooled task interdependence level they are mechanistic, highly differentiated and utilizing simple coordination mechanisms, and as task interdependence increases, they become more organic, less capable of differentiation, and require sophisticated coordination mechanisms (both system and people type mechanisms).

Nonroutine Technologies (Cells 4, 8, 12—Figure 5)

The last and lowest level of technological routineness is labeled nonroutine because the three technologies included are characterized by low task predictability and low problem analyzability. In other words, the nonroutineness arises both from the unexpected occurrence of problems and from the difficulty of resolving those problems once they occur. As with the last two technological levels, we proceed in task interdependence complexity from pooled to sequential to reciprocal in a comparative fashion, after first offering examples of the three technologies.

An example of the nonroutine-pooled technology (cell 4) would be the company research scientist who works on a problem small enough to handle alone or with a very small group of people. Examples of the nonroutine-sequential technology (cell 8) can be found in the aerospace industry where there is a sequential nature to the tasks that must be performed to produce subassemblies of a space vehicle, but the problems encountered along the way are frequent and difficult to resolve. Examples of the nonroutine-reciprocal technology (cell 12) would include an acute-patient ward in a hospital and a research team working on a relatively large research project.

All three of the nonroutine technologies require organic designs utilizing a great deal of discretion and power for both supervisors and unit workers in order to cope with the frequent, unpredictable and difficult problems which are encountered in performing the tasks (Perrow, 1970). Woodward (1965) concurs in showing that organizations which encounter relatively high levels of complexity need to be decentralized to be effective. Thus, a great deal of pressure is put on the worker with this decentralization and high levels of discretion and power, and this means that the workers need to have sophisticated technical skills.

Because of the high level of nonroutineness in these technologies, a high level of differentiation is desirable to try to bound and reduce the nonroutineness; however, the fact that the problems encountered are unpredictable and difficult to solve means that a high level of differentiation is possible only at the pooled task interdependence level. At the sequential level, moderate differentiation is possible, while at the reciprocal level only low differentiation is possible, given the high task interdependence.

On the other side, however, as task interdependence increases so does the need for integration, and the nonroutineness of these technologies means that the efforts directed at coordination will become increasingly difficult as we move from pooled to sequential to reciprocal interdependence. In fact, all three of these technologies require sophisticated coordination mechanisms (Galbraith, 1973). At the pooled level of task interdependence, integration can be accomplished via the hierarchy and vertical systems (e.g., computer support for the company research scientist in our example). The nonroutine-sequential technology can utilize lateral relations (e.g., project managers and matrix designs in aerospace firms). As Thompson (1967) suggests, the reciprocal technology places great demands on decision making and communications processes, and this is especially true in the nonroutine-reciprocal technology. Galbraith (1973) concurs in suggesting use of lateral relations (e.g., unit managers in hospitals and team managers for research teams) and use of vertical relations to involve all unit members in a give-and-take of decision making and communications in the effective nonroutine-reciprocal technology.

All of this emphasis on the difficulties of coordination in nonroutine technologies means that workers will need at least moderate interpersonal skills, and in the nonroutine-reciprocal they will need highly developed interpersonal skills. Both nonroutine-pooled and nonroutine-sequential require moderate levels of communications, and the communications tend to be verbal rather than written, especially unscheduled meetings between worker and supervisor (Randolph, 1975; Van de Ven, *et al.*, 1976). The studies by Randolph and Van de Ven support the fact that communications will be vertical in the nonroutine-pooled technology and both vertical and horizontal in the nonroutine-sequential technology.

In the nonroutine-reciprocal technology, communications will need to be frequent, largely verbal, and flowing in all directions. Van de Ven, *et al.* (1976) lend strong support to these recommendations in their findings that horizontal communications and meetings, both scheduled and unscheduled, increase dramatically in the effective units where high nonroutineness and task interdependence prevail, and Randolph (1977) lends support to the greater use of vertical communications in nonroutine-reciprocal technologies.

Overall, then, the nonroutine technologies need organic designs with decentralized decision making and high worker and supervisor discretion. Coordination of efforts should be a major concern, and coordination mechanisms include the hierarchy, vertical systems, and effective use of vertical and horizontal communications which are largely verbal.

CONCLUSION

In this paper we have provided a three-dimensional technology typology and, focusing on the unit level, have described unit designs to complement the resulting twelve technology types. The design problem at the unit level involves consideration of task, technology, structure, and processes, and it is not an easy task. We have not attempted to deal with the equally difficult task of developing an overarching structure connecting the units of the organization, but the work of Lawrence and Lorsch (1967) and Galbraith (1973) offer some guidance for this task. Our hope is that the unit design problem will be a little easier and more rational for those who follow the prescriptions described herein.

REFERENCES

Burns, T. and G. M. Stalker, *The Management of Innovation.* London: Tavistock Publications, 1961.

Davis, L. E., "Job Satisfaction Research: The Post-Industrial View," *Industrial Relations,* 1971, Vol. 10, p. 180.

Galbraith, J. *Designing Complex Organizations.* Reading, MA: Addison-Wesley, 1973.

Hall, R. H., "Intraorganizational Structure Variation: Application of a Bureaucratic Model," *Administrative Science Quarterly,* 1963, Vol. 7, pp. 295–308.

Hickson, D. J., O. S. Pugh, and D. C. Pheysey, "Operations Technology and Organization Structure: An Empirical Reappraisal," *Administrative Science Quarterly,* 1969, Vol. 14, pp. 378–397.

Khandwalla, P. N. "Mass Output Orientation of Operations Technology and Organizational Structure," *Administrative Science Quarterly,* 1974, Vol. 19, pp. 74–97.

Lawrence, P. and J. Lorsch, *Organization and Environment: Managing Differentiation and Integration.* Homewood, Ill.: Irwin, 1969.

Lupton, T. "Best Fit in the Design of Organizations," in Miller, E. J. (Ed.) *Task and Organization.* London: Wiley & Sons, 1976, pp. 121–149.

MILES, R. H., *Macro Organizational Behavior*. Santa Monica: Goodyear, 1980.

PERROW, C., "A Framework for the Comparative Analysis of Organizations," *American Sociological Review*, 1967, Vol. 32, pp. 194–208.

PERROW, C. *Organizational Analysis: A Sociological View*. Belmont, CA: Wadsworth, 1970.

PUGH, O. S., D. J. HICKSON, C. R. HININGS, and C. TURNER, "The Context of Organization Structures," *Administrative Science Quarterly*, 1969, Vol. 14, pp. 91–114.

RANDOLPH, W. A. "An In-Depth Analysis of Organizational Communication Patterns as Influenced by an Organization's Technology," unpublished dissertation, University of Massachusetts, 1975.

RANDOLPH, W. A. "The Relationship between Organization Technology and the Direction and Frequency Dimensions of Task Communications," *Human Relations*, 1977, Vol. 30, pp. 1131–45.

RANDOLPH, W. A. "Organization Technology and the Media and Purpose Dimensions of Organization Communications," *Journal of Business Research*, 1978, Vol. 6, in press.

THOMPSON, J. D. *Organizations in Action*. New York: McGraw-Hill, 1967.

THOMPSON, J. D. and F. L. BATES. "Technology, Organization and Administration," *Administrative Science Quarterly*, 1957, Vol. 2, pp. 325–342.

VAN DE VEN, A. H., A. L. DELBECQ, and R. KOENING, "Determinants of Coordination Modes within Organizations," *American Sociological Review*, 1976, Vol. 41, pp. 322–338.

WOODWARD, J. *Industrial Organization: Theory and Practice*. London: Oxford University Press, 1965.

How the Multidimensional Structure Works at Dow Corning

William C. Goggin

Although Dow Corning was a healthy corporation in 1967, it showed symptoms of difficulty that troubled many of us in top management. These symptoms were, and still are, common ones in U.S. business and have been described countless times in reports, audits, articles, and speeches. Our symptoms took such form as:

Executives did not have adequate financial information and control of their operations. Marketing managers, for example, did not know how much it cost to produce a product. Prices and margins were set by the division managers.

Cumbersome communications channels existed between key functions, especially manufacturing and marketing.

In the face of stiffening competition, the corporation remained too internalized in its thinking and organizational structure. It was insufficiently oriented to the outside world.

Lack of communication between divisions not only created the antithesis of a corporate team effort but also was wasteful of a precious resource—people.

Long-range corporate planning was sporadic and superficial; this was leading to overstaffing, duplicated effort, and inefficiency.

Fearing that our problems would become worse instead of better in the future, we undertook major changes in our organizational structure. We turned to a matrix concept of organization—what we later came to call the multidimensional organization.

We made this revolutionary and novel move with our fingers crossed. For one thing, we knew of no case where a full-fledged, permanent matrix organization was in successful operation. We knew that the matrix structures pioneered by the aerospace industry in the late 1950s and the 1960s had been successful, but they had been project expedients, not designs for permanent organizations. For another, the new pattern bore little resemblance to the existing one (see Part A of *Exhibit I*); we were committing ourselves to a drastic overhaul, not a modification.

This overhaul meant that communicating the purpose and nature of the change to employees would be very difficult and sometimes nearly impossible. However, we were confident that in the long run the matrix form would stimulate innovation and lead to increased emphasis on opportunities for profit rather than preoccupation with problems. And we were determined to make it succeed.

FOUR-DIMENSIONAL SYSTEM

As we first thought of it, the matrix organization was to be two-dimensional. As Part B of *Exhibit I* suggests, the different businesses in Dow Corning were seen as:

1. *Profit centers* — These were the different businesses the company was in. Businesses were defined along product lines—for instance, rubber, encapsulants and sealants; resins and chemicals; fluids, emulsions, and compounds; specialty lubricants; and consumer, medical, and semi-conductor products. In most of the cases each business's product line served a related group of industries, markets, or customers.

2. *Cost centers*—These were functional activities and included marketing, manufacturing, technical service and development, and research, as well as a number of supportive activities, such as corporate communications, legal

and administrative services, economic evaluation, the controller's office, the treasurer's office, and industrial relations.

But soon we came to see further dimensions of the system:

3. *Geographical areas*—Business development varied widely from area to area, and the profit-center and cost-center dimensions could not be carried out everywhere in the same manner. Part C of *Exhibit I* shows this dimension. Note that each area is considered to be *both* a profit and a cost center. Dow Corning area organizations are patterned after our major U.S. organization. Although somewhat autonomous in their operation, they subscribe to the overall corporate objectives, operating guidelines, and planning criteria. During the annual planning cycle, for example, there is a mutual exchange of sales, expense, and profit projections between the functional and business managers headquartered in the United States and the area managers around the world.

4. *Space and time*—A fourth dimension of the organization denotes fluidity and movement through time (see Part D). The multidimensional organization is far from rigid; it is constantly changing. Unlike centralized or decentralized systems that too often are rooted deep in the past, the multidimensional organization is geared toward the future. Long-term planning is an inherent part of its operation.

KEYS TO EFFECTIVENESS

In a multidimensional organization like the one we developed, decision making tends to be flattened out or spread across the organization. No longer is the chief executive or the president required to pass judgment on

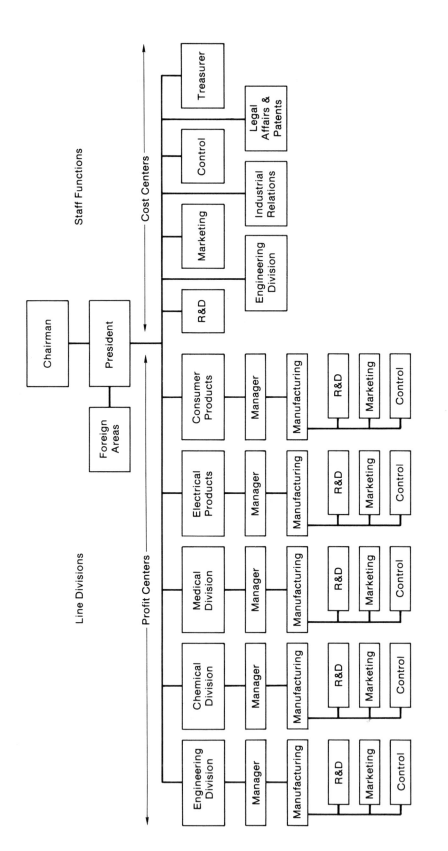

Exhibit I Evolution of a New Organization Concept   A. The divisionalized organization of early 1967

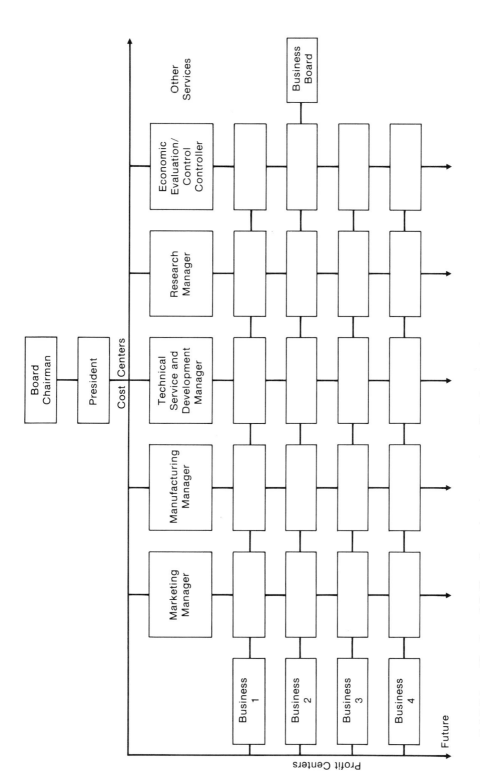

Exhibit I (Continued) B. Two-dimensional concept—profit and cost centers

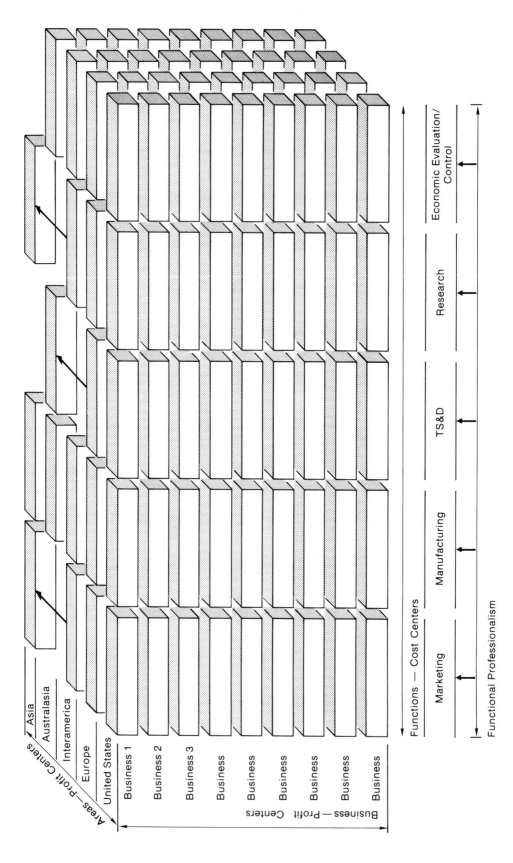

Exhibit I (Continued) C. Third dimension—areas

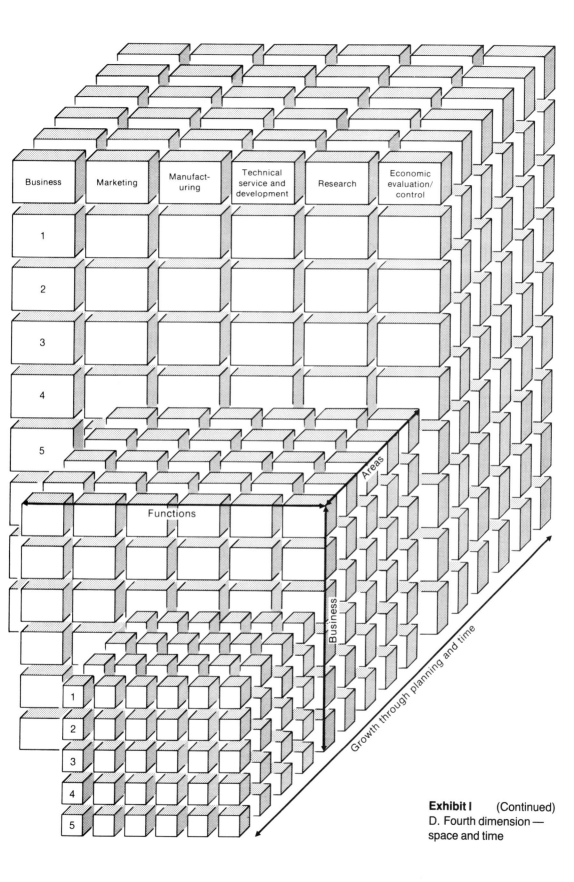

Business | Marketing | Manufact-uring | Technical service and development | Research | Economic evaluation/control

1
2
3
4
5

Functions

Areas

Business

Growth through planning and time

1
2
3
4
5

Exhibit I (Continued)
D. Fourth dimension — space and time

every important issue. Most of the decisions are made at the middle management level, but not unilaterally; the intent is to push decision making as far down into the organization as possible and encourage group consensus.

What are the requirements of making such a system work?

The first requirement is that communications within the corporation be thorough and complete. Timely and relevant data must go to all who have a *need to know*. A risk is attached to this: sensitive information often must be distributed well beyond the executive suite, leading to the ever-present danger that some data will find their way out of the corporation. Offsetting this concern is the fact that business conditions change so rapidly that today's confidential information may be virtually worthless tomorrow.

The second requirement is that those in charge of projects be able to understand and use the available data.

To appreciate what these requirements mean for managerial structure and reporting relationships, let us see how the Business Boards operate at Dow Corning.

Business Board Operation

There is a Business Board for each of the company's ten businesses. The only full-time board member is the manager of the business. His position in the organization is at once critical and tenuous. It is critical because his direct responsibility is the profit yield generated from the business he is charged with managing. It is tenuous because on paper he does not have direct control of the resources needed to accomplish his task. His operative body, his total resource, comprises representatives from the marketing, technical service and development, research, manufacturing, and economic evaluation/control functions (see *Exhibit II*). These are the Business Board members. They report *directly* to their functional group heads (vice president of marketing and distribution, director of technical service and development, and so on).

Organizationally, there is a strong dotted-line relationship running from the board member to the board manager. More important than organizational lines, however, is the clear understanding of where the profit responsibility lies. *Exhibit II* illustrates the structure and communications pattern of a board. Its manager reports directly to Dow Corning's top management. His primary task—to generate profits—is accomplished through the total and combined support of his board members.

At the outset, this setup created a stress-strain situation. Prior to 1968 the functional specialist at Dow Corning had concerned himself exclusively with maintaining and improving the professionalism of his function. Now, in addition, he was asked to lead in developing profits for his business. However, as his understanding of business goals increased and his comprehension of the workings of other functions increased, the stress began to dissipate.

The operation of each Business Board produces a healthy and invigorating power balance. The business manager must be a *leader,* not a dictator. He must work diligently toward sound economic decisions. Harmonious and productive Business Board activity is a tall order and does not happen automatically. Our experience is that teamwork rapidly improves with practice.

Cross-functional communications play a big part in the process. During the past six years, we have seen important changes in perspective. For example, in the early 1960s, an aggressive Dow Corning marketing manager would typically consider the generation of, say, 18% more sales dollars as *the* single most critical objective for the corporation. In line with this priority, he would make a strong case for allocating heavy marketing expenses to support sales objectives.

Today, the aggressive marketing manager who is on a Business Board is still concerned with the generation of increased sales dollars. But his overriding aim is generating the *most profitable* sales dollar.

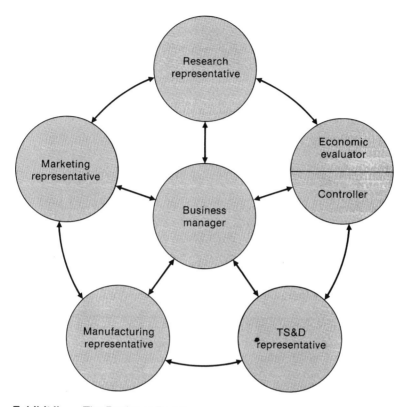

Exhibit II   The Business Board

In order to know and evaluate intelligently the profitability of products he is responsible for, he seeks to use the inputs of his functional colleagues in manufacturing, technical service and development, research, and economic evaluation. Our six-year history with the multidimensional organization indicates that similar advances in understanding have occurred among all the other functional representatives on each board.

Two-Boss System

A majority of the company's professional personnel work in dual authority relationships (see *Exhibit III*). While it may seem schizoid for a person to be responsible to two bosses, that is exactly what happens in a successful multidimensional operation— and it works well. Of course, the person must not become involved in a tug-of-war between his functional and Business Board bosses, or be given cause to despair over who is really appraising his day-to-day performance. To prevent that kind of situation, the functional and business managers are jointly responsible for periodic performance reviews that let the individual know exactly where he stands and what is expected of him.

Top management must also ensure that both the functional and the Business Board managers are given the authority, responsibility, and accountability for successfully attaining their objectives. The ultimate measurement is the long- and short-term rate of profit growth.

Making the two-boss system workable depends on the establishment of an environ-

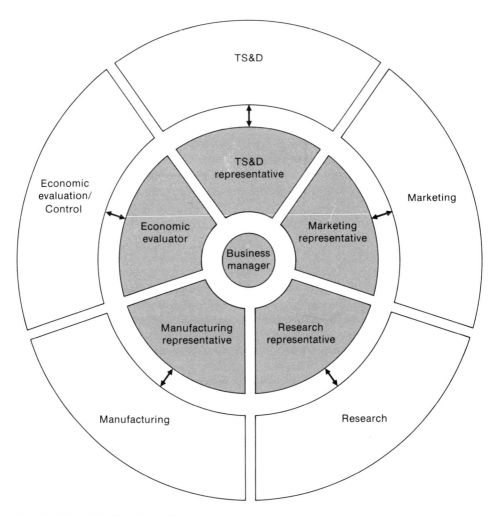

Exhibit III   The Two-Boss System

ment of trust and confidence. Nurturing and perpetuating this environment must begin at the very top of the organization. Corporate goals and objectives must be seen by every employee as good, proper, potentially achievable, and worthy of strong commitment. Only then can an individual commit himself with a clear conscience to achieving the goals while working in a complex system of interlocking responsibilities.

Supporting Subsystems

Another type of organization is the product management group (PMG). This is essentially a small Business Board devoted to long- and short-term planning for individual product families, or what we call business planning units (BPUs). A PMG comprises functional representatives, as does a Business Board, but its members may come from lower organizational levels. It is responsible for profits in its product area and is vested with the authority to bring its requests for resources to the appropriate Business Board. Once a request is approved, the PMG is fully responsible for wise investment of its resources so that corporate goals can be achieved. PMG managers often attend Business Board meetings, which is evidence of the vital contribution these people make to the company.

PMGs are usually permanent. However, the chairmanship of such a group is not a full-time responsibility, as it is on a Business Board. Personnel shifts within the PMGs are common, serving to bring fresh blood to the groups and to train lower-level management people for greater responsibilities.

Industry management teams are yet another subsystem. While the PMG concentrates its efforts on the management of individual product families, the industry management teams are concerned with the marketing of many products to a single major market or industry, such as the automotive market or the electronics industry.

In addition to the foregoing subsystems, Dow Corning has occasional need for short-term ad hoc task forces. Typical task force projects might be solving a product or processing problem, streamlining order entry and delivery procedures, resolving inventory problems, or developing a corporate safety promotion.

Corporate Business Board

I have described the flattened-out or egalitarian style of management and decision making that is built into the multidimensional organization. In order to keep the overall corporate direction well balanced and to prevent the potential splinter effect of several semiautonomous businesses zealously seeking to accomplish their individual goals and objectives, we have a guiding body called the Corporate Business Board. It comprises the chairman, president, vice presidents, and other functional heads; it is similar to executive committees in many corporations. As the top decision-making body in the corporation, this group provides cross-communications between businesses, functions, and areas. It influences and approves long- and short-range corporate objectives.

The Corporate Business Board meets at least once a month to review the sales and profit progress of each business against its projected plans. Progress in each geographical area is reviewed quarterly on the same basis. The board also meets as needed to review or initiate critical corporate projects and programs.

AREA MANAGEMENT

At this point in our organizational evolution, the geographical areas are at different stages of development. Within the next two to four years, however, all will be patterned closely after the U.S. organization. Each area has its own management, though corporate "ground rules" apply uniformly to all. Area managers must decide when modifications of these ground rules are absolutely necessary because of local customs and business practices, government regulations, and other considerations.

Close communication is maintained between area managers and the U.S. organization. The former must not function independently; at the same time the businesses and functions cannot do their jobs without intimate knowledge of area operations. The area managers work according to a plan for sales, expenses, and profits. The plan for each area is integrated into the plan for each business and function. Thus the area plan is viewed as a part of a larger corporate whole. This two-way system allows each area to maintain a viable cost-center/profit-center balance and to operate with a sufficient degree of autonomy.

Twice each year the area managers meet with the executive management to plan, review, and coordinate global plans and programs.

CRUCIAL SUPPORT SYSTEMS

The basic charter for each function at Dow Corning is clear and unequivocal:

Marketing—generation of sales volume, with a sharp eye on profitability.

Technical service and development—new-product commercialization and old-product maintenance.

Manufacturing—volume and efficiency in production, engineering, and technology.

Research—assurance of a steady flow of new products that can be commercialized.

Economic evaluation, control, and planning—development of a common corporate economic language and a uniform analytical system for evaluating capital expenditures and all strategic programs having an economic impact.

These functions are found in nearly all large U.S. corporations. In a multidimensional organization, however, they are perhaps more closely related, and it is especially important that they work together smoothly and productively. Consistent and uniform standards are essential.

To help achieve such coordination, our company maintains a number of support systems. Here I shall describe only six of them; the order of description is not intended to suggest relative priorities or importance. *Exhibit IV* lists the support systems and the operating entities they are designed to support.

Management by Objectives

One pillar of a multidimensional organization is MBO. At Dow Corning, MBO involves (a) a hierarchy of objectives, and (b) em-ployee *involvement, participation,* and *accountability* at all levels.

The objectives of each business, function, or support group are established on the basis of overall corporate objectives. A condensed version of our 1973 corporate objectives, with the confidential data excluded, appears in the ruled insert on page 139. Note that these objectives are simply stated, clear, and, for the most part, quantifiable. (Even Objective VIII will be stated in measurable terms before long, we hope; work toward that end is under way.) These objectives constitute the sum total of results that must be accomplished by members of the organization within given time periods, generally one year and five years.

To develop objectives in this way in every business, function, and area, a great amount of communication must go on throughout the planning cycle. For example, each Business Board must know what the marketing function's sales projections and expense requirements are. And marketing cannot make its projections without specific inputs from each business and area. Also, a PMG must develop its set of objectives in accordance with the goals of the parent business.

Four factors are critical to MBO effectiveness:

1. Individual *involvement* in preparing job objectives.

2. Active *participation* and decision making at every level in pursuit of established objectives.

3. Enough *autonomy* and *freedom* for employees to accomplish the goals set.

4. Periodic *measurement* of an employee's progress in attaining his or her goals.

Personnel Reviews

Reviews of employee performance are linked closely to the MBO approach. The fourth factor listed is the basis of a manager's discussion with a subordinate (such

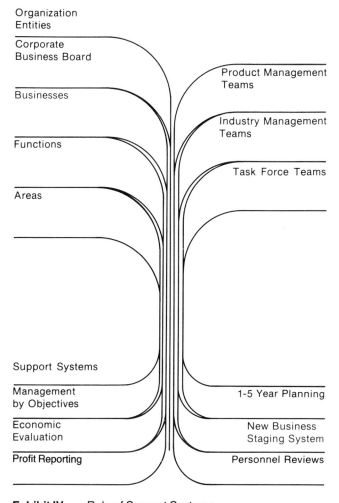

Organization
Entities

Corporate
Business Board

Product Management
Teams

Businesses

Industry Management
Teams

Functions

Task Force Teams

Areas

Support Systems

Management
by Objectives

1-5 Year Planning

Economic
Evaluation

New Business
Staging System

Profit Reporting

Personnel Reviews

Exhibit IV   Role of Support Systems

discussions occur at least once a year). For professional employees a 5-point rating scale is used, with 1 representing outstanding performance and 5 unsatisfactory performance.

Ideally, each professional employee understands that his rating is largely based on how well he achieved the results he was committed to achieve. Our experience strongly indicates that self-appraisals tend to be more critical and demanding than imposed, or autocratic, appraisals.

As one might expect, the two-boss system comes into play at review time. Both bosses evaluate an employee's performance and agree on the single rating that most fairly represents their judgment of his work.

Planning Process

The multidimensional organization has many moving and working parts, and planning how they are to fit together is a major activity. Our corporate planning department develops the format and planning cycle that guides the activities of the businesses, functions, and areas.

The planning department does not *do* the planning. It simply develops, administers, and communicates the corporate ground rules. Each business, function, and area must do its own planning. The total effort is funneled into one- and five-year corporate plans that are reviewed and approved by the Corporate Business Board before they are presented to the board of directors for final approval.

Economic Evaluation

Another extremely important support system is economic evaluation. This involves evaluating capital expenditures as well as any proposed strategic program that carries economic impact. Economic evaluation provides us with a common economic language. Each Business Board is staffed with an economic evaluator whose primary job is to measure the value of a new investment or new strategy to his business and to the corporation. The economic evaluator is generally the business's controller as well.

In a dynamic organization many options for new business development are considered, options which can originate from any source. Potentially, they must meet the ROI criteria set forth in the corporate objectives. It is up to the economic evaluator to assess objectively the investment proposals put before his business or the Corporate Business Board. His analysis includes the probable ROI, discounted cash flow, and net present value of the proposed investment. He is also expected to present alternatives to the proposed solution along with the appropriate economic justification.

Economic evaluation does not stifle thinking about new business opportunities; what it does do is vastly reduce the chance for error. It replaces investment decisions based on emotions and "gut feel" with economically sound and objective investment decisions.

Profit Reporting

All sales and expenditures are identified or assigned to a business or business planning unit. This allows the company's total profit before tax to be clearly identified by each geographic area as well as by each of the ten businesses. In the marketing function, for example, field salesmen are assigned specific business planning units or product lines for which they have sales responsibility. Selling costs are directly assigned to the business planning units of the products sold. The other cost center functions operate in a like manner.

In this direct-costing system we identify and separate both variable and fixed costs. This allows area and business managers to separate the planning and control of those costs which vary with volume from those which are fixed or subject to management decision. The system thereby provides a sure and uncluttered approach to profit determination. It also eliminates "hidden" expenses and greatly facilitates businesslike financial management.

New Business Staging

A company that stresses advanced technology naturally places much emphasis on new-product development and commercialization. Before the development of our multi-dimensional organization, an average of nearly eight years elapsed from the time a new product was conceptualized until it reached commercialization (if it ever did). In the light of encroaching competitive pressures, we realized we needed to reduce the commercialization time. As a result, our new business staging system was born.

This system provides a disciplined and organized approach to new product commercialization. As *Exhibit V* shows, seven stages of the product life cycle are identified, ranging from conception (Stage 1) through product obsolescence (Stage 7). The task is to identify and coordinate the efforts of many people. In each stage one function has the

1973 Corporate Objectives

I. *Profits*—Maintain rate of growth of pretax profits of at least A% per year.

II. *Sales*—Increase worldwide sales by at least B%.

III. *Share of market*—Increase market share by C%.

IV. *Productivity*—Improve productivity (total cost of employees divided by sales) by D%.

V. *Return on investment*—Increase ROI to E% after taxes and maintain it at that level.

VI. *New capital*—Expected return on new capital investment should be at least F% after taxes.

VII. *New products*—Products less than five years old should contribute a minimum of G% of total sales.

VIII. *Quality of life*—In all countries, Dow Corning should continue to fulfill its social responsibilities as a leading corporate citizen.

IX. *Safety*—Both corporate frequency and severity rates should be among the ten best reported to the Manufacturing Chemists Association each year.

---

major role to play and acts as the project quarterback. For example, in Stage 2 (feasibility), research is the prime mover. When a product moves to Stage 4 (commercialization), technical service and development assumes ball control. In Stage 5 (market expansion), it is marketing's ballgame.

But in no stage does the lead function have the only input. For instance, marketing is often much involved in Stage 4 commercialization projects, just as technical service and development is instrumental in keeping Stage 5 products properly maintained and free from operating defects.

The new business staging system is designed to produce a team effort, with clearly identified functional responsibilities. Using this system, the corporation hopes to reduce by 50%, before the end of this decade, the time that is traditionally required for the commercialization of a new product.

CONCLUSION

The advantages and disadvantages of a system such as Dow Corning's can be realistically evaluated only after manage-

ment has taken a rather exhaustive internal audit. I can personally attest to the difficulty of this task; it requires management to criticize a structure that many of its members have spent years developing.

By all quantitative and qualitative measurements, it can be stated, after five years of experience, that our multidimensional organization is successful. At the same time, however, even though I am an enthusiastic proponent of the system, I must be the first to caution that the multidimensional technique is not a panacea for all organization problems. And the dedication that top management must maintain during the long and arduous years of restructuring should not be underestimated.

What kinds of companies might benefit from a multidimensional organization? Those that meet all or most of the following conditions should be good prospects:

Developing, manufacturing, and marketing many diverse but interrelated technological products and materials.

Having market interests that span virtually every major industry.

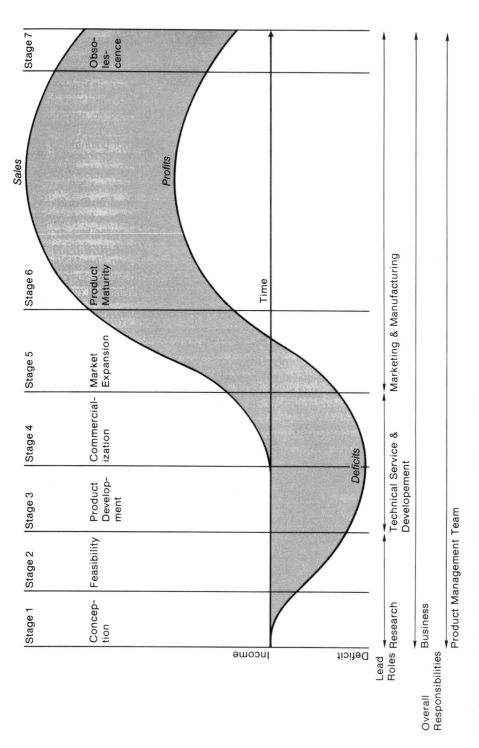

Exhibit V   Product Life Cycle and Management Responsibilities

Becoming multinational with a rapidly expanding *global* business.

Working in a business environment of rapid and drastic change, together with strong competition.

Conversely, a company with a limited product line, operating mostly in the United States, and serving a single industry or a limited number of customers would not have much use for this system. Nor would many service-oriented industries or manufacturing companies with nontechnical commodity-type products. I believe, however, that certain forward-thinking service-oriented industries (e.g., health management, education, and financial service) might use a modified version of the multidimensional organization quite effectively. My own experience and knowledge of service-related companies lead me to believe that many of the principles of multidimensional organization can be applied to non-manufacturing operations.

Costs and Benefits

The initiation fee to the multidimensional organization group is very high. Some costs to consider are:

1. Willingness to cope with resistance to change.

2. Top management dedication for years —and this means not one, but essentially all, top executives.

3. A highly intelligent and motivated middle management anxious to see the whole corporation progress — no freeloaders.

4. Determination to minimize internal politics—no empire builders.

5. An abundance of patience on the part of the board of directors, top management, and middle management.

At the outset, much of the existing organization may be uprooted, with functions and businesses redefined and realigned, and new geographic areas established. People movement soars to a high peak as many activities and jobs are phased out and new ones are created. At all levels, especially middle management, there is uncertainty and serious questioning of the "new" system.

Once operational, the system is surprisingly flexible, but at the outset it *appears* to be rigid. This is so because on paper a matrix structure clearly defines lines of authority. What cannot be clearly written into the scheme at the start is how free-flowing communication tends to soften the rigid-looking organizational lines once the system becomes operative. Also, in our own case, a number of subsystems that were not built into the original structure, such as the product management groups and the new business staging system, have tended to add flexibility and cross-communications throughout the entire corporation.

There is one final condition that should be considered by corporations desiring to explore the multidimensional concept further: the basic orientation of the *entire* organization must be psychologically attuned to results. Managers who have grown accustomed to rationalizing failure and near misses will find the climate of a dynamic multidimensional organization very uncomfortable because it is so results-oriented and facts-conscious. Those who prefer "telling it like it is" will find the system exciting and rewarding.

The break-in period for our new system was three to four years. The company did not suffer unduly as a result of the organizational upheaval. In fact, the economic downturn during 1970–1971 served to reinforce the system's potential for coping with difficulty.

What advantages stand to be gained from a multidimensional organization? Our experience points to the following:

Higher profit generation, even in an industry (silicones) price-squeezed by competition. (Much of our favorable profit picture seems due to a better overall understanding and practice of expense controls throughout the company.)

Increased competitive ability based on technological innovation and product quality without a sacrifice in profitability.

Sound, fast decision making at all levels in the organization, facilitated by stratified but open channels of communication and by a totally participative working environment.

A healthy and effective balance of authority among the businesses, functions, and areas.

Progress in developing short- and long-range planning with the support of all employees.

Resource allocations that are proportionate to expected results.

More stimulating and effective on-the-job training.

Accountability that is more closely related to responsibility and authority.

Results that are visible and measurable.

More top-management time for long-range planning and less need to become involved in day-to-day operations.

Perhaps the single most pressing problem that faces any industrial organization is how to cope effectively with change. The multidimensional organization is designed to combat that problem. Since change is constant, so must our organization be continually flexible and adaptive to changing conditions on all fronts. We perceive our organization to be a dynamic one, and, to date, our experience indicates that we do indeed have the ability to manage change rather than be managed by it.

On Concepts of Corporate Structure

Economic Determinants of Organization

Harold Stieglitz

Just about 25 years ago, General Motors announced one of its most important products—the GM Formula. Its wage escalation clause negotiated then with the UAW provided for a 1¢ increase in hourly wages for each 1.14 point rise in the BLS index. Confronted with the inflationary period of Korea, many company negotiators copied GM and adopted the 1 for 1.14 formula for escalating wages. The fact that the formula had a specific relevance to GM's employees —that it reflected the ratio of average wages of the GM employees to the cost-of-living index at the time of adoption—seemed beside the point. The fact that a different formula might have more appropriately reflected the wage-cost-of-living relationship of their employees deterred few from just going ahead with 1 for 1.14. Evidently what

Harold Stieglitz, "On Concepts of Corporate Structure: Economic Determinants of Organization," The Conference Board Record, *Feb. 1974, pp. 7–13*, © 1974 The Conference Board, Inc.

was good enough for the sophisticates at GM was good enough for most of its emulators.

More than 50 years ago, however, GM had developed another product that proved to have an even larger impact. This was a management concept labeled "centralized coordination, decentralized administration" —or, "decentralization with coordination and control." While adoption of this concept came less rapidly, many companies turned to it—especially in the post-World War II growth period, when diversification and greater complexity characterized an increasing number.

In application, the concept meant reorganizing operations into divisionalized profit centers that operated with a high degree of decentralization; setting up corporate staffs to provide centralized coordination and control under corporate-wide policies. Initially, the ambiguities and vagaries of the concept were not seen as deterrents to its adoption.

GM's success in the marketplace showed it must be doing something right. If "decentralization with centralized control" was good enough for GM, it was good enough for others.

Since the early 1920s, however, the concept was subject to adaptation and development at GM itself. Even during Alfred P. Sloan's tenure, changes in technology and the marketplace brought an ebb and flow to the degree of decentralization vs. centralized coordination—and, retrospectively, it's been more ebb than flow. But those who borrowed the concept sometimes missed the nuances of GM's later experience, so what seemed to work there didn't always work for them.

Emulation in structuring organization is not, of course, dead. Upon hearing of a major company that operates very effectively with a very small central staff, many a chief executive has envied the cost savings implicit in such a structure. Some have tried it. Similarly, the prospect of putting some young tigers at the head of their own decentralized profit centers has led others to reorganize. However, in more recent years, there is evidence that a more mature approach to organization planning has displaced such "me-too-ism."

THE REASONS FOR STRUCTURING ORGANIZATION

Sloan, the prime mover in the development and adaptation of GM's concept of organization, at the close of his long career, remarked, "An organization does not make decisions; its function is to provide a framework, based upon established criteria, within which decisions can be made."[1] The modifying phrase "based upon established criteria" is crucial, and maturity in corporate organization structuring has only developed as more top executives have been able to identify those criteria that condition the framework.

Admittedly, many a pragmatic top executive denies that there are any basic criteria that dictate key elements of the organization structure. The "situation," the "personalities," the "management style," and a host of other factors are presumably enough to make each organization and its structure unique.[2] Over the long run, however, one may observe that constant reorganizations and adaptation tend to move the structure in directions that seem almost independent of particular personalities or styles or whims.

Demonstrably, the spectrum of organizational structures throughout industry remains quite broad. It stretches from companies that are organized virtually like holding companies to those that operate, basically, like one-man businesses. There are companies that operate in a highly centralized manner, others that are highly decentralized—and all shades in between. Similarly, some are functionally organized, some have certain elements set up as divisions, some are mixed. And staff within these companies come in all shapes and sizes.[3]

Still, the patterns of organization structure that have emerged indicate that there are company characteristics that are at the root of the developments, and they are primarily economic. Moreover, those that are evidently most influential in shaping organization structure can be specified:

Degree of diversification in terms of the variety of goods and services produced and/or markets served.

Degree of interdependency, integration or overlap among the diversified operating components.

Such other factors as economies of scale, dispersion, or absolute size are significant, but largely to the extent that they affect diversification and overlap.[4]

The extent to which a company is diversified tends to determine whether its major operating activities will be structured by division or function and the nature of the groups that come into existence.

The extent to which the operations overlap—in terms of markets, technology, sources of supply, etc.—emerges as the key determinant of the degree of decentralization and the types and role of corporate staff.

In short, the emergence of the divisionalized decentralized form of organization is less a matter of managerial sophistication, more a matter of economic necessity. In an organizational sense, sophistication amounts to recognition of the inevitable.

A CONTINUUM OF ORGANIZATIONS

Relating structure to economic variables is more readily seen when the varieties of types of companies and apposite key structural elements are arrayed. Looking at diversity and overlap of operations, it's quite evident, for example, that companies range from those engaged in the production and/or sale of one good or service to those involved in a multiplicity of related and unrelated businesses. Indeed, when so arrayed, it is clear that the myriad variations form a continuum with no real discontinuities.

A company at point 1 of the continuum may be substantially different from one at point 10, but to distinguish too sharply between companies at points 4 and 5 would be fatuous. Even so, the continuum, as represented in the chart, can be divided for analytical purposes into four categories—each of which, in itself, covers a spectrum of companies:

I Single businesses—one company producing a single or homogeneous product for a single or homogeneous market.

II Multiple businesses, related—one company producing a variety of products for a variety of markets, but with a high degree of overlap in markets for the various products and/or a high degree of integration in materials or technology involved in manufacturing the products.

III Multiple businesses, unrelated—one company producing a variety of products for a variety of markets, but the overlap is absent. There are virtually no common denominators—no overlap—in the markets served or the resources or technology employed in producing the variety of goods or services.

IV Multiple businesses, unrelated (no corporate identity)—one company but little or no attempt to manage the unrelated businesses; little or no attempt to project a company identity. This, of course, is the holding company defined by Sloan as "a central office surrounded by autonomously operating satellites."

This continuum is not designed to suggest a strategy for growth. Nor does it imply that normal growth occurs through movement across the continuum. A company's growth pattern may keep it in Category I; move it from I to II; or from IV to III.

It bears repeating that the array is a continuum—there are no sharp discontinuities. For analytical purposes, a company can only be characterized as having "more or less" of the economic qualities of a particular category. Similarly, the key organizational elements that relate to these categories can also only be referred to in terms of degree—more or less—i.e., more or less decentralized, more or less divisionalized. Overall, the tendency to divisionalize increases as one moves from Categories I to IV; more significantly, the degree of decentralization decreases as one moves from IV to I. The major related structural elements—makeup of the divisions, types and roles of staff, nature of the groups—also vary.

FUNCTIONAL VS. DIVISIONAL FORM OF ORGANIZATION

It is no accident that companies, regardless of size, that fall into Category I tend to be organized on a functional basis. At the extreme left of the spectrum there is usually

A CONTINUUM OF CORPORATIONS AND RELATED ORGANIZATION STRUCTURES

Elements of Organization	Single Businesses (I)	Multiple Businesses Related (II)	Multiple Businesses Unrelated (III)	Multiple Businesses Unrelated (no corporate identity) (IV)
	1 2 3 4	5 6 7 8	9 10 11	12 13 14 15 16
Structure of Operations	Functional	Divisionalized	Divisionalized	Divisionalized (subsidiaries)
Functional elements within divisions	—	Prod. & Sales little staff	Prod. & Sales more staff	Prod. & Sales more complete staff
Degree of Decentralization	More Centralized	Decentralized	Highly Decentralized	Highly Decentralized (virtual autonomy for divisions)
Corporate Staff — Type	Administrative and Operational	Administrative and Operational	Administrative	Administrative (if any)
Role	Services Advisory Control	Advisory Control	Advisory (consultant)	—
Groups	—	Super-Divisions	Liaison	Unlikely

little basis for coordinating specialized activities in any other way. Thus, inasmuch as all manufacturing and engineering activities serve a common product, they are organized under one head. Inasmuch as all marketing activities are designed to promote one product, they too are most effectively coordinated by one head.

As the company finds either its product or market spectrum broadening—as it diversifies—it often is able to segregate either its production activities or its marketing activities by product or market. But in terms of who is accountable for what, it's still functional—until such time as increased diversity allows both marketing and production of a given product for a specified market to be linked.

This move to link production and sales of a given product under one head—thus divisionalizing and forming a "profit center," as opposed to a "cost center"—characteristically occurs in companies whose diversification efforts result in (a) more discrete technologies for each product, (b) more discrete markets for each product. Under these circumstances, whether diversification has come from internal product development or external mergers or acquisition, product divisions emerge as the more effective operating components. Again, it is no accident that companies whose operational characteristics are those of Categories II, III, or IV tend to organize them into product or so-called market divisions. In short, they divisionalize.[5]

However, the divisions that are so characteristic of the more diversified companies vary in terms of the more specialized functional components that are assigned or report to the division head. In Category II, for example, the divisions undoubtedly have their own production and sales units; they may very well have their own accounting and engineering units. But it is most likely that corporate units in various areas, e.g., marketing, manufacturing, purchasing, or research and development, will exist, in part,

to supply certain services that are common to several divisions. Thus the divisions of companies in Category II tend to truncate; they are not complete in terms of all the functions necessary to carry on their operations.

The divisions that make up companies in Categories III and IV, on the other hand, tend to be more self-sufficient, less reliant on common services. Indeed, in Category IV, many of the operating components exist as virtually self-sufficient subsidiaries. Obviously, the greater interdependence and overlap of markets, technology and resources in Category II accounts for the more truncated divisions in this class; the lack of commonality between the divisions or subdivisions of Categories III and IV makes for far greater self-sufficiency—at least in terms of functional components.

CENTRALIZATION-DECENTRALIZATION

Degree of overlap is even more closely related to the varying degrees of decentralization that is evident at various points in the continuum. Decentralization, in this context, has a specific meaning: the extent to which decision-making authority is delegated to lower levels of the organization and, by implication, the degree of constraint—of centralized control in the form, for example, of corporate-wide policies—that curtails the area of discretion left to lower-level managers.

Generally, it can be observed that three factors have a major effect on the degree of delegated authority and/or decentralization:

The confidence factor—the confidence of superiors in the competence of subordinates.

The information factor—the extent to which the organization has developed mechanisms to feed information to the decision-making points, and the extent to which feedback systems have developed that allow accountable managers to evaluate results of their decisions.

The scope-of-impact factor—the extent to which a decision made by one unit head affects the operations of another unit.

It is this third factor—the scope-of-impact of decision—that, in the long run, becomes the key ingredient in determining the degree of decentralization. And, clearly, the scope-of-impact of decisions is directly related to the degree of integration, or overlap, or interdependence of the company's varied operations. With a greater degree of interaction, less decentralization is possible. As the operations become more highly varied and opportunities for operational synergy decrease, the greater the possible degree of decentralization, the greater the toleration of differences in approaches to personnel, customers, and the public.[6]

In terms of the continuum, it is evident that the operation of companies in Category I encourages a higher degree of centralized decision-making than takes place in Category II. Similarly, companies in Category III can, and do, tolerate more decentralization than those in Category II. And while the operations, or the divisions of companies, in Categories III and IV might be very similar in terms of diversity and minimum overlap, the fact that companies in Category IV are not intent on projecting a corporate identity—and thus can eschew corporate-wide policies—makes for a degree of decentralization that verges on virtual autonomy for the operating divisions or subsidiaries.

CORPORATE STAFF: FUNCTIONS AND ROLES

Size is undoubtedly a key factor that determines whether and when a particular staff unit will emerge within the corporation. Until there is a continuing need for a particular functional expertise, the company may well make use of outside or part-time consultants or services. But once the need is felt and a full-time staff unit is created, whether it be one person or a larger unit, the nature of the operations and the degree of decentralization tend to be strong determinants of the types of specialized staff that come into being and their role relative to the rest of the company.

For analytical purposes, it is useful to distinguish between: (a) administrative staff, the functional (staff) units that derive from the fact that a corporation exists as a legal and financial entity (the legal, financial, and public relations staff are typical) and, (b) operational staff, the functional (staff) units that emerge because of the peculiar nature of the companies' operations (e.g., manufacturing, marketing, purchasing and traffic).

An even more substantive distinction can be drawn between the various roles that characterize staff in its varied relationships. Again, for analytical purposes, whether it be administrative or operational staff, three roles can be distinguished.[7]

Advisory or counseling role—the staff unit brings its professional expertise to bear in analyzing and solving problems. In this role, staff acts as a consultant; its relationship is largely that of a professional to a client.

Service role—the staff unit provides services that can be more efficiently and economically provided by one unit with specialized expertise than by many units attempting to provide for themselves. Its relationship in this role is largely that of a supplier to a customer.

Control role—because of its professional or specialized expertise in a given functional area, staff is called upon to assist in establishing the plans, budgets, policies, rules, standard operating procedures that act as major constraints on delegated authority; that set the parameters of decision-making at lower levels. And it sets up mechanisms to audit and evaluate performance vis-à-vis these controls. In exercising this role, its relationship to the rest of the organization is that of an agent for top management.

By combining the elements—type of staff and role — it is possible to draw a profile of corporate staff. And that profile tends to vary with companies in each of the four categories.

Thus the fact that Category I includes companies that are organized functionally, that are more centralized than decentralized, narrows the options for the character of staff units that come into being. Of necessity, staff units of both administrative and operational types become part of corporate structure—with the operational staff elements often reporting directly to the accountable operational head of manufacturing or sales. And while some staff units may be more service-oriented than advisory, others more advisory than control, the fact that the functional organization is virtually one large profit center makes advice, service and control a part of every staff unit's job.

Among Category II companies, whose diversification has fostered divisionalization and greater decentralization, the profile of corporate staff changes. The change is largely one of role rather than type.

Because the divisional operations are interdependent and overlap, there may well be need for operational staff as well as administrative units at the corporate level. But divisions may also have their own staff units to provide services that are unique to the division. Thus, in a divisionalized company there may be, for example, R&D at both corporate and division levels, with divisional staff emphasizing development, corporate staff emphasizing longer range research. However, because more staff is created within the divisions of Category II companies to provide services locally, the service role of the corporate staff declines.

As a result, the advisory and control roles of the corporate staff units assume primary emphasis.

However, this is not to suggest that the advisory and control role become dominant merely as residual factors. To the contrary, they gain emphasis because: (a) In companies with the economic characteristics of Category II, corporate top management becomes relatively more future-oriented; the divisions remain more oriented to the near term. The future emphasis underscores the corporate staff's advisory role in planning. (b) The decentralization occasioned by multiple profit centers heightens the need to discern areas of overlap as well as matters of overriding corporate concern that require consistency in decision-making, i.e., the generation of corporate policies. And it puts greater emphasis on discerning and establishing more sophisticated control procedures. Thus the greater emphasis on staff as an agency of control.

Moving to companies whose economic characteristics are those of Category III, the profile of corporate staff again changes— this time in both type and role. Because the operating divisions have little in common, they share no markets; they don't overlap in technology and resources; there is little need for corporate staff in operational areas. Rather, operational staff units are more often housed within the divisions or at the group level. The corporate staff units more often are those in the general areas of administration — financial, legal — and often those that are closely tied to future development of the corporation.

More significantly, the corporate staff's role as a control agency, prominent in both Categories I and II, fades among Category III companies. The far greater degree of decentralization possible in any such company is synonymous with fewer overall constraints in the form of corporate policies and procedures. This fact accounts for the change in role. For the most part, staff units in Category III companies, with the possible exception of finance and planning, are primarily advisory in role—captive consultants.

The diminished need for operational staff and the shift to a primarily consulting relationship that characterizes corporate staff in Category III companies becomes even more pronounced in Category IV. Indeed, it becomes difficult even to see corporate staff —in the sense so far discussed—in the company that operates like a holding company. The parent corporation may have a strong financial unit and legal unit, but these exist primarily to serve the parent. Since the divisions or subsidiaries are encouraged to operate in a manner that verges on autonomy, they establish their own controls, have their own staffs whose profile undoubtedly varies with the economic characteristics of the particular division or subsidiary. If there is such a thing as "corporate staff" in companies at the extreme of Category IV, it may very well exist as a separate "management service" subsidiary from which the other divisions may purchase services as required.

GROUP STRUCTURES

The increased use of groups, headed by group executives, is relatively recent. The increase has resulted largely from the proliferation of operating divisions within corporations. It's another level of management introduced to secure better coordination of several presumably separate divisions.[8] Almost by definition, the group mechanism is confined to the divisionalized companies of Categories II and III. But not quite.

There are ambiguities in the group concept and variations in the structure of groups that can be linked to the same factors accounting for variations in the role of corporate staff.

Starting with Category IV, in this instance, there is little evidence of attempts to link operating units into groups headed by a group executive. This seems consistent with

the parent corporation's hands-off approach to the highly independent divisions or subsidiaries.

In Category III companies, on the other hand, diverse though the divisions may be, there is an attempt to link the operations more closely with guidance from the corporation. There is an attempt to devise a corporate strategy and to project a corporate identity. Divisions very often are assembled into groups. But for the most part, the divisions within the groups have little in common— other than that they serve the "industrial market" or "consumer market" or operate under some such similarly broad umbrella. The group executive, in such instances, may serve as an advisor, a reviewer of plans, an appraiser of performance. But he is essentially a link pin between the division and their objectives and the corporation. His primary function may well be to plug the communication gap that emerges when the proliferation of divisions has caused too broad a span of control for the chief executive. Changes are such that a group will have no staff at the group level, or possibly just a controllership function that reports to the group executive.

Move to Category II companies and the character of the group and the function of the group executive change. Here, the groups that emerge tend to be more closely knit, comprised of divisions that invite synergistic development. Indeed, in many such situations the group structure develops as a pragmatic mechanism for dealing with the fact that the "discrete and separate" divisions are not really all that discrete or separate. In many such companies, the divisions do share markets or do overlap in technology. The pulling together of these overlapping divisions makes it more possible to develop a business strategy for a total market, or to pool certain production facilities, or share common staff services.

The group, in such instances, actually becomes more of a super-division composed of truncated or even functional divisions. And the group executive, rather than providing liaison between a series of unrelated divisions, becomes the head of a more encompassing profit center.

In Category I companies, the definition of group seems to preclude its existence—except possibly at point 4 in the spectrum where beginning attempts to diversify may lead to the creation of a group that pulls together newer businesses emerging as product divisions. The closest approximation of the group executive in the functionally organized company is the high level executive who coordinates related staff and operating functions—e.g., an executive vice president whose domain covers manufacturing, engineering, R&D, and purchasing. However, he is still primarily a functional executive.

THE MODELS IN PERSPECTIVE

These major elements of structure, when assembled by category, reveal organizational profiles that are significantly different. Each structural model is rooted in the dominant economic characteristics of the corporation as a total entity. It is worth underscoring the point that each category in itself covers a spectrum. The "more or less" caveat referred to earlier applies to each as well as the overall continuum. The profile of a company at point 13 may be more like one at point 12 than one at 16; or 5 and 4 may be more similar than 5 and 8.

Developments in organization structure make clear that companies, structurally, are trending toward more congruence with the economic realities of their businesses. But obviously there are more companies whose current structures seem to be at odds with their economic models. Indeed, complete congruence is more an ideal than a realizable goal.

In some companies, shorter term pressures, or more immediate advantages take priority over what seems more logical in the longer term. Immediate pressure to penetrate special markets may induce a divisionalized structure even though there are longer term advantages to greater integration on a functional basis. Or one phase of the company's operations, accounting for perhaps the larger part of the company's total sales and profits, may be so significant that the overall structure is organized functionally to accommodate it. Or the lack of management talent may require higher level management to make more decisions and thus force a greater degree of centralization than seems warranted by the character of the operations. For these and many more highly practical reasons, the longer term optimum organization structure is less than optimum to those whose performance is evaluated in the short term.

However, there is another set of factors, equally real, that impede achievement of the best fit. These lie in the psyche of the human organization. The incumbent staff may be so thoroughly familiar with the more specific organization problems of various elements of the organization that they have difficulty seeing the total corporation because of its divisions.

Even more inhibiting to achievement of the optimum structure are the inertial factors that restrict any major organization change—the comforts of sticking with past habits and traditions, of applying past practice to new situations.[9] A company's growth may be of a character that it moves from Category I to Category II. But the operating and staff personnel who move with it know how to operate in the environment of a functional organization with greater centralization and don't willingly assume new roles. As a result, some of the more poignant managerial tragedies, particularly those of chief executives, can be traced to their inability to mate individual "management styles" with the economic verities of the total company.

NOTES

1. Alfred P. Sloan, Jr., *My Years with General Motors* (New York, Doubleday, 1964).

2. See *The Chief Executive and His Job,* Studies in Personnel Policy, No. 214 (The National Industrial Conference Board, 1969).

3. For documentation of major organization trends see *Corporate Organization Structures,* Studies in Personnel Policy, Nos. 183 and 210 (The National Industrial Conference Board, 1961 and 1968), and *Corporate Organization Structures: Manufacturing* (1973). Also see *Organization Planning: Basic Concepts, Emerging Trends* (The National Industrial Conference Board, 1969).

4. See, for example, *Staff Services in Smaller Companies: The View from the Top,* Report No. 592 (The Conference Board, April 1973).

5. For a more complete analysis of divisionalization, see *Top Management Organization in Divisionalized Companies,* Studies in Personnel Policy, No. 195 (The National Industrial Conference Board, 1965).

6. Ibid.

7. For a more complete discussion, see also *Top Management Organization in Divisionalized Companies* (op. cit.), especially Chapter 7, "Staff."

8. Ibid. Chapter 4, "Group Executives."

9. For elaboration, see *Organization Change — Perceptions and Realities,* Report No. 561 (The National Industrial Conference Board, July 1972).

Conflict in Organization: A Re-examination

Joseph A. Litterer

The prevalence of conflict in organizations is only too apparent, not only from our personal experiences but also from literature of organizational studies.[1] All schools of thought on organizations have recognized that conflict exists. They have differed in how they looked at it. The writers of classical organization theory viewed conflict as undesirable, detrimental to the organization. Ideally it should not exist. Their prescription was simple. Eliminate it. This could be done by adequate job definition, detailed specification of relationships among positions, careful selection of people to fill positions, and thorough training of people once they had been assigned.[2]

This view of the classic organization writers paralleled the view of others on the handling of tension within people. A fundamental position of many who analyzed individual behavior was that individuals were motivated by a desire for tension reduction. The prescription in both therapy and organizational design therefore was to take steps or make arrangements which would reduce tension within individuals. More recently it has become accepted that tension is normal, even desirable, with the thought growing that "healthy" personalities actually seek to increase tension.[3]

This shift in thinking about personality has both a parallel and an impact on the thinking about conflict in organizations. If tension is not only

From *Academy of Management Journal* 9 (1966) pp. 178–86. Reprinted by permission.

acceptable but useful in individuals, then one source of individual tension, organizational conflict, may also be not only acceptable but useful. That, within certain bounds, conflict is acceptable and useful is the conclusion reached by a number of recent authors.[4] We therefore bring conflict from the role of a condemned, to that of a considered, variable.

While doubtless some forms and certain degrees of conflict are dysfunctional or "unhealthy," other types, to certain degrees, are useful. The questions then are how much conflict is functional and where are the limits beyond which it becomes dysfunctional. The problem before us is therefore much more complex than previously. At one time the ideal amount of conflict was zero and the common decision was "eliminate it." Now the questions are what are the limits within which conflict is useful and how does one manage conflict.

FUNCTIONS AND VARIABLES

The theme of this paper is to examine what is involved in managing conflict in organizations, given that it has both functional and dysfunctional potentialities. To reduce this to a manageable task, many important things will be excluded. We will not consider intrapersonal conflicts or conflicts between a person's self concept and the role which he occupies. Further, we will not even begin to explore the almost completely untapped area concerned with determining the type and degree of conflict which is functional and that which is dysfunctional. Our approach instead will be from the point of view of examining what conflict is and identifying the organizational elements that produce it. If we are to manage conflict within reasonable boundaries, it is to these elements that we have to look to find the levers and handles with which to do the job.

Functions of Conflict

Although the detrimental effects of conflict have been frequently cited, the advantages of conflict have received but scant attention. A number of different functions of conflict in organizations have been identified and discussed in the literature. Perhaps one of the most important cited by a number of investigators[5] is that conflict initiates a search for some way to resolve or ameliorate the conflict and therefore leads to *innovation* and *change*. It should also be noted at the same time that conflict not only leads to a search for change but it also makes change more acceptable, even desirable.

Closely related with the above is the observation that a conflict energizes people to activity, sometimes just to reduce the conflict and its concurrent displeasures, at other times because the conflict gives a zest to certain activities.

Conflict within an organization can be an essential portion of a cybernetic system. It often occurs at the point at which some other systems within the organization are functioning inadequately and therefore calls attention to these problem areas and generates a search for solutions or improvements. Conflict often leads to shifts or reallocations of existing or future rewards or resources, thereby fundamentally changing important aspects of the organization. Budget allocation and unions-management conflicts are among many widely recognized.

It should be pointed out that conflicts between units or people on one level in an organization will often keep them from effectively confronting units or people at different hierarchal levels. A manager at one level may have far more influence over subordinates if they are competing with each other than if they unite to work against him, as we are reminded by the old political adage "divide and conquer." We should not fail to recognize, however, that this also occurs in reverse, that subordinates may often achieve considerable autonomy when the superiors are in conflict and therefore have neither the time nor the energy to expend in dominating those at a lower level.

There are doubtless other functions that conflict serves in organizations. The point is, however, not to compile a list but to say that conflict can be of use to organizations and that some of these uses are of great importance.

Definition of Conflict

Let us examine the organization elements which cause interperson, person-unit and interunit conflict. First, conflict is a battle or clash involving two people or more in opposition to each other. From our point of view, it is an inter-personal or interunit event and involves a particular type of interaction. The roots of this particular type of interaction reveal most about conflict. Conflict occurs when one sees the prospect of relative deprivation resulting from the actions of or in interacting with the other. For example, to some people, having to take orders from a person whom they think to be in lower status would result in their losing some of their own status and hence they would be deprived. However, the loss can be relative since conflict can occur when both parties are gaining but one or both feel that the other may gain more. Then one or both may perceive the outcome as a second-best position.

Our definition of conflict, then, is that conflict is a *type of behavior which occurs* when two or more parties are in opposition or in battle *as a result* of a perceived relative deprivation from the activities of or interacting with another person or group.

FOUR CONFLICT SITUATIONS

The organizational causes of conflict are numerous. The particular organizational elements which lead to conflict do not bring this result about directly. Instead they create conditions which affect the perception and motivation of organizational members in such a way that conflict results. There are then a set of intervening variables which transform structural forms into behavioral outputs. The many organizational structures which produce conflict seem to feed four principal types of intervening variables or organizational situations. These are win-lose situations (or competition over position), competition over resources or work arrangements, status incongruencies, and perceptual differences.

Win-Lose Situations

This intervening variable develops when two people or two units have goals which cannot exist simultaneously. Surprisingly, organizations set up many circumstances which lead to this condition. This is commonly witnessed in inspection situations. The inspector is hired to find errors but errors are someone else's output. Therefore every time the inspector finds an error justifying his position's existence and opening the opportunity for praise and reward, someone else is losing. The latter's output is shown to be inadequate and his rewards are endangered. Formal inspection positions such as those of quality control inspectors come to mind most readily, but it should be recognized that many staff positions have inspection components which produce in part the conflict so frequently noted among line and staff positions. Accounting is one type of staff work with large inspection components.[6]

Inspection is one type of win-lose situation. There are others not so obvious, however. Not long ago a major airline was faced with considerable conflict between two of its managers at a western city. Upon investigation it was found that the Sales Manager, in order to increase his sales volume, wanted to provide certain services for customers. These, however, would be provided by the employees and from the budgets of the Ramp and Services Manager. There was considerable effort to decentralize and promote as much autonomy for individual managers as possible and handsome bonus systems were set up on certain standards of individual managerial performance. If the Sales Manager could increase his sales he would have many advantages. Conversely, if the Ramp Services Manager could keep his costs down he too would have many rewards coming to him. Hence the problem, and the conflict; the Sales Manager could not get his bonus unless the Ramp Services Manager were to forego some of his own. This condition, although not always clearly recognized, exists in many organizations where reward systems are based upon individual performances which are not independent but are very much interdependent.

Competition over Means Utilization

In this area, conflict occurs not over goals which may be similar, but stems from the fact that there are differing ideas as to what means are appropriate or who will have the means. French has shown that conflicts over the means to goal accomplishment are more disruptive of group cohesiveness than conflicts over differing goals.[7]

Another common source of conflict involves shared dependence on limited resources and scheduling problems.[8] Those that center on budgetary decisions, allocation of capital resources and the efforts made by certain departments to assure themselves that adequate supplies of scarce personnel are provided by the personnel department are recognized and common.

Scheduling problems are often not as clearly recognized and are perhaps more common. A common situation is cited by Whyte in a plant where a group of women workers was asked to participate in establishing new work norms.[9] As might be expected from previous studies, the standards they established were actually above those the industrial engineering department would have provided. However, worker-set performance standards 30–50 percent over engineering standards, instead of being a satisfactory situation, created numerous problems. The department following this one faced an avalanche of material which created considerable pressure. Departments preceding this one were placed under considerable pressure to produce more. Employees in these and other departments hearing of the high earnings in the initial department complained about inequities. The engineering department felt humiliated at having so badly misjudged workable standards. Management at several levels, seeing all these events, felt that somehow things were out of control and that their position was being eroded.

Status Incongruency

An often neglected but extremely pervasive influence on behavior stems from the fact that people want to know where they stand relative to others, that is, what their status is. This might not be too much of an issue if there were but one standard for evaluating a person. But actually there are numerous status hierarchies and one's position is never the same on them all. Further, it is often changing.

One set of status problems in industry arises from the impact of changing technology. Men who entered companies years ago and rose slowly through the ranks often feel that seniority and age justify fairly high status positions. However, they may find themselves superseded by younger men moved into higher level positions because their more recent technical training better fits them to cope with modern business problems.

Working for someone younger than themselves and with less seniority, these men feel their status has been eroded and often accept this with little grace.

There are many other things, however, which create status incongruencies. For example, it is generally felt that those who give orders or initiate action for others have higher status than those who receive the orders or have work initiated for them. Work-flow relationships can often cause difficulties, however. Whyte in his study of the restaurant industry found situations where waitresses or other women could initiate activities for men by transmitting orders to them.[10] In other situations cooks would have work initiated by runners. In each case, it appeared that low-status people were initiating work for those of higher status, in opposition to normal expectation, and much conflict arose.

Perceptual Differences

It has long been recognized that people who look at things differently often come into conflict. In organizations, people see things differently for a variety of reasons, among them locational factors. It is frequently observed that people in different functional departments will tend to have different views of what is good for the company and how things are to be done. The classic conflicts between marketing and production over such things as delivery times, quality and lengths of production runs are well known. People in these departments not only perform different types of work but also interact with different publics. Marketing people interact most frequently with people outside the company, customers and competitors; those in manufacturing interact mostly with other departments within the company or with the union. These differences in systemic linkages and activities lead to differences in perception of considerable magnitude.[11]

Hierarchal location also has an impact. The problems seen by the first line supervisor, faced with the enormous pressures of day-to-day operations, are quite different from those of the managers two and three levels above whose time perspectives are greater and whose pressures take a different form and come from different quarters. The manager looking at a long-range development may not want certain relationships established with the union. But the foreman, faced with the fact that he must meet a shipping date at the end of the month, may be much more prone to accept a short-term solution and worry about the future some other time.[12]

This scarcely exhausts all the intervening variables. Looking at the four, however, one can begin to understand which types of situations might be useful, that is, functional and which might lead to dysfunctional consequences.

FUNCTIONAL VERSUS DYSFUNCTIONAL

As pointed out earlier, conflict often leads to innovation. Innovation usually offers some way of resolving differences so that both parties gain more in the new arrangement than they lose.

With this in mind, it is fairly easy to see that incompatible goals are very difficult to resolve, in fact, often impossible. Often even mediation is impossible and the only thing that can take care of them is arbitration.[13] The other solution is to remove completely the element causing the incompatible goals. Such a solution was described by Argyris when a plant manager tried to find some way of assigning charges for a shipment of inferior products returned by a customer. The competition among the various foremen was fierce, each trying to avoid having the charges assigned to his unit. In the end the plant manager had to assign them to general plant overhead.[14]

Incompatible means leading to conflict can be reduced or eliminated by a search for another means set more acceptable to all parties concerned. This source of conflict seems to lead to creative resolutions far more frequently than any of the other types and therefore can most likely lead to invention and adaptation. This idea of finding or creating a third ground for resolving differences was an aspect of creativity that concerned Mary Parker Follett.[15]

Status incongruencies can be energizers in the sense that they may awaken a person to the fact that his performance and his background need improvement in order to secure a position more compatible with the status he would like to occupy. Not so much the source of innovation, this can be a source of motivation. On the other hand, status incongruency can produce a destructive form of conflict leading to long and bitter hostility rather than changes in individual talents or performance or advancement.

In almost any organization and certainly in large organizations, it is impossible for anyone to observe all the things which are relevant to the organization; hence, different perceptions are sure to exist. Such differences, when they culminate in broadening the view of the opposing parties or when they bring problems to the attention of higher individuals in the organization, may be very valuable in detecting serious breakdowns in the overall functioning of an organization. The problem, of course, is to keep these perceptions from becoming rigid and the conflicts from becoming fixed. This can be greatly facilitated in many ways, such as planned position rotation, training programs, committees and the like.

This has been an all too brief examination of how the intervening variables can be used to determine which are sources of useful conflict and how conflict can be managed in an organization. We still have one important topic to consider, the actions or programs to be taken to manage conflict.

MANAGING CONFLICT SITUATIONS

Three basic strategies have been proposed for handling conflict situations.[16]

Making the System Work. Let us consider the situation where people find themselves in what they deem to be a situation of status incongruency. One solution would be to work with the individuals to get them to accept that: Age is going to keep them from certain types of positions, or that if they are not going to work to learn new technologies, they cannot expect to get promoted and so on. The system essentially stays the same but some of the elements in it are modified to make the current arrangements more workable.

Developing Additional Machinery. An alternate to modifying some of the elements in the system is to alter the system by adding or replacing elements. For example, when conflicts develop because a low-status person is initiating action for one of higher status, the conflicts can be reduced in part by creating a buffer. Whyte described a situation where runners were to write an order on a slip of paper and place it on a hook from which the cooks could take it, thereby making the interaction less direct.[17] This reduction led to less conflict.

Changing Institutional Structure to Eliminate the Cause of the Conflict. Sometimes even modifying the system is not sufficient to reduce conflict and a major change is required in the organization, such as creating new positions or departments. For example, with the conflicts between the cook and runner, one solution proposed was to have the information on orders related to the book by a supervisor rather than by the runner. Even though this would require the creation of a special new supervisory position, the initiation of work would then be more in line with the usual expectations of status differences.

These three events in sequence constitute an overall mechanism for reducing conflict in organizations. We first try to make the system work, then try to develop additional machinery and when all else fails restructure the basic system.[18] To go from one event to another as a "natural" process can be wasteful and unnecessary. Our previous analysis showed that some situations can be corrected only by the latter step and others by only the last two. Hence, by analyzing the source of conflict, it is possible to choose the appropriate strategy in this sequence.

CONCLUSION

The intent of this paper was to explore conflict in organizations. It is not a single, simple, but a very complex, cluster of events. While it has detrimental effects, it can also have very useful consequences. The assumption that conflict was universally detrimental was consistent with earlier organizational models, given their basic concern with stable organizations and goal maximization. The functional possibilities of conflict became apparent in examining a system model of organizations, for here conflict's role as a control and innovation element can be considered.

This paper has examined only those portions of conflict most directly concerned with the questions of what use is conflict and how can it be managed. Even in this area, there are critical questions of how much conflict is useful and what forms of conflict are most useful. It has been shown that different organization arrangements produce different competitive situations, and that the effect of conflict depends to a considerable degree on the nature of the conflict.

It is concluded that conflict is a manageable organizational event producing both functional and dysfunctional effects. Conflict in this light is almost completely unexplored as a topic and therefore is one on which much constructive work can be expended.

NOTES AND REFERENCES

1. See for example: Chris Argyris, *The Impact of Budgets on People* (New York: The Controllers Institute Research Foundation, 1952), Alvin Gouldner, *Patterns of Industrial Bureaucracy* (Glencoe: The Free Press, 1954); Melville Dalton, *Men Who Manage* (New York: John Wiley & Sons, 1959); Peter Blau, *The Dynamics of Bureaucracy* (Chicago: University of Chicago Press, 1955).

2. With varying degrees of explicitness these points are made by many writers. See for example Frederick W. Taylor, *Scientific Management* (New York: Harper & Brothers, 1947); L. Urwick, *The Elements of Administration* (New York: Harper & Brothers, 1943); James Mooney, *Principles of Organization* (New York: Harper & Brothers, 1947).

3. See for example, Gordon W. Allport, "The Trend in Motivational Theory," *American Journal of Orthopsychiatry*, Vol. 23, (1953) pp. 107–119; Viktor E. Frankl, *From Death Camp to Existentialism* (Boston: Beacon Press, 1949); and William Wolf, "Wider Horizons in Psychotherapy," *American Journal of Psychotherapy*, Vol. 16, No. 1, January 1963, pp. 124–149.

4. Dalton, op. cit.; Kenneth Boulding, *Conflict Management and Organizations* (Ann Arbor: Foundation for Research on Human Behavior, 1961), p. 1 and Chris Argyris, *Integrating the Individual and the Organization* (New York, John Wiley & Sons, 1964), particularly Chapter 1.

5. Dalton, *op. cit.*; Peter Blau and William R. Scott, *Formal Organizations* (San Francisco: Chandler Publishing Company, 1962); James G. March and Herbert A. Simon, *Organizations* (New York, John Wiley & Sons, 1959).

6. March and Simon, *op. cit.*, p. 122.

7. John R. P. French, Jr., "The Disruption and Cohesion of Groups," *The Journal of Abnormal and Social Psychology*, Vol. 36, (1941), pp. 361–377.

8. March and Simon, *op. cit.*, p. 122.

9. William Foote Whyte, *Money and Motivation* (New York: Harper & Brothers, 1955).

10. William Foote Whyte, *Human Relations in the Restaurant Industry* (New York: Harper & Brothers, 1948).

11. See for example, DeWitt C. Dearborn and Herbert A. Simon, "Selective Perception: A Note on Departmental Identification of Executives," *Sociometry*, Vol. 21, (1958) pp. 140–144.

12. For an interesting discussion of this point see Norman H. Martin, "Differential Decisions in the Management of an Industrial Plant," *Journal of Business*, Vol. 29, (1956) pp. 249–260.

13. Bernard M. Bass, *Organizational Psychology* (New York: Allyn and Bacon, 1965), p. 336.

14. Argyris, *op. cit.*, (1952).

15. Metcalf and Urwick (eds.), *Dynamic Administration* (New York: Harper & Brothers, 1941).

16. Daniel Katz, "Approaches to Managing Conflict," in *Conflict Management and Organizations* (Ann Arbor: Foundation for Research on Human Behavior, 1961).

17. Whyte, (1948), *op. cit.* See also Elias Porter, "The Parable of the Spindle," *Harvard Business Review* (May–June, 1962).

18. There is a close parallel between the strategy sequence for conflict reduction proposed by Katz and the innovation process discussed by March and Simon, *op. cit.*

Organizational Conflict: Concepts and Models

Louis R. Pondy

There is a large and growing body of literature on the subject of organizational conflict. The concept of conflict has been treated as a general social phenomenon, with implications for the understanding of conflict within and between organizations.[1] It has also assumed various roles of some importance in attempts at general theories of management and organizational behavior.[2] Finally, conflict has recently been the focus of numerous empirical studies of organization.[3]

A WORKING DEFINITION OF CONFLICT

The term "conflict" has been used at one time or another in the literature to describe: (1) antecedent conditions (for example, scarcity of resources, policy differences) of conflictful behavior, (2) affective states (e.g., stress, tension, hostility, anxiety, etc.) of the individuals involved, (3) cognitive states of individuals, i.e., their perception or awareness of conflictful situations, and (4) conflictful behavior, ranging from passive resistance to overt aggression. Attempts to decide which of these classes—conditions, atti-

Abridged and reprinted by permission of the author and the publisher from *Administrative Science Quarterly*, 1967, Vol. 12, pp. 296–320.

tude, cognition, or behavior—is really conflict is likely to result in an empty controversy. The problem is not to choose among these alternative conceptual definitions, since each may be a relevant stage in the development of a conflict episode, but to try to clarify their relationships.

Conflict can be more readily understood if it is considered a dynamic process. A conflict relationship between two or more individuals in an organization can be analyzed as a sequence of conflict episodes. Each conflict episode begins with conditions characterized by certain conflict potentials. The parties to the relationship may not become aware of any basis of conflict, and they may not develop hostile affections for one another. Depending on a number of factors, their behavior may show a variety of conflictful traits. Each episode or encounter leaves an aftermath that affects the course of succeeding episodes. The entire relationship can then be characterized by certain stable aspects of conditions, affect, perception, and behavior. It can also be characterized by trends in any of these characteristics.

This is roughly analogous to defining a "decision" to include activities preliminary to and following choice, as well as the choice itself. In the same sense that a decision can be thought of as a process of gradual commitment to a course of action, a conflict episode can be thought of as a gradual escalation to a state of disorder. If choice is the climax of a decision, then by analogy, open war or aggression is the climax of a conflict episode.

This does not mean that every conflict episode necessarily passes through every stage to open aggression. A potential conflict may never be perceived by the parties to the conflict, or if perceived, the conflict may be resolved before hostilities break out. Several other alternative courses of development are possible. Both Coleman and Aubert make these points clearly in their treatments of the dynamics of conflict.[4]

Just as some decisions become programmed or routinized, conflict management in an organization also becomes programmed or institutionalized sometimes. In fact, the institutionalization of means for dealing with recurrent conflict is one of the important aspects in any treatment of the topic. An organization's success hinges to a great extent on its ability to set up and operate appropriate mechanisms for dealing with a variety of conflict phenomena.

Five stages of a conflict episode are identified: (1) latent conflict (conditions), (2) perceived conflict (cognition), (3) felt conflict (affect), (4) manifest conflict (behavior), and (5) conflict aftermath (conditions). The elaboration of each of these stages of a conflict episode will provide the substance for a working definition. Which specific reactions take place at each state of a conflict episode, and why, are the central questions to be answered in a theory of conflict. Only the framework within which those questions can be systematically investigated is developed here.

Latent Conflict

A search of the literature has produced a long list of underlying sources of organizational conflict. These are condensed into three basic types of latent conflict: (1) competition for scarce resources, (2) drives for autonomy, and (3) divergence of subunit goals. Later in the paper each of these fundamental types of latent conflict is paired with one of the three conceptual models. Briefly, competition forms the basis for conflict when the aggregated demands of participants for resources exceed the resources available to the organization; autonomy needs form the basis of conflict when one party either seeks to exercise control over some activity that another party regards as his own province or seeks to insulate itself from such control; goal divergence is the source of conflict when two parties who must cooperate on some joint activity are unable to reach a consensus on concerted action. Two or more types of latent conflict may, of course, be present simultaneously.

An important form of latent conflict, which appears to be omitted from this list, is role conflict. The role conflict model treats the organization as a collection of role sets, each composed of the focal person and his role senders. Conflict is said to occur when the focal person receives incompatible role demands or expectations from the persons in his role set.[5] This model has the drawback that it treats the focal person as merely a passive receiver rather than as an active participant in the relationship. It is argued here, that the role conflict model does not postulate a distinct type of latent conflict. Instead, it defines a conceptual relationship, the role set, which may be useful for the analysis of all three forms of latent conflict described.

Perceived Conflict

Conflict may sometimes be perceived when no conditions of latent conflict exist, and latent conflict conditions may be present in a relationship without any of the participants perceiving the conflict.

The case in which conflict is perceived when no latent conflict exists can be handled by the so-called "semantic model" of conflict.[6] According to this explanation, conflict is said to result from the parties' misunderstanding of each others' true position. It is argued that such conflict can be resolved by improving communications between the parties. This model has been the basis of a wide variety of management techniques aimed at improving interpersonal relations. Of course, if the parties' true positions *are* in opposition, then more open communication may only exacerbate the conflict.

The more important case, that some latent conflicts fail to reach the level of awareness also requires explanation. Two important mechanisms that limit perception of conflict are the suppression mechanism and the attention-focus mechanism.[7] Individuals tend to block conflicts that are only mildly threatening out of awareness.[8] Conflicts become strong threats, and therefore must be acknowledged, when the conflicts relate to values central to the individual's personality. The suppression mechanism is applicable more to conflicts related to personal than to organizational values. The attention-focus mechanism, however, is related more to organizational behavior than to personal values. Organizations are characteristically faced with more conflicts than can be dealt with given available time and capacities. The normal reaction is to focus attention on only a few of these, and these tend to be the conflicts for which short-run, routine solutions are available. For organizations successfully to confront the less programmed conflicts, it is frequently necessary to set up separate subunits specifically to deal with such conflicts.

Felt Conflict

There is an important distinction between perceiving conflict and feeling conflict. *A* may be aware that *B* and *A* are in serious disagreement over some policy, but it may not make *A* tense or anxious, and it may have no effect whatsoever on *A*'s affection towards *B*. The personalization of conflict is the mechanism which causes most students of organization to be concerned with the dysfunctions of conflict. There are two common explanations for the personalization of conflict.

One explanation is that the inconsistent demands of efficient organization and individual growth create anxieties within the individual.[9] Anxieties may also result from identity crises or from extra-organizational pressures. Individuals need to vent these anxieties in order to maintain internal equilibrium. Organizational conflicts of the three latent types described earlier provide defensible excuses for displacing these anxieties against suitable targets. This is essentially the so-called "tension-model."[10]

A second explanation is that conflict becomes personalized when the whole personality of the individual is involved in the relationship. Hostile feelings are most common in the intimate relations that characterize total institutions, such as monasteries, residential colleges, and families.[11] In order to dissipate accumulated hostilities, total institutions require certain safety-valve institutions such as athletic activities or norms that legitimize solitude and withdrawal, such as the noncommunication norms prevalent in religious orders.

Thus, felt conflict may arise from sources independent of the three types of latent conflict, but latent conflicts may provide appropriate targets (perhaps symbolic ones) for undirected tensions.

Manifest Conflict

By manifest conflict is meant any of several varieties of conflictful behavior. The most obvious of these is open aggression, but such physical and verbal violence is usually strongly proscribed by organizational norms. Except for prison riots, political revolutions, and extreme labor unrest, violence as a form of manifest conflict in organizations is rare. The motivations toward violence may remain, but they tend to be expressed in less violent form. Dalton has documented the covert attempts to sabotage or block an opponent's plans through aggressive and defensive coalitions.[12] Mechanic has described the tactics of conflict used by lower-level participants, such as apathy or rigid adherence to the rules, to resist mistreatment by the upper levels of the hierarchy.[13]

How can one decide when a certain behavior or pattern of behavior is conflictful? One important factor is that the behavior must be interpreted in the context in which it takes place. If *A* does not interact with *B*, it may be either because *A* and *B* are not related in any organizational sense, or because *A* has withdrawn from a too stressful relationship, or because *A* is deliberately frustrating *B* by withdrawing support, or simply because *A* is drawn away from the relationship by other competing demands upon his time. In other words, knowledge of the organizational requirements and of the expectations and motives of the participants appears to be necessary to characterize the behavior as conflictful. This suggests that behavior should be defined to be conflictful if, and only if, some or all of the participants perceive it to be conflictful.

Should the term manifest conflict be reserved for behavior which, in the eyes of the actor, is deliberately and consciously designed to frustrate another in the pursuit of his (the other's) overt or covert goals? But what of behavior which is not *intended* to frustrate, but does? Should not that behavior also be called conflictful? The most useful definition of manifest conflict seems to be that behavior which, in the mind of the actor, frustrates the goals of at least some of the other participants. In other words, a member of the organization is said to engage in conflictful behavior if he consciously, but not necessarily deliberately, blocks another member's goal achievement. He may engage in such behavior *deliberately* to frustrate another, or he may do so in spite of the fact that he frustrates another. To define manifest conflict in this way is to say that the following question is important: "Under what conditions will a party to a relationship *knowingly* frustrate another party to the relationship?" Suppose *A* unknowingly blocks *B*'s goals. This is not conflictful behavior. But suppose *B* informs *A* that he perceives *A*'s behavior to be conflictful; if then *A* acknowledges the message and *persists* in the behavior, it is an instance of manifest conflict.

The interface between perceived conflict and manifest conflict and the interface between felt conflict and manifest conflict are the pressure points where most conflict resolution programs are applied. The object of such programs is to prevent conflicts which have reached the level of awareness or the level of affect from erupting into noncooperative behavior. The availability of appropriate and effective administrative devices is a major factor in determining whether conflict becomes manifest. The collective bargaining apparatus of labor-management disputes and budgeting systems for internal resource allocation are administrative devices for the resolution of interest-group conflicts. Evan and Scott have described due process or appeal systems for resolving superior-subordinate conflicts.[14] Mechanisms for resolving lateral conflicts among the parties to a functional relationship are relatively undeveloped. Transfer-pricing systems constitute one of the few exceptions. Much more common are organizational arrangements designed to *prevent* lateral conflicts, e.g., plans, schedules, and job descriptions, which define and delimit subunit responsibilities. Another alternative is to reduce the interdependence between conflicting subunits by introducing buffers, such as inventories, which reduce the need for sales and production departments in a business firm to act in perfect accord.

The mere availability of such administrative devices is not sufficient to prevent conflict from becoming manifest. If the parties to a relationship do not value the relationship, or if conflict is strategic in the pursuit goals, then conflictful behavior is likely. Furthermore, once conflict breaks out on some specific issue, then the conflict frequently widens and the initial specific conflict precipitates more general and more personal conflicts which had been suppressed in the interest of preserving the stability of the relationship.[15]

Conflict Aftermath

Each conflict episode is but one of a sequence of such episodes that constitute the relationships among organization participants.[16] If the conflict is genuinely resolved to the satisfaction of all participants, the basis for a more cooperative relationship may be laid; or the participants, in their drive for a more ordered relationship may focus on latent conflicts not previously perceived and dealt with. On the other hand, if the conflict is merely suppressed but not resolved, the latent conditions of conflict may be aggravated and explode in more serious form until they are rectified or until the relationship dissolves. This legacy of a conflict episode is here called "conflict aftermath."[17]

However, the organization is not a closed system. The environment in which it is imbedded may become more benevolent and alleviate the conditions of latent conflict, for example, by making more resources available to the organization. But a more malevolent environment may precipitate new crises. The development of each conflict episode is determined by a complex combination of the effects of preceding episodes and the environmental milieu. The main ideas of this view of the dynamics of conflict are summarized in Figure 1.

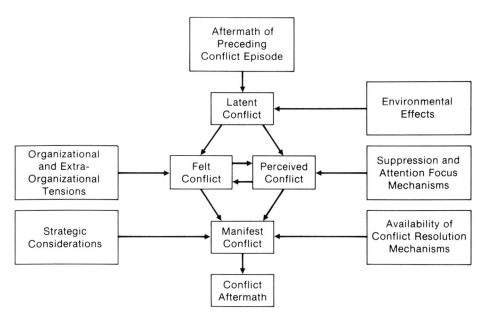

Figure 1   The Dynamics of a Conflict Episode

FUNCTIONS AND DYSFUNCTIONS OF CONFLICT

Few students of social and organizational behavior have treated conflict as a neutral phenomenon to be studied primarily because of scientific curiosity about its nature and form, its causes, and its effects. Most frequently the study of conflict has been motivated by a desire to resolve it and to minimize its deleterious effects on the psychological health of organizational participants and the efficiency of organization performance. Although Kahn and others pay lip service to the opinion that, "one might well make a case for interpreting some conflict as essential for the continued development of mature and competent human beings," the overriding bias of their report is with the "personal costs of excessive emotional strain," and, they state, "the fact that common reactions to conflict and its associated tensions are often dysfunctional for the organization as an on-going social system and self-defeating for the person in the long run."[18] Boulding recognizes that some optimum level of conflict and associated personal stress and tension are necessary for progress and productivity, but he portrays conflict primarily as a personal and social cost.[19] Baritz argues that Elton Mayo has treated conflict as "an evil, a symptom of the lack of social skills," and its alleged opposite, cooperation, as "symptomatic of health."[20] Even as dispassionate a theory of organization as that of March and Simon defines conflict conceptually as a *"breakdown* in the standard mechanisms of decision making"; i.e., as a malfunction of the system.[21]

It has become fashionable to say that conflict may be either functional or dysfunctional and is not necessarily either one. What this palliative leaves implicit is that the effects of conflict must be evaluated relative to some set of values. The argument with those who seek uniformly to abolish conflict is not so much with their *a priori* assertion that conflict is undesirable, as it is with their failure to make explicit the value system on which their assertion rests.

For the purposes of this research, the effects of organizational conflict on individual welfare are not of concern. Conflict may threaten the emotional well-being of individual persons; it may also be a positive factor in personal character development; but this research is not addressed to these questions. Intra-individual conflict is of concern only in so far as it has implications for organizational performance. With respect to organizational values, *productivity*, measured in both quantitative and qualitative terms, is valued; other things being equal, an organization is "better" if it produces more, if it is more innovative, and if its output meets higher standards of quality than other organizations. *Stability* is also valued. An organization improves if it can increase its cohesiveness and solvency, other things being equal. Finally *adaptability* is valued. Other things being equal, organizations that can learn and improve performance and that can adapt to changing internal and environmental pressures are preferred to those that cannot. In this view, therefore, to say that conflict is functional or dysfunctional is to say that it facilitates or inhibits the organization's productivity, stability, or adaptability.

Clearly, these values are not entirely compatible. An organization may have to sacrifice quality of output for quantity of output; if it pursues policies and actions that guarantee stability, it may inhibit its adaptive abilities. It is argued here that a given conflict episode or relationship may have beneficial or deleterious effects on productivity, stability, and adaptability. Since these values are incompatible, conflict may be simultaneously functional and dysfunctional for the organization.

A detailed examination of the functional and dysfunctional effects of conflict is more effectively made in the context of the three conceptual models. Underlying that analysis is the notion that conflict disturbs the "equilibrium" of the organization, and that the reaction of the organization to disequilibrium is the mechanism by which conflict affects productivity, stability, and adaptability.

CONFLICT AND EQUILIBRIUM

One way of viewing an organization is to think of each participant as making contributions, such as work, capital, and raw materials, in return for certain inducements, such as salary, interest, and finished goods. The organization is said to be in "equilibrium" if inducements exceed contributions (subjectively valued) for every participant, and in "disequilibrium" if contributions exceed inducements for some or all of the participants. Participants will be motivated to restore equilibrium either by leaving the organization for greener pastures, when the disequilibrium is said to be "unstable," or by attempting to achieve a favorable balance between inducements and contributions within the organization, when it is considered "stable." Since changing organizational affiliation frequently involves sizable costs, disequilibria tend to be stable.

If we assume conflict to be a cost of participation, this inducements-contributions balance theory may help in understanding organizational reactions to conflict. It suggests that the perception of conflict by the participants will motivate them to reduce conflict either by withdrawing from the relationship, or by resolving the conflict within the context of the relationship, or by securing increased inducements to compensate for the conflict.

The assumption that conflict creates a disequilibrium is implicit in nearly all studies of organizational conflict. For example, March and Simon assume that "where conflict is perceived, motivation to reduce conflict is generated," and conscious efforts to resolve conflict are made.[22] Not all treatments of the subject make this assumption, however. Harrison White attacks the March-Simon assumption of the disequilibrium of conflict as "naive."[23] He bases his assertion on his observation of chronic, continuous, high-level conflict in administrative settings. This, of course, raises the question, "Under what conditions *does* conflict represent a disequilibrium?"

To say that (perceived) conflict represents a state of disequilibrium and generates pressures for conflict resolution, is to say three things: (1) that perceived conflict is a cost of participation; (2) that the conflict disturbs the inducements-contributions balance; and (3) that organization members react to perceptions of conflict by attempting to resolve the conflict, *in preference to* (although this is not made explicit in the March-Simon treatment) other reactions such as withdrawing from the relationship or attempting to gain added inducements to compensate for the conflict.

1. Conflict as a Cost. Conflict is not necessarily a cost for the individual. Some participants may actually enjoy the "heat of battle." As Hans Hoffman argues, "The unique function of man is to live in close creative touch with chaos and thereby experience the birth of order."[24]

Conflict may also be instrumental in the achievement of other goals. One of the tactics of successful executives in the modern business enterprise is to create confusion as a cover for the expansion of their particular empire[25] or, as Sorensen observes, deliberately to create dissent and competition among one's subordinates in order to ensure that he will be brought into the relationship as an arbiter at critical times, as Franklin D.

Roosevelt did.[26] Or, conflict with an out-group may be desirable to maintain stability within the in-group.

In general, however, conflict can be expected to be negatively valued; particularly if conflict becomes manifest, and subunit goals and actions are blocked and frustrated. Latency or perception of conflict should be treated as a cost, only if harmony and uniformity are highly valued. Tolerance of divergence is not generally a value widely shared in contemporary organizations, and under these conditions latent and perceived conflict are also likely to be treated as costly.

2. Conflict as a Source of Disequilibrium. White's observation of *chronic* conflict creates doubt as to whether conflict represents a disequilibrium.[27] He argues that if conflict *were* an unstable state for the system, then only transient conflict or conflict over shifting foci would be observable. Even if organizational participants treat conflict as a cost, they may still endure intense, chronic conflict, if there are compensating inducements from the organization in the form of high salary, opportunities for advancement, and others. To say that a participant will endure chronic conflict is not to deny that he will be motivated to reduce it; it is merely to say that if the organization member is unsuccessful in reducing conflict, he may still continue to participate if the inducements offered to him exceed the contributions he makes in return. Although conflict may be one of several sources of disequilibrium, it is neither a necessary nor a sufficient condition of disequilibrium. But, as will be shown, equilibrium nevertheless plays an important role in organizational reactions to conflict.[28]

3. Resolution Pressures a Necessary Consequence of Conflict. If conflicts are relatively small, and the inducements and contributions remain in equilibrium, then the participants are likely to try to resolve the conflict within the context of the existing relationship.[29] On the other hand, when contributions exceed inducements, or when conflict is intense enough to destroy the inducements-contributions balance and there is no prospect for the re-establishment of equilibrium, then conflict is likely to be reduced by dissolving the relationship. Temporary imbalances, of course, may be tolerated; i.e., the relationship will not dissolve if the participants perceive the conflicts to be resolvable in the near future.

What is the effect of conflict on the interaction rate among participants? It depends on the stability of the relationship. If the participants receive inducements in sufficient amounts to balance contributions, then perception of conflict is likely to generate pressures for *increased* interaction, and the content of the interaction is likely to deal with resolution procedures. On the other hand, if conflict represents a cost to the participant and this cost is not compensated by added inducements, then conflict is likely to lead to *decreased* interaction or withdrawal from the relationship.

To summarize, conflict is frequently, but not always, negatively valued by organization members. To the extent that conflict *is* valued negatively, minor conflicts generate pressures towards resolution without altering the relationship; and major conflicts generate pressures to alter the form of the relationship or to dissolve it altogether. If inducements for participation are sufficiently high, there is the possibility of chronic conflict in the context of a stable relationship.

SUMMARY

It has been argued that conflict within an organization can be best understood as a dynamic process underlying a wide variety of organizational behaviors. The term conflict refers neither to its antecedent conditions, nor individual awareness of it, nor certain affective states, nor its overt manifestations, nor its residues of feeling, precedent, or structure, but to all of these taken together as the history of a conflict episode.

Conflict is not necessarily bad or good, but must be evaluated in terms of its individual and organizational functions and dysfunctions. In general, conflict generates pressures to reduce conflict, but chronic conflict persists and is endured under certain conditions, and consciously created and managed by the politically astute administrator.

Conflict resolution techniques may be applied at any of several pressure points. Their effectiveness and appropriateness depends on the nature of the conflict and on the administrator's philosophy of management. The tension model leads to creation of safety-valve institutions and the semantic model to the promotion of open communication. Although these may be perfectly appropriate for certain forms of imagined conflict, their application to real conflict may only exacerbate the conflict.

NOTES AND REFERENCES

1. Jessie Bernard, T. H. Pear, Raymond Aron, and Robert C. Angell, *The Nature of Conflict* (Paris: UNESCO, 1957); Kenneth Boulding, *Conflict and Defense* (New York: Harper, 1962); Lewis Coser, *The Functions of Social Conflict* (Glencoe, Ill.: Free Press, 1956); Kurt Lewin, *Resolving Social Conflict* (New York: Harper, 1948); Anatol Rapaport, *Fights, Games, and Debates* (Ann Arbor: University of Michigan, 1960); Thomas C. Schelling, *The Strategy of Conflict* (Cambridge, Mass.: Harvard Univ., 1961); Muzafer Sherif and Carolyn Sherif, *Groups in Harmony and Tension* (Norman, Okla.: University of Oklahoma, 1953); Georg Simmel, *Conflict,* trans. Kurt H. Wolff (Glencoe, Ill.: Free Press, 1955).

2. Bernard M. Bass, *Organizational Psychology* (Boston, Mass.: Allyn and Bacon, 1965); Theodore Caplow, *Principles of Organization* (New York: Harcourt,

Brace, and World, 1964); Eliot D. Chapple and Leonard F. Sayles, *The Measure of Management* (New York: Macmillan, 1961); Michel Crozier, *The Bureaucratic Phenomenon* (Glencoe, Ill.: Free Press, 1964); Richard M. Cyert and James G. March, *A Behavioral Theory of the Firm* (Englewood Cliffs, N.J.: Prentice-Hall, 1963); Alvin W. Gouldner, *Patterns of Industrial Bureaucracy* (Glencoe, Ill.: Free Press, 1954); Harold J. Leavitt, *Managerial Psychology* (Chicago: University of Chicago, 1964); James G. March and Herbert A. Simon, *Organizations* (New York: Wiley, 1958); Philip Selznick, *TVA and the Grass Roots* (Berkeley: University of California, 1949); Victor Thompson, *Modern Organization* (New York: Knopf, 1961).

3. Joseph L. Bower, The Role of Conflict in Economic Decision-making Groups, *Quarterly Journal of Economics,* 79 (May 1965), 253–257; Melville Dalton, *Men Who Manage* (New York: Wiley, 1959); J. M. Dutton and R. E. Walton, "Interdepartmental Conflict and Cooperation: A Study of Two Contrasting Cases," dittoed, Purdue University, October 1964; William Evan, Superior-Subordinate Conflict in Research Organizations, *Administrative Science Quarterly,* 10 (June 1965), 52–64; Robert L. Kahn, *et al., Studies in Organizational Stress* (New York: Wiley, 1964); L. R. Pondy, Budgeting and Inter-Group Conflict in Organizations, *Pittsburgh Business Review,* 34 (April 1964), 1–3; R. E. Walton, J. M. Dutton, and H. G. Fitch, *A Study of Conflict in the Process, Structure, and Attitudes of Lateral Relationships* (Institute Paper No. 93; Lafayette, Ind.: Purdue University, November 1964); Harrison White, Management Conflict and Sociometric Structure, *American Journal of Sociology,* 67 (September 1961), 185–199; Mayer N. Zald, Power Balance and Staff Conflict in Correctional Institutions, *Administrative Science Quarterly, 7* (June 1962), 22–49.

4. James S. Coleman, *Community Conflict* (Glencoe, Ill.: Free Press, 1957); Vilhelm Aubert, Competition and Dissensus: Two Types of Conflict and Conflict Resolution, *Journal of Conflict Resolution,* 7 (March 1963), 26–42.

5. Kahn, *et al., op. cit.,* pp. 11–35.

6. Bernard, Pear, Aron, and Angell, *op. cit.*

7. These two mechanisms are instances of what Cyert and March, *op. cit.,* pp. 117–118, call the "quasi-resolution" of conflict.

8. Leavitt, *op. cit.,* pp. 53–72.

9. Chris Argyris, *Personality and Organization: The Conflict Between the System and the Individual* (New York: Harper, 1957).

10. Bernard, Pear, Aron, and Angell, *op. cit.*

11. It should be emphasized that members of total institutions characteristically experience both strong positive *and* negative feelings for one another and toward the institution. It may be argued that this ambivalence of feeling is a primary cause of anxiety. See Coser, *op. cit.,* pp. 61–65; and Amitai Etzioni and W. R. Taber, Scope, Pervasiveness, and Tension Management in Complex Organizations, *Social Research,* 30 (Summer 1963) 220–238.

12. Dalton, *op. cit.*

13. David Mechanic, "Sources of Power of Lower Participants in Complex Organizations," in W. W. Cooper, H. J. Leavitt, and M. W. Shelly (eds.), *New Perspectives in Organization Research* (New York: Wiley, 1964), pp. 136–149.

14. Evan, *op. cit.;* William G. Scott, *The Management of Conflict: Appeals Systems in Organizations* (Homewood, Ill.: Irwin, 1965). It is useful to interpret recent developments in leadership and supervision (e.g., participative management, Theory Y, linking-pin functions) as devices for preventing superior-subordinate conflicts from arising, thus, hopefully, avoiding the problem of developing appeals systems in the first place.

15. See Coleman, *op. cit.*, pp. 9–11, for an excellent analysis of this mechanism. A chemical analogue of this situation is the supersaturated solution, from which a large amount of chemical salts can be precipitated by the introduction of a single crystal.

16. The sequential dependence of conflict episodes also plays a major role in the analysis of role conflicts by Kahn, *et al., op. cit.*, pp. 11–35. Pondy, *op. cit.* has used the concept of "budget residues" to explain how precedents set in budgetary bargains guide and constrain succeeding budget proceedings.

17. Aubert, *op. cit.*

18. Kahn, *et al., op. cit.*, p. 65.

19. Boulding, *op. cit.*, pp. 305–307.

20. Loren Baritz, *The Servants of Power* (Middletown, Conn.: Wesleyan University, 1960), p. 203.

21. March and Simon, *op. cit.*, p. 112, italics mine. At least one author, however, argues that a "harmony bias" permeates the entire March-Simon volume. It is argued that what March and Simon call conflicts are mere "frictions" and "differences that are not within a community of interests are ignored." See Sherman Krupp, *Pattern in Organization Analysis* (New York: Holt, Rinehart and Winston, 1961), pp. 140–167.

22. March and Simon, *op. cit.*, pp. 115, 129.

23. Harrison White, *op. cit.*

24. Quoted in H. J. Leavitt and L. R. Pondy, *Readings in Managerial Psychology* (Chicago: University of Chicago, 1964), p. 58.

25. Dalton, *op. cit.*

26. Theodore Sorensen, *Decision Making in the White House* (New York: Columbia University, 1963), p. 15. This latter tactic, of course, is predicated and the fact that, *for the subordinates*, conflict is indeed a cost!

27. Harrison White, *op. cit.*

28. Conflict may actually be a source of equilibrium and stability, as Coser, *op. cit.*, p. 159, points out. A multiplicity of conflicts internal to a group, Coser argues, may breed solidarity, provided that the conflicts do not divide the group along the same axis, because the multiplicity of coalitions and associations provide a web of affiliation for the exchange of dissenting viewpoints. The essence of his argument is that some conflict is inevitable, and that it is better to foster frequent minor conflicts of interest, and thereby gradually adjust the system, and so forestall the accumulation of latent antagonisms which might eventually disrupt the organization. Frequent minor conflicts also serve to keep the antagonists accurately informed of each other's relative strength, thereby preventing a serious miscalculation of the chances of a

successful major conflagration and promoting the continual and gradual readjustment of structure to coincide with true relative power.

29. For example, labor unions, while they wish to win the economic conflict with management, have no interest in seeing the relationship destroyed altogether. They may, however, choose to threaten such disruptive conflict as a matter of strategy.

Implications of Political Models of Organization

Michael L. Tushman

David A. Nadler

In the early 1970's, a leading food products manufacturer experimented by creating a new plant designed along lines of participative management. By mid 1977, reports indicated that the experiment was a success. Employee satisfaction was high, turnover was low, and the new system was credited with economic savings of approximately $1 million a year as compared to traditional factories. At the same time, however, reports filtering out from the company indicate that many of the key managers involved in the experiment have now left the company and that the experimental plant might be switched to a traditional system. As one ex-employee reported, "economically it was a success, but it became a power struggle. It was too threatening to too many people."

BusinessWeek, March 28, 1977

A large financial institution had experienced a long period of growth and prosperity under the leadership of a hard-driving CEO. After 13 years, the CEO retired. During the next 6 years, the firm went through 5 different CEO's. The senior staff, who advised the Board of Directors on executive selection, were reported to have chosen

Printed by permission of the authors.

individuals of limited power and/or ability. Organizational performance deteriorated. Finally, a CEO was brought in who was so universally perceived as lacking competence that the senior staff asked the Board to remove him. Only then was a concerted search made for a competent and powerful new CEO. By then, however, the organization had lost much ground.

These two episodes of organizational life are not atypical. As one observes the various events that occur within organizations, the frequency of events that seem to defy rationality is overwhelming. More importantly, many of the existing models of organization and management seem unable to explain why these events occur.

Recent work by those who study organizational behavior indicates that much of the seemingly "irrational" behavior can in fact be understood by making use of political models to analyze organizations. This paper builds on the growing work in the area of political approaches to organizations and is an attempt to define the political perspective in terms that may provide managers with insights into the actual workings of organizations. This will be done by examining several issues. First, the political perspective will be defined in contrast to existing views of organizations. Second, some emerging models of political processes in organizations will be presented as a complement to existing models of organizational behavior (such as Nadler and Tushman, 1977). Third, political models will be used as a basis for identifying some of the dynamics of managerial power and behavior within a political context.

A COMPLEMENTARY ORGANIZING PERSPECTIVE: A POLITICAL PERSPECTIVE ON ORGANIZATIONS

Rational Actor Approach

Many of the existing approaches to understanding organizational behavior implicitly build on rational models of behavior. From this point of view, the organization is seen as a system within which individuals and groups will act in internally consistent ways to reach explicit objectives. Thus, organizational structures and processes are deliberately planned and coordinated for the most efficient realization of explicit objectives.

A rational actor model takes dysfunctional behavior into account yet tends to assign these departures to either ignorance, miscalculation, or managerial error. Thus, inconsistent behaviors can be diagnosed, alternative interventions can be considered, and the best intervention selected. Individual organizational elements are subject to planned intervention, while the development of the organization as a whole is also regarded as subject to planned direction. The rational actor model views change as the rational adaptation by the organization to feedback from its environment. The role defined for the manager implied from the rational actor model follows the prescriptions of classical management theory: plan, organize, coordinate, and control based on clearly articulated and systematically derived objectives.

Organizational Politics Approach

As the examples cited above suggest, the rational actor approach often fails to predict or explain important aspects of organizational life. Frequently, individuals, groups, and organizations do not act in internally consistent ways. Public or explicit goals often have little relation to what actually brings about behavior. The resulting patterns of behavior are therefore often completely different than that which utility maximizing models would predict.

An interesting and dramatic example of the failure of the rational model is presented in Allison's (1971) book in which he examines the various decisions and events that were involved in the 1962 Cuban Missile Crisis. Allison reconstructs the events that led up to the crisis, and attempts to explain these events using several different models. His analysis indicates that the rational actor model fails to explain many of the critical incidents, and leaves unexplained questions like "why did the Russians put in the missiles," "why did Kennedy choose the embargo as a response," and "why did the Russians remove the missiles."

It is only when Allison develops a model which he labels as the political model that he is able to explain much of what occurred. The political model views behavior as the *result* of conflicts between different interest groups as opposed to a calculated plan to secure the State's interests. For example, the decision of the Russians to put missiles in Cuba makes most sense in light of the internal conflicts between the Russians' land forces and the Russian missile command over scarce resources.

Some Basic Concepts

What then is the political perspective? It is basically an orientation towards organizations as systems characterized by conflict, value dissensus, and bargaining. Some definitions are needed. *Politics* as referred to here indicates the structure and process of the use of authority and power to effect definitions of goals, directions, and other major parameters of the organization (Wamsley and Zald, 1973). The political perspective, therefore, emphasizes the view that a range of decisions in organizations are not made in a rational or formal way, but rather through compromise, accommodation, and bargaining. This occurs because different groups within the organization (subunits) have different preferences for outcomes and behave in ways that will enable them to realize their desired outcomes. Implicit in this conception of politics is the issue of *conflict*. Conflict (where one group seeks to advance its own interests at the expense of another group) arises in organizations when interdependent subunits either have inconsistent goals, have differing perceptions on how to reach a commonly held goal, or when they must share scarce resources (March and Simon, 1958; Schmidt and Kochan, 1972; Pfeffer, 1977).

Obviously, if one talks of political behavior, the question of *power* must also be considered. While many definitions exist, several converge on the notion that power is the potential (or capacity) of an actor to influence the behavior of another actor in a particular issue area (Crozier, 1973; Katz and Kahn, 1966).

The political perspective therefore views organizations as sets of groups or subunits which exercise different amounts of power and who are potentially in conflict with each other to obtain scarce resources and realize locally valued outcomes. The behavior of organizations (e.g. decision making, profit, innovation) is the result of these political processes operating inside the organization.

POLITICAL MODELS OF ORGANIZATIONS

The Need for Models

Having been sensitized to the political nature of organizations, most would agree that political behavior occurs and that being aware of the political nature of organizations could be helpful in understanding organizational behavior. On the other hand, the mere awareness of the political nature of organizations may not, in itself, be enough. Political behavior, as other phenomena, abound in organizations and seem to occur in random or unpredictable ways. For the manager to begin to function effectively within a political environment, he/she must have tools with which to analyze that environment. What this implies is the need for models of organizations as political systems that can aid the manager in understanding the regularities of political behavior, to diagnose the nature of political systems, and to aid in the formulation of managerial action.

Two recent models seem to provide some useful guides for the manager. The first, a network approach, provides a framework for looking at entire organizations as politically functioning systems. The second, based on intergroup conflict concepts, gives some idea as to how different groups within networks relate to each other.

A Network Model

A number of political scientists and sociologists have argued for the value of looking at communities and organizations as networks of individuals and groups linked together in various ways. A recent statement of this model by Tichy, Tushman, and Fombrun (1979) provides some useful terms and applies this specifically to the understanding of formal organizations.

Organizations are viewed as networks of individuals who can be linked in three different ways. Individuals can be linked together by information; simple flows of information between two individuals establish a link between them. Second, individuals can be linked by influence; the ability of one individual to induce behavior in another is another form of linkage. Third, individuals can be linked together through affect—positive or negative feeling. For diagnostic purposes, linkages can be identified by asking individuals within an organization whom they normally interact with the most (informational linkages), who they feel influences them the most, or whom they look to for help and guidance (influence linkages), or who they ideally like to interact with (affect linkage). With these pieces of information, it is possible to graphically plot the various relationships among a set of individuals. Such a plot yields what is called a network (see Figure 1) which represents the sum total of relationships (lines) among individuals (represented by the points).

Networks in organizations tend to display certain characteristics or patterns. First, when the network is plotted, there usually emerges sets of points (individuals) that are highly interconnected. These dense areas represent individuals who are collectively related by linkages of information,

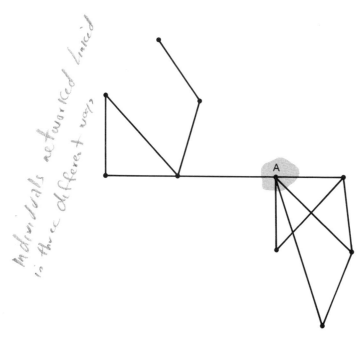

Figure 1   An Example of a Simple Network

influence, or affect (see, for instance Schwartz and Jacobson, 1977). They represent critical subunits of the political organization (analogous to the subunits of the formal organization) and are referred to as cliques (Tichy, 1973). Cliques are the basic building blocks of political organizations, much as the formal work group or subunit is seen as the major building block of formal organizations. Within these cliques one can also identify those individuals who have more frequent interactions with their peers (for example, person A in Figure 1). These sociometric stars tend to be more powerful than others in the clique and are a vital point in the organization's influence-information system. These key individuals may or may not have formal status or authority (Tushman, 1977; Pettigrew, 1972).

Over time, one can observe the functioning of cliques. One pattern that has been observed frequently is the tendency of different cliques to develop cooperative (or collusive) strategies of action. They tend to act in concert around a certain set of issues, activities, or decisions. When a set of cliques group together to take cooperative action, they are called a *coalition.* Coalitions, being sets of cliques, tend to be less stable than cliques (although some may endure over relatively long periods of time). Coalitions tend to develop around specific issues, values, decisions, etc. Thus, the nature and composition of coalitions may change over time as different issues become salient (Baldridge, 1971). For example, a set of cliques that cooperate around an important aspect of strategy may dissolve and reform with different composition around a question of executive succession. Thus, the membership of cliques in coalitions may be multiple and/or overlapping. A simple diagramatic representation of a set of cliques in coalition within a network is presented as Figure 2.

The network model therefore provides the manager with a way of beginning to identify what Tichy et. al (1979) call the "emergent" system as opposed to the formal or "prescribed" structure of the organization. Social networks are, then, a basic tool for identifying the structure of political relationships.

The Political Conflict Model

The network model enables identification of the system and outlines some broad parameters for understanding how the system functions. Another model, however, when combined with the network model provides a clearer picture of how cliques and coalitions relate to each other over time. This model, described by Tushman (1977) will be called the political conflict model, since it focuses on the interactions (typically conflict) among the various subunits of the organization (in the political sense, the various cliques and coalitions).

Drawing on the existing literature on political behavior in organizations, Tushman puts forth a set of propositions which he hypothesizes

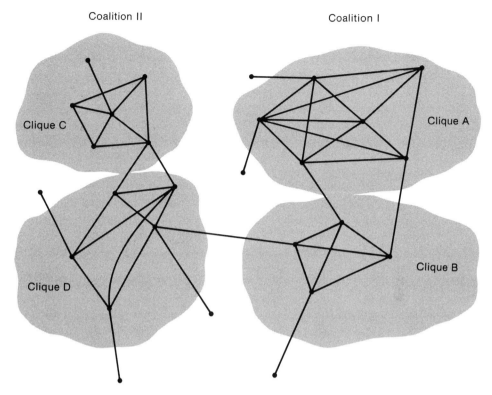

Figure 2   A Simple Graph of Cliques and Coalitions

describe the interaction of subunits (cliques and coalitions) within organizations. These propositions are as follows:

1. To understand the behavior of organizations, one must understand the dynamics and relationships among and between the subunits which make up the organization.

2. Subunits may not be equally powerful over different issues area; subunits which are better able to deal with critical sources of uncertainty in a particular decision making area will be more powerful than other subunits in that issue area.

   a. Since tasks and task environments are potentially unstable, the distribution of power and status within organizations will not be fixed or stable.

3. Subunits will act to decrease their internal dependence on others in order to limit the uncertainty which they must face and to increase their opportunities for growth and survival.

4. The greater the differentiation between subunits, the greater the difficulty of distortion-free communication and the greater the potential for organizational conflict.

These propositions thus present a picture of cliques involved in a constant interaction, with each clique attempting to maximize its own power (by minimizing its dependence on other groups), with shifting relationships, shifting coalitions, and differential power depending upon the realm of activity involved. Subunits that can deal with uncertainty tend to be more powerful and tend to engage in activity to maintain that power (Ritti and Gouldner, 1969).

This view supplements the network model and provides at least an initial picture of how the different components of the network interact with each other over time.

THE MANAGER WITHIN THE POLITICAL SYSTEM

The Managerial Role

Given a view of organizations as networks made up of interacting and conflicting groups, the role of the manager, sources of power for managers, and the kinds of tools that managers need must be re-examined. The first concern is to re-examine the aspects of the managerial role in light of political models.

Much of the leadership literature has focused on the relationship between the manager and his or her subordinates (see for example Stogdill, 1974). If, however, the political model has relevance, then one would expect that managers would spend a substantial amount of time outside their subunit developing or maintaining lateral relationships as well as working up the bureaucracy (e.g., persuading their superiors). Studies of what managers (and in particular top managers) actually do provide data in support of the political perspective. Research indicates that middle and upper level managers spend between 35 and 70 percent of their interaction time with subordinates (the higher the level, the less time with subordinates). Thus, a full 30 to 65 percent of their time was spent interacting with peers, professional colleagues, members of other departments, and outsiders (Sayles, 1979). Mintzberg's (1973) research suggests that this extra-unit managerial responsibility may be more important than is usually recognized. Of the ten basic roles Mintzberg argues typify most managerial jobs, only two deal with intra-unit activity.

Besides this dual focus of managerial activity, a number of studies indicate that managerial behavior is phrenetic; characterized by brevity, variety, and fragmentation. In Mintzberg's study, half of the executives' activities lasted nine minutes or less and only a tenth lasted more than an hour. Further, since managers have relatively little control of their pace of work, they are frequently forced to be "proficient at superficiality" (Mintzberg, 1973). To deal with this superficiality and yet attend to intra and extra unit decision making requirements, research emphasizes the importance of the manager's oral communication network. Managers simply do not utilize written or formal media. Oral communication is so heavily utilized in exchanging information, ideas, and live data since it is rapid, timely, and an efficient communication medium (Sayles, 1979; Keegan, 1974; Edstrom and Galbraith, 1977).

The growing mosaic of data on managerial behavior suggests that managers must be sensitive to both internal (supervisor-subordinate) as well as external (peer, cross departmental, extra-organizational) relations. Further, the available data indicates that in order to make sense out of their potentially overwhelming situation and to have the current data to make rapid yet informed decisions, managers must have extensive and well developed oral communication networks throughout the organization. More effective managers will have developed intra-unit *and* extra-unit oral communication networks. The higher up in the organization, the more critical external leadership roles become and the more the manager must be sensitive to his or her oral communication network.

Sources of Managerial Power

If the manager is to function within a network made up of cliques and coalitions, and if a large part of the interaction occurs with individuals other than subordinates, then the issue of managerial power (the capability of influencing the behavior of others) needs to be re-examined (Schein, 1977). French and Raven (1966) in their classic work provide a list of five "bases of power" which have often been applied to the managerial role. French and Raven see the bases of power as being:

1. Reward Power
2. Coercive Power
3. Legitimate Power
4. Referent Power
5. Expert Power

These bases of power continue to be operative within the political environments described above. However, there is a need to build on the French and Raven approach and identify other sources of power which are particularly salient within the context of political systems. Although some work on identifying sources of power has already been done, this list represents an early and probably incomplete conception of the additional bases of managerial power in organizations. Additional bases of power are as follows:

Control Over Critical Resources.   At different points in time, different sets of resources may be critical to an organization's effectiveness. Similarly, different groups within organizations have control over alternative resources. Putting this together, it follows that those groups that control resources that are critical to the organization's functioning will be those that exercise greatest power. This position has been developed by Hickson et. al (1971) and Salancik and Pfeffer (1977) in what they call the strategic contingency model of power within organizations. Several studies have demonstrated the validity of this model. As an example, within a university which was highly dependent upon outside funding (research grants) for a large portion of its operating budget, Salancik and Pfeffer found that knowing which departments brought in what amounts of research funds enabled the prediction of how much power they had in critical decisions. Thus, the power stemming from the control over a resource (for instance, money or information) is contingent on whether that resource is perceived as being critical to the organization.

Avoid Routinization.   An important source of power is the absence of routinization. To the extent that a manager's job (or the job of his or her unit) is routinizable or highly predictable, that manager has less power (Ritti and Gouldner, 1969). Sayles and Chandler's (1971) analysis of professionals working for NASA and Crozer's (1964) discussion of maintenance workers each demonstrate power accruing to individuals who work to make their tasks unpredictable yet important to the organization.

Access to Powerful Others.   In many organizations, one sees individuals and groups who are, on the face of it, not powerful, yet exercising great amounts of power. Newman and Warren (1977) have observed that a basis of power within political systems is access or proximity to others who have power. Individuals tend to perceive that proximity and access lead to transference of some power to the less powerful individual. Thus, those who have their office next to the chief executive, or those who have contact or connections with important others are perceived to have power, when in fact they may not. Obviously, access and proximity also tend to relate to issues of critical resource availability and control (Pettigrew, 1972).

Assessed Stature and Gaining Visibility.   From a political perspective, managers persuade, negotiate, and exercise power they can mobilize. Assuming the manager is able to identify important others, an important constraint on his or her ability to negotiate will be the manager's assessed stature or visibility (i.e. the process of positive impression formation or of developing positive feelings in the perceptions of relevant others). Assessed stature derives from the manager being able to identify what is salient in the other party's perspective, and from demonstrating technical or managerial competence in areas salient to the other party. Sayles (1979) and Pettigrew (1972) emphasize the importance of assessed stature by suggesting that the manager's ability to negotiate and persuade depends directly on his or her assessed stature with significant others in the political network.

Exchange as a Source of Power. Newman and Warren (1977) also point out that the ability to influence others often starts when one individual does a favor for another individual. This is consistent with concepts of exchange theory (Blau, 1962) and would indicate that when individuals provide resources, come to the assistance of others, do favors, etc., they set up a state of imbalance and obligation. This is what is frequently called the process of building up credits or points. The existence of such obligations, which can be called on in later time periods, is an additional source of power (Blau, 1963).

Group Support. To the extent that the manager has a cohesive work group, he or she will be better able to attend to inter-organizational issues. Conflict within a manager's work area will use up time, energy, and resources which could otherwise be used in developing inter-organizational linkages. In general, the more a manager has group support, the more he or she will be able to develop inter-organizational power.

The basic idea of this section is that if managerial behavior is embedded in a political network, and if power is an important resource in these systems, then managerial behavior can be facilitated by an awareness of different bases of power. Control of critical resources, avoiding routinization, control over information, access, exchange, assessed stature, visibility, and group support can each be seen as bases of power in organizations which go beyond formal bases of power which the organization gives the manager.

CONCLUSION—MANAGERIAL SKILLS

This paper has sought to emphasize the political nature of organizations and the idea that managerial behavior takes place in settings where struggles over power and control are pervasive and real. The organizational politics model was developed to serve as a counterpoint to the more traditional rational actor models of organizational behavior. It is the basic argument of this paper that the use of both models will provide managers with a perspective on organizations as mixed-motive situations.

The paper has focused on the organizational bases of political behavior and has suggested the following broad implications.

A. Importance of Diagnostic Models

Recent leadership research suggests that the demands on the managerial role are overwhelming. To deal with this complexity, managers need an organizing model to track the political topography, the dominant issues, key values and the flow of information in the system. A network based conceptual model was suggested. This approach focused on the dynamic of cliques, coalitions, and managers as they bargain and negotiate over scarce resources. It was suggested that the use of both the network model along with a general diagnostic model would provide an effective way of organizing organizational complexity.

B. The Importance of the Manager's External Role

If political behavior is an important aspect of organizational life, then managers must attend to organizational issues outside of their work area. To effectively deal with these external issues, managers must develop effective external communication networks. The importance of external information combined with the intensity of the managerial role suggests that managers must rely on well developed oral communication networks. Oral networks are best able to keep the manager current and permit rapid yet informed decision making, and are a source of potential allies throughout the organization. The challenge to the manager is to keep up with his or her oral network as well as to be able to use more formal and analytical informational inputs.

C. Bases of Power

Power is directly related to the manager's ability to produce outcomes consistent with his or her interests. Several bases of power have been discussed here; control of critical resources, control of information, avoiding routinization, access, exchange, assessed stature, visibility, and group support. These bases of power complement those suggested by French and Raven (1966) and indicate power resources beyond that defined by the formal organization.

These implications suggest that in order to be effective, managers must develop several distinct types of skills—analytic and interpersonal. *Analytic skills* are necessary so that the manager can develop models on how the organization and its components actually work (e.g., budget, financial, or inventory system). *Interpersonal skills* are critical if the manager is to be an effective actor within political systems. Decisions hinge on the ability to influence other actors. This influence will be contingent on the manager's power and on his or her ability to gain support, enthusiasm, and commitment from other, possibly indifferent, actors. Thus, more effective managers will have extensive contacts throughout the organization (possible allies and sources of information), and will be able to mobilize these actors for different issue areas. Vital interpersonal skills would include developing peer relations and information networks, carrying out negotiations, resolving conflicts, and developing cohesive teams (Sayles, 1979; Mintzberg, 1973).

In conclusion, the fact that political dynamics are ignored in much of the managerial literature does not detract from their importance. This paper has addressed itself to some aspects of the managerial role given a political perspective. The core idea of the paper is that in order to be successful, a manager must be aware of political constraints and opportunities. Managers can use diagnostic skills, network development, and developing power bases to take a proactive stance in implementing valued objectives. If this political involvement is not proactive, then it will be reactive, as the political behavior of others will act as a constraint on possible behavior and action.

REFERENCES

ALLISON, G. *Essence of Decision*. Boston: Little, Brown, 1971.

BALDRIDGE, V. *Power and Conflict in the University*. New York: Wiley and Sons, 1971.

BLAU, P. M. *Exchange and Power in Social Life*. New York: Wiley, 1967.

BLAU, P. M. *The Dynamics of Bureaucracy*. Chicago: University of Chicago Press, 1963.

CROZIER, M. "Problem of Power." *Social Research*, 1973, 40–43.

CROZIER, M. *The Bureaucratic Phenomenon*. Chicago: University of Chicago Press, 1964.

EDSTROM, A. and J. GALBRAITH. "Transter ot Managers as a Coordination and Control Strategy in Multinational Organizations." *Administrative Science Quarterly*, 22 (1977), 248–263.

FRENCH, J. and B. RAVEN. "The Bases of Social Power." In Cartwright, D. (ed.) *Studies in Social Power*. Ann Arbor: Institute for Social Research, 1966.

HICKSON, D., C. HINNINGS, R. LEE, R. SCHENCK, and J. PENNINGS. "A Strategic Contingencies Theory of Intra-Organizational Power." *Administrative Science Quarterly*, 16, (1971), 216–229.

KATZ, D. and R. KAHN. *The Social Psychology of Organizations*. New York: Wiley, 1966.

KEEGAN, W. "Multi-National Scanning: A Study of Information Sources Utilized by Executives in Multi-National Companies." *Administrative Science Quarterly*, 19 (1974), 411–421.

MARCH, J. and H. SIMON. *Organizations*. New York: Wiley, 1958.

MINTZBERG, H. *The Nature of Managerial Work*. New York: Harper & Row, 1973.

NADLER, D. A. and M. L. TUSHMAN. "Diagnostic Model for Organizational Behavior." In Hackman, J. R., E. E. Lawler, and L. W. Porter. *Perspectives on Behavior in Organizations*. New York: McGraw-Hill, 1977, 85–100.

NEWMAN, W. H. and E. K. WARREN. *The Process of Management* (Fourth Edition). Englewood Cliffs, N.J.: Prentice-Hall, 1977.

PETTIGREW, A. "Information Control as a Power Resource." *Sociology*, 6 (1972), 187–204.

PETTIGREW, A. "Towards a Political Theory of Organizational Intervention." *Human Relations*, 28 (1975), 191–208.

PFEFFER, J. "Power and Resource Allocation in Organizations." In Straw, M. B. and G. Salancik (eds.) *New Directions in Organizational Behavior*. Chicago: St. Clair Press, 1977.

RITTI, R. and F. GOULDNER. "Professional Pluralism in an Industrial Organization." *Management Science*, 16 (1969), B-233–246.

SALANCIK, G. R. and J. PFEFFER. "Who Gets Power and How They Hold on to it: A Strategic-Contingency Model of Power." *Organizational Dynamics*, 1977, 5 (3), 3–21.

SAYLES, L. *Leadership*. New York: McGraw-Hill, 1979.

SAYLES, L. and M. CHANDLER. *Managing Large Systems*. New York: Harper & Row, 1971.

SCHEIN, V. "Individual Power and Political Behavior in Organizations." *Academy of Management Review*, 2 (1977), 64–72.

SCHMIDT, S. and T. KOCHAN. "Conflict: Toward Conceptual Clarity." *Administrative Science Quarterly*, 17 (1972), 359–370.

SCHWARTZ, D. and E. JACOBSON. "Organizational Communication Network Analysis." *Organizational Behavior and Human Performance*, 18 (1977), 158–174.

STOGDILL, R. M. *The Handbook of Leadership*. New York: Free Press, 1974.

TICHY, N. M. "An Analysis of Cliques Formation and Structure in Organizations." *Administrative Science Quarterly*, 18 (1973) 194–208.

TICHY, N. M., M. L. TUSHMAN, and C. FOMBRUN. "Network Analysis in Organizations." *Academy of Management Review*, in press 1979.

TUSHMAN, M. L. "A Political Approach to Organizations: A Review and Rationale." *Academy of Management Review*, 2 (1977) 206–216.

TUSHMAN, M. L. "Special Boundary Roles in the Innovation Process." *Administrative Science Quarterly*, 22 (1977), 587–605.

WAMSLEY, G. and M. ZALD. *The Political Economy of Public Organizations*. Lexington: Heath Co., 1973.

Power, Dependence, and Effective Management

John P. Kotter

Americans, as a rule, are not very comfortable with power or with its dynamics. We often distrust and question the motives of people who we think actively seek power. We have a certain fear of being manipulated. Even those people who think the dynamics of power are inevitable and needed often feel somewhat guilty when they themselves mobilize and use power. Simply put, the overall attitude and feeling toward power, which can easily be traced to the nation's very birth, is negative. In his enormously popular *Greening of America*, Charles Reich reflects the views of many when he writes, "It is not the misuse of power that is evil; the very existence of power is evil."[1]

One of the many consequences of this attitude is that power as a topic for rational study and dialogue has not received much attention, even in managerial circles. If the reader doubts this, all he or she need do is flip through some textbooks, journals, or advanced management course descriptions. The word *power* rarely appears.

This lack of attention to the subject of power merely adds to the already enormous confusion and misunderstanding surrounding the topic of power and management. And this misunderstanding is becoming increasingly burdensome because in today's large and complex organizations the effective performance of most managerial jobs requires one to be skilled at the acquisition and use of power.

From my own observations, I suspect that a large number of managers—especially the young, well-educated ones—perform significantly below their potential because they do not understand the dynamics of power and because they have not nurtured and developed the instincts needed to effectively acquire and use power.

In this article I hope to clear up some of the confusion regarding power and managerial work by providing tentative answers to three questions:

1. Why are the dynamics of power necessarily an important part of managerial processes?
2. How do effective managers acquire power?
3. How and for what purposes do effective managers use power?

I will not address questions related to the misuse of power, but not because I think they are unimportant. The fact that some managers, some of the time, acquire and use power mostly for their own aggrandizement is obviously a very important issue that deserves attention and careful study. But that is a complex topic unto itself and one that has already received more attention than the subject of this article.

RECOGNIZING DEPENDENCE IN THE MANAGER'S JOB

One of the distinguishing characteristics of a typical manager is how dependent he is on the activities of a variety of other people to perform his job effectively.[2] Unlike doctors and mathematicians, whose performance is more directly dependent on their own talents and efforts, a manager can be dependent in varying degrees on superiors, subordinates, peers in other parts of the organization, the subordinates of peers, outside suppliers, customers, competitors, unions, regulating agencies, and many others.

These dependency relationships are an inherent part of managerial jobs because of two organizational facts of life: division of labor and limited resources. Because the work in organizations is divided into specialized divisions, departments, and jobs, managers are made directly or indirectly dependent on many others for information, staff services, and cooperation in general. Because of their organization's limited resources, managers are also dependent on their external environments for support. Without some minimal cooperation from suppliers, competitors, unions, regulatory agencies, and customers, managers cannot help their organizations survive and achieve their objectives.

Dealing with these dependencies and the manager's subsequent vulnerability is an important and difficult part of a manager's job because, while it is theoretically possible that all of these people and organizations would automatically act in just the manner that a manager wants and needs, such is almost never the case in reality. All the people on whom a manager is dependent have limited time, energy, and talent, for which there are competing demands.

Some people may be uncooperative because they are too busy elsewhere, and some because they are not really capable of helping. Others may well have goals, values, and beliefs that are quite different and in conflict with the manager's and may therefore have no desire whatsoever to help or cooperate. This is obviously true of a competing company and sometimes of a union, but it can also apply to a boss who is feeling threatened by a manager's career progress or to a peer whose objectives clash with the manager's.

Indeed, managers often find themselves dependent on many people (and things) whom they do not directly control and who are not "cooperating." This is the key to one of the biggest frustrations managers feel in their jobs, even in the top ones, which the following example illustrates:

> After nearly a year of rumors, it was finally announced in May 1974 that the president of ABC Corporation had been elected chairman of the board and that Jim Franklin, the vice president of finance, would replace him as president. While everyone at ABC was aware that a shift would take place soon, it was not at all clear before the announcement who would be the next president. Most people had guessed it would be Phil Cook, the marketing vice president.
>
> Nine months into his job as chief executive officer, Franklin found that Phil Cook (still the marketing vice president) seemed to be fighting him in small and subtle ways. There was never anything blatant, but Cook just did not cooperate with Franklin as the other vice presidents did. Shortly after being elected, Franklin had tried to bypass what he saw as a potential conflict with Cook by telling him that he would understand if Cook would prefer to move somewhere else where he could be a CEO also. Franklin said that it would be a big loss to the company but that he would be willing to help Cook in a number of ways if he wanted to look for a presidential opportunity elsewhere. Cook had thanked him but had said that family and community commitments would prevent him from relocating and all CEO opportunities were bound to be in a different city.
>
> Since the situation did not improve after the tenth and eleventh months, Franklin seriously considered forcing Cook out. When he thought about the consequences of such a move, Franklin became more and more aware of just how dependent he was on Cook. Marketing and sales were generally the keys to success in their

industry, and the company's sales force was one of the best, if not the best, in the industry. Cook had been with the company for 25 years. He had built a strong personal relationship with many of the people in the sales force and was universally popular. A mass exodus just might occur if Cook were fired. The loss of a large number of salesmen, or even a lot of turmoil in the department, could have a serious effect on the company's performance.

After one year as chief executive officer, Franklin found that the situation between Cook and himself had not improved and had become a constant source of frustration.

As a person gains more formal authority in an organization, the areas in which he or she is vulnerable increase and become more complex rather than the reverse. As the previous example suggests, it is not at all unusual for the president of an organization to be in a highly dependent position, a fact often not apparent to either the outsider or to the lower level manager who covets the president's job.

A considerable amount of the behavior of highly successful managers that seems inexplicable in light of what management texts usually tell us managers do becomes understandable when one considers a manager's need for, and efforts at, managing his or her relationships with others.[3] To be able to plan, organize, budget, staff, control, and evaluate, managers need some control over the many people on whom they are dependent. Trying to control others solely by directing them and on the basis of the power associated with one's position simply will not work—first, because managers are always dependent on some people over whom they have no formal authority, and second, because virtually no one in modern organizations will passively accept and completely obey a constant stream of orders from someone just because he or she is the "boss."

Trying to influence others by means of persuasion alone will not work either. Although it is very powerful and possibly the single and most important method of influence, persuasion has some serious drawbacks too. To make it work requires time (often lots of it), skill, and information on the part of the persuader. And persuasion can fail simply because the other person chooses not to listen or does not listen carefully.

This is not to say that directing people on the basis of the formal power of one's position and persuasion are not important means by which successful managers cope. They obviously are. But, even taken together, they are not usually enough.

Successful managers cope with their dependence on others by being sensitive to it, by eliminating or avoiding unnecessary dependence, and by establishing power over those others. Good managers then use that power to help them plan, organize, staff, budget, evaluate, and so on. *In other words, it is primarily because of the dependence inherent in managerial jobs that the dynamics of power necessarily form an important part of a manager's processes.*

An argument that took place during a middle management training seminar I participated in a few years ago helps illustrate further this important relationship between a manager's need for power and the degree of his or her dependence on others:

> Two participants, both managers in their thirties, got into a heated disagreement regarding the acquisition and use of power by managers. One took the position that power was absolutely central to managerial work, while the other argued that it was virtually irrelevant. In support of their positions, each described a very "successful" manager with whom he worked. In one of these examples, the manager seemed to be constantly developing and using power, while in the other, such behavior was rare. Subsequently, both seminar participants were asked to describe their successful managers' jobs in terms of the dependence *inherent* in those jobs.
>
> The young manager who felt power was unimportant described a staff vice president in a small company who was dependent only on his immediate subordinates, his peers, and his boss. This person, Joe Phillips, had to depend on his subordinates to do their jobs appropriately, but, if necessary, he could fill in for any of them or secure replacement for them rather easily. He also had considerable formal authority over them; that is, he could give them raises and new assignments, recommend promotions, and fire them. He was moderately dependent on the other four vice presidents in the company for information and cooperation. They were likewise dependent on him. The president had considerable formal authority over Phillips but was also moderately dependent on him for help, expert advice, the service his staff performed, other information, and general cooperation.
>
> The second young manager—the one who felt power was very important—described a service department manager, Sam Weller, in a large, complex, and growing company who was in quite a different position. Weller was dependent not only on his boss for rewards and information, but also on 30 other individuals who made up the divisional and corporate top management. And while his boss, like Phillips's was moderately dependent on him too, most of the top managers were not. Because Weller's subordinates, unlike Phillips's, had people reporting to them, Weller was dependent not only on his subordinates but also on his subordinates' subordinates. Because he could not himself easily replace or do most of their technical jobs, unlike Phillips, he was very dependent on all these people.
>
> In addition, for critical supplies, Weller was dependent on two other department managers in the division. Without their timely help, it was impossible for his department to do its job. These departments, however, did not have similar needs for Weller's help

and cooperation. Weller was also dependent on local labor union officials and on a federal agency that regulated the division's industry. Both could shut his division down if they wanted.

Finally, Weller was dependent on two outside suppliers of key materials. Because of the volume of his department's purchase relative to the size of these two companies, he had little power over them.

Under these circumstances, it is hardly surprising that Sam Weller had to spend considerable time and effort acquiring and using power to manage his many dependencies, while Joe Phillips did not.

As this example also illustrates, not all management jobs require an incumbent to be able to provide the same amount of successful power-oriented behavior. But most management jobs today are more like Weller's than Phillips's. And, perhaps more important, the trend over the past two or three decades is away from jobs like Phillips's and toward jobs like Weller's. So long as our technologies continue to become more complex, the average organization continues to grow larger, and the average industry continues to become more competitive and regulated, that trend will continue; as it does so, the effective acquisition and use of power by managers will become even more important.

ESTABLISHING POWER IN RELATIONSHIPS

To help cope with the dependency relationships inherent in their jobs, effective managers create, increase, or maintain four different types of power over others.[4] Having power based in these areas puts the manager in a position both to influence those people on whom he or she is dependent when necessary and to avoid being hurt by any of them.

Sense of Obligation

One of the ways that successful managers generate power in their relationships with others is to create a sense of obligation in those others. When the manager is successful, the others feel that they should—rightly—allow the manager to influence them within certain limits.

Successful managers often go out of their way to do favors for people who they expect will feel an obligation to return those favors. As can be seen in the following description of a manager by one of his subordinates, some people are very skilled at identifying opportunities for doing favors that cost them very little but that others appreciate very much:

> "Most of the people here would walk over hot coals in their bare feet if my boss asked them to. He has an incredible capacity to do little

things that mean a lot to people. Today, for example, in his junk mail he came across an advertisement for something that one of my subordinates had in passing once mentioned that he was shopping for. So my boss routed it to him. That probably took 15 seconds of his time, and yet my subordinate really appreciated it. To give you another example, two weeks ago he somehow learned that the purchasing manager's mother had died. On his way home that night, he stopped off at the funeral parlor. Our purchasing manager was, of course, there at the time. I bet he'll remember that brief visit for quite a while."

Recognizing that most people believe that friendship carries with it certain obligations ("A friend in need. . . ."), successful managers often try to develop true friendships with those on whom they are dependent. They will also make formal and informal deals in which they give something up in exchange for certain future obligations.

Belief in a Manager's Expertise

A second way successful managers gain power is by building reputations as "experts" in certain matters. Believing in the manager's expertise, others will often defer to the manager on those matters. Managers usually establish this type of power through visible achievement. The larger the achievement and the more visible it is, the more power the manager tends to develop.

One of the reasons that managers display concern about their "professional reputations" and their "track records" is that they have an impact on others' beliefs about their expertise. These factors become particularly important in large settings, where most people have only secondhand information about most other people's professional competence, as the following shows:

Herb Randley and Bert Kline were both 35-year-old vice presidents in a large research and development organization. According to their closest associates, they were equally bright and competent in their technical fields and as managers. Yet Randley had a much stronger professional reputation in most parts of the company, and his ideas generally carried much more weight. Close friends and associates claim the reason that Randley is so much more powerful is related to a number of tactics that he has used more than Kline has.

Randley has published more scientific papers and managerial articles than Kline. Randley has been more selective in the assignments he has worked on, choosing those that are visible and that require his strong suits. He has given more speeches and presentations on projects that are his own achievements. And in meetings in general, he is allegedly forceful in areas where he has expertise and silent in those where he does not.

Identification with a Manager

A third method by which managers gain power is by fostering others' unconscious identification with them or with ideas they "stand for." Sigmund Freud was the first to describe this phenomenon, which is most clearly seen in the way people look up to "charismatic" leaders. Generally, the more a person finds a manager both consciously and (more important) unconsciously an ideal person, the more he or she will defer to that manager.

Managers develop power based on others' idealized views of them in a number of ways. They try to look and behave in ways that others respect. They go out of their way to be visible to their employees and to give speeches about their organizational goals, values, and ideals. They even consider, while making hiring and promotion decisions, whether they will be able to develop this type of power over the candidates:

> One vice president of sales in a moderate-size manufacturing
> company was reputed to be so much in control of his sales force that
> he could get them to respond to new and different marketing
> programs in a third of the time taken by the company's best
> competitors. His power over his employees was based primarily on
> their strong identification with him and what he stood for. Emigrating
> to the United States at age 17, this person worked his way up "from
> nothing." When made a sales manager in 1965, he began recruiting
> other young immigrants and sons of immigrants from his former
> country. When made vice president of sales in 1970, he continued to
> do so. In 1975, 85% of his sales force was made up of people whom he
> hired directly or who were hired by others he brought in.

Perceived Dependence on a Manager

The final way that an effective manager often gains power is by feeding others' beliefs that they are dependent on the manager either for help or for not being hurt. The more they perceive they are dependent, the more most people will be inclined to cooperate with such a manager.

There are two methods that successful managers often use to create perceived dependence.

Finding and Acquiring Resources. In the first, the manager identifies and secures (if necessary) resources that another person requires to perform his job, that he does not possess, and that are not readily available elsewhere. These resources include such things as authority to make certain decisions; control of money, equipment, and office space; access to important people; information and control of information channels; and subordinates. Then the manager takes action so that the other person correctly perceives that the manager has such resources and is willing and ready to use them to help (or hinder) the other person. Consider the following extreme—but true—example.

> When young Tim Babcock was put in charge of a division of a large manufacturing company and told to "turn it around," he spent the first few weeks studying it from afar. He decided that the division was in disastrous shape and that he would need to take many large steps quickly to save it. To be able to do that, he realized he needed to develop considerable power fast over most of the division's management and staff. He did the following:

> He gave the division's management two hours' notice of his arrival.

> He arrived in a limousine with six assistants.

> He immediately called a meeting of the 40 top managers.

> He outlined briefly his assessment of the situation, his commitment to turn things around, and the basic direction he wanted things to move in.

> He then fired the four top managers in the room and told them that they had to be out of the building in two hours.

> He then said he would personally dedicate himself to sabotaging the career of anyone who tried to block his efforts to save the division.

> He ended the 60-minute meeting by announcing that his assistants would set up appointments for him with each of them starting at 7:00 A.M. the next morning.

> Throughout the critical six-month period that followed, those who remained at the division generally cooperated energetically with Mr. Babcock.

Affecting Perceptions of Resources. A second way effective managers gain these types of power is by influencing other persons' perceptions of the manager's resources.[5] In settings where many people are involved and where the manager does not interact continuously with those he or she is dependent on, those people will seldom possess "hard facts" regarding what relevant resources the manager commands directly or indirectly (through others), what resources he will command in the future, or how prepared he is to use those resources to help or hinder them. They will be forced to make their own judgments.

Insofar as a manager can influence people's judgments, he can generate much more power than one would generally ascribe to him in light of the reality of his resources.

In trying to influence people's judgments, managers pay considerable attention to the "trappings" of power and to their own reputations and images. Among other actions, they sometimes carefully select, decorate, and arrange their offices in ways that give signs of power. They associate with people or organizations that are known to be powerful or that others perceive as powerful. Managers selectively foster rumors concerning their own power. Indeed, those who are particularly skilled at creating power in this way tend to be very sensitive to the impressions that all their actions might have on others.

Formal Authority

Before discussing how managers use their power to influence others, it is useful to see how formal authority relates to power. By *formal authority*, I mean those elements that automatically come with a managerial job—perhaps a title, an office, a budget, the right to make certain decisions, a set of subordinates, a reporting relationship, and so on.

Effective managers use the elements of formal authority as resources to help them develop any or all of the four types of power previously discussed, just as they use other resources (such as their education). Two managers with the same formal authority can have very different amounts of power entirely because of the way they have used that authority. For example:

> By sitting down with employees who are new or with people who are starting new projects and clearly specifying who has the formal authority to do what, one manager creates a strong sense of obligation in others to defer to his authority later.

> By selectively withholding or giving the high-quality service his department can provide other departments, one manager makes other managers clearly perceive that they are dependent on him.

On its own, then, formal authority does not guarantee a certain amount of power; it is only a resource that managers can use to generate power in their relationships.

EXERCISING POWER TO INFLUENCE OTHERS

Successful managers use the power they develop in their relationships, along with persuasion, to influence people on whom they are dependent to behave in ways that make it possible for the managers to get their jobs done effectively. They use their power to influence others directly, face to face, and in more indirect ways.

Face-to-Face Influence

The chief advantage of influencing others directly by exercising any of the types of power is speed. If the power exists and the manager correctly understands the nature and strength of it, he can influence the other person with nothing more than a brief request or command:

> Jones thinks Smith feels obliged to him for past favors. Furthermore, Jones thinks that his request to speed up a project by two days probably falls within a zone that Smith would consider legitimate in light of his own definition of his obligation to Jones. So Jones simply calls Smith and makes his request. Smith pauses for only a second and says yes, he'll do it.
>
> Manager Johnson has some power based on perceived dependence over manager Baker. When Johnson tells Baker that he wants a report done in 24 hours, Baker grudgingly considers the costs of compliance, of noncompliance, and of complaining to higher authorities. He decides that doing the report is the least costly action and tells Johnson he will do it.
>
> Young Porter identifies strongly with Marquette, an older manager who is not his boss. Porter thinks Marquette is the epitome of a great manager and tries to model himself after him. When Marquette asks Porter to work on a special project "that could be very valuable in improving the company's ability to meet new competitive products," Porter agrees without hesitation and works 15 hours per week above and beyond his normal hours to get the project done and done well.

When used to influence others, each of the four types of power has different advantages and drawbacks. For example, power based on perceived expertise or on identification with a manager can often be used to influence attitudes as well as someone's immediate behavior and thus can have a lasting impact. It is very difficult to influence attitudes by using power based on perceived dependence, but if it can be done, it usually has the advantage of being able to influence a much broader range of behavior than the other methods do. When exercising power based on perceived expertise, for example, one can only influence attitudes and behavior within that narrow zone defined by the "expertise."

The drawbacks associated with the use of power based on perceived dependence are particularly important to recognize. A person who feels dependent on a manager for rewards (or lack of punishments) might quickly agree to a request from the manager but then not follow through—

EXHIBIT Methods of Influence

FACE-TO-FACE METHODS	WHAT THEY CAN INFLUENCE	ADVANTAGES	DRAWBACKS
Exercise obligation-based power.	Behavior within zone that the other perceives as legitimate in light of the obligation.	Quick. Requires no outlay of tangible resources.	If the request is outside the acceptable zone, it will fail; if it is too far outside, others might see it as illegitimate.
Exercise power based on perceived expertise.	Attitudes and behavior within the zone of perceived expertise.	Quick. Requires no outlay of tangible resources.	If the request is outside the acceptable zone, it will fail; if it is too far outside, others might see it as illegitimate.
Exercise power based on identification with a manager.	Attitudes and behavior that are not in conflict with the ideals that underlie the identification.	Quick. Requires no expenditure of limited resources.	Restricted to influence attempts that are not in conflict with the ideals that underlie the identification.
Exercise power based on perceived dependence.	Wide range of behavior that can be monitored.	Quick. Can often succeed when other methods fail.	Repeated influence attempts encourage the other to gain power over the influencer.
Coercively exercise power based on perceived dependence.	Wide range of behavior that can be easily monitored.	Quick. Can often succeed when other methods fail.	Invites retaliation. Very risky.
Use persuasion.	Very wide range of attitudes and behavior.	Can produce internalized motivation that does not require monitoring. Requires no power or outlay of scarce material resources.	Can be very time-consuming. Requires other person to listen.
Combine these methods.	Depends on the exact combination.	Can be more potent and less risky than using a single method.	More costly than using a single method.

INDIRECT METHODS	WHAT THEY CAN INFLUENCE	ADVANTAGES	DRAWBACKS
Manipulate the other's environment by using any or all of the face-to-face methods.	Wide range of behavior and attitudes.	Can succeed when face-to-face methods fail.	Can be time-consuming. Is complex to implement. Is very risky, especially if used frequently.
Change the forces that continuously act on the individual: Formal organizational arrangements. Informal social arrangements. Technology. Resources available. Statement of organizational goals.	Wide range of behavior and attitudes on a continuous basis.	Has continuous influence, not just a one-shot effect. Can have a very powerful impact.	Often requires a considerable power outlay to achieve.

especially if the manager cannot easily find out if the person has obeyed or not. Repeated influence attempts based on perceived dependence also seem to encourage the other person to try to gain some power to balance the manager's. And perhaps most important, using power based on perceived dependence in a coercive way is very risky. Coercion invites retaliation.

For instance, in the example in which Tim Babcock took such extreme steps to save the division he was assigned to "turn around," his development and use of power based on perceived dependence could have led to mass resignation and the collapse of the division. Babcock fully recognized this risk, however, and behaved as he did because he felt there was simply *no other way* that he could gain the very large amount of quick cooperation needed to save the division.

Effective managers will often draw on more than one form of power to influence someone, or they will combine power with persuasion. In general, they do so because a combination can be more potent and less risky than any single method, as the following description shows:

> "One of the best managers we have in the company has lots of power based on one thing or another over most people. But he seldom if ever just tells or asks someone to do something. He almost always takes a few minutes to try to persuade them. The power he has over people generally induces them to listen carefully and certainly disposes them to be influenced. That, of course, makes the persuasion process go quickly and easily. And he never risks getting the other person mad or upset by making what that person thinks is an unfair request or command."

It is also common for managers not to coercively exercise power based on perceived dependence by itself, but to combine it with other methods to reduce the risk of retaliation. In this way, managers are able to have a large impact without leaving the bitter aftertaste of punishment alone.

Indirect Influence Methods

Effective managers also rely on two types of less direct methods to influence those on whom they are dependent. In the first way, they use any or all of the face-to-face methods to influence other people, who in turn have some specific impact on a desired person.

> Product manager Stein needed plant manager Billings to "sign off" on a new product idea (Product X) which Billings thought was terrible. Stein decided that there was no way he could logically persuade Billings because Billings just would not listen to him. With time, Stein felt, he could have broken through that barrier. But he did not have

that time. Stein also realized that Billings would never, just because of some deal or favor, sign off on a product he did not believe in. Stein also felt it not worth the risk of trying to force Billings to sign off, so here is what he did:

On Monday, Stein got Reynolds, a person Billings respected, to send Billings two market research studies that were very favorable to Product X, with a note attached saying, "Have you see this? I found them rather surprising. I am not sure if I entirely believe them, but still. . . ."

On Tuesday, Stein got a representative of one of the company's biggest customers to mention casually to Billings on the phone that he had heard a rumor about Product X being introduced soon and was "glad to see you guys are on your toes as usual."

On Wednesday, Stein had two industrial engineers stand about three feet away from Billings as they were waiting for a meeting to begin and talk about the favorable test results on Product X.

On Thursday, Stein set up a meeting to talk about Product X with Billings and invited only people whom Billings liked or respected and who also felt favorably about Product X.

On Friday, Stein went to see Billings and asked him if he was willing to sign off on Product X. He was.

This type of manipulation of the environments of others can influence both behavior and attitudes and can often succeed when other influence methods fail. But it has a number of serious drawbacks. It takes considerable time and energy, and it is quite risky. Many people think it is wrong to try to influence others in this way, even people who, without consciously recognizing it, use this technique themselves. If they think someone is trying, or has tried, to manipulate them, they may retaliate. Furthermore, people who gain the reputation of being manipulators seriously undermine their own capacities for developing power and for influencing others. Almost no one, for example, will want to identify with a manipulator. And virtually no one accepts, at face value, a manipulator's sincere attempts at persuasion. In extreme cases, a reputation as a manipulator can completely ruin a manager's career.

A second way in which managers indirectly influence others is by making permanent changes in an individual's or a group's environment. They change job descriptions, the formal systems that measure performance, the extrinsic incentives available, the tools, people, and other resources that the people or groups work with, the architecure, the norms or values of work groups, and so on. If the manager is successful in making the changes, and the changes have the desired effect on the individual or group, that effect will be sustained over time.

Effective managers recognize that changes in the forces that surround a person can have great impact on that person's behavior. Unlike many of the other influence methods, this one doesn't require a large expenditure of limited resources or effort on the part of the manager on an ongoing basis. Once such a change has been successfully made, it works independently of the manager.

This method of influence is used by all managers to some degree. Many, however, use it sparingly simply because they do not have the power to change the forces acting on the person they wish to influence. In many organizations, only the top managers have the power to change the formal measurement systems, the extrinsic incentives available, the architecture, and so on.

GENERATING AND USING POWER SUCCESSFULLY

Managers who are successful at acquiring considerable power and using it to manage their dependence on others tend to share a number of common characteristics:

1.   They are sensitive to what others consider to be legitimate behavior in acquiring and using power. They recognize that the four types of power carry with them certain "obligations" regarding their acquisition and use. A person who gains a considerable amount of power based on his perceived expertise is generally expected to be an expert in certain areas. If it ever becomes publicly known that the person is clearly not an expert in those areas, such a person will probably be labeled a "fraud" and will not only lose his power but will suffer other reprimands too.

A person with whom a number of people identify is expected to act like an ideal leader. If he clearly lets people down, he will not only lose that power, he will also suffer the righteous anger of his ex-followers. Many managers who have created or used power based on perceived dependence in ways that their employees have felt unfair, such as in requesting overtime work, have ended up with unions.

2.   They have good intuitive understanding of the various types of power and methods of influence. They are sensitive to what types of power are easiest to develop with different types of people. They recognize, for example, that professionals tend to be more influenced by perceived expertise than by other forms of power. They also have a grasp of all the various methods of influence and what each can accomplish, at what costs, and with what risks. (See the *Exhibit* on pps. 202–3.) They are good at recognizing the specific conditions in any situation and then at selecting an influence method that is compatible with those conditions.

3. They tend to develop all the types of power, to some degree, and they use all the influence methods mentioned in the exhibit. Unlike managers who are not very good at influencing people, effective managers usually do not think that only some of the methods are useful or that only some of the methods are moral. They recognize that any of the methods, used under the right circumstances, can help contribute to organizational effectiveness with few dysfunctional consequences. At the same time, they generally try to avoid those methods that are more risky than others and those that may have dysfunctional consequences. For example, they manipulate the environment of others only when absolutely necessary.

4. They establish career goals and seek out managerial positions that allow them to successfully develop and use power. They look for jobs, for example, that use their backgrounds and skills to control or manage some critically important problem or environmental contingency that an organization faces. They recognize that success in that type of job makes others dependent on them and increases their own perceived expertise. They also seek jobs that do not demand a type or a volume of power that is inconsistent with their own skills.

5. They use all of their resources, formal authority, and power to develop still more power. To borrow Edward Banfield's metaphor, they actually look for ways to "invest" their power where they might secure a high positive return.[6] For example, by asking a person to do him two important favors, a manager might be able to finish his construction program one day ahead of schedule. That request may cost him most of the obligation-based power he has over that person, but in return he may significantly increase his perceived expertise as a manager of construction projects in the eyes of everyone in his organization.

Just as in investing money, there is always some risk involved in using power this way; it is possible to get a zero return for a sizable investment, even for the most powerful manager. Effective managers do not try to avoid risks. Instead, they look for prudent risks, just as they do when investing capital.

6. Effective managers engage in power-oriented behavior in ways that are tempered by maturity and self-control.[7] They seldom, if ever, develop and use power in impulsive ways or for their own aggrandizement.

7. Finally, they also recognize and accept as legitimate that, in using these methods, they clearly influence other people's behavior and lives. Unlike many less effective managers, they are reasonably comfortable in using power to influence people. They recognize, often only intuitively, what this article is all about—that their attempts to establish power and use it are an absolutely necessary part of the successful fulfillment of their difficult managerial role.

NOTES

Author's note: This article is based on data from a clinical study of a highly diverse group of 26 organizations including large and small, public and private, manufacturing and service organizations. The study was funded by the Division of Research at the Harvard Business School. As part of the study process, the author interviewed about 250 managers.

1. Charles A. Reich, *The Greening of America: How the Youth Revolution is Trying to Make America Liveable* (New York: Random House, 1970).

2. See Leonard R. Sayles, *Managerial Behavior: Administration in Complex Organization* (New York: McGraw-Hill, 1964) as well as Rosemary Stewart, *Managers and Their Jobs* (London: Macmillan, 1967) and *Contrasts in Management* (London: McGraw-Hill, 1976).

3. I am talking about the type of inexplicable differences that Henry Mintzberg has found; see his article, "The Manager's Job: Folklore and Fact," HBR July–August 1975, p. 49.

4. These categories closely resemble the five developed by John R. P. French and Bertram Raven; see "The Base of Social Power" in *Group Dynamics: Research and Theory*, Dorwin Cartwright and Alvin Zandler, eds. (New York: Harper & Row, 1968), Chapter 20. Three of the categories are similar to the types of "authority"-based power described by Max Weber in *The Theory of Social and Economic Organization* (New York: Free Press, 1947).

5. For an excellent discussion of this method, see Richard E. Neustadt, *Presidential Power* (New York: John Wiley, 1960).

6. See Edward C. Banfield, *Political Influence* (New York: Free Press, 1965), Chapter II.

7. See David C. McClelland and David H. Burnham, "Power Is the Great Motivator," HBR March–April 1976, p. 100.

Budgeting and Intergroup Conflict in Organizations

Louis R. Pondy

This paper was stimulated by field studies made by the author of capital budgeting practices in large manufacturing corporations. Capital budgeting is the process by which funds for plant and equipment are allocated to the various investment projects proposed by operating divisions or by functional departments (e.g., marketing, engineering). Budgeting is necessary because demands for capital funds invariably outrun the resources available. The budget provides a way of choosing among these competing claims for resources.

The engineering economics literature and the accounting literature usually treat the budgeting and resource allocation problem solely as a problem in economics, e.g., to choose those projects which will maximize the present value of invested capital. To

Louis R. Pondy, *"Budgeting and Intergroup Conflict in Organizations,"* Pittsburgh Business Review, *April 1964. Reprinted by permission.*

understand and explain the practices observed during the field studies, however, it became necessary to use additional concepts from the behavioral sciences. In brief, it proved helpful to interpret capital budgeting for resource allocation as a process of resolving intergroup conflict.

THE ORGANIZATION AS A CONFLICT SYSTEM

The classical bureaucratic way of describing an organization is as a hierarchy with each person responsible to the person directly above him in the authority structure. Through the pyramiding of this authority structure, each participant in the organization has eventual responsibility and loyalty to the organization's prime goal (presumably profit in the case of a business organization).

DEVELOPMENT OF SUBGROUP LOYALTIES

But each participant is a member not only of "the corporation," but also of the Marketing Department or of Division X, as well as of various professional organizations. In fact, because the Marketing Department is smaller and more congenial than "the corporation," there is a good chance that he has a closer identification with its immediate goals than with the long range goals of "the corporation."[1] This insight into the multiple membership and subgroup identifications of each organizational participant suggests the following alternative to the classical description: The organization is a collection of interest groups who have goals which may be only partially consistent with those of other interest groups and with the superordinate goal of the organization.[2]

Subgroup loyalties develop not only because of a common professional background of the subgroup members, not only because of a selective exposure of the business environment, not only because ingroup communication supports and reinforces subgroup goals, but also because each subgroup engages in competition with every other subgroup for an adequate share of the available resources.

EFFECT OF SUBGROUP LOYALTIES

The existence of subgroup loyalties has an important effect on the budgeting process. Characteristically each functional department either originates or participates actively in the organization and development of investment projects]. It is natural that the production department will be most energetic in the development of projects which improve production facilities, the marketing department in projects which improve product quality or customer service, and so on. "Thus each functional department has a vested interest in each of its projects considered for the budget, and will find it very

hard to be objective in judging the entire set of projects or in genuinely accepting the budgeting decisions of an impartial budget committee."[4]

Not only do subgroup loyalties distort the perceptions of the investment projects, but they lead subgroups to adopt political strategies for more nearly assuring approval of its projects. What strategies are adopted depends on the particular loopholes available in the budgeting system of the parent company.[5] For example, in companies which have long-range facilities plans, it is advantageous for an operating division or functional department to place a project in the long-range plan on a presumably tentative basis, only to have it gradually assume a more certain status. Or, if the budget committee requests the division to *rank* all of its proposed projects, the division will rank last those projects the budget committee is known to favor and is likely to approve regardless of the ranking, and rank first those projects the division favors most but which have the least chance of approval otherwise. Or again, if the budget committee sets up a minimum acceptable rate of return, the division is likely to "doctor" the economic analysis of marginal projects so that the target rate is met. In one case the division accounting department had been blocking a project for several years because the division manager could not prove rigorously that anticipated savings from a renovation would be assured. Eventually the division manager overrode the accounting department and made a rough guess of the savings so that the target rate of return would be exceeded by about three percentage points. The assistant to the division manager was quite candid in reporting the handling of this project.

THE BUDGET COMMITTEE AND CONFLICT RESOLUTION

In order to mediate this intense intergroup competition for funds most companies have set up budget committees, composed of functional representatives, to review the proposals made by the operating divisions or by the central staff. Representatives of the operating divisions are not usually members of the committee. That there is considerable conflict among the committee members is almost certain. To demonstrate the divergence of judgments and evaluations of projects in a large primary metal processing firm, the author asked two comparable members of the marketing and engineering-planning departments to make independent rankings from project summaries of nine projects from the company's previous budget. Though each man was familiar with all nine projects, the degree of agreement between their rankings was not statistically significant. These differences of course provide the basis for interfunctional conflict on the budget committee. Though no direct evidence is available on how these conflicts of project preference are settled, it is likely that bargaining and compromise take precedence over analytical efforts. This is true partially because group loyalties affect evaluation criteria as well as specific project preferences.

PROJECT CLASSIFICATIONS AS BARGAINING RESIDUES

The loyalties to evaluation criteria are reflected in the project classification system. Characteristically the accounting and finance representatives on the budget committee insist that all projects satisfy economic criteria, such as rate of return or payback. The legal representative of course will insist that compliance with government regulations (e.g., regarding smoke control or stream pollution) obviously is consistent with the firm's financial well-being and needs no economic justification. Similarly the marketing representative will insist that market share is really a more appropriate measure of the worth of a project than is rate of return. The production representative will push for operating efficiency criteria to supplement

the financial criteria, all the time arguing of course that his criteria, while superficially different, are really related to the financial criteria and, in fact, are more operational.[6] To avoid resurrecting the criterion conflict anew each time, the committee legitimizes the use of different criteria by defining different investment categories. A typical classification system comprises cost reduction, replacement, commercial, legal, and employee welfare categories. I choose to interpret these investment categories as "residues" from past conflict and bargaining among the functional departments over the issue of appropriate investment criteria.

Once formed, these investment categories provide an institutional framework for resolving the interfunctional conflict since each category requires a different set of criteria, so that the criterion conflict is repressed.[7] The project preference conflict is alleviated as follows: A rough, and more or less unintentional, balance is maintained among the various categories. There is no conscious attempt to allocate X percent of the budget to cost reduction projects, for example, but it does appear that, by unwritten rule, the share of the budget spent on cost reduction projects may legitimately range *only* between certain percentages of the total budget or between certain dollar amounts.

OTHER DEVICES FOR CONFLICT RESOLUTION

Two other miscellaneous devices for resolving conflict may be more accurately described as defense mechanisms for the budget committee. A complete ranking of the projects is not attempted, so that some unresolved conflict remains latent. A practice adopted by one company is to break the budget up into four priority increments to be authorized for expenditures in increments (if at all) by the board of directors.

The use of long-range plans is in some sense a defense mechanism. Suppose that only $10 million can be spent in each of the next three years, and each of these divisions has a prime project which will require the entire $10 million. Engineering economics or financial analysis may indicate which of the three projects to approve, but will provide no answer on how to handle the disappointment of the other two divisions. It is small consolation to the "losers" to know that they came out a close second. On the other hand, if the division knows that its project has been placed in a long-range plan for the next year hence, its feelings will at least be partially mollified, and the budget committee will experience less pressure from the divisional management.

CONCLUSION

We have argued that two factors are sufficient for intergroup conflict to exist: subgroup loyalties and intergroup competition. Both these factors were shown to be present in the budgeting-resource allocation process in the modern, large corporation. Budgeting can therefore be viewed as a process of resolving intergroup conflicts. This finding has crucial implications for the design of budgeting systems. Not only must the system provide procedures for the rational, economic analysis of budget proposals, but it must also provide procedures for the resolution of intergroup conflict over scarce resources that will inevitably arise.

NOTES

1. There are both motivational and cognitive processes producing subgroup identification. Examples of motivational factors are conformity of group goals and the self-image and affective ties with other group members. Examples of cognitive factors are the selective exposure to environmental cues (marketing personnel talk most to customers and therefore are most sensitive to marketing and commercial goals), reinforcement of group attitudes by ingroup communication, and uniform professional training and its effects on perception. See J. G. March and H. A. Simon, *Organizations* (New York: Wiley, 1958, pp. 93–106, 150–54.

2. See J. G. March, "The Business Firm as a Political Coalition," *Journal of Politics,* December 1962.

3. See Muzafer Sherif et al., *Intergroup Cooperation and Conflict: The Robbers Cave Experiment* (Norman, Okla.: Institute of Intergroup Relations, University of Oklahoma, 1961) for a description of the effect of intergroup competition on in-group loyalties in a boys' summer camp.

4. See Jane S. Mouton and Robert R. Blake, "The Influence of Competitively Vested Interests on Judgment," *Journal of Conflict Resolution* 6, no. 2 (June 1962): 149–53, for experimental documentation of the effects of subgroup loyalties on perception and satisfaction in a judgment situation.

5. Aaron Wildavsky has studied the use of subgroup strategies in the formation of the federal budget. In particular these include the cultivation of the "confidence" of the Budget Bureau and congressional committees, where confidence refers to affective ties and mutual rapport between the agency and the official group (private communication). See also his "Political Implications of Budgetary Reform," *Public Administration Review* 21, no. 4 (Autumn 1961): 183–90.

6. March and Simon *(Organizations,* pp. 156–57) assert that bargaining behavior will take precedence over analytic behavior in the absence of shared, operational goals. My own observations suggest that long-run profit maximization is *not* an operational goal when it comes to ranking complex capital investment projects.

7. One of the other strategies commonly employed by subgroups is to classify, with appropriate justifications, a marginal project in a category which is currently favored by the central staff of the firm. Once a project is placed in a certain category, it tends to be compared only with the other projects in that category.

The Rocky Road to the Marketplace

T. A. Wise

When Tom Watson Jr. made what he called "the most important product announcement in company history," he created quite a stir. International Business Machines is not a corporation given to making earth-shaking pronouncements casually, and the declaration that it was launching an entirely new computer line, the System/360, was headline news. The elaborate logistics that I.B.M. worked out in order to get maximum press coverage—besides a huge assembly at Poughkeepsie, I.B.M. staged press conferences on the same day in sixty-two cities in the U.S. and in fourteen foreign countries—underscored its view of the importance of the event. And the fact that the move until then had been a closely guarded secret added an engaging element of surprise. But it was the magnitude of the new line—Watson called System/360 "a sharp depar-

"The Rocky Road to the Marketplace," *Fortune* October 1966. Reprinted by permission.

ture from the concepts of the past"—that was really responsible for the reaction that ran through the computer industry. No company had ever introduced, in one swoop, six computer models of totally new design, in a technology never tested in the marketplace, and with programing abilities of the greatest complexity. Once the announcement was made, it is no wonder that, in the scattered locations where I.B.M. plans, builds, and sells its products, there was, on that evening of April 7, 1964, a certain amount of dancing in the streets.

By now, two and a half years later, it would seem that there was good reason for the celebrations. As Fortune related in Part I last month, I.B.M. was staking its treasure (some $5 billion over four years), its reputation, and its position of leadership in the computer field on its decision to go ahead with System/360. The current rate of shipments of the several models in the series is probably running close to 1,000 computers a month. Authoritative forecasts indicate that, on the basis of orders already on the books, over 26,000 members of the System/360 family will be operating around the world by the end of 1968. If these forecasts are correct, some $10 billion worth of I.B.M.'s new computing equipment will be in the field then. Even allowing for the fact that as many as 10 to 20 percent of the customers now signed up may cancel their orders, the results in hand by the end of this year would stamp the whole 360 venture as very successful.

The final verdict on I.B.M.'s wisdom, however, depends on a series of factors more complicated than the number of shipments. The programing of System/360 is one enormously difficult area and here much remains to be accomplished before the project can be rated a complete success. Moreover, there have been new developments in technology since System/360 was launched in 1964; will they enable competitors to leapfrog into something better? And the managerial and organizational changes that were brought about by the company's struggle to settle on, and then to produce and market, the new line are still having their effects. In each of these several aspects, past, present, and future are closely intertwined.

THE RISING COST OF ASKING QUESTIONS

No part of the whole adventure of launching System/360 has been as tough, as stubborn, or as enduring as the programing. Earlier this year, talking to a group of I.B.M. customers, Tom Watson Jr. said ruefully: "We are investing nearly as much in System/360 programing as we are in the entire development of System/360 hardware. A few months ago the bill for 1966 was going to be $40 million. I asked Vin Learson last night before I left what he thought it would be for 1966 and he said $50 million. Twenty-four hours later I met Watts Humphrey, who

is in charge of programing production, in the hall here and said, 'Is this figure about right? Can I use it?' He said it's going to be $60 million. You can see that if I keep asking questions we won't pay a dividend this year."

Watson's concern about programing, of course, goes back to the beginnings of the System/360 affair. By late in 1962 he was sufficiently aware of the proportions of the question to invite the eight top executives of I.B.M. to his ski lodge in Stowe, Vermont, for a three-day session on programing. The session was conducted by Fred Brooks, the corporate manager for the design of the 360 project, and other experts; they went into the programing in considerable detail. While the matter can become highly technical, in general I.B.M.'s objective was to devise an "operating system" for its computer line, so that the computers would schedule themselves, without manual interruption, and would be kept working continuously at or near their capacity. At the time it announced System/360, I.B.M. promised future users that it would supply them with such a command system.

Delivery on that promise has been agonizingly difficult. Even though Tom Watson and the other top executives knew the critical importance of programing, the size of the job was seriously underestimated. The difficulty of coordinating the work of hundreds of programers was enormous. The operating system I.B.M. was striving for required the company to work out many new ideas and approaches; as one company executive says, "We were trying to schedule inventions, which is a dangerous thing to do in a committed project." Customers came up with more extensive programing tasks than the company had expected, and there were inevitable delays and slowdowns. Even today, the difficulties of programing are preventing some users from getting the full benefit from their new machines. By I.B.M.'s own estimates, the company won't have most of the bugs out of programing the larger systems until the middle of 1967—at least a year behind its expectation.

In technology, I.B.M. was also breaking new ground. During the formative years of the decisions about the technology of System/360, a lengthy report on the subject was prepared by the *ad hoc* Logic Committee, headed by Erich Bloch, a specialist in circuitry for I.B.M. Eventually, the Logic Committee report led to the company's formal commitment to a new hybrid kind of integrated-circuit technology—a move that, like so many other aspects of the 360 decision, is still criticized by some people in the computer industry, both inside and outside of I.B.M.

The move, though, was hardly made in haste. The whole computer industry had raced through two phases of electronic technology—vacuum tubes and transistors—between 1951 and 1960. By the late 1950's it was becoming apparent that further technological changes of sweeping importance were in the offing. At that time, however, I.B.M. was not very much of a force in scientific research, its strengths lying in the assembling and marketing of computers, not in their advanced concepts. The company's management at the time had the wit to recognize the nature of the corporate deficiency, and to see the importance of correcting it. In 1956, I.B.M. hired Dr. Emanuel Piore, formerly chief scientist of U.S. naval research. Piore became I.B.M.'s director of research and a major figure in the technological direction that the company finally chose for its System/360.

THE COLD REALITIES OF CHOICE

Under Piore's direction, I.B.M.'s prestige in both pure and applied research rose dramatically. The company gained recognition as a leader in electronics, physics, and mathematics. It made efforts in many directions, including an important study into cryogenics—the behavior of materials at extremely low temperatures. At temperatures close to absolute zero ($-459.7°F.$) the resistance to electricity of certain metals, such as lead and tin, virtually vanishes. This means that cryogenic computer circuitry could be much faster, and the power required much smaller. Between 1958 and 1961, I.B.M. spent between $10 million and $15 million, including some government funds, in an attempt to perfect a computer technology based on cryogenics; at one point the company made what some regarded as an alarming laboratory discovery of a cryogenic process that might eventually make the manufacture of computers so cheap that I.B.M.'s profits would become very thin. (Watson turned to his marketing and manufacturing experts to find out what the company might do if this process were perfected. They assured him it was not about to happen.) For a long time some people at I.B.M. remained convinced that cryogenics would revolutionize their company and their industry. But when the company started working toward the practical choice of a technology for System/360, it leaned more heavily on its engineers than on its research scientists, and cryogenics died a sudden death.

In the end, as the report of the Logic Committee showed, the choice narrowed to two technologies. One was monolithic integrated circuitry: putting all the elements of a circuit —transistors, resistors, and diodes—on one chip at one time. The other was hybrid integrated circuitry—I.B.M. rather densely termed it "solid logic technology"—which means making transistors and diodes separately and then soldering them into place. In 1961 the Logic Committee decided that the production of monolithic circuits in great quantities would be risky, and in any case would not meet the schedule for any new line of computers to be marketed by 1964.

There was little opposition to this recommendation initially, except among a few engineering purists. Later, however, the opposition strengthened. The purists believed that monolithic circuits were sure to come, and that the company in a few years would find itself frozen into a technology that might be obsolete before the investment could be recovered. However, the Logic Committee's recommendation on the hybrid approach was accepted; since that time, Watson has referred to the acceptance as "the most fortunate decision we ever made." But some of the critics, at least, still persist in their disagreement with that judgment: their position is that if I.B.M. had put into monolithic circuits the effort it devoted to the hybrids, there would have been a monolithic success, and both company and industry would be better off.

THE SECRETS CIRCUITS HIDE

The decision to move into hybrid integrated technology accelerated I.B.M.'s push into component manufacturing, a basic change in the character of the company. In the day of vacuum tubes and transistors, I.B.M. had designed the components for its circuits, ordered them from other companies (a principal supplier: Texas Instruments), then assembled them to its own specifications. But with the new circuitry, those specifications would have to be built into the components from the outset. "Too much proprietary information was involved in circuitry production," says Watson. "Unless we did it ourselves, we could be turning over some of the essentials of our business to another company. We had no intention of doing that." In addition, of course, I.B.M. saw no reason why it should not capture some of the profit from the manufacturing that it was creating on such a large scale.

The company's turn to a new technology jibed neatly with a previous decision made in 1960 by Watson at the urging of the man who was then I.B.M. president, Al Williams, that the company should move into component manufacturing. By the time the decision to go into hybrid circuits was made, I.B.M. already had started putting together a component manufacturing division. Its general

manager was John Gibson, a Johns Hopkins Ph.D. in electrical engineering. Under Gibson, the new division won the authority, hitherto divided among other divisions of the company, to designate and to buy the components for computer hardware, along with a new authority to manufacture them when Gibson thought it appropriate.

This new assignment of responsibility was resented by managers in the Data Systems and General Products divisions, since it represented a limitation on their authority. Also, they protested that they would be unable to compare the price and quality of in-house components with those made by an outside supplier if they lost their independence of action. But Vincent Learson, then group executive vice president, feared that if they kept their independence they would continue to make purchases outside the company, and that I.B.M. as a consequence would have no market for its own component output. He therefore put the power of decision in Gibson's hands. I.B.M.'s board, in effect, ruled in Gibson's favor when, in 1962, it authorized the construction of a new manufacturing plant, and the purchase of its automatic equipment, at a cost of over $100 million.

While I.B.M. was making up its corporate mind about the technology for System/360, the delegation of specific responsibilities was going ahead. Learson designated Bob Evans, now head of the Federal Systems Division, to manage the giant undertaking. Under Evans, Fred Brooks was put in charge of all the System/360 work being done at Poughkeepsie, where four of the original models were designed; he was also made manager of the over-all design of the central processors. The plant at Endicott was given the job of designing the model 30, successor to the popular 1401, which had been developed there. And John Fairclough, a systems designer at World Trade, was assigned to design the model 40 at the I.B.M. lab at Hursley, England.

Out of the Hursley experience came an

interesting byproduct that may have significant implications for I.B.M.'s future. With different labs engaged in the 360 design, it was vital to provide for virtually instant communication between them. I.B.M. therefore leased a special transatlantic line between its home offices and the engineers in England, and later in Germany. The international engineering group was woven together with considerable effectiveness, giving I.B.M. the justifiable claim that the 360 computer was probably the first product of truly international design.

While dovetailing plans for the 360, I.B.M. also became involved at first hand with an international communication system for the processing of information. In 1961, I.B.M. used 28,900 miles of domestic telephone circuitry; by 1966 it was using 380,000 miles, and two voice channels across the Atlantic. On the basis of that volume, I.B.M. last year petitioned the FCC for the right to bypass the common carriers, A.T.&T. and I.T.T., and have direct access to the Comsat satellite. The petition was turned down in July of this year.

But the experience opened a new window to the future for the company. I.B.M. now has the vision of the communication of tomorrow, with machines talking to machines across the oceans. What that will mean in terms of the dollar volume of the market is still conjectural, but I.B.M. feels sure it is a market that does not have to be controlled completely by the entrenched carriers. I.B.M. makes a careful distinction between data transmission—the simple function of carrying electrical impulses—and data transformation, which it defines as the analyzing, correlating, and sorting of those impulses. I.B.M. does not want to be considered merely the manufacturer of a device that would be only a part of the common carriers' communication system, and so subject to conventional regulations and tariff schedules. It sees itself playing a critical role in a brand-new kind of international data communication, composed of computers

that work and talk with each other. And in such a vision compatibility is a necessary element. Compatibility is just what System/360 possesses.

IN A TUG-OF-WAR, ENOUGH ROPE TO HANG YOURSELF

Even in a corporation inured to change, people resist change. By 1963, with the important decisions on the 360 being implemented, excitement about the new product line began to spread through the corporation—at least among those who were privy to the secret. But this rising pitch of interest by no means meant that the struggle inside the company was settled. The new family of computers cut across all the old lines of authority and upset all the old divisions. The System/360 concepts plunged I.B.M. into an organizational upheaval.

Resistance came in only a mild form from the World Trade Corp., whose long-time boss was A. K. Watson, Tom's brother. World Trade managers always thought of European markets as very different from those in the U.S., and as requiring special considerations that U.S. designers would not give them. Initially they had reservations about the concept of a single computer family, which they thought of as fitted only to U.S. needs. But when I.B.M laboratories in Europe were included in the formulation of the design of some of the 360 models, the grumblings from World Trade were muted. Later A. K. Watson was made vice chairman of the corporation and Gilbert Jones, formerly the head of domestic marketing of computers for the company, took over World Trade. These moves further integrated the domestic and foreign operations, and gave World Trade assurance that its voice would be heard at the top level of the corporation.

The General Products Division, for its part, really bristled with hostility. Its output, after all, accounted for two-thirds of the company's revenues for data processing. It had a popular and profitable product in the field, the 1401, which the 360 threatened to replace. The executive in charge of General Products, John Haanstra, fought against some phases of the 360 program. Haanstra thought the new line would hit his division hard. He was concerned, from the time the System/360 program was approved, about the possibility that it would undermine his division's profits. Specifically, he feared that the cost of providing compatibility in the lower end of the 360 line (which would be General Products' responsibility) might price the machines out of the market. Later he was to develop some more elaborate arguments against the program.

For a while, some parts of I.B.M.'s marketing organization also resisted the new course. The marketers' concern was centered on one aspect of the 360 program: the central processor—i.e., the computer and its memory without any peripheral equipment—would sell for less than those in other I.B.M. lines. Some salesmen assumed that the difference threatened their commission structures. At I.B.M., salesmen are given quotas expressed in points, with one point representing one dollar's worth of additional net monthly rental income. If a salesman receives a quota of 1,000 points, and then manages to persuade a customer to replace equipment renting for $4,000 monthly with something renting for $5,000 monthly, he has met his quota (and earned a commission). Salesmen were haunted by the notion that lower prices would depress commissions. But this fear gradually dissolved, as it became clear that the lower prices for central processors would be more than offset by heavier sales of peripheral equipment—which were implied in the System/360's expanded capabilities.

THE BATTLE OF SAN JOSE

Long after the company's SPREAD committee had outlined the System/360 concept, and it had been endorsed by I.B.M.'s top

management, there were numerous development efforts going on inside the company that offered continuing alternatives to the concept—and they were taken seriously enough, in some cases, so that there were fights for jurisdiction over them. Early in 1963, for example, there was a row over development work at I.B.M.'s San Jose Laboratory, which belonged to the General Products Division. It turned out that San Jose—which had been explicitly told to stop the work—was still developing a low-power machine similar to one being worked on in World Trade's German lab. When he heard about the continuing effort, A. K. Watson went to the lab, along with Emanuel Piore, and seems to have angrily restated his demand that San Jose cut it out. Some people from San Jose were then transferred to Germany to work on the German machine, and the General Products effort was stopped. In the curious way of organizations, though, things turned out well enough in the end: the German machine proved to be a good one, and the Americans who came into the project contributed a lot to its salability. With some adaptations, the machine was finally incorporated into the 360 line, and now, as the model 20, it is probably selling better than any other in the series.

In the fall of 1963, Tom Watson acted in several ways to speed up work on the 360 program. First of all, he announced the abolition of the corporate management committee, a group of top executives functioning as the chief policy makers of the company. While the move was not formally linked to the 360, the fact was that Watson had become impatient with the excessively crowded agenda of the committee during the years when the 360 was being developed. He believed that too many of the vital decisions about the program were being "bucked upstairs" when they could have been settled at a lower level; abolishing the committee would force these earlier settlements.

Watson also made some new management assignments that reflected the impact of the 360 program on the corporation. Learson was shifted away from supervising product development and given responsibility for marketing, this being the next phase of the 360 program. Gibson took over Learson's former responsibilities. The increasing development of I.B.M. into a homogeneous international organization was reflected in the move up of A. K. Watson from World Trade (he is now corporate vice chairman); he was succeeded by Gilbert Jones, former head of domestic marketing. Piore became a group vice president in charge of research and several other activities.

One reason for Watson's interest in speeding up the 360 program in late 1963 was an increasing awareness that the I.B.M. product line was running out of steam. The company was barely reaching its sales goals in this period. Some of this slowdown, no doubt, was due to mounting rumors about the new line. But there was another, critical reason for the slowdown: major customers were seeking ways of linking separate data-processing operations on a national basis, and I.B.M. had limited capability along that line. Finally, I.B.M. got a distinctly unpleasant shock in December, 1963, when the Honeywell Corp. announced a new computer. Its model 200 had been designed along the same lines as the 1401—a fact Honeywell cheerfully acknowledged—but it used newer, faster, and cheaper transistors than the 1401 and was therefore priced 30 percent below the I.B.M. model. To make matters worse, Honeywell's engineers had figured out a means by which customers interested in reprograming from an I.B.M. 1401 to a Honeywell 200 could do so inexpensively. The vulnerability of the 1401 line was obvious, and so was the company's need for the new line of computers.

It was around this time that some I.B.M. executives began to argue seriously for simultaneous introduction of the whole 360 family. There were several advantages to the move. One was that it would have a tremendous public-relations impact and demonstrate the distinctive nature of I.B.M.'s

new undertaking. Customers would have a clear picture of where and how they could grow with a computer product line, and so would be more inclined to wait for it. Finally, there might be an antitrust problem in introducing the various 360 models sequentially. The Justice Department might feel that an I.B.M. salesman was improperly taking away competitors' business if he urged customers not to buy their products because of an impending announcement of his own company's new model. I.B.M. has long had a company policy under which no employee is allowed to tell a customer of any new product not formally announced by the management. (Several employees have, in fact, been fired or disciplined for violating the rule.) Still, introducing a long line of computers in sequence might put pressure on salesmen, many of whom would be closely questioned by anxious customers, to violate the rule. Announcing the whole 360 line at once would dispose of the problem.

LEARSON STAGES A SHOOT-OUT

Beginning in late 1963, then, the idea of announcing and marketing the 360 family all at once gained increasing support. At the same time, by making the 360 program tougher to achieve, the idea gave Haanstra some new arguments against the program. His opposition now centered on two main points. First, he argued that the General Products manufacturing organization would be under pressure to build in a couple of years enough units of the model 30 to replace a field inventory of the 1401 that had been installed over a five-yer period. He said that I.B.M. was in danger of acquiring a huge backlog, one representing perhaps two or three years' output, and that competitors, able to deliver in a year or less, would steal business away.

Haanstra's other objection in this period related especially to the 360-30, a model that I.B.M. hoped to sell heavily to its old 1401 customers. The trouble was, Haanstra said, that the 360-30 was noncompatible with the 1401; meanwhile Honeywell's 200, which was being sold with that company's new reprograming techniques, might tempt as many as three-quarters of the 1401 users —unless I.B.M. extended and improved its 1401 program. Specifically, he proposed a modernized version, using advanced transistor technology, the 1401-S.

But Haanstra's argument was countered to some extent by a group of resourceful I.B.M. engineers. They believed that the so-called "read-only" storage device could be adapted to make the 360-30 compatible with the 1401. The read-only technique, which involved the storing of permanent electronic instructions in the computer, could be adapted to make the model 30 act like a 1401 in many respects: the computer would be slowed down but the user would be able to employ his 1401 program. I.B.M. executives had earlier been exposed to a read-only device by John Fairclough, the head of World Trade's Hursley Laboratory in England, when he was trying (unsuccessfully) to win corporate approval for his Scamp computer.

Could the device really be used to meet Haanstra's objections to the 360-30? To find out, Learson staged a "shoot-out" in January, 1964, between the 1401-S and the model 30. The test proved that the model 30, "emulating" the 1401, could already operate at 80 percent of the speed of the 1401-S—and could improve that figure with other adaptations. That was good enough for Learson. He notified Watson that he was ready to go, and said that he favored announcing the whole System/360 family at once.

"GOING . . . GOING . . . GONE!"

Haanstra was still not convinced. He persisted in his view that his manufacturing organization probably could not gear up to meet the production demand adequately.

On March 18 and 19, a final "risk-assessment" session was held at Yorktown Heights to review once again every debatable point of the program. Tom Watson Jr., President Al Williams, and thirty top executives of the corporation attended. This was to be the last chance for the unpersuaded to state their doubts or objections on any aspect of the new program—patent protection, policy on computer returns, the company's ability to hire and train an enormous new work force in the time allotted, etc. Haanstra himself was conspicuously absent from this session. In February he had been relieved of his responsibilities as president of the General Products Division and assigned to special duty—monitoring a project to investigate the possibility of I.B.M.'s getting into magnetic tape. (He is now a vice president of the Federal Systems Division.) At the end of the risk-assessment meeting, Watson seemed satisfied that all the objections to the 360 had been met. Al Williams, who had been presiding, stood up before the group, asked if there were any last dissents, and then, getting no response, dramatically intoned, "Going . . . going . . . gone!"

Work on the pricing of the 360 line had already begun. IBM's marketing forecasters go through what is termed a "pricing loop" in determining the optimal price of their products. A price is first set tentatively on a model. Then the marketing organization gives an estimate of the number of models it can sell at that price. This estimate is fed back to the manufacturing group, which must itself estimate whether, given that volume of production, manufacturing costs might be lowered enough to warrant a lower price. This whole cycle is repeated several times, until the most desirable balance between price and volume is achieved. In the case of the 360, the pricing sessions were fairly hectic. One participant recalls, "We reviewed the competitive analysis for perhaps the fifteenth time. We had to take into consideration features that could be built in later with the turn of a screwdriver but that were not to be announced formally. We were pulling cost estimates out of a hat."

The April 7, 1964, announcement of the program unveiled details of six separate compatible computer machines; their memories would be interchangeable, so that a total of nineteen different combinations would be available. The peripheral equipment was to consist of forty different input and output devices, including printers, optical scanners, and high-speed tape drives. Delivery of the new machines would start in April, 1965.

THE NATURE OF THE RISK

With the April 7 announcement, I.B.M. was at last irrevocably committed to the risks that it had always recognized to be inherent in the 360 program. But in the summer of 1964 management was confident that it had made the right decision and had ample resources to see the program through. It was so confident, in fact, that it decided I.B.M. did not need all the cash it had on hand. Cash balances had been increasing for several years, and were approaching $1 billion at the end of 1963; meanwhile, there had been some trend toward increased purchases of equipment instead of rental, and so it was assumed that the need for cash would decline. For these reasons the company decided to prepay $160 million of loans from the Prudential Insurance Co., bearing an average interest rate of 3½ percent; Prudential waived the stipulated premium for prepayment. This stands as one I.B.M. decision about which there is, in retrospect, no controversy—it was a mistake. In 1966 the company has had to establish bank lines of credit totaling the same $160 million, and has to pay about two percentage points more for any of the funds that are used.

The basic announcement of the new line brought a mixed reaction from the competition. The implication that the 360 line would make obsolete all earlier equipment was derided and minimized by rival manufacturers, who seized every opportunity to argue that the move was less significant than it appeared. I.B.M.'s new technology was criticized for being less than pure microcircuitry. The competition also voiced doubts that I.B.M. could achieve any meaningful degree of compatibility in its line; that was unfeasible, they said, and even if achieved, it would be uneconomic for many customers

Despite these depreciatory words, the competition was concerned enough about the System/360 to respond to its challenge on a large scale. During the summer of 1964, General Electric announced that its 600 line of computers would have time-sharing capabilities. The full import of this announcement hit I.B.M. that fall, when M.I.T., prime target of several computer manufacturers, announced that it would buy a G.E. machine. I.B.M. had worked on a time-sharing program back in 1960 but had abandoned the idea when the cost of the terminals involved seemed to make it uneconomic. G.E.'s success caught I.B.M. off base and in 1964 and 1965 it was scrambling madly to provide the same capability in the 360 line. Late in 1964, R.C.A. announced it would use the pure monolithic integrated circuitry (i.e., as opposed to I.B.M.'s hybrid circuitry) in some models of its new Spectra 70 line. This development probably led to a certain amount of soul-searching at I.B.M.

In the end, however, I.B.M. seems to have decided that the threats posed by these new entries in the market were not disastrous. The company felt that the turn to monolithic circuitry did not involve capabilities that threatened the 360 line; furthermore, if and when monolithic circuitry ever did prove to have decisive advantages over I.B.M.'s hybrid circuitry, the company was prepared—the computers themselves and some three-quarters of the component manufacturing equipment could be adapted fairly inexpensively to monolithics. As for time sharing, any anxieties I.B.M. had about that were eased in March, 1965, when Watts Humphrey, a systems expert who had been given the assignment of meeting the time-sharing challenge (he is a nephew of President Eisenhower's Treasury Secretary, George Humphrey), got the job done.

The competitive challenge and its own new capabilities led I.B.M. to announce some additions to the 360 line in 1964 and 1965. One important addition was the model 90, a supercomputer type, designed to be competitive with Control Data's 6800. Another was the 360-44, designed for special scientific purposes. Also, there was the 360-67, a large time-sharing machine. Another, the 360-20, represented a pioneering push into the low end of the market. None of these are fully compatible with the models originally announced, but they are considered part of the 360 family.

THE FLYING SUITCASE SQUAD

It looked, at this point, as if the 360 program was well under control. Then some quite unforeseen troubles broke out in the manufacturing operation. One of the steps in making semiconductors was accomplished by an evaporation process, and the company had used small-capacity evaporators to test the technique. But when large-capacity evaporators were introduced to meet mass-production requirements, the I.B.M. engineers at East Fishkill, New York, ran into some problems, which had to do with metallurgical changes that took place in the larger units. Production at East Fishkill came to a virtual standstill. The company immediately rounded up all the smaller evaporators it could find and used them to work production back up to about 50 percent of the original goal. By the end of 1965 the metallurgical problems were finally solved—but by that time the original delivery schedule was unsustainable. I.B.M. had intended to deliver 1,000 of the new computers by December 31 but settled for 837.

Production of the 360 line was also held up by a maddening series of shortages. There were, for example, critical shortages of epoxy glass, copper laminate, and contact tabs. The tabs carry the connection between the printed circuits and the modules. Manufacturers of these tabs were scattered around the eastern part of the U.S., and none of them were prepared for the kind of demand I.B.M. was unleashing in their markets. In some periods of acute tab shortage, teams of I.B.M. engineers were being yanked off their jobs and sent to work with the suppliers to expedite production. I.B.M. representatives suddenly began appearing at tab plants late in the evening or early in the morning, with suitcases. They would pack all the tabs they could and then fly back to Endicott to keep the production line moving.

Around mid-1965, however, the company gradually became aware that production problems were not its only, or even its greatest, obstacle to getting the 360 program on schedule. While there had been no disposition to underrate the technical difficulties in preparing the programing, no one, it appears, foresaw the appalling management problems that would be associated with them. Part of the management problem was that programers who were desperately needed to develop improved software for the 360 line all during 1963 and 1964 were still spending a great deal of time improving the programs associated with the company's older computers. In any case, there was no real yardstick by which management could gauge the time and manpower required to develop the software for a unique venture like the System/360. Early this year the burden of this problem was thrust on Watts Humphrey, fresh from his triumph on time sharing.

The first thing Humphrey did was to order a complete review of all proposed programs; the second was to eliminate some of the more elaborate functions that had been promised. In I.B.M.'s rather euphemistic terminology, some thirty-one technical capabilities were "decommitted." This move helped to break one bottleneck, but it represented only a minor gain in the total software campaign.

I.B.M. had several managers trying to get the 360 program back on the track in 1964–65. Gibson, who had succeeded Learson in the job, was replaced late in 1964. His successor, Paul Knaplund, lasted about another year.

SHARING THE BAD NEWS

In March, Tom Watson Jr. visited California to address a meeting of "Share," which is a group of users of I.B.M. equipment who meet from time to time to exchange information and opinions about I.B.M. products. Some of the Share members had helped I.B.M. develop its new 360 computer language, and Watson doubtless felt a special obligation to be candid to the group; in any case, he made no effort to paper over his company's problems. Some of his listeners were then grumbling about the postponements of hardware delivery announced the previous October. Watson acknowledged the dissatisfaction of his customers, referred to the problems with software, and even conceded that the momentous decision to announce the entire 360 package at once in April, 1964, may have been "ill advised."

A month later there was another unscheduled development. Watson surprised the financial community by asking his stockholders for $371 million of equity capital. This financing partly reflected the needs that arose out of heavy demand for the 360 line, and in a sense, therefore, it was good news for the stockholders. In the prospectus, however, there was one item of unalloyed bad news: the company had suffered heavy setbacks at the high end of the 360 line— i.e., in its efforts to bring forth a great supercomputer in the tradition of Stretch. It was writing off $15 million worth of parts and equipment developed specifically for the 360-90.

There were signs at about this time that the 360 program was still generating major reshufflements of divisions and personnel. A new management committee had been formed. The corporate staff had been split into two sections, each headed by a group vice president. Dr. Piore had been freed from operational duties and responsibilities and given a license to roam the company checking on just about all technical activities. Some of his former duties are now in a division headed by Eugene Fubini, a former Assistant Secretary of Defense and the Pentagon's deputy director of research and engineering before he joined I.B.M. in 1965. Fubini was one of the first outsiders ever brought into the company at such a high executive level (he is a group vice president); his appointment would seem to confirm the continuing rise in influence of the technical men. Another change represented a comeback for Stephen Dunwell, who had managed the Stretch program and had been made the goat for its expensive failure to perform as advertised. When I.B.M. got into the 360 program, its technical men discovered that the work done on Stretch was immensely valuable to them; and Watson personally gave Dunwell an award as an I.B.M. fellow (which entitles him to work with I.B.M. backing, for five years, on any project of his choosing).

Still another change involved a new management review committee composed of the two Watsons, Learson, and Williams, which was created to help the chief executive run the corporation. Williams, who long had been planning to retire at fifty-five, was prevailed on by Watson to stay as chairman of the executive committee. Finally, Learson, the man who had sparked the 360 from the outset, was named president.

THE FUTURE OF A LINE

System/360 has undergone many changes since the concept was originally brought forth back in 1962 and even since Watson's announcement in 1964. Today nine central processors are being offered in the 360 line; some of them have memories that are much faster than those originally offered. The number of input-output machines jumped from the original forty to over seventy.

These changes should not be viewed as surprising because the 360 family was designed to be adaptable to new technologies and new kinds of peripheral equipment, and has been made adaptable to time sharing. It is still unclear how much of the equipment will ultimately provide this feature. I.B.M. estimates that time sharing will account for about 30 percent of the computer market; other manufacturers think it may take over the whole market.

To date, the 360 program seems, with one large reservation, to be a considerable success. The reservation concerns programing, where a lot of problems are yet to be licked. The company is currently investing very heavily in money and manpower to get them licked: some 2,000 programers and "support personnel" are on the job, and the cost of this effort may run over $200 million.

The payoff on the 360 program will take years to measure, of course. The payoff will involve not only direct System/360 orders (which have been pretty breathtaking so far), but the entire expansion of computer applications implicit in the line's burgeoning capabilities. The program has pushed I.B.M. itself into feats of performance in manufacturing, technology, and communications that its own staff did not believe were possible when the project was undertaken. Because of the 360, the company is a more sophisticated and more thoroughly integrated organization than it was in 1962.

At the same time, the massive difficulties associated with the project, and the retreats from some of the original goals, have led many businessmen to see I.B.M. in a new light. The difficulties have done something to that extraordinary I.B.M. mystique of success. The mystique is probably gone for good—although the successes may just go on becoming greater and greater.

Understanding and Managing Organization-Environment Relations

Relations between organizations and their external environments are the subject of Part III. The first section focuses on *understanding* the nature of organizational environments. Both the Jurkovich and the Emery and Trist articles identify key characteristics of these environments that must be appreciated and managed by organizational decision makers. The two management situations that follow provide concrete examples of how features of the external environment affect organizational decision making and planning processes.

The next section in Part III deals with the *management* of organization-environment relations. The first article by Lorsch sketches a general framework for establishing effective *fits* between organizations and their external environments. The next two articles by Kotter and Miles and his associates outline some *processes* by which these organization-environment fits may be achieved. Kotter deals with organizations' attempt to manage their dependence on outside elements, and Miles and his associates focus on the processes of strategic choice in which decision makers decide not only how to adapt to outside conditions, but what outside conditions they will operate under. The last article describes the emergence of organizational units that specialize in understanding and managing the organization-environment interface. Special attention is devoted to the conditions that create the need for these "boundary-spanning" units and contribute to their effective design and management.

The section on "Organization-Environment Relations" concludes with four managerial situations. The first, "Moving Money," focuses on the fit achieved between the task environment and the design of the "backroom" of a major New York City bank. Next, Mintzberg describes the processes governing strategy formation in Volkswagen and the United States government in Vietnam as they attempted to cope with changing environments. "Inside ITT's Washington Office" portrays the activities and management problems associated with a dynamic boundary-spanning unit. The situations close with an account of how boundary-spanning units may be used to facilitate organizational innovation.

In summary, the conceptual articles and management situations in Part III form a basis for understanding and managing relationships between complex organizations and their changing environments. This basis includes an appreciation not only of the important features of organizational environments together with effective organization-environment "fits," but also of the processes available to managers to achieve understanding and effectiveness in the external affairs domain.

The Causal Texture of Organizational Environments

F. E. Emery
E. L. Trist

IDENTIFICATION OF THE PROBLEM

A main problem in the study of organizational change is that the environmental contexts in which organizations exist are themselves changing, at an increasing rate, and towards increasing complexity. This point, in itself, scarcely needs labouring. Nevertheless, the characteristics of organizational environments demand consideration for their own sake, if there is to be an advancement of understanding in the behavioural sciences of a great deal that is taking place under the impact of technological change, especially at the present time. This paper is offered as a brief attempt to open up some of the problems, and stems from a belief that progress will be quicker if a certain extension can be made to current thinking about systems.

In a general way it may be said that to think in terms of systems seems the most appropriate conceptual response so far available when the phenomena under study—at any level and in any domain—display the character of being organized, and when understanding the nature of the interdependencies constitutes the research task. In the behavioural sciences, the

A paper read at the XVII International Congress of Psychology, Washington, D.C., U.S.A., 20–26 August 1963. A French translation appeared in *Sociologie du Travail*, 4/64. From *Human Relations*, vol. 18, no. 1, Feb. 1965, pp. 21–32. Reprinted by permission.

first steps in building a systems theory were taken in connection with the analysis of internal processes in organisms, or organizations, when the parts had to be related to the whole. Examples include the organismic biology of Jennings, Cannon, and Henderson; early Gestalt theory and its later derivatives such as balance theory; and the classical theories of social structure. Many of these problems could be represented in closed-system models. The next steps were taken when wholes had to be related to their environments. This led to open-system models.

A great deal of the thinking here has been influenced by cybernetics and information theory, although this has been used as much to extend the scope of closed-system as to improve the sophistication of open-system formulations. It was von Bertalanffy (1950) who, in terms of the general transport equation which he introduced, first fully disclosed the importance of openness or closedness to the environment as a means of distinguishing living organisms from inanimate objects. In contradistinction to physical objects, any living entity survives by importing into itself certain types of material from its environment, transforming these in accordance with its own system characteristics, and exporting other types back into the environment. By this process the organism obtains the additional energy that renders it 'negentropic'; it becomes capable of attaining stability in a time-independent steady state—a necessary condition of adaptability to environmental variance.

Such steady states are very different affairs from the equilibrium states described in classical physics, which have far too often been taken as models for representing biological and social transactions. Equilibrium states follow the second law of thermodynamics, so that no work can be done when equilibrium is reached, whereas the openness to the environment of a steady state maintains the capacity of the organism for work, without which adaptability, and hence survival, would be impossible.

Many corollaries follow as regards the properties of open systems, such as equifinality, growth through internal elaboration, self-regulation, constancy of direction with change of position, etc.—and by no means all of these have yet been worked out. But though von Bertalanffy's formulation enables exchange processes between the organism, or organization, and elements in its environment to be dealt with in a new perspective, it does not deal at all with those processes in the environment itself which are among the determining conditions of the exchanges. To analyse these an additional concept is needed—*the causal texture of the environment*—if we may re-introduce, at a social level of analysis, a term suggested by Tolman and Brunswik (1935) and drawn from S. C. Pepper (1934).

With this addition, we may now state the following general proposition: that a comprehensive understanding of organizational behaviour requires some knowledge of each member of the following set, where L indicates some potentially lawful connection, and the suffix 1 refers to the organization and the suffix 2 to the environment:

$$L_{11}, L_{12}$$
$$L_{21}, L_{22}$$

L_{11} here refers to processes within the organization—the area of internal interdependencies; L_{12} and L_{21} to exchanges between the organization and its environment—the area of transactional interdependencies, from either direction; and L_{22} to processes through which parts of the environment become related to each other—i.e. its causal texture—the area of inter-dependencies that belong within the environment itself.

In considering environmental interdependencies, the first point to which we wish to draw attention is that the laws connecting parts of the environment to each other are often incommensurate with those connect-ing parts of the organization to each other, or even with those which govern the exchanges. It is not possible, for example, always to reduce organization-environment relations to the form of 'being included in'; boundaries are also 'break' points. As Barker and Wright (1949), following Lewin (1936), have pointed out in their analysis of this problem as it affects psychological ecology, we may lawfully connect the actions of a javelin thrower in sighting and throwing his weapon; but we cannot describe in the same concepts the course of the javelin as this is affected by variables lawfully linked by meteorological and other systems.

THE DEVELOPMENT OF ENVIRONMENTAL CONNECTEDNESS (CASE I)

A case history, taken from the industrial field, may serve to illustrate what is meant by the environment becoming organized at the social level. It will show how a greater degree of system-connectedness, of crucial relevance to the organization, may develop in the environment, which is yet not directly a function either of the organization's own characteristics or of its immediate relations. Both of these, of course, once again become crucial when the response of the organization to what has been happening is considered.

The company concerned was the foremost in its particular market in the food-canning industry in the U.K. and belonged to a large parent group. Its main product—a canned vegetable—had some 65 per cent of this market, a situation which had been relatively stable since before the war. Believing it would continue to hold this position, the company per-suaded the group board to invest several million pounds sterling in erect-ing a new, automated factory, which, however, based its economies on an inbuilt rigidity—it was set up exclusively for the long runs expected from the traditional market.

The character of the environment, however, began to change while the factory was being built. A number of small canning firms appeared, not dealing with this product nor indeed with others in the company's range, but with imported fruits. These firms arose because the last of the post-war controls had been removed from steel strip and tin, and cheaper cans could now be obtained in any numbers—while at the same time a larger market was developing in imported fruits. This trade being seasonal, the firms were anxious to find a way of using their machinery and retaining their labour in winter. They became able to do so through a curious side-effect of the development of quick-frozen foods, when the company's staple was produced by others in this form. The quick-freezing process demanded great constancy at the growing end. It was not possible to control this beyond a certain point, so that quite large crops unsuitable for quick freezing but suitable for canning became available—originally from another country (the United States) where a large market for quick-frozen foods had been established. These surplus crops had been sold at a very low price for animal feed. They were now imported by the small canners—at a better but still comparatively low price, and additional cheap supplies soon began to be procurable from underdeveloped countries.

Before the introduction of the quick-freezing form, the company's own canned product—whose raw material had been specially grown at additional cost—had been the premier brand, superior to other varieties and charged at a higher price. But its position in the product spectrum now changed. With the increasing affluence of the society, more people were able to afford the quick-frozen form. Moreover, there was competition from a great many other vegetable products which could substitute for the staple, and people preferred this greater variety. The advantage of being the premier line among canned forms diminished, and demand increased both for the not-so-expensive varieties among them and for the quick-frozen forms. At the same time, major changes were taking place in retailing; supermarkets were developing, and more and more large grocery chains were coming into existence. These establishments wanted to sell certain types of goods under their own house names, and began to place bulk orders with the small canners for their own varieties of the company's staple that fell within this class. As the small canners provided an extremely cheap article (having no marketing expenses and a cheaper raw material), they could undercut the manufacturers' branded product, and within three years they captured over 50 per cent of the market. Previously, retailers' varieties had accounted for less than 1 per cent.

The new automatic factory could not be adapted to the new situation until alternative products with a big sales volume could be developed, and the scale of research and development, based on the type of market analysis required to identify these, was beyond the scope of the existing resources of the company either in people or in funds.

The changed texture of the environment was not recognized by an able but traditional management until it was too late. They failed entirely to appreciate that a number of outside events were becoming connected with each other in a way that was leading up to irreversible general change. Their first reaction was to make an herculean effort to defend the traditional product, then the board split on whether or not to make entry into the cheaper unbranded market in a supplier role. Group H.Q. now felt they had no option but to step in, and many upheavals and changes in management took place until a 'redefinition of mission' was agreed, and slowly and painfully the company re-emerged with a very much altered product mix and something of a new identity.

FOUR TYPES OF CAUSAL TEXTURE

It was this experience, and a number of others not dissimilar, by no means all of them industrial (and including studies of change problems in hospitals, in prisons, and in educational and political organizations), that gradually led us to feel a need for re-directing conceptual attention to the causal texture of the environment, considered as a quasi-independent domain. We have now isolated four 'ideal types' of causal texture, approximations to which may be thought of as existing simultaneously in the 'real world' of most organizations—though, of course, their weighting will vary enormously from case to case.

The first three of these types have already, and indeed repeatedly, been described—in a large variety of terms and with the emphasis on an equally bewildering variety of special aspects—in the literature of a number of disciplines, ranging from biology to economics and including military theory as well as psychology and sociology. The fourth type, however, is new, at least to us, and is the one that for some time we have been endeavouring to identify. About the first three, therefore, we can be brief, but the fourth is scarcely understandable without reference to them. Together, the four types may be said to form a series in which the degree of causal texturing is increased, in a new and significant way, as each step is taken. We leave as an open question the need for further steps.

Step One

The simplest type of environmental texture is that in which goals and noxiants ('goods' and 'bads') are relatively unchanging in themselves and randomly distributed. This may be called the *placid, randomized environment*. It corresponds to Simon's idea of a surface over which an organism can locomote: most of this is bare, but at isolated, widely scattered points there are little heaps of food (1957, p. 137). It also corresponds to Ashby's limiting case of no connection between the environmental parts (1960, S15/4);

and to Schutzenberger's random field (1954, p. 100). The economist's classical market also corresponds to this type.

A critical property of organizational response under random conditions has been stated by Schutzenberger: that there is no distinction between tactics and strategy, 'the optimal strategy is just the simple tactic of attempting to do one's best on a purely local basis' (1954, p. 101). The best tactic, moreover, can be learnt only by trial and error and only for a particular class of local environment variances (Ashby, 1960, p. 197). While organizations under these conditions can exist adaptively as single and indeed quite small units, this becomes progressively more difficult under the other types.

Step Two

More complicated, but still a placid environment, is that which can be characterized in terms of clustering: goals and noxiants are not randomly distributed but hang together in certain ways. This may be called the *placid, clustered environment,* and is the case with which Tolman and Brunswick were concerned; it corresponds to Ashby's 'serial system' and to the economist's 'imperfect competition'. The clustering enables some parts to take on roles as signs of other parts or become means-objects with respect to approaching or avoiding. Survival, however, becomes precarious if an organization attempts to deal tactically with each environmental variance as it occurs.

The new feature of organizational response to this kind of environment is the emergence of strategy as distinct from tactics. Survival becomes critically linked with what an organization knows of its environment. To pursue a goal under its nose may lead it into parts of the field fraught with danger, while avoidance of an immediately difficult issue may lead it away from potentially rewarding areas. In the clustered environment the relevant objective is that of 'optimal location', some positions being discernible as potentially richer than others.

To reach these requires concentration of resources, subordination to the main plan, and the development of a 'distinctive competence', to use Selznick's (1957) term, in reaching the strategic objective. Organizations under these conditions, therefore, tend to grow in size and also to become hierarchical, with a tendency towards centralized control and coordination.

Step Three

The next level of causal texturing we have called the *disturbed-reactive environment.* It may be compared with Ashby's ultra-stable system or the economist's oligopolic market. It is a type 2 environment in which there is more than one organization of the same kind; indeed, the existence of a number of similar organizations now becomes the dominant characteristic of the environmental field. Each organization does not simply have to take account of the others when they meet at random, but has also to consider that what it knows can also be known by the others. The part of the environment to which it wishes to move itself in the long run is also the part to which the others seek to move. Knowing this, each will wish to improve its own chances by hindering the others, and each will know that the others must not only wish to do likewise, but also know that each knows this. The presence of similar others creates an imbrication, to use a term of Chein's (1943), of some of the causal strands in the environment.

If strategy is a matter of selecting the 'strategic objective'—where one wishes to be at a future time—and tactics a matter of selecting an immediate action from one's available repertoire, then there appears in type 3 environments to be an intermediate level of organizational response—that of the *operation*—to use the term adopted by German and Soviet military theorists, who formally distinguish tactics, operations, and strategy. One has now not only to make sequential choices, but to choose actions that will draw off the other organizations. The new element is that of deciding which of someone else's possible tactics one wishes to take place, while ensuring that others of them do not. An operation consists of a campaign involving a planned series of tactical initiatives, calculated reactions by others, and counteractions. The flexibility required encourages a certain decentralization and also puts a premium on quality and speed of decision at various peripheral points (Heyworth, 1955).

It now becomes necessary to define the organizational objective in terms not so much of location as of capacity or power to move more or less at will, i.e. to be able to make and meet competitive challenge. This gives particular relevance to strategies of absorption and parasitism. It can also give rise to situations in which stability can be obtained only by a certain coming-to-terms between competitors, whether enterprises, interest groups, or governments. One has to know when not to fight to the death.

Step Four

Yet more complex are the environments we have called *turbulent fields*. In these, dynamic processes, which create significant variances for the component organizations, arise from the field itself. Like type 3 and unlike the static types 1 and 2, they are dynamic. Unlike type 3, the dynamic properties arise not simply from the interaction of the component organizations, but also from the field itself. The 'ground' is in motion.

Three trends contribute to the emergence of these dynamic field forces:

i. The growth to meet type 3 conditions of organizations, and linked sets of organizations, so large that their actions are both persistent and strong enough to induce autochthonous processes in the environment. An analogous effect would be that of a company of soldiers marching in step over a bridge.

ii. The deepening interdependence between the economic and the other facets of the society. This means that economic organizations are increasingly enmeshed in legislation and public regulation.

iii. The increasing reliance on research and development to achieve the capacity to meet competitive challenge. This leads to a situation in which a change gradient is continuously present in the environmental field.

For organizations, these trends mean a gross increase in their area of *relevant uncertainty*. The consequences which flow from their actions lead off in ways that become increasingly unpredictable: they do not necessarily fall off with distance, but may at any point be amplified beyond all expectation; similarly, lines of action that are strongly pursued may find themselves attenuated by emergent field forces.

THE SALIENCE OF TYPE 4 CHARACTERISTICS (CASE II)

Some of these effects are apparent in what happened to the canning company of case I, whose situation represents a transition from an environment largely composed of type 2 and type 3 characteristics to one where those of type 4 began to gain in salience. The case now to be presented illustrates the combined operation of the three trends described above in an altogether larger environmental field involving a total industry and its relations with the wider society.

The organization concerned is the National Farmers Union of Great Britain to which more than 200,000 of the 250,000 farmers of England and Wales belong. The presenting problem brought to us for investigation was that of communications. Headquarters felt, and was deemed to be, out of touch with county branches, and these with local branches. The farmer had looked to the N.F.U. very largely to protect him against market fluctuations by negotiating a comprehensive deal with the government at annual reviews concerned with the level of price support. These reviews had enabled home agriculture to maintain a steady state during two decades when the threat, or existence, of war in relation to the type of military technology then in being had made it imperative to maintain a high level of home-grown food without increasing prices to the consumer. This policy, however, was becoming obsolete as the conditions of thermonuclear stalemate established themselves. A level of support could no longer be counted upon which would keep in existence small and inefficient farmers —often on marginal land and dependent on family labour—compared with efficient medium-size farms, to say nothing of large and highly mechanized undertakings.

Yet it was the former situation which had produced N.F.U. cohesion. As this situation receded, not only were farmers becoming exposed to more competition from each other, as well as from Commonwealth and European farmers, but the effects were being felt of very great changes which had been taking place on both the supply and marketing sides of the industry. On the supply side, a small number of giant firms now supplied almost all the requirements in fertilizer, machinery, seeds, veterinary products, etc. As efficient farming depended upon ever greater utilization of these resources, their controllers exerted correspondingly greater power over the farmers. Even more dramatic were the changes in the marketing of farm produce. Highly organized food processing and distributing industries had grown up dominated again by a few large firms, on contracts from which (fashioned to suit their rather than his interests) the farmer was becoming increasingly dependent. From both sides deep inroads were being made on his autonomy.

It became clear that the source of the felt difficulty about communications lay in radical environmental changes which were confronting the organization with problems it was ill-adapted to meet. Communications about these changes were being interpreted or acted upon as if they referred to the 'traditional' situation. Only through a parallel analysis of the environment and the N.F.U. was progress made towards developing understanding on the basis of which attempts to devise adaptive organizational policies and forms could be made. Not least among the problems was that of creating a bureaucratic elite that could cope with the highly technical long-range planning now required and yet remain loyal to the democratic values of the N.F.U. Equally difficult was that of developing mediating institutions—agencies that would effectively mediate the relations between agriculture and other economic sectors without triggering off massive competitive processes.

These environmental changes and the organizational crisis they induced were fully apparent two or three years before the question of Britain's possible entry into the Common Market first appeared on the political agenda—which, of course, further complicated every issue.

A workable solution needed to preserve reasonable autonomy for the farmers as an occupational group, while meeting the interests of other sections of the community. Any such possibility depended on securing the consent of the large majority of farmers to placing under some degree of N.F.U. control matters that hitherto had remained within their own power of decision. These included what they produced, how and to what standard, and how most of it should be marketed. Such thoughts were anathema, for however dependent the farmer had grown on the N.F.U. he also remained intensely individualistic. He was being asked, he now felt, to

redefine his identity, reverse his basic values, and refashion his organization—all at the same time. It is scarcely surprising that progress has been,
and remains, both fitful and slow, and ridden with conflict.

VALUES AND RELEVANT UNCERTAINTY

What becomes precarious under type 4 conditions is how organizational
stability can be achieved. In these environments individual organizations,
however large, cannot expect to adapt successfully simply through their
own direct actions—as is evident in the case of the N.F.U. Nevertheless,
there are some indications of a solution that may have the same general
significance for these environments as have strategy and operations for
types 2 and 3. This is the emergence of *values that have overriding significance
for all members of the field.* Social values are here regarded as coping mechanisms that make it possible to deal with persisting areas of relevant uncertainty. Unable to trace out the consequences of their actions as these are
amplified and resonated through their extended social fields, men in all
societies have sought rules, sometimes categorical, such as the ten com-
mandments, to provide them with a guide and ready calculus. Values are
not strategies or tactics; as Lewin (1936) has pointed out, they have the
conceptual character of 'power fields' and act as injunctions.

So far as effective values emerge, the character of richly joined, turbulent fields changes in a most striking fashion. The relevance of large classes
of events no longer has to be sought in an intricate mesh of diverging
causal strands, but is given directly in the ethical code. By this transformation a field is created which is no longer richly joined and turbulent but
simplified and relatively static. Such a transformation will be regressive, or
constructively adaptive, according to how far the emergent values adequately represent the new environmental requirements.

Ashby, as a biologist, has stated his view, on the one hand, that
examples of environments that are both large and richly connected are not
common, for our terrestrial environment is widely characterized by being
highly subdivided (1960, p. 205); and, on the other, that, so far as they are
encountered, they may well be beyond the limits of human adaptation, the
brain being an ultra-stable system. By contrast the role here attributed to
social values suggests that this sort of environment may in fact be not only
one to which adaptation is possible, however difficult, but one that has
been increasingly characteristic of the human condition since the beginning
of settled communities. Also, let us not forget that values can be rational as
well as irrational and that the rationality of their rationale is likely to become more powerful as the scientific ethos takes greater hold in a society.

MATRIX ORGANIZATION AND INSTITUTIONAL SUCCESS

Nevertheless, turbulent fields demand some overall form of organization that is essentially different from the hierarchically structured forms to which we are accustomed. Whereas type 3 environments require one or other form of accommodation between like, but competitive, organizations whose fates are to a degree negatively correlated, turbulent environments require some relationship between dissimilar organizations whose fates are, basically, positively correlated. This means relationships that will maximize cooperation and which recognize that no one organization can take over the role of 'the other' and become paramount. We are inclined to speak of this type of relationship as an *organizational matrix.* Such a matrix acts in the first place by delimiting on value criteria the character of what may be included in the field specified—and therefore who. This selectivity then enables some definable shape to be worked out without recourse to much in the way of formal hierarchy among members. Professional associations provide one model of which there has been long experience.

We do not suggest that in other fields than the professional the requisite sanctioning can be provided only by state-controlled bodies. Indeed, the reverse is far more likely. Nor do we suggest that organizational matrices will function so as to eliminate the need for other measures to achieve stability. As with values, matrix organizations, even if successful, will only help to transform turbulent environments into the kinds of environment we have discussed as 'clustered' and 'disturbed-reactive'. Though, with these transformations, an organization could hope to achieve a degree of stability though its strategies, operation, and tactics, the transformations would not provide environments identical with the originals. The strategic objective in the transformed cases could no longer be stated simply in terms of optimal location (as in type 2) or capabilities (as in type 3). It must now rather be formulated in terms of *institutionalization.* According to Selznick (1957) organizations become institutions through the embodiment of organizational values which relate them to the wider society.[1] As Selznick has stated in his analysis of leadership in the modern American corporation, 'the default of leadership shows itself in an acute form when *organizational* achievement or survival is confounded with *institutional* success' (1957, p. 27). '. . . the executive becomes a statesman as he makes the transition from administrative management to institutional leadership' (1957, p. 154).

The processes of strategic planning now also become modified. In so far as institutionalization becomes a prerequisite for stability, the determination of policy will necessitate not only a bias towards goals that are congruent with the organization's own character, but also a selection of goal-paths that offer maximum convergence as regards the interests of other parties. This became a central issue for the N.F.U. and is becoming one now for an organization such as the National Economic Development Council, which has the task of creating a matrix in which the British economy can function at something better than the stop-go level.

Such organizations arise from the need to meet problems emanating from type 4 environments. Unless this is recognized, they will only too easily be construed in type 3 terms, and attempts will be made to secure for them a degree of monolithic power that will be resisted overtly in democratic societies and covertly in others. In the one case they may be prevented from ever undertaking their missions; in the other one may wonder how long they can succeed in maintaining them.

An organizational matrix implies what McGregor (1960) has called Theory Y. This in turn implies a new set of values. But values are psychosocial commodities that come into existence only rather slowly. Very little systematic work has yet been done on the establishment of new systems of values, or on the type of criteria that might be adduced to allow their effectiveness to be empirically tested. A pioneer attempt is that of Churchman and Ackoff (1950). Likert (1961) has suggested that, in the large corporation or government establishment, it may well take some ten to fifteen years before the new type of group values with which he is concerned could permeate the total organization. For a new set to permeate a whole modern society the time required must be much longer—at least a generation, according to the common saying—and this, indeed, must be a minimum. One may ask if this is fast enough, given the rate at which type 4 environments are becoming salient. A compelling task for social scientists is to direct more research onto these problems.

SUMMARY

(a) A main problem in the study of organizational change is that the environmental contexts in which organizations exist are themselves changing —at an increasing rate, under the impact of technological change. This means that they demand consideration for their own sake. Towards this end a redefinition is offered, at a social level of analysis, of the causal texture of the environment, a concept introduced in 1935 by Tolman and Brunswik.

(b) This requires an extension of systems theory. The first steps in systems theory were taken in connection with the analysis of internal processes in organisms, or organizations, which involved relating parts to the whole. Most of these problems could be dealt with through closed-system models. The next steps were taken when wholes had to be related to their environments. This led to open-system models, such as that introduced by

Bertalanffy, involving a general transport equation. Though this enables exchange processes between the organism, or organization, and elements in its environment to be dealt with, it does not deal with those processes in the environment itself which are the determining conditions of the exchanges. To analyse these an additional concept—the causal texture of the environment—is needed.

(c) The laws connecting parts of the environment to each other are often incommensurate with those connecting parts of the organization to each other, or even those which govern exchanges. Case history I illustrates this and shows the dangers and difficulties that arise when there is a rapid and gross increase in the area of relevant uncertainty, a characteristic feature of many contemporary environments.

(d) Organizational environments differ in their causal texture, both as regards degree of uncertainty and in many other important respects. A typology is suggested which identifies four 'ideal types', approximations to which exist simultaneously in the 'real world' of most organizations, though the weighting varies enormously:

1. In the simplest type, goals and noxiants are relatively unchanging in themselves and randomly distributed. This may be called the placid, randomized environment. A critical property from the organization's viewpoint is that there is no difference between tactics and strategy, and organizations can exist adaptively as single, and indeed quite small, units.

2. The next type is also static, but goals and noxiants are not randomly distributed; they hang together in certain ways. This may be called the placid, clustered environment. Now the need arises for strategy as distinct from tactics. Under these conditions organizations grow in size, becoming multiple and tending towards centralized control and coordination.

3. The third type is dynamic rather than static. We call it the disturbed-reactive environment. It consists of a clustered environment in which there is more than one system of the same kind, i.e. the objects of one organization are the same as, or relevant to, others like it. Such competitors seek to improve their own chances by hindering each other, each knowing the others are playing the same game. Between strategy and tactics there emerges an intermediate type of organizational response—what military theorists refer to as operations. Control becomes more decentralized to allow these to be conducted. On the other hand, stability may require a certain coming-to-terms between competitors.

4. The fourth type is dynamic in a second respect, the dynamic properties arising not simply from the interaction of identifiable compo-

nent systems but from the field itself (the 'ground'). We call these environments turbulent fields. The turbulence results from the complexity and multiple character of the causal interconnections. Individual organizations, however large, cannot adapt successfully simply through their direct interactions. As examination is made of the enhanced importance of values, regarded as a basic response to persisting areas of relevant uncertainty, as providing a control mechanism, when commonly held by all members in a field. This raises the question of organizational forms based on the characteristics of a matrix.

(e) Case history II is presented to illustrate problems of the transition from type 3 to type 4. The perspective of the four environmental types is used to clarify the role of Theory X and Theory Y as representing a trend in value change. The establishment of a new set of values is a slow social process requiring something like a generation—unless new means can be developed.

NOTE

1. Since the present paper was presented, this line of thought has been further developed by Churchman and Emery (1964) in their discussion of the relation of the statistical aggregate of individuals to structured role sets: "Like other values, organizational values emerge to cope with relevant uncertainties and gain their authority from their reference to the requirements of larger systems within which people's interests are largely concordant."

REFERENCES

ASHBY, W. ROSS (1960). *Design for a brain*. London: Chapman & Hall.

BARKER, R. G. & WRIGHT, H. F. (1949). Psychological ecology and the problem of psychosocial development. *Child Development* **20**, 131–43.

BERTALANFFY, L. VON (1950). The theory of open systems in physics and biology. *Science* **111**, 23–9.

CHEIN, I. (1943). Personality and typology. *J. soc. Psychol.* **18**, 89–101.

CHURCHMAN, C. W. & ACKOFF, R. L. (1950). *Methods of inquiry*. St. Louis: Educational Publishers.

CHURCHMAN, C. W. & EMERY, F. E. (1964). On various approaches to the study of organizations. Proceedings of the International Conference on Operational Research and the Social Sciences, Cambridge, England, 14–18 September 1964. To be published in book form as *Operational research and the social sciences*. London: Tavistock Publications, 1965.

HEYWORTH, LORD (1955). *The organization of Unilever*. London: Unilever Limited.

LEWIN, K. (1936). *Principles of topological psychology*. New York: McGraw-Hill.

LEWIN, K. (1951). *Field theory in social science.* New York: Harper.

LIKERT, R. (1961), *New patterns of management.* New York: Toronto, London: McGraw-Hill.

McGREGOR, D. (1960). *The human side of enterprise.* New York, Toronto, London: McGraw-Hill.

PEPPER, S. C. (1934). The conceptual framework of Tolman's purposive behaviorism. *Psychol. Rev.* **41**, 108–33.

SCHUTZENBERGER, M. P. (1954). A tentative classification of goal-seeking behaviours. *J. ment. Sci.* **100,** 97–102.

SELZNICK, P. (1957). *Leadership in administration.* Evanston, Ill.: Row Peterson.

SIMON, H. A. (1957). *Models of man.* New York: Wiley.

TOLMAN, E. C. & BRUNSWIK, E. (1935). The organism and the causal texture of the environment. *Psychol. Rev.* **42**, 43–77.

A Core Typology of Organizational Environments

Ray Jurkovich

This article presents a typology of organizational environments and discusses the more relevant relationships. Although environments have been receiving increasing attention, a set of widely accepted, related concepts which effectively describe the subject has not been developed (Organ, 1971). Theorists, in discussing environments, tend to deal in vague terms. A set of established, but more sharply defined terms are presented here in a structured manner, resulting in a core typology. This approach simplifies the subject area, avoiding the case in which the number of possible relationships between phenomena is so large that central issues are obscured by a mass of details.

Designing a typology under these conditions forces one to emphasize the descriptive and deemphasize—or avoid—the predictive features. Thus, a typology becomes an analytic tool that may be applied as an instrument to stimulate thinking on alternate directions in which decision makers can move their organizations. The results might lead them to make adjustments they would otherwise not attempt. Decision makers, of course, do this anyhow, but a good tool can facilitate the process. The next step is to develop predictive staements which, if empirically supported, can make a typology even more powerful.

From *Administrative Science Quarterly*, Vol. 19, no. 3 (September 1974), pp. 380–394. Reprinted by permission.

The main effort here is not to create new concepts. A few new notions are incorporated simply to provide analytical distinctions that are felt to be of importance. In addition, a lengthy review and comparison of the major terms is not undertaken. Some relevant concepts are borrowed from the most important works to date and these are modified for greater clarity. Integration with other concepts is undertaken for the purpose of broadening the current limited scope. Thus, this article is essentially an excursion in broadening and refining the existing parts of a conceptual puzzle and adding a few others to contribute to a better understanding of the whole.

THE EXTERNAL ENVIRONMENT

Two frequently cited works provide a basis for a general description. Thompson's (1967: 70–73) simple four-cell typology and Lawrence and Lorsch's (1967: 23–54) dichotomization of diversity and dynamic offer perceptions which appear to be the same:

Thompson

1. Homogeneous-stable
2. Homogeneous-shifting
3. Heterogeneous-stable
4. Heterogeneous-shifting

Lawrence and Lorsch

1. Low diversity and not dynamic
2. Low diversity and highly dynamic
3. High diversity and not dynamic
4. High diversity and dynamic

Both sets of authors discuss the problems of differentiation between and adaption to directly related organizational components having different kinds of environments. Presumably, the more disparate the environments with which two directly related components are confronted, the more difficult it is to integrate the components.

The typologies above are used here with revisions and additions. Homogeneity and heterogeneity, for instance, are included in the complexity continuum. Emery and Trist's (1965) typology is revised and incorporated in connection with the change rate continuum. The end result is 64 types, a list that can be further expanded by creation of additional categories. The reason for working with the chosen variables is that some of them occur persistently in the literature, but they are presented in a very restricted context. Frequently, attention has been concentrated on two major independent variables when in fact others play an equally important role.

The terms used can be arranged to form the matrix in Figure 1.

GENERAL CHARACTERISTICS

In designing action alternatives, decision makers or members of scanning units must analyze a variety of environmental factors or questions. Four major ones are (1) complexity (2) the routineness or nonroutineness of a problem-opportunity state (3) the presence of organized or unorganized sectors—elements or units of the environmental field (4) and the issue of whether such sectors are directly or indirectly related to the organization. Sectors refer to those elements or units of behavior—human and nonhuman—in the environment that decision makers perceive as relevant for the organization. Environment is the total set of sectors outside of the organization which, in turn, is a role cluster bound together by a set of rules that prescribes behavior and establishes sanctions when rules are violated.

COMPLEXITY

Child (1972: 3) provides a definition of environmental complexity that can be used here: "Environmental complexity refers to the heterogeneity and range of activities which are relevant to an organization's operations." In other words, the more diverse the relevant environmental activities and the more there are, the higher the complexity. His meaning of heterogeneity, however, is not clear. Duncan (1972) deals with environmental simplicity and complexity by considering the variety of locations of decision factors, but just how the various locations differ is assumed rather than explicitly stated. Duncan's finding that heterogeneity has little effect on uncertainty is hardly surprising if one interprets it on the basis of Simon's (1962) definition of complexity. Since in Simon's terms complexity consists of simple pieces added together, the effect of complexity on uncertainty will not be significant. The way in which Buckley defines environment perhaps offers another basis for the present purpose (1967: 62, italics his):

> The environment, however else it may be characterized, can be seen at bottom as *a set* or ensemble of more or less *distinguishable elements,* states, or events, whether these discriminations are made in terms of spatial or temporal relations, or properties. Such distinguishable differences in an ensemble may be most generally referred to as "variety."

Nevertheless, the meaning of variety is not simple. Complexity or noncomplexity is a question of perception and, as Starbuck (1973: 24)

Movement		General Characteristics																
		Noncomplex								Complex								
		Routine				Nonroutine				Routine				Nonroutine				
		Organized		Unorganized		Organized		Unorganized		Organized		Unorganized		Organized		Unorganized		
		*D	I	D	I	D	I	D	I	D	I	D	I	D	I	D	I
Low change rate	Stable	1																16
	Unstable																	
High change rate	Stable	49																
	Unstable																	64

* D = direct   I = indirect

Figure 1   A Core Typology of Organizational Environments

stated, "The same environment one organization perceives as unpredict-able, complex, and evanescent, another organization might see as static and easily understood." Any inductively derived definition of complexity results in a very abstract statement that is either too vague or too trivial or both. In this article the terms complex and noncomplex refer to whether or not decision makers perceive their environments as complex or noncom-plex; the terms do not refer to any universal operational definition that might be applied to a large sample of organizations.

Organizations dealing with noncomplex environments have one advantage: there are fewer critically important information categories necessary for decision making. When environmental sectors are essentially the same, the range of their expected behavior, strategies and tactics, and formal goals is easier to account for. Complex information systems are not required for environmental monitoring, since the critical information cate-gories are limited even though the range and size of the sectors can be large.

Organizations confronted with a complex environment must come to grips with a memory problem. Since the human brain has a limited capacity for retaining conscious information, special units that can monitor indi-vidual or clusters of sections are required (Thompson, 1967: 70). These units monitor the activities of others and routinely report the behavioral patterns to critical decision-making points that make decisions based on that information and/or feed back requests for further information and advice.

ROUTINE AND NONROUTINE
PROBLEM-OPPORTUNITY STATES

A decision maker can perceive parts of his environment as posing a prob-lem or offering an opportunity. The distinction between problems and opportunities need not be made here, since problems can be perceived as opportunities and opportunities can quickly present their share of prob-lems. Whatever the case, decision makers can look at environmental prob-lem-opportunity states as being approachable as routine or nonroutine activity. This idea is borrowed, with revisions, from Perrow (1970: 75–80) and March and Simon (1958). A decision maker can approach an opportu-nity or problem by asking whether his organization possesses the technol-ogies, people, cash reserves, and other resources to handle or solve a situ-ation without disturbing current activities. It can also be an uncertain or risky adventure he thinks the organization can handle but he is more speculative than realistic in his expectations.

Decision makers' perceptions of their environments depend upon conditions in their own organizations. The process of looking at the environment and comparing it with internal resources can suggest alternatives permitting the organization to take better advantage of opportunities it would otherwise have to pass up.

Problem-opportunity states assume varying degrees of uncertainty. If decision makers approach a situation and find that the analytical strategies resemble computational, judgmental or compromise, or inspirational strategies (Thompson, 1967: 134), they know, at least subjectively, what degree of uncertainty is attached to the problem. Computational strategies assume a high degree of certainty; judgmental and compromise strategies assume a moderate degree of uncertainty, but for different reasons; and an inspirational strategy assumes a high degree of uncertainty. One can ascertain quickly whether the organization can handle the situation as a routine or a nonroutine activity on the basis of the strategies which decision makers design.

The degree of routineness and nonroutineness might also be determined by the state of the information problems. These problems can take three forms: people complain that (a) they cannot gain access to critical information, (b) they cannot trust a significant portion of the information, or (c) the set of information categories they need for decision making is uncertain. The higher the percentage of members with information problems and the more severe those problems, the more nonroutine the problem-opportunity state is.

Where noncomplex routine sectors dominate the environmental field, the basis for decision rests more on deductions and inductions from the information itself. Specialists can exchange opinions and arrive at a consensus much more easily, rapidly, and completely and with greater certainty of having made the right decision. Frequently, nonspecialists can make the decisions, since there is an expected pattern for which standardized or programmed decisions are available.

Faced with complex routine sectors, decision makers primarily devote their attention to the decisions themselves, leaving the information gathering problems—mostly concerning quantity and range—to the decentralized monitoring units. Manageability is a secondary problem.

Organizations with predominantly noncomplex, nonroutine environmental sectors are faced with information problems that cannot always be solved with a data bank. In this situation there is reliance on noncalculable judgments or advice from specialists. Decision-making battles take place over opinions. Information is uncertain or incomplete and reliability and validity cannot be determined.

Faced with complex nonroutine sectors, decision makers concentrate less on the decision and more on the information: they must frequently negotiate, both directly and indirectly, with those at the information source in an attempt to extract better or more useful information than they have access to in order to develop standardized decision program packages.

Experience in earlier but similar situations whose abstract pattern resembles the current one is also an important resource here.

In this situation one indicator of managerial and executive frustration could be their turnover rate or expressions of a role occupant's continuous effort to establish alternative information sources in an attempt to reduce ambiguity in order to survive or perform adequately. The interaction frequency of the role occupant's information-monitoring units would be higher and more intense in this case. This would be indicated partly by the longer time involved and partly by a higher number of conflicts. Finally, individuals would work with exceptions more often than performing routine administrative tasks.

March and Simon (1958: 151) and Ashby (1968) have stated that there appear to be limits to the amount of routine and nonroutine activities and variety—complexity—that an individual can comfortably handle. This discussion suggests that complexity and nonroutineness can impose limits on each other. The amount of complexity might be limited by nonprogrammable activities and vice versa.

This notion may be equally valid when applied to the whole organization. In other words, what are the limits of environmental nonroutine complexity an organization can handle before entropy sets in? It could well be that the boundary of entropy is expanded by such techniques as decentralization. Centralization of large multigoal organizations requires much more rule enforcement, and once faced with an uncomfortable environment, it may be cheaper in the long run to allow specific decisions to be made at lower levels. The whole is greater than the sum of its parts. The boundary of entropy can be expanded without changing the fact that the organization as a whole remains.

ORGANIZED AND UNORGANIZED SECTORS

Another important aspect of the problem is whether sectors are organized or unorganized. Evan's (1966) discussion of organizational sets, an extension of Merton's role set, does not include more cumbersome, unorganized situations. Throughout this article the term sector is used to avoid excessive emphasis on interorganizational behavior. While almost everybody has an organizational role, he also plays nonorganizational roles. An important one, for instance, comes under the category of customer. We are not organized members of every organization. Almost everyone has only one central organization in which he earns money to exchange for products and services produced by others. Frequently, we must satisfy certain kinds of criteria to receive services—as patient or student, for instance—but customers and clients generally do not perform any of the essential activities of the supplying organization or strive for its goals, nor do those organizations demand that they do so. An organization's environment consists of more than organizational sets. Here, the term sector is used with a much broader meaning: both organizational sets and categories which represent unorganized individuals and groups are included. Some organizations must concern themselves with the young, old people, or housewives; people in these categories are not in an organizational role network in which interdependencies are present.

An organized sector refers to another organization or cluster of organizations covered by a formal rule set that is legitimate only for the role set intended by those rules. An unorganized sector refers to those actual or potential customers who use the organization's goods and services but are not bound together by formal or informal rules requiring patterned coordination interaction to reach formally defined goals.

The most important distinction between the two is that organized environments are generally easier to come to grips with than unorganized sectors. For example, Rickson and Simpkins (1972: 286) stated that "Firms are considerably more secure in dealing with a work force represented by a few unions than they would be if power among workers was more dispersed and 'wildcat' strikes were common." Information about the limits of what an organized sector can do and wants to do is more accessible and frequently is explicitly stated in records or by official spokesman. An amount and variety of information is generally available on a routine basis that is not available from unorganized sectors. With the latter, intervening organizations (for example, advertising and market research agencies) or an intervening subsystem of the organization is frequently required to conduct research to assess the attractiveness or legitimacy of goals. Once a goal has been assessed, decision makers can debate whether a decision program should be chosen and, if so, which one, after which they can discuss the necessary alterations or if necessary, design new ones. The question is not whether organized sectors exhibit more certain or uncertain behavior than unorganized sectors; the problem is to locate the sources of certainty or uncertainty in the exchange chain.

DIRECTLY AND INDIRECTLY RELATED SECTORS

The notion of directly related and indirectly related environments can contribute to the tracing of relevant problems. Direct environments refer to those sectors with which the organization exchanges without the use of intermediaries. Indirect environments refer to those sectors which produce goods and services or provide resources that must be acquired through intermediaries. An example of the latter is found in government agencies, which contract out to an organization which, in turn, contracts out to another to fulfill contractual agreements beyond its own capacity. Such subcontracting firms cannot handle large projects, but specialize in something that others do not. They can therefore get to the resource base indirectly. Wholesalers are intermediaries for retailers' organizations and retailers are often intermediaries between wholesalers and customers.

Indirect sectors can also eventually function as direct sectors. After an intervening market research organization has established which sectors have a need or desire for a particular activity, the organization can work directly with those sectors. This occurs frequently in multinational and intergovernmental relations where two, three, and sometimes even more parties are involved in negotiations. After the negotiations have been successfully completed through indirect contact, formal, direct relationships are often arranged. The fact that organizations can design ways to get to indirect sectors is important since there are all kinds of legal, political, ideological, and ethical problems that can allow or disallow desired exchanges. For instance, Perrow (1970: 126) cited a case showing how important it is to know the environment of a potential customer. A salesman from organization A wanted to sell something to C in a foreign country, but B was already doing so and B was also supplying inputs into A that might have been cut off had A decided to sell to C. Another good example, provided by Sethi (1972: 69–73), demonstrates the web of direct and indirect relationships in which Coca Cola became entangled between the United States and Israel when confronted with the decision to grant Israel a bottling franchise. The notion of direct and indirect relationships might also aid the theorist in defining the kinds of strategies and tactics that organizations use to avoid conflicting spheres of influence.

Finally, the more indirect an exchange sector is, the more difficult it is to exercise control over or act upon that sector. Identification of the interdependence series makes it possible to design methods to alter the interdependencies in a desired way. If the interdependencies cannot be altered or altered only partially, knowledge of them can lead to ideas about how the host organization could change its own structure, policies, and goals to become at least more responsive.

ENVIRONMENTAL CHANGE

Little has been said thus far about the movement of environmental sectors. On this point, Thompson (1967), Lawrence and Lorsch (1967), Burns and Stalker (1961), and Emery and Trist (1965) have made major contributions. Although there are undoubtedly many ways in which an organization might change, attention is limited here to formal goals, since information about organizational goals can be obtained from quarterly reports and other sources. This does not mean that a study concerned with organization environments should focus on goal changes. A change in the political situation, law revisions, and even the weather might be more relevant than goals. For example the 1972–1973 winter in the Netherlands was very mild and this just about put a few bootmaking companies out of business. A study of formal goal changes in environmental sectors might be relatively easy to conduct. Unorganized sectors, however—made up of customers, for example—have no such things as formal goals. One might then examine needs, but this could also prove to be extremely difficult to analyze. A more reasonable approach might be to ask decision makers and boundary agents about the kinds of ongoing changes that they perceive as the most relevant.

Environmental change—apart from internal influences—is an important determinant of internal behavior. Organizations are chiefly concerned with diagnosing changes, but they are no less concerned with change rates and their own change rate or timing capacity. One noticeable characteristic of the literature on organizational environments is the vagueness of the discussion on the meaning of the term change rate. This discussion attempts to bring operational clarity to the term. Internal change capacity is not explored here because the body of literature on the planning and the processes of internal change lies mainly outside the scope of this article. The term change rate will be used here in place of the notion of a stable-shifting or dynamic environment. Change rate takes into account the number of major goal alterations during a given period. The higher the number of major goal alterations over the same period, the higher the change rate; the lower the number, the lower the change rate.

Organizations can do one thing or a combination of things in conjunction with their goals: add new ones, drop some, and attempt to revise others. Consequently, change rates should be defined to reflect this behavior. Even a rough estimate of environmental change rates permits comparisons that can facilitate diagnosis. For example, two competitors may have completely different change rates, but the slower organization may actually be doing better. It might be doing the right thing at the right time, whereas the other may be frantically trying to catch up or wildly seeking a better survival base. Change rates are important indicators for the timing of the delivery of new goals and services to the market.

At a more abstract, theoretical level, one can study the expansion and contraction between the types of goals—societal, output, system, product, and derived—suggested by Perrow (1970: 126) and patterns between organizations. Knowing what one's exchange units are doing and how they are shifting can help an organization to keep up with its competitors.

Change rate can be dichotomized into low and high, with these terms being defined relative to one another. Clusters of organizations offering similar products and services may have high change rates in comparison with other clusters, but within clusters, too, there can be lows and highs, some of the lows being closely equivalent to a high in another cluster. Organizations should, however, be able to distinguish which sectors and groups of sectors are moving rapidly, to avoid competing with those whose pace could be difficult to equal.

Hage and Aiken (1970: 33–38) have suggested that internal complexity may lead to a high change rate, which implies that at least two of the variables here are causally related. But they speak of complexity among professional occupations that could cause high change rates. They offer an explanation for a certain type of situation. "However, the effect of this form of complexity," to use Hall's (1972: 151) words, "is minimized when other organizational characteristics are examined." Interest in defining complexity is relatively new in organizational theory. Hall's excellent summary points to the variety of sociological approaches that have produced a variety of results and interpretations, all of which are credible.

Stable and Unstable Change

Both low and high change rates can be dichotomized further into stable and unstable rates. Stable rates occur in a situation where most of the important factors influencing a situation are changing predictably in value and where the set of critical factors remains constant. Unstable rates take place when a situation is loose and erratic. Here, both the value of important variables —independent and intervening—and the kinds of relevant variables in the set are changing unpredictably. Instability can also be represented by an erratic step-function and as Boulding (1971: 20) notes: "Many real systems are governed by step-functions which at certain points display changes in the relation of inputs to outputs, and because you never quite know when steps are going to be taken, step-functions make the future terribly hard to predict." In addition, Ashby (1954: 53) states, "Every stable system has the property that if displaced from a resting state and released, the subsequent movement is so matched to the initial displacement that the system is brought back to the resting state." Thus, in unstable environmental conditions, unpredictability is increasing. While organizations may be rational, the participants can rationalize guesswork or speculate on outcomes that are rationally induced. Participants may also select information sets which, although originally perceived as relevant, become the cause of tension and conflict as the overlap between individual information sets diminishes. The conflict frequently takes the form of debating about the use of certain information units as well as about the outcomes.

The meaning of stability and instability is perhaps more problematic than organizational theorists are willing to admit. At times stability is perceived as the opposite of movement or change. Consider, for example, Thompson's stable-shifting and Duncan's static-dynamic continua. A good example of how theorists fuse the concepts of change rate and stable or unstable environments is found in a recent article by Child (1972: 3) who referred to environmental variability as the "degree of change that . . . in turn may be seen as a function of three variables: (1) the frequency of changes in relevant activities; (2) the degree of difference involved at each change; (3) the degree of irregularity in the overall patterns of change—in a sense the 'variability of change.'"

The first two variables are treated as change rate in the present article. The third involves the stability or instability of an environment. This distinction is made so that the importance of both can be appreciated.

There are four types of environmental movement: low, stable change; high, stable change; low, unstable change; and high, unstable change—all having different effects on an organization.

An organization with predominantly low but stable change rate environmental sectors would be one in which the planning of strategies, operations, and tactics can be expected to be essentially trouble free, since predictability is greater where uncertainty is low and fluctuates in a patterned way. Although the environment changes, it does not change quickly and long-range planning can be conducted without taking into account any major environmental alteration during any planned period.

Organizations with a low but stable change rate environment—the change rate remaining essentially constant but tending to change—will be able to pursue their intentions, but controlling the changing environmental factors become more difficult. Internal buffer mechanisms become broader; more roles are assigned to the filtering, coding, and interpreting of information; and current policies and technologies are manipulated so that they can still be used. Older forms are transformed into new versions under the mild threat of unfamiliar behavior. It is easier to rely on reformulated older techniques than to invent new ones, especially when there is a belief that they will work. In the absence of experience with innovations, reformulation is about the only thing an organization can resort to, and this is probably not dangerous.

Thus, with a low but unstable change rate, the planning of strategies, operations, and tactics is not a serious problem. It becomes more complex than dealing with a stable change rate but not uncomfortably problematic. There are more kinds of alternatives, the assumptions underlying each have to be clearly outlined, and assumptions about when to switch to other alternatives have to be more carefully examined. Boundary role activity increases, too, in time and content; the feedback interaction between boundary roles and buffer units increases in number and time and the coordination of feedback loops must be given more attention. Finally, managerial coalitions are farther apart than in an organization with predominantly low but stable changing environmental sectors. Under stable conditions, conflicts can be resolved more quickly and the resulting peace lasts longer. Under unstable conditions, conflict resolution is more difficult and the subsequent period of cooperation is much shorter. The basis of conflict lies in differences in the interpretation of information, the use of different kinds of information, and the assignment of different values, all of which appear appropriate. Political activity increases but can be controlled. Subordinates demand more responsibility in the form of contributing opinions. The status of boundary roles also increases and threatens the higher status role occupants unaccustomed to erratic environmental conditions.

High change rates and stable environments create difficult problems for organizations, too, but for different reasons. Since the change rate is increasing, timing and goal formulation—and reformulation—become crucial. Decisions about what goals and services to add, decrease, or completely drop, and how much of each and when, become frustrating. The design of strategies, operations, and tactics can still be accomplished, but the design itself becomes a goal, that is, it becomes a means of maintaining stability within the organization. Analytical methodologies gain in importance and both routine and nonroutine search behaviors are instituted to find newer or better methodologies offered in the environment; more emphasis is devoted to searching for new ideas within the organization.

Long-range planning is accomplished, but the plans become more general. Incremental planning is adopted to reach the alternative goals which have been generally outlined. The question becomes one of what short-range alternative strategies, operations, and tactics are needed to reach every step to every alternative goal and then when one step is completed, changes in the initially planned strategies, operations, and tactics must be considered. Plans are held open and subject to change, but they are not impossible to construct.

Conflict between coalitions arises not only over what and when but also the methodologies considered and stability within coalitions diminishes. Coalitions are loose and changing; they resemble the intersector change rate and instability in the environment (Cyert and March, 1963: 39).

Because the change rate is high, the frequency of interaction between occupants of boundary roles, decision-making centers, and buffer units is high. Whenever efficiently possible, information is sent directly to decision makers on a continuous basis so that changes in the environmental change rates can be detected with immediacy. Monthly and quarterly reports become old news as the emphasis is on shorter intervals. Decision makers often spend more time in familiarizing themselves directly with the sectors in order to better understand and anticipate changes. To facilitate muddling through, they attempt to assign subjective probabilities to possible changes sometimes by using industrial spies but more often by establishing informal contacts with executives in other organizations and with relevant, indirect information channels within sectors.

Organizations with environmental sectors characterized by instability and high change rates live on the brink of chaos. Rittel and Weber (1973) discussed the problems encountered in planning in this type of environment. Some of the following ideas resemble many of those they developed. Situations change rapidly and unpredictably. No matter how exhaustive and reliable information is, it tends to increase the potential for conflict. Strategies, operations, and tactics in environmental sectors reach such levels of generality and abstraction that counter moves cannot be specifically defined over the long run without allowing for radical, spontaneous revisions. Methodologies are sought which provide a neater, more complete picture. The rise of PPBS—Planning, Programming, Budgeting Systems—in the last 15 years represents an attempt to establish a more precise view of the general situation. Intensive effort to reduce or transform complexity, in unpredictable, rapidly changing organized and unorganized environmental sectors, is intended to yield a more certain view of the situation. Another indicator of the above is the growing interest and application of General Systems Theory, in which the study of wholes is stressed.

Organizations in this state design coping tactics, mainly in the form of decentralization and multidisciplinary research units, in the hope that more specific planning will emerge. Because of increasing interaction, the boundary roles, roles in buffer systems, and executive roles tend to fuse. This is by no means a stable fusion. The structure of the fused roles drifts in unstructured ways. Occasionally, boundaries are temporarily closed to permit analysis of what has taken place and to generate more standardized decision programs, however short lived they may be.

Frequently, when environmental sectors make impossible demands on the organization, the organization does nothing or repeats unsatisfactory, standardized behavior. When the organization does nothing, decision makers fear the risk involved in the disparity between its means and the demands made. A sort of cognitive dissonance develops and the decision makers retreat to safe ground. When organizations repeat standardized behavior, even though it is known to be unsatisfactory to the sectors, they are reflecting trained incapacity. Is it any wonder that organizations are charged with conservativism? In the face of instability and rapid change in the environment—mainly in the unorganized sectors of society—large investments or safe investments are made to stabilize the organization.

Each decision maker uses his own model of the situation, unrelated to the models of his peers, and consequent discussions become tense political debates. Internal and external consultants are often called for analysis and advice in an effort to keep the organization together. In the last few years process consultation (Schein, 1969) has been developed. One important purpose of this method is the cooling off of relations between people. This, of course, does not eliminate the basis of conflict, but it at least contributes to the development of mutual understanding and thus enhances the growth of the members' capacities for mutual tolerance.

When an organization is not afraid of its environment, it can and does plan strategies, operations, and tactics, but frequently on a coping basis. Problem solving is replaced by problem coping. Problems are never completely solved and people are forced to learn to live with the consequences of the unsolved aspects of problems. Some resources are always kept in reserve for investment in initially high-risk goals that start to prove themselves. New Venture Teams (Wileman and Freese, 1972) are set up solely to produce new ideas which keep the organization going.

Organizations generally gravitate towards stability or at least find it preferable. A highly unstable and rapidly changing environment can be perceived as dangerous. Most organizations try to avoid it and if that proves impossible, they either manipulate it to increase its stability or develop methods to maintain or restore internal stability. On the other hand, organizations may temporarily opt for a chaotic situation to loosen crystallized—ultrastable—or boring situations to get a larger share of a market, to create new ones, to extend services to other sectors, and so forth.

This discussion of change and stability resembles in part the notions offered by Emery and Trist (1965), who develop a typology consisting of four types: placid-random, placid-clustered, disturbed-reactive, and turbulent. They stated that the order of the four types constitutes an ascending order of uncertainty. Nevertheless, for the first and fourth types, the uncertainty seems to be about the same for different reasons. A placid-random environment is characterized by discrete sectors. There is no interdependency chain, but if there is, it is temporary and changes randomly. With a turbulent environment, the rapid movement and the complexity of relations are uncertainty sources.

There is a great deal of overlap between strategies and tactics associated with the first type. The fourth type is characterized as an environment in which general rules are substituted for strategies, operations, and tactics. The more general and abstract a discussion becomes, the more overlap there is between categories, thus further supporting the suggestion that the two types are similar. General rules and overlapping strategies and tactics appear to be essentially the same. If this is an ascending order of uncertainty, as the authors have suggested, why have they suggested an ascending order of more certain means to reduce the environmental uncertainty? The ascending order of certain organizational means with increasing environmental uncertainty applies only to the first three types: type 1, intermingling of strategies and tactics: type 2, development of strategies and tactics; and type 3, strategies, operations, and tactics. Organizational means become more complex in the face of environmental uncertainty, but not more certain. If one does not understand the situation with which he is confronted, he can expect to have problems in handling it (March and Simon, 1958: 140). It is reasonable to assume that under conditions of uncertainty,

TABLE 1   Environmental Effect on Planning

ENVIRONMENTAL MOVEMENT	DESIGN OF STRATEGIES, OPERATIONS, AND TACTICS
Low change rate/stable	Easily accomplished
Low change rate/unstable	More complex
High change rate/stable	Very complex—characterized by muddling through
High change rate/unstable	Most difficult—problem coping in the place of problem solving

goal setting and means are also more uncertain and complex, since there is an obvious resemblance to the problems of handling increasingly difficult environments.

In spite of these difficulties, some of the terms offered here suggest a revised scheme that makes use of a few of Emery and Trist's (1965) concepts.

SUMMARY AND CONCLUSIONS

The following four propositions will serve to sum up the extreme types of organizational environments discussed. (See figure.)

1. Organizations with type 1 environment have relatively minor information problems; can design long-range strategies, operations, and tactics more easily—more rapidly and in more detail—and implement them without major alterations; have relatively little internal conflict potential; possess a more mechanical structure; have clearly defined and predictable, gradually changing coalitions; and have relatively few problems with their existing decision-making programs when the environment changes.

2. Organizations confronted with a type 49 environment experience the same problems as do those with a type 1 environment, but they experience a higher degree of uncertainty concerning timing in the control of internal problem states.

3. Organizations confronted with a type 64 environment have major information problems; have very abstract, tentative sets of strategies, operations, and tactics and cannot execute them without expecting major alterations; have very vague coalitions that change unpredictably; and are constantly redesigning decision-making programs or constantly making exceptions to existing decision-making programs.

4. Organizations confronted with a type 16 environment have the same problems as are experienced by organizations with a type 64 environment, but they are able to predict and control internal problem states much more easily.

This typology is not a matrix of interdependencies; each cell represents a different situation. It is offered as a core typology, since other dimensions can be added. For example, the direct category might be further subtyped to include friendly competitor, unfriendly competitor, neutral competitor, and the like to obtain an even better idea of how organizations mutually adjust their negotiating styles.[1]

In addition, a typology of environments may be useful in bringing out the fact that certain classes or organizations more rightfully belong to certain kinds of environments. If this is true, a fresh start might be made with organizational typologies, arriving at something considerably more powerful than what is presently available. That is, more useful organizational typologies might be derived by first examining the different environmental situations organizations encounter and then and only then, constructing an organizational typology with types possessing internal organizational characteristics that are reasonably unique to a particular organization environment.

More than a decade ago Dill (1962) noted that typologies of environments were nonexistent. Even though the literature on organization-environment relationships has been growing and has added a great deal of useful information for both theory and practice, a reasonably comprehensible typology has yet to appear. The typology developed above can be seen as an instrument to map the rates and direction of environmental movements, that is, how different kinds of sectors in different locations are moving with respect to each other.

Knowing the environmental map or the direction of its movement may mean switching from one type of strategy and tactic to another. The decision to cooperate, coopt, by coopted, enter a coalition, drop out, or opt for conflict, could be partially dependent upon the environmental state (Thompson and McEwen, 1958). Lammers (1974) has developed a typology of strategies and tactics used by university authorities to counter student opposition. These strategies and tactics are applicable under certain kinds of conditions; mixed forms are also possible under mixed conditions and when the conditions destabilize or change, the mixed forms should congruently change.

General conditions can also influence environmental maps, as Hall (1972: 298–312) has pointed out. This effect is easily observed in cross-cultural studies. For instance, anyone familiar with the management journals knows that business negotiations with the Chinese and Russians are prolonged, detail-ridden exercises that appear to be attempts to keep an agreement stable even if conditions should happen to change. Recessions, inflations, changes in political regimes, and cultural factors can all cause organizations to change relations and alter the change rates. Even the possibility of an unfriendly political personality not yet formally in office can influence the situation. George McGovern's candidacy, for instance, was perceived by many people as one of the principal causes of a drop in the stock market. The launching of new products may be postponed because demand could diminish during a recession. On the other hand, new or revised products may be created to exploit whatever limited resources there are. Foreign investments may be curtailed in countries where a political regime is considering a nationalization program and this may create a partial chain reaction with directly and indirectly related sectors.[2]

Follett (Metcalf and Urwick, 1957) pointed to a dialectical phenomenon in organizational behavior: solved problems create new ones. With the suggested typology, one may be able to locate the source of problems to better study this phenomenon and to design appropriate models of problem states with a complex set of acceptable controls that could prevent the ongoing succession of crises.

Pushing problems off on other sectors only removes the symptoms from one sector and leaves the agony of treating the causes to someone else which may, in turn, create even larger problems for another sector. A good example of the latter occurs when measures to prevent robberies and stealing are instituted: it is hardly to be expected that criminals with criminal skills will change to honest work just because one kind of resource base has disappeared. Suppression of the symptom does not cure the disease; the suppressed symptoms simply appear elsewhere, compounding already existing problems or forming a new set.

NOTES

1. A set of formal operationalized hypotheses has not been developed here, because the purpose was to theoretically establish a descriptive core typology. Informal hypotheses have, however, been used to demonstrate how organizations might react to various kinds of environmental situations. Some of these informal hypotheses were supported by examples, others by reference to other studies, and a few by speculative logic.

2. The exchange currencies—power, status, money—and their combinations are not included, but it would be interesting to see how organizations and their sectors manipulate their resources and those of others within various situations. The ideas of Ilchman and Uphoff (1969), Haas and Drabek (1973: 224–228), and Blau (1966) provide a set of theoretical notions which, unfortunately, are too complex for this article.

REFERENCES

ASHBY, W. ROSS (1954). *Design for a Brain.* New York: Wiley.
———— (1968). "Principles of the self-organizing system." In Walter Buckley (ed.), *Modern Systems Research for the Behavioral Scientist:* 108–118. Aldine.
BLAU, PETER M. (1966). *Exchange and Power in Social Life.* New York: Wiley.
BOULDING, KENNETH E. (1971). "The dodo didn't make it: survival and betterment." *Bulletin of Atomic Scientists:* 27: 19–22.
BUCKLEY, WALTER (1967). *Sociology and Modern Systems Theory.* Englewood Cliffs, N.J.: Prentice-Hall.
BURNS, TOM, and G. M. STALKER (1961). *The Management of Innovation.* London: Tavistock.
CHILD, JOHN (1972). "Organizational structure, environment and performance: the role of strategic choice." *Sociology:* 6: 2–21.
CYERT, R. M., and J. G. MARCH (1963). *A Behavioral Theory of the Firm.* Englewood Cliffs, N.J.: Prentice-Hall.
DILL, WILLIAM R. (1962). "The impact of environment on organizational development." In Sidney Mailick and Edward H. van Ness (eds.), *Concepts and Issues in Administrative Behavior:* 94–109. Englewood Cliffs, N.J.: Prentice-Hall.
DUNCAN, ROBERT B. (1972). "Characteristics of organizational environments and perceived environmental uncertainty." *Administrative Science Quarterly,* 17: 313–327.
EMERY, F. E., and E. L. TRIST (1965). "The causal texture of organizational environments." *Human Relations,* 18: 21–32.
EVAN, WILLIAM M. (1966). "The organization set: toward a theory of interorganizational relations." In J. D. Thompson (ed.), *Approaches to organizational design:* 174–191. Pittsburgh: University of Pittsburgh.
HAAS, J. EUGENE, and THOMAS E. BRABEK (1973). *Complex Organizations: A Sociological Perspective.* London: Collier-Macmillan.
HAGE, JERALD, and MICHAEL AIKEN (1970). *Social Change in Complex Organizations.* New York: Random House.
HALL, RICHARD H. (1972). *Organizations: Structure and Process.* Englewood Cliffs, N.J.: Prentice-Hall.
ILCHMAN, WARREN, and NORMAN THOMAS UPHOFF (1969). *The Political Economy of Change.* Berkeley, Calif.: The University of California Press.
LAWRENCE, PAUL R., and JAY W. LORSCH (1967). *Organization and Environment.* Boston: Harvard Business School.
LAMMERS, C. J. (1974). "Tactics and strategies adopted by university authorities to counter student opposition." In Donald E. Light, Jr. (ed.), *The Dynamics of Protest* (forthcoming).
ORGAN, DENNIS (1971). "Linking pins between organization and environment." *Business Horizons,* 14: 73–80.
MARCH, JAMES G., and HERBERT A. SIMON (1958). *Organizations.* London: Wiley.
METCALF, HENRY C., and L. URWICK (eds.) (1957). *Dynamic Administration: The Collected Papers of Mary Parker Follett.* London: Pitman.
RICKSON, ROY E., and CHARLES SIMPKINS (1972). "Industrial organization and the ecological process: the case of water pollution." In Merlin Brinkerhoff and

Phillip R. Kunz (eds.), *Complex Organizations and Their Environments:* 282–292. Dubuque, Iowa: Brown.

RITTEL, HORST W. J., and MERLIN M. WEBER (1973). "Dilemmas in a general theory of planning." *Policy Sciences,* 4: 155–169.

SCHEIN, E. H. (1969). *Process Consultation: Its Role in Organizational Development.* Reading, Pa.: Addison-Wesley.

SETHI, S. PRAKASH (1972). "Coca-Cola and the Middle East crises: international politics and multinational corporations." In *Advanced Cases in Multinational Business Operations:* 69–73. Pacific Palisades, Calif.: Goodyear.

SIMON, H. A. (1965). "The architecture of complexity." *General Systems Review,* C: 63–76.

STARBUCK, WILLIAM (1973). *Organizations and Their Environments.* Berlin: International Institute of Management.

THOMPSON, JAMES D. (1967). *Organizations in Action.* London: McGraw-Hill.

THOMPSON, JAMES D., and WILLIAM J. McEWEN (1958). "Organizational goals and environment: goal setting as an interaction process." *American Sociological Review,* 23: 23–31.

WILEMAN, DAVID, and HOWARD FREESE (1972). "Problems new-venture teams face." *Innovation,* 28: 40–47.

When a Bank Tries to Change Neighborhoods

BusinessWeek

The pattern is painfully familiar. A major place of business finds itself trapped in a declining, predominantly black, inner-city area. The usual solution, of course, is to pack up and move to a more promising part of town. And that is exactly what South Shore National Bank of Chicago has decided to do, despite the protests of local residents that its departure would hasten their area's decline.

The difference is that South Shore National is federally regulated, and sometime within the next few weeks the Comptroller of the Currency is scheduled to hand down what could be a landmark decision on a ticklish question: Is a bank's major responsibility to its shareholders or to the community it serves?

Each side makes a compelling case. William Lloyd, a community activist and executive director of the South Shore Commission, claims that the bank's move would impose a "devastating psychological strain on the people here. The bank is the last bastion that represents stability. We're saying, 'Reach out to the little people who need you.'"

Bank officials, on the other hand, argue that because Illinois allows no branch banking, South Shore National must relocate to grow. President Leonard Musich adds that if his bank leaves the area, two other banks within a 1½-mi. radius will be able to compete more effectively and serve the needs of the community quite as well as South Shore National. The bank's attorney, Elmer Johnson, sums up the bank's position more pragmatically: "We are not a public agency established to solve community problems at the expense of stockholders."

BIG SAVERS

A few years ago, Chicago's South Shore was one of the city's most affluent communities, and the savings of its residents built $72-million in deposits for South Shore National, elevating it into the top 8% of the nation's banks. Today, however, working-class blacks have replaced the community's country club set, the bank's deposits have dwindled to $53-million, and the bank wants out. Its new home, pending approval of the Comptroller of the Currency, will be the Indiana Standard building in the $1.5-billion, 83-acre Illinois Center being built in downtown Chicago.

The first to benefit by the move would be the bank's older stockholders. They want to sell, but have been unable to negotiate a deal because of the bank's location. But if South Shore National moves, there are buyers for 80% of its 200,000 shares of stock, bringing in a total of $4.8-million. The prospective buyers include Indiana Standard, Illinois Central Industries, and the Pritzker family of Chicago.

Bank officials say that the 11,000 people who will work in the Indiana Standard building would provide an immediate market comparable to a city of 25,000. "We feel this is adequate to support a bank," Musich testified at recent public hearings on the proposed relocation.

women's specialty store insists that the loss of the bank would represent the loss of a major commercial lure. "It brings people in," she says of the bank. "On Wednesday when the bank is closed, we might as well close up shop."

Yet almost in the same breath, community residents complain that there is now a lack of services and marketing initiative at the bank. Activist Lloyd labels the bank's marketing policy a "programmed failure," deliberately aimed at losing deposits and producing a good reason to move.

One particularly soured retailer is Conrad Brown, owner of a food, liquor, and drug store near the bank. "A year ago when I wanted to open this store," he says, "I wanted to borrow $1,000. I wasn't a stranger, since I had banked there seven years." Yet, says Brown, South Shore National would only give him the money if he permitted the bank to freeze $1,000 in his savings account. "I went to another bank in Hyde Park where I had never done any business and got the money." Brown estimates that half of the businesses on his street take their deposits elsewhere, "because the bank only takes your money but won't give you anything for it." While other area banks demand only $50 to $200 in minimum deposits for high-interest accounts, another critic of South Shore National notes that it requires a $1,000 minimum.

RESIDENTS' CASE

The bank's position stirs angry responses among community residents. South Shore dentist Edward Schaaf claims that his practice is still "financially rewarding," but that having to open new business and personal accounts and take a safety deposit box in another bank "would place me at a great inconvenience." Sidney Tillis, manager of Kaplan Shoes, says, "If the bank leaves, I'll have to go with Brinks or Armour, and it will cost close to $100 a month." The owner of a

BANK'S REPLY

Bank officials argue that they have gone after new business—with few, if any, results. "We have done a lot of marketing," Musich insists—particularly in the installment loan area. He claims that the bank staged a city-wide radio promotion two years ago, but the results were "completely nil." This is one area, he adds, that "we could readily measure, since we offered premiums, and we still have most of them."

What do the bank's prospective buyers

think about it all? "Our only interest is downtown," says Jay Pritzker. Adds Indiana Standard's vice-president for finance, L. C. May: "The bank has been trying to survive in a declining neighborhood. A $1-million bank would provide all the banking services that the community would require. But the residents feel that the move is a slap in the face, a matter of pride. It's a tough situation, and I don't blame them for being concerned, but economics are economics."

The guess on both sides of the debate is that the Comptroller of the Currency will feel the same way. Says Lloyd resignedly: "The attitude of the buyers is—It's nothing personal, just business. It's been predicted that we won't win. I, for one, am also predicting this."

Piercing Future Fog in the Executive Suite

BusinessWeek

For corporate planners and the top executives who rely on their advice, the world has never looked as hostile or as bewildering as it does today. The very uncertainties, from the clouded economic outlook to the energy crisis, that make sophisticated forward planning more vital than ever before, also make accurate planning that much more difficult. "Annual financial plans for a number of companies are going to hell this year," says Jerome Jacobson, senior vice-president of Bendix Corp. "In a rapidly changing economic environment, some plans are out of date in three to six months."

So the very nature of corporate planning is undergoing a dramatic change, and the companies that fare best in coming years may well be the ones that adapt most quickly to the new styles in planning. Today's changes are most clearly visible in two areas:

FLEXIBILITY

Instead of relying on a single corporate plan with perhaps one or two variations, top management at more and more companies is now getting a whole battery of contingency plans and alternate scenarios. "We shoot for alternative plans that can deal with either/or eventualities," says George J. Prendergast, in charge of planning at chemical giant E. I. du Pont de Nemours & Co.

SPEED

Companies are reviewing and revising plans more frequently in line with changing conditions. Instead of the old five-year plan that might have been updated annually, plans are often updated quarterly, monthly, or even weekly. Arizona Public Service Co. last year adopted a "dynamic" budget that looks ahead two years but is rolled over every month. At Ralston Purina Co., a 1% change in the price of a prime commodity kicks off a change in the company's cost models and the whole corporate plan may change accordingly.

This is heady stuff for corporate planners, because it was not so long ago that planning was a marginal blue-sky sort of operation that seldom got more than a nod from top management. But forward planning became a crucial function and the planner a central figure in the company in the complex, fast-changing business world of the 1960s and 1970s. "Planning has become intimately associated with the whole management process," says George A. Steiner, professor of management at UCLA.

And the role of planning will continue to grow because the outlook is so hazy—not just for business but for all society. What worked before may not work in the future, and a company's very survival may depend on how well it gauges the future. "Many companies feel we are moving into a new era," says Alonzo L. McDonald, managing director of McKinsey & Co. "The 1950–70 assumptions probably will not be good guidelines for the 1970s on."

Indeed, the 1950–70 assumptions simply are not working today and virtually every company has had to rethink not only the content of its plan but also how it makes its plan.

Xerox Corp., for example, started taking a fresh look at its forward plan when "macroeconomics came thundering down at us," says George R. White, vice-president for product planning. The company's re-evaluation not only led to deferring the building of a new corporate headquarters and to the laying off of workers. Xerox also decided to issue, for the first time, a permanent straight debt issue—for $450-million. "It's a

straw in the wind," says White, "not as a short-term quick reaction but that the financial basis on which corporations of our size operate is changing."

AN UNCERTAIN FUTURE

For the short term, many companies have simply dusted off their "worst-case" scenarios, a process that C. A. Rundell, Jr., a Tyler Corp. executive vice-president, calls "stray bullet to the heart drills," while still clinging to a basic optimism. For the long term, an assortment of previously unthinkable assumptions, ranging from worldwide political upheaval to an end to economic growth, are all at once on everybody's mind.

Many planners, too, see the world at an economic and cultural watershed. American Standard, Inc., Vice-President Alan C. Root, the company's top planner, argues that while it is difficult to accept the idea of a long-term slowdown, "This is the beginning of a period of great change. It's a transition time for Western economies. What we are concerned with is the period of transition—the next five years."

For corporate planners, and even more for the senior executives who must act on their advice, the problem is not so much that some day they will have to deal with a future that may be cataclysmic, but that they must plan today for a future that has never been more uncertain. Nor are today's often conflicting economic forecasts—even for the immediate months ahead—of much real value to the planner. "Each time you get a forecast," says Glen L. Ryland, Frontier Airlines executive vice-president, "it sets the turnaround date back."

So planners are literally obliged to stress flexibility, which means multiple contingency plans, rather than a single forward plan, and more frequent revisions. It is not a very satisfactory solution, but as James E. Matheson, director of the Decision Analysis Group at Stanford Research Institute, says, "it is one way of coping with uncertainty." Henry M. Boettinger, corporate planning director at American Telephone & Telegraph Co., calls it "pulsing your way into the future."

In the end, of course, that puts more pressure on top management, which must operate with an eye to numerous plans instead of being able to follow a single scenario. At Exxon Corp., for instance, most-probable-case forecasts have been replaced by less definitive "envelopes" that include a range of possibilities. Says Brice A. Sachs, deputy corporate planning manager: "Today you still have to have a game plan. How do you get to that? Top management judgment and intuition. We don't really pin some things down anymore. There's a lot more thrown at the management."

LEARNING TO REACT QUICKLY

Not only is the decision harder to make, but the stakes at Exxon and elsewhere keep going higher. Until recently, for example, the investment necessary to procure a barrel of oil per day was about $350, says Sachs. Now, for the same amount of oil from the North Sea the investment will be some $9,000. Going to synthetic fuels, the cost could climb to $20,000. The executive must also look further into the future. Adding an additional 300,000 bbl. a day of productive capacity in Saudi Arabia could be carried out in a year or two. To provide for the equivalent capacity through a synthetic plant that converts coal to liquid form will take at least six years. As UCLA's Steiner says: "Time has telescoped. The longevity of a product is much shorter than ever before. But the period of research and development has stretched."

The shocker is the extent to which business did not see all of this coming. "We completely blew interest rates in 1974," admits John B. McKinnon, financial vice-president of Hanes Corp., the hosiery and apparel maker. "We projected a maximum rate of 8% and it was 12%. And we significantly missed our total figures for the fourth quarter. We were forecasting and budgeting for a 10% increase in sales and actually netted out a 7% decrease."

Inland Steel Co.'s director of corporate planning, Philip D. Block III, says his company undershot the mark on last year's sales volume. Both the volume of the steel business and its rate of return in the last two years exceeded the planning estimates. "There was no way we could foresee changes in exchange rates—which made U.S.-made steel more competitive with the foreign product in this country," he says. "Nor were we able to foresee how quickly we would be able to pass along the cost-increase pressures which built up during the period of controls," says Block.

But the downturn, if it threw everyone's primary plans out the window, did prove the value of contingency planning in helping companies turn on a dime, and today that is what planning is all about. "If you can't forecast, all you can do it react quickly," says Gary L. Neale, president of Planmetrics, Inc., a Chicago-based company that currently is helping 76 corporations computerize their planning process to speed up reaction time even more.

Except as theoretical exercises, multiple plans had little use in most companies until recently. Now that it is clear that no planner will ever bat 1.000, they are fast becoming standard operating procedure. "By January," says Hanes' McKinnon, "it appeared that the contingency plans [for recession] that the divisions had drawn up back in November were likely to be the real world." They assumed 15% sales drops and listed specific expense cuts to be made, ranked in six categories of priorities, with dollar figures attached to each. By January some of the divisions had already begun to implement the recession plans. All divisions were ordered to submit new budgets by Apr. 1— three months earlier than usual. The L'eggs division, the company's largest, already is implementing a "Mar. 1 plan" based on forecasts of still lower sales and earnings for the remainder of the year.

This year a lot of "worst case" contingency plans came off the shelf. Mead Corp. has three short-term contingency plans—A, B, and C, standing for aggressive, basic, and conservative. Mead's basic B plan, formulated last October, was scrapped very early. "We even felt our C plan was too optimistic," says Vice-Chairman William W. Wommack, who is in charge of strategy. "We tore everything up and asked for a new ABC, and our current B plan is even lower than our earlier C plan." Mead's new B plan, drawn in January, projects sales of $1.4-billion in 1975, down from the earlier B plan projection of $1.7-billion.

Xerox' White says that the company cannot operate by its originally devised 1975 budget. "We are not distraught at the fact that we have to replan early in the year, but we've never had to do it as broadly as we are having to do it now," he says. Indeed, Xerox now finds itself making and revising plans on almost a nonstop basis.

Similarly, says Bendix' Jacobson, "Our plan requires so many reviews today that it has become a continuous process. It is always being adjusted."

EXPLORING MORE ALTERNATIVES

Perhaps it is merely a reflection of today's pessimism, but most companies in their planning see less risk in cutting back too much than in pruning too little. Frontier Airlines developed a detailed plan for "reasonable size shrink" back in August, when it was in the midst of its best year in history but could see signs of a leveling off and decline in passengers. In mid-November the decision was made to "go down" and the planned shrinkage—a 6% cut in flying hours and a personnel reduction of 142—went into effect in January. A second "shrink" for

which planning began in January became effective this month. "We know how to go back up pretty fast," says Ryland. "Our strategy is to anticipate and lead on the downside and wait until we see positive action before we go up."

But contingency plans are flourishing not because business is bad, of course, but because it is so unpredictable. "In this age you can't plan on your plans," says SRI's Matheson. "You should be hedging your bets." Thomas H. Naylor, president of Social Systems, Inc., of Durham, N.C., found in a survey of 346 corporations that 73% were either using or developing a corporate planning model. The chief reason, cited by 78% of all the current users of models, was that they enabled the company to explore more alternatives in its planning.

The real problem arises, as Exxon's Sachs suggests, when it comes to deciding which plan to act upon. Sun Oil Co., which established a corporate planning department five years ago, still was projecting one scenario for the future until last fall. Now it has three. But managers are still asked to develop only one strategy from all those plans. "We formed a strategy sensitive to change that can accommodate a wide divergence of economic possibilities," says Rudolph Dutzman, Sun's director of corporate planning.

Daniel T. Carroll, president of Gould, Inc., says that "when your predictions don't work out you don't abort planning, you abort that plan. You also have to have a fire alarm of some sort that says now is the time a contingency has arisen. For example, if incoming orders fall below a certain level for three consecutive months, then implement Plan A. Sometimes we don't even wait for our own incoming orders to drop, but look at the incoming orders of our customers for a signal. That takes artistry."

What really takes artistry, though, is extending scenarios far into the future. It is necessary because today's complex investment and development decisions have longer lead times than ever. Xerox has pushed its long-range planning parameters out to 1990. "We've grown the length of the plan, and we now have five tracks plotted through 1990, where we used to have just one," says Michael A. E. Hughes, vice-president for marketing and technical services.

"The net of all this, when you come to some kind of bottom line, is that we have a company posture that has to be laid against a wider range of scenarios and outcomes than we've used in the past," says White. "This is a substantial change in planning style, because we used to feel comfortable enough about the center line to plan to it and say we'll adjust to discrepancies."

At General Electric Co., which has pioneered in corporate planning, the range of scenarios is also widening. "More than we've ever done before, we are developing this year a look at completely different views of future external environments over a five-year period, in the U.S. and the world," says Reuben Gutoff, senior vice-president for corporate strategic planning. "The point is to stretch our minds and really test."

GE might take a conventional "base" view of the economy that has a one in seven chance of happening and an alternate view that has only a one in ten chance, then synthesize elements of the alternate view with the most probable event. "That's a pretty tough thing to do," says Gutoff, "but that's the thing we're trying to do differently this year."

THE SCRAMBLE FOR NEW TECHNIQUES

The inability to project ahead with any certainty also lies behind the scramble for new techniques that allow plans to be "rolled over" more often. Companies increasingly are turning to the computer for help in assessing the impact of dozens of constantly changing variables on their businesses. While corporations can trace some effect from hundreds of factors, most concentrate their attention on the eight to twelve most crucial to their industry—rate of inflation, consumer spending on nondurables, interest rates, for example. At Tyler, managers have a list of 8 to 10 "key influencing factors" which they suggest their board members keep an eye on all year. The price of ammonium nitrate, an important ingredient for its newly acquired explosives business, currently is at the top of the list.

Even monitoring a dozen variables on a timely basis, though, and evaluating their cumulative effects, can tax a planning department. With a computer, suggests Planmetric's Neale, not only can long-range and short-range plans be updated continuously, so whenever managers refer to them they are current, but any number of what-if questions can be asked. The probable effect of a change to LIFO from FIFO accounting can be gauged, for example, or the actual effect of a rise in the cost of a critical component can be factored in. At Dow Chemical Co., 140 separate cost inputs—constantly revised—are fed into the corporate model. Such factors as major raw materials costs and prices by country and region are monitored weekly.

Hewlett-Packard Co., using its own H-P 2000 computer, runs as many as 50 different scenarios on four different models— economic statement, intermediate range plan, econometric, and aggregate sales. One major issue last year—whether to sell $100-million of long-term debt—involved some 100 different scenarios on the computer. The models helped the company finally decide to stay with in-house financing.

But planners today are also increasingly concerned about the kind of information that cannot be analyzed by a computer. They worry about the tendency of executives to extrapolate from the statistics of the past. "People tend to project from where they are today," says Mead's Wommack. "The truth of the situation is that the 1973 and 1974 period was an upward blip. On the other hand, 1975 will be way below the trend, and people may project off that."

In addition, the unique event changes everything. "Strategic planning is necessary precisely because we cannot forecast," says management philosopher Peter F. Drucker, noting that a single book, Rachel Carson's *Silent Spring* in the 1950s, changed the attitude of a whole civilization toward the environment. Last year, it was the oil crisis that forced everyone to rethink all their plans.

Chances are slim that planners will foresee world-shaking events sooner than anyone else, but most are trying. American Standard, for example, has factored into its plans the probability of a critical worldwide grain shortage in the late 1970s, in the wake of 5-degree wind changes that will reduce rain in the major producing areas of the world. "We're interested in the price of grains because if grains go up to $6 or $8 a bushel, it's inflationary and we'll have to pay more for money," explains American Standard's Root.

Projecting the effects of external imponderables can be a complex task. Atlantic Richfield Co. has an environmental analysis group that provides an overview, built upon surveys and interviews, of "social factors" such as predicted modes of transportation and consumer preferences. "You can't just extend the graphs on these things, you've got to really understand them," says Robert E. Wycoff, director of corporate planning. "They're not governed by economics."

Similarly, Dow Chemical has a product management team that analyzes new social and political pressures and relates them to its business. The result is what Dow calls its "ESP" (for economic, social, political) report, a formal document that attempts to evaluate risks from all of these factors.

With that kind of orientation, planning proves to be a kind of acid test for managers. "If you have a contributory planning process, then the quality of the five-year plan is a direct function of lower-level management. It is as strong or as weak as they

are," says Street. Fluor comptroller Ronald G. Cullis says that one unit's five-year plan was "so unsatisfactory that it forced a change in management at the unit." In another instance, two Fluor operating units spent so much time together developing their five-year plans that it prompted a consolidation and a reorganization of the corporate structure. "Corporate planning forces exposure of what really is," sums up Street.

If planning is now working its way up from the bottom in most large companies there still is a focal point of planning at the corporate level that is becoming increasingly significant—resource allocation among the units of a company. Frequently this is the key to the corporation's centralized authority.

At GE, for example, planning is carried out simultaneously but with a different perspective at corporate headquarters and in its 43 strategic business units. "Some type of corporate glue was necessary to tie these pieces together," says GE's Gutoff. "That recognition led to the planning work that pulled together these decentralized businesses. The business units were charged with doing their own planning, but overlaying that was planning at the corporate level, where we're going to have to make some tradeoffs, some resource allocations. It's really the interplay of these two activities that led to the functioning of the whole GE system."

Corporate planning at RCA Corp. also emphasizes determining which businesses will grow and which will not. "The top-down look on the businesses is as competitive investments," says George C. Evanoff, vice-president for corporate development at RCA, which has five major operating groups and 15 primary profit centers. "We're putting more emphasis on where the resource should be placed than how it should be applied. For example, do we back domestic satellites? Our essential plan is an articulation of strategies saying this area should receive more attention, this one less in terms of resource allocation."

This twin-planning technique—in which diverse business units plan their own futures but with an override by the corporation—may be the most effective answer yet to the increasingly knotty control problems facing complex companies spanning several industries. Professor James P. Baughman of Harvard Business School maintains that as business redefines its post-World War II assumptions, there is a rush away from decentralization to more centralized decision-making. Until recently, decentralization has been gospel and most middle managers were weaned on the concept. Now with the tightening of control, division managers in many corporations are beginning to complain about loss of autonomy. "It's cultural shock for a great many divisional executives," who see their previously delegated power eroding and even their pay threatened, says Baughman. "But it's also cultural shock for the top managers who aren't familiar with this sort of decision making."

WHEN PLANS GO OUT THE WINDOW

Wherever the authority lies, there is a perceptible trend toward caution in corporate planning, not so much for the coming year as for the long term. As risks mount, companies routinely demand of their businesses a higher return on investment. Although some executives, such as Rodney S. Gould, senior vice-president for corporate development at Dravo Corp., still see diversification as a hedge against uncertainty, much business planning seems more concerned with how to drop businesses, exit from markets, and retrench than with growing and expanding.

One way to reduce the danger, even for so strong a company as GE, is to take risks in bite sizes. "A decade ago our venture activity was pretty well tied up with major corporate ventures of very large size—nuclear, commercial jet engines, and com-

puters," says Gutoff. "In line with trying to reduce the risk exposure in the company, and at the same time not lose any of the entrepreneurship, we have moved toward more organically grown, smaller-in-size, larger-in-number ventures."

Many planners believe that changes facing corporations in the next few years will be fundamental. A whole new political dimension overlays much of their thinking, with a "government interference trend" expected to accelerate in the U.S. as well as elsewhere. Major societal changes such as the low-growth movement are anticipated. Monetary gyrations, rampant inflation, liquidity crises, and inadequate equity markets, while not expected to last indefinitely, are at least viewed as recurring threats to economic stability. Just predicting the future worth of the dollar is a major planning headache. American Standard encourages managers to translate dollars in forward plans into ounces of gold, not only to keep them aware of the continuing erosion of the dollar but to dramatize the need to look at market forecasts in terms of physical units (like thousands of square meters of cast-iron radiators) rather than paper money, which overstates market growth.

The expanding role of government creates new imponderables. Inland Steel has a $1-billion (by 1984) capital expansion program under way, but Block says: "We are wondering just what it is really going to cost us. We are trying to pay for it out of profits, but they depend on adequate selling prices. It is difficult to factor in government interference on pricing and the impact of controls of any kind—including 'jawboning'." Sun Oil is trying to factor into its planning such possibilities as postponement of certain Environmental Protection Agency regulations, removal of the oil depletion allowance and tax incentives, and imposition of a windfall profits tax.

In addition, some planners see a growing "politicization of capital allocations," as Xerox' White puts it, as the equity market dries up. In other words, government and not the markets would determine where capital should go. "We've seen it already," he says, citing Iran's planned rescue of Pan American World Airways and New York State's aid to the Urban Development Corp.

If political action is an imponderable in the U.S., it is doubly so abroad, and for some of the largest multinational corporations that is currently where most of the action is. Many companies are re-evaluating their prospects as the likelihood grows that foreign sources of raw materials may dry up.

Thus companies are trying to cut their risks in countries considered "difficult" or unstable. These days there are few exceptions. Some companies, for example, now avoid Great Britain, Japan, Italy, and even Australia, as well as the developing countries. "We had been regarding Canada as a jewel, but no more," says Xerox' Hughes.

In the past, executives could at least be reasonably confident about the long-term outlook and plan accordingly. Now many are not so sure. Depression strategies are coming in to fashion at least as alternate scenarios. Hewlett-Packard's Doyle, although he is paying a little more attention to H-P's exposure should things "really go sour" in the near future, says he does not expect a depression "this time around" because government pump-priming should get business moving again. But he thinks none of the underlying problems will have been solved and foresees a depression in 1978 or 1979. Some other planners are just as pessimistic.

In a recent planning conference in San Francisco attended by 65 corporate executives, the basic mood of the audience was one of gloom and the speakers did little to dispel it. As Stanford Business School economist Keith G. Lumsden put it, "there is no cure for the current dilemma." He and other panelists predicted continuing high inflation, only a temporary "whiff of enthusiasm" in the stock market, much lower growth rates in the next four or five years than in the past 15, continuing tight money, and high long-term interest rates. Even the possibility of this kind of long-term scenario complicates corporate planning efforts that in the past have been built on a straight course of optimism.

Risk-taking, then, might be characterized as riskier than ever, and even the most hopeful corporate planners and managers seem to be approaching the future warily. RCA's president, Anthony L. Conrad, has an "innate confidence in the economy, the progress of technology, and the growth of markets," but warns: "The businessman in the current climate has to be very agile. He's confronted with unexpected, unanticipated things. This makes long-range planning more critical, absolutely. As the fellow said, 'it's a very sporty course.'"

Organization Design: A Situational Perspective

Jay W. Lorsch

The approach to organization design I am going to advance is based upon a situational theory, not a theory that explains cause-and-effect relationships. It will not, for example, tell us that if we design a particular structural form it will cause a particular behavior. The state of existing knowledge, given the complexity of organizational phenomena, does not justify such theories. Rather, it is an explanatory theory or a conceptual framework intended to help us understand the complex interrelationship among variables that affect the way people behave in an organization.

DEFINITIONS

The phrases "organization design" and "situational" require definition. The term "situational" means that what are appropriate behavior patterns in an organization depend on the environment that confronts the organization and on the personalities of the members of the organization. Because organization design is an *important* means of influencing the pattern of behavior in an organization, it follows that what is an appropriate organization design also depends upon the nature of the organization's environment and the personality of its members.

"Organization design," like many managerial terms, has taken on several different meanings, and we want to be explicit here. An organization design is management's formal and explicit attempt(s) to indicate to organization members what is expected of them. It includes the following elements:

Organization Structure. The definition of individual jobs and their expected relationship to each other as depicted on organization charts and in job descriptions. In essence, this is management's attempt to draw a map of whom they want to do what.

Planning, Measurement, and Evaluation Schemes. The procedures established to define the organization's goals and the methods for achieving them, and the methods used to measure progress against these plans and to provide feedback about performance.

Rewards. The explicit rewards given by management in return for the individual's work. These include money, career opportunities, and other rewards. Of concern here is not only the "size" of such rewards but also how they relate to what results.

Selection Criteria. The guidelines used to select incumbents for various positions. These obviously affect the personalities, experience, and skills of organization members. They, in turn, can affect how these individuals respond to the signals conveyed by other design elements.

Training. The formally established educational programs, both on and off the job, that not only impart knowledge and skill but also provide another means for management to indicate how it expects organization members to behave on the job.

While my focus will be on these organization design elements, they are not the only ways managers communicate their expectations. Clearly, they do this through their own personal actions and contacts. The traditions or culture of an organization also consist of implicit messages about how members should behave. These, in turn, have a major impact on how people think and act. My focus on organization design stems from the fact that we now have available a theory and some experience that can help managers to understand better the substance and process of organization design decisions.

SOURCES OF IDEAS

Shortly, I shall elaborate more on situational theory and how it illuminates issues of organizational design. First, it is important to emphasize that the question of how to design organizations is one that traditionally concerned writers about management. The so-called classical writers on organizations had developed many principles from their own experience in a particular industry—for example, James Mooney in the automotive industry and Henri Fayol in mining. From them came ideas such as authority must equal responsibility, spans of control should be from six to nine people, and the staff advises, the line decides.

Managers also have always looked at the experience of other institutions for ideas about how best to organize their own companies. The Catholic Chuch and the military, for example, were early models for the way managers in private enterprise might think about organization design. Similarly, the early large companies, like the transcontinental railroads, became the source of organization design ideas for other firms. The same can be said for Du Pont and General Motors. How many company managements have borrowed the ideas of Pierre Du Pont and Alfred P. Sloan? And, of course, managers constantly look at the contemporary experiences of other firms, competitors and those in other industries, as models for their own thinking.

Another source of ideas for most managers is, of course, their own prior experience. The manager who has had a successful career at one company is tempted to apply the ideas he learned there with his new employer—sometimes with unfortunate results.

There is nothing inherently wrong with any of these ideas for designing organizations. Together, they provide a rich array of ideas about how to structure an organization, how to reward managers, how to evaluate their performance, and so on. The problem arises because managers have no systematic way of discriminating among the many ideas available and deciding which are relevant to their particular situation. The classical writers were interested in providing principles of organization that applied to most companies. The problem with ideas gleaned from one's own experience or the observation of other company practices is that they do not come with warning lights, whistles, or bells that assert that they work in this situation but not in that one or that this idea about structure will not work unless it is tied to that concept about measurement.

Variations in markets, in processing technology, in the state of scientific knowledge, and so on, all impose different requirements on organizational arrangements. So do the varying sizes of companies. Small companies, for example, can be managed with less formality and more emphasis on personal leadership than larger companies. Similarly, cultures in different countries provide different imperatives about how people expect to be rewarded, about how much they expect to be involved in decisions, and about other expectations.

During the last decade, academics have agreed on a set of ideas that together provide a theory for understanding the situational factors that affect organization design choices.

SITUATIONAL THEORY

Situational theory, as I suggested above, provides managers with a way to think about organization design issues in relation to the environmental and human characteristics of their situation. Even more important, perhaps, the theory enables managers to understand the complex causes of the organizational problems they face and can help them use their own creativity to invent new designs uniquely suited to their situation.

Since situation theory is a relatively new development, it has many of the problems of any young body of knowledge. It is not well integrated. There are still disputes about the relevant variables and the meaning of certain terminology. It is also a relatively complex set of ideas. So what follows is my own personal version of these ideas. It is based on the ideas gained in systematic research and in over ten years of applying these ideas to consulting problems. If the reader wants a different or more thorough perspective on these theories, the books listed at the end of this article can provide it.

At the outset, we need to define four terms:

1. The *environment* refers to the forces and institutions outside the firm with which its members must deal to achieve the organization's purposes. These include competitors' actions, customer requirements, financial constraints, scientific and technological knowledge, and so on. A common denominator is that all these elements provide information that is used to make and implement decisions inside the organization.

2. The organization's *strategy* is a statement of the environment(s) or business(es) relevant to the organization, the purposes of the organization within that context, and the distinctive means by which these goals will be achieved. In this sense, the strategy defines the environment in which an organization operates. A strategy may be explicitly stated or it may simply exist as an implicit idea based on the actions of the organization's managers over time.

3. A *task* is the actions members must take to implement the organization's strategy in a particular environment. The term *task* generally refers to the activities of a particular set of individuals in dealing with

the environment; for example, the task of a sales department or the task of division general managers.

4. *Psychological characteristics of members* are the enduring factors in an individual's personality that lead him or her to behave in a consistent fashion over time. It is not necessary to debate here about whether these should be labeled needs, values, interests, expectations, or all of these. The important point is that individuals do have qualities that vary greatly from those of other people, and organization design decisions must take these differences into account.

THE FIT BETWEEN TASK, PEOPLE, AND ORGANIZATION

With these definitions in mind, let us examine the first of several relationships that are important to understand in making organization design decisions—that between the individual member, his or her task, and the organization. Basically, research indicates that if there is a fit between the individuals' psychological makeup, the nature of their task, and the organization, two things are accomplished: first, the individuals gain a sense of competence, which is an important psychological reward, and, second, as they gain this sense of competence, they perform their work effectively and the organization achieves its goal. As the two-headed arrows in Figure 1 illustrate, this is not a simple cause-and-effect chain. Rather, as all the ideas I shall discuss indicate, organizations are complex social systems in which many variables interact to cause behavior.

Several points about these relationships are important to emphasize:

An individual's sense of competence is a self-reinforcing reward. As an individual performs a job successfully, feelings of competence encourage continued effort to do the job well.

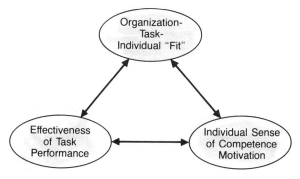

Figure 1   The Concept of Fit

Different tasks seem to be attractive to persons with different psychological makeups. For example, research scientists who work on uncertain, complex, and long-range tasks prefer to work alone, with freedom from supervision, and enjoy highly ambiguous and complex tasks. In contrast, factory managers, whose jobs are more certain, predictable, and short range, prefer more directive leadership, closer relationships with colleagues, and less ambiguity.

When I refer to the organization, I mean all the factors that influence an individual's behavior—leadership style, culture, *and* organization design. But the implication for organization design choices is clear. Design structure, measurement, and reward practices should fit the nature of the task to be done and the psychological makeup of the individuals selected to do the work. If they do, the probability is that the individuals will achieve the psychological rewards of feeling competent and will work effectively. This implies a management approach that acknowledges and appreciates differences in people. By recognizing different personality patterns, managers endow each individual with a sense of competence at work and highlight the dignity and worth of every man and woman in the organization.

DIFFERENTIATION OF UNITS

A second important relationship follows from the concept of fit. This is the fact that the performance of a functional unit (for example, sales, manufacturing, or R&D) is related to that unit's organization fitting the part of the environment with which it carries out transactions. As suggested above, a research laboratory whose numbers deal with an uncertain environment that provides feedback about results only after long intervals requires an organization design with low formality and infrequent but general measures of performance. On the other hand, a manufacturing plant in the same organization is faced with more rapid feedback and more certain information about its environment and requires more formality and more specific and frequent measures of performance. Figure 2 illustrates this contrast.

A research laboratory or manufacturing plant that does not provide the appropriate design is in for serious trouble. For example, take the comment of a researcher in a not very successful drug laboratory that required written progress reports every two weeks:

We're required to write a report on the progress of our work every two weeks. Sometimes there's not much new to talk about. We don't necessarily work on projects that you can make a breakthrough on every two weeks. But we know that we're being evaluated on our

Figure 2   Contrasting Organization Designs

DESIGN DIMENSION	R&D LAB	MANUFACTURING PLANT
Structure		
Spans of control	Wide	Narrow
Number of levels in hierarchy	Many	Few
Job definitions	General and broad	Specific and detailed
Measurement	General and less frequent (for example, quarterly)	Specific and frequent (for example, daily or even hourly)
Planning	General and as related to goals	Specific, with detailed methods
Rewards	Money, professional recognition, scientific careers	Money, management careers
Selection	Qualified technically Interest in industrial research	Leadership ability Process knowledge Cost analysis Scheduling and so on
Training	Professional conferences	Human skills Quantitative skills Technology

reports, so informal guidelines have developed. One guideline, for example, is that the less that's happened since the last report, the longer the current report is. It gets so you wrack your brain trying to write a report that makes you look good every two weeks rather than wracking your brain to crack open the research problem.

Any organization design has to permit differences between subunits. These differences in design are necessary, our research indicates, because they encourage the behavior that is required for the members of each unit to deal effectively with the specific nature of their part of the environment. The members of each unit must develop differential patterns of behavior and ways of thinking consistent with who they are and what tasks they must perform in dealing with their particular part of the environment. Although the above examples of R&D and manufacturing managers illustrate the point, I use such functional units as examples for two reasons. First, much of the research was conducted in such settings. Second, such functional units are the basic building blocks of even small business organizations, and they are also the basic units around which product divisions are structured in larger firms. However, the need for differentiation is also present among product divisions in multibusiness companies. Each product division must have an organization design, leadership style, and culture that fits its particular business environment.

Before concluding this discussion, it is important to emphasize that the amount of differentiation that is necessary will vary from one business environment to another. Three examples will illustrate the point:

1. As an example of minimal differentiation required across functions, take a firm in the business of producing corrugated containers—boxes and cartons. This firm has only two major functions—selling and manufacturing—and they have different goals. The sales personnel focus on prompt customer delivery and high quality as well as competitive pricing; the manufacturing managers are concerned with low cost and want to avoid quality and delivery requirements that affect costs adversely. Beyond these different goals there are few differences between the two functions. Both are focused on short-term results and are involved in relatively predictable tasks. Thus a more formal organization design and more directive leadership make sense to both production and sales personnel.

2. A company in the cosmetics industry requires more differentiation. It has four major functions—marketing, sales, manufacturing, and technical research. Each has a defined set of goals. Marketing personnel are concerned with advertising, sales promotion, and pricing policies that will lead to an expanding market share. Field sales personnel are, of course, concerned with market share, but their views on how to influence it focus on maintaining shelf space in retail outlets, keeping the channels of distribution well supplied, and so on. Manufacturing personnel are concerned with an efficient operation and the maintenance of product quality. The research personnel are aiming at new products. With the marketing personnel, they share a concern for intermediate and long-term results. Of course, the marketing personnel also share a concern for immediate results with the manufacturing and sales functions.

In addition to these differences, differences in management style and organization design across these functions will be important for the success of each function. In such a situation, management must act so that each of these units develops structures, measurement schemes, and reward practices that encourage their members to focus on the appropriate set of activities and issues.

3. Last, we can look at a business requiring even greater differentiation—a basic plastic materials business (for example, polystyrene or polyvinylchloride). Here we find the functions of sales, manufacturing, research, and technical services. The manufacturing personnel, like those in the previous examples, will be primarily concerned with near-term results in the areas of cost and quality. But since they are operating a much more capital-intensive technology, they may be much less flexible about interrupting product flows or making process changes than their counterparts in other businesses. The sales personnel will be concerned with customer relations and competitive pricing. Again, their focus will be largely on the near term, but they will also devote some attention to the future and to new

products. The technical services group will focus on providing technical services to the customer in support of the sales force, and thus will be primarily concerned with immediate results. At the same time, however, they are responsible for applied research aimed at developing new and improved products and processes and therefore must also focus some attention on the long term. Finally, the research unit will be involved in more basic research—understanding the structure of materials and using this understanding to develop entirely new products and processes as well as to improve existing ones. Their time horizon may be several years out. Each of these units needs to have an organization design and management style that will allow it to match its highly differentiated task and members.

While these models are drawn from manufacturing enterprises, similar examples can be found in retailing (merchants versus store operations personnel), insurance (sales versus underwriters), and banks (loan officers versus operations). These examples are also oversimplified in that, for instance, they have omitted the financial function, which has its own distinct point of view. Although these cases are drawn from single business organizations, varying degrees of differentiation also exist among the product divisions of multi-business firms, depending on how diversified the businesses are. For example, companies like Textron, Litton, and TRW require a high degree of differentiation among their various businesses. A company like General Foods needs less differentiation among the product divisions, because it is basically in the consumer food business.

Let us assume that an effective R&D laboratory and an effective manufacturing plant are in the same organization. We would expect the points of differentiation to be diverse. Leadership styles would differ: R&D managers would lead by encouraging participation in decision making; by contrast, the plant managers, although not completely autocratic, would take a more directive approach to supervision and coordination. Units would also differ, not only in the formality of organization practices and in members, goals, time, and interpersonal relations, but also in the goals and time dimensions implicit in formal practices. Members would also tend to different predispositions, including different cognitive styles, different levels of tolerance for ambiguity—stronger among the R&D managers—and different attitudes toward authority and toward people in general.

DIFFERENTIATION AND INTEGRATION

There is a cost connected with differentiation. This becomes clear in examining the relationship between differentiation and integration.

Differentiation, as previously described, means that members of each unit will see problems that involve them with other units primarily from their own point of view. It is not surprising, therefore, that differentiation produces conflict. The sales manager wants to move up scheduling an order from a big customer. The plant manager is opposed because such an interruption will lead to higher manufacturing costs. Resolving such conflicts is the stuff of which management is made.

The more differentiation, the more varied the viewpoints of the units involved in decisions and, therefore, the more difficult it is to achieve integration. (By integration we mean simply the quality of the necessary relationships among the units of the organization if the organization's overall goals are to be achieved.) Stated more formally, the more differentiated the units are, the more difficult it is to achieve integration among them —that is, the more difficult it is to coordinate their efforts to achieve higher-level goals. Research findings show that a high quality of integration is related to goal achievement for an organization.

The difficulty in achieving integration is also affected by several other factors (see Figure 3). First and most obvious is the number of units whose activities must be integrated. The more units that are involved, the more difficult collaboration becomes. Second is the pattern of interdependence. As Figure 4 suggests, we can identify three patterns.

1. *Pooled.* Subsidiary units are each interdependent with a central unit. The best example of this is the relationship between the corporate headquarters and product divisions in a diversified company in which no attempt is made at interdivisional integration.

2. *Sequential.* As the term implies, each unit is interdependent with the unit ahead of it in the flow. An example is production departments in a manufacturing plant.

3. *Reciprocal.* This is the final pattern and, as the diagram indicates, it is one of mutual interdependence among all the units. An example is the relationship among marketing, R&D, and manufacturing in product innovation.

Figure 3   Factors Affecting the Difficulty of Achieving Integration

FACTOR	DIFFICULTY OF ACHIEVING INTEGRATION	
	Low	*High*
Degree of differentiation	Small	Large
Number of units requiring integration	Few	Many
Pattern of integration	Pooled	Reciprocal
Frequency of integration required	Infrequent contact	Frequent contact— daily or more often
Importance of integration to organization's strategy	Marginal	Critical
Complexity and uncertainty of information	Simple and highly certain	Highly complex and uncertain

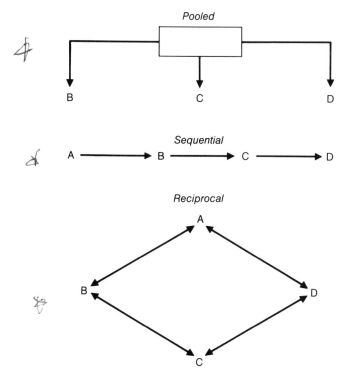

Figure 4   Patterns of Required Integration

James Thompson reported that it is increasingly difficult to achieve integration as one moves from pooled to sequential to reciprocal interdependence because of the growing number and complexity of the relationships involved.

A third factor is the frequency of interaction required among units. Other things being equal, the more frequently contact is necessary, the harder it is to achieve integration. Thus it is probably relatively easier to achieve integration around issues of production scheduling between sales and manufacturing if such schedules can be set on a quarterly basis. If the environment calls for more frequent—say, monthly—schedule adjustments, the problems of integration will increase.

The importance of integration in the organization's strategy is another factor that bears on the difficulty of achieving it. If the issues are central to the firm's strategic goals, it may be necessary to expend more effort to integrate than would be desirable if only peripheral issues were involved.

Last, the complexity and uncertainty of the information involved have an effect on the problems of integrating. The more uncertain or complex the information, the more time and effort must be expended to sort out, understand, and resolve conflicting points of view.

ACHIEVING INTEGRATION

Two sets of factors determine how well an organization achieves integration, given the difficulties imposed by its environment and strategy. First are the design elements intended to foster integration. These can cover a wide range. At one extreme are integrating departments, which may be labeled product management or program management. Such departments are separate units under their own managers created to facilitate cross-unit integration.

Integrative roles can also be established. These differ from integrative departments in that the role players, whatever their titles, report directly to the general manager in charge of the total organization. Both devices move the organization into a matrix structure in which one dimension is responsible for cross-unit integration while the other is responsible for the management of the differentiated units.

Cross-unit teams or committees are another structural device for achieving integration. They can be used in lieu of or in addition to integrating roles and departments. The planning and measurement scheme, as well as financial rewards and recognition, also can be designed to encourage personnel to make a collaborative effort. The best-known example of such attempts are the profit- or investment-center measurement and reward schemes used in most multibusiness firms. In essence, they motivate the managers in a particular business, whatever their functional allegiance, to work collaboratively toward the superordinate goal of that business.

Which and how many of the devices should be designed into a particular organization depends first on how difficult the integrative task is. But this decision also depends upon which of the factors shown in Figure 3 are present. For example, integration may require sales and manufacturing to decide production schedules and inventory levels on a quarterly basis. A planning scheme and an occasional meeting between representatives of the two units may be all that's needed.

On the other hand, in a high-technology business, integration around new product development needs may involve completely different requirements. Probably sales, manufacturing, and research and development engineering will take part. There will be a great deal of uncertainty and complexity in the information. Integrative devices that encourage face-to-face contact among representatives of the units involved will have to be used on a continuing basis.

Since these units are apt to be highly differentiated, it may also be necessary to assign a specific person to an integrative role. Such a person should be someone who commands the respect of those whose efforts he is integrating and should have some familiarity with the problems and points of view of the various units with which he is working. In this way, the integrator will have a relatively balanced viewpoint about the issues involved and, equally important, is apt to be perceived as neutral and objective by the others. Finally, such a person should have the interpersonal skills necessary to help resolve the conflicts that emerge from the different points of view.

Resolving Interunit Conflicts

The second set of factors related to an organization's effectiveness in achieving integration is how its managers go about resolving interunit conflicts. Many factors are involved, but two seem most important. The first is the pattern of behavior used to resolve conflict. If the managers work in a problem-solving mode to get the various viewpoints out on the table and work through to the best overall solution, our evidence indicates they will be most effective at achieving integration. If, on the other hand, they smooth over or avoid conflict or let a party with greater power force a solution on others, their efforts at achieving integration will be less effective.

Similarly, conflict resolution is more effective when the distribution of real influence in the organization is consistent with the knowledge and ability to contribute to decisions. For example, if one unit's members have much to contribute to decisions but are not allowed to make this contribution, conflict will not be resolved in a manner that leads to effective integration.

When I speak of "real influence," I mean influence as it is actually deployed in the company, not just as it is reflected in an organization chart or position description. Of course, the latter can have an impact on the distribution of influence. But so do the culture of the organization, the nature of the business, and other organization design elements. For example, in many consumer product firms, marketing personnel have an inordinate amount of influence compared with their peers in research and development. Their influence is based on the key role they must play in formulating strategy in this environment and is exacerbated by the fact that top management is often recruited from marketing personnel. All this leads to a culture in which marketing is expected to be king, adding further to its influence.

If management desires to improve conflict resolution practices, one design element that can be effective is training and education programs. Through such programs, managers can be educated to the need for changes in the way conflict is resolved and can develop skill in more effective practices. Of course, the way rewards are distributed and jobs are defined can also affect the balance of influence, if this is a desired goal. However, in my experience, bringing about a desired change in conflict resolution practices is very difficult because, as was pointed out above, they are so intertwined with the culture and leadership style in the organization.

PROBLEMS OF APPLICATION

In applying these ideas, the organization designer must deal with certain issues. First, he must assess the environmental requirements faced by his organization. Some instruments have been developed to do this, but in my experience, the best data can be obtained from careful interviews with knowledgeable executives. How certain are the various units about their part of the environment? What is the time frame within which results can be assessed? What are their goals? What units require integration around which issues? How frequently?

A similar set of issues presents itself in assessing individual needs. Again, instruments are available for this purpose, but knowledgeable managers make their own assessments. They only need to step back and think about what the personnel in different units prefer in terms of their relations with supervisors and peers, what the rapidity of feedback is, and how much tolerance they have for ambiguity.

We shouldn't forget to take account of both the culture of the organization and the leadership style of top management. While there has been little systematic research into the relationship between these factors and organization design, it seems clear that decisions about organization design must be consistent with top management's style of leadership. It is doubtful that an organization design can be implemented effectively if top management finds it at odds with its own preferences.

The question of culture and organization design is more complicated. The first problem is understanding what the culture is. What is the traditional pecking order among units? What are the norms for interpersonal interaction, conflict resolution, behavior that will be rewarded, and so on? When they can answer these questions, those involved in designing the organization must then ask themselves if they want to support the existing culture or move the culture in some new direction. The answer, of course, will determine how closely the organization design conforms to the existing culture.

A final issue is the necessity of arranging the various elements in the organization design to make them consistent with each other. Too often, for example, the personnel function designs a reward scheme and the controller's staff designs a measurement scheme, and the two schemes present contradictory signals to line management. If the underlying premise of the situational approach is followed, the organization design must fit both the environment and the individual member's needs. All the elements of an organization's management processes should fit together to produce the desired result—an effective organization.

In sum, the organization designer must create a structure, rewards and measurements, and other elements compatible with the external environment, strategy, tasks, organization members, top-management style, and existing culture. This may seem like an impossible task, but it really resembles an architect planning a house. The architect starts with the character and shape of the land and the requirements of the occupants and then considers costs, building codes, and other relevant factors. To pursue this analogy, the requirements based on the character of the land and the occupants are like the environmental, strategic, task, and individual requirements facing the organization designer. Once he understands what the ideal organization to meet these conditions would be, the designer can begin to consider alternatives and trade-offs that are more suitable to the style of top management. Similarly, he can make judgments about the extent to which the design is compatible with the existing culture and which changes in the design should be used to shift the culture.

Perhaps the architectural analogy is not a perfect one, but it does emphasize once again that the ideas we have described are only tools. Managers, like architects, must be skilled in using their tools and must enjoy the process of creative problem solving. Without these ingredients in their makeup, they will be unable to take advantage of the tools available to them.

SELECTED BIBLIOGRAPHY

John Child's *Organization: A Guide for Managers and Administrators* (Harper & Row, 1977) is a recent book that provides an interesting overview of the ideas discussed here plus others. It provides a number of newer ideas and techniques for applying these ideas as well. Jay Galbraith's *Designing Complex Organizations* (Addison-Wesley Publishing Company, 1973) contains a brief overview of how to use the perspective discussed in this paper with particular emphasis on the organization as an information-providing system. Paul R. Lawrence and Jay W. Lorsch's *Organization and Environment: Managing Differentiation and Integration* (Division of Research, Graduate School of Business Administration, Harvard University, 1967) was one of the first books to articulate the contingency or situational approach to organization theory. It provides a contrast with the prior principles of organization and behavioral science research. Jay W. Lorsch and Stephen A. Allen, III's *Managing Diversity and Interdependence: An Organizational Study of Multidivisional Firms* (Division of Research, Graduate School of Business Administration, Harvard University, 1973) builds on the earlier work of Lawrence, Lorsch, and Thompson and applies their ideas to the problems of organizing large multibusiness companies. It could be particularly helpful to persons concerned with corporate-divisional relationships. Jay W. Lorsch and John J. Morse's *Organizations and Their Members: A Contingency Approach* (Harper & Row Publishers, 1974) adds the issue of individual motivation to the situational approach. It provides useful ideas for thinking about how organizational design decisions affect individual performance. James D. Thompson's *Organizations in Action* (McGraw-Hill Book Company, 1967), one of the early books in the situational tradition, provides interesting ideas for thinking about the problems of achieving integration.

Managing External Dependence

John P. Kotter

Theorists interested in explaining or predicting organizational behavior have focused on a variety of factors, including employee characteristics, internal social structure and culture, formal organizational arrangements, leadership, technology, and the external environment. For a recent overview of the literature, see Kotter (21). The one factor which received the least attention until the mid-1960s was external environment. Since then a growing number of people have been exploring different aspects of how formal organizations interact with, shape, and are shaped by their environments.

One important part of this organization environment literature has focused on organizational dependence on environmental entities (1, 2, 3, 4, 12, 18, 19, 20, 25, 33, 37, 44). The theoretical argument which emerges from the literature, especially from the work of Pfeffer, Salancik, Aldrich, and Thompson, can be summarized as follows:

1. All organizations find themselves dependent, in varying degrees, on some elements in their external environments. This dependence is usually based on the external elements' control of some resources which the organization needs, such as land, labor, capital, informa-

From *Academy of Management Review*, Vol. 4, no. 1. Reprinted by permission.

tion, or a specific product or service. The importance of the resource to the organization, the number of potential supplies, and the cost of switching suppliers all affect the degree of dependency. In some instances, organizations can be dependent on external elements because those elements have some legal authority, or because they can influence other elements upon which the organization is dependent legally or for resources. Figure 1 illustrates one organization's network of dependence on environmental elements.

2. If the dependencies are of some size, they can pose a threat to an organization's survival and autonomy. For example, an accreditation agency could close a hospital, and the bank that holds a large loan for a small company could refuse to renew unless the company drops its plans to pursue a new product line.

3. To avoid having to cater to the desires of those they are dependent upon, risk their organization's demise, accomplish their goals, and to obtain discretion in setting goals, those who are in positions of authority in organizations generally try to direct their organizations to somehow actively *manage* their external dependence.

4. As a result, a significant amount of organizational behavior that cannot be accounted for by focusing entirely on internal factors (employee characteristics, leadership, social interactions and culture, or formal structure) can be understood if one recognizes how organizations tend to manage external dependence.

Figure 1 One Organization's Network Of Dependence On External Elements

EXTERNAL ELEMENT	DEPENDENCE ON	BASIS OF DEPENDENCE
1. Customers & potential customers in Industry X	Low on any single one but overall, very high	All revenues come from customers, but largest customer over last 4 years supplied only 3% of company's revenue.
2. Retired entrepreneur	High	Owns 65% of all stock.
3. Competition in Industry X	Medium	25 firms make similar products. A major technical breakthrough by any one could hurt, especially in the short run.
4. One bank	Medium-low	$200,000 loan, but could go to another bank (at a cost).
5. Labor Markets	Low	The skills they require are in limited supply, but that supply is considerably larger than their needs.
6. Material Suppliers	Very low	There are plenty of suppliers for almost all parts.

This article argues for the usefulness of this external dependence perspective. More importantly, it provides a simple way of conceptualizing how organizations manage external dependence. It also demonstrates how literature from interorganizational relations, business policy, economics, political science, and organizational design can be integrated within that framework. The most important prior discussion of this perspective is in the recent book by Pfeffer and Salancik (37). It does not, however, provide such a simple yet compelling framework.

BASIC APPROACHES TO MANAGING
EXTERNAL DEPENDENCE

Logically, there are two ways that an organization can manage external dependence:

1. It can try to reduce demands made by external elements by reducing its dependence on those elements and/or by gaining some counter-vailing power over them.
2. It can try to minimize the cost of complying with the demands made by those external elements.

Evidence exists that organizations use both of these strategies in managing external dependence. Specifically:

1. Organizations reduce external demands through: (a) the choice of a domain; (b) the establishment of favorable relationships with external elements; (c) the control of who operates and how they operate in the chosen domain.
2. Organizations minimize the cost of complying with external demands through organizational design.

Selecting a Domain

One way in which organizations manage external dependence is through their choice of which products or services to offer, how to provide them, and to whom (11, 44). Specifically:

1. They modify their current domain by seeking environmental niches, where external dependence is easy to manage. For example, a popu-lar (and profitable) strategy among business firms is to seek domains where they can have a dominant position—little or no competition, barriers keeping out competitors, little regulation, yet plenty of sup-pliers and customers (38). In such a domain, they face relatively little

environmental dependence because of the lack of competitors and regulators, yet they have considerable countervailing power over the suppliers and customers.

2. They expand their domains through diversification (9). This can take the form of vertical integration, geographical expansion, or the adoption of new and different products and services through internal development or through merger and acquisition (30). If successful, diversification helps them to reduce their dependence on any single product, service, market, or technology (37).

3. While seeking niches and diversifying, organizations tend to move with relatively small incremental steps (42). For example, an organization that produces a narrow line of electronic motors is much more likely to diversify into other electronic products than into financial services. Organizations behave this way largely to avoid moving where dependence is difficult for them to manage.

Not all organizations use these approaches as aggressively as others, because of internal or external constraints. *First,* some legal charters (a privately owned manufacturing firm) allow much more freedom in selecting a new domain than others (a nonprofit hospital). In addition, some organizations possess more resources (surplus cash, top management talent, etc.) than others that can be used to expand or shift a domain.

Establishing External Linkages

A *second* way that organizations cope with external dependence is by establishing favorable relationships with those they are dependent upon and with alternative sources of support in their domain. They do so in five different ways.

1. Investing resources in advertising and public relations (7, 13) in order to establish favorable attitudes toward the organization.

2. Creating a large number of boundary spanning roles (18, 29) and recruiting individuals from external elements in order (6, 35) to establish personal linkages.

3. Negotiating contracts (45) to give them some legal power over the external elements.

4. Co-opting key members of external elements, often through directorships (29, 30).

5. Establishing joint ventures and other complex coalitions with other organizations (25, 34, 36).

All organizations use these methods to some degree. Organizations that are not able easily to use the domain-choice strategy to help manage external dependence, such as public, nonprofit, and highly regulated prof-it-making organizations, probably use these methods more often than organizations that can easily shift or expand their domains. Once again, richer organizations are better able to use these methods than poorer ones (8, 15), especially the first two. These five methods form a continuum of sorts, with respect to their cost. At one end, advertising costs a good deal of money, but it does not make the organization even more dependent on eternal entities. At the other extreme, joint ventures may actually save a firm money, but they cost the organization in terms of increased external dependence. The methods in between, in varying degrees, include both kinds of costs.

Controlling Who Operates in the Domain And How

A *third* way in which organizations attempt to manage external depend-ence is by attempting to control who operates in their domain and/or how they can operate. For example, methods used include:

1. Forcing out competition (10, 30), thus reducing their dependence on competition and increasing their countervailing power over clients and customers.
2. Creating, joining, and participating in trade associations and coordi-nating councils to help reduce competition (37).
3. Attempting to influence legislation and regulation (30, 43), usually to limit competition (14, 27).
4. Attempting to influence informal norms in their industry (29, 37), again usually to limit competition.

Richer organizations are better able to use these methods than poorer organizations. But due to antitrust laws and contemporary social norms and values, very few organizations use these methods extensively. Those that do are often forced to because they have been unable to manage external dependence successfully in other ways. For a description of the aggressive use of these tactics at the end of the nineteenth century, before antitrust legislation, see Chandler and Salisbury (10).

Designing the Organization

A way in which organizations will often attempt to manage external de-pendence is through organizational design. Unlike the previous approach-es, this strategy is aimed more at adapting to, rather than changing, the external environment. Specifically:

1. Organizations will usually create separate subunits to deal with each major source of external dependence (22, 44). In a business firm, these

might include a purchasing department, a marketing department, a labor relations department, a public relations department, etc.

2. They generally staff and organize these subunits differently so that each is capable of effectively understanding and managing its environmental entity (22).

3. They establish mechanisms for resolving conflicts among the different subunits, and thus for dealing with the conflicting demands made by those external entities they are dependent upon (22). In doing so, they will often try to see that the distribution of power among subunits corresponds to the degree the organization is dependent on each of their subenvironments (17, 29). When successful, internal decision making then reflects the relative importance of various environmental entities to the organization.

Once again, some organizations are much more aggressive and/or successful than others in using this approach to managing external dependence for a variety of reasons, some of which relate to success in using the other three management strategies. Some evidence suggests if an organization is extremely successful in using the first three strategies and dominates its external environment, it will rely less and less on this final adaptive strategy (21). Without the pressing need to use the organizational design strategy, organizations often seem to eschew this method to avoid the costs associated with making organizational changes. At the other extreme, evidence exists that if an organization is completely unsuccessful in its use of the first three strategies, and as a result is extremely dependent on many environmental entities, it will have great difficulty using the final strategy to help the situation (21). With many important external dependencies, an organization might find that it is simply unable to create separate subunits to deal with each, and if it does, it might well find that it is unable to integrate the internal conflicts among those subunits.

SUMMARY AND DISCUSSION

The external dependence perspective pulls together in a dynamic way much of what we currently know about how organizations shape and are shaped by their immediate external environments. It does so by integrating the work of economists, organization theorists, management theorists, interorganizational theorists, business policy specialists, and sociologists. It offers ways both for explaining and predicting many aspects of organizational behavior and organizational dynamics.

For example, the framework can help explain why specific firms or certain types of organizations rely heavily on boundary spanning roles or pay special attention to EEOC regulations while others do not. It can also help to predict an organization's future behavior in areas of diversification, political activities, joint ventures, board appointments, or changes in the design of the organization.

The framework presented here offers a simple, logical way of thinking about the dozens of tactics or actions that managers sometimes use to cope with external dependence and therefore highlights the basic choices or alternatives managers possess. Specifically, the framework identifies four major strategic alternatives and about a dozen more detailed tactics. In doing so, it helps us to see how seemingly unrelated managerial actions (such as increasing advertising expenditures, on the one hand, and altering the design of the production subunit, on the other) are often closely related.

The framework also suggests one direction for future research. Most of the research on the tactics described in this paper has focused on one or a very limited number of them. The typical research question has been "When, why, and under what circumstances do organizations advertise, acquire other organizations, or enter into joint ventures?" While clearly valuable, research that focuses on one method at a time, unless it controls for all the others, is not able to take into account the interaction effects. The framework presented here suggests that those effects could be very important. More research is needed in the future that focuses on all of the potential strategies and tactics, but for a limited set of organizations, such as those in an industry (as Hirsch (19) has argued).

Finally, the framework provides insight into the question of organizational effectiveness. It takes us beyond the recognition that organization-environment compatibility often seems to be associated with positive results. It suggests reasons why those in an organization might not try or might be unable to create an organization-environment fit. It also enlightens theories regarding adaptation and dominance. Organizational literature all too often suggests that behavior aimed at adaptation is good while behavior oriented toward dominance is bad. The framework suggests that both types of behavior are probably needed for an organization to survive and to be socially effective.

REFERENCES

1. Aiken, M., and J. Hage. "Organizational Interdependence and Intra-organizational Structure," *American Sociological Review*, Vol. 33 (1968), 912–930.

2. Aldrich, Howard. "Cooperation and Conflict between Organizations in the Manpower Training System: An Organization-Environment Perspective," in Anant R. Negandhi (Ed.), *Conflict of Power in Complex Organizations: An Inter-Institutional Perspective* (Kent, Ohio: Comparative Administration Research Institute, Center for Business and Economic Research, Kent University, 1972).

3. ALDRICH, HOWARD. "Resource Dependence and Interorganizational Relations: Relations between Local Employment Service Offices and Social Services Sector Organizations," *Administration and Society*, Vol. 7 (1976), 419–455.

4. ALDRICH, H. E., and J. PFEFFER. "Environments of Organizations," *Annual Review of Sociology*, Vol. 2 (1976), 79–105.

5. ALLEN, M. P. "The Structure of Interorganizational Elite Cooptation: Interlocking Corporate Directorates," *American Sociological Review*, Vol. 39 (1974), 393–406.

6. BATY, G., W. M. EVAN, and T. ROTHERMEL. "Personnel Flows as Interorganizational Relations," *Administrative Science Quarterly*, Vol. 16 (1971), 430–443.

7. CARLSON, R. O. "Public Relations," in D. L. Sills (Ed.), *International Encyclopedia of the Social Sciences*, Vol. 13 (New York: Macmillan and The Free Press, 1968), 208–217.

8. CAVES, RICHARD E. "Uncertainty, Market Structure, and Performance: Galbraith as Conventional Wisdom," in J. W. Markham and G. F. Papanek (Eds.), *Industrial Organization and Economic Development* (Boston: Houghton Mifflin, 1970), 283–302.

9. CHANDLER, A. *Strategy and Structure* (Cambridge: MIT Press, 1962).

10. CHANDLER, A. D., Jr., and STEPHEN SALISBURY. *E. I. Report and the Making of the Modern Corporation* (New York: Harper and Row, 1971).

11. CHILD, J. "Organizational Structure, Environment and Performance: The Role of Strategic Choice," *Sociology*, Vol. 6 (1972), 1–22.

12. CLARK, PETER, and JAMES WILSON. "Incentive Systems: A Theory of Organizations," *Administrative Science Quarterly*, Vol. 6 (1961), 29–166.

13. COMANOR, W. S., and T. A. WILSON. "Advertising, Market Structure and Performance." *Review of Economics and Statistics*, Vol. 49 (1967), 425–440.

14. EPSTEIN, EDWIN M. *The Corporation in American Politics* (Englewood Cliffs, New Jersey: Prentice-Hall, 1969).

15. GALBRAITH, J. K. *The New Industrial State* (Boston: Houghton Mifflin, 1967).

16. HICKSON, D. J., C. R. HININGS, C. A. LEE, R. E. SCHNECK, and J. M. PENNINGS. "A Strategic Contingencies Theory of Intraorganizational Power," *Administrative Science Quarterly*, Vol. 16 (1971), 216–229.

17. HININGS, C. R., D. J. HICKSON, J. M. PENNINGS, and R. E. SCHNECK. "Structural Conditions of Intraorganizational Power," *Administrative Science Quarterly*, Vol. 19 (1974), 22–44.

18. HIRSCH, P. M. "Processing Fads and Fashions: An Organization-Set Analysis of Cultural Industry Systems," *American Journal of Sociology*, Vol. 77 (1972), 639–659.

19. HIRSCH, P. M. "Organizational Effectiveness and the Institutional Environment," *Administrative Science Quarterly*, Vol. 20 (1975), 327–344.

20. JACOBS, DAVID. "Dependency and Vulnerability: An Approach to the Control of Organizations," *Administrative Science Quarterly*, Vol. 19 (1974), 45–59.

21. KOTTER, JOHN P. *Organizational Dynamics* (Reading, Mass.: Addison Wesley, 1978).

22. LAWRENCE, P. R., and J. W. LORSCH. *Organization and Environment* (Cambridge: Graduate School of Business Administration, Harvard University, 1967).

23. LEARNED, EDMUND P., C. R. CHRISTENSEN, K. R. ANDREWS, and W. D. GUTH. *Business Policy: Text and Cases*, rev. ed., (Homewood, Ill.: Richard D. Irwin, 1969).

24. LEVINE, S., and P. E. WHITE. "Exchange as a Conceptual Framework for the Study of Interorganizational Relationships," *Administrative Science Quarterly*, Vol. 5 (1961), 583–601.

25. LEVINE, S., P. E. WHITE, and B. D. PAUL. "Community Interorganizational Problems in Providing Medical Care and Social Services," *American Journal of Public Health*, Vol. 53 (1963), 1183–1195.

26. MACAULAY, S. "Non-contractual Relations in Business: A Preliminary Study," *American Sociological Review*, Vol. 28 (1963), 55–67.

27. MACAVOY, PAUL W. *The Economic Effects of Regulation* (Cambridge, Mass.: MIT Press, 1965).

28. PATE, J. L. "Joint Venture Activity, 1960–1968," *Economic Review, Federal Reserve Bank of Cleveland*, (1969), 16–23.

29. PERROW, C. "Departmental Power and Perspective in Industrial Firms," in M. N. Zald (Ed.), *Power in Organizations* (Nashville, Tenn.: Vanderbilt University Press, 1970), 58–89.

30. PFEFFER, JEFFREY. "Merger as a Response to Organizational Interdependence," *Administrative Science Quarterly*, Vol. 18 (1972), 382–394.

31. PFEFFER, JEFFREY. "Interorganizational Influence and Managerial Attitude," *Academy of Management Journal*, Vol. 15 (1972), 317–330.

32. PFEFFER, JEFFREY. "Size, Composition and Function of Hospital Boards of Directors: A Study of Organization-Environment Linkage," *Administrative Science Quarterly*, Vol. 18 (1973), 349–364.

33. PFEFFER, JEFFREY. "Beyond Management and the Worker: The Institutional Function of Management," *Academy of Management Review*, Vol. 1, No. 2 (1976), 36–46.

34. PFEFFER, JEFFREY. "Patterns of Joint Venture Activity: Implications for Antitrust Policy," Testimony presented before the Subcommittee on Monopolies and Commercial Law of the House Committee on the Judiciary, February 11, 1976.

35. PFEFFER, JEFFREY, and HUSEYIN LEBLEBICI. "Executive Recruitment and the Development of Interfirm Organizations," *Administrative Science Quarterly*, Vol. 18 (1973), 449–461.

36. PFEFFER, JEFFREY, and PHILIP NOWAK. "Joint Ventures and Interorganizational Interdependence," *Administrative Science Quarterly*, Vol. 21 (1976), 398–418.

37. PFEFFER, JEFFREY, and G. R. SALANCIK. "Organizational Context and the Characteristics and Tenure of Hospital Administrators," *Academy of Management Journal*, Vol. 20 (1978), 74–88.

38. PORTER, M. E. "Note on the Structural Analysis of Industries," Harvard Business School, 9–376–054 (1975).

39. PUGH, D. S., D. J. HICKSON, C. R. HININGS, and C. TURNER. "The Context of Organization Structures." *Administrative Science Quarterly*, Vol. 14 (1969), 91–114.

40. Salancik, G. R. "The Role of Interdependencies in Organizational Responsiveness to Demands from the Environment: The Case of Women versus Power," Unpublished manuscript, University of Illinois.

41. Schein, E. *Organizational Psychology* (Englewood Cliffs, New Jersey: Prentice-Hall, 1965).

42. Starbuck, W. "The Organization and Its Environment," in M. Dunnette (Ed.), *Handbook of Industrial and Organizational Psychology* (Chicago: Rand McNally, 1976).

43. Stigler, G. L. "The Theory of Economic Regulation," *Bell Journal of Economics and Management Science*, Vol. 2 (1971), 3–21.

44. Thompson, J. D. *Organizations in Action* (New York: McGraw-Hill, 1967).

45. Thompson, J. D., and W. J. McEwen. "Organizational Goals and Environment: Goal Setting as an Interaction Process," *American Sociological Review*, Vol. 23 (1958), 23–31.

Organizational Strategy, Structure, and Process

Raymond E. Miles

Charles C. Snow

Alan D. Meyer

Henry J. Coleman, Jr.

An organization is both an articulated purpose and an established mechanism for achieving it. Most organizations engage in an ongoing process of evaluating their purposes—questioning, verifying, and redefining the manner of interaction with their environments. Effective organizations carve out and maintain a viable market for their goods or services. Ineffective organizations fail this market—alignment task. Organizations also constantly modify and refine the mechanism by which they achieve their purposes—rearranging their structure of roles and relationships and their managerial processes. Efficient organizations establish mechanisms that complement their market strategy, but inefficient organizations struggle with these structural and process mechanisms.

For most organizations, the dynamic process of adjusting to environmental change and uncertainty—*of maintaining an effective alignment with the environment while managing internal interdependencies*—is enormously complex, encompassing myriad decisions and behaviors at several organization levels. But the complexity of the adjustment process can be penetrated: by searching for patterns in the behavior of organizations, one can describe and even predict the process of organizational adaptation. This article presents a theoretical framework that managers and students of management

Reprinted by permission from the *Academy of Management Review*, July 1978, pp. 546–62.

can use to analyze an organization as an integrated and dynamic whole—a model that takes into account the interrelationships among strategy, structure, and process. (For a complete discussion of the theoretical framework and research studies, see (15)). Specifically, the framework has two major elements: (a) a general model of the process of adaptation which specifies the major decisions needed by the organization to maintain an effective alignment with its environment, and (b) an organizational typology which portrays different patterns of adaptive behavior used by organizations within a given industry or other grouping. But as several theorists have pointed out, organizations are limited in their choices of adaptive behavior to those which top management believes will allow the effective direction and control of human resources (4, 5, 6). Thus the theoretical framework to prevailing theories of management is also related. An increased understanding of the adaptive process, of how organizations move through it, and of the managerial requirements of different adjustment patterns can facilitate the difficult process of achieving an effective organization-environment equilibrium.

In the following sections, a typical example of organizational adaptation drawn from one of our empirical research studies is first presented. Second, a model of the adaptive process that arose from this research is described and discussed. In the third section, four alternative forms of adaptation exhibited by the organizations in our studies are described. Finally, the relationship between the organizational forms and currently available theories of management is discussed.

AN EXAMPLE OF ORGANIZATIONAL ADAPTATION

As an example of the problems associated with the adaptive process, consider the experience of a subsidiary of one of the companies in our studies.

Porter Pump and Valve (PPV) is a semi-autonomous division of a medium-sized equipment-manufacturing firm, which is in turn part of a large, highly diversified conglomerate. PPV manufactures a line of heavy-duty pumps and components for fluid-movement systems. The company does most of its own castings, makes many of its own parts, and maintains a complete stock of replacement parts. PPV also does special-order foundry work for other firms as its production schedule allows.

Until recently, Porter Pump and Valve had defined its business as providing quality products and service to a limited set of reliable customers. PPV's general manager, a first-rate engineer who spent much of his time in the machine shop and foundry, personified the company's image of quality and cost efficiency. In the mid-seventies corporate management became concerned about both the speed and direction of PPV's growth. The management and staff at corporate headquarters began considering two new product and market opportunities, both in the energy field. Fluid-movement systems required for nuclear power generation provided one of these opportunities, and the development of novel techniques for petroleum exploration, well recovery, and fluid delivery provided the second. PPV had supplied some components to these markets in the past, but it was now clear that opportunities for the sale of entire systems or large-scale subsystems were growing rapidly.

PPV's initial moves toward these new opportunities were tentative. The general manager discovered that contract sales required extensive planning, field-contact work, and careful negotiations—activities not within his primary area of interest or experience. Finally, in an effort to foster more rapid movement into these new markets, executives in the parent organization transferred the general manager to a head-office position and moved into the top spot at PPV a manager with an extensive background in both sales and engineering and who was adept at large-scale contract negotiations.

Within a year of the changeover in general managers, PPV landed several lucrative contracts, and more appeared to be in the offing. The new business created by these contracts, however, placed heavy coordination demands on company management, and while the organization's technology (production and distribution system) has not been drastically revised over the past two years, workflow processes and the operational responsibilities of several managers have changed markedly. Materials control and scheduling, routine tasks in the past, are now complex activities, and managers of these operations meet regularly with the executive planning committee. Moreover, a rudimentary matrix structure has emerged in which various line managers undertake specific project responsibilities in addition to their regular duties. Key personnel additions have been made to the marketing department and more are planned, with particular emphasis on individuals who are capable of performing field planning and supervising and who can quickly bring new fluid systems to full operation. Budgets of some of the older departments are being cut back, and these funds are being diverted to the new areas of activity.

As illustrated, Porter Pump and Value experienced changes in its products and markets, in the technological processes needed to make new products and serve new markets, and in the administrative structure and processes required to plan, coordinate, and control the company's new operations. None of the usual perspectives which might be used to analyze such organizational changes—for example, economics, industrial engineering, marketing, or policy—appears to address all of the problems experienced by Porter Pump and Valve. Therefore, how can the adaptive process which occurred at PPV be described in its entirety?

THE ADAPTIVE CYCLE

We have developed a general model of the adaptive process which we call the *adaptive cycle*. Consistent with the strategic-choice approach to the study of organizations, the model parallels and expands ideas formulated by theorists such as Chandler (9), Child (10), Cyert and March (11), Drucker (12, 13), Thompson (18), and Weick (19, 20). Essentially, proponents of the strategic-choice perspective argue that organizational behavior is only partially preordained by environmental conditions and that the choices which top managers make are the critical determinants of organizational structure and process. Although these choices are numerous and complex, they can be viewed as three broad "problems" of organizational adaptation: the *entrepreneurial problem*, the *engineering problem*, and the *administrative problem*. In mature organizations, management must solve each of these problems simultaneously, but for explanatory purposes, these adaptive problems can be discussed as if they occurred sequentially.

The Entrepreneurial Problem

The adaptive cycle, though evident in all organizations, is perhaps most visible in new or rapidly growing organizations (and in organizations which recently have survived a major crisis). In a new organization, an entrepreneurial insight, perhaps only vaguely defined at first, must be developed into a concrete *definition of an organizational domain: a specific good or service and a target market or market segment.* In an ongoing organization, the entrepreneurial problem has an added dimension. Because the organization has already obtained a set of "solutions" to its engineering and administrative problems, its next attempt at an entrepreneurial "thrust" may be difficult. In the example of Porter Pump and Valve, the company's attempt to modify its products and markets was constrained by its present production process and by the fact that the general manager and his staff did not possess the needed marketing orientation.

In either a new or ongoing organization, the solution to the entrepreneurial problem is marked by management's acceptance of a particular product-market domain, and this acceptance becomes evident when management decides to commit resources to achieve objectives relative to the domain. In many organizations, external and internal commitment to the entrepreneurial solution is sought through the development and projection of an organizational "image" which defines both the organization's market and its orientation toward it (e.g., an emphasis on size, efficiency, or innovation).

Although we are suggesting that the engineering phase begins at this point, the need for further entrepreneurial activities clearly does not disappear. The entrepreneurial function remains a top-management responsibility, although as Bower (7) has described, the identification of a new opportunity and the initial impetus for movement toward it may originate at lower managerial levels.

The Engineering Problem

The engineering problem involves the creation of a system which *operationalizes management's solution to the entrepreneurial problem.* Such a system requires management to select an appropriate technology (input-transformation-output process) for producing and distributing chosen products or services and to form new information, communication, and control linkages (or modify existing linkages) to ensure proper operation of the technology.

As solutions to these problems are reached, initial implementation of the administrative system takes place. There is no assurance that the configuration of the organization, as it begins to emerge during this phase, will remain the same when the engineering problem finally has been solved. The actual form of the organization's structure will be determined during the administrative phase as management solidifies relations with the environment and establishes processes for coordinating and controlling internal operations. Referring again to Porter Pump and Valve, the company's redefinition of its domain required concomitant changes in its technology —from a pure mass-production technology to more of a unit or small-batch technology (21).

The Administrative Problem

The administrative problem, as described by most theories of management, is primarily that of reducing uncertainty within the organizational system, or, in terms of the present model, of rationalizing and stabilizing those activities which successfully solved problems faced by the organization during the entrepreneurial and engineering phases. Solving the administrative problem involves more than simply rationalizing the system already developed (uncertainty reduction); it also involves formulating and implementing those processes which will enable the organization to continue to evolve (innovation). This conception of the administrative problem, as a pivotal factor in the cycle of adaptation, deserves further elaboration.

Rationalization and Articulation—In the ideal organization, management would be equally adept at performing two somewhat conflicting functions: it would be able to create an administrative system (structure and processes) that could smoothly direct and monitor the organization's current activities without, at the same time, allowing the system to become so ingrained that future innovation activities are jeopardized. Such a perspective requires the administrative system to be viewed as both a *lagging* and *leading* variable in the process of adaptation. As a lagging variable, it must rationalize, through the development of appropriate structures and processes, strategic decisions made at previous points in the adjustment process. As a leading variable, the administrative system must facilitate the organization's future capacity to adapt by articulating and reinforcing the paths along which innovative activity can proceed. At Porter Pump and Valve, management modified its planning, coordination, and control processes substantially in order to pursue the company's newly chosen areas of business (the "lagging" aspect of administration). At the same time, key personnel were added to the marketing department; their duties included product development, market research, and technical consulting. These activities were designed to keep PPV at the forefront of new product and market opportunities (the "leading" aspect of administration).

THE STRATEGIC TYPOLOGY

If one accepts the adaptive cycle as valid, the question becomes: How do organizations move through the cycle? That is, using the language of our model, what strategies do organizations employ in solving their entrepreneurial, engineering, and administrative problems? Our research and interpretation of the literature show that there are essentially three *strategic* types of organizations: Defenders, Analyzers, and Prospectors. Each type has its own unique strategy for relating to its chosen market(s), and each has a particular configuration of technology, structure, and process that is consistent with its market strategy. A fourth type of organization encountered in our studies is called the Reactor. The Reactor is a form of strategic "failure" in that inconsistencies exist among its strategy, technology, structure, and process.

Although similar typologies of various aspects of organizational behavior are available (1, 2, 3, 15, 16, 17), our formulation specifies relationships among strategy, technology, structure, and process to the point where entire organizations can be viewed as integrated wholes in dynamic interaction with their environments. Any typology is unlikely to encompass every form of organizational behavior—the world of organizations is much too changeable and complex to permit such a claim. Nevertheless, every organization that we have observed appears, when compared to other organizations in its industry, to fit predominantly into one of the four categories, and its behavior is generally predictable given its typological classification. The "pure" form of each of these organization types is described below.

Defenders

The Defender (i.e., its top management) deliberately enacts and maintains an environmental for which a stable form of organization is appropriate. Stability is chiefly achieved by the Defender's definition of, and solution to, its entrepreneurial problem. Defenders define their *entrepreneurial* problem as *how to seal off a portion of the total market in order to create a stable domain,* and they do so by producing only a limited set of products directed at a narrow segment of the total potential market. Within this limited domain, the Defender strives aggressively to prevent competitors from entering its "turf." Such behaviors include standard economic actions like competitive pricing or high-quality products, but Defenders also tend to ignore developments and trends outside of their domains, choosing instead to grow through market penetration and perhaps some limited product development. Over time, a true Defender is able to carve out and maintain a small niche within the industry which is difficult for competitors to penetrate.

Having chosen a narrow product-market domain, the Defender invests a great deal of resources in solving its *engineering* problem: *how to produce and distribute goods or services as efficiently as possible.* Typically, the Defender does so by developing a single core technology that is highly cost-efficient. Technological efficiency is central to the Defender's success since its domain has been deliberately created to absorb outputs on a predictable, continuous basis. Some Defenders extend technological efficiency to its limits through a process of vertical integration—incorporating each stage of production from raw materials supply to distribution of final output into the same organizational system.

Finally, the Defender's solution to its administrative problem is closely aligned with its solutions to the entrepreneurial and engineering problems. The Defender's *administrative* problem—*how to achieve strict control of the organization in order to ensure efficiency*—is solved through a combination of structural and process mechanisms that can be generally described as "mechanistic" (8). These mechanisms include a top-management group heavily dominated by production and cost-control specialists, little or no scanning of the environment for new areas of opportunity, intensive planning oriented toward cost and other efficiency issues, functional structures characterized by extensive division of labor, centralized control, communications through formal hierarchical channels, and so on. Such an administrative system is ideally suited for generating and maintaining efficiency, and the key characteristic of stability is as apparent here as in the solution to the other two adaptive problems.

Pursued vigorously, the Defender strategy can be viable in most industries, although stable industries lend themselves to this type of organization more than turbulent industries (e.g., the relative lack of technological change in the food-processing industry generally favors the Defender strategy compared with the situation in the electronics industry). This particular form of organization is not without its potential risks. The Defender's *primary risk* is that of *ineffectiveness*—being unable to respond to a major shift in its market environment. The Defender relies on the continued viability of its single, narrow domain, and it receives a return on its large technological investment only if the major problems facing the organization continue to be of an engineering nature. If the Defender's market shifts dramatically, this type of organization has little capacity for locating and exploiting new areas of opportunity. In short, the Defender is perfectly capable of responding to today's world. To the extent that tomorrow's world is similar to today's, the Defender is ideally suited for its environment. Table 1 summarizes the Defender's salient characteristics and the major strengths and weaknesses inherent in this pattern of adaptation.

Prospectors

In many ways, Prospectors respond to their chosen environments in a manner that is almost the opposite of the Defender. In one sense, the Prospector is exactly like the Defender: there is a high degree of consistency among its solutions to the three problems of adaptation.

Generally speaking, the Prospector enacts an environment that is more dynamic than those of other types of organizations within the same industry. Unlike the Defender, whose success comes primarily from efficiently serving a stable domain, the Prospector's prime capability is that of finding and exploiting new product and market opportunities. For a Prospector, maintaining a reputation as an innovator in product and market development may be as important as, perhaps even more important, than high profitability. In fact, because of the inevitable "failure rate" associated with sustained product and market innovation, Prospectors may find it difficult consistently to attain the profit levels of the more efficient Defender.

Defining its *entrepreneurial* problem as *how to locate and develop product and market opportunities*, the Prospector's domain is usually broad and in a continuous state of development. The systematic addition of new products or markets, frequently combined with retrenchment in other parts of the domain, gives the Prospector's products and markets an aura of fluidity uncharacteristic of the Defender. To locate new areas of opportunity, the Prospector must develop and maintain the capacity to survey a wide range

TABLE 1   Characteristics of the Defender

ENTREPRENEURIAL PROBLEM	ENGINEERING PROBLEM	ADMINISTRATIVE PROBLEM
Problem:	*Problem:*	*Problem:*

How to "seal off" a portion of the total market to create a stable set of products and customers.	How to produce and distribute goods or services as efficiently as possible.	How to maintain strict control of the organization in order to ensure efficiency.
Solutions:	*Solutions:*	*Solutions:*
1. Narrow and stable domain. 2. Aggressive maintenance of domain (e.g., competitive pricing and excellent customer service). 3. Tendency to ignore developments outside of domain. 4. Cautious and incremental growth primarily through market penetration. 5. Some product development but closely related to current goods or services.	1. Cost-efficient technology. 2. Single core technology. 3. Tendency toward vertical integration. 4. Continuous improvements in technology to maintain efficiency.	1. Financial and production experts most powerful members of the dominant coalition; limited environmental scanning. 2. Tenure of dominant coalition is lengthy; promotions from within. 3. Planning is intensive, cost oriented, and completed before action is taken. 4. Tendency toward functional structure with extensive division of labor and high degree of formalization. 5. Centralized control and long-looped vertical information systems. 6. Simple coordination mechanisms and conflict resolved through hierarchical channels. 7. Organizational performance measured against previous years; reward system favors production and finance.
Costs and Benefits:	*Costs and Benefits:*	*Costs and Benefits:*
It is difficult for competitors to dislodge the organization from its small niche in the industry, but a major shift in the market could threaten survival.	Technological efficiency is central to organizational performance, but heavy investment in this area requires technological problems to remain familiar and predictable for lengthy periods of time.	Administrative system is ideally suited to maintain stability and efficiency but it is not well suited to locating and responding to new product or market opportunities.

of environmental conditions, trends, and events. This type of organization invests heavily in individuals and groups who scan the environment for potential opportunities. Because these scanning activities are not limited to the organization's current domain, Prospectors are frequently the creators of change in their respective industries. Change is one of the major tools used by the Prospector to gain an edge over competitors, so Prospector managers typically perceive more environmental change and uncertainty than managers of the Defender (or the other two organization types).

To serve its changing domain properly, the Prospector requires a good deal of flexibility in its technology and administrative system. Unlike the Defender, the Prospector's choice of products and markets is not limited to those which fall within the range of the organization's present technological capability. The Prospector's technology is contingent upon both the organization's current *and* future product mix: entrepreneurial activities always have primacy, and appropriate technologies are not selected or developed until late in the process of product development. Therefore, the Prospector's overall engineering problem is *how to avoid long-term commitments to a single type of technological process,* and the organization usually does so by creating multiple, prototypical technologies which have a low degree of routinization and mechanization.

Finally, the Prospector's *administrative* problem flows from its changing domain and flexible technologies: *how to facilitate rather than control organizational operations.* That is, the Prospector's administrative system must be able to deploy and coordinate resources among numerous decentralized units and projects rather than to plan and control the operations of the entire organization centrally. To accomplish overall facilitation and coordination, the Prospector's structure-process mechanisms must be "organic" (8). These mechanisms include a top-management group dominated by marketing research and development experts, planning that is broad rather than intensive and oriented toward results not methods, product or project structures characterized by a low degree of formalization, decentralized control, lateral as well as vertical communications, and so on. In contrast to the Defender, the Prospector's descriptive catchword throughout its administrative as well as entrepreneurial and engineering solutions is "flexibility."

Of course, the Prospector strategy also has its costs. Although the Prospector's continuous exploration of change helps to protect it from a changing environment, this type of organization runs the *primary risk of low profitability and overextension of resources.* While the Prospector's technological flexibility permits a rapid response to a changing domain, complete efficiency cannot be obtained because of the presence of multiple technologies. Finally, the Prospector's administrative system is well suited to maintain flexibility, but it may, at least temporarily, underutilize or even misutilize physical, financial, and human resources. In short, the Prospector is effective—it can respond to the demands of tomorrow's world. To the extent that the world of tomorrow is similar to that of today, the Prospector cannot maximize profitability because of its inherent inefficiency. Table 2 summarizes the Prospector's salient characteristics and the major strengths and weaknesses associated with this pattern of adaptation.

Analyzers

Based on our research, the Defender and the Prospector seem to reside at opposite ends of a continuum of adjustment strategies. Between these two extremes, a third type of organization is called the Analyzer. The Analyzer is a unique combination of the Prospector and Defender types and represents a viable alternative to these other strategies. A true Analyzer is an organization that attempts to minimize risk while maximizing the opportunity for profit—that is, an experienced Analyzer combines the strengths of both the Prospector and the Defender into a single system. This strategy is difficult to pursue, particularly in industries characterized by rapid market and technological change, and thus the word that best describes the Analyzer's adaptive approach is "balance."

The Analyzer defines its *entrepreneurial* problem in terms similar to both the Prospector and the Defender: *how to locate and exploit new product and market opportunities while simultaneously maintaining a firm core of traditional products and customers.* The Analyzer's solution to the entrepreneurial problem is also a blend of the solutions preferred by the Prospector and the Defender: the Analyzer moves toward new products or new markets but only after their viability has been demonstrated. This periodic transformation of the Analyzer's domain is accomplished through imitation—only the most successful product or market innovations developed by prominent Prospectors are adopted. At the same time, the majority of the Analyzer's revenue is generated by a fairly stable set of products and customer or client groups—a Defender characteristic. Thus, the successful Analyzer must be able to respond quickly when following the lead of key Prospectors while at the same time maintaining operating efficiency in its stable product and market areas. To the extent that it is successful, the Analyzer can grow through market penetration as well as product and market development.

The duality evident in the Analyzer's domain is reflected in its *engineering* problem and solution. This type of organization must learn *how to achieve and protect an equilibrium between conflicting demands for technological flexibility and for technological stability.* This equilibrium is accomplished by partitioning production activities to form a dual technological core. The stable component of the Analyzer's technology bears a strong resemblance to the Defender's technology. It is functionally organized and exhibits high levels of standardization, routinization, and mechanization in an attempt to approach cost efficiency. The Analyzer's flexible technological compo-

TABLE 2   Characteristics of the Prospector

ENTREPRENEURIAL PROBLEM	ENGINEERING PROBLEM	ADMINISTRATIVE PROBLEM
Problem:	*Problem:*	*Problem:*
How to locate and exploit new product and market opportunities.	How to avoid long-term commitments to a single technological process.	How to facilitate and coordinate numerous and diverse operations.
Solutions:	*Solutions:*	*Solutions:*
1. Broad and continuously developing domain. 2. Monitors wide range of environmental conditions and events. 3. Creates change in the industry. 4. Growth through product and market development. 5. Growth may occur in spurts.	1. Flexible, prototypical technologies. 2. Multiple technologies. 3. Low degree of routinization and mechanization; technology embedded in people.	1. Marketing and research and development experts most powerful members of the dominant coalition. 2. Dominant coalition is large, diverse, and transitory; may include an inner circle. 3. Tenure of dominant coalition not always lengthy; key managers may be hired from outside as well as promoted from within. 4. Planning is comprehensive, problem oriented, and cannot be finalized before action is taken. 5. Tendency toward product structure with low division of labor and low degree of formalization. 6. Decentralized control and short-looped horizontal information systems. 7. Complex coordination mechanisms and conflict resolved through integrators. 8. Organizational performance measured against important competitors; reward system favors marketing and research and development.
Costs and Benefits:	*Costs and Benefits:*	*Costs and Benefits:*
Product and market innovation protect the organization from a changing environment, but the organization runs the risk of low profitability and overextension of its resources.	Technological flexibility permits a rapid response to a changing domain, but the organization cannot develop maximum efficiency in its production and distribution system because of multiple technologies.	Administrative system is ideally suited to maintain flexibility and effectiveness but may underutilize and misutilize resources.

nent resembles the Prospector's technological orientation. In manufacturing organizations, it frequently includes a large group of applications engineers (or their equivalent) who are rotated among teams charged with the task of rapidly adapting new product designs to fit the Analyzer's existing stable technology.

The Analyzer's dual technological core thus reflects the engineering solutions of both the Prospector and the Defender, with the stable and flexible components integrated primarily by an influential applied research group. To the extent that this group is able to develop solutions that match the organization's existing technological capabilities with the new products desired by product managers, the Analyzer can enlarge its product line without incurring the Prospector's extensive research and development expenses.

The Analyzer's administrative problem, as well as its entrepreneurial and engineering problems, contains both Defender and Prospector characteristics. Generally speaking, the *administrative* problem of the Analyzer is *how to differentiate the organization's structure and processes to accommodate both stable and dynamic areas of operation.* The Analyzer typically solves this problem with some version of a matrix organization structure. Heads of key functional units, most notably engineering and production, unite with product managers (usually housed in the marketing department) to form a balanced dominant coalition similar to both the Defender and the Prospector. The product manager's influence is usually greater than the functional manager's since his or her task is to identify promising product-market innovations and to supervise their movement through applied engineering and into production in a smooth and timely manner. The presence of engineering and production in the dominant coalition is to represent the more stable domain and technology which are the foundations of the Analyzer's overall operations. The Analyzer's matrix structure is supported by intensive planning between the functional divisions of marketing and production, broad-gauge planning between the applied research group and the product managers for the development of new products, centralized control mechanisms in the functional divisions and decentralized control techniques in the product groups, and so on. In sum, the key characteristic of the Analyzer's administrative system is the proper differentiation of the organization's structure and processes to achieve a balance between the stable and dynamic areas of operation.

As is true for both the Defender and Prospector, the Analyzer strategy is not without its costs. The duality in the Analyzer's domain forces the organization to establish a dual technological core, and it requires management to operate fundamentally different planning, control, and reward systems simultaneously. Thus, the Analyzer's twin characteristics of stability and flexibility limit the organization's ability to move fully in either direction were the domain to shift dramatically. Consequently, the Analyzer's *primary risks* are both *inefficiency and ineffectiveness* if it does not maintain

TABLE 3   Characteristics of the Analyzer

ENTREPRENEURIAL PROBLEM	ENGINEERING PROBLEM	ADMINISTRATIVE PROBLEM
Problem:	*Problem:*	*Problem:*
How to locate and exploit new product and market opportunities while simultaneously maintaining a firm base of traditional products and customers.	How to be efficient in stable portions of the domain and flexible in changing portions.	How to differentiate the organization's structure and processes to accommodate both stable and dynamic areas of operation.
Solutions:	*Solutions:*	*Solutions:*
1. Hybrid domain that is both stable and changing.	1. Dual technological core (stable and flexible component).	1. Marketing and engineering most influential members of dominant coalition, followed closely by production.
2. Surveillance mechanisms mostly limited to marketing; some research and development.	2. Large and influential applied engineering group.	2. Intensive planning between marketing and production concerning stable portion of domain; comprehensive planning among marketing, engineering, and product managers concerning new products and markets.
3. Steady growth through market penetration and product-market development.	3. Moderate degree of technical rationality.	3. "Loose" matrix structure combining both functional divisions and product groups.
		4. Moderately centralized control system with vertical and horizontal feedback loops.
		5. Extremely complex and expensive coordination mechanisms; some conflict resolution through product managers, some through normal hierarchical channels.
		6. Performance appraisal based on both effectiveness and efficiency measures, most rewards to marketing and engineering.
Costs and Benefits:	*Costs and Benefits:*	*Costs and Benefits:*
Low investment in research and development, combined with imitation of demonstrably successful products, minimizes risk, but domain must be optimally balanced at all times between stability and flexibility.	Dual technological core is able to serve a hybrid stable-changing domain, but the technology can never be completely effective or efficient.	Administrative system is ideally suited to balance stability and flexibility, but if this balance is lost, it may be difficult to restore equilibrium.

the necessary balance throughout its strategy-structure relationship. Table 3 summarizes the Analyzer's salient characteristics and the major strengths and weaknesses inherent in this pattern of adaptation.

Reactors

The Defender, the Prospector, and the Analyzer can all be proactive with respect to their environments, though each is proactive in a different way. At the extremes, Defenders continually attempt to develop greater efficiency in existing operations, while Prospectors explore environmental change in search of new opportunities. Over time, these action modes stabilize to form a pattern of response to environmental conditions that is both *consistent* and *stable*.

A fourth type of organization, the Reactor, exhibits a pattern of adjustment to its environment that is both *inconsistent* and *unstable*; this type lacks a set of response mechanisms which it can consistently put into effect when faced with a changing environment. As a consequence, Reactors exist in a state of almost perpetual instability. The Reactor's "adaptive" cycle usually consists of responding inappropriately to environmental change and uncertainty, performing poorly as a result, and then being reluctant to act aggressively in the future. Thus, the Reactor is a "residual" strategy, arising when one of the other three strategies is improperly pursued.

Although there are undoubtedly many reasons why organizations become Reactors, we have identified three. First, *top management may not have clearly articulated the organization's strategy*. For example, one company was headed by a "one-man" Prospector of immense personal skills. A first-rate architect, he led his firm through a rapid and successful growth period during which the company moved from the design and construction of suburban shopping centers, through the construction and management of apartment complexes, and into consulting with municipal agencies concerning urban planning problems. Within ten years of its inception, the company was a loose but effective collection of semi-autonomous units held together by this particular individual. When this individual was suddenly killed in a plane crash, the company was thrown into a strategic void. Because each separate unit of the company was successful, each was able to argue strongly for more emphasis on its particular domain and operations. Consequently, the new chief executive officer, caught between a number of conflicting but legitimate demands for resources, was unable to develop a unified, cohesive statement of the organization's strategy; thus, consistent and aggressive behavior was precluded.

A second and perhaps more common cause of organizational instability is that *management does not fully shape the organization's structure and processes to fit a chosen strategy*. Unless all of the domain, technological, and administrative decisions required to have an operational strategy are properly aligned, strategy is a mere statement, not an effective guide to behavior. One publishing company wished, in effect, to become an Analyzer

—management had articulated a direction for the organization which involved operating in both stable and changing domains within the college textbook publishing industry. Although the organization was comprised of several key Defender and Prospector characteristics such as functional structures and decentralized control mechanisms, these structure-process features were not appropriately linked to the company's different domains. In one area where the firm wished to "prospect," for example, the designated unit had a functional structure and shared a large, almost mass-production technology with several other units, thereby making it difficult for the organization to respond to market opportunities quickly. Thus, this particular organization exhibited a weak link between its strategy and its structure-process characteristics.

The third cause of instability—and perhaps ultimate failure—is *a tendency for management to maintain the organization's current strategy-structure relationship despite overwhelming changes in environmental conditions.* Another organization in our studies, a food-processing company, had initially been an industry pioneer in both the processing and marketing of dried fruits and nuts. Gradually, the company settled into a Defender strategy and took vigorous steps to bolster this strategy, including limiting the domain to a narrow line of products, integrating backward into growing and harvesting, and assigning a controller to each of the company's major functional divisions as a means of keeping costs down. Within recent years, the company's market has become saturated, and profit margins have shrunk on most of the firm's products. In spite of its declining market, the organization has consistently clung to a Defender strategy and structure, even to the point of creating ad hoc cross-divisional committees whose sole purpose was to find ways of increasing efficiency further. At the moment, management recognizes that the organization is in trouble, but it is reluctant to make the drastic modifications required to attain a strategy and structure better suited to the changing market conditions.

Unless an organization exists in a "protected" environment such as a monopolistic or highly-regulated industry, it cannot continue to behave as a Reactor indefinitely. Sooner or later, it must move toward one of the consistent and stable strategies of Defender, Analyzer, or Prospector.

MANAGEMENT THEORY LINKAGES TO ORGANIZATIONAL STRATEGY AND STRUCTURE

Organizations are limited in their choices of adaptive behavior to those which top management believes will allow the effective direction and control of human resources. Therefore, top executives' theories of management are an important factor in analyzing an organization's ability to adapt to its environment. Although our research is only in its preliminary stage, we have found some patterns in the relationship between management theory and organizational strategy and structure.

A theory of management has three basic components: (a) a set of assumptions about human attitudes and behaviors, (b) managerial policies and actions consistent with these assumptions, and (c) expectations about employee performance if these policies and actions are implemented (see Table 4). Theories of management are discussed in more detail in Miles (14).

During the latter part of the 19th Century and the early decades of the 20th, mainstream management theory, as voiced by managers and by management scholars, conformed to what has been termed the *Traditional* model. Essentially, the Traditional model maintained that the capability for effective decision making was narrowly distributed in organizations, and this approach thus legitimized unilateral control of organizational systems by top management. According to this model, a select group of owner-managers was able to direct large numbers of employees by carefully standardizing and routinizing their work and by placing the planning function solely in the hands of top managers. Under this type of management system, employees could be expected to perform up to some minimum standard, but few would be likely to exhibit truly outstanding performance.

Beginning in the twenties, the Traditional model gradually began to give way to the *Human Relations* model. This model accepted the traditional notion that superior decision-making competence was narrowly distributed among the employee population but emphasized the universality of social needs for belonging and recognition. This model argued that impersonal treatment was the source of subordinate resistance to managerial directives, and adherents of this approach urged managers to employ devices to enhance organization members' feelings of involvement and importance in order to improve organizational performance. Suggestion systems, employee counseling, and even company unions had common parentage in this philosophy. The Depression and World War II both acted to delay the development and spread of the Human Relations model, and it was not until the late forties and early fifties that it became the prime message put forth by managers and management scholars.

Beginning in the mid-fifties, a third phase in the evolution of management theory began with the emergence of the *Human Resources* model which argued that the capacity for effective decision making in the pursuit of organizational objectives was widely dispersed and that most organization members represented untapped resources which, if properly managed, could considerably enhance organizational performance. The Human Resources approach viewed management's role not as that of a controller (however benevolent) but as that of a facilitator—removing the constraints that block organization members' search for ways to contribute meaningfully in their work roles. In recent years, some writers have questioned the extent to which the Human Resources model is applicable,

TABLE 4   Theories of Management

TRADITIONAL MODEL	HUMAN RELATIONS MODEL	HUMAN RESOURCES MODEL
Assumptions	*Assumptions*	*Assumptions*
1. Work is inherently distasteful to most people. 2. What workers do is less important than what they earn for doing it. 3. Few want or can handle work which requires creativity, self-direction, or self-control.	1. People want to feel useful and important. 2. People desire to belong and to be recognized as individuals. 3. These needs are more important than money in motivating people to work.	1. Work is not inherently distasteful. People want to contribute to meaningful goals which they have helped establish. 2. Most people can exercise far more creative, responsible self-direction and self-control than their present jobs demand.
Policies	*Policies*	*Policies*
1. The manager's basic task is to closely supervise and control his (her) subordinates. 2. He (she) must break tasks down into simple, repetitive, easily learned operations. 3. He (she) must establish detailed work routines and procedures and enforce these firmly but fairly.	1. The manager's basic task is to make each worker feel useful and important. 2. He (she) should keep his (her) subordinates informed and listen to their objections to his (her) plans. 3. The manager should allow his (her) subordinates to exercise some self-direction and self-control on routine matters.	1. The manager's basic task is to make use of his (her) "untapped" human resources. 2. He (she) must create an environment in which all members may contribute to the limits of their ability. 3. He (she) must encourage full participation on important matters, continually broadening subordinate self-direction and control.
Expectations	*Expectations*	*Expectations*
1. People can tolerate work if the pay is decent and the boss is fair. 2. If tasks are simple enough and people are closely controlled, they will produce up to standard.	1. Sharing information with subordinates and involving them in routine decisions will satisfy their basic needs to belong and to feel important. 2. Satisfying these needs will improve morale and reduce resistance to formal authority—subordinates will willingly cooperate and produce.	1. Expanding subordinate influence, self-direction, and self-control will lead to direct improvements in organizational performance. 2. Work satisfaction may improve as a "by-product" of subordinates making full use of their resources.

arguing for a more "contingent" theory emphasizing variations in member capacity and motivation to contribute and the technological constraints associated with broadened self-direction and self-control. The Human Resources model probably still represents the leading edge of management theory, perhaps awaiting the formulation of a successful model.

Linking the Strategic Typology to Management Theory

Are there identifiable linkages between an organization's strategic type and the management theory of its dominant coalition? For example, do top executives in Defenders profess Traditional beliefs about management and those in Prospectors a Human Resources philosophy? The answer to this question is, in our opinion, a bit more complex than simply "yes" or "no."

One of our studies investigated aspects of the relationship between organizational strategy-structure and management theory. Although the results are only tentative at this point, relatively clear patterns emerged. In general, Traditional and Human Relations managerial beliefs are more likely to be found in Defender and Reactor organizations, while Human Resources beliefs are more often associated with Analyzer and Prospector organizations. But this relationship appears to be *constrained in one direction;* it seems highly unlikely that a Traditional or Human Relations manager can function effectively as the head of a Prospector organization. The prescriptions of the Traditional model simply do not support the degree of decentralized decision making required to create and manage diversified organizations. It is quite possible for a Human Resources manager to lead a Defender organization. Of course, the organization's planning and control processes under such leadership would be less centralized than if the organization were managed according to the Traditional model. Using the Human Resources philosophy, heads of functional divisions might either participate in the planning and budgeting process, or they might simply be delegated considerable autonomy in operating their cost centers. (In Defender organizations operated according to the Human Resources philosophy, human capabilities are aimed primarily at cost efficiency rather than product development.)

The fit between management theory and the strategy, structure, and process characteristics of Analyzers is perhaps more complex than with any of the other types. Analyzers, as previously described, tend to remain cost efficient in the production of a limited line of goods or services while attempting to move as rapidly as possible into promising new areas opened up by Prospectors. Note that the organization structure of the Analyzer does not demand extensive, permanent delegation of decision-making authority to division managers. Most of the Analyzer's products or services can be produced in functionally structured divisions similar to those in Defender organizations. New products or services may be developed in separate divisions or departments created for that purpose and then integrated as quickly as possible into the permanent technology and structure. It seems likely to us, although our evidence is inconclusive, that various members of the dominant coalition in Analyzer organizations hold moderate but different managerial philosophies, that certain key executives believe it is their role to pay fairly close attention to detail while others appear to be more willing to delegate, for short periods, moderate amounts of autonomy necessary to bring new products or services on line rapidly. If these varying managerial philosophies are "mismatched" within the Analyzer's operating units—if, for example, Traditional managers are placed in charge of innovative subunits—then it is unlikely that a successful Analyzer strategy can be pursued.

Holding together a dominant coalition with mixed views concerning strategy and structure is not an easy task. It is difficult, for example, for managers engaged in new product or service development to function within planning, control, and reward systems established for more stable operations, so the Analyzer must be successfully differentiated into its stable and changing areas and managed accordingly. Note that experimentation in the Analyzer is usually quite limited. The exploration and risk associated with major product or service breakthroughs are not present (as would be the case in a Prospector), and thus interdependencies within the system may be kept at a manageable level. Such would not be the case if Analyzers attempted to be both cost-efficient producers of stable products or services and active in a major way in new product and market development. Numerous organizations are today being led or forced into such a mixed strategy (multinational companies, certain forms of conglomerates, many organizations in high-technology industries, etc.), and their struggles may well produce a new organization type and demands for a supporting theory of management. Whatever form this new type of organization takes, however, clearly its management-theory requirements will closely parallel or extend those of the Human Resources model (15).

CONCLUSIONS

Our research represents an initial attempt: (a) to portray the major elements of organizational adaptation, (b) to describe patterns of behavior used by organizations in adjusting to their environments, and (c) to provide a language for discussing organizational behavior at the total-system level. Therefore, we have offered a theoretical framework composed of a model of the adaptive process (called the adaptive cycle) and four empirically determined means of moving through this process (the strategic typology). In addition, we have related this theoretical framework to available theories of management (Traditional, Human Relations, Human Resources). Effective organizational adaptation hinges on the ability of managers to not only envision and implement new organizational forms but also to direct and control people within them.

We believe that managers' ability to meet successfully environmental conditions of tomorrow revolves around their understanding of organizations as integrated and dynamic wholes. Hopefully, our framework offers a theory and language for promoting such an understanding.

REFERENCES

1. ANDERSON, CARL R., and FRANK T. PAINE. "Managerial Perceptions and Strategic Behavior," *Academy of Management Journal*, Vol. 18 (1975), 811–823.
2. ANSOFF, H. IGOR. *Corporate Strategy* (New York: McGraw-Hill, 1965).
3. ANSOFF, H. IGOR, and RICHARD BRANDENBURG. "A Language for Organizational Design," *Management Science*, Vol. 17 (1971), B717–B731.
4. ANSOFF, H. IGOR, and JOHN M. STEWART. "Strategies for a Technology-Based Business," *Harvard Business Review*, Vol. 45 (1967), 71–83.
5. ARGYRIS, CHRIS. "On Organizations of the Future," *Administrative and Policy Study Series*, Vol. 1, No. 03–006 (Beverly Hills, Calif.: Sage Publications, 1973).
6. BEER, MICHAEL, and STANLEY M. DAVIS. "Creating a Global Organization: Failures Along the Way," *Columbia Journal of World Business*, Vol. 11 (1976), 72–84.
7. BOWER, JOSEPH L. *Managing the Resource Allocation Process* (Boston: Division of Research, Harvard Business School, 1970).
8. BURNS, TOM, and G. M. STALKER. *The Management of Innovation* (London: Tavistock, 1961).
9. CHANDLER, ALFRED D., JR. *Strategy and Structure* (Garden City, N.Y.: Doubleday, 1962).
10. CHILD, JOHN. "Organizational Structure, Environment, and Performance—The Role of Strategic Choice," *Sociology*, Vol. 6 (1972), 1–22.
11. CYERT, RICHARD, and JAMES G. MARCH. *A Behavioral Theory of the Firm* (Englewood Cliffs, N.J.: Prentice-Hall, 1963).
12. DRUCKER, PETER F. *The Practice of Management* (New York: Harper & Brothers, 1954).
13. DRUCKER, PETER F. *Management: Tasks, Responsibilities, Practices* (New York: Harper & Row, 1974).
14. MILES, RAYMOND E. *Theories of Management* (New York: McGraw-Hill, 1975).
15. MILES, RAYMOND E., and CHARLES C. SNOW. *Organizational Strategy, Structure, and Process* (New York: McGraw-Hill, 1978).
16. ROGERS, EVERETT M. *Communication of Innovations: A Cross-Cultural Approach*, 2nd ed. (New York: Free Press, 1971).
17. SEGAL, MORLEY. "Organization and Environment: A Typology of Adaptability and Structure," *Public Administration Review*, Vol. 35 (1974), 212–220.
18. THOMPSON, JAMES D. *Organizations in Action* (New York: McGraw-Hill, 1967).
19. WEICK, KARL E. *The Social Psychology of Organizing* (Reading, Mass.: Addison-Wesley, 1969).
20. WEICK, KARL E. "Enactment Processes in Organizations," in Barry M. Staw and Gerald R. Salancik (Eds.), *New Directions in Organizational Behavior* (Chicago: St. Clair, 1977), pp. 267–300.
21. WOODWARD, JOAN. *Industrial Organization: Theory and Practice* (London: Oxford University Press, 1965).

Boundary Spanning Roles and Organization Structure

Howard Aldrich
Diane Herker

A minimal defining characteristic of a formal organization is the distinction between members and non-members, with an organization existing to the extent that some persons are admitted, while others are excluded, thus allowing an observer to draw a boundary around the organization (61, pp. 139–146). Defining organizations in terms of boundaries to interaction also allows a parsimonious definition of the role of formal authority in an organization: authorities are persons who apply organizational rules in making decisions about entry and expulsion of members (6, p. 283). In this sense, organizational behavior (OB) has always contained an implicit "open systems" view, although few theorists or researchers have studied boundary-maintaining or boundary-crossing (5).

The definition and location of a specific boundary may be possible only given a specific conceptual and empirical context. This article takes the existence of boundaries as given, while treating boundary spanning activity as problematic. Specifically, it examines functions served by boundary roles, the generation of boundary units and roles relating organizations to their environments, and the environmental and organizational sources of variation in the structure of boundary roles. Use is made of existing literature, but the argument is speculative at many points.

Reprinted by permission from the *Academy of Management Review*, April 1977, pp. 217–230.

Although most investigators agree on the importance of focusing on relations between organizations and their environments, there is little agreement on the degree of autonomy of action organizations have vis-à-vis their environments. At the extreme are two positions: a natural selection model, laying heavy emphasis on the dominance of environmental constraints on behavior, and a strategic choice or resource dependence model, emphasizing the active role organizational administrators play in shaping outcomes. As these two macro-theoretical positions are reviewed elsewhere (9), and there is no prospect of reconciling them in this paper, we concentrate on propositions and hypotheses of the middle-range.

FUNCTIONS OF BOUNDARY ROLES

Two classes of functions are performed by boundary roles: information processing and external representation. Information from external sources comes into an organization through boundary roles, and boundary roles link organizational structure to environmental elements, whether by buffering, moderating, or influencing the environment. Any given role can serve either or both functions.

The Information Processing Function

In focusing on the information processing function, we are following the lead of Dill (24), who suggested that the environment of an organization could be treated as information available to the organization through search or exposure. Thompson and McEwen discussed the organization's need for information to judge the amount and sources of support for its goals (63, p. 30). Terryberry argued that viable organizations are characterized by "an increase in the ability to learn and to perform according to changing contingencies in the environment" (60, p. 660).

Boundary role incumbents, by virtue of their position, are exposed to large amounts of potentially relevant information. The situation would be overburdening if all information originating in the environment required immediate attention. Boundary roles are a main line of organizational defense against information overload (17, 42). Expertise in selecting information is consequential, since not all information from the environment is of equal importance. External information can be conceptualized in terms of a three-part hierarchy, corresponding to Parsons' (47) distinction between three levels of authority in organizations: strategic, managerial, and technical information (17, p. 325). Their relative importance varies by type of environment and technology; e.g., in stable homogeneous environments and organizations with highly routinized technology, strategic information is less important.

The process by which information filters through boundary positions into the organization must be examined. Boundary roles serve a dual function in information transmittal, acting as both filters and facilitators. Information overload would still be a problem if all relevant information had to be immediately communicated to internal members. Accordingly, boundary role personnel selectively act on relevant information, filtering information prior to communicating it (23, 40). They act autonomously on some information, and consolidate, delay, or store other information, thus alleviating the problem of overloading communication channels (although perhaps incurring other costs to the organization in the process). Information is summarized and directed to the organizational units that need it.

Boundary role personnel may act on information requiring an immediate response, as when a sales department responds to a customer inquiry about product specifications. They may store information for future use, as when a purchasing department files information on a new supplier's products, to be referred to at re-order points. Boundary personnel in marketing may uncover trends in the demand for their organization's products which will have a major impact on the mix of resources required, and communicate this information to purchasing. Boundary units may also summarize information and communicate it to other units on a regularized basis (41).

The expertise of boundary role occupants in summarizing and interpreting information may be as important to organizational success as expertise in determining who gets what information, depending upon the uncertainty in the information processed. Information to be communicated often does not consist of simple verifiable "facts." If the conditions beyond the boundary are complexly interrelated and cannot be easily quantified, the boundary role incumbents may engage in "uncertainty absorption," —drawing inferences from perceived facts and passing on only the inferences (40, p. 189).

Consider the case of a lobbyist formulating a report on a bill and amendments that will differentially affect the operations of his or her organization. The lobbyist will have to summarize information about the bill's progress, testimony in hearings, and apparent predispositions of committee members and other legislators, as well as making the entire situation meaningful to his or her superiors. If these superiors cannot understand the interrelationships and implications of the raw data, they will not be able to use the information. Some simplification is necessary and the relationships of events in Washington to organizational operations will have to be clearly specified. In short, the lobbyist must put the information in usable form (67).

Innovation and structural change are often alleged to result from information brought into the organization by boundary personnel (11, 28). All complex organizations have a tendency to move toward an internal state of compatibility and compromise between units and individuals within the organization, with a resultant isolation from important external influences (18). This trend can jeopardize the effectiveness and perhaps the survival of the organization, *unless* the organization is effectively linked to the environment through active boundary personnel. By scanning the environment for new technological developments, innovations in organizational design, relevant trends in related fields, etc., boundary personnel can prevent organizations from becoming prematurely ossified and mismatched with their environments (20).

This review of the information processing function of boundary roles may be summarized in the following hypothesis:

H1: *An organization's ability to adapt to environmental contingencies depends in part on the expertise of boundary role incumbents in selecting, transmitting, and interpreting information originating in the environment.*

The External Representation Function

External representation can be viewed in terms of an organization's response to environmental influence. Environmental constraints and contingencies can be adapted to in at least three ways: (a) by internal structural differentiation to match the pattern of the relevant environment, which requires information about environmental characteristics; (b) by gaining power over relevant elements of the environment, manipulating it to conform to the organization's needs; and (c) a compromise position, the modal pattern of use of boundary personnel in "normal" boundary spanning roles. Included under the external representation function are all boundary roles that involve resource acquisition and disposal, political legitimacy and hegemony, and a residual category of social legitimacy and organizational image.

Boundary roles concerned with resource acquisition and disposal include purchasing agents and buyers, marketing and sales representatives, personnel recruiters, admissions officers, and shipping and receiving agents. In these roles the organization is represented to the environment, because the normal flow of authoritative commands is from the core of the organization to these boundary roles. The behavior of personnel in these roles is supposed to reflect the policy decisions of decision makers in line roles.

This usual flow of directives to boundary roles presents two problems for boundary personnel. First, much of the information they attend to has an external origin, and it occasionally becomes apparent that policy directives are based on information that is no longer relevant. This poses a dilemma for the conscientious boundary spanner, especially in organizations with a high degree of decentralization—should behavior be immediately modified to correspond to latest developments, or should action be delayed until the information has "gone through channels"? Second, as Strauss (59) pointed out in his study of purchasing agents, some boundary personnel are not satisfied with their subordinate position on the vertical axis of the organization, given their self-evident horizontal location of equality with other departments. Thus dissatisfied boundary spanners take the intiative to increase their power vis-à-vis other units. For example, personnel officers suggest changes in job descriptions before agreeing to post them; admissions or intake staff develop their own criteria of "worthy" applicants (14); and purchasing agents make informal compacts with salespersons from outside firms to push products which their production department "really" needs (59).

Boundary roles involved with maintaining or improving the political legitimacy or hegemony of the organization not only represent the organization but also mediate between it and important outside organizations. The term "mediate" refers here to aspects of the boundary role involving negotiations that will eventually affect the power of the focal organization vis-à-vis another organization or group. Kochan (36) notes that city governments have created collective bargaining units as a response to threats to the city's control over its employees. The role of the corporate lawyer is perhaps the most clear example of the necessity and difficulty of preserving at least an equal balance of rights and responsibilities between business organizations (38).

Boundary spanning personnel can help maintain the legitimacy of the organization by providing information to important client groups, specially adapted for them. Aldrich and Reiss (10) note that police officers on the beat transmit an image of city law enforcement capabilities to small *businesspersons* independent of the *businessperson's* attitudes toward the police themselves. Information transmittal is facilitated because both police and small business are exposed to environmental forces that make their commonality of interest highly salient. Adair's (1) study of the use of Navajo Indians as health aides for their own communities found that the Indians functioned as mediators in their boundary roles, drawing the doctor and the Navajo patient closer together. The Indian health worker offers a different side to each party involved, finding a middle ground to settle discords between them. Detached school workers perform the same sort of representation function for school systems.

Maintaining the organizational image and enhancing its social legitimacy are less a matter of mediating contacts than of simply making the organization visible. Advertising and public relations specialists try to influence the behavior of target groups in ways that benefit the focal organization, without bargaining or negotiating with the target group. The flow of intra-organizational influence to these roles is much more one-sided than in the boundary roles described above; one apparent consequence is a high rate of turnover.

One function of boards of directors and public advisory commissions is to link the organization to target groups in the environment in a highly visible way, so that they will feel their interests are being represented. Thus, women and blacks are being appointed in increasing numbers to corporate boards, and students now serve as trustees on university boards. Fulfilling this function requires recruiting people who are already members of or in contact with specific target groups. Maniha and Perrow (39) describe the formation of a Youth Commission's board in terms of such community interest groups as Catholics, the university, and youth-oriented voluntary associations.

These three varieties of external representation functions can be related to organizational effectiveness in the second hypothesis:

H2: *An organization's ability to cope with environmental constraints depends in part on the ability of boundary role incumbents to achieve a compromise between organizational policy and environmental constraints, to choose strategic moves to overcome constraints, or to create conditions in which the organization's autonomy is seldom challenged.*

CREATION OF BOUNDARY ROLES

By definition all organizations have some boundary spanning roles, if only at the level of the organization head or chief executive. But some have an elaborate set of boundary roles while others have only a few. In some cases boundary roles are formalized into full-time organizational positions, while in others they are only part-time activities. This section examines the generation and formalization of boundary roles as explicit organizational roles, with references to organizational size and technology, and various characteristics of organizational environments. To understand the process of boundary spanning *behavior*, an interactive model of the kind developed by Adams (2) is needed, but such models are highly specific to the particular pair-wise relationship being examined. Here we are concerned with the general features of the boundary role while recognizing that actual behavior in boundary roles will vary from context to context.

The extent to which organizational positions involve interaction with external elements varies greatly. Many positions outside the technical core involve some extra-organizational interaction, but only a few involve intensive interaction. As an empirical test of arguments in this article we would need a measure providing better than a "yes-no" categorization of roles as either boundary spanning or not. This would require determining the proportion of time spent with outsiders, the number of outside contacts, the importance of each contact, etc., as Whetten (65) has recently done in a study of manpower organizations.

The number of formally designated boundary spanning roles in an organization is partially dependent on organizational size (5). A small organization is able to survive with a fairly simple structure, with relatively few differentiated roles and functions (16, 21, 22). Its structure may be less formalized and more amenable to restructuring to achieve and maintain a satisfactory position vis-à-vis its environment. A small organization might be willing and able to rely on information brought to it informally by its members. This tendency is more marked among organizations that have highly committed members or that are not highly dependent on their environment for survival (6), such as a small religious sect (29). As organizational and environmental complexities increase, organizations can no longer afford non-differentiated boundary spanning activities.

Technology and Boundary Role Differentiation

Holding size constant, boundary spanning units or roles should be expected to increase as a proportion of all roles as organizations differentiate in response to the interaction of technology and environment, and under the direct impact of environmental pressure. In the following discussion, technology is treated as a source of internal differentiation generating boundary roles to the extent that varying technology types create different patterns of organization-environment interaction. Thompson's categories of mediating, long-linked and intensive technology capture the implications of various technology types for the generation of boundary roles (62, pp. 15–18).

Organizations with a *mediating technology* link clients or customers with each other, as in the case of banks, insurance companies, or the post office; or they link clients with other organizations, thus serving a "people-processing function" (30). Such organizations should have the highest proportion of boundary roles, as boundary roles are their line roles. The wholesaler of small consumer goods has boundary personnel who purchase goods from producers and sell them to organizations which, in turn, sell them to retail customers. An investment banking firm contracts with a client to put together a "package" of investment instruments that satisfy financial needs and then sells the "package" to other organizations with funds to invest. Boundary personnel similarly serve a line function in the people processing component of organizations such as schools and government agencies.

A study of organizations using a mediating technology in the book publishing and record producing industries found that they allocated a large proportion of their personnel to boundary spanning roles, on the input side to contract for and supervise the production of raw material, and on the output side to promote the cultural products and achieve optimal distribution (32). These boundary roles also monitored the environment and provided information quickly to managers and executives, apparently as a strategy to help the organization hold its position in a very uncertain environment.

Organizations with a *long-linked technology* attempt to buffer most of their units and roles from the environment, and have a lower proportion of boundary roles. Since the various organizational units are serially inter-dependent, there are many boundary roles between intraorganizational components, but the focus here is on roles at the external boundary. Specif-ic boundary roles are important for such organizations. First, long-linked technology gains maximum efficiency through standardized production of large volumes of output (to take advantage of economies of scale) and so such organizations need an effective marketing and sales force (35, 51). Second, Thompson (62, p. 40) argues that "organizations employing long-linked technologies and subject to rationality norms seek to expand their domains through *vertical integration*," and thus the legal and accounting departments of such organizations interact fairly intensively with potential acquisitions in the environment (50).

Organizations using an *intensive technology*, which depends on the object being worked on, also buffer most of their roles from the environ-ment. They often achieve this by temporarily drawing the object or the client into the organization. In intensive technology organizations con-cerned with people-changing activities, the client is temporarily assigned an organizational role, and must change behavior to suit norms which preclude appealing to his or her environmental role relative to the organi-zation. The boundary personnel who engage in initial interaction with potential clients affect the organization's subsequent internal operations if they have the power to admit or reject clients, e.g., the physician associ-ated with a hospital or the admissions officer at a private college. By detect-ing a violation and making an arrest, a police officer provides the rest of the criminal justice system with raw material to be processed (55).

Thompson argues that these organizations seek to expand their do-mains by incorporating the object worked on, with "total institutions" (26) placing an almost impenetrable boundary around clients. The people-changing organizations that use an intensive technology (e.g., hospitals) have one characteristic that opens them to environmental influence—their high degree of professionalization. Aiken and Hage (4) assert that profes-sionals in organizations engage in a great deal of boundary-spanning con-tact because of the need to maintain contact with a professional reference group and keep abreast of changing technology in their field.

In intensive technology organizations not concerned with people-changing activities, the clients often become a temporary part of the organi-zation's administrative structure and thus need a liaison person to repre-sent them, as in the construction industry (62, p. 44). Thus, while it is clear that mediating technology organizations have proportionately more boundary spanning roles than other organizations, the relative ranking of organizations with long-linked and intensive technology cannot be determined without further empirical research.

H3: *Organizations using a mediating technology will have the highest proportion of boundary roles, while organizations using long-linked and intensive technologies will have a smaller proportion of boundary roles.*

H4: *Organizations using long-linked or intensive technologies will departmentalize and otherwise separate boundary spanning units from their core technical units.*

Environment and Boundary Role Differentiation

Environmental pressures are responsible for much of the observed differentiation in organizations, after technology is taken into account. Some theories of organization-environment interaction posit that maintenance of a high degree of internal organizational complexity occurs only in response to environmental pressures that tolerate nothing less (9, 18). The concentration of important environmental elements into an organized form may promote a matching organizational response, in the form of more boundary units or more formalized and centralized boundary spanning activities (52). Kochan points out that:

> A number of collective bargaining researchers have noted the proliferation of specialized labor relations units in city governments in response to the increased unionization of public employees (36, p. 7).

Wilson (67) discusses the growth of lobbying efforts of unions, trade associations, and other organizations representing vested interests, in response to the growth in power of the federal government. The consumer, ecology, and other movements have brought pressure on corporations, which have responded by establishing public relations units to deal with pressure groups. The same type of response occurred among public agencies in the President's Office for Consumer Affairs and similar offices in HEW, HUD, etc. (45).

H5: *Organizations in environments where important elements are concentrated will have a higher proportion of boundary roles than organizations in environments where important elements are dispersed.*

Heterogeneous environments should evoke more organizational boundary spanning units and roles, as organizations "seek to identify homogeneous segments and establish structural units to deal with each" (62, p. 70). Separate units, whether established on the basis of heterogeneity in a client population or in the geographical domain served, lead to a higher proportion of boundary roles than in organizations of comparable size serving a homogeneous domain. Hospitals establish separate units for obstetrics, contagious diseases, and out-patient services. Auto manufacturing firms respond to heterogeneity in client income distribution by divisionalizing operations around products with different selling prices, but not necessarily costs (19).

H6: *Organizations in heterogeneous environments will have a higher proportion of boundary roles than organizations in homogeneous environments.*

Stable environments, which presumably call for less frequent monitoring, should evoke fewer boundary roles than unstable environments, although much depends on whether change is occurring at a constant or variable rate (62, pp. 71–72). In the cultural industry (books, records, films) where fashions change rapidly, we would expect to find proliferation of boundary roles on both input and output sides of the organization (32). In organizations producing for a stable market, we would expect most roles to be related directly to the production process, although an unexpected shift in the market can change the situation dramatically, as in Emery and Trist's (25) example of a food canning firm. Some theorists have argued that the most salient characteristic of organizational environments today is their rate of change (60), a purported trend which should cause an increase in the proportion of boundary spanning roles in most organizations.

H7: *Organizations in rapidly changing environments will have a higher proportion of boundary roles than organizations in stable environments.*

A final dimension to be considered is the extent to which the environment is rich or lean in resources (7, 12, 25). In rich environments, holding competition constant, we would expect to find fewer boundary roles, since environmental search and monitoring would be less critical for organizational survival than in environments where lack of resources prevents the accumulation of a "resource cushion." At a time of international or interorganizational hostility, the environment becomes less rich in information and so nations and organizations have to allocate more roles to their boundaries to make use of what little information is available (66).

H8: *Organizations in lean environments will have a higher proportion of boundary roles than organizations in rich environments.*

Environment and Boundary Role Formalization

If internal complexity is associated with environmental pressures and demands, organizational boundary roles will be officially recognized full-time roles, especially if decision makers recognize the existence of such contingencies. Whether boundary roles will be thus formalized depends upon organizational recognition of potentially costly contingencies that may arise from failure to maintain effective links to elements in the environment. But such recognition need not be based on intelligence that organization itself has accumulated, as professional education (e.g., MBA programs), professional and trade publications (e.g., *Business Week*), and informal inter-firm contact (51) all keep organizational decision-makers abreast of new developments in the design and administration of formal organizations (12,

58). The following discussion focuses on direct, rather than indirect, recognition of environmental contingencies and constraints.

Most large organizations formally designate such roles as labor negotiators and corporate lawyers responsible for transactions in the labor relations sector, since strikes and law suits might cripple an organization. Labor contracts are negotiated for fairly long periods of time and the organizational costs of mistakes in boundary-spanning negotiation with unions are fairly high. Smigel's (57) discussion of staff recruitment in large Wall Street law firms indicates that firms became aware of a variety of changes in their environment, including the small output of prestigious law schools, students' wariness of accepting positions with large firms, and the increasing demand for trained lawyers. One result was creation of the formal position of "hiring partner" to scan the potential output of top ranking law schools, sell students on advantages of employment in the firm, and thus improve recruitment of desirable graduates.

The more critical the contingency, the more attention is paid to explicit formalization of the role and selection of an incumbent. This is particularly evident with regard to the composition of boards of directors of large organizations, as Pfeffer argues that organizations:

> use their boards of directors as vehicles through which they co-opt, or partially absorb, important external organizations with which they are interdependent (50, p. 222).

Price (53), in a study of state wildlife governing boards, found that one major function of board members was to serve as a buffer group between the full-time staff and the public. Zald points to the external representation functions of boards of directors:

> They promote and represent the organization to major elements of the organizational set, for example, customers, suppliers, stockholders, interested agencies of the state, and the like. That is, they defend and support the growth, autonomy, and effectiveness of their agencies vis-à-vis the outside world (68, p. 99).

Another critical contingency for large corporations involves managing reciprocal relations with other large firms; a trade relations person is alerted to look for opportunities to cooperate with other firms when it could be to their mutual advantage. Perrow notes that:

> the practice of reciprocity is so extensive that about 60 percent of the top 500 corporations have staff members who are explicitly assigned to trade relations. Of course, any smart sales executive or top executive can serve in this capacity. However, it is striking that the practice is sufficiently common to justify so many special positions among the giants (48, p. 122).

Pursuing leads on possible acquisition of other companies is an important function assigned to corporate development units. Aguiler notes that the high volume of acquisition leads generated by this staff:

> demonstrates how the formalization of a search procedure can significantly increase a company's relative involvement with a particular kind of information (3, p. 47).

H9: *Boundary roles are most likely to be formalized when crucial environmental contingencies have been explicitly recognized by organizational decision makers, or the organization is structured in a way that facilitates the adoption of structural innovations through imitation and borrowing from other organizations or other external sources.*

ROUTINIZATION, DISCRETION, AND POWER

The degree of role specificity (31) of boundary roles varies considerably, with some being highly routinized and others highly non-routine. Thompson (61) identified two conditions leading organizations to increase specificity of control over boundary role personnel. First, organizations that provide services for large numbers of persons and thus face many non-members (relative to members) at the boundaries of the organization must either substantially increase the number of personnel in boundary positions or else routinize the tasks of existing staff so they can handle a higher volume of work. Second, organizations using a mechanized production technology which places a premium on large runs of standardized products depend upon a large volume of standardized transactions per member at the organization's output boundary. Pressures for routinization are somewhat lessened when the non-members dealt with have little or no discretion to participate in a relationship. Later Thompson identified a third condition, in that stable environments are likely to produce boundary roles governed by rules, whereas unstable environments are likely to increase flexibility in the specificity of boundary role routines (62, p. 71).

Purchasing agents and sales personnel interact frequently with suppliers and buyers and usually deal with fairly homogeneous groups of organizations and individuals. A high frequency of interaction and homogeneity of elements at the boundary allows behavior in these roles to be highly routinized (27, p. 24; 62, p. 111). Routinization is reflected in the existence of standard purchase and sales forms or contracts, standard operating procedures for soliciting and accepting bids, and standard operating procedures for calling on customers and closing sales. A classic example is the retail salesperson who knows the one proper way to record a cash sale and the one proper way to record a credit transaction.

Routinization of roles at the organization's boundary not only increases efficiency in handling predictable relationships and large numbers of repetitive transactions, but also serves a social control function. The programmed nature of these activities is partial insurance of boundary spanner consistency with organizational procedures, norms, and goals. Members who interact freely with non-member groups, particularly homogeneous sets, are likely to develop attitudes consistent with those of the non-members, rather than of their focal organization. The existence of standard operating procedures partially protects the organization against attitudes and behaviors that are not consistent with organizational objectives.

MacAuley (38) noted different behavioral orientations among boundary and non-boundary personnel in the use of contracts among business firms. Sales departments tended to display non-organizational norms that made them willing to conduct transactions without legally binding contracts. Members of the controllers and legal departments upheld the organizational norm of using contracts, which also happened to be the norm of their professional reference group.

Mathiesen's (41) study of prison staff members identified the boundary role of "social worker" as a position that was difficult to routinize.

> Though almost all staff members claimed there were few or no
> specific rules or regulations guiding their communications, the social
> workers appeared particularly vehement about it, and included
> relations to official organizations. They stressed that here they had to
> be extremely flexible, that they had to organize the work on a
> day-to-day basis and according to the unique circumstances of the
> individual case (41, p. 76).

Telephoning was preferred to the use of letters, and when complex cases arose, face-to-face meetings were arranged. Boundary roles (once created) that deal with heterogeneous elements must contain a minimal degree of routinization to maximize flexibility in dealing with special cases.

The degree to which boundary roles are routinized thus is a function of both the need to adapt to environment contingencies and constraints, and the need to control behavior of potentially deviant members. Routinization can serve as a social control mechanism when the organization does not or cannot assume normative commitment of members to organizational procedures. Similar mechanisms would be the use of uniforms to reinforce organizational identification, or frequently shifting employees between boundary roles and core roles to prevent development of identification with elements in the environment (27, p. 21).

H10: *Boundary role routinization will vary directly with the volume of repetitive work, the predictability of outcomes, the homogeneity and stability of the environment, and the need to control the behavior of organizational members.*

Power in Boundary Roles

Thompson (62) noted that where the environment is heterogeneous and shifting and where contingencies are important to the organization, boundary personnel are expected to exercise discretion and develop expertise, and to the extent they are successful in recognizing contingencies, they may become powerful within the organization. The potential power position of boundary spanners was evident in discussion of their information-processing function. The information that filters into the organization through boundary positions is often not raw data, but the inferences of boundary role incumbents. This type of information is difficult for anyone removed from the boundary to verify. The process of uncertainty absorption is a case of creation of organizational intelligence; and once created, intelligence tends to be accepted (66).

The organization thus relies upon the expertise and discretion of its boundary role personnel. They have a gatekeeper's power, and may become even more powerful if they make correct inferences and if the information is vital for organizational survival (40). Their power is further enhanced to the degree that the nature of the task assigned the boundary role makes routinization of the role difficult, if not impossible.

Pettigrew (49, p. 190) showed how the "self-interested filtering of information during a decision process by a gatekeeper" enabled a boundary spanner to consolidate and enhance his or her power. To the extent that information access and control is a power resource, boundary spanners are in an excellent structural position to convert this resource into actual power.

Labor negotiators provide an example of a boundary role that is difficult to routinize, thus leading to de facto concentration of power in the role. Even though negotiators may deal with fairly homogeneous groups, the outcomes are not highly predictable and the costs to the organization may be high. Therefore, negotiators require some degree of discretionary power. Their power is enhanced to the extent that the group they are negotiating with is powerful.

> Specifically, a number of components of union power that derive from the tactics or activities of the union—involvement in city elections, use of strike threats in bargaining—all are associated with a higher degree of power in the boundary unit in city governments (34, p. 27).

H11: *The power of boundary role incumbents will vary inversely with boundary role routinization, and directly with their own expertise in accomplishing role requirements and with the costliness and unpredictability of interorganizational transactions.*

Organizational dependence on boundary role personnel raises the issue of their commitment to and integration into the organization. The least costly monitoring mechanism is for the organization to rely on the professional identification and ethics of the boundary personnel. More obtrusive strategies include attempts to indoctrinate boundary personnel in organizational policies, norms, and goals, prior to their engaging in inter-organizational contacts. Rotation of members among boundary roles is another active strategy, although it has costs in terms of disrupting local adaptations that have been made by boundary spanners. An organization might grant powerful boundary personnel higher positions within the organizational structure to reinforce commitment, although such positions may be a result of the power these members develop through successful interaction on behalf of the organization, e.g. the common practice of picking top management out of the sales division of an organization.

Many studies emphasize the stress and conflict felt by personnel in boundary roles (33, 46), but overlook the positive potential inherent in their role accumulation prospects. Sieber (56) has recently argued that multiple relationships with diverse role partners provide numerous sources of gratification, rather than strain, to individuals such as boundary personnel. He notes that role rights and privileges may accumulate more rapidly than duties, that overall status security may be enhanced by means of buffer roles, that multiple roles can serve as resources for status enhancement and role performance, and finally that multiple roles may enrich one's personality and enhance one's self-conception. While this article is not addressed to the issue of costs and benefits to individuals who occupy boundary roles, the positive side of boundary spanning activities should be seen as a counter to the negative image currently portrayed in the literature.

Two recent studies in a research and development organization and a large manufacturing company report positive correlations between boundary spanning activity and several dimensions of job satisfaction (34, 35). These studies also found very small or insignificant correlations between role conflict, role ambiguity, and boundary spanning activity. The authors argue that boundary spanning jobs, to the extent they enable role incumbents to reduce uncertainties for others, permit boundary spanners to gain power, improve their bargaining position, and hence increase their job satisfaction and perhaps even gain better jobs.

IMPLICATIONS

The picture of boundary spanning roles portrayed in this article has two implications for the study of formal organizations. First, this view of organization-environment interaction is a decidedly disaggregated one, in contrast to current literature which sees organizations responding as "wholes" to environmental influence (15, 25). We treat boundary spanning roles as the critical link between environmental characteristics and organizational structure, with the further stipulation that organizations face multiple environments and thus can have a variety of boundary roles of units with different structural characteristics. This implies, for example, that when an investigator studies the impact of interorganizational dependence on organizational structure, the place to begin is with its impact on boundary spanning roles in the immediate vicinity of the dependence relationship, rather than with the structure of the organization as a whole (8, 43).

Second, more empirical studies are needed of how personnel in boundary spanning units or roles carry out their duties, and in particular how such role performance varies under different environmental conditions and over time. This would mean more studies of the type carried out by Mintzberg (44), on the day-to-day behavior of managers, or Mathiesen (41) on the day-to-day behavior of staff members in two Scandinavian prisons. Both studies make extensive use of non-participant observation and detailed first-hand knowledge of the actual, rather than self-reported, behavior of those persons studied. The cumulation of such studies would enable us to understand the process by which boundary spanning roles are generated, elaborated, and used by their incumbents.

REFERENCES

1. ADAIR, ROSS. "The Indian Health Worker," *Human Organization,* Vol. 19 (1960), 59–63.

2. ADAMS, J. STACY. "The Structure and Dynamics of Behavior in Organizational Boundary Roles," in M. Dunette (Ed.), *Handbook of Organizational and Industrial Psychology* (Chicago: Rand McNally, 1976), pp. 1175–1199.

3. AGUILER, FRANCIS. *Scanning the Business Environment* (New York: MacMillan, 1967).

4. AIKEN, MICHAEL, and JERALD HAGE. "Organizational Interdependence and Intraorganizational Structure," *American Sociological Review,* Vol. 33 (1968), 912–930.

5. AIKEN, MICHAEL, and JERALD HAGE. "Organizational Permeability." Paper presented at the 1972 Meetings of the American Sociological Association.

6. ALDRICH, HOWARD. "Organizational Boundaries and Inter-organizational Conflict," *Human Relations,* Vol. 24 (1971), 279–287.

7. ALDRICH, HOWARD. "An Organization-Environment Perspective on Cooperation and Conflict in the Manpower Training System," in A. Negandhi (Ed.), *Conflict and Power in Complex Organizations* (Kent, Ohio: C.A.R.I., Kent State University, 1972), 11–37.

8. ALDRICH, HOWARD. "Organization Sets, Action Sets, and Networks: Making the Most of Simplicity," in P. Nystrom and W. Starbuck (Eds.), *Handbook of Organizational Design* (Amsterdam: Elsevier, 1977).

9. ALDRICH, HOWARD, and JEFFREY PFEFFER. "Environment of Organizations," in A. Inkeles (Ed.), *Annual Review of Sociology, Vol. II* (Palo Alto, Calif.: Annual Review Inc., 1976), 79–105.

10. ALDRICH, HOWARD, and ALBERT J. REISS, JR. "Police Officers as Boundary Personnel," in H. Hahn (Ed.), *Police in Urban Society* (Beverly Hills, Calif.: Sage Publications, 1971), 193–208.

11. BENNIS, WARREN. *Beyond Bureaucracy* (New York: McGraw-Hill, 1966).

12. BENSON, J. KENNETH. "Models of Structure Selection." Unpublished paper, University of Missouri–Columbia, 1971.

13. BENSON, J. KENNETH. "The Interorganizational Network as a Political Economy," *Administrative Science Quarterly*, Vol. 20 (1975), 229–249.

14. BLAU, PETER. *The Dynamics of Bureaucracy* (Chicago: University of Chicago Press, 1957).

15. BLAU, PETER, and RICHARD SCHOENHERR. *The Structure of Organizations* (New York: Basic Books, 1971).

16. BLAU, PETER, and W. RICHARD SCOTT. *Formal Organizations* (San Francisco: Chandler, 1962).

17. BROWN, W. B. "Systems, Boundaries, and Information Flow," *Academy of Management Journal*, Vol. 9 (1966), 318–327.

18. CAMPBELL, DONALD. "Variation and Selective Retention in Socio-Cultural Evolution," *General Systems*, Vol. 16 (1969), 69–85.

19. CHANDLER, ALFRED. *Strategy and Structure* (Cambridge: MIT Press, 1962).

20. CHILD, JOHN. *The Business Enterprise in Modern Industrial Society* (London: Collier MacMillan, 1969).

21. CHILD, JOHN. "Parkinson's Progress: Accounting for the Number of Specialists in Organizations," *Administrative Science Quarterly*, Vol. 18 (1973), 328–348.

22. CHILD, JOHN. "Participation, Organization and Social Cohesion," *Human Relations*, forthcoming.

23. CYERT, RICHARD, and JAMES MARCH. *A Behavioral Theory of the Firm* (Englewood Cliffs, N.J.: Prentice-Hall, 1963).

24. DILL, WILLIAM. "The Impact of Environment on Organizational Development," in S. Mailick and E. Van Ness (Eds.), *Concepts and Issues in Administrative Behavior* (Englewood Cliffs, N.J.: Prentice-Hall, 1962).

25. EMERY, FRED, and ERIC TRIST. "The Causal Texture of Organizational Environments," *Human Relations*, Vol. 18 (1965), 21–31.

26. GOFFMAN, ERVING. "On the Characteristics of Total Institutions," in D. Cressey (Ed.), *The Prison* (New York: Holt, Rinehart, and Winston, 1961).

27. GUETZKOW, HAROLD. "Relations Among Organizations," in R. Bowers (Ed.), *Studies on Behavior in Organizations* (Athens, Georgia: University of Georgia Press, 1966).

28. HAGE, JERALD, and MICHAEL AIKEN. *Social Change in Complex Organizations* (New York: Random House, 1970).

29. HARRISON, MICHAEL. "The Adjustment of a Social Movement to Its Organizational Environment." Unpublished paper, Department of Sociology, SUNY, Stony Brook, 1972.

30. HASENFELD, YEHESKEL. "People Processing Organizations: An Exchange Approach," *American Sociological Review*, Vol. 37 (1972), 256–263.

31. HICKSON, DAVID. "A Convergence in Organization Theory," *Administrative Science Quarterly*, Vol. 2 (1966), 224–237.

32. HIRSCH, PAUL. "Processing Fads and Fashions: An Organizational Set Analysis of Cultural Industry Systems," *American Journal of Sociology*, Vol. 77 (1972), 639–659.

33. KATZ, DANIEL, and ROBERT KAHN. *The Social Psychology of Organizations* (New York: John Wiley and Sons, 1966).

34. KELLER, ROBERT, and WINFORD HOLLAND. "Boundary-Spanning Roles in a Research and Development Organization: An Empirical Investigation," *Academy of Management Journal*, Vol. 18 (1975), 388–393.

35. KELLER, ROBERT, ANDREW SZILAGYI, and WINFORD HOLLAND. "Boundary-Spanning Activity and Employee Reactions: An Empirical Study," *Human Relations*, forthcoming.

36. KOCHAN, THOMAS. "Determinants of the Power of Boundary Units in an Interorganizational Bargaining Relation," *Administrative Science Quarterly*, Vol. 20 (1975), 434–452.

37. LAWRENCE, PAUL, and JAY LORSCH. *Organization and Environment* (Cambridge, Mass.: Graduate School of Business Administration, Harvard University, 1967).

38. MACAULAY, STEWART. "Non-contractual Relations in Business: A Preliminary Study," *American Sociological Review*, Vol. 28 (1963), 55–67.

39. MANIHA, JOHN, and CHARLES PERROW. "The Reluctant Organization and the Aggressive Environment," *Administrative Science Quarterly*, Vol. 10 (1965), 238–257.

40. MARCH, JAMES, and HERBERT SIMON. *Organizations* (New York: John Wiley and Sons, 1958).

41. MATHIESON, THOMAS. *Across the Boundaries of Organizations* (Calif.: Glendessary Press, 1972).

42. MEIER, RICHARD. "Information Input Overload," in F. Massarik and P. Ratoosh (Eds.), *Mathematical Explorations in Behavioral Sciences* (Homewood, Ill.: Richard Irwin, Inc., 1965).

43. MINDLIN, SERGIO, and HOWARD ALDRICH. "Interorganizational Dependence: A Review of the Concept and a Re-examination of the Findings of the Aston Group," *Administrative Science Quarterly*, Vol. 20 (1975), 382–392.

44. MINTZBERG, HENRY. *The Nature of Managerial Work* (New York: Harper and Row, 1973).

45. NADEL, MARK. *The Politics of Consumer Protection* (Indianapolis: Bobbs-Merrill, 1971).

46. ORGAN, DENNIS. "Linking Pins Between Organizations and Environment," *Business Horizons*, Vol. 14 (December 1971), 73–80.

47. PARSONS, TALCOTT. "Suggestions for a Sociological Approach to Theory of Organizations," *Administrative Science Quarterly*, Vol. 1 (1956), 63–69.

48. PERROW, CHARLES. *Organizational Analysis* (Belmont, Calif.: Wadsworth Publishing Company, 1970).

49. PETTIGREW, ANDREW. "Information Control as a Power Resource," *Sociology*, Vol. 6 (1972), 187–204.

50. PFEFFER, JEFFREY. "Size and Composition of Corporate Boards of Directors," *Administrative Science Quarterly*, Vol. 17 (1972), 218–228.

51. PFEFFER, JEFFREY, and HUSEYIN LEBLEBICI. "Executive Recruitment and the Development of Interfirm Organization," *Administrative Science Quarterly*, Vol. 18 (1973), 449–461.

52. PFEFFER, JEFFREY, and HUSEYIN LEBLEBICI. "The Effect of Competition on Some Dimensions of Organizational Structure," *Social Forces*, Vol. 52 (1973), 268–279.

53. PRICE, JAMES. "The Impact of Governing Boards on Organizational Effectiveness and Morale," *Administrative Science Quarterly*, Vol. 8 (1963), 361–368.

54. PRUDEN, H., and R. REESE. "Interorganizational Role-Set Relations and the Performance and Satisfaction of Industrial Salesmen," *Administrative Science Quarterly*, Vol. 17 (1972), 601–609.

55. REISS, ALBERT J. *The Police and the Public* (New Haven: Yale University Press, 1971).

56. SIEBER, SAM. "Toward a Theory of Role Accumulation," *American Sociological Review*, Vol. 39 (1974), 567–578.

57. SMIGEL, ERWIN. "The Impact of Recruitment on the Large Law Firm," *Human Relations*, Vol. 25 (1960), 56–65.

58. STARBUCK, WILLIAM. "Organizations and Their Environments," in M. Dunnette (Ed.), *Handbook of Organizational and Industrial Psychology* (Chicago: Rand McNally, 1976), 1069–1124.

59. STRAUSS, GEORGE. "Tactics of Laterial Relationship: The Purchasing Agent," *Administrative Science Quarterly*, Vol. 7 (1962), 161–186.

60. TERRYBERRY, SHIRLEY. "The Evolution of the Organizational Environments," *Administrative Science Quarterly*, Vol. 12 (1968), 590–614.

61. THOMPSON, JAMES. "Organizations and Output Transactions," *American Journal of Sociology*, Vol. 68 (1962), 309–325.

62. THOMPSON, JAMES. *Organizations in Action* (New York: McGraw-Hill, 1967).

63. THOMPSON, JAMES, and WILLIAM McEWEN. "Organizational Goals and Environment," *American Sociological Review*, Vol. 23 (1958), 23–31.

64. WEBER, MAX. *The Theory of Social and Economic Organization* (New York: The Free Press, 1947).

65. WHETTEN, DAVID. *Predicting Organization-Set Dimensions: An Inter-organizational Study of the Effectiveness of Manpower Programs in New York State* (Ph.D. Thesis, Cornell University, 1974).

66. WILENSKY, HAROLD. *Organizational Intelligence* (New York: Basic Books, 1967).

67. WILSON, JAMES Q. *Political Organizations* (New York: Basic Books, 1973).

68. ZALD, MAYER. "The Power and Functions of Boards of Directors," *American Journal of Sociology*, Vol. 75 (1969), 97–111.

Moving Money

Barry Newman

"The truly crucial prerequisite is the conviction, on the part of every manager, that he CAN control ALL factors relevant to his operation."

—From a speech by Bob White, Operating Group Head.

"It's kind of like the Marine Corps."
—A worker

NEW YORK—At the foot of Wall Street, near the docks and the heliport and the canvas-domed tennis courts, there is a factory. It is in a tall building sheathed in smoky glass and concrete that from the outside looks like any other 24-story stack of offices. But when the businessmen and stenographers are filing from the other downtown towers at the end of the day, the factory at 111 Wall St. is still rattling away.

Forty-foot-long sorting machines are roaring and hissing like high-speed locomotives.

Robot forklift trucks are carrying trays of work from station to storage bin, from storage bin to station. Trucks laden with the night's raw materials are descending on the loading docks. And in several large rooms, workers flailing furiously at electric machines are raising a din equal to a barrage from a hundred burp guns.

"MOVING MONEY"

The business volume here is high by most factory standards: $20 billion a day. Of course, the factory doesn't make that much money; it moves it. "Money that is not moving," a hurrying worker says, "is useless."

Eighteen billion of those dollars are symbolically shuffled among the world's financial institutions. Two billion are "machined" in the form of three million checks and 104,000 corporate documents. Twelve million lines are printed; phones ring and phones are dialed 139,000 times.

In a year, $2.5 trillion ebb and flow through the white corridors of 111 Wall St., where 6,500 laborers in the Operating Group of First National City Bank perform the physical acts of the otherwise-ephemeral business of banking. They debit or credit accounts. They send checks drawn on other banks through the clearing houses and back to their original writers. They file checks written by Citibank's own customers and, once a month, wrap them up in a bank statement and drop them in the mail.

There are others like them at any big bank, buildings full of them elsewhere in New York's financial district. Those buildings, though, have somewhat stronger ties than 111 Wall St. to the traditional "back office" of the days when banking rooms were furnished with deep-grained Windsor chairs and bankers were men who drank Madeira after dinner from crystal decanters.

INSPIRATION: DETROIT

First National City Bank's Operating Group isn't like that. It derives its inspiration not from Greek pediments and cutaway coats but from the assembly line, from Detroit. There is a passion for efficiency here that by most accounts makes this operating group the most intensively managed banking operation anywhere, and one that in the last five years of relentless inflation has hammered its costs absolutely flat. Depending on where you stand, 111 Wall St. radiates an aura that can be electrifying or frightening, aggressive or compulsive, disciplined or ironhanded.

Anyone hired as a manager by the group must be a person, as the recruiting literature puts it, "who can flourish in a crisp, quantitative environment." The best kind of line worker, one manager says, "is someone with the ability to think like the system, to think like the machine. They're very unique individuals; they're valuable to us."

They speak a patois of acronyms and computer talk: Marti means Machine Readable Telegraphic Input; an employe's ASR is his Annual Salary Rate; when one "blips," he falls short of his goal; when he makes "a save," he has cut a cost. Work is capacitized, prioritized and recapacitized.

Channels (the word for departments) try to "interface" better, while managers "face off, one on one, to dimension a rock (a tough problem) and tighten up their indicators." The verb "to paradise" refers to a reorganization program in the group, as in: "If you two channels can get your seamless processing recapacitized, you can both be paradised."

"WIN," "PASS" OR "FAIL"

Each Operating Group worker knows precisely what is expected of him. Each job has a standard. Doing better than standard is "a win," meeting the standard is "a pass," falling below standard is "a fail." A worker who fails risks "documentation"—his incapacity is immortalized on a permanent record. The same is true for managers; each has an objective, always intended to pare costs. Forecasts are made and performance is measured—annually, monthly, and, in many instances, daily or hourly. A 2% variation is considered significant. "You sort of expect to meet the forecasts or else," a young manager says.

"No excuses or rationalizations of events 'beyond one's control' are accepted," Operating Group Head Bob White said in a three-year-old speech his employes still study. Failing, he said, isn't always an offense, but "hiding a fail is much more serious than a fail itself." Workers at 111 Wall St. all sit at tables, never at desks, because, as Mr. White said, "you can't hide things in tables."

Bob White—who is blond, healthy-looking and 39 years old—came to Citibank in 1970, not from another bank but from Ford Motor Co. Citibank was looking for people to process bank statements with the same hard-nosed rigor that Detroit uses to process station wagons. The Operating Group in 1970 was a discordant tangle of old-fashioned banking functions swamped by frantically accelerating volume; it cried out for austerity.

Costs were rising 15% a year; the backlog of uncorrected errors had topped 25,000; work-force turnover was at 50%. A decision was made to lower the boom: There would be no cost increases in 1970. "We squeezed out the fat," Mr. White says. "We became kind of serious. Whatever we forecast, we were going to make."

Quality standards were imposed, then time standards. And 111 Wall St. was pulled apart and nailed together again as 23 separate assembly lines, one for each kind of bank transaction. New generations of computers were spawned; overtime was slashed; turnover dropped to 10% while total Operating Group employment fell from more than 10,000 to the current 6,500. As efficiency increases, "the processing becomes clearer, more understandable, and hence better," Mr. White says. "Service to customers is improved."

The "heavy" of this drama was Bob White; he got things done. The power behind him was a man named John Reed, who was 30 years old in 1970, when the country's second-largest bank put him in charge of its operations. (He has since moved on to another of Citibank's groups, and Mr. White has taken his place. But the two still drive to work together every morning from Connecticut—arriving at their desks between 6 and 7 a.m.)

Mr. Reed works in a big room almost completely filled by an enormous round table. "I get my biggest jollies out of getting together with a bunch of people with the same objectives and just getting there," he says. But revamping the operating group was "analogous to a heart transplant," Mr. Reed says. "There were a lot of rejection phenomena." It was his job to give Mr. White elbow room:

"I held a cultural umbrella over White's head so he wouldn't have to realize he was working in a bank. If he knew, it would have scared the hell out of him. I protected him from the bankers. If we had to lay anybody off, I said, 'Do it,' and let the personnel office run up and down my back with spikes on."

OF PEOPLE AND PAPER

Cost cutting, it seems, will end for Bob White and John Reed only when there aren't any costs left to cut. The Operating Group consists of people processing paper. Its managers' ultimate vision is the elimination of people and the elimination of paper. All that will remain is the process: electronic blips coursing through electronic brains.

A unit manager: "I'm not processing paper; I'm processing information. If I could have my way, I'd never see paper at all."

An operations head: "I have 130 people. If I automate the way I want to, there won't be any left."

For the moment, however, there are still people at 111 Wall St. and a great deal of paper. The icy efficiency envisioned in the upper reaches of management isn't achieved without a fair infusion of sweat and muscle.

About 300 of the people and 2,500 pounds of the paper pass each day through what is known as the Branch Channel of Check Processing Operations. The Branch Channel is on the eighth floor, a cross-hatching of glass partitions enclosing large, red-carpeted rooms. The rooms are flanked by corridors lined with narrow metal lockers that the workers use—instead of desks—to store their belongings. What happens here, in simplest terms, is this: Checks deposited by customers of the 245 New York-area branches of First National City Bank are sorted, credited to the proper accounts, and sent to the banks they were drawn on.

Each day about 1.5 million checks are deposited, worth perhaps $1 billion. The branches stuff them into purple canvas bags, and in late afternoon they are collected by a fleet of 38 trucks and dumped on the loading docks of 111 Wall St. If all goes well, the last check will be put through the mill by 6 a.m. The trick is to send out as many checks as came in.

"CRISP INTERACTION"

One of those responsible for doing that is operations head Bill Czerniewicz (which sounds like Chenevitz), a round-faced, 31-year-old "production man" who came to Citibank from the lunar module program at Grumman Aerospace. As the check bags are carted up the freight elevators on a recent evening, he and six of his unit managers are sitting at a round table having a "crisp interaction" about the previous day's performance:

"How was the cumus?" Mr. Czerniewicz asks.

"Improved," a unit manager says.

"Number of trays out of proof?"

"Increased. We're getting worse."

"So we blew one standard last night, huh?" the boss says. "By the way, the 10th floor got murdered on housekeeping. They think we'll get murdered. So we better get moving on that. . . ."

The check bags are dumped in the encoding rooms where dozens of people sit jabbing the keyboards of noisy machines that translate the amount on every check into a trail of squarish magnetic-ink numbers along the bottom edge of each—a language computers can read. These workers are paid on an "incentive" system, which is another word for piecework. The objective is to encode as many checks as possible. The acceptable standard is 1,200 an hour. The record is 2,400.

One of the fastest encoders is a young man of Chinese descent. His secret is to minimize movement: Two fingers tweeze each check and drop it into a slot; the arm never moves. The other hand flies over the keys as the eyes dart from check to check. The mouth hangs slightly open; the rest of the body is frozen.

"KEEP WORKING"

"You don't really see the check," another encoder says. "You don't really read the number. You sense it. It doesn't go through your brain. Your fingers feel it." This encoder makes $15,000 a year, averaging 2,000 checks an hour. But the work is less than enjoyable. "We have to keep working," he says. "We can't afford to take a coffee break. They push us. They push us hard."

When the encoders are finished, the checks are blocked and batched and placed into "trays" that look like shoe boxes by workers sitting at high tables at the end of each room. (They also catch customers' addition errors on deposit slips, 1,200 of them a night.) Then the checks are "handed off" to the climate-controlled computer room, where four 40-foot "Trace" machines sort them for delivery to dozens of institutions, from Chase Manhattan Bank to the Bank of China.

At 40 miles an hour the checks shoot through the machines in a white blur. A tape records them, a microfilm camera takes their pictures and a spray gun dots them with a series of identifying numbers and an orange bar code. The machines spit them out into 24 bins, the last for "rejects" the computer couldn't read. These are bundled off to the "reject repair" room, where women are sitting in front of machines that flash pictures of the problem checks every second or two. Signs on the machines light up to indicate the problem, and the women punch the information into the computer by hand.

Once the rejects return to the mainstream of checks, the totals that come out of the computer are compared with the totals that went in. Invariably there are mistakes—a check dropped, or chewed up, or a number misprinted. A roomful of "reconcilers" try to find out what happened by matching print-outs. If they can't iron out a "difference," a staff of investigators takes over. This happens about 300 times a night. The investigators dig through the actual checks, searching for the one that went wrong.

Emil Garcia is an on-line investigator, whose job is to catch as many differences as possible before the first crucial deadline of the night at 11:30, when a shipment of checks must arrive at the Federal Reserve Bank a few blocks away. For every $1 million that doesn't make the Fed on time, Citibank takes a fine of $167 from the budget of Branch Channel; that is the amount the parent company stands to lose in potential interest.

"A DIFFERENCE IS A DIFFERENCE"

As the deadline approaches, Mr. Garcia is agitatedly in quest of a missing check for $11.85. "A difference is a difference," he says, pawing through a tray. "You gotta follow your instincts. If it didn't go where it should have gone, you've got to figure out where it did go." He puts the tray back and fumbles through the racks for another one. "Let's not panic now," he says. "The bloody thing's got to be somewhere. . . ."

At 11 p.m. the first wave of checks appears in the dispatch room. They are bagged in clear plastic and marked with the name of the Federal Reserve Bank that will be their ultimate destination. At 11:05 the bank's driver, Robert Edmonds, arrives and crams the plastic bags into canvas sacks. He loads them onto a cart and pushes it on the run to the elevator. A battered, unmarked panel truck is waiting at the loading dock. Mr. Edmonds, a young man with a red bandana around his neck, heaves the sacks inside for the short trip. "Hope you have your crash helmet on," he says.

The truck lurches onto the potholed street, jouncing heavily as the bags stuffed with $100 million in checks toss about inside. Mr. Edmonds screeches around the corner and gets hung up at a red light. When it changes, he floors the accelerator. "Go, car. Go," he says in a tense whisper. A garbage truck is blocking the street ahead. Mr. Edmonds jumps the curb and drives around it on the sidewalk. At last he storms down Gold Street and into the Fed.

After a frustrating wait for the freight elevator, he wheels his cart into the freight room upstairs, where several men immediately pull open the sacks and start wrapping the checks for mailing. It is precisely 11:29. Mr. Edmonds pushes the cart slowly toward the elevator. "We've never missed a shipment," he says, taking a deep breath. "I never know whether it's good management or luck."

Patterns in Strategy Formation

Henry Mintzberg

The literature on strategy formation is in large part theoretical but not empirical, and the usual definition of "strategy" encourages the notion that strategies, as we recognize them ex post facto, are deliberate plans conceived in advance of the making of specific decisions. By defining a strategy as "a pattern in a stream of decisions," we are able to research strategy formation in a broad descriptive context. Specifically, we can study both strategies that were intended and those that were realized despite intentions. A research program suggested by this definition is outlined, and two of the completed studies are then reviewed — the strategies of Volkswagenwerk from 1934 to 1974 and of the United States government in Vietnam from 1950 to 1973. Some general conclusions suggested by these studies are then presented in terms of three central themes: that strategy formation can fruitfully be viewed as the interplay between a dynamic environment and bureaucratic momentum, with leadership mediating between the two forces; that strategy formation over time appears to follow some important patterns in organizations, notably life cycles and distinct change-continuity cycles within these; and that the study of the interplay between intended and realized strategies may lead us to the heart of this complex organizational process.

From *Management Science*, vol. 24, no. 9 (May 1978). Copyright © 1978, The Institute of Management Sciences. Reprinted by permission.

What are strategies and how are they formed in organizations? A large body of literature, under the title of strategy formulation in the private sector, and policy making in the public sector, addresses the question of how organizations make and interrelate their significant (that is, strategic) decisions. A brief review [14] has suggested that a good deal of this literature falls distinctly into one of three theoretical groupings, or "modes." The *planning mode,* comprising the largest body of published materials and in the tradition of both management science and bureaucratic theory, depicts the process as a highly ordered, neatly integrated one, with strategies explicated on schedule by a purposeful organization [2], [17]. In sharp contrast, the *adaptive mode,* popularized by writers such as Lindblom [4], [12], [13] in the public sector and Cyert and March [8] in the context of business, depicts the process as one in which many decision-makers with conflicting goals bargain among themselves to produce a stream of incremental, disjointed decisions. And in some of the literature of classical economics and contemporary management, the process is described in the *entrepreneurial mode,* where a powerful leader takes bold, risky decisions toward his vision of the organization's future [6], [9].

Some interesting research has been undertaken to put the theory into empirical context, for example, Allison's development of three models to explain policy making perceptions during the Cuban Missile Crises [1], Collins and Moore's description of the entrepreneurial personality [7], and Bowman's investigation into strategic effectiveness [3]. But most of the literature remains theoretical without being empirical, and the contradictions among these three modes remain to be investigated.

This paper presents the results of the first stage of a research project begun in 1971, and continuing, to study patterns in the process of strategy formation. The first section describes the term "strategy," and shows how the definition leads naturally to the choice of a research methodology. This methodology is described in the second section. A third section then describes briefly the results of the formation of strategies in two organizations, and a final section presents some theoretical conclusions about strategy formation that arise from these results.

DEFINITION OF STRATEGY

The term *strategy* has been defined in a variety of ways, but almost always with a common theme, that of a deliberate conscious set of guidelines that determines decisions into the future. In Game Theory, strategy represents the set of rules that is to govern the moves of the players. In military theory, strategy is "the utilization during both peace and war, of all the nation's forces, through large-scale, long-range planning and development, to ensure security and victory" (Random House Dictionary). And in management theory, the Chandler definition is typical: ". . . the determination of the basic long-term goals and objectives of an enterprise, and the adoption of courses of action and the allocation of resources necessary for carrying out these goals" [5, p. 13]. All these definitions treat strategy as (a) explicit, (b) developed consciously and purposefully, and (c) made in advance of the specific decisions to which it applies. In common terminology, a strategy is a "plan."

The position taken here is that this definition is incomplete for the organization and nonoperational for the researcher. It conceals one important side of the decisional behavior of organizations that all of the above theorists would likely consider strategic (that is, important). And by restricting strategy to explicit, a priori guidelines, it forces the researcher to study strategy formation as a perceptual phenomenon, all too often reducing his conclusions to abstract normative generalizations.

In this paper, the concept defined above will be referred to as *intended* strategy. Strategy in general, and *realized* strategy in particular, will be defined as a *pattern in a stream of decisions.*[1] In other words, when a sequence of decisions in some area exhibits a consistency over time, a strategy will be considered to have formed. A few examples will clarify this definition. When Richard Nixon, early in his first term of office, made a number of decisions to favor Southern voters (appointment of Supreme Court justices from the South, interference with school integration plans, etc.), the press quickly coined the phrase "Southern strategy." Their action corresponded exactly to ours as researchers: despite no explicit statement of intent, the press perceived a consistency in a stream of decisions and labeled it a strategy. To take a very different illustration, art critics seek to delineate distinct periods during which the works of great artists (and, by imputation, their decisions about those works) exhibited certain consistencies in their use of form, color and so on. Again, the procedure corresponds to ours: Picasso's "Blue Period" would be our "Blue Strategy"!

Defining strategy as we do enables us to consider both sides of the strategy formation coin: strategies as intended, a priori guidelines as well as strategies as evolved, a posteriori consistencies in decisional behavior. In other words, the strategy-maker may *formulate* a strategy through a conscious process before he makes specific decisions, or a strategy may *form* gradually, perhaps unintentionally, as he makes his decisions one by one. This definition operationalizes the concept of strategy for the researcher. Research on strategy formation (not necessarily formu*lation*) focuses on a tangible phenomenon—the decision stream —and strategies become observed patterns in such streams.

THE RESEARCH METHODOLOGY

This definition of strategy necessitated the study of decision streams in organizations over time periods long enough to detect the development and breakdown of patterns.

Furthermore, because there was little precedent for such research, wherein the basic parameters were defined and operationalized, and because the process of strategy formation appeared to be an extremely complex one, it was evident at the outset that our research would have to be exploratory and as purely inductive as possible. Thus it was decided to concentrate on intensive historical studies of single organizations over periods of decades. These studies proceeded in four steps.

Step 1: Collection of Basic Data

All studies began with the development of two chronological listings over the whole period, one of important decisions and actions by the organization, the other of important events and trends in the environment. The choices of what decisions and events to study, as well as the sources of the data, varied considerably from one study to another. Our task was to uncover whatever traces were left of decisions and events that had taken place as many as fifty years earlier. In one case, back issues of a magazine served as the trace of its decisions on content; in another case, newspaper reports served in part to reveal military decisions of a government. Other sources included product catalogs, minutes of executive meetings, interviews, and so on.

Step 2: Inference of Strategies and Periods of Change

From the chronology of decisions, divided into distinct strategic areas (in the case of the magazine, for example, content, format, and administration), various strategies were inferred as patterns in streams of decisions. These strategies were then compared with each other, as well as with other data such as sales, budgets, and staff levels, in order to identify distinct periods of change in the formation of strategy. Some periods of change were *incremental,* during which new strategies formed gradually; others were *piecemeal,* during which some strategies changed while others remained constant; and still others were *global,* during which many strategies changed quickly and in unison. In addition, we identified periods of *continuity,* during which established patterns remain unchanged; periods of *limbo,* during which the organization hesitated to make decisions; periods of *flux,* during which no important patterns seemed evident in the decisions streams, and so on.

Step 3: Intensive Analysis of Periods of Change

At this point the study shifted from the broad perception of overall patterns to the intensive investigation of specific periods of change. Here we relied on in-depth reports and, where possible, interviews with the original strategy-makers.

Step 4: Theoretical Analysis

At this point a report was written and a group then met in a series of brainstorming sessions to generate hypotheses to explain the findings. These sessions were guided by a list of open-ended questions designed to focus attention and stimulate the flow of ideas, for example: When is a strategy made explicitly that controls subsequent decisions, and when does a strategy evolve implicitly as a convergence in a stream of ad hoc decisions? When do intended strategies differ from realized ones? What is the role of planning, leadership, shared goals, and bargaining in integrating different strategies? Under what conditions are formal analysis and planning used? (Indeed, what does the term "planning" mean in the context of strategy formation?) What are the relative influences of external forces, organizational forces, and leadership in strategy formation? When and why are organizations proactive and reactive? How do organizations balance change with stability? What overall patterns does the process of strategy formation follow? These questions stimulated debate and discussion, which in turn led to the generation of hypotheses. These

in turn are on their way to being woven into theories, the skeletons of which are reported here.

PATTERNS IN TWO STUDIES

Four major studies, each involving some significant portion of one man-year of funded research, have been completed, involving a large automobile company, a government military strategy, a magazine, and a national film agency. In addition, over twenty smaller studies have been carried out as graduate student term papers and theses, ranging from an expansion period in a hockey league to the development of a university's strategy across a century and a half. The major periods of two of the intensive studies are reviewed briefly below, using the terminology of the research.

THE STRATEGIES OF VOLKSWAGENWERK, 1920 TO 1974

This study divides into seven distinct periods, as follows:

Before 1948: Flux

Ferdinand Porsche conceived the idea of a "people's car" in the 1920s; in 1934, the German Nazi government decided to support the project, and in 1937, with the problems worked out of the design, construction was begun on a large automobile manufacturing plant at Wolfsburg. Just as the plant was to go into full operation war was declared, and it was immediately converted to production of war vehicles. By 1945 the plant was largely destroyed.[2] The British occupation forces used it to service their vehicles. Later there began some primitive production of Porsche's "Volkswagen," using in large part East German refugees as the labor force, with many of the raw materials procured by barter. The plant was offered to various Allied interests (including Henry Ford), but all declined, seeing no value in the Volkswagen. In 1948 the British selected Heinrich Nordhoff, a former division chief of Opel, to run the operations.

1948: Global Change

Nordhoff inherited half an intended strategy—Porsche's design and his concept of the market (an inexpensive automobile for the common man). To this he added the other components of an intended strategy —an emphasis on quality and technical excellence, aggressive exporting, and rigorous service standards, all integrated around the dominant element of the "people's car."

1949 to 1958: Continuity

This intended strategy was ideally suited to the environment of post-war Germany as well as to world-wide export markets. For the next ten years, Nordhoff realized his intended strategy, building up the central organization and expanding manufacturing capacity and distribution channels very rapidly. Two new models were introduced (work on both having begun in 1949), but these were really modifications of the basic Volkswagen. (In 1954 Nordhoff ordered work halted on the design of a completely new model.)

1959: Minor Change

Increasing competition and changing consumer tastes in Germany and abroad spurred Volkswagen to make some minor modifications in its strategies around 1959. Advertising was introduced in the United States in anticipation of the compacts; design of the first really new model, the medium-priced 1500, was pursued; the firm was about to go public and investment was increased sharply in anticipation of a dividend load. But all essential aspects of the original strategy remained unchanged; only some new, essentially peripheral elements, were grafted on to the old strategy.

1960 to 1964: Continuity

The Volkswagen strategy remained essentially the same in almost all respects, although profits were being squeezed by competitive pressures and increasing costs despite increasing sales. The larger 1500 model was introduced, but it again emphasized durability, economy, and unexcelled appearance.

1965 to 1970: Groping

Facing ever more severe pressures, the firm finally reacted in the form of an anxious and disjointed search for new models. Many were introduced in this period, some in contrast to Volkswagen's economy-car image. Some the firm designed itself; others were acquired. Nordhoff died in 1968, and Kurt Lotz became managing director. By 1970, profits were down for the third straight year. The old strategy had clearly disintegrated, but a clear new one had yet to emerge.[3]

1971 to 1974: Global Change

An experienced Volkswagen executive, Rudolf Leiding, replaced Lotz in 1971 and immediately began a period of consolidation of the new acquisitions and the development of a new integrated turnaround strategy. The new product strategy was modeled around the successful Audi—stylish, front-wheel drive, water cooled. Accordingly, a host of existing lines were dropped, a few new ones being concentrated on to avoid direct competition between models. Complementarity was stressed in their design to assure reliable, economic assembly, and attempts were made to rationalize production on a world-wide basis and to build plants abroad, in low wage areas where possible. Marketing strategy emphasized performance, reliability, and service. Capital expenditures were very large throughout the period. (These strategies were pursued in what proved to be a period of continuity after 1974, despite Leiding's resignation, with the new products selling well. After large losses in 1974, Volkswagenwerk became profitable again in the second half of 1975.)

U.S. STRATEGY IN VIETNAM, 1950 TO 1973

It is impossible, in a few lines, to review comprehensively a situation as complex as the U.S. experience in Vietnam from 1950 to 1973. (Our chronology record alone numbers 101 pages.) Nevertheless, the central themes can be reviewed briefly, in ten distinct periods, to show the main patterns of change and continuity.

1950: Global Change

Until 1950, the United States government refused requests by France to aid its forces fighting in Indochina. Shortly after Communist forces took over the Chinese government, however, the U.S. changed its strategy and began a program of direct monetary aid to the French.

1950 to 1953: Continuity

For three and a half years, the U.S. followed a more or less uninterrupted strategy of steadily increasing aid to the French in Indochina. This was accompanied, particularly at the outset, by a strategy of encouraging the French to reduce their colonial ties to the so-called "Associated States." Neither strategy accomplished its purpose. By the end of 1953, despite a massive infusion of U.S. aid, the French military position was weaker than in 1950.

1954: Flux, then Global Change

Late in 1953 the French military position began to disintegrate. Before and during the multination Geneva conference in April, Secretary of State John Foster Dulles negotiated with the allies of the U.S. in order to reach agreement, but his efforts were not successful. The day before the Indochina phase of the conference opened on May 8,

the French garrison at Dien Bien Phu fell. At a press conference on June 8, Dulles claimed there was no plan to ask Congress for authorization of American aid to Indochina, a position confirmed two days later by President Eisenhower. Shortly thereafter the French government fell, and Pierre Mendès-France became Premier on a platform of ending the war by July 20. At Geneva a settlement was reached, among other points dividing Vietnam in two. In the aftermath of Geneva, the French left Vietnam and the U.S. began a program of direct aid to the South Vietnamese, with the intended strategy of democratizing the government of Premier Diem.

1955 to 1961: Continuity

To the end of the Eisenhower administration, the U.S. pursued an uninterrupted strategy of direct aid to the South Vietnamese, while the intended strategy of democratization was neither realized nor vigorously pursued.

1961: Global Change

The change in strategy in 1961 was the first time the U.S. government acted in a purely proactive manner, without tangible external stimulus. The new Kennedy team in Washington chose to change the intended strategy from passive aid to active support. On May 11, 1961, a contingent of Special Forces was dispatched to Vietnam to advise and train the Vietnamese. Kennedy also approved the initiation of a covert warfare campaign against North Vietnam. At the end of the year, under pressure from Diem, Kennedy agreed to a build-up of support troops.

1962 to 1965: Incremental Change Leading to Global Change

The number of U.S. advisors increased from 948 at the end of November, 1961, to 2,646 by January, 1962, to 5,576 by June 30, and to 11,000 by the end of 1962. In 1963, public manifestations began against the Diem government, and the U.S. strategy of support for Diem gradually changed (apparently in contradiction of intentions). First, Washington brought economic pressures to bear on the Diem government, by the deferring of decisions on aid, and eventually, it tacitly supported the coup that overthrew him (after considerable confusion between Washington, the military, and the CIA). With the assassination of Kennedy less than a month later, Lyndon Johnson became president. From the early days of his administration, the debate within the U.S. government over the intended strategy for Vietnam (bombing, escalation, etc.) grew more intense. As the debate went on, the realized strategy began to change to one of escalation of the U.S. war effort. For example, in February 1964, clandestine American attacks began, including patrols and air operations in Laos against the North Vietnamese. Then in August 1964 the first spate of bombings was carried out against the North in reprisal for the attack on U.S. destroyers in the Gulf of Tonkin. And in October 1964 the covert air war in Laos was intensified. Meanwhile the debate over the official (intended) strategy continued, with various options debated in meeting, memo and report. Throughout the period, Johnson seemed uncertain how to proceed and reluctant about approving large-scale bombings. But events were dragging him along. Opinion within the government was more and more favoring bombing and escalation; the government crisis in Saigon was worsening; the Viet Cong was stepping up its harassment. On February 6, 1965, after the Viet Cong had attacked American personnel at Plei Ku, Johnson ordered a major retaliatory strike on the North. On February 11, another similarly justified attack was launched. And on February 13 Johnson ordered sustained bombing on a non-retaliatory basis. Thereafter, with the bombing seeming to prove relatively ineffective, the debate over troop deployment began in earnest. Under pressure from the Pentagon, Johnson approved in April 1964 the first ma-

jor troop increases and "a change of mission for all Marine battalions deployed in Vietnam to permit their more active use. . . ." By June the "search and destroy" strategy had begun to replace the "enclave" strategy, and in July Johnson approved General Westmoreland's request for 44 battalions.

1965 to 1967: Continuity

Three strategies were pursued in parallel during this period. First, the land war was escalated until the U.S. troop level in Vietnam reached a peak of over half a million in 1967. Second, the bombing campaign was intensified sporadically throughout the period. And third, Johnson put pressure on the North Vietnamese, through periodic variations in the bombing campaign, to come to the negotiating table. Meanwhile, pressures began to build in Washington, notably from McNamara, for a reassessment of the whole strategy. Although this may have constrained the escalation decisions Johnson made, it did not change the basic course of the strategy. By the end of 1967, the ground war was being fought extensively, the air war was being widened slowly, and diplomatic activity went on at a furious pace.

1968: Global Change

A series of factors apparently stunned Johnson into a major reassessment of the strategy. One was the Tet offensive, begun on January 31, 1968, which for the first time provided tangible evidence of the military reality (a stalemate) in Vietnam. Second was the military request, on February 28, for 206,756 more troops, which according to the *Pentagon Papers* would have meant the call-up of reserve forces. Third, a new Secretary of Defense, Clark Clifford, was working behind the scenes for a bombing halt. And fourth, the New Hampshire presidential primary, and other manifestations of public sentiment, made clear the great resistance to the war effort that was growing among the U.S. population. On March 13, 1968, Johnson decided to deploy 30,000 more troops, but then a few days later a massive change in the strategy was signaled. On March 22, General Westmoreland was recalled to Washington and on March 31 Johnson announced a partial bombing halt, a reduction of the latest deployment to 13,500 troops, and his intention not to seek re-election. Three days later he announced North Vietnam's readiness to meet with American negotiators.

1968 to 1969: Limbo, then Global Change

After a brief period of limbo to the end of 1968, ending the term of the lame-duck president, Richard Nixon took over the presidency and initiated global change in strategy. In effect, Johnson's global change was to halt an old strategy; Nixon's was to replace it with a new one. His was a proactive, integrated strategy—he referred to its goal as "peace with honor"—consisting of the following elements: "Vietnamization," which meant the withdrawal of U.S. troops and the equiping of the South Vietnamese to take over the fighting; active peace initiatives to negotiate a settlement, alternated with military pressure (based on air and naval power, to replace the withdrawn land power) to encourage the North Vietnamese to undertake serious negotiations; and "linkage," the bringing of pressure on the Russians—by threatening a withdrawal of cooperation on other East-West negotiations—to influence the North Vietnamese to reach a settlement.

1970 to 1973: Continuity

That strategy remained intact into 1973, with only the emphasis of its various components changed from time to time to gain advantage. U.S. troop withdrawals continued rather steadily throughout the period. So did U.S. military pressure, which consisted primarily of periodic bombing offensives, but also included a ground excursion into Cambodia in mid 1970 and air support

for a South Vietnamese one into Laos in early 1971, as well as the mining of North Vietnamese ports in mid 1972. Political pressure was maintained on the Soviet Union during the entire period. And negotiation also continued throughout, although sporadically. An agreement was finally reached in January 1973, at which time the U.S. halted all offensive military activity. (The heaviest bombing of the war took place in North Vietnam just three weeks prior, after an earlier agreement fell apart.) By March 29, 1973, all American combat and support forces had left Vietnam, and effective August 15, all funding for American military activity in or over Indochina was ended. (Fighting, however, continued, the South Vietnamese army and government finally collapsing in April, 1975.)

SOME GENERAL CONCLUSIONS ABOUT STRATEGY FORMATION

Three themes will be pursued in this section. The first is that strategy formation can fruitfully be viewed as the interplay between a dynamic environment and bureaucratic momentum, with leadership mediating between the two. Second, strategy formation over periods of time appears to follow distinct regularities which may prove vital to understanding the process. And third, the study of the interplay between intended and realized strategies may lead us to the heart of this complex organizational process.

STRATEGY FORMATION AS THE INTERPLAY OF ENVIRONMENT, LEADERSHIP AND BUREAUCRACY

In general terms, strategy formation in most organizations can be thought of as revolving around the interplay of three basic forces: (a) an *environment* that changes continuously but irregularly, with frequent discontinuities and wide swings in its rate of change, (b) an organizational operating system, or *bureaucracy,* that above all seeks to stabilize its actions, despite the characteristics of the environment it serves, and (c) a *leadership* whose role is to mediate between these two forces, to maintain the stability of the organization's operating system while at the same time insuring its adaptation to environmental change. Strategy can then be viewed as the set of consistent behaviors by which the organization establishes for a time its place in its environment, and strategic change can be viewed as the organization's response to environmental change, constrained by the momentum of the bureaucracy and accelerated or dampened by the leadership.

Both Volkswagen and Vietnam are above all stories of how bureaucratic momentum constrains and conditions strategic change, at least after the initial strategic direction has been set. Any large automobile company is mightily constrained by its technical system. Retooling is enormously expensive. This helps to explain Volkswagen's slow response to the environmental changes of the 1960s. But this explanation is not sufficient. Volkswagen was clearly constrained by momentum of a psychological nature as well. The very success of its unique and integrated strategy seemed to reinforce its psychological commitment to it, and to act as a great barrier to the consideration of strategic change.

Even leadership was absent when needed in the 1960s. Nordhoff's period of great leadership began in 1948, when there was little to lose by acting boldly and when little bureaucratic momentum was present. That leadership lasted for the next ten years. But by the early 1960s, when bold action was needed in the face of an increasingly changed environment, the central leadership was not forthcoming. Quite the contrary, instead of pushing the bureaucracy to change, Nordhoff became a force for continuity. When change did come, it was late and it lacked a conceptual focus. The organization groped awkwardly in its new en-

vironment, until a new, dynamic leader came on the scene with a fresh strategy in 1971.

Bureaucratic momentum played a major role in the U.S. strategy in Vietnam as well. Earlier in our discussion, the periods 1954, 1961, and 1965 were labeled as global change because various strategies changed quickly and in unison. But in a broader perspective, all of these changes were incremental. The precedent of resisting Communist expansion in Southeast Asia—"the metastrategy" (a strategy of strategies)—was set in 1950. After that, the changes of 1954, 1961, and 1965, while substituting one means for another, simply reinforced the basic direction; they did not change it. Each escalation step seemed to be a natural outgrowth of the last one, one commitment leading to the next. (A management scientist might be tempted to describe this as exponential smoothing, in which the current strategy was always some exponentially weighted sum of past ones.) Only in 1968, when the organization was faced with a massive failure, was there a truly global change in strategy.

At no time was bureaucratic momentum more evident than during the great debate of 1963–1965. The pressures on Johnson to do more of the same—to escalate—became enormous. One could even argue that the creation of the Special Forces by Kennedy became a self-confirming contingency plan. In effect a guerilla fighting force, created in case it might be needed, found a way to make itself needed. It came to be used because it was there. This suggests that strategies can be evoked by available resources (as in the case of the employees, factory, and people's car of Volkswagenwerk of 1948 looking for something to do),[4] and that contingency plans, a favorite prescriptive tool of planning theorists in time of environmental turbulence, may have a habit of making themselves self-confirming, whether they are needed or not.

Of course the environment played a major

role in Vietnam too. The U.S. altered its strategy in 1954 and 1965, albeit within the metastrategy, because the changed environment was proving inhospitable to its existing strategy. And the global changes of 1950 and 1968 were certainly evoked by environmental change, in these two cases rather specific events—the fall of the Chinese government and the Tet offensive.

What of leadership? The real tragedy of Vietnam is that, up until 1968, the leadership never seemed to mediate appropriately between the bureaucracy and the environment. In 1961, for example, leadership acted proactively in the absence of either significant environmental change or bureaucratic momentum. Kennedy voluntarily escalated the war in a way that made the 1965 escalation all but inevitable. "All but" because sufficiently strong leadership in 1965 might have been able to resist the environmental and bureaucratic pressures. But the cards were stacked against Johnson. Both the environmental change and the bureaucratic momentum were pulling him in the same direction, each suggesting more of the same (escalation) as the natural next step. It would have taken very powerful leadership indeed to resist these forces, and Johnson did not exhibit it. Only in 1968, facing the most dramatic failure of all and a markedly changed domestic environment, did Johnson finally exert the leadership initiative that reversed the eighteen-year course of the metastrategy.

Thereafter, Nixon exhibited strong leadership too, introducing proactive change in 1969 and pursuing it vigorously to the end. But again, admittedly in retrospect, that proactivity served only to prolong what was inevitably a lost cause. And bureaucratic momentum seemed to play a minor role in the Nixon years, his strong chief advisor Kissinger, standing in place of the policy-making machinery of government. But those two men also fell prey to psychological momentum, pursuing their costly and ultimately futile strategy against public and congressional resistance.

PATTERNS OF STRATEGIC CHANGE

There is no need to dwell on the point that strategy formation is not a regular, nicely sequenced process running on a standard five-year schedule or whatever. An organization may find itself in a stable environment for years, sometimes for decades, with no need to reassess an appropriate strategy. Then, suddenly, the environment can become so turbulent that even the very best planning techniques are of no use because of the impossibility of predicting the kind of stability that will eventually emerge. (What kind of strategic plan was John Foster Dulles to carry in his briefcase to Geneva in 1954?) In response to this kind of inconsistency in the environment, patterns of strategic change are never steady, but rather irregular and ad hoc, with a complex intermingling or periods of continuity, change, flux, limbo, and so on.

But that should not lead to the conclusion that patterns in strategy formation do not exist. Indeed, if we are to make any normative headway in this area, we must find consistencies that will enable organizations to understand better their strategic situations. Thus the prime thrust of our research has been to identify patterns of strategic change.

Most of our studies show evidence of two main patterns, one superimposed on the other. The first is the life cycle of an overall strategy—its conception, elaboration, decay, and death. The second is the presence of periodic waves of change and continuity within the life cycle. (Longer cycles of this kind could be identified as well, from one life cycle to the next.) What this second pattern suggests is that strategies do not commonly change in continuous incremental fashion; rather, change—even incremental change —takes place in spurts, each followed by a period of continuity. Nowhere is this better demonstrated than in the stepwise escalation of the Vietnam metastrategy in 1950, 1954, 1961, and 1965.

Why do organizations undergo distinct

periods of change and continuity? For one thing, such a pattern seems to be consistent with human cognition. We do not react to phenomena continuously, but rather in discreet steps, in response to changes large enough for us to perceive. Likewise, strategic decision processes in organizations are not continuous, but irregular [15]. They must be specifically evoked; they proceed for a time; and then they terminate. Furthermore, consistent with the Cyert and March notion of sequential attention to goals [8], the leadership of an organization may choose to deal with the conflicting pressures for change from the environment and continuity from the bureaucracy by first acceding to one and then the other. To most bureaucracies—for example, the automobile assembly line—change is disturbing. So the leadership tries to concentrate that disturbance into a specific period of time, and then to leave the bureaucracy alone for a while to consolidate the change. But of course, while the bureaucracy is being left alone, the environment continues to change, so that no matter how well chosen the strategy, eventually a new cycle of change must be initiated.

With these two patterns in mind, we can now consider the patterns of strategic change in both studies. Volkswagen began its life (or at least left the incubation stage) in 1948 with what we call a *gestalt* strategy, defined as one that is (a) unique and (b) tightly integrated (in the sense that its elements are mutually complementary, or *synergistic,* in Volkswagen's case fusing around the dominant element of the people's car). The first feature, uniqueness, means that the gestalt strategy deposits the organization in a *niche,* a corner of the environment reserved for itself. If well chosen, therefore, that strategy can protect the organization from attack for a period of time. That is exactly what happened in the case of Volkswagen. But the second feature, tight integration, makes a gestalt strategy difficult to change. The changing of a single dimension may cause *dis*integration of the whole

strategy. That also became clear when Volkswagen had to change, when competitors moved into its niche and the market moved away from it. Volkswagenwerk's initial response to the changes in environment was two-fold. Before 1959, and after 1959 until 1965, it essentially ignored the changes. And in the 1959 period it resorted to a *grafting* procedure, adding a new piece to its existing gestalt strategy, but avoiding any fundamental change in it. When Volkswagen finally did begin to respond seriously in 1965, that response was an awkward one, a *groping* procedure with no clear focus. After seventeen years with one gestalt strategy, the organization was not accustomed to making major changes in strategy. It was only in the 1970s that Volkswagen was able to develop a clear new strategy, in part, we shall soon argue, a result of its groping procedure.

A few words on gestalt strategies are in order, since they appear frequently in organizations. First, they seem to develop at one point in time, most frequently when the organization is founded. That is when bureaucratic momentum is weakest, leadership typically strong (entrepreneurial), and environments rather tolerant. In contrast, achieving a gestalt strategy is difficult in an ongoing organization, which has a great deal more bureaucratic momentum. Yet both the Volkswagenwerk of 1971 and the United States Government of 1969 seemed able to, no doubt because both faced environments beginning to settle down after periods of great turbulence that had severely disrupted their bureaucratic momentum.

Second, gestalt strategies seem to be associated with single, powerful leaders. This is especially true of the two periods mentioned above, as well as that Volkswagenwerk of 1948. Perhaps the sophisticated integration called for by such strategies can be effected only in one mind. The development of a gestalt strategy requires innovative thinking, rooted in synthesis rather than analysis, based on the "intuitive" or inexplicit processes that have been associated with the brain's right hemisphere [16]. Thus we are led to hypothesize that gestalt strategies are the products of single individuals, and only appear in organizations with strong leadership, in effect, those that use the entrepreneurial mode. It is difficult to imagine one coming out of a decentralized organization, unless all the decision-makers follow the conceptual lead of one creative individual. Nor can one be imagined resulting from a formal management science or planning process per se, these being essentially analytic rather than synthetic. (That is not to say, of course, that a synthesizer cannot parade under the title of planner or management scientist, or for that matter, advisor, as in the case of Kissinger.) We hypothesize then that the planning mode will normally lead to what can be called *mainline* strategies, typical and obvious ones for the organization to adopt (for example, because the competitors are using them).

Vietnam represents the classic strategic life cycle, although the pattern differs somewhat from that of Volkswagen. The Vietnam metastrategy had a clearly identifiable birthdate, 1950, and unlike that of Volkswagen, which grew rapidly from the outset, this one grew slowly, receiving three distinct boosts, in 1954, 1961 and 1965. It was only after this third boost, however, fifteen years after its birth, that the metastrategy really underwent rapid expansion. Its demise also differed from that of Volkswagen. Whereas the Volkswagen strategy experienced a long, agonizing death, like a developing cancer, the U.S. metastrategy in Vietnam experienced one major setback, like a massive stroke, in 1968, and thereafter remained in a coma until 1973, when it finally expired. (The new gestalt strategy that arose in 1969 served only to bury it. In Volkswagen, of course, only the strategy expired; out of its ashes a new one emerged, and the automobile operations carried on. The Vietnam operations did not.)

The change-continuity cycles were also very marked in the case of Vietnam. Except

for the period of 1962 to 1965, when the change was gradual, and largely out of control of the central leadership, periods of change and continuity were always evident. And in the broad perspective, as noted earlier, up to 1968 that change was always incremental. Vietnam in fact represents a classic case of incrementalism, and exhibits profoundly its dangers. Each escalation step was taken without an assessment of what the next step might have entailed, with the result that Lyndon Johnson in 1968 found himself in a situation that Harry Truman, the President under whom the first step was taken in 1950, as well as all the Presidents in between (including the Lyndon Johnson of 1965), would have considered inconceivable. Strategy-makers seem prepared to assume positions in incremental steps that they would never begin to entertain in global ones. On the other hand, some of our other studies, notably of the magazine, show that even in simple situations global strategy is very difficult to conceive and execute successfully. This, perhaps, is the strategy-maker's greatest dilemma—the danger of incremental change versus the difficulty of global change.

DELIBERATE VERSUS EMERGENT STRATEGIES

Earlier it was claimed that the definition of strategy used in this research opens up the other side of the strategy formation question, strategies as ex post facto results of decisional behavior as well as strategies as a priori guidelines to decision-making. Two kinds of strategies were identified: intended and realized. These two, at least in theory, can now be combined in three ways, as shown in Figure 1 and listed below:

1. Intended strategies that get realized; these may be called *deliberate* strategies.

2. Intended strategies that do not get realized, perhaps because of unrealistic ex-

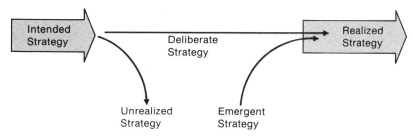

Figure 1   Types of Strategies

pectations, misjudgments about the environment, or changes in either during implementation; these may be called *unrealized* strategies.

3. Realized strategies that were never intended, perhaps because no strategy was intended at the outset or perhaps because, as in (2), those that were got displaced along the way; these may be called *emergent* strategies.

The Volkswagen strategy of 1948 to 1958 is perhaps the best illustration of a deliberate strategy, both intended and realized. Kennedy's intended strategy of 1961 of advising the Vietnamese is probably the best example of an unrealized strategy. And the subsequent United States strategy of finding itself in a fighting instead of advising role is probably the best example of an emergent strategy, realized despite intentions. (Note the association of these last two with Kennedy's proactive strategy making.)

But practice is always more complicated —and more interesting—than theory, and despite our neat trichotomy, we found a number of other relationships between intended and realized strategies. These include intended strategies that, as they get realized, change their form and become, in part at least, emergent; emergent strategies that get formalized as deliberate ones; and intended strategies that get overrealized.

Planning theory postulates that the strategy-maker "formulates" from on high while the subordinates "implement" lower

down. Unfortunately, however, this neat dichotomy is based on two assumptions which often prove false: that the formulator is fully informed, or at least as well informed as the implementor, and that the environment is sufficiently stable, or at least predictable, to ensure that there will be no need for *re*formation during implementation. The absence of either condition should lead to a collapse of the formulation-implementation dichotomy, and the use of the adaptive mode instead of the planning one. Strategy formation then becomes a learning process, whereby so-called implementation feeds back to formulation and intentions get modified en route, resulting in an emergent strategy.

The failure to so adapt is dramatically illustrated in a paper by Feld [10]. He describes the problems that arise in military organizations that hold rigidly to this dichotomy, "The command function of planning and coordination [being] considered to require a sheltered position" despite the fact that "The conditions of combat are fluid and haphazard in the extreme" (p. 17). Thus, in the infamous battle of World War I, where the British casualties numbered 300,000:

No senior officer from the Operations Branch of the General Headquarters, it was claimed, ever set foot (or eyes) on the Passchendaele battlefield during the four months the battle was in progress. Daily reports on the condition of the battle-field were first ignored, then ordered discontinued. Only after the battle did the Army chief of staff learn that he had been directing men to advance through a sea of mud. (p. 21)

The most successful deliberate strategies of our two studies—the gestalt ones of Nordhoff and later Leiding in Volkswagenwerk —were both formulated by men who knew their industry intimately and who were able to predict conditions in environments that were settling down after periods of great turbulence. In sharp contrast is the Vietnam strategy of 1962–1965, the most costly emergent strategy of our studies—one realized in a form totally different and far more involving than that intended. Both Kennedy and Johnson had only the most cursory knowledge of the real conditions in Vietnam [11], and neither was able to predict the conditions of an environment that was becoming increasingly turbulent. As Halberstam notes in his detailed study of the U.S. experience in Vietnam:

> ... it was something they slipped into more than they chose; they thought they were going to have time for clear, well-planned choices, to decide how many men and what type of strategy they would follow, but events got ahead of them. The pressures from Saigon for more and more men would exceed Washington's capacity to slow it down and think cooly, and so the decisions evolved rather than were made, and Washington slipped into a ground combat war. [11, p. 544]

What can we say then about Johnson's decisions to escalate the war in 1965? Here we have a situation, apparently a common one if our other studies can be used as a guide, where an emergent strategy became a deliberate one. Johnson's decisions of 1965, unlike those of 1968, did not break any pattern. Quite the contrary, they formalized one that was becoming increasingly evident since 1962. The U.S. was fighting a war in 1965, no longer advising an ally. In other words, the strategy-maker perceived an unintended pattern in a stream of deci-

sions and made that pattern the intended one for the future. An emergent strategy, once recognized, became a deliberate strategy. (Thus not only we, but also the leaders we studied, were perceivers of patterns in decision streams.) A similar phenomenon—although less pronounced— seemed to be at play in Volkswagen in the 1970s. Out of the groping of the 1960s, Leiding perceived an emergent pattern, which we might call the Audi strategy. One car—stylish, front-wheel drive, water cooled —seemed to be most successful in the new environment. And so he built the new gestalt around it. The general conclusion seems to be that new strategies sometimes have incubation periods. While the old strategy is decaying, one or more emergent strategies are developing peripherally in the organization. Eventually one is selected and formalized as the new, intended strategy. Decisional behavior in effect coalesces around what seems to have worked for the organization—and perhaps also what lends coherence to the frustrating years of failing to realize intentions.

But the formalization of an emergent strategy is hardly incidental to the organization. As the Vietnam period of 1965 to 1968 shows so clearly, the very act of explicating an implicit strategy—of stating clearly and officially that it is to be the intended strategy —changes profoundly the attitude of the bureaucracy and of the environment to it. Johnson's decisions of 1965 opened the flood-gates of escalation. Had he remained in limbo, refusing to make a decision (all the while, the decisions in fact being made for him on the battlefield), it is doubtful that the military bureaucracy could have pursued escalation so vigorously. In effect, the very fact of making a strategy explicit—even an implicit one that is evident to all—provides a clear and formal invitation to the bureaucracy to run with it. (One could of course make the reverse point, that the very fact of his having remained in limbo for two years built up a charge in the military establishment that went off with that much more explosive force when the detonator was finally released.)

To overstate the bureaucracy's position, it says to its top management: "Our business is running the operations; yours is formulating the strategy. But we need a clearly defined, intended strategy to do our job—to buy our machines, hire our workers, standardize our procedures. So please give us such a strategy—any strategy—so long as it is precise and stable [and lets us grow]." The danger in this innocent statement, of course, is that the bureaucracy runs like an elephant. The strategy that gets it moving may be no more consequential than a mouse, but once underway there is no stopping it. As Halberstam notes about Kennedy in 1963 and Johnson after 1965: ". . . the capacity to control a policy involving the military is greatest before the policy is initiated, but once started, no matter how small the initial step, a policy has a life and a thrust of its own, it is an organic thing" [11, p. 209]. Bureaucratic momentum takes over, happy to have a clear strategy, never stopping to question it. The strategy-maker may awake one day—as did Lyndon Johnson in 1968—to find that his intended strategy has somehow been implemented beyond his wildest intentions. It has been *overrealized.* Thus, "make your strategy explicit" may be a popular prescription of the management consultant [18], but in the light of this research it can sometimes be seen to constitute questionable advice indeed.

CONCLUSION

This article has been written with the intention of bringing a new kind of description to the much misunderstood process of strategy formation in organizations. A few descriptive studies—two of which are reported here—constitute a limited data base, but they do call into question a number of assumptions about the process, at least in certain con-

texts. A strategy is not a fixed plan, nor does it change systematically at pre-arranged times solely at the will of management. The dichotomy between strategy formulation and strategy implementation is a false one under certain common conditions, because it ignores the learning that must often follow the conception of an intended strategy. Indeed the very word "formu*lation*" is misleading since we commonly refer to as "strategies" many patterns in organizational decisions that form without conscious or deliberate thought. Even Chandler's well known edict of structure follows strategy [5] must be called into question because of the influence of bureaucratic momentum on strategy formation. The aggressive, proactive strategy-maker—the hero of the literature on entrepreneurship—can under some conditions do more harm than the hesitant, reactive one. Contingency planning, a popular prescription in times of environmental turbulence, can be risky because the plans may tend to become actualized, whether needed or not. And so too can it sometimes be risky to make strategy explicit, notably in an uncertain environment with an aggressive bureaucracy. In general, the contemporary prescriptions and normative techniques of analysis and planning—and the debate that accompanies them—seem unable to address the complex reality of strategy formation. To tell management to state its goals precisely, assess its strengths and weaknesses, plan systematically on schedule, and make the resulting strategies explicit are at best overly general guidelines, at worst demonstrably misleading precepts to organizations that face a confusing reality.

There is perhaps no process in organizations that is more demanding of human cognition than strategy formation. Every strategy-maker faces an impossible overload of information (much of it soft); as a result he can have no optimal process to follow. The researcher or management scientist who seeks to understand strategy formation is up against the same cognitive constraints, but with poorer access to the necessary information. Thus he faces no easy task. But proceed he must, for the old prescriptions are not working and new ones are badly needed. These will only grow out of a sophisticated understanding of the rich reality of strategy formation, and that will require an open mind, a recognition of how little we really know, and intensive, painstaking research.[5]

NOTES

1. Where a decision is defined as a commitment to action, usually a commitment of resources [15].
2. The war production period could also have been viewed as one of continuity in strategy.
3. This is called a period of flux in the sense that Volkswagenwerk was looking haphazardly for a replacement for its beetle. It could also be called a period of continuity in the sense that the firm pursued a strategy of model diversification.
4. Chandler [5] makes the same point to explain the expansion of the DuPont company after World War I, when it found itself with excess capacity.
5. The author wishes to acknowledge the contributions of Ron Wilson, Danny Miller, Bill Litwack, and Bob Woolard, who carried out the studies associated with this research; the Canada Council which funded them; Andre Theoret and later Roger Gosselin, who joined the group for the hypotheses-generating sessions; and Jim Waters who commented on an earlier draft of the paper.

REFERENCES

1. Allison, G. T., *Essence of Decision,* Little Brown, Boston, Mass., 1971.
2. Ansoff, H. I., *Corporate Strategy,* McGraw-Hill, New York, 1965.
3. Bowman, E. H., "Strategy and the Weather," *Sloan Management Review,* (Winter, 1976), pp. 49–58.
4. Braybrooke, D. and Lindblom, C. E., *A Strategy of Decision,* Free Press, New York, 1963.
5. Chandler, A. D., *Strategy and Structure,* MIT Press, Cambridge, Mass., 1962.
6. Cole, A. H., *Business Enterprise in a Social Setting,* Harvard Univ. Press, Cambridge, Mass., 1959.
7. Collins, O. and Moore, D. G., *The Organization Makers,* Appleton-Century-Crofts, New York, 1970.
8. Cyert, R. M. and March, J. G., *A Behavioral Theory of the Firm,* Prentice-Hall, Englewood Cliffs, N.J., 1963.
9. Drucker, P. F., "Entrepreneurship in the Business Enterprise," *Journal of Business Policy,* Vol. 1, No. 1 (1970), pp. 3–12.
10. Feld, M. O., "Information and Authority: The Structure of Military Organization," *American Sociological Review,* Vol. 24 (1959), pp. 15–22.
11. Halberstam, D., *The Best and the Brightest,* Random House, New York, 1972.
12. Lindblom, C. E., "The Science of 'Muddling Through'," *Public Administration Review,* Vol. 19 (1959), pp. 79–88.
13. ———, *The Policy-Making Process,* Prentice-Hall, Englewood Cliffs, N.J., 1968.
14. Mintzberg, H., "Strategy-Making in Three Modes," *California Management Review,* Vol. 16, No. 2 (1973), pp. 44–53.
15. ———, Raisinghani, D. and Théorêt, A., "The Structure of 'Unstructured' Decision Processes," *Administrative Science Quarterly,* Vol. 21, No. 2 (1976), pp. 246–275.
16. Ornstein, R. E., *The Psychology of Consciousness,* Freeman, San Francisco, Calif., 1972.
17. Steiner, G. A., *Top Management Planning,* Macmillan, New York, 1969.
18. Tilles, S., "How to Evaluate Corporate Strategy," *Harvard Business Review,* Vol. 41 (July–August, 1963), pp. 111–121.

Inside ITT's Washington Office

Thomas S. Burns

If the brains of ITT were in New York City in the late sixties, the heart of the company was in the nation's capital. The ITT Washington office was staffed by a colorful lot of lobbyists, technical specialists, marketeers, consultants, and sales representatives, all living in a loose confederation of cliques and tribes. The ITT Building on L Street was the main area of activity. Adjacent to the Mayflower Hotel and strategically located in downtown Washington, it commanded the network of satellite offices scattered around the city.

With representatives from divisions in many industries and experts in a broad

Excerpted from Tales of ITT: An Insider's Report by Thomas S. Burns. Copyright © 1974 by Thomas S. Burns. Reprinted by permission of the publisher, Houghton Mifflin Company. Burns is a former vice president of International Telephone and Telegraph (ITT).

spectrum of technologies, the cumulative clout of the ITT Washington organization was awesome indeed. When all the forces cooperated and an objective was clearly identified, no task seemed beyond accomplishment. However, intercompany politics, feuds, divisional competition, and personal ambition were always in evidence. The effectiveness of the organization was far below what the money poured into its coffers should have commanded. There were simply too many people representing diverse and overlapping interests to achieve much harmony of purpose. Dog was always eating dog, or at least sharpening a fang or two.

The Washington office proper and the entire capital show for ITT was run by William R. Merriam. Bill was the scion of an old Washington family, well connected enough socially to give ITT the aura of respectability it so badly needed in some circles.

MERRIAM'S PRAETORIAN GUARD

The so-called corporate people were Merriam's Praetorian Guard. They reported only to him. Each was chosen for a special talent or skill and usually had connections with either the Democratic or Republican party. Most were sensitive political specialists who could be relied on like secret agents. They occupied the coziest offices, had the largest expense accounts, and were asked the fewest questions about their activities. In more humble circumstances in the organizational scheme were the marketing people and technical specialists. They represented divisions and subsidiaries that leased space from Grand Landlord Merriam. At the bottom of the social scale was a mysterious group of technical experts and liaison people who rotated in and out of the Washington office on short tenure.

Typical of "corporate people" was the Lone Ranger and Tonto team of Tom Casey and Tom Gallagher. Gallagher was one of a large number of military retirees who became "commercial representatives." They were an unusual lot. Although sales was their function, they were prevented by law from actively selling to the military for three years after discharge or retirement. But, being clever in the methods of Pentagon procurement, they found ways around such awkward regulations. Lunch and cocktail hours were used to maximum advantage, as were the golf course and private club. By and large, they performed their marketing chores without setting foot inside the Pentagon. Their techniques might be shabby and inept by professional standards, but they relied on personal equations to overcome the limitations of marketing finesse and product knowledge.

It was a lucrative game—for a while. The "representatives" exploited contacts and an intimate knowledge of certain military programs for as long as both lasted. The span was usually two to three years. Wild parties, magnificent expense accounts; weekends at game preserves and on the sea in yachts. Always lots and lots of money. Then, as had to happen, friends retired or were transferred and new programs formed. The "representative" became ineffective and was gradually removed from the scene to be replaced by a more recent model. He had been milked of his useful information, and his contacts had lost their influence. Paradoxically, he was put out to pasture just at the time when he could have legally started to ply the selling trade.

THE SURVEILLANCE SYSTEM

To achieve a grass-roots control, ITT established a unique surveillance system for politicians. Every senator, congressman, governor, and important state official was assigned to a senior ITT manager for "cognizance" on a geographical basis. The manager was responsible for making the politician's acquaintance and being available on any occasion when he might require some service. A routine report was made to the ITT manager concerning the activities, disposition, and temper of his charge. The system was worked out by Senior Vice-President Gerrity, to be sure that an ITT political "button man" could be activated on short notice whenever and wherever needed. Cumbersome, perhaps, but effective—and most ITT managers enjoyed their small political intelligence contribution to the great scheme.

RELATIONS BETWEEN HEADQUARTERS STAFF AND WASHINGTON LOBBYISTS

The New York staff disliked the Washington corporate people, but admired them grudgingly. "The bastards spend money like it was going out of style, but they deliver the goods," a staff controller said. "So when we bitch, we are told to cover it up and forget it."

. . . So, cuss them out and disparage their roles as we did, when the going got tough, ITT division managers ran to seek the advice of an ITT lobbyist—and usually the result was a ploy that worked.

On one occasion when my Cable Division marketeers had exhausted all strategies and were about to show a white feather in a contract dispute, I turned to one of Merriam's lieutenants for help. We had trooped the line, ensign through admiral, in an attempt to sell our system. But it soon became apparent that the web of Navy protection was being spun around the contracting officer and the award was about to be made to our competitor. Merriam blew the whistle, and an ITT lobbyist took a week to study our "case," then called us in for a consultation.

He was less than impressed with our efforts: "You're overmatched. No matter how technically effective you think you are, it is stupid trying to go this on your own. You need some muscle, and the sooner we bring it to bear, the better."

With our fate in the balance, he began the sideshow. Feet on the desk, he drew a yellow legal pad out of his drawer and began to doodle. He drew three lines on the paper and, as we watched patiently, he began filling the columns with names of senators, administration officials, congressmen, and one or two senior military officers.

THE GUYS WE OWN

. . . "First list are the guys we own. Second list are the guys we can usually count on, people who owe us something. Third list are just influential guys, not friends but people who will negotiate for a deal."

He ticked off a dozen names, skipping from column to column.

"These are the congressional types who will influence the procurement," he said. "Lucky for you boys we have some kind of major manufacturing facility in just about every one of their states."

He waved his pencil and continued the lecture.

"When you work with these politicians, remember you have to prepare the whole goddamned smear. Write the letters, the "off the cuff" comments, the press releases, everything. Believe me, they use most of our stuff; some don't even proofread what we write for them. More often than not we arrange for releases. The responsibility we accept is to keep them out of trouble and to be sure that ITT is not embarrassed."

He paused for dramatic effect, looked out the window and studied a heap of rubble someday destined to be a subway terminal. Finally he said, "We can line up most of the guys you need and neutralize the ones that might come out against you. You really are lucky—we have one hell of payroll in some of these states." He handed me the list. "Take this along and learn something about the legislators I've checked. I'll arrange some meetings in the next couple of weeks."

. . . As the Eastern Airlines shuttle plane lurched through the sky from Washington to New York, I reread the list. With most of the people on the list pulling for us we could have arranged a war with Red China or an embargo on Japanese transistor radios. I wondered how it was possible to broker so much power so casually.

Dita Beard played her politics as a commercial enterprise.

"These guys are businessmen, pure and simple. They are in the business of getting reelected; and if you are ever in doubt as to how to deal with the bastards, keep that in mind. It is a very rare son-of-a-bitch here in Washington who is so entrenched that his reelection is not the first consideration in any goddamn thing he does."

"Don't use amateurs," was an ITT Washington office dictum. "Wait until a guy has been around long enough to know the tricks of the trade. The pros know how to get elected, how to stay elected, and how to get their bills paid in the process."

So much for freshman congressmen and newly appointed department undersecretaries.

ITT'S WASHINGTON WEIRDOS

The weird personalities patrolling the beat for ITT in Washington were stashed in the nooks and crannies of the Washington office, out of the way of the normal traffic. "Eddie the Expediter" was such a geek. Eddie was an emaciated, gray-haired marketeer with a consumptive appearance and an irritating apologetic manner. But to ITT top management involved in Pentagon affairs, Eddie was a most valuable "marketing" man to have around. His specialty was the covert acquisition of classified information. Eddie had built a career on his intelligence contacts in the military establishment. His reputation for acting as a double agent between ITT and the Pentagon had been passed on for several generations of senior officers. He represented the generosity of ITT. Eddie would pay handsomely for significant bits of information and would always protect his source.

His credits were impressive. He could come up with a Top Secret Defense Concept Paper, sensitive memorandum, or unpublished budget projections almost on request. Eddie never obtained anything officially so there was no accountability—and he was most careful to dispose of all documents once the information was viewed by the requesting party. ITT, of course, took no official responsibility for Eddie or his activities. In the finest tradition of the espionage agent, he was alone.

The information relating to budgets, projects, and military planning that Eddie dealt in was absolutely essential to the ITT scheme of obtaining business. The future must be known. Geneen (president of ITT) would not be surprised. So, never mind that Eddie was, in fact, a spy; he was a credit to the Washington office, a hero first-class—

an ITT patriot who would crawl all the way out on the national security limb, whenever and however requested.

ESPIONAGE ACTIVITIES

Geneen had a penchant for such espionage activities. High on the list of Washington people for ITT executives to acquire socially were agents of the FBI, CIA, and the military groups in the intelligence community. The ITT board of directors and top management were liberally sprinkled with ex-government security people, ex-CIA chief John McCone being the most celebrated. Anyone who had held a position in military or government intelligence was an employment candidate. The presence of these people seemed to give Geneen a sense of security and fitted with his belief that business success relies heavily on a maximum of insider information—and no surprises.

WASHINGTON OFFICE BECAME RESPONSIBLE ONLY TO ITSELF

Gradually over the years the Washington office became an entity responsible primarily to itself. These professionals kept only a few people completely informed. They realized that only success counted, the "go/no-go" of obtaining contracts and arranging appointments, guiding legislation and securing patronage—only specifics. If they performed well, they survived; if they failed, they were cashiered. And there were few questions asked as to how they had achieved the objectives.

Backed by the company's carte blanche, the ITT Washington lobbyists became some of the most formidable hucksters in the capital during the sixties and early seventies. With more and more cold cash poured into the quest for favorable antitrust solutions to the company's problems, the senior lobbyists worked at creating their own spheres of influence and a powerful base of support for Geneen's acquisition plans.

Lobbyists with weekly payments to deliver were used to passing money around without much thought of the consequences of their actions—just as an espionage officer probably regards political murder in the same class with the audit of a saboteur's expense account. All in a day's work.

Boundary Spanning Units: Organizational Implications for the Management of Innovation

Robert Callahan
Paul Salipante, Jr.

Can those responsible for an organization's personnel management help their firm meet a strong challenge to its market? The study reported here found that creative human resource management was indeed critical to one firm's successful adoption of a new technology in its major product line. This success rested on the development of several new organizational units and the effective selection and management of their personnel. The type of new units developed are generally termed *boundary spanning units* and are defined as any group or department whose primary responsibilities are to deal with parties outside the organization, such as clients, suppliers, and research institutions.

The firm that was the focus of this study successfully utilized special boundary spanning units to help it develop a new product line while retaining its capabilities in established markets. In investigating the firm's

From *Human Resources Management,* Spring 1979, vol. 18, no. 2, pp. 26–31.

transition to the new technology and products, three specific conclusions emerged. First, new boundary spanning units established on a temporary basis can be effective in managing adaptation to an innovation, yet leave intact the basic structural and procedural nature of the organization. Second, these units require creative staffing procedures and dispensation from normal organizational rules. Third, the organization must isolate the units' personnel from the rest of the organization; however, opportunities for transfer of their expertise to the organization's regular employees must be provided as the work shifts from creative uncertainty to routine certainty.[1]

ORGANIZATIONAL ADAPTATION TO INNOVATIONS

Over the last fifteen years a number of organizational theorists have noticed that those organizations successfully operating in rapidly changing environments tend to have more "organic," flexible structures.[2] Such findings, combined with the perception that change is occurring at an accelerating rate, have supported the call by several writers for substantial modifications in organizational structures and the basic nature of the employment relationship.[3] It was argued that these modifications would improve organizations' ability to manage the adoption of innovations. The continued success of bureaucratic organizations, however, has served to argue against the need for massive structural change.[4]

A more recent view is that only the organizational departments which span the boundary between the organization and the parts of its environment which are rapidly changing need to be highly adaptive.[5]

Such boundary spanning departments serve to buffer the core of the organization from the need for constant and rapid change. It is these units which have proven to be a valuable mechanism for managing innovations arising from environmental changes.

THE RESEARCH

Investigating organizational adaptation—a shifting and dynamic condition—with traditional survey methods such as questionnaires,[6] has been the approach of most studies. The research on which this study is based was designed to study the dynamics and to investigate processes in sufficient depth to assess individual events, specific management decisions and changes in organizational practices. The dynamics of managing the innovation process were explored primarily through a "real time" (rather than retrospective) study of an organization facing a major change in its environment. This type of research[7] requires close, inside contact with an organization and its personnel. The study covered one and a half years and entailed three major stages, the first

being a historical perspective through interviews and document analysis to determine the status of the adaptation process. This was important since the decision makers had already decided to set up new units to handle the innovation and had just begun to select their managers. The second and more important stage utilized observation, interviews and document analysis covering the nine month period of organizational life during which the new departments were staffed and put into operation.

OVERVIEW OF THE FIRM'S MANAGEMENT OF INNOVATION

The firm studied is multi-divisional and bureaucratic in basic structure. With well over $100 million in annual sales, its major product line is X-ray equipment used in medical diagnosis. The organizations which started the X-ray industry in the early 1900's were very small and founded by engineers. The equipment's initial development was a joint effort of medical people with backgrounds in physics and the engineers. Over the years the X-ray technology became more and more standardized in terms of equipment, procedures, and product (X-ray films). Additional equipment designed for specific purposes (e.g., chest, internal organs, head, cardiac systems) utilized the same basic technology. During this evolution the physicians retained a scientific orientation to the equipment and its usage. In contrast, this firm's personnel became more sales-oriented and not technically skilled because of the standardized performance of the equipment.

A major technical innovation now promises to revolutionize the X-ray equipment industry. The innovation (Computerized Tomography or C.T.) uses a computer to assemble more data than conventional X-ray equipment can. The C.T. is several times more costly than conventional equipment and more complicated mechanically and electronically. Its output is also different, so physicians must undergo retraining to accurately interpret the diagnostic results.

One element in merging this technology into the current business was to determine how best to design, develop, and market this innovation. Management in the organization, therefore, evaluated the capabilities of their existing departments, including the boundary spanning units (specifically, sales and service). They found that the sales and service departments did not possess the technical qualifications or personal status required to market the C.T. or to collect and transfer technical knowledge to the designers. The new technology required extensive knowledge of computers, computer programming, and modern electronics. High personal status vis-a-vis physicians was needed, since the medical profession had to be re-educated before they could make intelligent purchasing and utilization decisions. In addition, the actual performance and technical options were extremely soft in design and continually needed to be reevaluated and updated. Given the deficiencies in the existing boundary spanning departments, one option considered by the firm's management was hiring new personnel into existing units. This was rejected, however, because of the existing units' low perceived status overall and the jealousy that would likely be created by not retraining existing personnel.

The firm's decision makers selected the alternative of creating new but temporary boundary spanning departments for C.T. sales and service. Part of the rationale for establishing new departments centered around the type of work to be performed. These new units would be responsible for sensing changes in different environmental segments, both technically (in terms of product performance and product option design), and marketability (required characteristics to satisfy customer needs and remain competitive). This type of work is creative and uncertain and predominantly determined by the environment. In contrast, the existing boundary spanning departments perform more routine and certain work, since the product line is limited and the technology relatively static and well known to the customer. The basic tasks for the existing sales and service units, then, were quite routine, while the new units had to constantly develop new procedures.

Critical to management decision-making was the view that the tasks of the new unit would become more routine and prescribed over time. It was anticipated that the innovation would eventually become standardized, as had previously occurred with X-ray equipment. In consequence, management decided that the new boundary spanning units would be temporary, gradually transferring responsibility for the innovation to the existing boundary spanners as the work became more prescribed. Thus, the organization gained short-term adaptability without sacrificing its inherently bureaucratic form and without creating unnecessary permanent units.

As a rough measure of the efficacy of creating the new units, it must be noted that several organizations without this form of boundary spanning have dropped their own C.T. introductions. Several other competitors initially attempted to utilize their existing boundary spanning departments. Within six months, three of these created new units, even attempting to hire away the new personnel from the original organization.

Given this overview of the organization's process of adopting an innovation, let us now examine more closely the new sales department, its personnel (termed product specialists), their relation to management, and the organizational practices applied to the department.

BOUNDARY SPANNING PERSONNEL

The firm's management determined that the new sales department required personnel with a unique combination of skills in computer technology and the medical field. Having a medical background was critical because the computer hardware and software suppliers have not specialized in medical applications of computers. The application of computer technology to the medical field is new and controversial. Consequently, there is a scarcity of skilled personnel, creating search problems for the organization. The problem was handled by contacting one former employee who was known to have been working in a computer firm for several years. He was offered the position of manager of this newly created unit and charged with the reeponsibility of hiring other members. His contacts outside the X-ray industry proper provided a list of potential candidates. In addition, he perceived the need to hire personnel with advanced degrees as well as specific technical competencies. Unlike the present sales force who possess "associate degrees" or some medical school training, the new units' personnel had a minimum of a master's degree with several possessing Ph.D.'s. All had the formal teaching experience which was required to reeducate some of the medical personnel on C.T. technology and usage. In addition, all had some medical background and extensive experience in the computer field.

The new personnel reflected more the values and technical competencies of the client group they were serving (radiologists) than their own organizational personnel. Their personal and professional qualifications gave them prestige and status in the eyes to their clients. Instead of status due to organizational position (e.g. Vice-president), their status was professionally oriented in the form of advanced education and demonstrated competence in the critical aspect of the technical innovation—computers. An attempt to heighten this group's uniqueness was the use of the title "Product Specialist," rather than the conventional "sales personnel." As a result of these characteristics, the boundary spanners could legitimately educate the clients to utilize the C.T. product. It was critical that the flow of technical information be valued as well as accepted in an area where not only is little technical knowledge available and constantly changing but, in comparison, existing technology is very certain and predictable.

The education of the medical profession was also viewed as part of the eventual standardization process and as such will allow the firm's existing sales group to make the C.T. sales in the future. In addition, the new boundary spanners' high status would aid them in gradually training the existing sales personnel on the C.T.'s computer technology. Some of this had begun by the time the follow-up search was concluded. The new boundary spanners had interviewed and selected several existing sales personnel to assist in future sales. Those selected received several weeks of technical training to assist in this potential reintegration of the C.T. sales function.

In reviewing these personnel developments, the critical factor was the hiring of experts to serve the role of temporary boundary spanners. Their expertise in several fields allowed them to interface with key technical development staff in their own organization, as well as with experts in the client organization. Their specialized knowledge of the innovation and their high personal status permitted their taking a dominant role in interactions with clients and those whom they train in their own organization. If management sees the boundary spanners as temporary, it may be more willing to pay the high wages necessary to attract a small group of highly qualified individuals.

MANAGEMENT RELATIONS

Another consideration in the organization's management of the innovation process was the relationship between itself and the new boundary spanners. One specific distinction was the pattern of hierarchical communications. Existing boundary personnel used well-defined and concise channels for reporting and communicating. At each step in the hierarchy, the manager would seek permission from the next level to proceed further up the hierarchy. In most situations, the regular sales personnel were limited to written forms of communication which were handled by each sequential level, perhaps being interpreted and modified as they were passed up the hierarchy. In contrast, the new boundary spanners went directly to any level of the hierarchy, including the President, without special permission or the normal appointment procedure. In fact, each member was permitted this freedom without checking with the new unit's head. He encouraged their direct communication throughout the hierarchy.

Another aspect of this same freedom from hierarchical and structural constraints existed whenever the new boundary spanner felt that a specific piece of information was critical to another organizational unit concerned with the innovation. For example, if the product specialist felt that a certain programming aspect was needed to make the equipment more accurate or competitive, he would immediately seek out the engineering design head and make the data known directly. In fact, many potential design changes were submitted to these product specialists by the design personnel before a final decision was needed. Only if a manager were convinced of its relevancy would such information usually proceed through existing organizational channels until it met the proper recipient. Normally, such information is viewed skeptically by those technical units because of the lack of formal technical training by the existing boundary spanners.

Another fact of management relations with the new boundary spanning group was the frequency of informal invitations by higher management for the new boundary spanners to participate in meetings, design reviews, and strategies sessions, In these frequent contacts information flowed freely between the groups in order to handle any contingencies which might arise. For example, the heads of C.T. production or design admitted to possible flaws in the products and asked for opinions from the product specialists as to the consequences. In addition, the product specialists related the new options which they felt would allow the company to maintain a competitive edge.

ORGANIZATIONAL RULES

The research revealed several distinctions between the rules applied to the new boundary spanners and those applied to the existing personnel. The budget process was one such distinction. While the new department had a budget, the dollar figures were not as rigid as in the budgets of existing departments. If variances occurred, they were merely noted to top management, while other departments had to report and justify all variances in writing. One specific example of this tolerance was the abnormally high phone bill (4 to 1 ratio); other groups were strongly encouraged to use written correspondence.

Procedures for reassignment to other positions also differed. Each new product specialist was promised a two-year contract no matter what the success of the innovation. After two years, the individual could select another organizational position of his choice or continue in the present role even though it would resemble a traditional selling function over time. The existing personnel were routinely reassigned to other functions or positions at the discretion of the organization.

Finally, the new personnel were paid largely on a fixed salary no matter how many units were sold. A small commission was started which gave everyone an equal bonus based on total units sold. This was in recognition that the product specialists called upon each other extensively during the education and negotiation process with potential clients. In contrast, the existing sales personnel received individual commissions as their compensation. With salary, the new boundary spanners were protected financially from the high uncertainty of sales during the two-year contract.

As these examples indicate, the new personnel were protected from usual organizational rules and regulations. The new rules or the flexible application of old regulations were a recognition of this department's relevant system being not just the larger organization, but rather the temporary system containing the new department and the relevant organizations in its environment. One example highlighting this concept was the manager remaining in a physical location of his choice (over 2,000 miles from headquarters and not near any other office of the firm) while carrying out his responsibilities.

IMPLICATIONS FOR THE MANAGEMENT OF INNOVATION

Clearly, it is hazardous to generalize from a study based on one firm's experience and limited data on a few other firms in the same industry. On the other hand, by using a methodology which allows one to trace the dynamics of the innovation process, we are able to establish the feasibility of temporary boundary spanning units and gain insight into how they can be managed. From this one study, it appears that temporary boundary spanning units can be effective. The firm, largely bureaucratic in form, entered the field late, as would perhaps be predicted by those stressing the need for an organic organizational structure in a changing environment. Nevertheless, once the firm decided to adopt the innovation, it quickly developed a quality product and achieved a degree of sales success at a time when some other firms were forced out of the market. Regarding generalization, then, the key factors in determining the appropriateness of temporary boundary spanning units would appear to be an organization that is highly structured and an innovation that is ex-

pected to move quite rapidly from a state of high technical and market uncertainty to one of reasonable certainty. Let us consider each of these factors in turn.

While much literature in organizational behavior propounds massive and permanent organizational change as a response to environmental uncertainty, many organizations—especially bureaucratic organizations, based on cross-sectional research—have the opposite bias of maintaining the status quo in structure. Especially for bureaucratic organizations then, temporary boundary spanning units can balance this tension between adaptation of an innovation and maintenance of existing systems, structures and procedures. Specifically, creating new boundary spanning units obviates the need for rapid large scale changes in personnel and operating rules in the organization. The major part of the organization and its personnel are protected from the uncertainty of the innovation and exposed to new procedures gradually and only after they have attained a higher degree of certainty. Further, the new personnel can manage part of the innovation adoption process for the firm by providing informal training of the existing organizational members and by supplying critical technical information to relevant organizational subunits.

Turning to the nature of the innovation itself, the uncertainty can be perceived as temporary or long-term in nature. If it is long-term, the organization should set up permanent departments to deal with the relevant environmental forces.[8] If it seems temporary, then a permanent change in organizational structure is unwarranted. Temporary change accompanied by planning for eventual reintegration is preferable. Further, some unique implications for the organization's decision-makers arise in terms of managing a new group of boundary spanners. Part of this uniqueness can be described in terms of work performed by these individuals in contrast to existing personnel.

Much of the routine organizational work is prescribed in nature by the organizational norms, management policies and procedures, as well as the certainty of the technology and resulting products. The boundary spanners, however, will be dealing with continual uncertainty. Their work can be described as entailing an emergent quality. The work is not totally determined by the boundary spanners themselves, but to a great degree by the environment and its representatives. For example, during the development and production of the C.T. many new technological problems were found where no proven solution existed. However, over time the technology has been developed and standardized. This brings the control of the product and the work increasingly under the discretion of the organization.

It is the contention of the authors that the work performed by the organizational member needs to be congruent with the work agreement or norms under which the work itself is performed. From this case it was obvious that the existing boundary spanners were performing prescribed work and that the normal organizational rules and procedures applied to them. In contrast, the technical innovation created a situation where the work was predominantly emergent and unpredictable. Under these conditions, the organization needs individuals who can respond and translate the environmental uncertainties into forms manageable by other organizational departments. To accomplish this emergent form of work, the personnel need to utilize creative and unproven methods. The mere definition of emergent work requires a more flexible work procedure. Therefore, a new relationship and work agreement between the organization proper and the new boundary spanners is necessary. In effect, the new boundary spanning department should be organic in form and procedures. Also, the boundary spanners should be given clear indication that their roles and the existence of their department will change when the work shifts from emergent to prescribed.

One possible criticism of the points made in this paper is that they would be self-evident to organizations faced with managing the innovation process. Historical analysis suggests this is not so; managers of even the most successful enterprises have not recognized that strategic changes such as innovating in terms of product or market called for structural changes.[9] The current problems of some major firms with a process of diversification suggests that structural change is still a hazy area for many management teams. Once managers (and consultants) realize the need for change, they appear ready to embrace a particular remedy or approach advocated by other organizations or in the literature.[10] It would be preferable to adopt an experimental approach whereby the remedy is chosen to fit the organization's particular circumstances. The common managerial axiom of making the least change needed to successfully meet one's goal seems appropriate in this context. Thus, if the organization is faced with adopting an innovation which will bring a temporary increase in uncertainty, the creation of temporary boundary spanning units seems appropriate. Since it is the solution having the least impact on existing organizational units, an experimental approach is facilitated; if the new units are not successful they can be easily dismantled without disrupting the rest of the organization. This advantage might even lead one to initially adopt boundary spanning units on a temporary basis until an evaluation of the units' success can be performed.

There are a number of circumstances, then, in which the establishment of temporary boundary spanning units would be an effective mechanism for an organization to quickly adopt a new innovation. The key advantage of this approach is that it buffers most organizational units from change, allowing them a longer time period to adapt to the innovation.

NOTES

1. T. G. Cummings and S. Srivastva, *Management of Work* (Kent, Ohio: Comparative Administration Research Institute of Kent State University, 1977).

2. J. Woodward, *Industrial Organization* (London: Oxford University Press, 1965).

3. For example, W. Bennis, "The Decline of Bureaucracy and Organizations of the Future" in Bennis. *Beyond Bureaucracy* (New York: McGraw-Hill, 1966); R. Likert, *The Human Organization* (New York: McGraw-Hill, 1967); H. A. Shepard, "Changing Interpersonal and Intergroup Relationships in Organization" in March, (ed.), *Handbook of Organizations* (Chicago: Rand McNally, 1965).

4. W. Bennis, "A Funny Thing Happened on the Way to the Future," *American Psychologist,* 1970.

5. J. Thompson, *Organizations in Action* (New York: McGraw-Hill, 1967); P. R. Lawrence and J. W. Lorsch, *Developing Organizations: Diagnosis and Action* (Reading, Mass.: Addison-Wesley, 1969).

6. For representative research, see M. Aiken and J. Hage, "Organizational Interdependence and Intra-Organizational Structure," *American Sociological Review, 33* (1968): 912–930; W. B. Brown, "System, Boundaries, and Information Flow" *Academy of Management Journal, 9* (1966): 318–327; H. Guetzkow, "Relations Among Organizations" in Bowers, (ed.), *Studies on Behavior in Organizations* (Athens, Ga.: University of Georgia Press, 1966).

7. W. E. Moore, *Man, Time and Society* (New York: Wiley, 1963); U. L. Olesen and E. W. Whittaker, *The Silent Dialogue: A Study in the Social Psychology of Professional Socialization* (San Francisco: Jossey Bass, 1968); A. M. Pettigrew, *The Politics of Organizational Decision-Making* (London: Troistock, 1973).

8. P. R. Lawrence and J. W. Lorsch, *Organization and Environment* (Graduate School of Business Administration: Harvard University, 1967).

9. A. D. Chandler, *Strategy and Structure* (Cambridge, Mass.: M.I.T. Press, 1964); N. M. Sapolsky, "Organizational Structure and Innovation," *Journal of Business,* 40 (1967): 497–510.

10. See J. Waters, W. Notz and P. Salipante, "The Experimenting Organization," *Academy of Management Journal,* in press. For an interesting case of this phenomenon, see the Northern Electric Case in Lorsch, and Lawrence, *Organizational Planning* (Homewood, Ill.: Irwin Co., 1979).

PART IV

Emerging Perspectives and New Frontiers in Macro Organizational Behavior

Organizational effectiveness is perhaps the most important yet one of the least understood concepts in the field of macro organizational behavior. Some theorists assess the effectiveness of organizations by looking backward, judging them in terms of the degree to which they have achieved their goals. Other theorists take a forward-looking view, judging the effectiveness of organizations in terms of their survival and growth potentials in the future. And, these represent only two of the many competing views of organizational effectiveness. What is certain is that the nature of effectiveness of organizations is not constant, but will vary with the goals they set for themselves and with the changes taking place as part of the evolution of the external environments in which they are embedded.

The first article on organizational effectiveness, by Steers, reviews the competing criteria used to assess organizations and proposes a framework for analysis that emphasizes the major processes involved in effectiveness. The other article, by Child, distills some predictors of organizational effectiveness from a study of 82 companies operating under different environmental conditions. The two managerial situations also included in this section provide additional insight into the nature of organizational effectiveness.

The problems encountered by the "Coors dynasty" in maintaining the effectiveness of their famous brewing operations are revealed in the first situation. The second situation describes the multiple, often conflicting constituencies that place demands on the modern corporation. The management of this mix of competing expectations constitutes what Burck describes as the "politics" of the corporation, and signals yet another perspective on organizational effectiveness: the ability to minimally satisfy the expectations of important constituencies located both within and outside the organization.

The second section of Part IV focuses on some new frontiers in macro organizational behavior that are having, or soon will have, an effect on the nature and effectiveness of complex organizations. Featured in this section are articles and situations describing the form and essence of emerging alternative organizations both in the United States and abroad.

Mills outlines developments in Europe's industrial democracy movement and their implications for enterprise in the United States, and Moch and Fox create an analytical framework for comparing the form and content of these alternative organizations. The situations that follow describe alternative organizations in the United States and identify some factors that encourage or retard the diffusion of a successful organizational innovation.

When Is an Organization Effective?

Richard M. Steers

While most organizational analysts agree that the pursuit of effectiveness is a basic managerial responsibility, there is a notable lack of consensus on what the concept itself means. The economist or financial analyst usually equates organizational effectiveness with high profits or return on investment. For a line manager, however, effectiveness is often measured by the amount and quality of goods or services generated. The R&D scientist may define effectiveness in terms of the number of patents, new inventions, or new products developed by an organization. And last, many labor union leaders conceive of effectiveness in terms of job security, wage levels, job satisfaction, and the quality of working life. In short, while there is general agreement that effectiveness is something all organizations should strive for, the criteria for assessment remain unclear.

In view of the many different ways in which managers and researchers conceptualize organizational effectiveness, it comes as no surprise that there is equal disagreement over the best strategy for attaining effectiveness. A principal reason for this lack of agreement stems from the parochial views that many people harbor about the effectiveness construct. As mentioned, many define effectiveness in terms of a single evaluation criterion (profit or productivity, for example). But it is difficult to conceive of an organization that would survive for long if it pursued profits to the exclusion of its employees' needs and goals or those of society at large. Organizations typically pursue multiple (and often conflicting) goals—and these goals tend to differ from organization to organization according to the nature of the enterprise and its environment.

Another explanation for the general absence of agreement on the nature of effectiveness arises from the ambiguity of the concept itself. Organizational analysts often assume, incorrectly, that it's relatively easy to identify the various criteria for evaluating effectiveness. In point of fact, such criteria tend to be somewhat intangible; indeed, they depend largely on who is doing the evaluating and within what specific frame of reference.

A number of organizational analysts have tried to identify relevant facets of effectiveness that could serve as useful evaluating criteria. I recently reviewed 17 different approaches to assessing organizational effectiveness and found a general absence of agreement among them. Figure 1 summarizes the criteria used in the 17 models and notes the frequency with which each is mentioned. As this table reveals, only one criterion (adaptability-flexibility) was mentioned in more than half of the models. This criterion was followed rather distantly by productivity, job satisfaction, profitability, and acquisition of scarce and valued resources. Thus there is little agreement among analysts concerning what criteria should be used to assess current levels of effectiveness.

PROBLEMS IN ASSESSMENT

This absence of convergence among competing assessment techniques poses a serious problem for both managers and organizational analysts. If appropriate assessment criteria cannot be agreed upon, it would be manifestly impossible to agree completely on an evaluation of an organization's success or failure. This inability to identify meaningful criteria to be used across organizations results in part from ignoring several questions (or problems) that must be resolved if we are to derive more meaningful approaches to assessing organizational effectiveness. Eight such issues are:

1. *Is there any such thing as organizational effectiveness?* It is only logical to ask whether there is indeed empirical justification for any such construct. In the absence of any tangible evidence, it may be that organizational effectiveness exists only on an abstract level, with little applicability to the workplace and its problems. But if effectiveness is indeed a viable concept from a managerial standpoint, its definition and characteristics must be made more explicit.

2. *How stable—consistently valid—are the assessment criteria?* A second problem encountered in attempts to assess effectiveness is that many of the

Figure 1   Frequency of Occurrence of Evaluation Criteria in 17 Models of Organizational Effectiveness

EVALUATION CRITERIA	NO. OF TIMES MENTIONED (N = 17)	PERCENT OF TOTAL
Adaptability-flexibility	10	59
Productivity	6	35
Job satisfaction	5	29
Profitability	3	18
Acquisition of scarce and valued resources	3	18
Absence of organizational strain	2	12
Control over external environment	2	12
Employee development	2	12
Efficiency	2	12
Employee retention	2	12
Growth	2	12
Integration of individual goals with organizational goals	2	12
Open communication	2	12
Survival	2	12
All other criteria	1	6

Source: R. M. Steers, "Problems in the Measurement of Organizational Effectiveness," *Administrative Science Quarterly*, 1975, vol. 20, pp. 546–558.

assessment criteria change over time. In a growth economy, for example, the effectiveness of a business firm may be related to level of capital investment; during a recession or depression, however, capital liquidity may emerge as a more useful criterion, and high fixed investment may shift from being an asset to being a liability. Clearly, such criteria do not represent permanent indicators of organizational success. In fact, it is probably this transitory nature of many effectiveness criteria that has led some investigators to suggest that adaptability or flexibility represents the key variable in any model of effectiveness.

3. *Which time perspective is most appropriate in assessment?* Contributing to the problem of criterion instability is the question of which time perspective to take in assessing effectiveness. For example, if current production (a short-run criterion) consumes so much of an organization's resources that little is left over for investment in R&D, the organization may ultimately find itself with its products outmoded and its very survival (a long-term criterion) threatened. Thus the problem for the manager is how best to

allocate available resources between short- and long-term considerations so that both receive sufficient support for their respective purposes.

4. *Are the assessment criteria related positively to each other?* Most approaches to assessing effectiveness rely on a series of relatively discrete criteria (for example, productivity, job satisfaction, profitability). The use of such multiple measures, however, often leads to situations in which these criteria are in conflict. Consider, for instance, an organization that uses productivity and job satisfaction as two of its criteria. Productivity can often be increased (at least in the short run) by pressuring employees to exert greater energy and turn out more goods in the same period of time. Such managerial efforts are likely, however, to result in reduced job satisfaction. On the other hand, it's possible to increase job satisfaction by yielding to employee demands for increased leisure time and reduced production pressures—but at the price of lower productivity. Thus, while the use of multiple evaluation criteria adds breadth to any assessment attempt, it simultaneously opens the door to conflicting demands that management may not be able to satisfy.

5. *How accurate are the assessment criteria?* A further problem in assessing organizational effectiveness is how to secure accurate measures for assessment purposes. How does an organization accurately measure managerial performance or job satisfaction, if these are to be used as effectiveness criteria? And how consistent are such measures over time? In point of fact, we tend to measure the performance of the individual manager loosely in terms of an overall rating by his superior and to measure job satisfaction frequently interms of turnover and absenteeism rates. Such operational definitions have their obvious limitations. Performance ratings, for example, may be skewed by personality factors, and a low turnover rate may indicate low performance standards born of a complacent or indifferent management.

6. *How widely can the criteria be applied?* A major problem with many of the criteria suggested for assessing effectiveness is the belief that they apply equally in a variety of organizations. Such is often not the case. While profitability and market share may be relevant criteria for most business firms, they have little applicability for organizations like a library or a police department. Thus, when considering appropriate criteria for purposes of assessment, we should take care to ensure that the criteria are consistent with the goals and purposes of a particular organization.

7. *How do such criteria help us understand organizational dynamics?* The organizational analyst of necessity is concerned with the utility of the effectiveness construct. What purposes are served by the existence of evaluation criteria for assessing effectiveness? Do they provide insight into the dynamics of ongoing organizations? Do they help us make predictions concerning the future actions of organizations? Unless such models facilitate a better understanding of organizational structures, processes, or behavior, they are of little value from an analytical or operational standpoint.

8. *At which levels should effectiveness be assessed?* Finally, managers face the problem of the level at which to assess effectiveness. Logic suggests evaluating organizational effectiveness on an organizationwide basis. Such an approach, however, ignores the dynamic relationships between an organization and its various parts. We must bear in mind that the individual employee ultimately determines the degree of organizational success. If we are to increase our understanding or organizational processes, we must develop models of effectiveness that enable us, to the greatest extent possible, to identify the nature of the relationships between individual processes and organizational behavior. Moreover, a comparison of the relative effectiveness of various departments or divisions is also useful. It is highly likely that certain of these subunits (for example, sales) may be more successful than others within the same organization. The existence of such differences complicates even further any attempts to draw firm conclusions concerning the effectiveness of a given organization.

Even a cursory examination of these problems reveals the magnitude and complexity of the subject. If managers are to reduce their dependence on simplistic criteria for evaluating effectiveness, we must provide them with a framework for analysis that surmounts these problems.

One solution that at least minimizes many of the obstacles to assessing effectiveness is to view effectiveness in terms of a process instead of an end state. Most of the earlier models of effectiveness place a heavy emphasis on identifying the criteria themselves (that is, the end state). Although such criteria may be useful, they tell us little about the ingredients that facilitate effectiveness. Nor do they help the manager better understand how effectiveness results. Hence it appears that we need to re-examine our notions about the concept of organizational effectiveness and about the kinds of analytical models managers require to help them make their own organizations effective.

A PROCESS MODEL FOR ANALYZING EFFECTIVENESS

From a static viewpoint, it may be enough to define effectiveness in terms of attaining operative goals. However, if we are to understand more fully the processes involved in bringing about an effective level of operations, it is necessary to take a more dynamic approach to the topic. The approach suggested here is essentially a "process model" of effectiveness. Its aim is to provide managers with a framework for analysis of the major *processes* involved in effectiveness. This approach contrasts sharply with earlier models that merely listed the requisite criteria for assessing organizational success.

The process model that is proposed here consists of three related components: (1) the notion of goal optimization; (2) a systems perspective;

and (3) an emphasis on human behavior in organizational settings. I believe that these three components, taken together, provide a useful vehicle for the analysis of effectiveness-related processes in organizations. This multidimensional approach has several advantages over earlier models—in particular, the advantage of increasing the comprehensiveness of analysis aimed at a better understanding of a highly complex topic.

Goal Optimization

If we examine the various approaches currently used to assess organizational effectiveness, it becomes apparent that most ultimately rest on the notion of goal attainment. A primary advantage of using the operative goal concept for assessing levels of effectiveness is that organizational success is evaluated in the light of an organization's behavioral intentions. In view of the fact that different organizations pursue widely divergent goals, it is only logical to recognize this uniqueness in any assessment technique.

The goal optimization approach has several advantages over conventional approaches: First, it suggests that goal maximization is probably not possible and that, even if it were, it might be detrimental to an organization's well-being and survival. In most situations, for example, there appears to be little chance for a company to maximize productivity and job satisfaction at the same time. Instead, compromises must be made—compromises that provide for an optimal level of attainment of both objectives. Thus the use of a goal optimization approach permits the explicit recognition of multiple and often conflicting goals.

Second, goal optimization models recognize the existence of differential weights that managers place on the various goals in the feasible set. For instance, a company may place on the pursuit of its profit goal five times the weight, and resources, that it puts on its affirmative-action employment goal or its job satisfaction goal.

Third, the model also recognizes the existence of a series of constraints that can impede progress toward goal attainment. Many of these constraints (for example, limited finances, people, technology, and so on) may be impossible to alleviate, at least in the short run.

Fourth, this approach has the added advantage of allowing for increased flexibility of evaluation criteria. As the goals pursued by an organization change, or as the constraints associated with them change, a new optimal solution will emerge that could represent new evaluation criteria. Hence the means of assessment would remain current and would reflect the changing needs and goals of the organization.

Last, from the standpoint of long-range planning, weighted goals and their relevant constraints could be modeled by using computer simulations to derive optimal solutions for purposes of allocating future resources and effort.

Systems Perspective

The second important aspect of a process model of organizational effectiveness is the employment of an open-systems perspective for purposes of analysis. Such a perspective emphasizes interrelationships between the various parts of an organization and its environment as they jointly influence effectiveness.

If we take a systems perspective, we can identify the four major categories of influences on effectiveness: (1) organizational characteristics, such as structure and technology; (2) environmental characteristics, such as economic and market conditions; (3) employee characteristics, such as level of job performance and job attachment; and (4) managerial policies and practices. While the precise manner in which these variables influence effectiveness goes beyond the scope of this article, it is suggested that these four sets of variables must be relatively consonant if effectiveness is to be achieved.

Thus managers have a responsibility to understand the nature of their environment and to set realistic goals that accommodate and/or exploit that environment. Given these goals, the more effective organizations will tend to be those that successfully adapt structure, technology, work effort, policies, and so on to facilitate goal attainment.

Behavioral Emphasis

A final aspect of the process approach to understanding and analyzing effectiveness is the emphasis on the role of individual behavior as it affects organizational success or failure. The position taken here is in opposition to the stand taken by many that effectiveness is best examined exclusively on a "macro" (or organizationwide) basis. Instead, it appears that greater insight can result if analyses include consideration of how the behavior of individual employees impacts upon organizational goal attainment. If an organization's employees largely agree with the objectives of their employer, we would expect them to exert a relatively high level of effort toward achieving those goals. If, on the other hand, organizational goals largely conflict with employees' personal goals, there is little reason to believe that employees would exert their maximum effort.

As an interesting example of the importance of individuals in goal attainment, consider the controversy over automobile seat belts. In an effort to improve traffic safety, the federal government initially passed a law that required auto manufacturers to install seat belts in all new cars. When this action failed to have the desired consequences (many people simply did not use them), additional laws were passed requiring manufacturers to install warning lights, buzzers, and so forth to remind drivers to use seat belts. Finally, when these measures also proved ineffective, laws were passed requiring manufacturers to install devices that made it mandatory to use seat belts before the ignition could be activated—although even these devices could be circumvented with a degree of ingenuity. While the initial goal was laudatory, the processes (means) used to achieve this goal were largely ineffective because they ignored the predispositions and behavior patterns of most drivers. Perhaps a more effective strategy (certainly in terms of time and cost) would have been simply to pass a law nullifying accident insurance claims for drivers injured while not wearing seat belts.

Hence when we examine organizational effectiveness, it is important to recognize and account for the people who ultimately determine the quality and quantity of an organization's response to environmental demands.

CONCLUSION

Most contemporary organizations exist in turbulent environments in which threats to survival and growth are relatively commonplace. Within such environments, managers must try to secure and properly utilize resources in an effort to attain the operative goals set forth by the organization. The process by which they do so—or fail to do so—is at the heart of the concept of organizational effectiveness.

In the above discussion, I have tried to review the various approaches that have been taken to evaluating organizational effectiveness. Little homogeneity exists between the various approaches. This lack of consensus, in turn, results from the existence of at least eight problems inherent in the existing models. In an effort to overcome many of these problems, I have proposed a process model of organizational effectiveness.

The model described differs from the earlier models. Instead of specifying the criteria for effectiveness (for example, when is an organization effective?), this model focuses on the process of becoming effective (for example, what conditions are most conducive to effectiveness?). It is argued that the actual criteria for evaluation vary depending on the particular operative goals of the organization. Because of this, it appears appropriate to place greater emphasis on understanding the dynamics associated with effectiveness-oriented behavior.

It is further recommended that one way to conceptualize organizational effectiveness *as a process* is to examine three related factors. First, optimized goals (that is, what an organization is capable of attaining) can provide realistic parameters for the assessment process. Given an organization's operative goals, we can ask intelligent questions about the appropriateness of managerial resource-allocation decisions. In other words, is there a better way for managers to expend their limited resources?

Important questions to consider in connection with this first factor include the following:

To what extent are we applying our limited resources toward the attainment of our various goals? In point of fact, organizations often make resource-allocation decisions independent of goal decisions, resulting in "unfunded" goals and "funded" nongoals. This behavior is perhaps most clearly exemplified in the practice by various state and federal legislatures of passing authorization bills and appropriation bills separately. Thus it is possible (and, in fact, it often happens) that a bill (goal) becomes law without the appropriation of resources to implement it.

Is there a clear relationship between the amount of resources we spend on the various goals and the importance of each goal? If, for example, an organization truly believes it places equal weight on making a profit and on improving quality of working life, are such beliefs reflected in the allocation of resources? This does not suggest that equivalent amounts of resources must be spent on each goal. Instead, it implies that sufficient resources be spent to bring about the attainment of both goals.

What kind of return on investment, per goal, are we getting on our resources? If organizations pursue multiple goals, it would seem logical to examine the efficiency of effort invested in each goal. It may be that an organization is highly efficient in realizing its less important goals and relatively inefficient in realizing its more important goals. Where such inefficiencies are noted, decisions must be made concerning the desirability of continuing the pursuit of a goal. Where a goal is viewed as worthwhile (for example, hiring the hard-core unemployed), companies may pursue the goal despite a low return on investment.

Is the entire organization working together for goal attainment? There are instances in which an organization's existing marketing channels are not suited to newer products—a "bad fit" that leads to suboptimal results. Moreover, a fairly common complaint against research and development departments is that scientists stress basic research projects at the expense of applied projects that generally have more immediate and more certain payoffs.

Is the "fit" between the organization and its environment changing? Organizations should continually raise questions concerning their place in the external environment. A relatively successful example of such organization-environment fit can be seen in American Motors Corporation (AMC), which for many years has specialized in small cars and jeeps while the "Big Three" stressed medium- and large-sized cars. As the other auto makers shift their focus toward smaller cars, however, AMC (with fewer resources) may find it necessary to adjust its efforts toward newer markets. Hence flexibility in the face of environmental change remains an important area of concern for effective organizations.

Second, it has been stressed throughout our discussion that the use of a systems perspective allows for the explicit recognition of the ways in which various organizational factors blend together to facilitate or inhibit effectiveness-related activities. This approach forces managers to employ more comprehensive analytical models when they ask questions about why the organization achieved or failed to achieve a particular goal. It facilitates a broader perspective both on the nature of the problem and on its possible solutions.

Third, it is highly desirable to recognize the important link between individual behavior and organizationwide performance. That is, any consideration of how organizations become effective (or more effective) must account for the primary determinant of ultimate organizational performance: the employees of the organization. Recent efforts to institute management-by-objectives programs in organizations represent one such attempt to coordinate the efforts of various employees toward specific organizational objectives. Taken together, these three related factors should help managers and organizational analysts understand the various ways in which organizations move toward or away from goal attainment and organizational effectiveness.

SELECTED BIBLIOGRAPHY

Several interesting pieces exist on the subject of organizational effectiveness. For a review of some early formulations of effectiveness that have greatly influenced our current thinking, the reader is referred to Basil S. Georgopoulos and Arnold S. Tannenbaum's "A Study of Organizational Effectiveness," *American Sociological Review*, Vol. 22, pp. 534–540, 1957; Ephraim Yuchtman and Stanley E. Seashore's "A System Resource Approach to Organizational Effectiveness," *American Sociological Review*, Vol. 32, pp. 891–903, 1967; and Thomas A. Mahoney and Peter J. Frost's "The Role of Technology in Models of Organizational Effectiveness," *Organizational Behavior and Human Performance*, Vol. 11, pp. 127–138, 1974. Also of importance is James Price's *Organizational Effectiveness: An Inventory of Propositions* (Irwin, 1968).

A systematic review and analysis of the major problems encountered in attempts to assess effectiveness can be found in a recent article by the author, "Problems in the Measurement of Organizational Effectiveness," *Administrative Science Quarterly*, Vol. 20, pp. 546–558, 1975. A more complete description of the process model of organizational effectiveness, along with a review of the major determinants of effectiveness, is presented in a forthcoming book by the author entitled *Organizational Effectiveness: A Behavioral View* (Goodyear, in press).

Several excellent books on organizations are available that are consistent with the process view of effectiveness. In particular, Alfred D. Chandler's *Strategy and Structure* (Anchor, 1964) reviews in detail the growth and adaptation of several major corporations. Chandler's basic hypothesis is that successful organizations structure themselves in accordance with their chosen strategy (goals) for responding to the environment. Paul R. Lawrence and Jay Lorsch's book, *Organization and Environment* (Harvard Business School, 1967), takes a similar stand.

For a somewhat more theoretical treatment of a process model, the reader is referred to Daniel Katz and Robert L. Kahn's *The Social Psychology of Organizations* (Wiley, 1966) and Richard Hall's *Organizations: Structure and Process* (Prentice-Hall, 1972).

What Determines Organization Performance? The Universals vs. the It-All-Depends

John Child

Background: This article is largely based on a research program involving 82 British companies selected among six industries to provide contrasting environments. Two of the industries were in the service sector: advertising and insurance (predominantly ordinary life insurance). Four were manufacturing, with two of these being science based—electronics (predominantly instruments and components) and pharmaceuticals. The other two manufacturing industries were chocolates-and-sweets and family newspapers. The companies chosen provided a clustering within each industry around six different size levels, of 150, 300, 500, 1,000, 2,500, and 6,000 employees.

Information on the organization, technology, location, scale, ownership, policy, and background of each company was obtained chiefly through interviews with its senior managers and specialists. In 78 of the companies, the researchers followed up this investigation within one to two weeks with a questionnaire to senior and departmental managers asking them about the nature of their jobs, their personal attitudes toward matters such as change and innovation, and how they would characterize typical behaviors at their level in the company. Completed replies returned by 787 of the 888 managers contacted were the source of data on managerial characteristics. Statistics on the profit and growth performance of the companies were collected from their internal records and accounts.

One school of management thought maintains that, irrespective of the circumstances, certain factors, attributes—call them what you will—universally determine the performance of any organization. The opposing school (newer, and perhaps for that reason just as doctrinaire) argues that universals are not reflections of reality, that the effect of any factor on organizational performance varies with the objectives, size, markets, and other characteristics of the particular organization. This is the contingency school.

Which school is correct? Research, including our own investigations, discourages dogmatism, permits tentative generalizations, and indicates strongly the need for further research. Based on the research to date, however, ten propositions are advanced here about the factors that determine organizational performance; half of these propositions refer to universal attributes, while the other half lend themselves to a contingency approach to organizational performance.

But first, a few caveats that quality what follows.

The question of what determines the levels of performance achieved by organizations still defies a sure answer. The problem is extremely complex because, as Jonathan Boswell said in his *The Rise and Fall of Small Firms,* "A vast number of influences on performance are at work. Some of these are quantifiable, others aren't; some are external to the firm, others are internal and managerial, and of the latter many are subtly interwoven."

Both universalistic and contingency perspectives assume that it is possible to identify factors that will to some degree determine levels of performance. A major difficulty, however, lies in the fact that performance is not simply a dependent variable. The performance levels achieved by an organization constitute a vital input of information to its managers that is likely to stimulate them to make adjustments in policies and modes of operation. These adjustments may be an attempt to correct a poor level of performance or to accommodate the consequences of good performance, such as a growth in scale, and so to sustain the favorable trend. In other words, it is unrealistic to regard performance *only* as a variable dependent on other factors.

This conclusion has important implications for the interpretation of the kind of data it has been practicable to obtain in most research studies. These data are cross-sectional in nature, deriving from measurements taken in a single time period, rather than from a close examination of how performance and other variables change in association with one another over time. Within certain limits, such studies can provide useful clues as to what factors are associated with different levels of performance, but they cannot address the question of how performance acts as part of a continuing cycle of organizational change. This means that they cannot demonstrate what causes good or bad performance. Problems of interpretation will therefore arise.

For instance, in my own research into 82 British companies, I found that less profitable and slower-growing firms used manpower budgets and other cost controls more than did high performers. The implications of this correlation are ambiguous. To what extent do manpower budgets contribute to lower performance because of their intrinsic inflexibility and because they focus managers' attention on departmental considerations, rather than on broader needs? On the other hand, to what extent is manpower budgeting instituted or intensified as a response to poor performance, in an attempt to keep manpower costs to a minimum and to control a staffing situation that may be getting out of hand? My impression is that in practice a period of poor performance often stimulated an intensification of financial controls.

These introductory remarks contain the elements of a simple framework that will be used to bring together the more salient research findings on the performance of organizations. This framework is sketched out in Figure 1 in terminology that applies particularly to business organizations. Briefly, the strategy and plans that are formulated are regarded as major determinants of an organization's activities, and hence a critical influence on its eventual performance. Strategic decisions are responses to pressures imposed on managers by the various participants within the organization and its environment, with managers' own stakes in ownership being a strongly influencing factor. The design of organization structure in the light

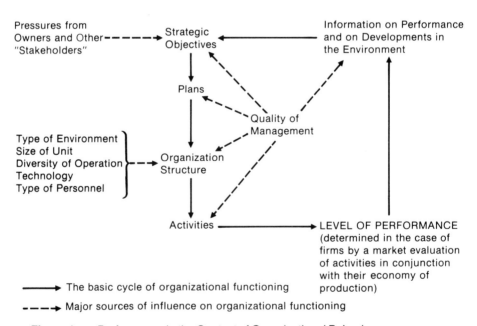

Figure 1 — The basic cycle of organizational functioning

Major sources of influence on organizational functioning

Figure 1   Performance in the Context of Organizational Behavior

of situational contingencies is included as a potential determinant of how effectively the tasks of the organization are carried out. The quality of management is regarded as a pervasive element that can affect all aspects of organizational behavior.

The managerial, strategic, and organizational factors that have emerged as correlates of performance will now be discussed separately, with research findings organized around the ten major propositions mentioned earlier.

MANAGERIAL CORRELATES OF PERFORMANCE

"The good manager" is the keynote of one of the most popular universalistic theories about performance. This theory holds that the successful leadership of any organization will depend on the presence of certain qualities of character, drive, competence, and dedication among its managers. Thus, a British survey carried out in the early 1960s concluded that "thrusting" managerial attitudes "are considerably more likely to lead to high and profitable growth than are the sleepy attitudes and practices with which they are contrasted."

Youth, technical qualification, and a stake in the ownership of the organization are among the factors often thought of as promoting more effective management. For example, in recruiting, the relative merits of youth, with its supposed adaptability and energy, as against the experience of more mature applicants, have often occasioned debate. What are the facts?

Proposition 1: Organizations run by younger teams of top managers will tend to achieve higher levels of performance.

The journal *Management Today* found in its 1973 survey of the boards of the 200 largest British companies that those having the oldest boards showed lower profitability and growth than companies with the youngest directors. As the journal put it, there was no refutation here of "the common-sense view that companies dominated by conservatively reared older men are less likely to produce dynamic performance."

Our research at the Aston Management Centre did not find that the age of senior managers correlated systematically with company profits, but it did relate to growth in sales, income, and assets measured over a five-year period. In each one of six industries sampled, younger managements typically achieved higher rates of company growth. At their best, the "young Turks" achieved quite outstanding growth performances. Although there was a lot of variation in the levels attained, the least successful young teams did no worse than the least successful older managements. Two economists, Peter Hart and John Mellors, have also independently looked at the age of company chairmen and the growth of net assets in four British industries and reached the same conclusion: The growth of companies controlled by older men tends to be slower, although less volatile.

So a fairly general link seems to exist between youthful management and more rapid growth. But how should we interpret this observation? After all, it may signify little more than that faster-growing companies recruit and promote younger people more rapidly into senior vacancies. Is youth among managers just a consequence of growth already achieved?

Favoring this argument is the fact that managers in faster-growing companies tended to have had shorter periods of service with the company and to have reached their present posts via fewer intermediate positions. On the other hand, they had not on the whole been in their present jobs for any less time than had managers in slow-growing companies.

The personal qualities that we found to characterize younger managers support the view that age is, indeed, an operative influence. Younger managers were more likely to press actively for change and innovation within their companies. They questioned prevailing systems of formal rules and authority more keenly. They also had greater confidence in their own abilities to succeed in the high positions they held than did older managers. The confident attitudes and behavior found among younger managers are just the kind likely to promote a striving for innovation and rapid growth.

Comparisons of individual companies illustrate these general findings. An example is the best and the worst performers among the 15 insurance companies in the Aston study. Let us call them Company A and Company B. These two organizations had such distinctive climates that they were immediately apparent to the visitor. In Company A, the high performer, there was an atmosphere of busyness, yet the staff appeared relaxed, friendly, and well turned out. Despite the hustle and bustle, appointments were always kept punctually and staff members seemed to know of and take an interest in each other's movements. The initial appearance of Company B to the visitor was in marked contrast. Staff members were casual to the point of indifference; there was little animation in their behavior; the whereabouts of senior managers were often unknown (particularly around the middle of the day); and appointments were not kept on several occasions.

Company A's senior management team had an average age of 34 years, compared with 50 years in Company B. When we applied statistical measurements of attitudes and behavior, the managers in the two companies contrasted sharply. In Company A, formal rules and routines were adhered to with less than half the degree of rigidity found in Company B. Some 50 percent more pressure for change and innovation was reported among managers in Company A. The young management team in that company expressed itself as being almost twice as ready to take risks when necessary, and also preferred to have more variety and challenge in its work. It is worth noting that a study by Victor Vroom and Bernd Pahl of 1,500 managers from 200 U.S. companies found a consistent and significant relationship between younger age and a greater willingness to take risks.

I have devoted some space to the question of youthful management because it may be an influence on performance that applies in most types of organization and upon which managers can act. Research findings to date point to the need for career systems that allow young people of proven ability and appropriate experience to advance rapidly to senior positions. The other side of this coin is the justification of the practice found in some American corporations where, after the age of 50 or so, senior executives may be transferred into less demanding positions.

In British industry, the rapid promotion of able men and women who are still in their prime is slowly becoming more usual, but a planned transfer of older people to less responsible positions, as opposed to more brutal methods like dismissal or compulsory early retirement, is not. This always tends to be resisted by the older executives who hold power in company managements, and it is important for transfers of this kind not to entail a loss of remuneration and privilege. The question remains, nevertheless, whether holding down top management positions is to be primarily a reward of age and long service or a recognition of who is best able to meet the requirements of the job—quite possibly a relatively young man.

Proposition 2: Organizations run by formally better-qualified teams of top managers will tend to achieve higher levels of performance.

The reasoning behind this proposition is the straightforward notion that the possession of formal qualifications is likely to indicate that managers have a certain level of attested expertise and ability. This potential influence on levels of performance cannot, of course, be entirely separated from the age factor, since younger managers tend more often to possess these formal qualifications than do older managers.

Some evidence emerges from British studies that the financial success of companies is generally greater when a relatively high proportion of their directors have formal professional qualifications. D. P. Barritt found this to be the case after studying the profits of larger British companies in the 1950s. More recently, in the mid-1960s, a study by Roger Betts of 23 companies, chiefly in construction and plastics, found that those achieving a higher rate of growth in profits had a greater average number of formal qualifications held per director. In both industries, the successful companies had a significantly higher proportion of directors concerned with research and development and (it appeared) possessing scientific qualifications.

There is some support, then, for the proposition that formally qualified management teams will achieve superior performance. And the balance within top executive or directorial teams of types of qualifications may also relate to success. For example, in the study of Betts just cited, there was evidence that poor-performing companies had a heavy weighting of men with production and engineering backgrounds. Another study of 93 major British companies achieving the highest and lowest rates of return on capital during the period 1966–72 found that the high performers had more directors with accounting qualifications, while the low performers had more directors with engineering qualifications. This proportionate relationship of directors' qualifications appeared to be more closely associated with organizational performance than the total number of qualifications within the board.

Proposition 3: Organizations run by managers with a substantial personal stake in their ownership will tend to achieve higher levels of performance.

A major theme in writings on the "managerial revolution" is that managers who do not have a significant personal stake in the ownership of corporations will devote more attention to objectives other than the maximization of profit. One such objective is growth, which many commentators have concluded will furnish considerable advantages to managers in terms of higher remuneration, prestige, sense of achievement, and so on.

A number of studies have been made in the United States and Britain of the relation between the control of companies and their levels of performance. Overall, the results suggest that companies with a concentration of ownership control (rather than dispersed ownership) tend to have higher rates of profit *and* higher rates of growth, but differences in levels of performance have often not been significant, and the measures of ownership influence have been formalistic and indirect.

In our studies, we have found that where there was a greater concentration of ownership control, chief executives attached particularly great importance to maximizing profits and growth: There were, however, no significant links between the ownership control factor and rates of profit actually achieved, and the only significant link with growth was found in the tendency for owner-controlled companies to have a more rapid growth in net assets over a five-year period.

Rather fewer studies have looked at managers' stockholdings in relation to company performance, but the results that emerge are more clear-cut, indicating that when managers have greater personal stake in ownership, the performance of companies tends to be superior. For example, a study by Steve Nyman of the 100 largest British commercial and industrial companies found that higher levels of stockholding by directors were significantly associated with higher rates of growth. A larger stake in ownership was also associated with the achievement of higher rates of profit, although this result was only just statistically significant. Given higher growth and higher profitability, it is not surprising that a greater stake in ownership was also associated with a higher stock market rating and a higher price-earnings ratio.

In short, there is a clear tendency for the company in which control is linked with a stake in ownership to be a superior performer. The motivational implications of this relationship for all types of organizations are significant, since they suggest that whenever managers have a direct personal stake in the success of an undertaking, its performance will be enhanced. There is also a suggestion here that the objectives held by managers may influence the performance of their organizations, which leads us to a consideration of strategic factors.

Proposition 4: The performance standards set by an organization's management will be influenced by the norms of performance among other organizations of a similar type.

Strategy deals with the objectives established for an organization and the effort to attain them. For example, if we establish the objective of sustaining a given annual rate of growth, this may mean diversification into a faster-growing industry in order to achieve the objective. There is ample evidence that normal rates of profit and growth vary among industries and that these variations can have an important influence on the performance of firms, especially smaller ones whose activities are usually confined to a single industry. In addition to reflecting certain shared economic circumstances having to do with size of markets, growth of overall demand, structure of the industry, and so forth, the differentiation of company performance levels by industry also reflects the presence of shared standards by which many firms are content to judge themselves. This phenomenon—of managements' assessing performance against localized, rather than general, standards—is likely to be even more widespread outside the business sphere, where mechanisms to enforce universal economic standards such as stock market ratings are absent. It is this consideration that underlies the proposition made above.

We also expect that the mix of objectives held by an organization's senior managers will have an impact on its performance. The exact formulation of objectives may well result from an appraisal of what can realistically be attained in the light of the organization's previous performance. The type of objectives held by top management is, nevertheless, likely to be an active influence upon performance because of the ways in which objectives shape plans and activities. Moreover, the singlemindedness of management is important, first because efforts may be dissipated in trying to achieve too many different aims at once, and second, because the more conflict among senior managers over objectives, the less integrated will be their efforts toward reaching a common goal. Hence, we arrive at the fifth proposition.

Proposition 5. The less dispersed top-management objectives are and the more agreement there is among senior managers as to which objectives have priority, the more successful the organization will be in attaining them.

Chief executives in our study of British firms were asked to rate the importance to their companies of ten possible objectives, scoring each of them separately along five-point scales. Nearly all of the respondents gave very high priority to maximizing net profit over the long term (five years) and to achieving a high rate of growth. Because of this strong measure of agreement, the rating of these objectives did not discriminate between successful companies and others.

The evaluation of certain other objectives did differentiate. In the more profitable companies, with above-average rates of return for their industries on sales and on net assets, chief executives attached lower importance to a high level of distributed dividends, but greater importance to a high level of rewards and benefits for employees. In more profitable firms they also showed less concern for the company's prestige. In the faster-growing companies, chief executives attached low importance to maximizing short-term profits over a 12-month period, to paying out a high level of dividends, and to "service to the wider community."

A comparison of three sugar confectionary companies with contrasting performance profiles illustrates these points in greater detail. Company X was a poor performer by any criterion. Company Y had an outstanding growth record and had maintained an average level of profitability. Company Z was highly profitable and had achieved an average level of growth. As **Figure 2** shows, the chief executives of all three companies attached considerable importance to major objectives such as maximizing long-term profitability, growth, and market share. In Company X, however, the chief executive hardly discriminated in his assessment among these objectives and others in the list we gave him. In the two better-performing companies, less importance was attached to objectives like prestige, a high dividend payout, and service to the community. In growth-Company Y, innovation was given a high rating. In Company Z, which was securing high margins on high-quality traditional lines, less emphasis was given to growth and market share than in Company Y, and somewhat more stress was placed on maximizing profits in the short term.

Findings like these, even though they concern chief executives' views alone, suggest that the mix of strategic objectives selected for a business may influence its performance. In the sample as a whole, the companies achieving greater commercial success were those whose top managements were more singleminded in pursuing longer-term profit and growth objectives. Chief executives in these companies also paid considerable attention to the building up of internal strengths, such as providing favorable conditions for employees and retaining surpluses within the business to finance further profitable expansion.

In companies where chief executives attach more importance to external points of reference, such as prestige, serving the community, and paying higher dividends, financial performance tends to be poorer. Whether this association between a lower concern for external interests and superior performance can continue through the 1970s, with the present

Figure 2   Rating of Objectives in Three Confectionary Companies*

OBJECTIVE	RATINGS OF IMPORTANCE**		
To maximize	Company X	Company Y	Company Z
1. Net profit over five years	5	5	5
2. Rate of growth	5	5	4
3. Market share	4	5	4
4. Employee rewards	4	5	5
5. Net profit over one year	5	3	4
6. Prestige	5	3	2
7. Innovation	4	5	2
8. Assets and reserves	4	2	1
9. Dividends distributed	4	2	1
10. Service to the wider community	4	1	1

*Company X was a small, famliy firm with low profitability and low growth, old product and old technology. Company Y was an American-owned firm of small to medium size, with average profitability and rapid growth, some new products and advanced technology. Company Z was a medium-size subsidiary, with high profitability and average growth, and traditional high-quality products, enjoying high margins on low-cost technology.

**5—extremely important
   4—very important
   3—moderately important
   2—not very important
   1—not at all important

growth insistence on company social responsibility, remains to be seen. On the whole, though, the message of these findings seems clear: If you want to manage a successful business, concentrate on a few key objectives and avoid distractions. This also implies, of course, that careful thought should be given to the selection of key objectives in the first place.

Further support for Proposition 5 comes from a study by David Norburn, who compared 21 British companies with varying levels of financial performance. He found that the more successful companies were characterized by a greater degree of consensus among top executives about who was responsible for setting long-term objectives and about the priority of objectives their organizations should follow. In poor-performing organizations he found both more disagreement and a wider spread of objectives. Norburn also found that successful company managements possessed better information on their environments. It is likely that superior, well-integrated information will assist managers to agree on which objectives deserve priority.

There are more strategic factors associated with performance than can be considered here, but there is enough evidence to indicate that as a general rule, attention to the formulation of strategy will have beneficial effects on performance. For instance, the systematic planning of expansion policies among American firms is related to superior economic performance. A comparative study of acquisition behavior among American companies carried out by Igor Ansoff and his colleagues lends further support to Proposition 5, because the firms more successful in terms of profit and growth were found to have restricted their attention to a more limited range of possible acquisitions and to have evaluated these more thoroughly.

ORGANIZATION STRUCTURE AND PERFORMANCE

Managerial attributes and the quality of strategy appear to have some relation to levels of performance in most organizations, even though the organizations differ in their environment, diversity, size, technology, and personnel. When we turn to a third possible influence on performance, the design of organization structure, we find most authorities taking the view that the type of situation is vital. This is the contingency approach mentioned earlier, which states that the design of organization most appropriate for high performance can be formulated only with contingent circumstances in mind. According to this theory, there are no general principles of organization.

The argument goes as follows: Contingent factors such as the type of environment or the size of the organization have some direct influence on levels of success. There may, for example, be economies of scale open to the larger organization. Certain environments, such as particular industries, may be more beneficent and provide greater opportunity. Second, it is assumed that a set of structured administrative arrangements consciously adapted to the tasks that are to be done, to the expectations and needs of people performing the tasks, to the scale of the total operation, to its overall complexity, and to the pressures of change being encountered will themselves act to promote a higher level of effectiveness than will a structure ill-suited to these contingencies. Organization structure is seen in this way to modify the effects of contingencies upon performance. Last, the all-pervasive quality of management affects both strategic decisions as to the type of conditions under which the organization will seek to operate and the design of its internal structure.

Environment

According to contingency theory, different approaches to organizational design are conducive to high performance, depending on whether or not the environment in which the organization is operating is variable and complex in nature, or stable and simple. Variability in the environment refers to the presence of changes that are relatively difficult to predict, involve important departures from previous conditions, and are likely, therefore, to generate considerable uncertainty.

Complexity of the environment is said to be greater the more extensive and diversified the range of an organization's activities, which correspondingly take it into more diverse sectors of the environment. These diverse sectors are all relevant areas of external information that it should monitor. There is evidence that the degree of environmental variability is a more important contributor to uncertainty among managerial decision makers than is complexity. I shall discuss variability now and return to complexity in a later section on diversity of opeations.

Proposition 6: In conditions of environmental variability, successful organizations will tend to have structures with the following characteristics: (1) arrangements to reduce and to structure uncertainty; (2) a relatively high level of internal differentiation; and (3) a relatively high level of integration achieved through flexible, rather than formalized, processes.

This mouthful of a proposition attempts to distill the essence of what we know so far about a highly complex issue. Among possible arrangements to reduce and structure the uncertainty generated by a changing environment are a closer liaison with the separate independent organizations upon which one's own organization is highly dependent as supplier or customer (even to the extent of vertical or horizontal integration), and attempts to secure a better quality of intelligence from outside the organization.

The critical nature of a variable environment and the need for liaison with outside organizations and for a significant intelligence activity all mean that an organization is under pressure to employ specialist staff in boundary or interface roles—that is, in positions where they form a link with the outside world, scooping in and evaluating relevant information. This may well take the form of setting up more specialist departments and thereby increasing the internal differentiation of the organization.

If there are many new significant external changes to which an organization has to adapt, and if it has become fairly differentiated to cope with these, then there will be all the more need to achieve a degree of integration among its personnel that not only offsets their specializations from one another but, over and above this, permits them to react swiftly to new developments in a coordinated manner. Flexible, rather than highly formalized, methods of coordination and information-sharing will be required. This generally means a greater amount of face-to-face participation in discussions and decision making, with an emphasis on close lateral relations among members of different departments instead of formal links up and down hierarchies or via periodic formal meetings. This mode of working also implies a higher degree of delegation, particularly when it comes to operational decisions.

Various studies that have examined organizational performance in relation to structure and variable environments have produced sufficiently consistent findings to support the conclusions we have just made. Each study, of course, examines the structural elements I have mentioned in more detail. In the United States there is the well-known work of Paul Lawrence and Jay Lorsch, as well as studies by Robert Duncan, Pradip Khandwalla, Anant Negandhi, and Bernard Reiman, among others. Of British studies, Tom Burns' and G. M. Stalker's is the best known.

Our own research at Aston indicated that companies in the variable science-based environment characterizing electronics and pharmaceuticals that were achieving above-average levels of growth tended to rely less on formal procedures and documentation than did slow-growing companies. Among firms in more stable environments, high-growth companies relied more (but only marginally so) on formalized methods of integration than did less successful firms.

These organizational differences between high- and low-growth companies located in contrasting environments were most marked in certain areas of management. Within the stable sector, faster-growing companies had significantly more formalization in the production area, especially in matters like defining operator tasks, training operators, and recording their performance. The faster-growing companies in variable environments particularly made little use of formal training procedures, standardized routine personnel practices, and formal hierarchical channels for communication or seeking and conveying decisions.

Size of Unit

Here the major proposition is this:

Proposition 7: Organizations that increase their degree of formalization to parallel their growth in size will tend to achieve higher levels of performance.

Critics contend that the problem of the large organization is the dead weight of bureaucratic administration that it takes on. In an attempt to hold together its many divisions and departments, the large organization emphasizes conformity to the rules, a trait that has prompted the observation that "a new idea has never come out of a large corporation." Many studies of organization have confirmed that large scale does indeed breed bureaucracy in the form of highly compartmentalized jobs and areas of work, elaborate procedural and paperwork systems, long hierarchies, and delegation of routine decisions to lower-level managers within precise discretionary limits.

Much as critics may decry bureaucracy, we found that in each industry the more profitable and faster-growing companies were those that had developed this type of organization in fuller measure with their growth in size above the 2,000-or-so employee mark. At the other end of the scale, among small firms of about 100 employees, the better performers generally managed with very little formal organization. The larger the company, the higher the correlation between more bureaucracy and superior performance.

Poorly performing large companies tend to specialize their staff less, to have less developed systems and procedures, and to delegate decision making less extensively. It is also worth noting that among the poorly performing companies the strength of the relation between changes in size and changes in structure is noticeably reduced, compared with that among high performers.

Comparisons of larger companies within the same industry clearly illustrate this trend. For example, we studied three of the largest national daily newspaper groups. One was the superior performer by a substantial margin, in terms of growth, return on net assets, and return on combined circulation plus advertising sales. Although this particular group was the smallest of the three big companies in numbers employed, it operated a highly formalized type of organization—it had developed a more elaborate set of procedures and systems covering a wider range of activities than had the other two companies, and it relied heavily on written communication and records. Indeed, its most distinguishing feature lay in this heavier use of documentation, especially job descriptions, manuals, work records, and the like.

The newspaper industry represents a relatively stable environment. When the nature of each organization's environment is taken into account, as well as its size, the association between organization and performance becomes more complicated. The need for companies operating in a more variable environment to keep a check on the formality in their organization, especially its routine-enforcing elements, probably explains why it is the successful companies in a more stable environment that most rapidly take on a formal bureaucratic type of structure as they grow larger. The rate at which companies tend to develop bureaucratic structures as their size increases varies according to the environment and performance in the following sequence from low to high: below-average performers in stable environments; below-average performers in variable environments; above-average performers in variable environments; above-average performers in stable environments.

Managers, it appears from our research, have to take note of multiple contingencies, such as environment plus size, when planning the design of their organization. When there is not much variability in the environment, the need to develop organization to suit size becomes relatively more dominant. In this environment, the better-performing companies tend to develop formalized structures at a faster rate as they grow than do poor performers. When the environment is a variable one, however, these differences in structural development are reduced, because the contingency of coping with uncertainty tends to offset the contingency of coping with large scale. We found that in a variable environment, the rate of increase in formalization accompanying growth in scale is higher for good performers, but the absolute level of their formalization only reaches that of poor-performing companies at a size approaching 10,000 employees. The picture is complex indeed, as most practical managers are well aware!

Diversity of Operations

Now comes the eighth proposition:

Proposition 8: Organizations that group their basic activities into divisions once these activities become diversified will tend to achieve higher levels of performance.

This proposition expresses the fundamental argument for the divisionalized organizational structure that has become the dominant form among large business firms today and that can also be seen in some large public undertakings. Organizations having a spread of different products or services, and having outlets in a number of regions, operate in a complex total environment. Such organizations are also likely to be large. Because of both their size and their diversity, they will almost certainly experience communications difficulties.

To overcome these problems, it is logical to create decentralized, semi-autonomous operating units or divisions, for these can group formal relationships in a way that reflects the necessities of exchanging information and coordination around common problems. These commonalities may center around product groups, favoring a product division type of organization, or they may center on geographical regions, favoring an area division structure. If both product and regional coordination are equally vital, then a mixed, or "grid," structure may be logical.

The detailed research of John Stopford and Louis Wells supports the argument that these divisionalized arrangements work. American multinational corporations that have divisionalized their structures in response to a diversity of activities tend to be superior performers. The more successful firms have in most cases adopted the kind of divisionalization— international divisions, global area divisions, global product divisions, mixed or grid structures—that considerations such as product diversity and level of involvement in foreign business would logically dictate.

Technology

This brings us to the ninth proposition:

Proposition 9: Organizations that design their work flow control and support structures to suit their technologies will tend to achieve higher levels of performance.

The term technology is employed in almost as many different senses as there are writers on the subject. The analyses offered by Charles Perrow and Joan Woodward are the best known and best developed. Perrow's definition of technology in terms of variability of inputs and availability of known techniques to handle these comes close to what most have in mind when they speak of variability in the environment and its generation of uncertainty. To this extent, Perrow's recommendations for structural design tend to be borne out by the findings of studies on organizational performance under different environmental conditions.

Woodward's view of technology is based on the physical organization of work flows. Does the organization have heavy plant and a rigid sequence of production, as in car assembly? Or does if have fairly light plant and flexible production, as in the manufacture of some electronic instruments and in service industries? Woodward's pioneering studies suggested that when organizations design structural attributes to fit their technologies, they secure a superior level of performance. Unfortunately, neither Woodward nor subsequent investigators adopting her approach have employed precise measures of performance.

The research we conducted indicated that the pattern of specialization in production and ancillary areas such as production control and maintenance was predictable in terms of the technology employed. In addition, the proportion of total employment allocated to some of the ancillary functions varied along with differences in technology. For example, more rigid technologies, such as those of a process type, tend to have relatively few production control specialists and internally specialized production control departments. Most control is actually built into the technology itself.

These associations between technology and the structure of employment lead one to ask whether, along with environment, size, and diversity, there is some logic of adjustment to contingencies here. If there is, does the extent to which organizations adapt to the logic predict differences in their performance?

The closeness of fit between technology and the pattern in which roles were specialized did not vary significantly between good- and poor-performing companies. What did distinguish the more successful firms was that they tended to vary their investment in manpower devoted to production support activities according to differences in their technology. For instance, among companies using heavy plant and more rigid production systems, the more profitable and faster-growing ones had significantly larger percentages of their total employment given over to maintenance activities. In other words, allocation of manpower in relation to technological requirements appears to improve performance.

Type of Personnel

Now let's consider the last proposition:

Proposition 10: Organizations that adapt forms of administrative structure consistent with the expectations and perceived needs of their personnel will tend to achieve higher levels of performance.

This proposition is a cornerstone of the behavioral study of organizations. Readers of *Organizational Dynamics* will already be familiar with the work of Chris Argyris, Frederick Herzberg, Rensis Likert, Douglas McGregor, and others who have argued for structures and styles of management that secure a higher degree of commitment to the organization from employees by more adequately meeting their expectations and their needs as mature adults. In a broader context, moves to enrich jobs and the developments in industrial codetermination now under way in Europe also reflect an implicit faith in Proposition 10, since they start from the premise that employees' expectations and perceived needs are not being fulfilled adequately by existing organization forms.

The results of many research studies indicate that the proposition is valid. Indeed, some would call it a truism. While it is unnecessary to review familiar ground, some qualifications are in order. The proposition refers to the expectations and perceived needs of personnel. This reference to the perceptual level is important, for whatever the order of man's universal psychological needs, it is clear that different types of people do not have the same requirements of their work at the conscious perceptual level. One has only to compare the professional employee with the manual worker to realize that sociocultural factors are crucial in shaping different expectations as to what constitute legitimate conditions of work. Similarly, research of a cross-cultural nature has indicated that different supervisory styles are effective with employees located in different cultural milieux where different attitudes toward work and authority are evident. In short, Proposition 10 indicates the managements need to spend time ascertaining the expectations of different groups among their employees if they want to have a reliable idea of which arrangements will secure the willing commitment of those employees.

CONCLUSION

I have discussed ten propositions, of which half support the universalistic argument on organizational performance and half support the contingency argument. These two arguments have sometimes been regarded as completely opposed, but the findings of research indicate several ways in which they are compatible.

In essence, the contingency approach stresses that managers should secure and evaluate information on their operating situation and that they should adapt the design of their organizational structure when necessary. It will quite possibly prove to be a general rule that managerial qualities such as the personal flexibility and drive associated with youth or the thrust for performance spurred on by a personal stake in stock appreciation enhance a company's ability to adjust to new contingencies. This is a universalistic type of statement, which includes two of the propositions I have advanced; it is nevertheless quite compatible with a contingency view of organizational design.

A further example of compatibility between the two arguments can be provided. The priority top managements give to different objectives is probably a factor that always influences the performance profiles that they attain. At the same time, the performance of any two companies having identical sets of objectives is unlikely to be the same, because this will also be determined by how they decide to adjust to prevailing contingencies.

The practical implications of the first five universalistic propositions have already been discussed. The first two draw attention to the desirability of selecting and developing managers who possess a combination of relative youth and relevant qualifications. Proposition 3 supports the general thrust of research on motivation and reward by indicating that the performance of organizations is enhanced when they grant their managers a sizable personal stake in their development. The fourth and fifth propositions indicate how the objectives management selects can shape performance, and how a greater degree of boardroom consensus over objectives will increase the chances of achieving good performance. These last two propositions speak for the practical importance of good communication, information sharing, and other hallmarks of effective integration among top executives.

The thrust of the last five propositions, and supporting research, is that the design of organization is likely to influence a company's performance. The problem has to be worked out in the context of each company's own circumstances. Several evaluations have to be made before deciding on the form of organization that is most appropriate. First, we must assess the nature of present and future contingencies. In other words, just what kind of institution are we, and what do we want to be in terms of markets, size, type of production, and so on? Second, what are the organizational requirements imposed by relevant contingencies? For example, a large unit will have particular problems of coordination and communication. What alternative organizational designs might satisfy these requirements?

Third, if different contingencies pose the dilemma of conflicting requirements, what policies could we formulate to modify the contingencies themselves? Some companies, for example, that seek to enter a faster-growing but more variable market or that seek to combine successful new product development with economies of large-scale, standardized "bread and butter" operations are finding that they can circumvent the size contingency by setting up small, internally flexible, venture-management units or similar companies-within-companies.

The important point is that there are usually several ways of securing an effective match between a company's internal organization and the contingencies it faces. This fact tends to be overlooked by those who share the present-day public concern about large bureaucratic firms and other institutions. A bureaucracy can be operated in different ways, and not necessarily with the proverbial "dead hand." And even if large scale brings too much bureaucracy to permit desirable levels of participation and sensitivity to change, there are in most areas of activity various possibilities for devolving units into smaller ones without incurring any loss in their efficiency.

SELECTED BIBLIOGRAPHY

Most writings on the performance of organizations have been by economists, who have only infrequently examined managerial or organizational factors. Robin Morris and Adrian Wood, in editing *The Corporate Economy* (Macmillan, 1971) have, however, drawn together recent theoretical and empirical studies that take such factors into account. Jonathan Boswell's *The Rise and Decline of Small Firms* (Allen and Unwin, 1973) examines the performance of small firms in Britain, giving particular attention to problems of management succession. *Attitudes in British Management* (Penguin, 1966) contrasts "thrusting" and "sleeping" managerial attitudes, which it claims are associated with marked differences in company performance. Paul R. Lawrence and Jay W. Lorsch, in *Organization and Environment* (Harvard Business School, 1967), provides a classic statement of the contingency approach. Within the contingency school, Tom Burns and G. M. Stalker, in *The Management of Innovation* (Tavistock, 1961), consider the implications of environmental differences. John M. Stopford and Louis T. Wells, in *Managing the Multinational Enterprise* (Basic Books, 1972), concentrate on diversity of operations, while Joan Woodward's *Industrial Organization: Theory and Practice* (Oxford University Press, 1965) reports studies on technology, organization, and performance. More detailed accounts of the author's own research into performance will appear in the *Journal of Management Studies* in October 1974 and February 1975.

A Test for the Coors Dynasty

BusinessWeek

William Coors, 61, and his brother Joseph, 60, both lean and over 6 ft. tall, favor windbreakers to suit jackets and look every inch the rugged Westerners they are. "Coors folk are dead honest about everything," says an associate, "and they are very proud of what they do."

What they do is brew beer. As the third generation of the Golden (Colo.) family that has always worried more about making beer than about selling it, Bill and Joe Coors are firmly, if belatedly, beginning to deal with the social pressures and more competitive marketplace that have pushed Coors beer from fourth place to fifth among the nation's brewers. "Making the best beer we can make," says the usually blunt Bill Coors, "is no longer enough."

The problems of Adolph Coors Co. stem from the ingrown nature of the operation: 85% of the stock is controlled by the Coors family. With an inside board that is more knowledgeable about Coors' operations than about changes in the industry, the company failed to gird for the marketing onslaught triggered by Miller Brewing Co.'s determination to become No. 1.

And the family's proclivity for privacy has ruled out publicizing the company's good works, while leaving the field clear for attacks on Joe Coors' conservative political beliefs. Coors concedes that a union boycott helped pare sales 5.3% last year. Revenues dipped only slightly, to $593.1 million, but net profit dropped 11.5% to $67.7 million. The Coors say sales bottomed out in the first quarter of 1978. This week they announced that an 18.5% drop in barrels of beer sold in the quarter pushed sales down 14% and knocked net income back nearly 70%, to $4.9 million.

Coors' return on operating capital still is the best in the business: 13.5% last year, compared with 10% at Miller and Anheuser-Busch Inc., according to Emanuel Goldman, senior analyst at Sanford C. Bernstein & Co. But it has slipped more as the company slugs it out in the marketplace.

The Coors are determined to give the fight their all. "Their problems are unique in that they are absolutely correctable," says Robert S. Weinberg, a beer industry consultant. "The problems they have they can solve with money."

That money is being put into advertising, public relations, and new products. To carry out the spending, the brothers last year brought in the highest level of outside experts they have ever hired to handle marketing and public relations. New product development is being directed by Joe Coors' son, Peter, 31.

Their efforts are starting to show. Coors is beginning to do market research, and for the first time in 35 years, Coors is putting people back into its ads. The company adopted another promotional ploy long used by the big brewers last winter with its sponsorship of the Colorado Coors Pro Ski Tour.

In a further departure for a company that has made only one beer for 20 years, Coors next month will introduce a new light beer. And Coors is experimenting with a super-premium brew.

Coors also plans to publicize its positive side to offset current protests. Joe Coors' politics and what Bill Coors calls an "absolute refusal to bend to any kind of coercion" have made the company an easy target. "The problem is their name is Coors, and that's the name on the can of beer," says William Peniche, a J. Walter Thompson Co. executive retained to help improve the Coors corporate image.

Such plans will cost plenty. But with no long-term debt, Coors can afford it. Indeed, for years the company was the envy of the brewing industry. Sales grew steadily from 1941 to 1975, doubling between 1968 and 1973. "You could have sold Coors beer in

Glad bags," says Leland Shalton, a marketing vice-president.

Adolph Coors Co. built that success on good beer. The mystique that developed around the Rocky Mountain brew, which even today is sold in only 14 states, helped make the company the only regional brewer among the top five. "Joe and Bill never believed that mystique bit," says Franklin W. Hobbs IV, vice president of Dillon Read & Co., the investment banking house that took Coors public in 1975. "They genuinely believe they simply make a better product, and that is why it sold."

That emphasis on quality was handed down from their grandfather, Adolph Coors, who founded the brewery in 1873. Bill and Joe, whom most employees call by their first names ("Our father was Mr. Coors," says Joe), also inherited a penchant for hard work and a dislike of frills. They lunch almost daily at the "residence," a Victorian house their grandfather built on the brewery grounds, and share a spartan single-room office. Before the kidnapping and murder of their older brother, Adolph Coors III, in 1960, the three brothers worked together in a slightly larger room.

The company has an unusual management style. Adolph III was nominally to have held the top spot. Now Bill, as the elder of the two surviving brothers, is chairman and chief executive; Joe holds the title of president. But there are no formal lines of responsibility. Bill handles the technical side and has a reputation for near-genius within the brewing industry. Joe oversees financial and administrative functions. But each brother can act in any area. "People know they can talk to either one of us and get decisions," says Joe Coors.

The brothers' apparent lack of rivalry amazes outsiders, although such smooth relations postdate their early years. "There was an intense amount of sibling rivalry when we were young," says Bill Coors, "and in subtle ways my father encouraged it. It was a great motivation for all three of us. But we have suppressed it. We believe in the philosophy of our grandfather and our father that we must perpetuate this great institution, and this comes first."

The brothers also have adhered to their forefathers' distaste for self promotion. "We've been secret about our affairs," says Bill. "That was the nature of our grandfather and father, and it is my brother's and mine."

But with unsought—and unfavorable—publicity cutting into sales, the Coors brothers are changing. Joe has long been known locally as an arch-conservative. He sees his political views as a natural outgrowth of his business philosophy. For, above all, Joe Coors is a compleat capitalist, dedicated to the free enterprise system. To drive home the government's growing role in U.S. life some years back, the company paid its workers in full, withholding no taxes, for two months. It then deducted three month's worth of taxes from one paycheck to emphasize the magnitude of the government's take.

The Politics

Joe Coors' political views came to national attention in 1975 when *The Washington Post* ran four lengthy stories about his efforts to nudge the U.S. toward the political right. Joe had been nominated for a seat on the board of the Corporation for Public Broadcasting by President Richard Nixon the day before his resignation; Gerald Ford resubmitted the nomination, which was never acted on. A key complaint was that Joe was using his company to further his own political views. At issue was Television News Inc., a broadcast news agency set up in 1972 under the corporate umbrella of Adolph Coors Co. The *Post* said that its output had no discernible conservative slant, but that reporters felt restrained in their choice of stories to cover. The money-losing subsidiary has since been closed.

A Claim to Rights

The Coors remain as outspoken as ever. "They're from the West and they speak straight. And they suffer for it," says John H.

Mullin III, a Dillon Read senior vice president. Brewery workers struck a year ago over seniority and human rights, primarily the Coors' insistence on polygraph tests before hiring. More than 1,000 of the 1,472 workers who walked out have been replaced. But a union boycott of Coors beer, which has been supported by minority groups, has hurt sales.

The brothers claim seniority is a minor issue and defend their right to use lie-detector tests. "The New World Liberation Front says it is going to get Joe Coors," says the intended victim. "I don't want a member here with that opportunity." The front is a Maoist terrorist group, with ties to the Symbionese Liberation Army, which claims responsibility for 100 bombings over the past four years, including one at Coors facility in California. Such adverse publicity overshadows Coors' history of good labor relations.

During Prohibition, a hefty chunk of the family fortune went toward keeping the brewery open. And the company has a good record on minority hiring. Through an Outward Bound program, it has had considerable success with hard-core unemployables. Still, says Dillon Read's Hobbs, "it's crazy how these undercurrents stay."

Last year the Coors were believed to be providing financial support to Anita Bryant's anti-gay campaign. In the past the brothers would have ignored such talk. But this time Bill Coors gave an interview to *The Advocate,* a Los Angeles gay community newspaper, in which he denied the rumor and added: "I have a first cousin who is gay. He's a good friend, welcome in my house. I regard his life as strictly his business." The paper dropped its support of a boycott against Coors beer, and the company claims sales to gays are up.

The Family

This kind of straightforward talk comes just as easily to the fourth generation which, in addition to Peter, includes his brothers, Jeffrey, 33, and Joseph Jr., 36, and his cousin Adolph IV, 32. Jeffrey, who is vice-president for quality assurance and research and development, and Peter are directors. Joe Jr. runs an industrial porcelain operation; Adolph IV is a chemist.

Like Bill and Joe Coors, whose first work for the company was as pre-schoolers painting the brewery fence for 12½¢ an hour, the younger Coors have worked at odd jobs since they were children. But they were under far less pressure to join the family business than their fathers had been. Joe nonetheless worked as a chemical engineer for DuPont for three years after graduating from Cornell. Bill Coors, an accomplished pianist, joined the company when he graduated from Princeton, but he seriously considered careers in both music and medicine.

Though both Bill and Joe Coors are in their sixties, neither is thinking of retirement. "Our father died at 86 with his boots on," says Bill, who is as interested in nutrition and dealing with executive stress as Joe is in politics. "I see a similar role for myself."

The future management of Coors will not be determined by primogeniture, claims Bill Coors, although it is unlikely the reins will pass from family hands. Noting that Peter and Jeffrey have moved up almost in tandem, Joe Coors muses: "We might even have another brother team."

The Intricate 'Politics' of the Corporation

Charles G. Burck

One weekend recently, the chief executive of one of the country's biggest industrial corporations pulled Oswald Spengler's *Decline of the West* from his bookshelves and reread it. Spengler, as the executive knew from reading him years before, predicted that Western civilization would end in a bitter struggle in which raw Caesarean power would triumph over money. The businessman did not and does not share the German philosopher's pessimism, but he wanted to check—just in case he'd overlooked something the first time around.

The environment in which the corporation finds itself these days encourages a certain amount of gloomy speculation. American manufacturers are not earning enough to replace their deteriorating plants and equipment, and their productivity is lagging. With the stock market drying up as a source of

equity capital, companies have fallen heavily into debt to the banks. The interest charges on that debt were easy enough to support in an era of rapid growth, but now have become an onerous burden. The explosive leap in energy costs, along with the relentlessly advancing expense of recovering other resources, has raised serious questions as to whether yesterday's glorious growth rates will ever return again.

These problems, while worrisome, are at least conventional and familiar. More difficult may be the newer problems caused by changes in what U.S. society demands from the corporation. Consumers, once docile in the marketplace, have discovered their discontent and are uniting to attack the corporation in adversary proceedings. Environmentalists have called it to account for ravaging the landscape and befouling the air and water. Local communities that provide a home for company plants are loudly asserting their claim that the corporation owes them something. In Detroit a public outcry against the impending loss of jobs forced financially troubled Chrysler to reverse an earlier decision to close down an obsolete plant.

ELEVATED DESIRES

Management has to concern itself a great deal more with how employees feel about their work. Says Irving Shapiro, chairman of Du Pont: "In the past, people wanted a steady job, and income was all-important. In the future, people will want a sense of participation, satisfaction, contribution." No less difficult to manage than blue-collar workers are executives who no longer tend, with single-minded dedication, to sacrifice everything for their careers. They are increasingly inclined, for example, to turn down promotions that would require them to uproot their families or move to an "undesirable" city.

Corporations, to be sure, have been adjusting to new demands for many years. Classically, these demands have arisen mainly from the marketplace, either in the expressed desires of consumers or in some inchoate yearning for a product or service that was not yet in existence. The most successful corporations have been those whose leaders anticipated these demands and marshaled the capital, technology, and people needed to produce what was wanted. Thus Andrew Carnegie, foreseeing what a large and integrated steel industry could do for the world, brought the Bessemer process together with coke, iron ore, and manpower to build what in 1901 became U.S. Steel.

HOW IT GOT TO BE "HUMANE"

As it evolved, the corporation gradually began to encounter a greater number of demands emanating from outside the classic marketplace. Around the time of the nation's birth, when the small, atomistic firm described by Adam Smith fought it out in a rowdy free market, the sole obligation of the business enterprise was to produce goods and charge what the traffic would bear. Conflicts between this narrow economic interest and broader social expectations began to arise in the late nineteenth century, but did not become pervasive until the 1930's. It was not until 1938, for example, that the first federal child-labor law went into effect.

With some pain, corporations learned to live with the growing power of unionized labor and laws guaranteeing a minimum wage, unemployment compensation, and safer working conditions. Through each round of new requirements, the corporation took on greatly enlarged responsibilities. It also became more "humane."

The process of hanging a greater variety of diverse obligations upon the corporation might be viewed, in one sense, as a radical expansion of its marketplace. Every choice a corporation makes these days—to close a plant, to fill a swamp, to hire a quota of blacks—affects thousands of people who had no voice in the classical marketplace but who are increasingly creating new market conditions through social pressure, moral suasion, and law. Simply trying to gauge the corporation's responsibility to these diverse interests is still a relatively new job for management. It may also be the most complicated.

Though few executives are apt to think of it this way, the corporation has in fact become a "political" institution. Before acting, managers must weigh a multitude of interests, including those of employees, creditors, customers, suppliers, shareholders, and the public at large. All these "constituencies" assert claims that are valid, though often conflicting. In the end, the manager, like the politician, has to resolve the competing claims of his constituents and do something.

"THE FUTURE IS A WHOLE NEW GAME"

In the process, corporations have possibly become the nation's most pragmatic, most adaptable, and most successful instruments of change. Privately owned, individualistically managed, and free to try a wide variety of approaches, they are essential elements of democratic pluralism, critical institutions in the American System.

For all the corporation's past ability to master change, though, there remain real questions about how well it can meet the challenges of today. Its varied constituencies are changing more dramatically than ever—sometimes unpredictably, often with enormous consequences. The Arab oil embargo, for example, represented what might be called the revolt of a constituency of suppliers, but it produced more than a simple extra cost of doing business in classical-market terms. "Everything before it is history," remarks Irving Shapiro. "The future is a whole new game."

BEYOND EFFICIENCY LIES EFFECTIVENESS

Clearly, managements have to rethink their whole function. Peter Drucker, that most prolific of writers on the subject, says, "The assumptions of all the work of management during the past century are being put into doubt by new developments demanding new vision, new work, and new knowledge." Meeting problems is only part of the challenge; seizing opportunities is of equal or greater importance. For every Xerox that grasped the immense opportunities beckoning from an unexploited market, scores of other corporations have bogged down in what Drucker identifies as a preoccupation with efficiency.

To be sure, efficiency—the art of doing the same thing with less effort or fewer re-sources—is one of the corporation's great and singular contributions to the advancement of mankind. But it is not enough. Management's new goal, says Drucker, must be "effectiveness," which is a shorthand way of describing the *optimum* use of all the resources available to pursue *extraordinary results*. To be "effective," the manager must somehow infuse the whole corporate organization with the intuitive sense that a good entrepreneur has for identifying problems—and opportunities—beyond the horizon.

The notion of seeking extraordinary results is hardly radical, but it can get lost in large organizational superstructures. Does this mean that big corporations are necessarily inflexible and unresponsive? Those who argue in the affirmative rest their case to some degree on circumstantial evidence. Small, innovative companies sometimes seem better adapted to serving markets overlooked by big firms, and have a powerful track record for pioneering new technologies ignored by the giants. Indeed, great numbers of small corporations are flourishing. In addition, some of the suspicion of bigness springs from emotional sources—the traditional American distrust of large agglomerations of power, and the Chaplinesque vision of man crushed in the cogs.

THE FLEXIBLE TITAN

But size need not be an obstacle to flexibility or responsiveness. Where it leads to incapacity, the blame rests with management, rather than the phenomenon of bigness itself. I.B.M., after all, was a well-established maker of business machines, with revenues of $410 million and comfortable profits, when it shifted its entire corporate strategy to make the computers that changed the world.

Sophisticated management will scale down the oversized division or department into a number of profit centers or other sub-enterprises, some of them highly autonomous. The pragmatic manager adapts to whatever works best, a process that extends all the way down to dealing with the consumer. For example, many large retailers have demonstrated their "effectiveness" by restructuring their giant department stores and emporiums into smaller units, such as boutiques, shops, and arcades. This meets the consumer's demand for a more intimate shopping environment, while enabling the store owner to make the most of computer technologies that afford more sensitive and precise inventory control. By fragmenting the mass market into many little individual markets, the companies give the consumer a wider choice and spread their own risks in the fickle world of fashion.

PUTTING OFF THE IMPORTANT JOBS

But to be effective, the manager must also overcome some habits of thinking that have little to do with whether his corporation is large or small. Harold J. Leavitt, professor of organizational behavior and psychology at the Stanford Business School, has identified

An Alternative to Smith and Galbraith

CHARACTERISTIC	CLASSICAL-MARKET MODEL	MANAGERIAL MODEL	SOCIAL-ENVIRONMENT MODEL
Nature of the economy	Perfectly competitive	Monopolistic-oligopolistic	Effectively competitive
Level of profits	Normal	Supernormal	Normal
Enterprise goal	Short-run profit maximization	Security and growth of business volume	Long-run profit maximization
Locus of decision-making power	Entrepreneurs	Managers	Stockholders—board of directors
Nature of competition	Price	Price Product variation Selling costs	Multivectored dynamic process
External constraints on enterprise behavior	Markets	Markets	Markets Public opinion Political pressures
Determinants of social activity	None	Social and charitable propensities of managers	Long-run profit maximization

The corporate executive knows that his company behaves according to neither the Adam Smith nor the John Kenneth Galbraith description, but he may be hard put to find a theoretical model that will do justice to reality. Neil H. Jacoby, founding dean of the U.C.L.A. Graduate School of Management, offers one in his book, *Corporate Power and Social Responsibility*.

Of the three models above, the classical-market model sums up the corporation as Smith saw it—the small, owner-managed firm purveying simple products in a perfectly competitive market. The managerial model, developed during the 1940's and

one of these habits as the tendency of managers to "respond to the programmed tasks facing them before responding to the unprogrammed ones."

The programmed tasks are the routine, familiar jobs. The unprogrammed work is creative: identifying potential problems and seizing opportunities generally apprehended only by the skillful entrepreneur or intuitive executive. One unprogrammed area of inquiry, for example, might be trying to find out how the corporation should structure itself in the future to satisfy the human needs of its employees.

Because unprogrammed work is unusual-

ly challenging, managers tend to postpone it while they perform routine tasks instead. Leavitt thinks a kind of Gresham's law applies: programmed tasks chase away unprogrammed tasks like bad money chasing out good. If boredom in the factory appeared to be a major long-range problem, a manager might nevertheless prefer the status quo to restructuring operations, which would involve experimentation and a degree of risk. While some workers might thrive on greater responsibilities, such as they have in Sweden, others might agree with the American auto worker who, upon returning from an experimental stint at Saab, said, "If I've

---

1950's, was, as Jacoby says, "carried to an extreme by Galbraith in *The New Industrial State.*" In it, management is divorced from ownership and the corporation is run not so much to optimize profits for stockholders as to satisfy the managers' own desires for security, power, and prestige. Companies compete by varying their product styles and spending money on advertising and other marketing devices. But since competition is muted by oligopoly, profits are "abnormally" high.

Jacoby's social-environment model reflects the corporation's status as a political institution. Legislation and the prodding of public opinion induce large companies to allocate resources to social purposes they might ignore if they were responding solely to classical-market forces. Because the corporation is financially more secure than Adam Smith's merchant, its managers can afford to look beyond the quick dollar to maximize long-run profits.

Jacoby's formidable phrase to describe competitive forces—the "multivectored dynamic process"—includes four major categories of competition—intraproduct (within the same industry), interproduct (across industry lines), potential (from companies that might enter the business), and international. These categories in turn break down into several subcategories. Interproduct competition, for example, involves not only price, product variation, and selling costs, but also services, credit terms, trade-in allowances, warranties, and competition from secondhand products.

Not everyone will agree with all of Jacoby's conclusions. There is little evidence, for example, that stockholders constitute an effective locus of decision-making power for most corporations. And boards of directors are too often creations of the managements they are supposed to oversee. Jacoby himself recognizes the weaknesses of boards, and proposed they be strengthened. He says the majority of directors should be well-paid outsiders with an independent staff to examine corporate affairs. Since few managers will willingly undertake reforms that would bring them tougher overseers, Jacoby advocates that corporations be chartered nationally, with stringent requirements about their boards' independence written into the charters.

got to bust my ass to be meaningful, forget it. I'd rather be monotonous."

In this case, the plant manager's programmed task is to meet a near-term production schedule, and he is reluctant to sacrifice it to reorganize the work, though that might make for a greater long-run profit. Unfortunately, most of the unprogrammed jobs that are shunted aside this way do affect the corporation's long-run prospects. The long-range planning of corporate strategy is the premier unprogrammed task.

Techniques of planning have been substantially improved in recent years, and a growing number of corporations at least attempt to set goals for five or more years ahead. Multinational oil companies and electric utilities have been among the most assiduous long-run planners; it was easy for them to plan because until recently they enjoyed relatively stable growth rates and predictable markets. But managers are quite naturally chary of getting locked into strategies based on abstractions. They know that the best-laid plans, even when formulated on I.B.M. 360's, gang aft a-gley. The markets of the oil companies and utilities have been disrupted by unforeseen events, which caused a dramatic decline in the forecasts for oil consumption and the postponement of power-plant construction that had been on the drawing boards for years.

SOME THINGS WE'D RATHER NOT KNOW

Another impediment to serious long-range planning is the natural human tendency not to think about things that make one uncomfortable. Asbestos manufacturers are about as eager to dwell on the carcinogenic properties of their product as the fat man is to contemplate atherosclerosis. Even the pragmatic businessman tends to find improbably optimistic scenarios less "unthinkable" than more probable pessimistic alternatives. So executives assigned to planning all too often remain sealed off in their departments—

consulted occasionally by someone who wants extrapolations of the past rather than troublesome departures from convention.

The result is a dismaying abundance of corporate problems that could have been avoided, and not just in hindsight. For several years, for instance, there have been indications that something of fundamental importance was happening in the oil business. If U.S. automakers had studied the distribution of world petroleum reserves and the course of politics in the Middle East, they might have been better able to anticipate the big price rise. If they had then turned their full resources to designing cars that would run on less gasoline, they would probably be selling more cars today.

The troubles of Reserve Mining Co. provide another case in point. When Reserve's owners, Armco and Republic Steel, chose to fight for the freedom to continue dumping taconite tailings into Lake Superior, they must have been counting, against all probability, on the evaporation of environmentalism. Since 1969, Reserve has earned a reputation for flagrantly opposing the public interest, has spent $6 million in legal battles, and is bound to spend a lot more. It could have filtered the water supplies of affected communities in the first place for an estimated $12 million.

THE MANAGEMENT OF CHANGE

What's needed is not so much new planning techniques as better application of the ones that exist. Peter Gabriel, dean of the Boston University School of Management and a former partner of McKinsey & Co., thinks that "the often spectacular failure in so much of what still parades as—and on occasion even is—highly sophisticated planning largely results from confusion between process and substance." The central need, says Gabriel, is for corporate managers to better understand what it is they need to plan for.

Managers have to stretch their minds to assess the changes taking place in all of the corporation's interrelated constituencies. In doing this, says Gabriel, they must understand that the events of tomorrow may be shaped by "ideological" factors, which have become as important as material considerations in influencing everything from oil supplies to employee relations. They also have to shift their emphasis from "the identification of opportunities specific to the individual company—like new products and new markets within traditional lines of business—to problems related to whole industries, if not the entire economy." In sum, he says, the corporation has to plan "for the management of change, rather than the administration of steady-state operations."

A fine example of long-range planning is the exercise conducted by J. C. Penney last year. Chairman Donald Seibert formed a number of groups of from five to eight middle-management people, each member of a group from a different area of the company. Provided with general guidance on source material, access to libraries and files, and plenty of time to work, the groups independently assessed the company's future. Seibert then commissioned outside consultants to work out future scenarios, and asked the in-house groups to chew over the professionals' work. The exercise, which took four months, contributed an unusually broad range of ideas to what became Penney's own long-range plan.

"A MULTIPLICITY OF IMAGINATIVE VENTURES"

One difficult strategy to plan is how to deal with all those new social forces that have become such a familiar part of the corporation's environment. The concept of corporate "social responsibility" has recently been expanded to include a list of demands as long as the attention spans of business's most vociferous critics. Some of these de-

mands are ridiculous, others seriously important, and still others fall in between. The manager who simply writes off the whole problem of social responsibility does so at his peril. Most often, he has failed to take the time to sort out the issues.

A lot of fruitless verbiage could be stricken from the social-responsibility debate if corporate executives had a clear idea of what their responsibilities really are. Thornton Bradshaw, president of ARCO, puts the case succinctly by defining the corporation's two major obligations as "one, to operate to the full extent within the rules, and two, to create as many experimental situations as possible so that the new approaches can be picked up and become a part of our social pattern."

By creating "experimental situations," Bradshaw means things like trying new approaches to training the "unemployable," providing incentives for employee car pools, and so on. Such experiments, conducted pragmatically and in the corporation's own interest, are among the corporation's contributions to democratic pluralism. As Eli Goldston, the late chairman of Eastern Gas & Fuel Associates in Boston, once put it: "It's probably a good thing in any democratic society to have a multiplicity of decision makers—even if you take a scattering of not-so-bright and awfully conservative and somewhat eccentric executives. There's going to be 5,000 of them, each with a little pot of money to do something with. I'd sooner have them than Congress if what I was looking for was a multiplicity of imaginative ventures. And it is the multiplicity of decision spots that creates a wonderful opportunity for innovation."

Many of the corporation's social experiments are purely discretionary—charitable support for the arts, for example. Others, such as opening up jobs to minorities and women, are mandatory, but the means of implementing them afford the corporation some discretion. And the question of closing down a plant or moving a headquarters is broadly discretionary, though corporate executives must decide whether they need to make some effort to ease the impact of the move on employees, or even, in some cases, forgo it for the sake of the community.

There are no sure formulas for dealing with such issues. The corporation's leaders can only apply their own ethics. Taking refuge in the letter of the law begs the question and is self-destructive. The abdication of ethics will inevitably lead to a situation where every corporate decision will be judged by the applicable legal paragraph, and business will be buried under a mountain of regulations.

HOW TO KEEP AHEAD OF THE LAW

Bradshaw's other maxim of corporate behavior—"to operate to the full extent within the rules"—is not quite the obvious advice it appears to be. It is in the nature of the System that the rules are repeatedly being rewritten as people's expectations change. And as new responsibilities are placed on the corporation (say, to stop polluting the air), managers have to add the costs involved (to install and operate antipollution devices) to the price of the goods produced.

The attitude of corporate managers is most critical during the period leading up to the time when the rules are rewritten and set in concrete. During this period of awakening, when people are beginning to discern that some costs of production are being borne by the public, the wise course for the manager may well be to go to the government and say, "We think you should work up some industry regulations on this." It may be that the public will be willing to bear some of the costs.

But whatever the outcome, blindly resisting reform is no answer at all. The automobile industry, for example, fought emission controls at first, and upon losing the battle found itself painted into a corner—

having to build all of its cars to standards stricter than are needed by most of the nation, and on a crash schedule too short for the best application of engineering talent.

TESTING A DOOMSDAY PREDICTION

By contrast, Du Pont seems to be handling the fluorocarbon issue with far greater dexterity. Fluorocarbons are a class of chemical products that includes the Freons, the principal gases used as aerosol propellants, as well as in refrigeration and air-conditioning systems. Freons are an invention of Du Pont and have become one of its many profitable businesses. The company estimates that the industries directly dependent on fluorocarbon production contribute $8 billion to the economy and employ 200,000 people.

During the past year, several scientists have, on the basis of computer models, suggested that fluorocarbons rising into the upper atmosphere may damage the ozone layer that shields the earth from excessive ultraviolet radiation. The scientists warn that the consequences would probably be disastrous—including increased incidences of skin cancer and substantial biological and climatic changes. Their work is highly speculative at this point, however, as they themselves have acknowledged.

No rational manager would halt production of a major product on mere speculation. Not with the premature and costly elimination of phosphates from most laundry detergents still fresh in his memory. "The fluorocarbon issue troubles me greatly," says Du Pont Chairman Shapiro. "I hear the theory doesn't hold water, but there is great alarm that the atmosphere will be destroyed."

Under these trying circumstances, Du Pont appears to be doing about the best it can. Along with other fluorocarbon manufacturers, it is supporting research sponsored by the National Academy of Sciences and the Manufacturing Chemists Association.

The latter group alone has funded, to the tune of $1.5 million, atmospheric measurements to test the hypothesis, and it plans to begin work in the stratosphere this year. Finally, Du Pont has made it unmistakably clear that it will stop production if, as it says, "any creditable scientific data show that any fluorocarbons cannot be used without a threat to health."

Particularly now, when their credibility is so low, corporations need to show convincingly that they can move quickly and conscientiously when such problems of potential public concern arise. Environmentalists tend to set standards of minimum or even zero risk to public health and safety. But decisions about risk are too important to be weighed in an atmosphere that pits environmental crusaders against corporate villains. The crusaders are apt to win most of the battles, and society will pay enormously for unrealistically risk-free production.

THE DICTATORIAL BOSS IS DEAD

Another area where there are few clear-cut rules for achieving effectiveness is in the art of managing the corporation's people. "Job satisfaction" is the catchall label that defines the primary task, and it is increasingly important to workers and managers at all levels of the corporation. Too much can be made— and has been—of the idea that the new attitudes of workers will cause the withering away of traditional economic disciplines and organizational constraints. The Age of Aquarius is *not* dawning, at least within the institutions that will carry society through whatever we will call the age that is coming upon us.

Nevertheless, the corporation cannot hope to escape some of the very real changes in values and work habits that are the inevitable outgrowth of increased affluence and education. "The leading motivators of the new work force are achievement, recognition, and the nature of the work,"

says Reginald Jones, chairman of General Electric. "The new management has to set reasonable goals, and encourage and challenge the work force."

This is by no means an altruistic exercise. Gone forever are the days when a dictatorial boss could elicit performance by barking at his workers. Corporate organization has become too complex for that, the boss too dependent on the knowledge and skills of his employees, who themselves have become power centers in the operation. If a corporation is to achieve extraordinary results, its employees have to *want* to take the initiative, to be creative.

WORKERS WANT MORE THAN MAYOISM

From the factory floor up through middle management, jobs in American industry still too frequently owe more than a trace of their structure and definition to the prescriptions issued at the turn of the century by Frederick W. Taylor, the original efficiency expert. Taylor viewed the worker as basically a mechanical being, and his system for organizing work was to carefully delineate all duties, breaking jobs down into the minutest motions and steps, in order to extract from each worker the maximum in efficiency.

Lingering Taylorism has not been particularly ameliorated by the efforts of the "human relations" school of management, which dates back to the Twenties and the work of industrial psychologist Elton Mayo. Stroking the workers' egos may have represented an improvement over the reductiveness of Taylorism. But apart from its doubtful ethical underpinnings (the stroking was calculated, not sincere), it was not particularly productive.

The company that can pinpoint and eliminate residual Taylorism generally finds that it creates not only better employee morale but higher productivity. The tendency for jobs in complex organizations to become highly specialized, and therefore fragmented, can rob the worker of the satisfaction that comes from completing an entire task. For more than thirty years at A.T.&T., the service representatives in business departments were limited to processing new phone orders and the like. Any decision to grant a customer extra time to pay a bill or to require a deposit for a new account had to be made by supervisors. In 1966, the company decided to give the more able and motivated service representatives these decision-making powers. Chairman John DeButts says that "we did it with some misgivings, but it worked out very well. We said, in effect, 'We trust you.' They did a better job, were extremely conscientious, and were proud that they could do the *whole* job."

Innovations in the workplace can do a good deal more than simply lift the mind-numbing restrictions from jobs at the lower corporate levels. Managers, no less than workers, can benefit from imaginative departures from convention and return the rewards to the enterprise as a whole. J. C. Penney's long-range planning effort is a case in point. Besides helping to shape the company's thinking about its future, it dealt a large number of middle line managers into the planning process, making concern about the corporation's ultimate destiny a part of their own job experience.

A LESSON FROM THE ORIENT

The old-line manager may doubt that there is any positive correlation between job enrichment and higher productivity, particularly in such areas as middle management, where productivity is hard, if not impossible, to measure accurately. But the examples of success continue to multiply at a rate that makes a causal relationship almost impossible to doubt.

The Japanese offer perhaps the most prominent body of evidence—and they have begun exporting their techniques to the plants they own in the U.S. (See "The Japanese Are Coming—with Their Own Style of Management," *Fortune,* March.) They have run their enterprises with an almost intuitive understanding of the connection between employee satisfaction and enhanced productivity. They shape benefits to the needs of specific groups in the work force, foster team spirit through informal relations between management and empoyees, and involve all members of a division or company in detailed planning.

BACK TO A SENSE OF LEGITIMACY

Here in America (and of late even in Japan as well), the corporation has become widely mistrusted. That is unfortunate for a number of reasons. Several other institutions that once served as anchors for the society, including the family and the church, have also undergone long-term erosion, leaving lots of Americans with the feeling that they have been cut adrift from solid values. Many of these people devote a large part of their lives to their work. For that work to be perceived by the public, and by themselves, as something less than a force for good, is psychologically debilitating. Yet the work of the corporation is often so perceived. Norman Podhoretz, editor of the intellectual journal *Commentary,* notes: "A lot of businessmen are full of self-hate and are lacking a sense of legitimacy." Others wonder why they are so little appreciated.

Perhaps thinking clearly about the corporation as a "political" institution can help return some of the sense of legitimacy. Certainly, that view of the corporation today is more realistic than Adam Smith's description (the merchant who promotes society's interests only because he is unwittingly led to do so by the "invisible hand") or John Kenneth Galbraith's model (the oligopolist who controls his markets and assures his own perpetuation).

The goals of the "political" corporation can be defined in many ways: satisfying consumers as well as stockholders, allocating resources, marshaling talents, providing jobs, bearing a fair share of the total costs of production. Broadly, these are society's goals. If the corporation is effective, it will make a profit. That remains the unique yardstick for measuring the corporation's success in meeting its goals at the lowest possible cost, not only to itself but to all of society.

Europe's Industrial Democracy: An American Response

Ted Mills

The decade of the 1970s in Europe has witnessed one of the more remarkable transformations in the nature, structure, and direction of industrial society in the 200-year-old history of the industrial age.

Quietly, without revolutionary incident or fanfare, industrial Europe in this decade has witnessed a startling shift of influence and power in European economic organizations, which—for lack of a better term—I call the "industrial democracy" phenomenon.

Industrial democracy in Europe has been politically sought—and won—essentially as a power transfer away from the few to the many, away from the owners and the means of production of goods and services (and the managers who serve their interests) to the working men and women who produce those services (and the unions that serve their interests). Already, that transfer has begun to alter social expectations, power balances, political direction and debate, and the very value system of European industrial societies.

True, the term industrial democracy implies significantly different things in various European countries. To oversimplify, it is used here to describe the many differing outcomes of a political thrust toward greater guarantees, provided by law, of social and economic entitlements. The source, I suggest, has been public hunger for the same democratizing influence inside economic organizations that has already been won outside.

The result has been in five basic "faces," or forms, politically proposed and government sanctioned by law. These forms are (1) codetermination, or workers on boards, (2) works councils, (3) shop-floor participation, (4) financial participation, and (5) collective bargaining (see the appendix on page 434–36 for a general description of each form).

Industrial democracy, however, is not new; its roots can be traced to the late nineteenth century, when—particularly in Britain's Fabian Society—the notion of democracy at work caught the fancy of many of Europe's leading intellectuals, including—of all people—George Bernard Shaw and his intimate friends, Sidney and Beatrice Webb.

In the late 1970s, there are many people in industry, labor, and government in European countries who claim that the future of capitalism in Europe, and perhaps the world, may lie in the eventual outcomes of the sweep of industrial democracy in Europe. And, curiously, even the most ardent advocates of the sweeping changes in the conduct of European industrial organizations, almost to a man or woman, characterize themselves as strong stakeholders in the survival of that system and its free-market economic rewards.

Unlike the radicals of the extreme European left (who despise and deplore the industrial democracy phenomenon), advocates of industrial democracy seek neither to destroy the free-market system nor to replace it with other systems, such as the state-owned systems advanced by most socialists and all communists. Rather, they seek to preserve it through reforming it. Their announced goal is to make the existing system more responsive to the powerful participative pressures in today's restive European societies. They would permit more—many more—of the system's stakeholders a greater voice in determining its future, like a kind of social safety valve.

There are many in European management, however, who claim that the shapers of the industrial democracy movement will succeed (or have succeeded) in destroying the very system that they seek to preserve, by making it economically unmanageable through participative overload. Already, up to 45% of European labor costs today go to paying for social benefits—30-day vacations with pay in most countries, free health care for all, paid absenteeism, and other costly benefits that employers and/or governments must pay. The results, such managers claim, with arguments sometimes not unlike those advanced by advocates of Proposition 13 in California, is untenable taxation, and untenable real income at *every* level of American society, including taxes.

Companies *and* countries so heavily taxed, this argument runs, will result in economies—already ravaged by the 1975–1977 recession and still shaky—which will eventually fall apart, inviting Communist takeover and social and economic disaster.

To Americans, who view with alarm what has happened so fast in Europe in this decade, such arguments seem both plausible and frightening. The U.S. business rumor mill is rife with stories of German, Dutch, and Scandinavian companies, intolerably burdened and slowed by the new regulatory "codetermination" laws, seeking escape to the United States or elsewhere for survival. Yet, on the reverse side of the coin, the three European countries with far and away the most stringent regulatory industrial democracy laws—Holland, West Germany, and Sweden—were the three strongest economies in Europe in 1977 (although Sweden's was faltering), and all three countries had relatively the smallest and most toothless Communist parties in Europe.

By contrast, the two countries with the least stringent (or absent) regulatory industrial democracy laws in Europe—France and Italy—both had weak economies, and both had the largest and most powerful Communist parties in all of free Europe. Possibly, on close inspection, the apparent correlation between industrial democracy reform and imminent economic disaster or Communist takeover does not necessarily hold water.

For any number of reasons, such as its quiet evolutionary nature, its many faces in many countries (see the *Exhibit*), its social (as distinct from economic) nature, its focus on labor-management issues, or simply because it is happening in Europe and seems irrelevant, this major shift of social and economic power has until very recently been astonishingly under-reported and even ignored by the American media. It is possible that an American reader of this article will be learning, for the first time, of the profound societal implications of the birth (almost all of it in this decade) of the industrial democracy phenomenon across the Atlantic.

Will the wind of major social change in the twentieth century be a prevailing westerly and arrive here across the Atlantic in a decade or so? If yes, the complex and varying European laws now on the books requiring 33% to 50% worker participation on governing boards, the imposition of mandatory works councils, and especially Sweden's historic Democracy at Work Act of 1977, which gave the unions the right to bargain over almost anything management might want to do, might give cause for serious alarm in U.S. management and (particularly) in union circles.

It is the contention of this article, however, that Americans should not draw too hasty or facile a parallel between the new industrial relations structures in Europe today and those of the United States tomorrow. Such parallel drawing may be dangerous. For, basically, what has happened so fast in Europe in this decade has been a wholly European political phenomenon. What has happened has been bred in and of the political nature, processes, and societal realities of Europe, not America. It is the contention of this article that the basic European industrial democracy phenomenon of the 1970s—the legislative, regulatory part—is, like certain European wines which turn to vinegar in passage, not transportable.

THE EUROPEAN ETHOS

As most Americans would quickly agree, the United States is not Europe. U.S. management is very different and far more democratic than that of Europe. U.S. labor unions, and the American AFL-CIO labor confederation, are very different and significantly more democratic than those of their European brothers. Most important of all, the people of Europe are hugely different culturally, politically, and economically from Americans.

Gertrude Stein once remarked that the United States is the oldest society on earth because it was the first to enter the twentieth century. In at least one sense she was right. It was not until after World War II that other industrialized societies, particularly those of Europe and Japan, took a quantum leap toward the standards of living and consumption increasingly enjoyed by most Americans for the first five decades of the century.

If measured in the overnight rush to consumption of things like automobiles, refrigerators, and even bathrooms, the postwar explosion in Europe of what the French call *la société de consommation* was and still is astonishing. Paris or Rome at rush hour have become a far worse experience than anything Americans know of; an American driving for the first time through downtown Frankfurt or Milan is startled at the resemblance to downtown Houston or Atlanta. The apparent surface homogenization of free Western societies in the third quarter of the twentieth century was one of the striking aspects of that period, and will become more so in the quarter century ahead.

Behind the chrome-and-concrete current similarities, however, and despite America's genealogical debt to the countries of Europe, our cultural roots are hugely different. Centuries of clinging European social and political history, of embedded European traditions, class structures and hatreds, idiosyncratic cultural and parochial attitudes and behaviors, economic beliefs, and particularly the European manifests of right, middle, and left, are vastly different in heritage from ours.

To attempt to identify in a paragraph or two the essential American ethos and its considerable differences from those of each European country is as foolhardy as to attempt similarly to condense the nature and dimensions of the European industrial democracy phenomenon of the 1970s into a single chart. Yet if the tens of thousands of books by observers of the American scene, from de Tocqueville on, would agree on any predominant and distinguishing feature of the American character, it would quite prob-

EXHIBIT Significant European "Industrial Democracy" Legislation

DATE	COUNTRY	LAW/ACTIVITY
1945	France	Works councils mandatory
1946	Sweden	Works councils mandatory
1947	Germany	Codetermination (iron and steel 33%)
1951	Belgium	Works councils mandatory
1951	Germany	Parity codetermination (iron and steel 58%)
1952	Germany	First works constitution act
1967	France	Financial participation (profit sharing) act

1970s

DATE	COUNTRY	LAW/ACTIVITY
1970	Italy	Worker's charter act
1971	Norway	Codetermination law (33%)
1971	Holland	First works council act
1972	Sweden	First codetermination act (33%)
	European Economic Community	Fifth directive (two-tier boards in Eurocompanies)
1972	Germany	Second works constitution act
1973	Austria	Labor constitution act (councils, codetermination)
1973	Norway	Codetermination act (33%)
1973	Holland	Two-tier board act
1973	Sweden	Worker dismissal protection act
1973	Germany	Metalworker "Humanization of Work" strike
1974	United Kingdom	Bullock Commission authorized
1974	United Kingdom	British Work Research Unit established
1974	France	Sudreau Commission report
1974	France	A.N.A.C.T. established
1974	Denmark	Codetermination act (33%)
1975	European Economic Community	"Gundelach Report" (two-tier boards)
1975	France	Cosurveillance proposed
1975	Sweden	Meidner (financial profit-sharing proposed)
1976	Germany	Parity codetermination act (50%)
1976	United Kingdom	Employment protection act
1976	Sweden	"Democracy at Work" act (unrestricted bargaining)
1976	Denmark	Work environment act (psychological welfare)
1976	Norway	Work environment act (psychological welfare)
1976	Holland	Second works council act (tougher)
1976	France	Manual worker protection act
1976	Italy	FLM/Fiat contract (union rights in management)
1977	United Kingdom	Bullock Commission report

ably be the driving force of our pioneer-bred veneration of individualism and personal liberty, notions only superficially understood in Europe.

Like no other society in world history Americans have, for two centuries, believed to the depths of their beings that individual freedom of choice and action is our most precious and desirable covenant with one another. This belief is enshrined in our constitution and the political system it provides. Accompanying this deep faith is a demonstrable conviction that liberty works as a way of running our lives, our enterprises, our local, state, and federal governments.

For all the many ills that currently confront Americans—the alleged decline in our practice of cherished individualism; the alarming and growing gap between rich and poor in our incredibly affluent society; and the incursions of an ever more centralized and regulatory government in Washington—we, nevertheless, are still unqualifiedly, both individually as citizens and collectively as institutions and enterprises, the freest, most libertarian society in world history. Whatever its merits or defects, California voters' ringing approval of Proposition 13 in its mid-1978 referendum is as natural to the yeasty individualistic American character as it would be alien to Europeans.

In that essential individualistic quality of ours as a people lies the fingerpost to the uniquely American response to the industrial democracy phenomenon of the 1970s in Europe. For in many ways, much of the "democracy" in industrial life that Europeans have sought and achieved through legislation, we either correctly believe we already have, or we do not view what has happened over there as really democratic (as we define the term) at all.

Much of what the various European industrial democracy laws have achieved in such a rush neither our workers nor our unions—to say nothing of our managers—really want. Such mandated innovations as workers on governing boards or works councils do not excite us. We do not need them. We do not want them. And, to an extent astonishing to Europeans, our managements and unions rely strongly on the power of our legally sanctioned collective bargaining process, American-style, for arriving at what we do want.

More important, however, though often our various special-interest groups run to Washington for protective cover for their best interests (not necessarily those of the nation), as a people we basically still deeply resent government telling us what we must do. As individualists, as pragmatists, as libertarians, we really believe we can best get what we want ourselves, through and in our still largely free institutions. That is where we differ most, at all levels of our society, from our European cousins.

And that is why industrial democracy, as it gains momentum on this side of the Atlantic, will differ essentially in form, structure, and method of appearance from the European version of the 1970s. Despite our European genesis, most of us are not European. We are American.

Class and the Political Solution

Two basic and lingering aspects of the European ethos wholly or essentially absent in the United States tell most of the story of why the difference is and will be great.

First, even in progressive Scandinavia, the ancient notion of class by birth still clings to most contemporary social and economic European institutions like an unscourable bathtub ring. Class is still as manifest in the jealously guarded social caste system of most European managements as it is in the fierce class-consciousness of European workers. Continuing European awareness of class—and its political mirror image, class struggle—may well be the seminal social essence of the European version of industrial democracy.

Second, and certainly in large measure deriving from the deep sense of class itself (so basically absent in the twentieth-century United States), is the turn-to-government-for-what-you-need syndrome characteristic of most European electorates. To a degree astounding to many constitutionally protected, liberty-cherishing Americans, it is a centuries-old fact of European political life that the electorates simply assume that if there is a problem, government will fix it.

The "political solution" urge of the European electorates reaches back in time two centuries or more to the days of the unwritten "social contract" between the class-conscious disenfranchised masses and the reigning duke or king or parliament, in which there was a noblesse oblige responsibility—assumed by both governed and governing—that "father will fix," since only father could bridge the class chasm. Social and economic redress, protection of social rights, demands from under and consequent decrees down from the top—even in such matters, in our time, as a 30-day paid vacation for all, now mandatory law of the land in almost every European country—are matters that every European assumes government should concern itself with in Europe. And so it does.

An illuminating example of the persistent turn-to-government syndrome in the European character was recounted to me in 1978 by a Swedish union friend close to the seats of power in Stockholm. The imminent, possibly already begun, deterioration of the long-healthy planned Swedish economy has become stunningly evident to employers, unions, and all political parties. With massive unemployment already, and more looming, particularly in Sweden's shipbuilding and aerospace industries, the clear and present need for immediate strong remedial action, such as all-out pursuit of alternate products, is manifest to all.

Yet in mid-1978, the Swedish labor confederations and their powerful Social Democratic political allies are hanging back from active commitment to tangible action. They are searching instead for a "political solution" to Sweden's bleak economic future. Their faith is in some form of new legislation, like the hugely controversial and politically charged Meidner wealth-redistribution plan, to avert the disaster. Father should fix.

The lingering sense of class, and its accompanying belief in a political solution, have been powerful social stimuli, among many others, to the industrial democracy phenomenon of the 1970s in Europe. And the evident results have been a mounting transfer of influence power from the few to the many in European capitalist structures, achieved politically, which is the hallmark of the phenomenon.

DEMOCRACY AMERICAN-STYLE

There is no industrial democracy of moment (of the political 1970s' European kind) in the United States in the late twentieth century. Nor are there any discernible pressures seeking its emergence.

To begin with, to many in American labor as well as in management, the term "industrial democracy" smacks of "communistic" thinking. To understate the case, industrial democracy is not a term bandied about American corporate executive suites these days—as it is in Europe—nor is it likely to be heard either in most American union halls or in the high places of U.S. unionism.

Yet a clear, obdurate fact remains: the freedom of choice, liberty, and individualism we Americans so cherish politically still tends to stop at the plant gate or office door in most American enterprises, public and private. For the most part the influence, to say nothing of the rights, of employees at every level in the decision-making powers of our economic insitutions is somewhere between minimal and nonexistent.

Until recently, when the nose dive of U.S. productivity increases became alarmingly evident and remedies increasingly desirable, the absence of employee liberty at work was not a matter of serious moment, or even noteworthy, to most U.S. mangements. Traditionally, in the United States—in a kind of double standard so widespread in our culture that we give it no heed—life at work simply has not been a locus for the individualism, dualism, and liberty we care so fiercely about outside the work place and pontificate about in our Fourth of July speechifying. At work, in private enterprise, profit and economic growth is the name of the game for managers, and U.S. unions have traditionally perceived their role as seeking for their members an ever-increasing piece of both, as joint stakeholders in the free enterprise system (which they cherish as fully as does U.S. management).

Notions such as individual life space, human rights at work, trust, cooperation, personal dignity, and personal growth (as distinct from skill growth) have until very recently seemed somehow irrelevant to the ends of our for-profit enterprises, and the key actors in their maintenance. Democratic, individualistic, and participative concerns have seemed somehow to be incompatible with efficient profitable management in the United States.

Very much like most pre-1970s European managers, private-sector U.S. managers until the mid-1970s still primarily viewed their employees simply as a third resource, after raw materials and capital, whose essential function was to help the organization maximize its return on investment for its stockholder-owners. And in the United States those employees, until very recently, largely agreed. American preoccupation with "economic man"—human beings perceived and valued by their purely economic worth and potential—has long been, and still largely is, the most prevalent and pervasive in the world.

Very *unlike* most European unions and labor confederations, however, most U.S. labor unions and our one labor confederation (the AFL-CIO) are not profoundly concerned about either worker or union influence in winning increased rights or participation in the decision-making processes of American work organizations, for all their strong fight for safer and more humane physical working conditions. What has become in the 1970s a matter of high moment and political activity for their European brothers is simply not a principal concern of union members or their leaders in the United States.

In fact, somewhat the reverse is true. Deeply embedded in the philosophy of U.S. "job unionism," as enunciated to an international labor conference in May 1976 by Thomas Donahue, executive assistant to AFL-CIO president George Meany, is the conviction that the management of business neither is nor should be a union concern.[1]

"We do not seek to be a partner in management," Donahue said, "to be, most likely, the junior partner in success and the senior partner in failure. We do not want to blur in any way the distinction between the respective roles of management and labor in the plant. We guard our independence fiercely—independent of government, independent of any political party, and independent of management."

Noting, with understatement, that Americans have developed "the world's most elaborate, extensive, and complex [he could have added "and most effective"] system of collective bargaining" agreements across the country (each negotiated separately), Donahue stressed and restressed American job unionism's unique and consistent devotion to the legal bargaining process "by equals" as the pervasive hallmark of U.S. trade unionism today and in the future.

Conspicuously absent from Donahue's summation of current U.S. labor policy was reference or even allusion to increased influence, or increased individual liberty at work for union members, as a goal of American labor. He did underscore emergent "social unionism," defining it as the significant and growing union-initiated intent to contribute to communities, and to improve health and safety in work places, as well as the "conditions of work" (which he defined, as noted earlier, in a physical, as distinct from social or political, sense of the term).

Donahue's remarks even more conspicuously avoided any advocacy of greater worker participation in management decisions, increased U.S. worker/union influence through works councils or membership on boards, the "right to be consulted and advised," or, in fact, *any* of the faces of industrial democracy in Europe except collective bargaining, on which his case rested solely. Curiously, in Donahue's "separate but equal" pronouncements there is unmistakable congruence between the late-1970s position of U.S. labor and U.S. management in at least one critically important area: unions and workers should stay the hell out of management.

In a labor movement whose leadership is publicly resolved to be independent from government, from political parties, and particularly from management, the future for industrial democracy, European-style, would seem slim indeed. Such a perception is given even more ballast when one realizes that very much unlike Europe, most U.S. industrial relations policies and agreements are forged not in political or government milieux, not even by the AFL-CIO, but primarily at 150,000 different bargaining tables around the country.

Individualism and Collective Bargaining

On closer examination, however, the future of a form of industrial democracy, uniquely American in character and deriving from American individualism, may not be quite as dim (or undesirable to management and labor) as appearances in 1978 would lead one to believe.

To advance such a hypothesis, it is necessary to emphasize three points:

First, as already noted, most major unions in the United States already are considerably more democratic than their European counterparts. U.S. union members have far greater influence on, and direct participation in, local union policy and bargaining than can be found in almost any European union structure, except in Britain, where, as one U.S. labor leader notes, unionism is "*too* democratic, and uncontrollable."

In a 1977 article in the labor magazine *The Federationist,* AFL-CIO spokesman James Ellenburger noted that in many respects the powerful works councils in Germany—created by a strong 1972 law—are in the most ways the equivalent of a union local in the United States, a structure absent in the German [DGB] trade union federation.[2] In almost every West European country, labor-management policy making, with its omnipresent political aspects, is largely determined not at the local level, as in the United States, but by the labor confederation elite. And very often, it is determined by tripartite commissions consisting of top management, top labor confederation leaders, and the (usually prolabor) leaders of the reigning government.

In 1975, a handful of U.S. union autoworkers visited the Saab-Scania plant in Sweden, presumably to see Swedish industrial democracy at work. The U.S. workers were loudly vocal in their concern at the political distance they saw between the Swedish worker on the floor and his or her shop steward—often only one to a plant—to say nothing of their dismay at the even greater distance of the stewards from the centralized locus of decision making in the labor confederations. As anyone who has attended or been involved in one or more feisty American union elections will testify, the individualistic, libertarian traditions of democracy are alive and well—very well indeed—in American unionism.

To state the first point briefly, the strength of basic industrial democracy vigor within American labor was already way ahead of Europe's when the 1970s began. Wishful thinkers in American management who predict union softening or demise are somewhat badly informed, as those who fought the labor reform legislation in Congress will quite probably discover in 1979.

Second, in the past two decades there have been considerable social fissures and major value reappraisals in American working society, including management, of a magnitude and import often significantly underestimated. The largely uneducated immigrant American worker, for whom the complexity of mass production was divided down into dumb, repetitive simplicity by Taylorian "scientific management" half a century or more ago, is mostly gone now from the work force. He has been replaced by his more educated children and still more educated grandchildren—with all the value shifts, expectations, and impatience with dumb work and police-like authority that "education," regardless of its quality, tends to bring in its wake.

Where there used to be a huge disparity between the complex requirements of modern technology and the abilities of the worker, the situation has flip-flopped; today, the disparity is between the stupidity and lack of challenge in the divided-down work and the status expectations of the educated American employee entering the work force.

To this important and uniquely American phenomenon (European mass education, while increasing, is in most countries half a century behind ours in sheer percentages of population finishing the equivalent of high school) must be added another of equal or greater importance: the startling and dramatic shift of the *nature* of the work in America in the past two decades.

Thanks partially to technology and partially to the emerging information-based shape of so-called "postindustrial society," over two-thirds of all Americans at work today are involved in service instead of manufacturing tasks, and the trend is growing. This shift in itself is pregnant with implications for what tomorrow's "age of information" worker will do—and seek.

Third, and perhaps most significant of all, an ever-growing number of managements and unions, separately and together, have begun exploring an actually age-old but, in the Taylorized twentieth century, startlingly new notion. This notion is that the best work organization for all, employee and employer alike, in our fast-changing society with its ever-rising individual expectations, is a structure in which the individualism, liberty, life space, and dignity of every employee—from worker to senior manager —become critically important concerns and goals of the total organization.

It is a notion which postulates that untapped, dormant, and latent in our work organization lie major reservoirs of now-educated employee expertise, which if tapped through new decision-making decentralization could and would arrest the decline of the productivity of American work organizations.

In the 1970s in the United States—curiously synchronizing in a point of time with the wholly different, politicized phenomenon in Europe—the old preindustrial-age notions of the medieval guilds began to reappear. In the guilds, the head man was the most expert, the leader, not merely boss, and cooperation by all was the guiding principle of work. In U.S. work places, this notion masquerades today under an opaque new term, "quality of work life."

In March 1977, George Morris, vice president of industrial relations for the largest enterprise in the United States—General Motors— summarized the basic premise of the wholly "made-in-USA" form of work place democracy, as practiced at GM. Speaking to the Society of Automotive Engineers, on the same rostrum with his union counterpart Irving Bluestone, vice president of the United Automobile Workers (UAW), Morris explained the U.S. quality of work life approach. He defined it not just as it applies to labor-management relations but as a *philosophy of management* to which the UAW not only totally subscribes but which it also has *demanded through collective bargaining*.

After describing that quality of work life must (in unionized organizations) be a joint union-management process of learning and growth, Morris said:

"When we began applying organization development principles about seven years ago, our focus was on improving organizational effectiveness. We saw improvements in the work climate as naturally flowing from these efforts. I think now we have reversed those objectives. Our primary objective is to improve the quality of work life. We feel that by concentrating on the quality of work life and wisely managing the systems that lead to greater job satisfaction and feelings of self-worth that improvements in the effectiveness of the organization will follow."[3]

Clearly, at least to one not unsubstantial American organization and its equally giant union, concern—and one should add *operational* or *functional* concern—for feelings of self-worth, human dignity, and the life space of every individual in work organizations is perceived as a goal worth pursuing. And this pursuit is fully congruent with that organization's pragmatic, bottom-line goals, and its effectiveness as the profit-making institution its stockholders expect it to be.

It is also intriguing to note in Morris's statement that, in recent years, GM has essentially reversed its basic management priorities. Morris placed primary management emphasis on human growth and dignity at work with an assumption that the secondary payoffs, or necessarily following results, is improved profitability, which is the organization's basic end.

In May 1977, at a conference in Washington convoked to examine the emergent American quality of work life movement, over 100 U.S. workers, stewards, and managers, representing 17 organizations, with a total of more than 300,000 employees, met to attempt to define the basic components of quality of work life. An English-speaking European manager or union leader witnessing that meeting (there were none) would have been startled by the glaring absence of prevalent European industrial democracy buzz words.

Absent in toto from the American vocabulary—or interests—were the European buzz words and concerns such as *codetermination, works councils, worker participation, self-management, worker influence, rights to consultation, financial participation*, or even *shop-floor democracy*. Political issues, positions, affiliations, or advocates were not once mentioned. The prevalent words emanating from that conference were American words and concerns: *cooperation, dignity, trust, experiment, shared, collective bargaining, contract* (the legal collectively bargained agreement), *involvement, human*, and other words reflecting the heart of the American individualistic libertarian tradition. It was an American meeting. The intensity of the conference and its videotaped discussions made it very manifest that to those working men and women already active in it, the quality of work life approach had become a vital, fast-emerging, operational reality of U.S. industrial life.

Ruth Wilder, a participant in that conference, is a GM worker and a UAW shop committee person in a Fisher Body plant, in Grand Rapids, Michigan. She has been working in (and for) a quality of work life environment for several years. Like her fellow American workers, she used unambiguous forthright American terms connoting her personal feelings as a union steward about individual liberty at work:

"The [GM's quality of work life] program was initially explained to us that it would make a worker feel as important when he walked through the door of a plant as he felt before he walked in there. It dignified him. It made him feel important where he's working as well as in his community. Why should walking through the door of a factory—or whatever—change you suddenly into a nothing, when you're someone?"

Another American unionist, the late labor leader "Gundy" Gundvaldson, then president of the Northwest Region of the International Woodworkers of America, who voluntarily joined as a cosponsor with the

Weyerhauser Corporation in a quality of work life project undertaken jointly by the union and company, told an interviewer shortly before his death:

"The workers see many ways of improving the quality of a product and improving productivity at the same time. If a mangement climate can be developed in which workers are encouraged and rewarded for taking an interest in worksite improvement; if communication structures are set up to invite meaningful participation arriving at work-related decisions; if it stimulates a reduction in absenteeism; if the quality of the product improves; if the safety record improves; if the worksite becomes more pleasant; if the workers begin to feel a sense of ownership, then a quality of work life project is a success."

For all the mushrooming emergence of quality of work life activities in the United States, the number of public and private organizations and unions jointly involved in late 1978 in quality of work life activities is still ridiculously small. The 200 to 500 organizations now involved in exploring are relatively little more than a handful of the three million companies in the United States, although among them are some of the largest and best-managed companies and some of the strongest and best-managed unions in the country.

It is noteworthy in the way the United States seems to be moving toward its own kind of industrial democracy that, consistent with the American tradition of liberty of choice and action, all quality of work life activities to date have been wholly voluntary. None has been mandated by government. None has been regulated or supervised or inspected by federal, state, or local officials. More important, particularly to unions in the United States, not one cooperative quality of work life project in existence has contravened, or changed, or weakened the collective bargaining process.

TRIAL AND ERROR

What is happening across the United States, in sum, is wholly different in character, in dimension, in nature, in form, in language, and to a considerable degree, in union and management intent, from what has happened with a rush in the Europe of the 1970s.

Missing from the American response to what seems to be a world-wide phenomenon of work place democratization are government intervention, workers on boards (actual or sought), works council structures, increased union influence in management decision making, and union clamor for major expansion of the areas permissible for collective bargaining. *Not one of these items* was included in the proposed 1978 labor law reform legislation, which was filibustered to death in Congress to U.S. management's temporary delight.

Most important of all the differences present in the American response, and largely missing in most of the European "advances" documented in this article, is a basic focus on individual worker involvement in day-to-day decision making, or union-management cooperation on a voluntary basis. What most strongly identifies the American response, and distinguishes it from the European phenomenon, however, is its pragmatic, uniquely American sense of trial-and-error growth without preconceived, statutory legal prescriptions therefor.

What has happened in Europe has been discrete, fixed, finalized, and legalized, often in hundreds of pages of complex legislation.[4] What has happened in America has been open, groping, growing—a *process*, without discrete boundaries or manuals or formulas. That American response has been defined as "faith in human nature, faith in human intelligence, and the power of pooled and collective experience. It's not belief that these things are complete but that if given a show, they will grow and generate the knowledge and wisdom needed to guide collective action."

One final observation. The foregoing definition was written by a uniquely American philosopher, John Dewey.[5] It should further be noted that Dewey's definition, written in 1929, was not about quality of work life at all. The term had not even been invented yet. It was Dewey's definition of political democracy, American-style.

Just possibly, remembering Dewey's definition of democracy as a process that is never complete may help the reader judge the European phenomenon, and whether, in its various faces, it is "industrial democracy" at all.

NOTES

1. Thomas Donahue, remarks to the International Conference on Trends in Industrial and Labor Relations, Montreal, Canada, May 26, 1976.
2. James Ellenberger, "The Realities of Codetermination," *The Federationist*, AFL-CIO Vol. 84, No. 10 (Washington, D.C.: October 1977), p. 10.
3. George B. Morris, Jr., "A Management-Union Approach to Improving Quality of Work Life," remarks to the Society of Automotive Engineers, March 2, 1977.
4. *Industrial Democracy in Europe: A 1977 Survey* (Washington, D.C.: American Center for the Quality of Work Life, 1978).
5. John Dewey, *Democracy and Education* (New York: The Macmillan Co., 1929).

APPENDIX: THE FIVE FACES OF EUROPEAN INDUSTRIAL DEMOCRACY

1. Codetermination: Workers on Boards

First instance: 1947 in German coal and steel industries as anti-Nazi device (50% workers).

By 1974, minority representatives on boards (usually 33%) required by law in Germany, Austria, Denmark, Sweden, Holland. Upped to 50% in

Germany, 1977 (private companies with 2,000+ employees). German formula, roughly, proposed for Britain by Bullock Committee, 1977, but no legislation in sight.

Worker polls (1976) in Britain, Denmark, France showed workers do not feel it very important. Not much interest in form in Scandinavia. Many people everywhere feel it is essentially cosmetic.

EEC proposed two-tier structure: (1) 50% owners–50% workers, (2) 100% management, latter reporting to former, for all Eurocompanies in future.

Generally conceived/perceived as "communications" structure against worker "control" device; no known instance in Europe (yet) of workers on boards blocking management decisions, or seeking to.

In Britain, Germany, much publicized by press (in Britain as "industrial democracy").

Wherever present, achieved by legislative process, or national law. Opposed by Communists.

2. Works Councils

Since World War II, either through legislation or collective bargaining, works councils mandatory in all European countries in varying degrees and strengths. Stated functions: to improve company performance, working conditions, security.

In some companies, worker/union-run; in some, management chairs. Usually, mostly workers, some stewards; usually members elected democratically from workplace.

In France, where legally mandated, weak discussion groups without power. In Britain, nonmandated wide variance between weakness and strength. In Holland and Germany, where mandated, powerful and legally protected. In Scandinavia, where mandated, not considered important structures. In Italy, where not mandated, extremely powerful.

Generally, particularly Holland and Germany, growing in influence (and achievements) over factory-level management decision making, performance, and productivity.

Usually achieved, in most countries, through legislative process, or national law.

3. Shop-Floor Particiation

Other names: work place democracy, quality of work life, job enrichment.

Seminal efforts: Britain's Tavistock Institute, Norway's Work Research Institute, notably latter.

Various notions/restructuring processes designed to provide workers with greater participation in decisions affecting day-to-day performance of work.

British Work Research Unit (1974), A.N.A.C.T. in France (1974), Work Research Unit in Sweden (1977).

Unilateral (management only) "job enrichment" activities increasingly unpopular with unions, particularly in Sweden and Holland, as "union-busting"; bilateral, joint union-management participative activities, particularly in Germany, increasingly popular with both unions and managements.

German Humanization of Work Act (1974); $109,000,000 over five years for experimentation in this area. Almost no legislative mandates; almost wholly private/voluntary, wherever found.

4. Financial Participation

Other names: profit sharing with unions/workers.

Except for scarce voluntary plans, nonexistent in Europe outside France, although much discussed/advocated by unions, notably in Sweden.

Under French law (1973), most workers get nothing, the few get pittances; considered a farce.

Swedish Meidner Plan (1976) proposed giving 20% of all private profits to unions; considered a key reason for voters' ouster (1976) of Social Democrats who endorsed it.

Most proposed financial participation plans suggest laws mandating percentages of all private profits going into centrally administered fund, dominated or controlled by union confederation (e.g., Meidner Plan: Sweden). Most seen as union ploy to dominate economy over long run as profits accrue; in most, payouts to workers small or even nonexistent.

Union advocates call such plans "capitalist alternative to socialism," but voters are not buying, hence absence of legal achievements in this face.

Opposed by Communists.

5. Collective Bargaining

Still number one mainstay of industrial democracy in Europe in all countries; notably weak in France and Britain; notably strong in Germany, Holland, Italy, Belgium, and Sweden.

Worth noting: "faces" above, and laws creating same, carefully avoid any intrusion on rights of collective bargaining, or relationship thereto. Such laws, as noted, tend to provide new "social" rights; collective bargaining is (except in Italy and Sweden) economic.

In Italy, where no industrial democracy legislation exists, unions (notably powerful metal workers) have used bargaining to achieve industrial democracy gains won politically elsewhere.

In Sweden, new 1977 Democracy At Work law radically opens collective bargaining to matters traditionally considered management prerogative for first time, down to local union levels.

The Industrial Relations Setting, Organizational Forces, and the Form and Content of Worker Participation

James L. Koch
Colin L. Fox

One of the most striking phenomena in Western industrial states today is wide-spread experimentation with programs aimed at increasing worker participation in organizational decision making. These experiments, many of recent vintage, are as diverse as the causal textures (13) in which they are embedded. From a comparative, or cross national perspective, they tend to reflect institutionalized aspects of divergent industrial relations systems. Within nations, they reflect the varied socio-technical pressures and constraints of specific organizations. This article identifies factors in industrial relations systems and within organizations which might be included in a midrange theory of forces influencing the form and content of worker participation. Two forms of participation are considered—direct and indirect, in addition to three decision making content levels—technical, managerial, and institutional (32).

Industrial democracy is a multi-faceted concept. According to Bernstein (4), its elements include participation in decision making, economic return, sharing information, guaranteeing individual rights, establishing fair judicial procedures, and creating "a participatory democratic consciousness." This article is concerned with the first of these elements— participation in decision making. To the extent that these elements are

From the *Academy of Management Review*, July 1978, pp. 572–83. Reprinted by permission.

interrelated (i.e., mutually reinforcing in a systemic manner), this article has relevance to the broader issue of industrial democracy.

As Table 1 indicates, technical level participation entails workforce involvement in immediate job-related problem solving. In its indirect form, participation at this level might involve individuals influencing working conditions through elected shop stewards. Job enrichment (increasing the planning and controlling activities in a task) is an illustration of direct participation at the technical level.

Managerial or mid-level participation tends to encompass work and administrative control systems for an entire department, workshop, or factory (50). Content for shared decision making at this level includes the determination of layout, equipment specifications, work scheduling, employee selection, and raw material acquisition. Workers' councils, and, to a lesser extent, trade unions provide illustrations of indirect, or representational, participation at the managerial level. Workers' cooperatives and semi-autonomous groups are illustrations of direct participation.

TABLE 1   Forms and Content of Worker Participation

CONTENT LEVELS	FORMS OF PARTICIPATION	
	Indirect/ Representational	*Direct*[a]
Institutional (Higher Level Decisions): Overall organizational policy and strategy.	A Worker Representatives on Boards of Directors.	D Advisory influence of Hospital Physicians and Faculty Senates. Worker Cooperatives
Managerial (Mid-Level Decisions): Control/ administration of technical sub-organization.	B Workers' Councils.[b] Trade Unions.	E Semi-autonomous units—worker roles encompass department operation, staffing levels, determination of rewards (50). Scanlon Plans. Worker Cooperatives.
Technical (Job-Level Decisions): Material/ resource processing and service delivery.	C Trade Unions	F Job restructuring/ enrichment, MBO, Likert's System IV Management.

[a]Participation is considered direct at the institutional level if formal or informal processes exist to insure on-going rank-and-file influence over decisions at this level.

[b]Under some circumstances, Workers' Councils may have mechanisms which insure *direct* participation (e.g., obligatory referendums, democratic elections, rotation of worker representatives, and a participatory democratic ethos). This appears to be the case in Yugoslavia.

Worker involvement in institutional or higher level decisions has not achieved broad legitimacy in the United States, a marked contrast with developments in Europe and Scandinavia. There are a few notable exceptions, among them workers' cooperatives in the Northwest plywood industry and, the long-established custom of participation by hospital physicians and university faculties in the decision processes of their respective institutions. U.S. trade unions have had only a minor influence at this level.

THE INDUSTRIAL RELATIONS SETTING

While differences exist between nations in form and content of participation, organization theory has yet to encompass the industrial relations forces which account for these differences and to shape evolving patterns of participation. What, for example, accounts for emergence of Workers' Councils and maintenance of viable worker roles on Boards of Directors? Will these forms of participation evolve in the U.S.? These questions can best be answered by a comparative examination of industrial relations systems, the factors which reinforce their characteristics, and the transitional elements (13) which create pressure for change to more democratic/participative modes of decision making. In each of the following sections, the U.S. experience is posed against the experience of other Western Nations, and testable propositions are developed concerning the relationship between industrial relations contexts and worker participation.

The Employment Relationship: A Mirror of Dominant Values

Centers of manufacturing and mercantilism emerged in the U.S. during a period in which the country was largely unsettled and lacking in deeply-felt traditions. This enabled relations between individuals and work organizations to be shaped by the dominant values of enterprise. Waves of immigrants, seeking a stake in the U.S. economic system, were eager to people a growing factory system, and hard work was placed on a par with duty to God (48). This contrasts with the influence of industrialism in more established societies.For example, in Norway, industrialism was forced to adapt to a social ecology characterized by the long-standing traditions of independent farmers and fishermen (44).

Throughout the 18th, 19th and early 20th centuries, the economic values of individualism, private property, and competition predominated in U.S. courts. Employee efforts to influence working conditions through unionization were branded a criminal conspiracy and later an unfair form of collusion in restraint of free trade. Throughout this early period, wage earners lacked formal power or legitimate informal influence over conditions in their immediate work environment. For malcontents, the only means of seeking a better lot was through upward or geographic mobility. Both forms of mobility traditionally have been markedly more constrained in European nations, contributing to labor's more aggressive stance in seeking through industrial democracy a more classless society (3, 14).

The U.S. industrial relations system has not been shaped by the larger social purpose of a classless society but by economic values and beliefs which viewed work as a means of subsistence and material achievement. In this regard, "bread and butter" unionism has brought a fuller measure of individual well-being through such factors as job security, wage increases, and reduced working time. In contrast with Europe and Scandinavia, the U.S. labor movement has not seriously questioned management's right to manage. Most of its impact has occurred through representational processes at the technical and managerial levels of organizational decision making.

Pressure to increase direct participation is likely to come from an emergent value system which emphasizes quality of life and personal growth (7, 20, 40) over material achievement. This shift in values reflects both an intergenerational transition (20) and a broad-based secular change away from the historically rooted values and beliefs which legitimized fragmented work and hierarchical means of insuring worker compliance (7). Worker interest in *direct* participation at technical and managerial levels of organizational decision making (17) poses a threat to the traditional roles of union leaders and managers alike. Nonetheless, disparity between emergent and traditional economic values and beliefs represents a transitional element which is creating pressure to expand individual participation at all levels of organizational decision making.

P1: *The greater the inconsistency between emergent and traditional values the greater the pressure for reforms in the industrial relations system, and the greater management's interest in self-initiated experiments to increase direct participation at the technical and managerial levels.*

Union Ideologies

Trade union ideologies vary broadly between nations, and these differences have a significant influence on whether or not unions press for participation in managerial and institutional decisions (22). In Britain, the Trade Union Confederation has taken an active stance in support of nationalization of key industries and broadened forms of codetermination (3), while in France unions are the principal force in efforts to achieve the long term Marxist goal of a new society based on collective ownership. Ironically, in France, centralized industry-wide agreements, together with strong ideological conflicts between labor and management, have hampered the emergence of worker participation in managerial decisions within organizations (3).

The ideology of trade unionism in Sweden presents yet another climate for industrial relations. Despite the election of a more conservative Prime Minister, broad support exists for extending social democracy to the work place. Both blue- and white-collar trade confederations (representing 95 and 70 percent of their respective constituencies) and the Swedish Employers Confederation support broadened forms of worker participation.

The underlying ideology of U.S. unionism is far more conservative than the British, French, or Swedish examples. Trade union officials are skeptical of work reforms and would prefer to steer bargaining away from difficult-to-measure issues like variety of work, autonomy, and initiative. They tend to view job enrichment and worker participation programs as a way of exploiting workers in order to increase profits. One top union official has said: "If you want to enrich the job, enrich the pay check. The better the wage, the greater the job satisfaction. There is no better cure for the 'blue-collar blues'" (51).

With their own industrial engineering departments, unions are prepared to address concrete issues arising out of the efficiency tenets of scientific management and modern operations management. But they are far less prepared and more skeptical when it comes to the "soft" technology involved in assessing social science effectiveness criteria associated with participation.

Union officials, having come up through the ranks, have a scarcity consciousness (33). They tend to see a world of limited opportunity, a world in which securing a share of economic prosperity is more important and prudent than taking risks to fulfill higher needs. From a practical perspective, they would rather be critics than partners in management, exerting influence "almost exclusively by negotiation and grievance handling, rather than by representation on managerial bodies" (40, p. 184). Officially, the position of the AFL-CIO is that it does "not want to blur in any way the distinctions between the respective roles of management and labor in the plant" (9). But the autonomy of national and local unions in the U.S. creates the potential for considerable variance in commitment to this conservative ideology. Thus, the following proposition applies to both cross-national and within-nation differences in worker participation:

P2: *The more conservative the union ideology the more dampened the response of union leaders to rank-and-file interest in expanding participation beyond institutionalized arrangements for indirect participation at the technical and managerial levels.*

Labor Markets

Quality of work issues like participation is not of compelling interest to labor or management at times of high unemployment. The U.S. labor movement today is concerned with quantity of jobs, and expanding participation at managerial or institutional levels is far down on the list of priorities. Moreover, U.S. employers, faced with a loose labor market, have few problems in attracting sufficient labor supplies.

In Sweden and West Germany, like post–World War I Japan, chronic labor shortages have increased management interest in exploring reforms which might enhance abilities to attract and maintain a stable workforce. Since the early 1960s, these nations have periodically resorted to extensive use of guest workers for many low-skill, monotonous jobs in manufacturing. In Sweden, employer resistance to worker participation was softened by increased turnover, growing social problems in the assimilation of guest workers, and evidence that less than four percent of graduating high school students were willing to take a factory job (21).

The presence of a secondary labor market (8) in the U.S. has made it comparatively easy for management to staff monotonous dead-end jobs (although turnover is high in these positions). The large pool of unemployed and casually employed workers in secondary jobs acts like a buffer in the U.S. economy, enabling employers to transfer seasonal or cyclical peaks in demand to workers who are willing to accept low wages, poor working conditions, and little employment security. Moreover, it precludes a broad-based union interest in qualitative aspects of work such as greater self-determination.

P3: *The more closely a national economy approaches zero unemployment the greater the importance of increased workforce participation as a union goal, and the less management's resistance to this goal.*

Dominant Power of Labor in the Political Process

Although the U.S. labor movement has been very influential in the political process, it is not dominant in either party over management or capital. This is not the case in Western Europe or Scandinavia where trade unions dominate social democratic parties and where socialism or fear of socialism has tended to promote reforms aimed at increasing industrial democracy. Labor's political "clout" and its ability to win legislative reforms which extend industrial democracy into traditional management decision domains is enhanced by high degrees of unionization. Thus, political support for participation in managerial and institutional decisions is greater in Sweden where 90 percent of all workers belong to unions, West Germany (50 percent unionized) and even Great Britain (40 percent unionized) than in the U.S. (25 percent unionized).

P4: *The greater the degree of unionization the greater the scope of legally sanctioned worker participation.*

Laws and Rules of the Industrial Relations System

Scope of Bargaining Units—Representational participation in institutional decision making is fostered by broad, industry-wide bargaining units (e.g.,

Norway, Sweden, and France). Conversely, narrow bargaining structures, covering a single job category, tend to limit opportunities for participation in managerial and institutional decision.

In the U.S., the National Labor Relations Board's "community of interests" criterion has encouraged decentralized and often fragmented bargaining structures. At the job level, this has contributed to narrow and carefully defined work roles and increased potential for structural conflict between interdependent tasks. At the institutional level, this criterion has contributed to jurisdictional conflicts and reduced potential for trade unions to become a unified political force as they are in Europe. Moreover, it has forced elected union officials to focus bargaining on *quantifiable* economic outcomes where they will be subject to invidious comparisons by the rank-and-file (27).

P5: *Decentralized and fragmented wage bargaining reduces the propensity of unions to seek increased workforce participation in managerial and institutional decisions.*

Rules Influencing Change Processes—Throughout the term of a union-management contract, daily adaptations are made in work scheduling and job assignments, and major developmental programs which will significantly impact on the work place are initiated. In both day-to-day and long term changes, there is no provision in the U.S. industrial relations system for direct worker involvement in the process by which plans are formulated. A legitimate forum for participation exists at the bargaining table, but its *post hoc* nature tends to limit the options of elected representatives.

Once a contract is signed, management is free under the reserved rights doctrine to initiate changes which are within the contract's parameters. This characteristic of the U.S. industrial relations system contrasts with the case in nations where workers' councils are a mainstay or where legislation insures workforce involvement in problem solving and decision processes *throughout the course of a contract.* The following selected aspects of Swedish industrial relations law illustrate this contrast (21).

1. Works councils (since 1946) have established the principle of shop floor participation involving up to twenty members in on-going, joint explorations directed at improving productivity and job satisfaction. These groups openly share what in the U.S. would be privileged management information.

2. The 1972 "Rationalization Agreement" states that changes in production methods must be aimed at four goals, all of *equal* weight: increased productivity; increased job satisfaction; a better working environment; and job security. All such change must come about through prior consultation with employees.

3. 1973 legislation gave employees two voting memberships on Boards of Directors and restricted rights of employers to dismiss employees.

4. A 1974 law granted employee safety representatives the right to shut-down operations they believed to be dangerous.

5. A 1975 Swedish Employer Confederation–LO agreement created works council financial subcommittees with the right to examine virtually all company books and hire outside consultants for interpretation if necessary.

6. Legislation presently is pending which would provide employees the right to examine drawings of new plants and obligate employers to consider physical and psychological demands of work on the human organism.

Taken together, these provisions suggest the key role that legislated mechanisms might play in insuring viable forms of worker participation at the managerial and institutional levels. Clearly, decentralized power and the sharing of information are essential.

P6: *If institutionalized mechanisms exist to insure that power and information are shared, workers will be more likely to perceive that they have genuine influence in managerial and institutional decisions.*

Maturity of Union-Management Relations

In the early stages of bargaining relationships, goals of the two parties tend to be fixed and fundamentally in conflict. Selekman (37) described a six-state evolutionary process which ranged from an initial *containment-aggression* stage to a final *cooperation* stage. In the beginning of a bargaining relationship, his theory posits that union leaders will aggressively pursue an extended voice in company operations while management tries equally hard to keep the union in check. In an ultimate stage of maturity (cooperation), relations will stabilize and mutual problem solving may occur in matters beyond conventional distributive issues of wages, hours, and working conditions (e.g., waste, efficiency, technological change, quality of working life). Harbison and Coleman (16) also argue that union-management relations will tend to evolve toward increasing cooperation. In this stage, parties will be more likely to settle grievances without resort to arbitration; they will deemphasize crisis bargaining through frequent mutual discussions of problems at all levels; and they will be willing to engage in joint fact gathering and joint exploration of problems through study committees (30). As union-management relations mature, management will be more willing to share power and information concerning higher level decisions.

P7: *In unionized organizations, the correlation between rank and file interest in participation and actual participation will be moderated by the maturity of bargaining relationships.*

ORGANIZATIONAL FORCES

While the industrial relations context institutionalizes broad differences between nations in form and content of employee participation, equally important forces within organizations also influence patterns of employee participation. In addition to managerial values and worker attitudes, these forces include organizational size and centralization, technology, and clarity of possible payoffs from sharing power.

Interaction of Size and Centralization

Indik's (19) review of studies of participation in organizations of varying size identified a rather consistent relationship between size and feelings of alienation, impersonality, and remoteness. While individuals in large organizations express a strong desire for greater involvement in mid- and higher level decisions (17), if size is accompanied by centralized decision making, the degree to which individuals and work groups can put their ideas into practice will be greatly constrained.

Hierarchy and bureaucracy emerge out of organizational attempts to gain control over variances from desired states in core operations or processes. These classical elements of organization design facilitate unity of direction, consistency, and fairness in administration of work rules. But they can also have debilitating consequences for participation in work organizations. Robert Hoxie (18), a labor theorist, was one of the first to comment on these consequences. He argued that scientific management and bureaucracy enabled management to monopolize knowledge and prevented workers from having a clear conception of the organization's overall activities. In this way, Hoxie contended, management could exercise complete control over workers' activities.

P8: *Large, centralized organizations limit the potential for direct participation in technical, managerial and institutional decision processes and increase employee interest in seeking representational participation through trade unions.*

Technology

Direct participation in technical and managerial decisions is far more important to the individual than representational forms of participation at the institutional level (12, 17). Nonetheless, participation in decisions which have an immediate impact on the individual's day-to-day work activities is often constrained by technology.

Contingency theories posit that organizational structure, authority relationships, and amounts of participation are a function of technology (6, 29, 52). According to Perrow (34), the latitude for participation is greatest in nonroutine technologies. Nonuniformity in raw materials and high variability in transformation processes tends to encourage broader task scope. Thus, workers in nonroutine jobs will tend to have a higher degree of influence due to the responsibility and autonomy associated with their work roles.

Individuals in interdependent tasks also may have greater opportunities for participation. Reciprocal interdependence necessitates coordination through feedback (45), and this tends to open channels of communication both laterally and vertically. As with nonroutine technologies, reciprocal task interdependence tends to encourage flexible, decentralized work structures (e.g., education, counseling, medical services).

By contrast, routine technologies tend to result in narrow, regimented tasks. In these tasks, the individual has very little influence over work pace and working methods and lacks a clear conception of overall operations. In addition, supervisory styles, one way communications, and other facets of organizational climate which characterize routine technologies are generally not conducive to direct participation at any decision level.

P9: *Opportunities for direct participation at the technical and managerial levels are greatest in nonroutine technolgies.*

Conceptualizations of Control

Scientific management and human relations approaches have been used more extensively in the U.S. than in Western Europe or Scandinavia as means of further legitimizing management's authority and control (14). Human relations interventions have tended to accept existing work and authority structures as a given and endeavored to make them more palatable by improving the organizational climates which surround them. Significantly, recent efforts to increase employee participation in managerial decisions through job and work system redesign have been described by U.S. managers as "experiments" (14). As with earlier human relations interventions, where these programs are imposed by management, they are more likely to increase management's control than to result in shared influence (46).

Managers who conceptualize control as a function of rationality, unilateral decision making, and centralization tend to reinforce dependencies on hierarchical administrative structures and standardized operating procedures. They may also lack confidence in the ability of employees to exercise responsibility and good judgment, a factor which has been associated with the failure of some Scanlon Plans (36). For these managers, control is a zero sum concept; if the share at lower levels is enlarged, management's own share is reduced. This orientation can be contrasted with normative models of management which view control as an additive factor. These models suggest that control which is exercised at lower system levels actually facilitates control of the larger organization (1, 2, 5, 25, 28, 31, 35, 38, 41, 43). As Strauss and Rosenstein argued, this nonzero-sum conceptualization of control supports the view that participation is "another forum for the resolution of conflict as well as another means by which management can induce compliance with its directives" (39, p. 198).

P10: *Within organizations, the propensity to share influence and power with employees will be greatest at those levels where managers perceive participation as a means of increasing control over system variances and improving overall operating effectiveness.*

Worker Attitudes: Self-Investment in Occupational Roles

Significant differences in work-related self-investment exist between occupational groups. Among industrial workers work is not a central life interest, neither is it a source of primary relationships (1), nor the most important basis of self-esteem (10). This contrasts with the case for professionals who tend to be deeply committed and involved in their occupational roles (24).

According to Dubin, individuals in routine jobs with early career ceilings tend to adjust to these otherwise debilitating work roles by becoming neutral and indifferent. This was illustrated in Walker and Guest's (47) classic depth interviews of assembly line workers. These workers voiced their disdain for mass production characteristics (mechanical pacing, repetitiveness, minimum skill requirements, etc.), but indicated a willingness to accept these conditions to obtain the higher pay levels afforded by work on auto assembly lines.

P11: *Factors associated with higher personal status (e.g., skill levels, professionalism, occupational or organizational identification, and occupational communities) increase worker pressure for direct and indirect forms of participation at all decision levels.*

The Clarity of Possible Payoffs

Improvements in work satisfaction and economic or operating effectiveness gains are both possible payoffs which might be associated with participation. But empirical evidence on both counts is weak. Evidence linking satisfaction with participation is based largely upon correlational studies in which perceived participation and satisfaction have been correlated (38). Results from field experiments are far less conclusive (7, 12, 15, 23, 26). Although subjects indicate a reluctance to return to nonparticipative methods once they have had an opportunity to influence mid- or higher-level decisions, they do not necessarily express greater satisfaction when objective increases in participation occur at these levels (23, 42).

Evidence on economic improvements through participation in mid- and higher level decisions is also sparse. In the U.S., Donnelly Mirrors is often referred to as one of the long standing success stories, but even in this case evidence is largely anecdotal. Quantified results from field experiments with longitudinal control group designs are conspicuously absent from the literature. Surprisingly, Europe's extensive *Mitbestimmung* or codetermination phenomenon has also failed to provide concrete evidence of real payoffs (11). This lack of clarity concerning differential consequences of alternatives for increasing participation necessitates use of inspiration as a basis for taking action to increase employee influence (45). It requires a systemic appreciation of overlooked alternatives to conventional work arrangements. It also demands availability of internal O.D. skills, an organizational change which encourages innovation, and a reward system which recognizes managers for their efforts to enhance participation.

P12: *The greater the critical mass of supporting organizational development skills and the greater the organization's rewards for innovation in managerial processes the greater the likelihood of significant employee participation at all decision levels.*

CONCLUSION

Whyte (49) argued that job enrichment, with its narrow focus on task design, should be viewed only as a first step in reforming the nature of work. This stage, in his view, must be followed by reassessments of total organizational reward systems and a redefinition of the individual's role to include fuller participation in higher management decisions. Others have argued that the contemporary cultural, social, and psychological milieu is greatly increasing the external pressure experienced by union officials and managers. Even where broadened models of participation have a long history (for example, in West Germany, Yugoslavia, and Israel Kibbutzim), discrepancies still remain between desired and perceived amounts of participation (42).

Will Scandinavian or European models of codetermination diffuse in the U.S.? Not in the present industrial relations setting. Labor lacks the political clout to establish enabling legislation, and such a movement would be inconsistent with its present ideologies and goals. With high unemployment, rank and file pressure for job security has, for the moment, supplanted concern for job quality. Moreover, the self-realization values which emerged in the 1960s and which appeared to compel the U.S. society toward broader models of industrial democracy are constrained in some organizations by entrenched attributes of advanced industrialism (see Figure 1).

U.S. industrialism has crystallized many aspects of the social fabric: large scale urbanization; hardened union-management relations; and a separation of work and non-work roles. In this context, self-realization values for most employees tend to be channeled in the direction of non-

Industrial Relations Setting

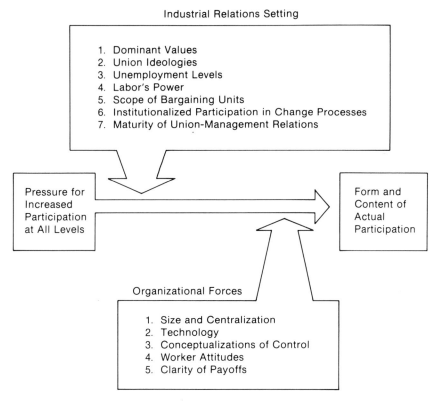

Figure 1 The Industrial Relations Setting, Organizational Forces, and the Form and Content of Worker Participation

work activities. They work in fragmented jobs, in bureaucratically and hierarchically controlled organizations. Representation on works councils or boards of directors will not change this.

From a labor market perspective, U.S. employers are in a far more favorable position than their counterparts in European or Scandinavian countries. With high levels of unemployment and a large pool of workers trapped in secondary labor markets, there is little reason to support mid- and higher-level models of participation as a means of attracting a work force. Moreover, with one in eight Americans below the poverty level in 1975 (U.S. Census Bureau) and serious problems in restoring full employment, worker alienation is not a priority social issue.

For those who have jobs, an instrumental orientation toward work has been institutionalized by our industrial relations system. Contract clauses have tended to strengthen narrow job jurisdictions and to become yet another layer of bureaucracy in the employment relationship. Moreover, fragmented bargaining structures make it politically untenable for union officers to compromise quantifiable economic gains for "soft" quality of life improvements. It is on the former issue that their effectiveness will be assessed by the rank-and-file members who elect them. From a pragmatic perspective, collective bargaining and protection of rights through grievance procedures represent tested forms of industrial democracy. The benefits and risks of participation in higher level decisions are unknown.

There is also a welter of factors within organizations which constrain prospects for employee participation in mid- and higher level decisions. Centralization and routine technologies greatly narrow the latitude for meaningful participation, and zero sum conceptualizations of control erode legitimacy of efforts to share influence. As a part of the overall gestalt, these and other organizational characteristics make it difficult for employees in many occupational groups to conceive of increasing their levels of self-investment in work roles.

In this general milieu, there are "pockets" within which enabling conditions may exist to support experiments in much broader forms of worker participation. In less centralized organizations, and in more autonomous work units or agencies, potential for meaningful mid-level participation exists. If these organizations employ nonroutine technologies, more organic and participative structures are likely to be an important key to organizational effectiveness. Finally, where self-investment in occupational roles is high, there will continue to be pressure to increase opportunities for participation in mid- and higher level decisions. Whether durable organizational innovations will be fashioned in these contexts remains to be seen.

REFERENCES

1. ARGYLE, MICHAEL. *The Social Psychology of Work* (Great Britain: Penguin Books, 1974).

2. ARGYRIS, CHRIS. *Integrating the Individual and the Organization* (New York: Wiley, 1964).

3. BARKIN, SOLOMON. (Ed.) *Worker Militancy and Its Consequences, 1965–75* (New York: Praeger Publishers, 1975).

4. BERNSTEIN, PAUL. *Workplace Democratization: Its Internal Dynamics* (Kent State University Press, 1976).

5. BLAKE, ROBERT, and JANE S. MOUTON. *The Managerial Grid* (Houston, Texas: Gulf, 1964).

6. BURNS, TOM, and G. M. STALKER. *The Management of Innovation* (London: Oxford University Press, 1965).

7. DAVIS, LOUIS E., and ALBERT CHERNS. *The Quality of Working Life Vol. 1 & 2* (New York: The Free Press, 1975).

8. DOERINGER, PETER B., and MICHAEL J. PIORE. *Internal Labor Markets & Manpower Analysis* (Lexington, Mass.: D.C. Heath and Company, 1971).

9. DONAHUE, THOMAS R. "Collective Bargaining, Codetermination, and the Quality of Work," *World of Work Report,* Vol. 1 (August 1976), 1, 6–7.

10. DUBIN, ROBERT, JOSEPH E. CHAMPOUX, and LYMAN W. PORTER. "Central Life Interests and Organizational Commitment of Blue-Collar and Clerical Workers," *Administrative Science Quarterly,* Vol. 20 (1975), 411–421.

11. ELLIS, HARRY B. "Workers on the Board: Productivity Help or Hindrance?" *The Christian Science Monitor* (May 18, 1977).

12. EMERY, FRED E., and D. E. THORSRUD. *Form and Content in Industrial Democracy* (London: Tavistock Publications, 1969).

13. EMERY, FRED E., and ERIC L. TRIST. "The Causal Texture of Organizational Environments," *Human Relations,* Vol. 18 (1965), 21–32.

14. FOY, NANCY, and HERMAN GADON. "Worker Participation: Contrasts in Three Countries," *Harvard Business Review,* Vol. 54 (1976), 71–83.

15. GOLEMBIEWSKI, ROBERT, KEITH BILLINGSLEY, and SAMUEL YEAGER. "Measuring Change and Persistence in Human Affairs: Types of Change Generated by O. D. Designs," *Journal of Applied Behavioral Science,* Vol. 12 (1976), 133–157.

16. HARBISON, FREDERICK H., and JOHN R. COLEMAN. *Goals and Strategy in Collective Bargaining* (New York: Harper & Row, 1951).

17. HESPIE, GEORGE, and TOBY WALL. "The Demand for Participation Among Employees," *Human Relations,* Vol. 27 (1976), 411–428.

18. HOXIE, ROBERT F. *Scientific Management and Labor* (New York: D. Appleton, 1915).

19. INDIK, B. P. "Organization Size and Member Participation: Some Empirical Tests of Alternative Explanations," *Human Relations,* Vol. 18 (1965), 339–349.

20. INGLEHART, RONALD. *The Silent Revolution: Changing Values and Political Styles Among Western Publics* (Princeton University Press, 1977).

21. JENKINS, DAVID (Ed.) *Job Reform in Sweden* (Stockholm: Swedish Employers' Confederation, 1975).

22. KERR, CLARK, JOHN T. DUNLOP, FREDERICK HARBISON, and CHARLES A. MYERS. *Industrialism and Industrial Man* (Cambridge: Harvard University Press, 1960).

23. KOCH, JAMES L. "Effects of Feedback on Job Attitudes and Work Behavior: A Field Experiment," *Technical Report No. 6* (Eugene, Ore.: Office of Naval Research and University of Oregon, 1976).

24. KORNHAUSER, WILLIAM. *Scientists in Industry* (Berkeley: University of California Press; Institute of Industrial Relations, 1962).

25. LIKERT, RENSIS. *The Human Organization: Its Management and Value* (New York: McGraw-Hill, 1967).

26. LISCHERON, J. A., and T. D. WALL. "Employee Participation: An Experimental Field Study," *Human Relations,* Vol. 28 (1975), 863–884.

27. MARSHALL, F. RAY, ALLAN M. CARTTER, and ALLAN KING. *Labor Economics, Wages, Employment, and Trade Unionism,* 3rd Ed. (Homewood, Illinois: Richard D. Irwin, 1976).

28. MCGREGOR, DOUGLAS. *The Human Side of Enterprise* (New York: McGraw-Hill, 1960).

29. MOBERG, DENNIS, and JAMES L. KOCH. "A Critical Appraisal of Integrated Treatments of Contingency Findings," *Academy of Management Journal*, Vol. 18 (1975), 109–124.

30. National Center for Productivity and Quality of Working Life. *Recent Initiatives in Labor-Management Cooperation* (Washington: U.S. Government Printing Office, 1976).

31. ODIORNE, GEORGE. *Management by Objectives* (New York: Pitman, 1965).

32. PARSONS, TALCOTT. *Structure and Process in Modern Societies* (New York: Free Press, 1960).

33. PERLMAN, SELIG. *A Theory of the Labor Movement* (New York: Augustus M. Kelley, 1949).

34. PERROW, CHARLES. "A Framework for the Comparative Analysis of Organizations," *American Sociological Review*, Vol. 32 (1967), 195–208.

35. PORTER, LYMAN, EDWARD E. LAWLER, and J. HACKMAN. (Eds.), *Behavior in Organizations* (New York: McGraw-Hill, 1975).

36. RUH, ROBERT A., ROBERT L. WALLACE, and CARL F. FROST. *Management Attitudes and the Scanlon Plan* (Lansing, Mich.: Midwest Scanlon Associates and the Michigan State University, 1972).

37. SELEKMAN, BENJAMIN M. *Labor Relations and Human Relations* (New York: McGraw-Hill, 1947).

38. STEERS, RICHARD M. *Organizational Effectiveness: A Behavioral View* (Santa Monica, Calif.: Goodyear, 1977).

39. STRAUSS, GEORGE, and ELIEZER ROSENSTEIN. "Worker Participation: A Critical View," *Industrial Relations*, Vol. 9 (1970), 197–214.

40. STURMTHAL, ADOLPH. "Workers' Participation in Management: A Review of United States Experience," *International Institute for Labor Studies, Bulletin 6* (Geneva, Switzerland: June 1969), pp. 149–186.

41. TANNENBAUM, ARNOLD S. *Control in Organizations* (New York: McGraw-Hill, 1968).

42. TANNENBAUM, ARNOLD S., BOGDAN KAVCIC, MENACHEM ROSNER, MINO VIANELLO, and GEORG WIESER. *Hierarchy in Organizations: An International Comparison* (San Francisco: Jossey-Bass, 1974).

43. TANNENBAUM, ROBERT, and WARREN SCHMIDT. "How to Choose a Leadership Pattern," *Harvard Business Review*, Vol. 51 (1973), 162–180.

44. THORSRUD, D. E. *Workers' Participation in Management in Norway* (Geneva, Switzerland: Institute for Labor Studies, 1972).

45. THOMPSON, JAMES D. *Organizations in Action* (New York: McGraw-Hill, 1967).

46. TICHY, NOEL M., and JAY N. NISBERG. "When Does Work Restructuring Work? Organizational Innovations at Volvo and G.M.," *Organizational Dynamics*, Vol. 5 (1976), 63–80.

47. WALKER, CHARLES, and ROBERT GUEST. *The Man on the Assembly Line* (Boston: Harvard University Press, 1952).

48. WEBER, MAX. *The Protestant Ethic and the Spirit of Capitalism*. Translated by Talcott Parsons (New York: Charles Scribner's Sons, 1958).

49. WHYTE, WILLIAM F. "Organizations for the Future," in Gerald Somers (Ed.), *The*

Next Twenty-Five Years of Industrial Relations (Madison: Industrial Relations Research Association, 1973), 129–140.

50. WILD, RAY. *Work Organization* (London: John Wiley & Sons, 1975).

51. WINPISINGER, WILLIAM W. "Job Satisfaction: A Union Response," *AFL-CIO American Federationist,* Vol. 79 (1972), 1–7.

52. WOODWARD, JOAN. *Industrial Organization: Theory and Practice* (London: Oxford University Press, 1965).

Workplace Democratization: The Case of the U.S. Plywood Industry

Paul Bernstein

Eighteen plywood manufacturing firms in Oregon and Washington are fully owned by their employees and to varying degrees, are also managed by them. These companies make up about one-eighth of the American plywood industry. They range in size from 80 to 450 owner-workers and in gross annual earnings from $3 million to $15 million. They range from nineteen to thirty-three years of continuous operation.

FOUNDING OF WORKER-OWNED FIRMS

The first, Olympia Plywood, was founded in 1921. A group of lumbermen, carpenters, and mechanics pooled their resources and built a plant by their own labor in Olympia, Washington. Most of the workers were heirs

Adapted by permission of Paul Bernstein, Workplace Democratization: Its Internal Dynamics (Edison, N.J.: Trans-action Books, 1978).

to a Scandinavian tradition of cooperative enterprise, common to that immigrant population of the Pacific Northwest. To assemble the materials and to purchase a site, the 125 workmen had to contribute $1,000 each, which they raised by cashing in savings bonds, borrowing from friends, pledging future wages, or mortgaging personal property. In return for their individual contribution each worker received by contract a share in the new company entitling him to employment, and an equal vote in directing all company affairs. The company commenced manufacture in August with workers electing a board of directors from their own number to manage affairs, although the whole body of workers frequently reassembled to receive information on the state of the enterprise and to set policy in matters that immediately affected them, such as pay. After the initial sacrifice, the company prospered. Plywood was then a relatively new industry with a steadily increasing demand, and Olympia quickly developed a reputation for high-quality products. Three other worker-owned companies were established just before World War II in much the same way. They, too, found a ready market for plywood, which was being further boosted by wartime demand.

A few years after the war a private plywood company became the first to convert to worker-ownership. As the market price of plywood was then declining and there were problems getting logs, the owner of Oregon-Washington Plywood Co. in Tacoma decided to sell his business. A few workers in this firm were aware of the four successful worker-owned mills and began a campaign to convince their fellow employees to buy the company. Though raising the money would be a hardship and the project itself risky, about three-fifths of the firm's employees pledged their support. The original owner not only agreed to the arrangement, but even offered to stay on as sales broker for the first six months.

Again, $1,000 was the sum set for each member to contribute. Since more than twice that amount was needed to buy the company, each worker bought a second share on time. The new shareowners also decided to lower their wages to create operating capital for the first few months. The market price of plywood continued to decline during the first year, and the going was rough. But the men worked hard and were willing to defer payment of part of their wages. The next year brought a boom market for plywood, and the company, renamed North-Pacific Plywood, Inc., has prospered ever since.

Indeed, the ability of worker-owned mills to survive the severe price-swings characteristic of the plywood market helped lead to the creation of over twenty worker-owned companies by the mid-fifties. Shares of the prewar firms had risen in value from the initial $1,000 to $40,000 or $50,000 and this gave other workers more confidence in their ability to buy and successfully operate closed or bankrupt conventional firms. Some nonworkers became attracted to the idea too, and a curious new breed of business promoter cropped up. These promoters arranged the establishment of worker-owned companies, taking a cut of the profits as their service fee. Some of the agent-created companies quickly failed, and a few agents were taken to court for fraud. The resulting scandal somewhat cooled local ardor for launching any more worker-owned firms. After 1955, none seem to have been founded.

SYSTEM OF SELF-GOVERNMENT

The organization of the plants varies from one to another, but all reflect the same general process. Employee-shareholders meet annually to select from their own number a board of directors (which could just as accurately be termed a workers' council). The board makes most policy decisions, but its power is checked by the whole group: for example, expenditures over $25,000 must be approved by the entire membership of the company. Similarly, any major decision to invest, build a subsidiary plant, borrow a large sum of money, open a sales contract, or sell a sizable asset must be voted on by all the workers. In some companies the rank-and-file can challenge a board decision by collecting a petition of 10 to 20 percent of the membership and calling a special shareholders' meeting to decide the issue.

A president, vice-president, and secretary-treasurer are also elected yearly. In several mills, the president is the worker who received the most votes in the board election. The elections themselves seem to be partly a popularity contest, partly the selection of genuine business-leadership talent, and partly an expression of task-group friendships. This last factor means there are representatives on the board from different parts of the productive process. This is true in many mills and is usually considered by managers to be an advantage. It gives them an accurate picture of opinion throughout the company and makes it easier to circulate information back to every task group. Also, managers expressed satisfaction in the interviews that this mechanism allows each group to learn directly from each other about problems of the plant, rather than having to be told by the managers themselves.

The board of directors appoints a general manager to coordinate day-to-day affairs. He is the company's expert on business matters and usually comes from outside the firm. The rest of the administrative staff consists of a plant supervisor, sales manager, logs purchaser, accountant, shipping expediter, and their assistants, usually all shareowners.

The governing process in the mills is based on a circular pattern of authority (see Figure 1). The workers hire the manager, set his salary, and make all decisions on company expansion, modernization, diversification, and so forth. Yet on a day-to-day basis they work under the manager's direction. The directors, elected by their fellow workers, receive neither deference nor extra pay, and continue to work in the plant while serving on the board. Thus it becomes impossible for them to avoid suggestions from other workers. Several directors commented on the number of times they are "told off" by their fellow workers in the course of the week. Worker-owners feel free to walk into the general manager's office as well, with complaints and suggestions. If for some reason he is not available, they can ask the company president, a fellow worker, to speak to the manager for them. In contrast to many political democracies, participation remains at a high level after elections.

Of course, some workers are more involved than others. These workers feel a strong responsibility to make the company succeed; they learn all they can about the company's problems; and they run for director. Others who are known to be talented refuse to take on leadership responsibility.

"Why bother? It's too much of a hassle," is their attitude. A good number of workers feel incapable of being leaders and offer only a suggestion or two. Almost all, however, feel willing to complain to any director or officer. Finally, there are some worker-owners who do not participate at all. They consider their company to be like any other mill except that it provides more take-home pay. On the whole, then, the worker-owned mill exhibits a gradation in participation and political maturity somewhat like that reported by political scientists for political democracies in general: a proportion of activists, a proportion of "occasionals" and a proportion of "apathetic." Also the flow of criticism upwards is strikingly greater in these mills and the sense of alienation from top decisions that is common in regular politics is almost entirely absent.

To supplement the informal communication network where worker-directors talk with their friends back on the production line, company issues are presented to shareowners in more formal ways. In the most concerned companies, monthly reports are sent to each worker's home. These reports give the company's profit-and-loss statement, its output, inventory, sales situation, and other crucial economic transactions usually reserved for top executives in the standard corporation. In less diligent worker-owned firms, a shorter statement is prepared quarterly and left in a stack on a table for interested workers to pick up. Reports from the twice-monthly board meetings are posted in most companies. At year's end the company financial statement is circulated to all worker-owners, and in at least one firm, a complete audit is mailed to each member, revealing exactly what has been paid to every other member of the firm.

Members report that they had no trouble being prepared for a general shareholders' meeting. Even if the agenda were not printed up, everyone knew what matters were at hand. "Regular talk in the plant is about the company," they reported.

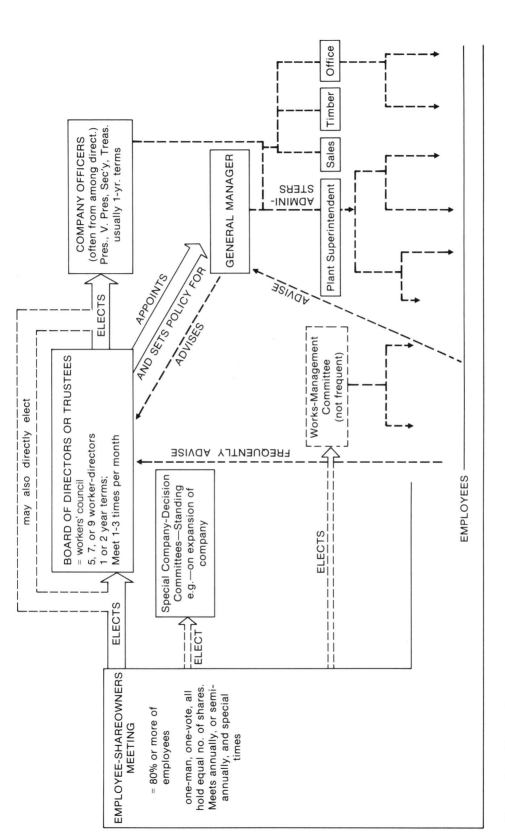

Figure 1 Flows of Authority and Communication in Worker-Managed Plywood Firms (Reprinted by permission from Bernstein, 1976, p. 16.)

Much of the success or failure of the worker-owned mill depends upon the general manager. He needs both sound business sense and the ability to present his viewpoint convincingly to the directors. His relationship with the members affects their motivation in the mill as workers. It also affects their flexibility and wisdom in making long-run business decisions as owners.

Many a manager has found himself caught between the workers' wants and his own judgment of what is best for the firm. He must deal with a basic tension between the workers' interests as wage-earners and their interests as owners. The first interest focuses on the short-run: "Give me my income now—as big a share of this year's surplus as possible." The other interest is long-term; for example: "We must reserve fifty to sixty percent of this year's surplus to purchase timberland so we'll have an assured supply of raw material in years to come."

Another tension exists between the workers' expertise about their specific jobs in the plant and their minimal knowledge about outside factors to be considered in collective decisions. Generally, leaders' complaints reflected this particular contradiction of interests:

"It's hard to follow a good business practice in this company. The share-owners take a limited approach to things."

"Our firm needs to learn how good businesses can grow. Expansion is virtually nil in most worker-owned mills. The men want to work with what's closest to them. For instance, they've never entertained the thought of going beyond plywood (into other wood products)."

"The men are too conservative about going into debt. They resist borrowing funds for plant improvement even after they agree that the upgrading should be done. They'd rather wait until we had enough cash on hand to pay for it."

"The workers need to learn the value of risk-taking."

Two methods are relied upon to solve this problem. One is for the manager to show the workers clearly how their short-run interests depend on the firm's long-run investment. The other is to have many workers learn the facts of business directly by becoming directors. "I think every worker should be elected to the board at least once," remarked one old man in overalls, working by a board conveyor. "I was a director once, and really learned the problems of the company." A manager agrees: "There's a tremendous increase in the individual worker's understanding of business just from serving on the board."

PRODUCTIVITY

In spite of such difficulties the firms prosper. Evidently, considerable forces of productivity are released by the self-management process which can outweigh the inefficiencies of semi-amateur management. Worker-owned mills have demonstrated their higher productivity compared to conventionally owned firms in the following ways:

1. Workers' collectives have many times taken bankrupt or losing private plywood firms and converted them into successful enterprises.

2. Worker-owned firms' output averaged 115–120 square feet of plywood per man-hour in contrast to conventional firms' 80–95 square feet, during the 1950s. During the 1960s, they were producing 170 square feet per man-hour compared to 130 square feet for conventional firms.

3. When worker-owned firms were challenged by the Internal Revenue Service for paying their members higher than industry-level wages and for deducting those as labor costs, the companies were able to demonstrate to the satisfaction of the IRS auditor and the tax court judges that these higher wages were justified by their workers' 25 to 60

percent greater productivity than the plywood industry's average.

4. In general, worker-owned mills operate at a higher percentage of capacity than do conventional mills.

5. Whenever the entire industry has suffered from a slump in demand and private firms have thus had to lay off workers, worker-owned firms have been able to keep their men on the job. (They have thereby added to "social productivity" also, by saving state agencies or the community the burden of paying out unemployment compensation, and by sparing their workers' families the interpersonal problems that can accompany unemployment).

Motivations behind this greater productivity are apparent in the attitudes of members, as expressed in these comments:

"When the mill is your own, you really work hard to make a go of it."

"Everyone digs right in—and wants the others to do the same. If they see anybody trying to get a free ride, they get on his back right quick."

"Group pressure here is more powerful than any foreman could be."

"If a guy held back, he didn't feel right. Actually, he was stealing from the others."

Thus pride of ownership motivates the majority to produce more than hired workers, and mutual supervision keeps potential laggards from lowering the standard.

The effect of the self-management system on supervision and productivity is demonstrated by the experience of a firm whose worker-owners recently sold their company to a large conglomerate. Under the new owner, eight more foremen are needed, though there are 100 fewer workers. The plant superintendent, who had worked under both systems, was asked if there were any differences now that the firm was no longer worker-owned:

"Oh, certainly, people were eager then. They were more efficient. You could depend on them to stay often beyond five o'clock. Nobody worried about time—their aim was just to finish the product."

The workers expressed similar feelings:

"Before a guy took real pride in his work. Now we come just for the money."

"The men used to boast about their output. Now no one cares."

EARNINGS

Because their roots are in a cooperative, egalitarian philosophy, the plywood mills pay all members an equal wage: floor-sweeper, skilled panel-finisher, and accountant alike. Since certain jobs may take longer than others, or a machine may be shut down for repairs and put someone off work for a few hours, a sophisticated system of record-keeping has evolved to equalize the final take-home pay. Every week or month a person's hours at work are totaled and whoever has less than the standard is given first bid for weekend work to bring his total pay up to equality. He need not actually work then if he prefers not to, but he must be offered the opportunity. Likewise, those whose weekly or monthly totals exceed that period's standard must reduce their hours during the next period to the level which allows for equal income.

Highly skilled workers sometimes resent not receiving more pay than men who do the simplest jobs in the firm. And some members regard equal wages as unrealistic, especially because in low-profit years a few workers may leave the company for higher paying jobs elsewhere. (In those years the fixed wage of the highest non-scale job in other plants may be better than the variable wage in a hard-hit worker-owned mill.) In order not to lose men in bad years from certain crucial jobs such as electrician or mechanic, some firms have made these into nonowner positions. Members are hired for those posts at higher salaries than the egalitarian pay. However, most worker-owners are reluctant to create hired, salaried jobs, so the practice is strictly limited to a few positions, most often the general manager.

During all but the worst market times, average pay is almost always higher in worker-owned plywood companies than in other firms, not only on an hourly basis (which usually averages twenty-five percent higher) but also because of the year-end division of the profits. The latter has run to several thousand dollars per person in good years. Sometimes a portion of the bonus is retained in a pension fund, managed by a bank to increase its value. Sometimes a portion is converted into certificates used by the company to generate significant amounts of capital, in effect borrowing from its worker-owners. The certificates are redeemable within three to ten years, paying four to eight percent interest. And finally, each worker receives the full value of his share when he leaves the company, either by selling it to an incoming worker or to the company itself. Such shares typically bring in $20,000 to $40,000.

There are other material benefits as well for worker-owners, which vary somewhat from firm to firm: free lunches in the company's own restaurant; full medical care, including dental and eye care, and coverage for each family, the workers' own gasoline supply at wholesale prices; and company-paid life insurance. All of these fringe benefits were obtained years before unions were able to secure just a few of them for workers in regular plywood mills.

Cooperation in these firms includes the freedom to take time off when needed. From one day to three months can be requested in addition to the worker's paid vacation. The requests are usually granted because the flexibility of work assignments in the firm allows other workers to take over the missing person's responsibilities. The only restriction is that he not use his time off for moonlighting because then he would be violating one basic obligation of his stock-ownership: to contribute equal labor to the common enterprise.

One complaint in the firms is that the older workers do not, in effect, live up to this obligation because they are kept on beyond their usefulness to the company. Retirement is not compulsory, and the employment of older members who are less efficient is criticized by some as a form of featherbedding. Of course, one might regard the employment of older workers who want to continue working to be far more humane than the forced retirement characteristic of conventional companies. Workers in the plywood firms can continue their life-long trade among close friends during their last years instead of being forced into involuntary idleness.

THE NON-OWNING WORKER

In addition to using one or two highly paid, nonowning, skilled workers, many mills employ ordinary workers on a much larger scale. This practice seems contrary to their egalitarian philosophy. The number of these nonowning workers varies from season to season and from firm to firm. It can be as high as a third of a mill's workforce, but most often it is around 10 or 15 percent. Some of the hired employees are sons or sons-in-law of current shareowners, interested in temporary employment during the vacation months and not in ownership. A few others were considered too old when they joined to be able to complete payments on a share before retirement. Others are temporary workers hired during peak-demand seasons, who then stay with the company for years if the sales level stays higher than when they were first hired.

The most basic reason nonowning workers are not brought in as equal partners is that shareowners fear their stock must be devalued in order to add more shareowners to the fixed asset-value of the firm. High demand for a job at the mill can drive the price higher than that minimum value, which accounts for the prices cited earlier. "You'd be cutting the melon into thinner slices," explained one worker. For this reason worker-owners prefer to let a new person purchase a share only when a current member leaves. A second major reason for the accumulation of nonowning workers is that sometimes, even when a share is available, a job-seeker cannot afford it. A down payment of $2,000 at least is normally required, and there is a monthly deduction from wages to complete the purchase of a share. These installments can run $150 to $250 per month for up to ten years.

A third group of nonowning workers are hired on at special plants at forest sites. At these plants logs are cut into thin sheets of veneer, the first step in plywood manufacture. Worker-owned companies seem always to have treated their veneer plants as subsidiaries, never having opted for multiple-plant democracy or for a federation of self-governing plants. A few share-owners are stationed at these forest mills as supervisors, but the remainder of the workforce are hired hands.

Non-owning employees at the plywood companies do not receive the same fixed, egalitarian wage as shareowners; they are paid according to the prevailing industry-wide union scale. However, they usually enjoy the same fringe benefits as shareowners: paid holidays, life insurance, medical plans, and a Christmas bonus. And they have the same physical working conditions. Nevertheless, they cannot participate in any of the firm's self-government. The other workers are their bosses, not partners, and usually they are not protected by a union.

PROBLEMS OF CONTINUITY

At least twenty-six worker-owned mills have been in operation, but today there are only eighteen. What happened to the others?

Two failed economically, one because the former parent company reneged on its agreement to set up a national sales organization for the fledgling enterprise. Another relied too heavily on a self-aggrandizing general manager, and by the time the worker-directors realized what he was doing, they were unable to rescue the firm from bankruptcy.

Aside from economic failures, there are three or four worker-owned firms whose demise was caused ironically by their economic success. These firms continue as prosperous plywood mills but are no longer self-managed. Their worker-owners, nearing retiring age, sold their firms to conglomerates, to convert their individual share values into cash, and as a result transformed their cooperatives into standard corporations.

Successful firms are the most vulnerable to this, because their high value keeps the price of their shares high, out of the reach of most workers seeking employment yet within the range of big corporations who can offer to purchase many shares at once. This may be the only effective offer received by the members in a long time. Thus, wealthy conglomerates like ITT and the Times-Mirror Corporation have been attracted by the success of prosperous plywood firms and have made offers as high as $100,000 for each individual worker's share.

Even in companies where a majority of shareowners are not ready to retire, there may be incentive to accept a corporate offer. The higher price of shares in successful companies often means that each individual who does buy in must take a longer time to complete payment on his share. When a large number of shareowners are on such time-payments, they may see a generous takeover offer as an opportunity to be relieved of further payments and even to make a substantial profit. When this "unpaid-up" faction is added to those nearing retirement, a majority of shareowners may wish to accept a conglomerate's offer. A third factor in workers' decisions is the fluctuating price of plywood; for example, two firms were sold after the two-year slump of 1967–1968 had put real hardships on the worker-owners. Thus, three of the oldest and most successful worker-owned mills have sold out to larger corporations (in 1954, 1969 and 1970). The life-span of each was about thirty years.

Despite their general laxity about corporate takeovers, the worker-owned mills have given careful attention to ensuring their continuity insofar as sale of shares to individuals is concerned. In all the firms it is a basic rule that the company has first option to buy the share when an individual member decides to sell. If the company declines the option and the member finds a buyer, the board of directors still has the right to veto the new person. "After all," one president explained, "we're not just hiring; we're taking on a new partner."

Additionally, most companies have an informal trial period for new members. They are taken around the plant to work at various jobs alongside as many shareholders as possible. Some firms also put great store in having prospective members "sponsored," by being a friend or relative of a current (or outgoing) member. In firms that are not very careful in their selection procedures, one heard complaints about the younger generation: "They're not hard workers. They've grown up in the affluent era and don't have the same attitudes about the value of work." Younger people who were hard-working, however, were quickly recognized and respected.

The foregoing remarks refer only to the continuity of existing firms. Why have no new firms been added since the mid-1950s? One reason is that to start a new mill has become economically more difficult. The price of plywood is no longer steadily rising; instead, it cycles drastically. Over the same period the cost of the raw material, timber logs, has soared, and other employment has become available in the area (in particular, the aerospace and electronics industries).

No longer are there community leaders or business agents offering to organize worker-owned mills. And perhaps the present generation is less willing than the past one to sacrifice a decent income during the two to four years of hardship usually required to get a self-managed mill fully underway.

Although there are a few leaders in these mills who expressed a desire to see their form of self-management spread, most worker-owners view their company not as a specimen of self-government to be preserved for its own sake, but primarily as a means for their own livelihood. There have been one or two instances of a new worker-owned mill spinning off from a parent collective, but no general procedure has been developed by the worker-owned mills for significant proliferation.

MANAGERIAL IMPLICATIONS OF THE PLYWOODS EXAMPLE

The unique experience of these worker self-managed firms in the United States has made evident the possibilities for advanced democratization of the workplace. The following factors characterize these alternative organizations and the context which facilitated their development:

1. The invention of the "working share" which secures for each person the rights of ownership, and self-government and does so on an egalitarian basis.

2. The existence already within the present legal environment of a space for workers' self-management within state law through incorporation either as a cooperative or as a jointly-held corporation, and within federal law, after a series of battles with the Internal Revenue Service to define a mutually acceptable status under the tax laws.

3. The creation of a "workers' council" structure and process in the United

States without the prelude of a socialist revolution and without waiting for a supportive change in labor union ideology.

4. Development of a mechanism to equalize the distribution of incomes between managing and working classes, again without waiting for government compulsion.

5. At the same time, the equalization of income was not gained at expense of lessening employee motivation or productivity, as other incentives were generated which yielded equal or greater output.

Moreover, the creation and early years of these plywood companies offer some guidelines for those who would implement worker owned and managed organizations in a non-socialist context:

1. *Timing.* Workers seem most willing to depart from the prevailing system and launch into self-management when the traditional system is obviously failing them. A good proportion of the mills were founded either during the Depression or when workers in a private mill saw their own employers about to close shop. When closures are imminent and management is already relinquishing its power, there is no need for workers to force it out or coerce it into sharing power by a strike.

2. *Economic Attributes.* One major reason self-management was able to succeed in the plywood industry is that the manufacturing process is labor intensive and requires relatively low levels of capital. The capital required was within the range of what a group of highly motivated workers could assemble. A lot of the machinery they could even construct themselves. This offers a clue toward distinguishing which industries offer greater probabilities of success for the launching of worker-owned enterprises today (e.g., perhaps service sector and retail trades).

Another economic fact important to the establishment of self-management in plywood was that the earliest collectives began when the market was first developing. Market entry is a crucial factor in the fate of any enterprise, and the lesson implied by these mills is that persons interested in launching a worker-managed firm would do well to select as their product one whose market is still young and has plenty of potential for expansion.

3. *Size.* Manufacturing plywood does not require teams larger than are feasible for direct self-government. Apparently a self-governing manufacturing unit cannot go much above 350–400 members without encountering serious discontinuities of communication, interpersonal knowledge, interaction, etc. Larger collectives that aim for self-government usually find they have to segment themselves into units of this size or smaller, and then send delegates from each unit to a coordinating council.

Successful Strategies for Diffusing Work Innovations

Richard E. Walton

In a previous article, the analysis presented showed that in seven of eight companies studied, the success of work restructuring in a single plant was *not* accompanied by wide diffusion of the innovation to other plants in the firm, even though, in most cases, there was a stated company policy favoring diffusion.[1]

Since completion in 1974 of the studies on which the earlier article was based, the size of the sample of innovating companies has grown substantially. Each year practitioners in the field of work restructuring are learning more about how to diffuse these complex social innovations. As of 1977, there were a number of diffusion programs that were successful or very promising.

This paper will analyze in detail three such programs which are particularly instructive. The three cases include the most successful

From Journal of Contemporary Business, *Spring 1977,
vol. 6, no. 2, pp. 1–22. Reprinted by permission.*

diffusion firm in the earlier sample, Volvo, whose program has continued to expand. The other cases are TRW, Inc., which has a promising diffusion record to date in a program started in 1974; and a company we shall call "ABC" which has the longest and most impressive record in this field. Both TRW and ABC are United States firms.

The "work restructuring" approach pursued in some cases over the years has the dual goal of improving productivity and improving the quality of work life. It embraces many aspects of work, including the content of the job, compensation schemes, social structure, status hierarchy, scope of worker responsibility for supervision and decision making. The design of each element is intended to contribute to an internally consistent work culture—typically one that enlarges workers' scope of influence, enhances their mastery of new skills, strengthens their sense of association with co-workers, increases their identification with the product and promotes their sense of dignity and self-worth.

In gross terms, the present rate of work restructuring in the United States seems satisfactory. Given the current state of the art of tailoring work structures to particular technologies, work forces and economic frameworks, and given our present capacity to implement them, a much faster growth of restructuring activity throughout U.S. industry might inhibit the longer-run diffusion of the innovations. In the process, we would be exposed to too many abortive innovations —ones that either are ill-conceived or poorly implemented.

Hence, at this time, it is more interesting to describe diffusion within a firm than in the spread of work restructuring throughout industry. Diffusion within a firm has advantages. The expertise gained in earlier projects can be applied more readily to subsequent ones. Moreover, the spread of innovation within a system is almost essential for the long-term thriving of the initial innovation, which otherwise tends to become isolated and then threatened.

By "diffusion of work restructuring with a firm," we do not necessarily mean that a particular work design is adopted by other plants in the system, although this could be the firm in which diffusion takes place. Rather, here it means that at least the same general approach used initially in one or several plants also is utilized in other plants. In the latter case, the similarity across projects may be confined to the fact that diagnoses and changes are made within the same philosophical framework.

ABC DIVISION

The diffusion record. Here we present analysis of diffusion within ABC, a relatively autonomous division of a large firm. The division has a dozen plants today. In 1977, roughly a decade after the first major effort was launched in one new plant, the division

had seven more new plants that had incorporated the innovations throughout all their operations. Three of the older plants, all unionized, had adopted work innovations in one or more departments. Only one plant had no significant work innovations. The twelve plants have a range of from several hundred to more than a thousand employees. These plants are characterized by a very high average capital investment per employee. No other manufacturing system of this size has utilized innovative work structures as effectively and as systematically as ABC division. Without question, the innovations have contributed significantly to the performance of the division and have made these plants unusually attractive work places within their communities.

The division has not been without its abortive efforts, but those efforts are a small minority of the projects undertaken. Only one of the eight plants in which innovation was introduced at start-up has not realized its potential, generally, and its innovative work system has not been particularly successful. In the older plants where innovations have taken place on a departmental basis, the "batting average" is not as high, but it is still impressive.

The innovations in all of the start-up plants incorporated a central principle of compensation, that is, a skill-based pay scheme. Management's elements of the work structure were important too, for example, formation of work teams; integration of set-up, maintenance and inspection into the duties of operating teams; mechanisms for worker involvement in addressing plant-wide issues; symbols of a more egalitarian community, for instance, common cafeteria and parking privileges; and major investments in training. Some of the new plants, particularly the third and fourth, were more ambitious than others in their goals for developing and utilizing the capacities of workers. Still, the pattern of these innovations is remarkably uniform throughout the system. Even in the existing plants in which the innovations tend to be less comprehensive at the start, they still fall into the same conceptual pattern.

How do we explain the widespread use of work innovations throughout this multiplant system in ABC?

Situational Factors, Strategies and Tactics

The first major factor is the division's growth pattern. A decade ago the division had four plants in two locations. Success in the marketplace has required the addition of geographically dispersed facilities at a rate of one new plant about every 1½ years.

After the first new plant featured an innovative work structure that was deemed successful, management incorporated it into the design of the next new plant, with modifications based on the experience. This process has repeated itself as each new plant has started.

The rate of addition of new plants created an excellent opportunity for diffusion, but other management choices ensured that the opportunity was used. After the first new plant, the management of each new plant included many people with positive experiences in one of the earlier innovative plants. Thus they came to a new plant determined both to incorporate the best of the innovations in which they had been involved and to improve on them. One plant manager, in particular, played an instrumental role in several new plants, carrying his personal experience from one start-up situation to the next.

The division's ability to develop a sufficient pool of experienced managers to staff an additional new plant every 1½ years requires explanation. The division used first-line supervisory positions as the gateway to assimilate and develop large numbers of college graduates each year. The growth rate, in turn, made this initial assignment, which included working rotating shifts with the work teams they supervised, acceptable to the college graduates. The growing demand for managers assured them that after

a couple of years they would be promoted from shift work. This supervisory assignment policy ensured that those who were hired into one of the innovative plants would have first-hand understanding of the innovations as they moved to higher management positions.

The rate of growth of the division and the promotion-from-within policy did more than enable management to field good plant start-up teams; it brought to the top of the division the managers who had direct experience, often first-line, with the plant-level innovations. Thus, by 1976 one could observe a high degree of consensus within management about the type of organizational culture that is desirable and the work structures that tend to create that work culture.

An interesting question arises here: Why didn't the ABC's initial project experience the same tendency toward "self-encapsulation" which existed in many of the pilot projects studied earlier? Ironically, the very success of the pilot projects in these other cases had created organization dynamics that discouraged rather than encouraged diffusion. There was a "star-envy" phenomenon, whereby the attention given pilot units "turned off" managers of peer units and made them disinclined to follow the example. Also the more impressive the pioneer's results, the less favorable were the career payoffs for success and the greater the risks for failure for those managers who followed suit. In addition, the extraordinary esprit de corps and sense of being special that tended to develop in the pilot unit made the work innovations appear less generalizable to other plant managers. ABC neatly bypassed all of these organization dynamics when they used a core group of managers who had major roles in the first innovative plant to design and start up the second new plant organization.

Thus, several growth-related policies combined to drive and support the diffusion process: the rate of growth; the fact that growth took the form of constructing new plants rather than acquiring them; the start-up of new plants by managers experienced with work innovations; the promotion-from-within policy; and the use of the first-line role as the entry position.

The second major factor affecting diffusion is the nature of the division's products and manufacturing processes. The division's technologies, although diverse in appearance and in the skills and knowledge they require, all tended to be continuous and capital-intensive in nature. In these and other respects, the work situation was such that there was significant economic leverage if employees had positive attitudes and if they developed more than customary operational knowledge and skills. In turn, the work situation had the potential to be relatively satisfying.

As stated earlier, the new plants were added to meet growth in demand for existing product lines. Hence, though not all plants were identical in output and technologies, almost all products were produced at several plants. The resulting similarity among plants had certain consequences for diffusion. There was a presumption that an effective work innovation developed at one plant deserved serious consideration at other plants. Also, because each plant made products which also were produced at other plants in the system, division management was able to compare and rank the cost, delivery and quality performance among those plants producing any particular line.

The growth-related policies discussed earlier were especially relevant to the diffusion via the *new* plants added to the system, but they were less relevant to introducing change in *existing* plants, which is a much more difficult task. It is more difficult because attitudes, behavior and relationships already are established there, whereas a brand-new unit has no history and, thus, individuals' expectations can be influenced readily as they enter into the organization. Moreover, a less obvious but important dif-

ference between introducing work innovations into the design of a new plant and the redesign of an existing plant is the presence of a natural deadline in the new plant and the absence of the deadline in the old one. A plant management team of an established plant may be genuinely interested in work innovations and may see significant potential, but because the payoff from this activity tends to be longer run, management may tend to procrastinate.

Nevertheless, the innovations pioneered in the new ABC plants gradually are being adapted and utilized in the three established, unionized plants mentioned earlier. The need to compete with directly comparable operations in the newer, higher-performing plants has been an important stimulus to innovation in the older plants. This stimulus has been aided by the transfer of some managers from new plants to the established plants and by the support given by division management for the innovations.

Also facilitating innovation in existing plants have been the constructive labor relations that management has developed over the years. This made it natural for the managers to consult with the union on the particular innovations they wanted to introduce.

In addition, plant managers have been astute in choosing the time and place for introducing innovations into existing plant organizations—for example, to coincide with an important change in product or processes; with the establishment of a new department required by a new product; or with major renovations of physical plant. Such changes in existing plants provide a measure of the same advantages offered by a new plant, because there are firm deadlines established for planning and implementing the social innovation. Physical changes can help unfreeze an established culture.

Another strategic dimension of the ABC diffusion was its pragmatic orientation. In many work innovation programs studied earlier, diffusion was inhibited by the use of concepts which, although inspiring, were unrealistic, such as using "autonomous groups" as a term for work teams to which some self-supervisory responsibilities were delegated. A second inhibiting tendency was for advocates of the new work structures to develop a missionary zeal, which often caused others to take the innovations less seriously. Unrealistic concepts and missionary zeal were absent from almost all ABC projects; they were moderately present in only two of them.

ABC's innovative plants were given little or no external publicity, which further increased the tendency for the managers involved to view them as a way of doing business rather than as social experiments.

Within this pragmatic framework, ABC made excellent use of specialists in organization change. The division has a good record, not only in being well managed but also in using methods of organization development in a balanced and tailored way. Management often had made effective use of external consultants and had reduced its reliance upon them by developing internal consulting expertise as a particular methodology of organization development matured.

An example of the strategic contribution of ABC's consulting staff is a methodology for designing new plants, which includes an intensive 2-week meeting of the nucleus of the new plant management to examine alternative organization designs, to formulate performance goals and to gain cohesion and common commitment. This methodology was utilized designing the third new plant and all subsequent new plants.

VOLVO

The Diffusion Record

Volvo's earliest diffusion efforts began about 1970. Two pioneering projects previously had occurred more or less spontaneously in the auto assembly plant at Torslanda and at a neighboring truck assembly plant.

By 1975, work improvements had been undertaken in at least eight different locations.[2] Common to each of the following was the development of mechanisms for enabling large numbers of workers to participate in the consideration of a range of issues on which they previously had not been consulted. The following descriptions identify particularly the variety of other work improvements that distinguish the projects.

At the Torslanda auto plant which employed 8,000 workers, changes have been occurring incrementally since the earlier experiments. However, except for a few relatively small departments which have employed a more comprehensive approach to restructuring, the program has been characterized by a variety of modest changes made on the margin. These include: (1) physical renovation in the body shop to control noise and to improve ventilation and the plant's color scheme, (2) job enlargement in the assembly plant and (3) delegation of responsibility for quality in the paint shop.

At factories in Oofström and Konga, which employ 5,000 workers and produce auto body components and some of Volvo's own manufacturing machinery, changes have occurred in many departments. The changes have centered on the actual design of work activity, including enlargement of individual jobs, rotation among jobs, formation of work groups and the delegation of supervisory tasks and responsibilities to the work groups. These changes have been accompanied by major training investments to upgrade the participative skills of supervisors and to increase the job-design knowledge of industrial engineers. Engineering efforts have resulted in mechanizations of monotonous work stations; they have also resulted in the insertion of buffer inventories that reduce the rigidity of the tie between workers and production speed

At Bergslag, where 4,000 workers are employed in the production of transmission components, much of the work improvement has taken the form of mechanization. The plant has made imaginative use of industrial robots, inventing a mechanical hand to do work that is dirty, heavy or monotonous.

At the Arvika foundry, which employs 500 workers, the physical environment for certain work stations has been upgraded significantly.

At Kalmar, Volvo designed a truly revolutionary plant, which began production in the Spring of 1974. Assembly work at Kalmar is performed by about twenty-five groups, each typically composed of about fifteen workers. A group has responsibility for a complete component of the car, such as the electrical system, instrumentation or wheels and brakes. Employees can develop professional pride as they acquire expertise in an entire subsystem of the automobile. The members of the team can influence the working procedures, the internal distribution of jobs and variation in the rate of work. The team is responsible for supplies of materials and plays an active part in quality inspection. The foreman can devote more time to long-range planning and coordination among areas.

The building has been designed to create a small workshop atmosphere. Each group has at its disposal a floor area screened from the view of the other teams, and each has a separate place for relaxation. Instead of moving on a conveyor line, car bodies are transported on battery-driven trolleys, carefully designed to provide more flexibility in the work organization. Buffer areas that hold two trolleys separate groups, providing each group with a measure of independence from the larger system and permit it to vary its pace without affecting down-stream operations. The trolleys permit two different work arrangements within an assembly group: straight assembly in which each worker can specialize in tasks with 5-minute cycle times, and dock assembly, in which each worker performs work with a 20- to 30-minute cycle time as a member of a 3-man team that performs all the work for which the 15-person group is responsible.

At the large engine complex in Skövde, similarly comprehensive innovations have occurred in a new unit put in operation in late 1974. The unit eventually will employ about 900 workers. Most of the work structure principles which characterize the Kalmar plant also were incorporated in the design of both the machinery and assembly areas of this unit.

Volvo has planned a final assembly plant to help serve the U.S. market in Chesapeake, Virginia. The intention there is to build upon the Kalmar work innovations.

How impressive is the record just outlined? The author's judgment is that, on the one hand, when compared with ABC a smaller proportion of Volvo workers is affected less dramatically, their mental capacities are less fully utilized in the regular work activities and the economic payoff to the firm (for example, savings as a percentage of payroll costs) is probably much less. On the other hand, there can be no question that Volvo's achievements are extraordinary. The production technologies of the auto industry lend themselves much less naturally to the types of restructuring employed by ABC in all its plants. Moreover, Volvo's diffusion program is of more recent origin. Perhaps the best appraisal is that the work innovations at Volvo were as attuned to the concerns of its work force in Sweden as ABC's were to its work force in America.

How do we explain Volvo's diffusion record? At least seven explanatory factors can be identified.

Situational Factors, Strategies and Tactics

First, the particular impetus to action was by its nature, a relatively effective one. In the late 1960's turnover in Volvo's plants was very high and rising. One could state dramatically, as Volvo's president did. that unless auto work was made more hospitable to Swedish workers, auto makers could not continue to operate in Sweden. Thus, turnover became the primary target for work innovations and their diffusion.

The turnover target had several characteristics that were conducive to an action-oriented work improvement program. It is a direct symptom of the quality of work life and yet also is linked readily to a variety of business costs. The objective to reduce turnover is neutral ideologically and absolutely uncontroversial—and turnover rate is one of the more readily measured symptoms in the work place.

The turnover focus had other advantages. Turnover was a symptom common to all plants. No plant management could argue that their turnover need not or could not be reduced. Turnover also was a type of target that could be attacked in many ways —from spending large sums on the physical environment to the imaginative reconception of work organization. Thus, improving work to reduce turnover was a game in which everyone had to play—and one in which everyone could play.

Second, the characteristics of some of the particular work improvements which emerged help explain why so many plants could participate in the program within a short period of time. Some work improvements, such as those made in the Arvika Foundry, were relatively straightforward changes in work procedures and physical environment that required no new social or technical skills for implementation. They are simpler to diffuse than the complex and innovative work organizations in Skövde and Kalmar. Other work improvements involved robots, buffers and maneuverable trolleys in lieu of conveyors. The strictly technical aspects of these improvements can be diffused without simultaneously implementing significant social changes, but once installed these devices permit, indeed invite, the development of different organizational forms. Moreover, there is operating in a company like Volvo a technological imperative, such that, once developed, technologies like the engine trolley for Skövde and the larger car

trolley for Kalmar undoubtedly will be diffused to all new facilities and progressively introduced in the renovation of existing ones. In many respects the diffusion of these technical innovations will spearhead the diffusion of more advanced work organizations with which they are compatible.

Third, a cooperative union-management framework was a major enabling factor. Union officials supported the projects described above, in part because they could emphasize the worker consultation dimension of these projects as a step toward the union's own objective of creating industrial democracy, and in part because of the care which management took to involve the union at each stage of a project.

Fourth, one cannot explain the diffusion at Volvo without acknowledging the positive leadership provided by the firm's president, Mr. Pehr Gyllenhammar, who articulated in a dramatic way the turnover threat to the Swedish auto industry. Gyllenhammar has been in the forefront among businessmen in western countries in calling for humanization of work, both for the benefit of the human beings themselves and for businesses that employ them. Moreover, he has played a direct role in insisting that the project teams associated with Kalmar and Skövde think boldly and that they not confine themselves to making changes on the margin. Thus Mr. Gyllenhammar deserves some personal credit for the technical innovations which enabled Volvo to break out of the constraints of the conventional conveyor-belt assembly line. He also has backed his rhetoric by approving substantial funds for the work projects.

Such public statements have served as a model for subordinates; equally important, they have publicly committed the firm to a leadership position in addressing the issue. Once established, this public image increased the cost of not following through— to the firm in terms of public relations and to Mr. Gyllenhammar in terms of personal credibility.

Fifth, some features of the Swedish society seem to help explain the amount of diffusion in Volvo. During 1970–76, there was more general interest and support for work innovations in Sweden than in the United States. Also, Sweden has institutional processes for translating general concern into action. There is a pattern in Sweden of responding to guidance from central authorities. At the national level, this has given the Swedish Employers' Federation more leverage over Swedish employers in fostering work innovations throughout Swedish industry than we can ever imagine happening in U.S. industry. At the firm level, the fact that top leadership in Volvo made it company policy to humanize work had more leverage over plant management than it would have in the United States.

Sixth, the organizational mechanisms for pursuing work improvement were apparently effective ones. In existing plants, special working groups were formed to gather data, consult with others and define problems or opportunities. In planning for the new facilities, project organizations were formed to involve managers, union officials, workers and specialists from various industries and academic disciplines. After providing initial impetus and perhaps early guidance, these special units typically were dissolved and their functions absorbed in the line organization.

The communication efforts designed to aid diffusion have included circulation of working papers on technical and other ideas, exchange visits between plants and a conference in 1974 to compare project experiences.

Note that several of the existing plants began their exploration of work improvement in 1970 and 1971 and that both of the new plants at Skövde and Kalmar were being planned in the same time period, that is, during 1972–73. The more dramatic innovations in new plants occurred *after*—and built upon—the experiments previously conducted in existing plants. These patterns avoided the pilot-project syndrome.

Seventh, special note must be made of the importance to Volvo's diffusion (present and potential) of the reorienting and educating of industrial engineers and then making an important part of their task the humanization of work and the physical environment. Swedish engineering ingenuity has led Swedish industry in other respects. Volvo's channeling of this ingenuity into the work improvement program was an important facet of its diffusion program.

TRW, INC.

Though ABC, Volvo and TRW are all treated here as positive examples of diffusion, their records are not comparable. The innovations at ABC and Volvo have proven viable over an extended period of time. TRW appears to be on a relatively impressive path of diffusion, but the projects started are generally too young to be termed viable.

The Diffusion Record

Early in 1974, the Vice President and Director of Organization Development and Vice President and Director of Industrial Relations, with the active support of their common superior who heads the corporate personnel function in TRW, launched a work restructuring effort.[3] They were assisted initially by a team of several internal professionals and a few external consultants with experience in the field.

In the background at the time the program began was a work restructuring experiment in a small department of one TRW plant, although it did not appear to serve as a pilot project for the program. The program consultants were more oriented to plant-wide projects and to tapping the experience of other firms with projects on that scale.

Thus, a general approach to innovation rather than a specific innovation was to be tried initially and improved upon as it was diffused more widely.

By early 1977 the following initiatives had

occurred. In eighteen separate locations, one or more exploratory sessions had occurred between a top plant team (or comparable unit[4] of knowledgeable workers) and members of the consulting team. Typically these sessions were intended to clarify the philosophy of the TRW program, to familiarize members of the plant team with the many forms that work restructuring can take, to illustrate how the ideas might be applied to the plant in question and, finally, to leave the plant team with an approach for determining the feasibility and desirability of undertaking a project there. The following quote is illustrative of the message left with a plant team:

Your answers to the following questions are relevant not only to whether a project is feasible, but also to how the work organization should be designed or redesigned. Preliminary answers to these questions are required in the feasibility phase. More thorough answers are needed in developing and refining a tentative design.

First, are the productivity and quality of work life objectives understood and shared within the team considering work restructuring?

Second, are work restructuring ideas applicable to the technology and work force in question? How?

Third, are there significant potential economic benefits? How much? And how are they estimated?

Fourth, are there significant potential benefits to the employees affected? In what form?

Fifth, can management become committed? Does it have or can it acquire requisite attitudes and skills?

Sixth, can the union, as well as employees, be expected to support the project?

In fourteen out of eighteen cases, the initial visit was followed up by serious explora-tion on the part of the plant team and by additional consulting visits. Of these fourteen cases, twelve remained active after an initial test of feasibility. One of the two dropouts resulted when the union membership failed to vote a sufficient majority for establishing a plant-wide productivity bonus, which had been conceived as the most appropriate initial step in the work restructuring plan. The second dropout occurred after a plant study team had investigated two different approaches; these investigations came to a halt when an economic recession began to preoccupy plant mangement. These two plants may yet resume their exploration of work restructuring.

Of the twelve projects which remained active after an initial testing phase, there were actual steps to restructure work in nine. However, one of the nine projects essentially was nullified when the plant's business dropped off sharply. The other three projects were still in the study stage early in 1977.

Thus in the spring of 1977 it was appropriate to count eight work-restructuring projects which were being facilitated by the corporate-level program. Four of the projects involved new plants; two other projects were in established manufacturing plants with unions; and, finally, two of the "plants" had major departments which employed professionals. Each of those plants employing professionals involved less than fifty people. The other six projects ranged from slightly less than 100 people to just under 1,000.

The nature of these innovations varied widely. The work structures in the four new plants have similar features, conceptually; that is, skill-based pay schemes, work teams, support activities integrated into the line and lean supervisory arrangements. However, the translation of these concepts into operational systems with actual procedures and roles has created a variation in design considerably greater than in the case of the new plants in the ABC Division.

One of the projects in an established unionized plant started with a plant-wide productivity bonus. By 1977 this step not only had achieved gains in productivity and quality of work life, but also had created a favorable climate in which other work restructuring steps could be considered, for example, formation of work teams that can assume more self-supervisory responsibility.

The other project in a unionized plant had as its initial focus the development of trust and problem-solving between union and management officials. This was followed by an open process of eliciting ideas for quality of work life and productivity improvement from the shop floor and then by the negotiation of an agreement to allow work restructuring experiments to occur on a departmental basis.

Without describing the two other projects which involved professionals, it is important to note that they take forms different from any of the above. This adds further to the diversity of forms which work restructuring has taken in the TRW program.

As indicated earlier, most of the innovations in these eight projects were not yet well established, and a few projects took only one or two steps toward comprehensive work restructuring. Nonetheless, most and maybe all of the eight reasonably may be counted as instances of diffusion. Failure, if it occurs, probably will be due to deficiencies in design and implementation or bad luck rather than to the fact that diffusion did not take place.

A 3-day "Plant Managers' Workshop" held in February 1977, attended by teams from seven of the projects where work restructuring was underway, confirmed for all participants as well as for other observers that the TRW work restructuring program was well launched and that it was entering a new stage.

How do we explain this diffusion within TRW? First it is important to understand how the strategy relates to background factors; then it is relevant to consider the elements of the diffusion strategy and the functions they are intended to perform. However, any assessments offered about the actual effects of particular elements of the diffusion strategy or related background factors are hypotheses and are offered in advance of systematic evidence.[5]

Situational Factors, Strategies and Tactics

The TRW firm is a large manufacturing plant which is highly diversified. Its growth pattern historically had been by acquisitions as well as by internal growth.

Each of these factors had implications for diffusion. First, because there were more than 100 plants, even if only a small fraction of the firm's plants were ready to explore innovations, it still would be possible to achieve a critical mass of effort to create a corporate program with momentum. Also if the initial innovations proved effective, the large number of remaining plants would provide a correspondingly large opportunity to achieve a return on the initial effort and risk.

Second, the fact that it was a manufacturing-based firm means that innovations that promised advantage in the manufacturing arm of the business could, and perhaps would need to, receive top management attention.

Third, because the manufacturing system was highly diversified, the learning in one plant was not necessarily directly applicable to other plants. TRW, Inc. businesses included electronics and computer-based services; car and truck production and replacement parts; spacecraft and propulsion products; fasteners, tools and bearings; and energy products and services. Some plants were capital-intensive, others were labor-intensive. Some were characterized by assembly or batch processes, others by continuous-process technology. Some were marginal plants that produced for a commodity market, while others were highly profitable plants that served a unique niche in the marketplace. For some plants cost was the basic competitive factor; for others delivery and quality were strategic. Some plants were characterized by mature technologies; others were distinguishable by relatively rapid rates of technological change. Thus in contrast to the ABC situation, the economic payoffs and improved quality of work life that derived from innovation in one plant could not be assumed to be available in the next plant in the same order of magnitude.

This meant that there was greater need for a methodology for assessing the size of the dollar stakes and psychological stakes associated with a particular project and also for an educational effort to ensure that project-by-project assessments would be made.

Moreover, again in contrast to ABC, the work structure that proved effective in one plant (for example, team composition, compensation scheme, training investment, supervisory roles) was not necessarily appropriate in the next plant. The learning transferred from one plant to the next had to occur at a higher level of abstraction (principles of design rather than designs themselves).

Fourth, to the extent that growth had been achieved through acquisition rather than from within, TRW was a mosaic of management sub-cultures, in contrast to the more or less uniform management cultures found in Volvo. The varied management philosophies meant that different management groups in TRW would approach the question of plant floor innovations very differently, thus requiring a diffusion strategy that recognized "market segments"—to borrow an important principle from marketing science.

The first two background factors, size and the manufacturing dominance, had positive implications for the diffusion effort. On the other hand, diversification and the acquisitions history complicated the diffusion task in TRW (relative to that faced by ABC and Volvo) and required a more deliberate program for promoting diffusion.

When the program was launched in 1974, it included an objective to initiate several projects more or less simultaneously. One rationale for this was to avoid the self-encapsulation tendency of a single pilot proj-

ect. By the same logic, the aim was to have a project in each of four major business groups; the company wished to overcome a proclivity to concentrate resources in groups which were characterized by management philosophies most receptive to the innovations.

Additional considerations argued for initiating on several fronts at once. Because of the size of the firm, in order for a program to be taken seriously as a corporate program, it had to quickly achieve a level of activity and results that would be associated with a portfolio of plant projects rather than a pilot project. Also, because of the diversity of the large TRW plant system which constituted the eventual market for work innovations, to achieve diversity became the goal in the initial wave of projects along as many of the following dimensions as possible: new and established plants; unionized and nonunionized plants; white-collar and blue-collar work forces; and assembly, batch and continuous-process technology.

The fact that this corporate-wide program was launched in 1974 after there was some credible experience outside TRW and at least one instructive grass-roots experiment in one location within TRW was important because it enabled those who conceived of a corporate-wide progarm to be bold and ambitious.

The objective of launching a number of projects in a relatively short period of time was achieved. This relatively rapid development of momentum had important consequences beyond those reported above as part of the rationale. The momentum had a very favorable impact on the commitment of several types of groups associated with the program—the participating plants which were reassured by the fact that there are other innovating plants; the internal and external consultants whose efforts were reinforced by the evidence of progress; and the top corporate supporters of the program who could better justify the attention and priority being given it.

The parallel progress of several projects provided both an advantage and a disadvantage for the process of cross-project learning. The advantage was that what was learned in one innovating plant could be considered quickly in another plant. The disadvantage was that sometimes the things learned in one plant occurred too late to prevent another plant from making the same mistake.

The above discussion had addressed the overall diversity of TRW's plant system, but within any one of the firm's twelve operating divisions, there often were several plants producing the same product or similar products. Hence, within a division one aspect of the strategy used at ABC could be employed, namely, after a new plant pioneers the innovations and demonstrates its effectiveness, the established plants begin to take more interest in the innovation. By early 1977 this process already had worked in one division and had potential in several others.

Another strategic dimension of the diffusion program was its pragmatic versus romantic orientation. The pragmatic formulation of the TRW program was reflected in the fact that initially projects were called "productivity projects," although it was understood from the outset that they were designed to promote both productivity and quality of work life. Later the rhetoric referring to the goals of the program became more balanced.

From the beginning, it was understood by all concerned that to be successful, projects must be owned by line management. Plant managers, for example, must see the work innovations as an integral component of how they manage their business, not as a personnel policy or practice that could be designed or implemented by others.

The pragmatic orientation was reflected in a growing recognition of several "realities." First, different projects would and should take quite different forms. Second, comprehensive change in existing plants might often require a period of several years and might involve several steps, each more or less "digested" before the next is undertaken. Third, highly positive work cultures, characterized by self-management capabilities, cannot be created overnight but must be instituted progressively, hand-in-hand with the development of the work culture which it contemplates.

Although pragmatic, the program was based on two articles-of-faith assumptions which formed the basis of all activities of the program. The first idea was that in a large fraction of work organizations today there exists a significant potential for improving business results and quality of work life by modifying the work organization. The magnitude of this potential must be assessed on a case-by-case basis. The second idea was that all elements of the work system need to reinforce one another.

The program structure and its activities were designed to fit the background factors and strategic objectives of the program described above. The activities and the functions they were intended to perform are presented in Figure 1.

The diagram is to some degree self-explanatory. Many of the activities and their functions already have been referred to above. Four structural elements of the program, however, deserve comment: first is the cochairmanship of the program by the top organizational development executive and the top industrial relations executive, who clearly communicated their joint commitment to the program. This joint commitment was especially important in the case of diffusion to unionized plants. Second is the project liaison manager, for example, the person on the program consulting team who was responsible for providing lead consultation to the project, monitoring and reporting developments in the project and coordinating all outside assistance provided to the project. Third, a structural element that has been used in some projects is a "project steering committee," comprised of members

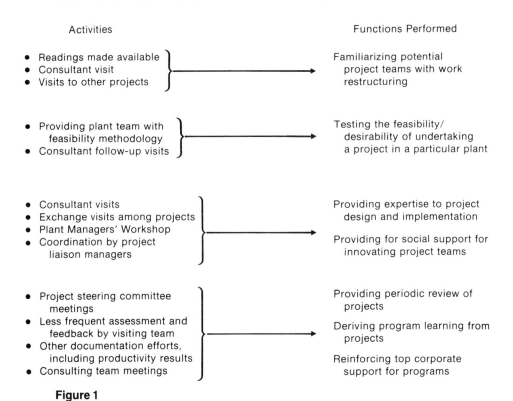

Activities   Functions Performed

- Readings made available
- Consultant visit
- Visits to other projects

Familiarizing potential project teams with work restructuring

- Providing plant team with feasibility methodology
- Consultant follow-up visits

Testing the feasibility/desirability of undertaking a project in a particular plant

- Consultant visits
- Exchange visits among projects
- Plant Managers' Workshop
- Coordination by project liaison managers

Providing expertise to project design and implementation

Providing for social support for innovating project teams

- Project steering committee meetings
- Less frequent assessment and feedback by visiting team
- Other documentation efforts, including productivity results
- Consulting team meetings

Providing periodic review of projects

Deriving program learning from projects

Reinforcing top corporate support for programs

Figure 1

of plants and division management, one or more consultants and perhaps others. The idea is to provide for a periodic review of the progress of a project, to provide a sounding board for the project team and to ensure that the team is getting the outside support it required from the division and consultants. More frequent meetings were especially useful during the late design stage and during approximately the first year of implementation. A fourth important and unique structural element of the program is a "consulting team" which had held 2-day meetings, twice a year since mid-1974. The consulting team included (1) the cochairmen of the program and their superior; (2) the several internal consultants who report to them and who spend full-time on the project activities; (3) corporate-level staff specialists on compensation, communication, finance and manufacturing; (4) a number of division and group-level personnel managers; and (5) a few outside consultants. All are considered program "consultants" who may be deployed to contribute to a particular project or to contribute to the development of a methodology which can be used across many projects, for example, the assessment methodology referred to above.

Of course, as intended, the consulting team has helped ensure that project-level learnings are shared, that consulting resources are deployed strategically and that the need for new program methodologies is identified and then met.

An additional effect of creating this forum of interdisciplinary specialists and personnel generalists from various business groups in TRW has been to create a broad base of ownership for the program. That they have been used as consultants has reinforced a basic tenet of the program, which is that "consultants" should be referred to with a small "c"—that is, they are where you find them, which is not always represented by a shingle or a business card.

CONCLUSIONS

What can we learn from these three cases of diffusion? At the first level, these cases demonstrate that it *is* possible to diffuse work innovations systematically and effectively throughout a multiplant system.

At the second level, we can learn something about a number of issues that must be considered in formulating a diffusion strategy. Perhaps the three cases can shed light on each of seven issues framed below as questions:

1. In what types of firms can ambitious work restructuring programs be undertaken?

The most striking similarity of these firms is that all three are well managed and their managements are relatively attuned to the human dimension. Perhaps those are two prerequisites. The dissimilarities among the three systems in other respects are equally interesting, indicating the variety of firms that can undertake work restructuring on an ambitious scale. Their competitive orientations vary—ABC is marketing-oriented, Volvo is engineering-oriented and TRW is manufacturing-oriented—although their business orientations do not necessarily cover a broad spectrum. The fact that impressive diffusion occurred in multiplant systems with three types of interdependence among plants is also significant: ABC plants comprised a series of parallel production capacities not linked by product flow but often "competitively" producing the same product for the market; Volvo was a highly integrated system with the products of one plant flowing to another; the plants within

one of TRW's more than twenty divisions or groups typically were interdependent in one of the above ways, but these divisions and groups themselves were generally unrelated, making the system, as a whole, rate low on interdependence among its parts.

2. Toward what goals should the work restructuring program be directed?

At one level of abstraction the goals were the same in all three cases—namely, the innovations should serve the business needs of the organization and the human needs of the members of the organization. In none of the cases was there any attempt to blur the fact that the managers associated with the program saw the innovations as good business. The pragmatic orientation was essential for the diffusion achieved.

At a more concrete level the three cases had different foci: increasing "productivity" was the by-word in TRW; "turnover" was the frequently cited target in Volvo; and something like "system performance," including high utilization of a very expensive technology, was always in the minds of ABC innovators. As argued in the case of Volvo, the selection of concrete goals can be an important tactical choice in implementing a diffusion program.

3. Where should program leadership emanate from?

Although top leadership seemed critically important in Volvo, the absence of any comparable public commitment by the top executives in ABC and TRW was not disabling. Leadership for the innovations in ABC resided for a long period in managers of innovative plants. Eventually the innovations merely became a pervasive part of the total division culture and leadership equally diffused. Leadership in TRW at the program level was provided by the corporate personnel function, and at the project level, it was provided by plant managers.

Significantly all three firms took an inclusive, constructive stance toward the unions when innovations were contemplated in unionized plants.

4. How concretely versus abstractly should one characterize the innovative approach one wants to diffuse?

In the ABC case in which the plants were very similar to each other, the innovations were transferred from one plant to the next with relatively little variation. Thus, the characterization of the innovations being diffused could be and were at a relatively concrete level. TRW offered a contrasting case. The system was highly diversified and the forms which work restructuring took were highly varied. Therefore, the innovations needed to be characterized at a higher level of generality. Concreteness in the case of TRW had to be achieved by pointing to several specific alternatives.

As a general proposition it may be desirable not to go to a higher level of abstraction than necessary, but that level itself depends on the diversity of the system.

5. Which is better—a single pilot project or several projects initiated simultaneously?

ABC avoided the self-encapsulating tendency of a single pilot project by drawing managers for the second project from the pool of managers involved in the first project. Both Volvo and TRW avoided this by initiating multiple projects. The latter strategy is more available today because more design knowledge and experience are available to draw on.

6. Is it better to start with existing plants or to wait for a new plant start up?

Volvo was able to make marginal innovations in large departments and more comprehensive experiments in small departments in existing plants during 1970–73 be-
fore its more radical innovations in two new facilties which began operations in 1974. ABC began with a new plant, and only after several new plants had adopted the new work structure did some innovations begin to spread to the older plants. TRW, in effect, started with both. Thus, it appears that either way can work well. It would appear that one can afford to be opportunistic on this dimension.

7. What should be the core methodology for transmitting innovations?

The vehicles for diffusion varied across the three cases, each a natural fit to the situation.

ABC illustrates the powerful effect of moving managers who have direct experience with work innovations into other units of the organization. Volvo illustrates the potential effect of developing technological innovations that are interrelated with work arrangements. The channels and roles within a firm that normally ensure the diffusion of technical innovations are added to those which one otherwise might have used to promote the social innovation by itself.

TRW illustrates the potential in certain circumstances for using a plant-wide productivity bonus as the leading edge for change in existing plants in a way analogous to Volvo's use of a technological device like trolleys, buffers or robots. TRW's plant-wide productivity bonus has its own effect, but even more importantly it enabled other restructuring steps to happen—as does Volvo's technological devices.

TRW also best illustrates the development of explicit structures, roles and activities that may be used to implement a diffusion strategy; indeed, that are required if diffusion is to occur at a reasonable rate throughout a system comprised of highly diversified parts—diversified in terms of technologies, business strategies and management cultures.

Assistance from a central group was more pronounced in TRW than in either ABC or Volvo.

The answers to many of the seven questions strike a theme—that is, "it depends." This theme signals a third level of learning about diffusion programs.

ABC management achieved an impressive record of diffusion by certain conscious steps, in particular, interplant transfers of personnel and interplant comparisons. Why these steps were effective only could be understood in reference to the division's growth patterns and the nature of its products.

The Volvo and TRW situations differed in important respects, requiring that the diffusion strategy be formulated differently. Their strategies appear to be as well suited to their respective situations as the ABC strategy was to its own.

The general lesson that emerges is that although a corporate program may usefully borrow elements from the successful programs of other firms, the overall strategy must be developed on the basis of a thorough understanding of the firm, for example, the larger social context, the firm's patterns, products, technologies, management culture and prior experience in organization development.

NOTES

I wish to acknowledge the assistance of two colleagues: Mr. Sheldon Davis, with whom I share an intellectual and practical interest in this subject, and Mr. Max Hall, who offered criticism of an earlier draft of this paper. Research support was provided by the Division of Research, Harvard Graduate School of Business Administration.

1. Richard E. Walton, "The Diffusion of New Work Structures: Explaining Why Success Didn't Take," *Organizational Dynamics* (Winter 1975).

2. Rolf Lindholm and Jan-Peder Norstedt, *The Volvo Report* (Stockholm: Swedish Employers' Confederation, 1975).

3. The purpose and approval of the TRW effort is outlined in "Employee Productivity Projects," a working paper drafted in 1974 by Mr. Sheldon A. Davis and Mr. Robert Hauserman and periodically revised on the basis of experience and input from members of the consulting team.

4. For easy reference we refer to all of the TRW units as "plants."

5. A more systematic assessment of the extent and determinants of TRW's diffusion of work restructuring as well as of two other organization development methodologies, namely "team building" and "organization sensing," is being conducted by Ove Myrseth, a doctoral student at the Harvard Business School.